D0849046

THE QUR'AN

The Qur'an

A new translation by
M. A. S. ABDEL HALEEM

OXFORD
UNIVERSITY PRESS

OXFORD
UNIVERSITY PRESS

Great Clarendon Street, Oxford OX2 6DP

Oxford University Press is a department of the University of Oxford.
It furthers the University's objective of excellence in research, scholarship,
and education by publishing worldwide in

Oxford New York

Auckland Bangkok Buenos Aires Cape Town Chennai
Dar es Salaam Delhi Hong Kong Istanbul Karachi Kolkata
Kuala Lumpur Madrid Melbourne Mexico City Mumbai Nairobi
São Paulo Shanghai Taipei Tokyo Toronto

Oxford is a registered trade mark of Oxford University Press
in the UK and in certain other countries

Published in the United States
by Oxford University Press Inc., New York

British Library Cataloguing in Publication Data

Data available

Library of Congress Cataloging-in-Publication Data

Koran. English.
The Qur'an/a new translation by M. A. S. Abdel Haleem.
p. cm.
Includes bibliographical references and index.
I. Haleem, M. A. S. Abdel. II. Title.

BP109 2004
297.1′22521–dc22   2004041455

ISBN 0–19–280548–7

1

Typeset in Ehrhardt
by RefineCatch Limited, Bungay, Suffolk
Printed in Great Britain by
Clays Ltd, St Ives plc

CONTENTS

Introduction   ix

   The Life of Muhammad and the Historical Background   x
   The Revelation of the Qur'an   xiv
   The Compilation of the Qur'an   xv
   The Structure of the Qur'an: Suras and Ayas   xvi
   Stylistic Features   xix
   Issues of Interpretation   xxi
   A Short History of English Translations   xxvi
   This Translation   xxix

A Chronology of the Qur'an   xxxvii

Select Bibliography   xxxix

Map of Arabia at the Time of the Revelation   xliii

THE QUR'AN

  1. The Opening (*Al-Fatiha*)   3
  2. The Cow (*Al-Baqara*)   4
  3. The Family of 'Imran (*Al 'Imran*)   34
  4. Women (*Al-Nisa'*)   50
  5. The Feast (*Al-Ma'ida*)   67
  6. Livestock (*Al-An'am*)   80
  7. The Heights (*Al-A'raf*)   94
  8. Battle Gains (*Al-Anfal*)   110
  9. Repentance (*Al-Tawba*)   116
 10. Jonah (*Yunus*)   128
 11. Hud (*Hud*)   136
 12. Joseph (*Yusuf*)   145
 13. Thunder (*Al-Ra'd*)   153
 14. Abraham (*Ibrahim*)   158
 15. Al-Hijr (*Al-Hijr*)   162
 16. The Bee (*Al-Nahl*)   166
 17. The Night Journey (*Al-Isra'*)   175
 18. The Cave (*Al-Kahf*)   183
 19. Mary (*Maryam*)   191

20. *Ta Ha* (*Ta Ha*)   196
21. The Prophets (*Al-Anbiya'*)   203
22. The Pilgrimage (*Al-Hajj*)   209
23. The Believers (*Al-Mu'minun*)   215
24. Light (*Al-Nur*)   220
25. The [Scripture that] Shows the Difference (*Al-Furqan*)   227
26. The Poets (*Al-Shu'ara'*)   232
27. The Ants (*Al-Naml*)   239
28. The Story (*Al-Qasas*)   245
29. The Spider (*Al-'Ankabut*)   252
30. The Byzantines (*Al-Rum*)   257
31. Luqman (*Luqman*)   261
32. Bowing down in Worship (*Al-Sajda*)   264
33. The Joint Forces (*Al-Ahzab*)   266
34. Sheba (*Saba'*)   272
35. The Creator (*Fatir*)   277
36. *Ya Sin* (*Ya Sin*)   281
37. Ranged in Rows (*Al-Saffat*)   285
38. *Sad* (*Sad*)   290
39. The Throngs (*Al-Zumar*)   295
40. The Forgiving One (*Ghafir*)   301
41. [Verses] Made Distinct (*Fussilat*)   307
42. Consultation (*Al-Shura*)   311
43. Ornaments of Gold (*Al-Zukhruf*)   316
44. Smoke (*Al-Dukhan*)   321
45. Kneeling (*Al-Jathiya*)   324
46. The Sand Dunes (*Al-Ahqaf*)   327
47. Muhammad (*Muhammad*)   331
48. Triumph (*Al-Fath*)   334
49. The Private Quarters (*Al-Hujurat*)   338
50. *Qaf* (*Qaf*)   340
51. Scattering [Winds] (*Al-Dhariyat*)   343
52. The Mountain (*Al-Tur*)   345
53. The Star (*Al-Najm*)   347
54. The Moon (*Al-Qamar*)   350
55. The Lord of Mercy (*Al-Rahman*)   353
56. That which is Coming (*Al-Waqi'a*)   356
57. Iron (*Al-Hadid*)   359
58. The Dispute (*Al-Mujadala*)   362

59. The Gathering [of Forces]   (*Al-Hashr*)   365
60. Women Tested   (*Al-Mumtahana*)   368
61. Solid Lines   (*Al-Saff*)   370
62. The Day of Congregation   (*Al-Jumu'a*)   372
63. The Hypocrites   (*Al-Munafiqun*)   374
64. Mutual Neglect   (*Al-Taghabun*)   376
65. Divorce   (*Al-Talaq*)   378
66. Prohibition   (*Al-Tahrim*)   380
67. Control   (*Al-Mulk*)   382
68. The Pen   (*Al-Qalam*)   384
69. The Inevitable Hour   (*Al-Haqqa*)   387
70. The Ways of Ascent   (*Al-Ma'arij*)   389
71. Noah   (*Nuh*)   391
72. The Jinn   (*Al-Jinn*)   393
73. Enfolded   (*Al-Muzzammil*)   395
74. Wrapped in his Cloak   (*Al-Muddaththir*)   397
75. The Resurrection   (*Al-Qiyama*)   399
76. Man   (*Al-Insan*)   401
77. [Winds] Sent Forth   (*Al-Mursalat*)   403
78. The Announcement   (*Al-Naba'*)   405
79. The Forceful Chargers   (*Al-Nazi'at*)   407
80. He Frowned   (*'Abasa*)   409
81. Shrouded in Darkness   (*Al-Takwir*)   411
82. Torn Apart   (*Al-Infitar*)   412
83. Those who Give Short Measure   (*Al-Mutaffifin*)   413
84. Ripped Apart   (*Al-Inshiqaq*)   415
85. The Constellations   (*Al-Buruj*)   416
86. The Night-Comer   (*Al-Tariq*)   417
87. The Most High   (*Al-A'la*)   418
88. The Overwhelming Event   (*Al-Ghashiya*)   419
89. Daybreak   (*Al-Fajr*)   420
90. The City   (*Al-Balad*)   422
91. The Sun   (*Al-Shams*)   423
92. The Night   (*Al-Layl*)   424
93. The Morning Brightness   (*Al-Duha*)   425
94. Relief   (*Al-Sharh*)   426
95. The Fig   (*Al-Tin*)   427
96. The Clinging Form   (*Al-'Alaq*)   428
97. The Night of Glory   (*Al-Qadr*)   429

98.	Clear Evidence (*Al-Bayyina*)	430
99.	The Earthquake (*Al-Zalzala*)	431
100.	The Charging Steeds (*Al-'Adiyat*)	432
101.	The Crashing Blow (*Al-Qari'a*)	433
102.	Striving for More (*Al-Takathur*)	434
103.	The Declining Day (*Al-'Asr*)	435
104.	The Backbiter (*Al-Humaza*)	436
105.	The Elephant (*Al-Fil*)	437
106.	Quraysh (*Quraysh*)	438
107.	Common Kindnesses (*Al-Ma'un*)	439
108.	Abundance (*Al-Kawthar*)	440
109.	The Disbelievers (*Al-Kafirun*)	441
110.	Help (*Al-Nasr*)	442
111.	Palm Fibre (*Al-Masad*)	443
112.	Purity [of Faith] (*Al-Ikhlas*)	444
113.	Daybreak (*Al-Falaq*)	445
114.	People (*Al-Nas*)	446

Index   447

INTRODUCTION

THE QUR'AN is the supreme authority in Islam. It is the funda-
mental and paramount source of the creed, rituals, ethics, and laws
of the Islamic religion. It is the book that 'differentiates' between
right and wrong, so that nowadays, when the Muslim world is
dealing with such universal issues as globalization, the environment, combating terrorism and drugs, issues of medical ethics, and
feminism, evidence to support the various arguments is sought in
the Qur'an. This supreme status stems from the belief that the
Qur'an is the word of God, revealed to the Prophet Muhammad via
the archangel Gabriel, and intended for all times and all places.

The Qur'an was the starting point for all the Islamic sciences:
Arabic grammar was developed to serve the Qur'an, the study of
Arabic phonetics was pursued in order to determine the exact pronunciation of Qur'anic words, the science of Arabic rhetoric was
developed in order to describe the features of the inimitable style of
the Qur'an, the art of Arabic calligraphy was cultivated through
writing down the Qur'an, the Qur'an is the basis of Islamic law and
theology; indeed, as the celebrated fifteenth-century scholar
and author Suyuti said, 'Everything is based on the Qur'an'. The
entire religious life of the Muslim world is built around the text of
the Qur'an. As a consequence of the Qur'an, the Arabic language
moved far beyond the Arabian peninsula, deeply penetrating many
other languages within the Muslim lands—Persian, Turkish, Urdu,
Indonesian, and others. The first *sura* (or section) of the Qur'an,
al-Fatiha, which is an essential part of the ritual prayers, is learned
and read in Arabic by Muslims in all parts of the world, and many
other verses and phrases in Arabic are also incorporated into the
lives of non-Arabic-speaking Muslims.

Muslim children start to learn portions of the Qur'an by heart in
their normal schooling: the tradition of learning the entire Qur'an by
heart started during the lifetime of the Prophet and continues to the
present day. A person attaining this distinction becomes known as a
hafiz, and this is still a prerequisite for admission to certain religious
schools in Muslim countries. Nowadays the Qur'an is recited a
number of times daily on the radio and television in the Muslim

world, and some Muslim countries devote a broadcasting channel for long hours daily exclusively to the recitation and study of the Qur'an. Muslims swear on the Qur'an for solemn oaths in the lawcourts and in everyday life.

The Life of Muhammad and the Historical Background

Muhammad was born in Mecca in about the year 570 CE. The religion of most people in Mecca and Arabia at the beginning of Muhammad's lifetime was polytheism. Christianity was found in places, notably in Yemen, and among the Arab tribes in the north under Byzantine rule; Judaism too was practised in Yemen, and in and around Yathrib, later renamed Madina (Medina), but the vast majority of the population of Arabia were polytheists. They believed in a chief god *Allah*, but saw other deities as mediators between them and him: the Qur'an mentions in particular the worship of idols, angels, the sun, and the moon as 'lesser' gods. The Hajj pilgrimage to the Ka'ba in Mecca, built, the Qur'an tells us, by Abraham for the worship of the one God, was practised but that too had become corrupted with polytheism. Mecca was thus an important centre for religion, and for trade, with the caravans that travelled via Mecca between Yemen in the south and Syria in the north providing an important source of income. There was no central government. The harsh desert conditions brought competition for scarce resources, and enforced solidarity within each tribe, but there was frequent fighting between tribes. Injustices were practised against the weaker classes, particularly women, children, slaves, and the poor.

Few hard facts are known about Muhammad's childhood. It is known that his father Abdullah died before he was born and his mother Amina when he was 6 years old; that his grandfather Abdul Muttalib then looked after him until, two years later, he too died. At the age of 8, Muhammad entered the guardianship of his uncle Abu Talib, who took him on a trade journey to the north when he was 12 years old. In his twenties, Muhammad was employed as a trader by a wealthy and well-respected widow fifteen years his senior named Khadija. Impressed by his honesty and good character, she proposed marriage to him. They were married for over twenty-five years until Khadija's death when Muhammad was some 49 years old. Khadija was a great support to her husband. After his marriage, Muhammad lived in Mecca, where he was a respected businessman and peacemaker.

Muhammad was in the habit of taking regular periods of retreat and reflection in the Cave of Hira outside Mecca. This is where the first revelation of the Qur'an came to him in 610 CE, when he was 40 years old. This initiated his prophethood. The Prophet was instructed to spread the teachings of the revelations he received to his larger family and beyond. However, although a few believed in him, the majority, especially the powerful, resented his calling them to abandon their gods. After all, many polytheist tribes came to Mecca on the pilgrimage, and the leaders feared that the new religion would threaten their own prestige and economic prosperity. They also felt it would disturb the social order, as it was quite outspoken in its preaching of equality between all people and its condemnation of the injustices done to the weaker members of the society.

The hostility of the Meccans soon graduated from gentle ridicule to open conflict and the persecution of Muhammad's followers, many of whom Muhammad sent, from the fifth year of his preaching, to seek refuge with the Christian king of Abyssinia (Ethiopia). The remaining Muslims continued to be pressurized by the Meccans, who instituted a total boycott against the Prophet's clan, refusing to allow any social or economic dealings with them. In the middle of this hardship, Muhammad's wife, Khadija, and his uncle, Abu Talib, died, so depriving the Prophet of their great support. This year became known as the Year of Grief. However, events were soon to take a change for the better. The Prophet experienced the event known as the Night Journey and Ascension to Heaven, during which Muhammad was accompanied by Gabriel from the sanctuary of Mecca first to Jerusalem and then to Heaven. Soon afterwards, some people from Yathrib, a town some 400 km north of Mecca, met Muhammad when they came to make the pilgrimage and some of these accepted his faith; the following year more returned from Yathrib, pledged to support him, and invited him and his community to seek sanctuary in Yathrib. The Muslims began to migrate there, soon followed by the Prophet himself, narrowly escaping an attempt to assassinate him. This move to Yathrib, known as the Migration (Hijra), was later adopted as the start of the Muslim calendar. Upon arrival in Yathrib, Muhammad built the first mosque in Islam, and he spent most of his time there, teaching and remoulding the characters of the new Muslims from unruly tribesmen into a brotherhood of believers. Guided by the Qur'an, he acted as teacher, judge, arbitrator, adviser, consoler, and father-figure to the new community. One of the reasons the people of Yathrib invited the Prophet to migrate there was the hope that he would be a good arbitrator between their warring tribes, as indeed proved to be the case.

Settled in Yathrib, Muhammad made a pact of mutual solidarity between the immigrants (*muhajirun*) and the Muslims of Yathrib, known as the *ansar*—helpers. This alliance, based not on tribal but on religious solidarity, was a departure from previous social norms. Muhammad also made a larger pact between all the tribes of Yathrib, that they would all support one another in defending the city against attack. Each tribe would be equal under this arrangement, including the Jews, and free to practise their own religions.

Islam spread quickly in Yathrib, which became known as Madinat al-Nabi (the City of the Prophet) or simply Medina (city). This was the period in which the revelations began to contain legislation on all aspects of individual and communal life, as for the first time the Muslims had their own state. In the second year at Medina (AH 2) a Qur'anic revelation came allowing the Muslims to defend themselves militarily (22: 38–41) and a number of battles against the Meccan disbelievers and their allies took place near Medina, starting with Badr shortly after this revelation, Uhud the following year, and the Battle of the Trench in AH 5. The Qur'an comments on these events.

In AH 6 the Meccans prevented the Muslims from undertaking a pilgrimage to Mecca. Negotiations followed, where the Muslims accepted that they would return to Medina for the time being but come back the following year to finish the pilgrimage. A truce was agreed for ten years. However, in AH 8 a Meccan ally broke the truce. The Muslims advanced to attack Mecca, but its leaders accepted Islam and surrendered without a fight. From this point onwards, delegations started coming from all areas of Arabia to meet the Prophet and make peace with him.

In AH 10 the Prophet made his last pilgrimage to Mecca and gave a farewell speech on the Mount of Mercy, declaring equality and solidarity between all Muslims. By this time the whole Arabian peninsula had accepted Islam and all the warring tribes were united in one state under one head. Soon after his return to Medina in the year 632 CE (AH 10), the Prophet received the last revelation of the Qur'an and, shortly thereafter, died. His role as leader of the Islamic state was taken over by Abu Bakr (632–4 CE), followed by 'Umar (634–44) and 'Uthman (644–56), who oversaw the phenomenal spread of Islam beyond Arabia. They were followed by 'Ali (656–61). These four leaders are called the Rightly Guided Caliphs.

After 'Ali, the first political dynasty of Islam, the Umayyads (661–750), came into power. There had, however, been some friction within the Muslim community on the question of succession to the Prophet after his death: the Shi'is, or supporters of 'Ali, felt that 'Ali and not Abu Bakr was the appropriate person to take on the mantle of head of the community. They believed that the leadership should then follow the line of descendants of the Prophet, through the Prophet's cousin and son-in-law 'Ali. After 'Ali's death, they adopted his sons Hasan and then Husayn as their leader or imam. After the latter's death in the Battle of Karbala in Iraq (680 CE/AH 61), Husayn took on a special significance for the Shi'i community: he is mourned every year on the Day of 'Ashura. Some Shi'i believe that the Prophet's line ended with the seventh imam Isma'il (d. 762 CE/AH 145); others believe that the line continued as far as a twelfth imam in the ninth century.

The Islamic state stretched by the end of its first century from Spain, across North Africa, to Sind in north-west India. In later centuries it expanded further still to include large parts of East and West Africa, India, Central and South-East Asia, and parts of China and southern Europe. Muslim migrants like the Turks and Tartars also spread into parts of northern Europe, such as Kazan and Poland. After the Second World War there was another major influx of Muslims into all areas of the world, including Europe, America, and Australia, and many people from these continents converted to the new faith. The total population of Muslims is now estimated at more than one billion (of which the great majority are Sunni), about one-fifth of the entire population of the world,[1] and Islam is said to be the fastest-growing religion in the world.

---

[1] See http://www.iiie.net/Intl/PopStats.html.

The Revelation of the Qur'an

Muhammad's own account survives of the extraordinary circumstances of the revelation, of being approached by an angel who commanded him: 'Read in the name of your Lord.'[2] When he explained that he could not read,[3] the angel squeezed him strongly, repeating the request twice, and then recited to him the first two lines of the Qur'an.[4] For the first experience of revelation Muhammad was alone in the cave, but after that the circumstances in which he received revelations were witnessed by others and recorded. When he experienced the 'state of revelation', those around him were able to observe his visible, audible, and sensory reactions. His face would become flushed and he would fall silent and appear as if his thoughts were far away, his body would become limp as if he were asleep, a humming sound would be heard about him, and sweat would appear on his face, even on winter days. This state would last for a brief period and as it passed the Prophet would immediately recite new verses of the Qur'an. The revelation could descend on him as he was walking, sitting, riding, or giving a sermon, and there were occasions when he waited anxiously for it for over a month in answer to a question he was asked, or in comment on an event: the state was clearly not the Prophet's to command. The Prophet and his followers understood these signs as the experience accompanying the communication of Qur'anic verses by the Angel of Revelation (Gabriel), while the Prophet's adversaries explained them as magic or as a sign of his 'being possessed'.

It is worth noting that the Qur'an has itself recorded all claims and attacks made against it and against the Prophet in his lifetime, but for many of Muhammad's contemporaries the fact that the first word of the Qur'an was an imperative addressed *to* the Prophet ('Read')

[2] These words appear at the beginning of Sura 96 of the Qur'an.

[3] Moreover, until the first revelation came to him in the cave, Muhammad was not known to have composed any poem or given any speech. The Qur'an employs this fact in arguing with the unbelievers: 'If God had so willed, I would not have recited it to you, nor would He have made it known to you. I lived a whole lifetime among you before it came to me. How can you not use your reason?' (10: 16). Among other things this is taken by Muslims as proof of the Qur'an's divine source.

[4] The concepts of 'reading', 'learning/knowing', and 'the pen' occur six times in these two lines. As Muslim writers on education point out (e.g. S. Qutb, *Fi Dhilal al-Qur'an* (Cairo, 1985), vi. 3939), the revelation of the Qur'an began by talking about reading, teaching, knowing, and writing.

linguistically made the authorship of the text outside Muhammad. Indeed, this mode is maintained throughout the Qur'an: it talks to the Prophet or talks about him; never does the Prophet pass comment or speak for himself. The Qur'an describes itself as a scripture that God 'sent down' to the Prophet (the expression 'sent down', in its various forms, is used in the Qur'an well over 200 times) and, in Arabic, this word conveys immediately, and in itself, the concept that the origin of the Qur'an is from above and that Muhammad is merely a recipient. God is the one to speak in the Qur'an: Muhammad is addressed, 'Prophet', 'Messenger', 'Do', 'Do not do', 'They ask you . . .', 'Say' (the word 'say' is used in the Qur'an well over 300 times). Moreover, the Prophet is sometimes even censured in the Qur'an.[5] His status is unequivocally defined as 'Messenger' (*rasul*).

The first revelation consisted of the two lines which began the Qur'an and the mission of the Prophet, after which he had no further experience of revelation for some while. Then another short piece was revealed, and between then and shortly before the Prophet's death in 632 CE at the age of 63 (lunar years), the whole text of the Qur'an was revealed gradually, piece by piece, in varying lengths, giving new teaching or commenting on events or answering questions, according to circumstances.

The Compilation of the Qur'an

With every new revelation, the Prophet would recite the new addition to the Qur'an to those around him, who would eagerly learn it and in turn recite it to others. Throughout his mission the Prophet repeatedly recited the Qur'an to his followers and was meticulous in ensuring that the Qur'an was recorded,[6] even in the days of persecution. As each new piece was revealed, Gabriel instructed the Prophet as to where it should go in the final corpus. An inner circle of his followers wrote down verses of the Qur'an as they learned them from

---

[5] 9: 43; 80: 1–11.

[6] The word *qur'an* means 'reading/reciting' and came to refer to 'the text which is read/recited'. The Muslim scripture often calls itself *kitab* 'writing', and this came to refer to 'the written book'. Thus the significance of uttering and writing the revealed scripture is emphasized from the very beginning of Islam, and is locked in the very nouns that designate the Qur'an.

the Prophet and there are records of there being a total of twenty-nine scribes for this. By the end of the Prophet's life (632 CE) the entire Qur'an was written down in the form of uncollated pieces. In addition, most followers learned parts of it by heart and many learned all of it from the Prophet over years spent in his company.[7] They also learned from the Prophet the correct ordering of the Qur'anic material.[8] They belonged to a cultural background that had a long-standing tradition of memorizing literature, history, and genealogy.

The standard Muslim account is that, during the second year after the Prophet's death (633 CE) and following the Battle of Yamama, in which a number of those who knew the Qur'an by heart died, it was feared that with the gradual passing away of such men there was a danger of some Qur'anic material being lost. Therefore the first caliph and successor to the Prophet, Abu Bakr, ordered that a written copy of the whole body of Qur'anic material as arranged by the Prophet and memorized by the Muslims should be made and safely stored with him.[9] About twelve years later, with the expansion of the Islamic state, the third caliph, 'Uthman, ordered that a number of copies should be made from this to be distributed to different parts of the Muslim world as the official copy of the Qur'an, which became known as the 'Uthmanic Codex. This codex has been recognized throughout the Muslim world for the last fourteen centuries as the authentic document of the Qur'an as revealed to the Prophet Muhammad.

The Structure of the Qur'an: Suras and Ayas

As explained above, Qur'anic revelation came to the Prophet gradually, piece by piece, over a period of twenty-three years. Material was placed in different sections, not in chronological order

[7] See Subhi al-Salih, *Mabahith fi 'Ulum al-Qur'an* (Beirut, 1981), 65–7.

[8] During the last twenty-five years there have been some views contesting this traditional history of the Qur'an and maintaining that it was canonized at a later date. The reader can consult a survey and discussion of these views in Angelika Neuwirth, 'The Qur'an and History: A Disputed Relationship', *Journal of Qur'anic Studies*, 5/1 (2003), 1–18. Also see H. Motzki, 'The Collection of the Qur'an: A Reconsideration of Western Views in Light of Recent Methodological Developments', *Der Islam* (2001), 2–34.

[9] The written fragments were another important source for the collation of this 'canonical' document.

of revelation, but according to how they were to be read by the Prophet and believers. The Qur'an is divided into 114 sections of varying lengths, the longest (section 2) being around twenty pages in Arabic, the shortest (sections 108 and 112) being one line in Arabic each. These sections are each known in Arabic as *sura*, and we will use this word to refer to them.

Each sura (with the exception of Sura 9) begins with 'In the Name of God, the Lord of Mercy, the Giver of Mercy', and a sura consists of a number of verses each known in Arabic as an *aya*. Again, an aya can run into several lines and consist of several sentences, or it can be one single word, but it normally ends in Arabic with a rhyme.

The titles of the suras require some explanation. Many suras combine several subjects within them, as will be explained below under 'Stylistic Features', and the titles were allocated on the basis of either the main theme within the sura, an important event that occurs in the sura, or a significant word that appears within it. The introductions to the suras in this translation are intended to help the reader in this respect.

Meccan and Medinan Suras

The Qur'anic material revealed to the Prophet in Mecca is distinguished by scholars from the material that came after the Migration (Hijra) to Medina. In the Meccan period, the Qur'an was concerned mainly with the basic beliefs in Islam—the unity of God as evidenced by His 'signs' (*ayat*),[10] the prophethood of Muhammad, and the Resurrection and Final Judgement—and these themes are reiterated again and again for emphasis and to reinforce Qur'anic teachings. These issues were especially pertinent to the Meccans. Most of them believed in more than one god. The Qur'an refers to this as *shirk* (partnership): the sharing of several gods in the creation and government of the universe. The reader will note the frequent use of 'partnership' and 'associate' throughout the Qur'an. The Meccans also initially denied the truth of Muhammad's message, and the Qur'an refers to earlier prophets (many of them also mentioned in the Bible, for instance Noah, Abraham, Jacob, Joseph,

---

[10] See e.g. 25: 1–33; 27: 59 ff.; 30: 17 ff.; 41: 53.

Moses, and Jesus),[11] in order both to reassure the Prophet and his followers that they will be saved, and to warn their opponents that they will be punished. The Qur'an stresses that all these prophets preached the same message and that the Qur'an was sent to confirm the earlier messages. It states that Muslims should believe in all of them without making any distinction between them (2: 285). The Meccans likewise could not conceive of the Resurrection of the Dead. In the Meccan suras the Qur'an gives arguments from embryology and from nature in general (36: 76–83; 56: 47–96; 22: 5–10) to explain how the Resurrection can and will take place; the Qur'an seeks always to convince by reference to history, to what happened to earlier generations, by explanations from nature, and through logic.

In the Medinan suras, by which time the Muslims were no longer the persecuted minority but an established community with the Prophet as its leader, the Qur'an begins to introduce laws to govern the Muslim community with regard to marriage, commerce and finance, international relations, war and peace. Examples of these can be found in Suras 2, 3, 4, 6, 8, and 9. This era also witnessed the emergence of a new group, the *munafiqun* or hypocrites, who pretended to profess Islam but were actually working against the Islamic state, and these 'hypocrites' are a frequent theme in the Medinan suras. We also see here discussion of the 'People of the Book' with particular reference to Jewish and Christian communities, both those contemporary with the Prophet and those in the past. It will be seen that the Qur'an tends to speak of groups or classes of people rather than individuals.

Throughout the Meccan and Medinan suras the beliefs and morals of the Qur'an are put forward and emphasized, and these form the bulk of Qur'anic material; the percentage of strictly legal texts in the Qur'an is very small indeed. The Qur'an contains some 6,200 verses and out of these only 100 deal with ritual practices, 70 verses discuss personal laws, 70 verses civil laws, 30 penal laws, and 20 judiciary matters and testimony.[12] Moreover, these tend to deal with general principles such as justice, kindness, and charity, rather than detailed laws: even legal matters are explained in language that appeals to the emotions, conscience, and belief in God. In verses dealing with retaliation (2: 178–9), once the principles are established

---

[11] See e.g. 2: 136; 3: 84–5; 6: 83–90; 42: 13.

[12] A. Khallaf, *A Concise History of Islamic Legislation* [Arabic] (Kuwait, 1968), 28–9.

the text goes on to soften the hearts of both parties: offender and victims. In introducing the obligation of the fast of Ramadan (2: 183–7), the aim throughout is to make the fast seem easy and highly desirable, and it is indeed perceived this way by Muslims. The month of Ramadan is a time of festivity and rejoicing.

Stylistic Features

The Qur'an has its own style. It may be useful to readers to mention some of the important features of this style. The reader should not expect the Qur'an to be arranged chronologically or by subject matter. The Qur'an may present, in the same sura, material about the unity and grace of God, regulations and laws, stories of earlier prophets and nations and the lessons that can be drawn from these, and descriptions of rewards and punishments on the Day of Judgement. This stylistic feature serves to reinforce the message, to persuade and to dissuade. This technique may appear to bring repetition of the same themes or stories in different suras but, as the Qur'an is above all a book of guidance, each sura adds to the fuller picture and to the effectiveness of the guidance. For instance, in the midst of discussion about divorce and settlements, it suspends the introduction of regulations and instructs the believers to keep up prayer and stand in obedience to God (2: 237–8), later to resume discussion of the divorce regulations. While urging people to give in charity, before the day comes when there will be no trade and no help from friends or intercessors, it shifts to the Throne verse (2: 255) to describe the glory of God and refer to the time when no one can intercede for anyone else. Afterwards, having reminded people of God's power, it resumes its injunctions to give in charity. In a religion that seeks to affect people's beliefs and behaviour in all aspects of life it is never sufficient to say something once or twice, and if the material on God, on earlier prophets, or on the Day of Judgement were each dealt with only once, the effect would not be so all-pervasive. This technique compresses many aspects of the Qur'anic message into any one sura, each forming self-contained lessons. This is particularly useful as it is rare for anyone to read the whole Qur'an at once: it is mainly used in short sections during worship and preaching, as well as by individuals or on television and radio in daily readings.

A central feature of Qur'anic style is contrast: between this world and the next (each occurring exactly 115 times), between believers and disbelievers, between Paradise and Hell. This has been studied in great detail, and scholars have found truly remarkable patterns of contrasts: angels and devils, life and death, secrecy and openness, and so on, occurring exactly the same number of times.[13] This sense of balance in the text is continued in passages where the Prophet is instructed to say, 'Now the truth has come from your Lord: let those who wish to believe in it do so, and let those who wish to reject it do so' (18: 29) and 'There is no compulsion in religion: true guidance has become distinct from error' (2: 256) (one of the names the Qur'an gives for itself is *al-Furqan*—the book that distinguishes [right from wrong] (25: 1)).

One stylistic feature that makes the Qur'an particularly effective is that God speaks directly to people (e.g. 56: 57–73) and to the Prophet, often using 'We', the first person plural of majesty, to represent Himself. It involves the readers/listeners by questioning, directing, and urging them, alternating this with information (e.g. 56: 47–74). The Qur'an is also full of dialogue between God and His prophets (e.g. Abraham in 2: 260; Noah in 11: 45–8), between prophets and their audiences (e.g. Salih and the Thamud people in 11: 61–5), and between different individuals (e.g. Solomon and the hoopoe, Solomon and his chieftains, and the Queen of Sheba talking to her advisers, all in 27: 19–44).

One of the obvious stylistic features of the Qur'an is the use of grammatical shifts from one personal pronoun to another (e.g. third to second to first person speaker; from singular to plural of majesty), and in the tenses of verbs. This is an accepted rhetorical practice in Arabic, similar to features used in some European literature. It is called in Arabic *iltifat* (i.e. 'turning' from one thing to another). One example (4: 114) is changing from talking about God, in the third person, to God Himself speaking in the first person plural of majesty: 'There is no good in most of their secret talk, only in commanding charity, or good, or reconciliation between people. To anyone who does these things, seeking to please God, We shall give a rich reward.' Instead of saying 'He will give him . . .', God speaks in the plural of majesty to give His personal guarantee of reward.[14]

[13] A. Nawfal, *al-I'jaz al-'Adadi lil-Qur'an il-Karim* (Cairo, 1976).
[14] M. Abdel Haleem, *Understanding the Qur'an: Themes and Style* (London: I.B. Tauris, 2001), 187–208.

The Qur'an always offers justification for its message, supporting it with logical argument, for example in explaining the unity of God (e.g. 21: 21–2; 23: 91; 36: 78–83). The Qur'an supports its statements with reference to the past (the history of earlier nations and prophets), to the present (to nature as a manifestation of God's wisdom, power, and care), and to the future (life in the Hereafter and Judgement), in addition of course to reminding people constantly of God and His attributes.

Another feature of the Qur'an is that it does not name individuals, with a few rare exceptions such as prophets and angels, but consistently uses techniques of generalization. One method of achieving this is the use of general words like 'those who' or 'whoever', giving the message universal application. Thus, in permitting Muslims to defend themselves, it gives permission generally to 'those who have been driven unjustly from their homes . . .' (22: 40 ff.). This will apply at any time or place. When it urges the Prophet to deliver the message, even when dealing with his own personal situation and feelings, instead of saying 'You should deliver the message and fear none but God', it speaks of 'those who deliver God's messages and fear only Him and no other: God's reckoning is enough' (33: 39). Reformers, preachers, and anyone standing for the truth can apply this readily to themselves, because such statements are put in a proverbial style. Verses of the Qur'an are therefore readily quoted and inscribed on plaques which can be hung on the walls of offices, houses, courtrooms, and so on as an inspiration or a reminder.

Issues of Interpretation

Over the years, a large body of commentaries on the Qur'an has accumulated, and differences in interpretation can be observed both between the various traditions within Islam (such as Sunni, Shi'i, or Sufi),[15] and between different periods in history. It is not the intention here to go into detail (see the Bibliography to this volume for useful works for further reading), but some illustrative examples may give the reader some understanding of the complexity and sophistication of views that arise from reading the Qur'an.

---

[15] For a definition of these terms see I. R. Netton, *A Popular Dictionary of Islam* (London: Curzon Press, 1992).

An important feature of the Qur'anic style is that it alludes to events without giving their historical background. Those who heard the Qur'an at the time of its revelation were fully aware of the circumstances. Later generations of Muslims had to rely on the body of literature explaining the circumstances of the revelations (*asbab al-nuzul*),[16] and on explanations and commentaries based on the written and oral records of statements by eyewitnesses. These oral testimonies were collected and later written down.

Interpretation is further complicated by the highly concise style of the Qur'an. A verse may contain several sentences in short, proverbial style, with pronominal references relating them to a wider context. Moreover, proverbial statements can be lifted from the text and used on their own, isolated from their context and unguided by other references in the Qur'an that might provide further explanation. Both non-Muslims eager to criticize Islam and some Islamic extremists have historically used this technique to justify their views.

Some examples will illustrate this feature, for instance the verse 'Slay them wherever you find them' (2: 191),[17] thus translated by Dawood and taken out of context, has been interpreted to mean that Muslims may kill non-Muslims wherever they find them. In fact the only situations where the Qur'an allows Muslims to fight are in self-defence and to defend the oppressed who call for help (4: 75), but even in the latter case this is restricted to those with whom the Muslims do not have treaty obligations (8: 72). The pronoun 'them' here refers to the words 'those who attack you' at the beginning of the previous verse. Thus the Prophet and his followers are here being allowed to fight the Meccans who attack them. The Qur'an makes many general statements but it is abundantly clear from the grammar and the context of this statement that this is not one of them.

'Wherever you find them' or 'come up against them' is similarly misunderstood. As exegetes and commentators explain, the Muslims

[16] The *asbab al-nuzul* are found in Qur'an commentaries. They identify the circumstances of the revelations and refer to names and details of what actually happened.

[17] N. J. Dawood's translation, *The Koran*, Penguin Classics (Harmondsworth, 1990). This has been used as the title of an article, ' "Slay them wherever you find them": Humanitarian Law in Islam', by James J. Busuttil of Linacre College, Oxford, in *Revue de droit pénal militaire et de droit de la guerre* (1991), 113–40.

were anxious that if their enemies attacked them in Mecca, which was and is a sanctuary (in which no Muslim is allowed to fight, or kill even an animal or plant), and they retaliated and killed, they would be breaking the law. The Qur'an simply reassured the Muslims that they could defend themselves when attacked, even if they killed their attackers, whether within the sanctuary or outside it. However, the six verses that concern war (2: 190–5) contain many restrictions and are couched in restraining language that appeals strongly to the Muslims' conscience. In six verses we find four prohibitions; seven restrictions (one 'until', four 'if', two 'who fight you'); as well as such cautions as 'in God's cause', 'be mindful of God', 'God does not love those who overstep the limits', 'He is with those who are mindful of Him', loves 'those who do good', and 'God is most forgiving and merciful'. The prevalent message of the Qur'an is one of peace and tolerance[18] but it allows self-defence.

Equally misinterpreted and taken out of context is what has become labelled as 'the sword verse' (9: 5) although the word 'sword' does not appear in the Qur'an: 'When the [four] forbidden months are over, wherever you find the polytheists, kill them, seize them, besiege them, ambush them'. The hostility and 'bitter enmity' of the polytheists and their *fitna* (persecution: 2: 193; 8: 39) of the Muslims during the time of the Prophet became so great that the disbelievers were determined to convert the Muslims back to paganism or finish them off: 'They will not stop fighting you [believers] until they make you revoke your faith, if they can' (2: 217). It was these hardened polytheists in Arabia, who would accept nothing other than the expulsion of the Muslims or their reversion to paganism, and who repeatedly broke their treaties, that the Muslims were ordered to treat in the same way—either to expel them or to accept nothing from them except Islam. But, even then, the Prophet and the Muslims were not simply to pounce on such enemies, reciprocating by breaking the treaty themselves: an ultimatum was issued, giving the enemy notice that, after the four sacred months mentioned in 9: 5 above, the Muslims would wage war on them.

Yet the main clause of the sentence—'kill the polytheists'—is singled out by some non-Muslims as representing the Islamic attitude to war; even some Muslims take this view and allege that

---

[18] See Abdel Haleem, *Understanding the Qur'an*.

this verse abrogated many other verses, including 'There is no compulsion in religion' (2: 256) and even, according to one solitary extremist, 'God is forgiving and merciful'. This far-fetched interpretation isolates and decontextualizes a small part of a sentence and of a passage, 9: 1–15, which gives many reasons for the order to fight such polytheists: they continually broke their agreements and aided others against the Muslims, they started hostilities against the Muslims, barred others from becoming Muslims, expelled them from the Holy Mosque and even from their own homes. At least eight times the passage mentions the misdeeds of these people against the Muslims. Moreover, consistent with restrictions on war elsewhere in the Qur'an, the immediate context of this 'sword verse' exempts such polytheists as do not break their agreements and who keep the peace with the Muslims (9: 7); it orders that those enemies seeking safe conduct should be protected and delivered to the place of safety they seek (9: 6). The whole of this context to verse 5, with all its restrictions, is ignored by those who simply isolate one part of a sentence to build on it their theory of war and violence in Islam.

One further cause for misinterpretation is the lack of awareness of the different meanings of a given term in different contexts (see below, 'This Translation: Identifying Aspects of Meaning'). Thus, for example, in Dawood's translation: 'He that chooses a religion other than Islam, it will not be accepted of him and in the world to come, he will be one of the lost' (3: 85),[19] it has to be borne in mind that the word *islam* in the Arabic of the Qur'an means complete devotion/submission to God, unmixed with worship of any other. All earlier prophets are thus described by the Qur'an as *muslim*. Those who read this word *islam* in the sense of the religion of the Prophet Muhammad will set up a barrier, illegitimately based on this verse, between Islam and other monotheistic religions. The Qur'an clearly defines its relationship with earlier scriptures by saying: 'He has sent the Scripture down to you [Prophet] with the Truth, confirming what went before: He sent down the Torah and the Gospel earlier as a guide for people' (3: 3–4). Indeed it urges the Christians and the Jews to practise their religion (5: 68, 45, 47). They are given the honorific title of 'People of the Book', and the Qur'an appeals to

---

[19] *The Koran*, translated by N. J. Dawood, Penguin Classics.

what is common between them: 'Say, "People of the Book, let us arrive at a statement that is common to us all: we worship God alone, we ascribe no partner to Him, and none of us takes others beside God as lords" ' (3: 64).

The Qur'an forbids arguing with the People of the Book except in the best way and urges the Muslims to say: 'We believe in what was revealed to us and in what was revealed to you; our God and your God are one [and the same]' (29: 46). God addresses Muslims, Jews, and Christians with the following: 'We have assigned a law and a path to each of you. If God had so willed, He would have made you one community, but He wanted to test you through that which He has given you, so race to do good: you will all return to God and He will make clear to you the matters you differed about' (5: 48). The Qur'an allows Muslims to eat the food of the People of the Book and marry their women (5: 5). These are explicit statements which Muslims involved in interfaith dialogue rely upon.

Misinterpretation is also observed with regard to the status of women. For example, 2: 228 'husbands have a degree [of right] over them [their wives]' has been variously interpreted by Muslims and non-Muslims to relegate women in general to a lower status, when in fact this cannot be based on this verse. The reference here is not to 'women' and 'men' but to 'wives' and 'husbands'. The context is in questions of divorce, between wives and husbands. Partly based on a misinterpretation of this verse, for example, most traditional scholars came to the view that Muslim women could not be judges, whereas Abu Hanifa (d. AH 150/767 CE), the founder of one of the four main schools of Islamic law, and modern jurists in many Muslim countries (although not all) do also allow women to be judges.

A further example of discrimination against women due to disregard of context is found in the way some scholars interpreted 2: 282. In urging the recording of a debt in writing, the Qur'an says: 'Call in two men as witnesses. If two men are not there, then call one man and two women out of those you approve as witnesses, so that if one of the two women should forget the other can remind her.'[20] The majority view was to generalize this to all testimony and all

---

[20] Many translate *tadilla* as 'err', not realizing that one of the many meanings (*wujuh*) of the verb is 'forget'.

other situations. The fact is that the verse should be seen in its context, where the Qur'an is insisting on the protection of people's property. In the preceding pages, it urges wealthy people to give in charity, but it then turns in the above verse to ensure that their money is not taken fraudulently or through neglect. After urging the wealthy to give free loans (as opposed to charging interest) for the sake of God, it urges in the strongest manner the recording of any loan agreement. In the longest verse in the Qur'an (twelve lines in Arabic) it gives instructions on how to secure the agreement in writing and by testimony to avoid conflict or loss of the lender's money. It calls on people to do this in a cultural environment where women generally were less involved in money matters and calculations than men, and less literate. Modern interpreters take the view that the cultural context is different now and that a woman can be as well educated as a man, or even better. Therefore they confine this verse to its cultural context and allow a woman now to give witness alone, just as she is allowed to be a judge on her own.

It is in the nature of central religious scriptures to be open to endless interpretation and enlisted to justify all shades of opinion, and these are just a few examples of misinterpretation, which can become further complicated with mistranslation. The Qur'an itself predicts in 3: 7 that some people will deliberately interpret certain verses in a skewed way; the Arabic of the Qur'an is very concise and attracted a sophisticated body of exegesis and commentary, including interpretations by those wishing to derive authoritative foundations for their sometimes extremist ideologies. It is the job of the translator to bring his or her reader as close as is possible to the meaning of the original Arabic, utilizing the tools of solid linguistic analysis and looking at it in the context of its own stylistic features, but in a language that is comprehensible to the non-specialist majority. The Qur'an was after all first addressed to the Arabs in their own language, 'to make things clear' (see for example 12: 2; 43: 3).

A Short History of English Translations

The history of translation of the Qur'an is a long and interesting one. The title itself has often been rendered in English as 'Koran', but this older Anglicized form is gradually being replaced by 'Qur'an', which reflects the correct Arabic transliteration and pronunciation of the word. The first translation into English was done in 1649 by Alexander Ross, a grammar school teacher in Southampton. However, Ross unfortunately did not know Arabic and made his translation from one in French by André du Ryer. The translation is at times widely different from the original. Ross's title is indicative of his attitude. He describes it as *The Alcoran of Mahomet translated . . . and newly Englished, for the satisfaction of all that desire to look into the Turkish vanities*. A century later, in 1734, George Sale's Protestant translation was the next version of the Qur'an to be presented in English, and his italicized commentaries, embedded in the text, helped to make the Qur'an more understandable to an English-speaking audience. For centuries this was one of the most successful translations, in both the UK and the USA, and it continued to be printed throughout the first half of the twentieth century. It is still available for consultation in many academic libraries.

In 1861 the Revd J. M. Rodwell undertook a translation of the Qur'an. His perspective on the Qur'an was a strongly biblical one.[21] One oddity is his disregard for the traditional Muslim arrangement of the suras, rearranging them into what he thought to be the chronological order; moreover some of his footnotes include material that is incorrect and offensive to Muslims. Nonetheless he had a linguistic talent that enabled him to come up with innovative solutions to previously intractable problems. It is easy to perceive the influence of Rodwell's work on many subsequent translators. Rodwell also instigated the practice of partial numbering of Qur'anic verses, providing some help to those wishing to cite passages from his translation.

The next translator of the Qur'an into English, E. H. Palmer (1840–82), is claimed to be the first who had direct and long-lasting contact with Arabs and sought, in style, to retain some of the 'rude, fierce eloquence' of the Qur'an but without becoming 'too rude or familiar'. His translation appeared in 1880. He was the first to reflect, in his footnotes, some real respect for the text and the Prophet of Islam. The first British Muslim to translate the Qur'an, however, was the novelist and vicar's son Muhammad Marmaduke

---

[21] In his notes he is over-eager to claim biblical sources for Qur'anic material, and quick to claim that there are contradictions between verses where none exists.

Pickthall. He undertook a new translation (published in 1930) after observing that some of the earlier translations included 'commentation offensive to Muslims and employed a style of language which Muslims at once recognise as unworthy'. Although his language may now seem almost artificially archaic, his translation keeps close to the original Arabic, and is still very popular among Arabs and Muslims. The next significant translation was written by Abdullah Yusuf Ali, an Indian Muslim, and appeared in 1934. This text, entitled *The Holy Qur'an: Text, Translation and Commentary*, has appeared in numerous editions, normally including the Arabic text parallel with the translation, along with 6,310 explanatory notes, 300 pieces of running commentary in blank verse, fourteen appendices and indices. It is an extremely useful work, especially his notes and indices, for those who want a fuller and more guided understanding of the background and text of the Qur'an. His language contains poetic features and archaic words that make the style outdated.

Arthur J. Arberry's translation, *The Koran Interpreted*, appeared in 1955 and is undoubtedly one of the most respected translations of the Qur'an in English. Arberry shows great respect towards the language of the Qur'an, particularly its musical effects. His careful observation of Arabic sentence structure and phraseology makes his translation very close to the Arabic original in grammatical terms. To those unfamiliar with the text itself, this feature, along with the lack of any notes or comments, can make the text seem difficult to understand and confusingly unidiomatic. However, it remains a popular version of the text, particularly in academic circles.

In the following year (1956), N. J. Dawood produced his translation for Penguin Books. His stated aim was above all to make the language modern and readable, and he certainly succeeds in this, when one compares it with the translations available at the time. However, from the beginning his translation was seen to take too many liberties with the text of the Qur'an and to contain many inaccuracies, as was immediately pointed out by reviewers; moreover, many Muslims were deeply offended by the way he translated key terms and by some of the notes to the translation.

In 1980 an English translation by Muhammad Asad was published. He was an Austrian (Leopold Weiss) who converted to Islam. He called it *The Message of the Qur'an, Translated and Explained*. It contains a parallel Arabic text, 5,371 very useful notes, and four appendices. Asad is one of the most original translators, who did the background research for himself in the original lengthy Arabic exegeses. His language and choice of words too are original, but he inserts many bracketed explanatory words which, though useful, make his sentences cumbersome. Also his 'rationalistic' approach leads him to translations that some Muslim theologians disagree with: for example, his translation of 50: 17 as 'the two demands of his nature . . .' rather than 'recording [angels]', or *hammim* in 56: 93 as 'burning despair' rather than 'scalding water'.

There is not enough space here for an exhaustive survey of all English translations; we have mentioned only some important or popular ones from the past and present.

This Translation

General Style

This translation is intended to go further than previous works in accuracy, clarity, flow, and currency of language. It is written in a modern, easy style, avoiding where possible the use of cryptic language or archaisms that tend to obscure meaning. The intention is to make the Qur'an accessible to everyone who speaks English, Muslims or otherwise, including the millions of people all over the world for whom the English language has become a lingua franca. The message of the Qur'an was, after all, directly addressed to all people without distinction as to class, gender, or age: it does not rely on archaisms or pompous language for effect. Although the language of the present translation is simple and straightforward, it is hoped that it does not descend to an inappropriate level.

Special attention has been paid to certain criteria which, if ignored, could have led to confusion, misrepresentation of the Arabic meaning, or a translation comprehensible only to an academic or enthusiast. The present translator fully recognizes how very difficult the task is of translating the Qur'an, and the following remarks are not meant to belittle the efforts or qualities of previous translators, all of whom have made a useful contribution, but merely to illustrate how the methodology utilized in this present translation can lead to enhanced accuracy and clarity of meaning.

Intertextuality

It has frequently been remarked that different parts of the Qur'an explain each other, and utilization of the relationship between the parts of the Qur'an was considered by Ibn Taymiyya (d. 1328 CE) to be the most correct method. He explained: 'What is stated in a general way in one place is explained in detail in another; what is stated briefly in one place is explained at length in another.' The reader will find in the footnotes to the translation examples of how useful this technique is in explaining the meaning of ambiguous passages of the Qur'an.

Context

Context is crucial in interpreting the meaning of any discourse, Qur'anic or otherwise. For instance, when the Prophet was fleeing from Mecca for his life, he hid with Abu Bakr in a cave on the route to Medina. His Meccan enemies were pursuing him, but they passed by the mouth of the cave and lost the trail, enabling the Prophet eventually to reach Medina unharmed. In this translation the Qur'anic passage that describes the Prophet's experience as he waited tensely in the cave is rendered: 'God sent His calm down to him, aided him with forces invisible to you, *and brought down the disbelievers' plan*. God's plan is higher' (9: 40), but Dawood pursues the warlike metaphor implied in 'forces invisible to you' (understood by the commentators to include a spider that distracted the pursuers from looking into the cave by weaving a cobweb across the entrance to it) to render the passage as: 'God caused His tranquillity to descend upon him and sent to his aid invisible warriors so that *he routed the unbelievers* and exalted the Word of God.' He takes the subject of routed/brought down to be Muhammad rather than the contextually evident God, and consequently produces an incorrect translation of the Arabic text which does not match the context of the passage, in which the Prophet was utterly helpless, taking refuge in the cave.

Identifying Aspects of Meaning

Key terms are frequently used in the Qur'an with different meanings for different contexts, a feature known in Arabic as *wujuh al-Qur'an*. These were recognized from the early days of Qur'anic exegesis and have been highlighted in many publications.[22] As will be shown later, ignoring this feature and forcing upon a word one single meaning for the sake of consistency results in denial of the context and mis-representation of the material. There are numerous concepts of the Qur'an which illustrate this feature, including *amr*, *jihad*, *awliya*, and *taqwa*. Thus *amr* is commonly translated as 'command' when in many situations it has other meanings, including 'matter' and 'affair'; *jihad* is commonly translated as 'fighting', although in cer-tain situations it is more appropriate to render it as 'struggle'; *awliya* is commonly translated as 'friends' when it in fact generally means 'allies' or 'supporters'; and *taqwa* is commonly translated as 'fear of God', but the true meaning is closer to the concept of 'being mindful of God'. It is important for the translator to recognize when it is appropriate to be consistent in the translation of a repeated term, and when to reflect the context. This also applies to such funda-mental terms as *islam*, *muslimun*, *kafirun*, *fasiqun*, *dhalimun*, and *din*. Arabic classical dictionaries include varieties of meanings for these terms.

Arabic Structure and Idiom

Throughout this translation, care has been taken to avoid unneces-sarily close adherence to the original Arabic structures and idioms, which almost always sound unnatural in English. Literal translations of Arabic idioms often result in meaningless English. Moreover, the Arabic language at the time of the Qur'an was very concise. Parts of the sentence could be omitted because they were well understood from the context, and elision is a marked feature in the Qur'an: sometimes whole clauses are elided. This type of elision is particu-larly noticeable in conditional sentences, in oaths, and in contrasts (e.g. 11: 17; 50: 1; 13: 31; and 38: 9). In some cases it is possible to use dots to indicate that something is missing. In others it is better to supply the omitted clause.

Another example where adhering to Arabic can be misleading is in the description of Paradise, regularly described in the Qur'an as

---

[22] For classical studies see Bibliography: Ibn Sulayman; al-Mubarrad; and Ibn al-Jawzi. A useful modern study that recognizes this feature is Toshihiko Izutsu, *The Structure of the Ethical Terms in the Koran: A Study in Semantics* (Tokyo: Keio University, 1959).

having streams. A literal translation of the Arabic phrase *tajri min tahtiha al-anhar* is thought by some to be 'under which rivers flow'. This may, however, suggest to the English reader that the rivers flow underground, which is not what is meant in Arabic; rather the image is of a shady garden watered by many streams. The present translation gives 'graced with flowing streams'. 'Graced' was intended to convey the generosity in God's gift to the people of Paradise implicit in the Qur'anic text; the adjective 'flowing' is taken from the Arabic verb *tajri* used in connection with these 'rivers'; while 'streams' was chosen above the more general 'rivers' as the impression is one of many small rivulets coursing throughout the garden, keeping it watered, beautiful, and fresh. In classical Arabic, the term *nahr* applies to any body of running water, from the smallest of streams to the widest of rivers. In modern Arabic the term has become restricted to rivers and this may in some cases have led to a misunderstanding of the term.

Also problematic can be a particular kind of rhetorical question, frequent in the Qur'an, which expresses disapproval through its grammatical structure rather than by any lexical addition. It was decided for this translation to use 'How' to convey this sense of disapproval. For instance, in describing the actions of the disbelievers in 16: 72 the present translation gives 'How can they believe in falsehood and deny God's blessings?'; in the question posed by the disbelievers in 17: 94, 'How could God have sent a human being as a messenger?' The literal translations 'Do they believe in falsehood?' or 'Has God sent a human being?' would not convey the disapproval inherent in the Arabic original.

In other instances a literal translation of the Arabic would produce a text incomprehensible to most readers. Thus for example 20: 113, which describes the contents of the Qur'an, translated literally as 'We have turned about in it something of threats', is here rendered as 'We have . . . given all kinds of warnings in it.' Or 74: 45 'we plunged *along with the plungers*' has been adapted in this translation to 'we indulged with others [in mocking the believers]'.

Pronouns

Identifying the proper reference of pronouns is problematic in the Qur'an since these sometimes shift in the same verse with the risk of ambiguity and distortion of meaning if these shifts are not correctly identified. There are numerous examples in the Qur'an where there is a change of addressee from Prophet to believers and others and vice versa. Like many other languages, Arabic distinguishes between 'you' singular and 'you' plural; in modern English 'you' is used for singular and plural without distinction. Yet in the Arabic of the Qur'an, in almost all cases where 'you' is used in the singular it is the Prophet who is being addressed. In this translation, therefore, 'Prophet' is added to the English text where it is clear that it is he who is being addressed, to make the passages as clear in English as they are in Arabic. This is particularly important in passages where, within the same verse, there is a shift between plural and singular address. For example in 10: 61 the Arabic reads 'In whatever matter you (singular, therefore addressing the Prophet) may be engaged and whatever part of the Qur'an you (singular, therefore addressing the Prophet) are reciting, whatever work you (plural, therefore addressing the whole community) are doing, We witness you (plural) when you (plural) are engaged in it.'

Classical Usage

It is important to identify the meaning of Arabic words as used at the time of the revelation of the Qur'an rather than the one(s) they have acquired in modern Arabic. The present translation has placed great emphasis on information gleaned from classical Arabic dictionaries, including the *Lisan al-'Arab* by Ibn Mandhur, *al-Qamus al-Muhit* by al-Fayruzabadi, and *al-Mu'jam al-Wasit* by the Arabic Language Academy in Cairo. It is interesting to give an example of how the semantic spread of a certain key term has changed: *walad* in classical (Qur'anic) Arabic means the non-gender-specific 'child' or 'children', while in modern Arabic it can only mean 'boy' or 'son'. The claim of the pagan Arabs that God has *walad* is repeated several times in the Qur'an. As the Meccans believed that the angels were the daughters, not the sons, of God, it is immediately evident that the modern meaning of *walad* is too restrictive to express accurately the intended meaning of the classical Arabic original in this context. Although later, in Medina, references were made to the Christian belief that Jesus was the son of God, to use 'son' when talking about the beliefs of Meccan Arabs is incorrect and misleading.

Paragraphing and Punctuation

The Arabic convention throughout the ages has been to put each sura in one continuous paragraph, however many pages this may entail. This is clearly not normal usage in English. It can furthermore make the volume seem overwhelming to someone not familiar with its contents. In order to clarify the meaning and structure of thoughts and to meet the expectation of modern readers, the present translation divides the material into paragraphs. We have also marked the beginning of each verse with its number in superscript small type so as to aid those who wish to consult specific passages (while not, we hope, interrupting the flow or distracting the reader). This combination is new in presenting the Qur'an and should add to the clarity and help quick reference to every verse in the Qur'an. Among the current translations there are two conventions, either to break each sura into individual verses given on separate lines, or to use free-flowing paragraphs but to give the verse numbers only at intervals of five or ten verses. Neither of these systems is satisfactory: the first makes the translations look, in places, more like a list than a text and interrupts the flow and indeed the understanding of the text as a whole, while the second system leaves the reader unable to ascertain where the intervening verses begin and end, something which is extremely important for the referencing and cross-referencing which contributes so much to understanding the meaning of the text.

Nor does the Arabic Qur'an use a system of punctuation in the same way as modern English. The Qur'an has its own system of marking pauses, indeed a whole branch of study is devoted to it,[23] but the now conventional system of commas, full stops, colons and semicolons, question marks, dashes, quotation marks, etc. is not used in the Qur'an. These have been carefully and consciously introduced into this translation. The quotation marks are important because the Qur'an very frequently presents dialogue and direct speech, sometimes not introduced or even attributed, yet it is imperative to identify in the translation where one speaker ends and another begins. Dashes have frequently been used because there is a feature of Qur'anic language, long recognized by Arab scholars, where for

---

[23] *'Ilm al-waqf wa 'l-ibtida'.*

instance the Qur'an will report the views of disbelievers and inter-rupt their statement with comments such as 'so they claim'. Also, sometimes it will break the expounding of a general argument with a more detailed episode, before going back to the general argument. Such material is placed between dashes in this translation in order to make the sentence structure and the flow of ideas clearer. Colons are used especially near the end of verses, where a short statement concludes and comments on the sentence.

Sometimes it has been necessary to break what might appear to be a single sentence into smaller units, in order to avoid creating sen-tences that were several lines long, and in order to solve problems of shifting pronouns in Arabic: an important stylistic feature of the Qur'an called *iltifat* (grammatical shifts for rhetorical purposes) mentioned earlier. Thus, in one verse, there can be shifts in pro-nouns from first to second to third person or changes in tense from present to future. This clearly does not correspond to the norms of English sentence structure. One solution was to break up even short verses which have been traditionally kept together to the detriment of clarity. Sometimes it happened that a new paragraph was even started mid-verse in an attempt to solve stylistic difficulties.

Footnotes and Explanatory Introductions

In order not to overburden or overzealously guide the reader with extensive commentaries, only short introductions to the suras have been supplied. These are designed to help the reader by identifying where the title comes from, and giving some information on the background and the general structure of the sura. The footnotes are meant to be minimal, and to explain allusions, references, and cul-tural background only when it was felt these were absolutely neces-sary to clarify meaning and context. Sometimes the footnotes explain reasons for departing from accepted translations, give alter-natives, or make cross-references. The footnotes also give explan-ations (where they are considered to be helpful or of interest) of ambiguous passages which are made clear in the Arabic commentar-ies on the Qur'an, classical and modern. Particular use was made of Fakhr al-Din al-Razi's twelfth-century *Mafatih al-Ghayb*, Abu Hayyan's early fourteenth-century *al-Bahr al-Muhit* (Beirut, 1993), and Baydawi's late fourteenth-century *Anwar al-Tanzil wa Asrar al-Ta'wil*.

Razi must be singled out as the most useful tool in understanding the Qur'an. He is an all-round linguist *par excellence*, noting and discussing linguistic questions missed by perhaps all the others, and opening up areas for discussion where others do not. He is always aware of the context and the position of the verse in the whole structure of the sura. His mind is mathematical, analytical, as he spells out the linguistic function of each verse or statement. He cites as many references and opinions as possible and normally evaluates them, using other verses of the Qur'an and references to Arabic poetry as well as other commentaries. All these qualities mark his thought patterns as the most 'modern' of all the commentators, his linguistic analysis illuminated by philosophy, logic, and reason.

ACKNOWLEDGEMENTS
In preparing this translation the intention was to produce easily readable, clear contemporary English, as free as possible from the Arabism and archaism that marked some previous translations, while remaining true to the original Arabic text. With these aims, it was necessary to have the text read by native speakers of English, mainly graduates in English and Arabic, including some of my former MA students. I am especially grateful to the following individuals, who have provided very useful suggestions: Matthew Shorter, Maureen O'Rourke, James Howarth, and in particular Marianna Klar, whose acute attention to detail and meticulous accuracy were most import-ant in adding corrections to the typescript and in reading the whole text more than once. I am also grateful to Gemma Tighe, who typed the first draft, to Elsaid Badawi and Abdel Rahman Haleem for helpful discussions and suggestions, but above all, I am most indebted to my wife, Harfiyah, for her invaluable work throughout the editorial process, and for her assiduous proof-reading. Finally, I would like to mention with appreciation the highly professional, thorough, and painstaking treatment the text has received from Judith Luna, Elizabeth Stratford, and other OUP staff. Judith Luna, as commissioning editor, has encouraged me throughout, with patience, understanding, and enthusiastic commitment to the project.

M. A. S. Abdel Haleem

A CHRONOLOGY OF THE QUR'AN

*c.*570   Birth of Muhammad (his father died before his birth)

576   Death of Muhammad's mother when he is 6

578   Death of Muhammad's grandfather

595   Muhammad's marriage to Khadija

*c.*610   First revelation of Qur'an

615   First migration of Muslims to Abyssinia seeking refuge from persecution in Mecca

615   'Umar ibn al-Khattab converts to Islam after reading a written Qur'anic passage his believing sister was trying to hide from him

619   Death of Khadija and Abu Talib (the Prophet's uncle and support)

620   Muhammad's 'Night Journey to Jerusalem and Ascension to Heaven'

622   Migration to Medina (Hijra) and starting date of Muslim calendar

624   Battle of Badr: the Muslims defeat the much larger Meccan army

625   Battle of Uhud: Meccan army defeat Muslims

627   Battle of the Trench—Meccans fail to take Medina and retreat

628   Treaty of Hudaybiyya: truce with the Meccan alliance, allowing peaceful preaching of Islam and so many converts

630   Truce broken by a tribe allied to Mecca; Mecca's surrender to the Muslims and acceptance of Islam

630   Battle of Hunayn

631   Expedition to Tabuk

631   The Year of Embassies—Islam accepted by all the Arabian tribes. Muhammad concludes treaties of peace with the Christian chief of al-Aqaba and the Jewish tribes in the oases of Maqna, Adhruh, and Jarba to the south

632   Muhammad's farewell pilgrimage to Mecca

      8 June   Death of Muhammad in Medina

633   Qur'an collected into one volume by Abu Bakr

645   'Uthman commissions copies of the Qur'an to be made and circulated

1153   First Latin translation of the Qur'an

1543   First printed edition (Basle) with a preface by Martin Luther

1649   Alexander Ross makes first translation of the Qur'an into English (from French)

1734   George Sale's translation of the Qur'an
1861   J. M. Rodwell's translation of the Qur'an
1880   E. H. Palmer's translation of the Qur'an
1930   Muhammad Marmaduke Pickthall's translation of the Qur'an
1934   Abdullah Yusuf Ali's translation of the Qur'an
1955   Arthur J. Arberry's translation of the Qur'an
1956   N. J. Dawood's translation of the Qur'an
1980   Muhammad Asad's translation of the Qur'an

SELECT BIBLIOGRAPHY

General Reference Works

Beeston, A. F. L., Johnstone, T. M., Serjeant, R. B., and Smith, G. R. (eds.), 'Bibliography of Translations of the Qur'an into European Languages', in *Arabic Literature to the End of the Umayyad Period*, Cambridge History of Arabic Literature (Cambridge: Cambridge University Press, 1983).

Esposito, John L., *Oxford Encyclopaedia of the Modern Islamic World* (Oxford: Oxford University Press, 1999).

Hazard, Harry W., *Atlas of Islamic History* (Princeton: Princeton University Press, 1954).

McAuliffe, J. D. (ed.), *Encyclopaedia of the Qur'an* (Leiden: E. J. Brill, 2001), vols. i and ii (A–D; E–I). Two more volumes to follow.

Robinson, Francis, *An Atlas of the Islamic World since 1500* (Oxford: Oxford University Press, 1982).

Other Translations

For extensive commentaries in English:

Asad, M., *The Message of the Qur'an, Translated and Explained* (Gibraltar: Dar al-Andalus, 1980; repr. 1997).

Yusuf Ali, A., *The Holy Qur'an: Text, Translation and Commentary* (1934; many editions).

Studies of the Qur'an

Abbott, N., *Studies in Arabic Literary Papyri*, ii. *Qur'anic Commentary and Tradition* (Chicago: University of Chicago Press, 1967). See also *Studies in Arabic Literary Papyri*, iii. *Language and Literature* (Chicago: University of Chicago Press, 1972).

Abdel Haleem, M., *Understanding the Qur'an: Themes and Style* (London and New York: I.B. Tauris, 2001).

—— (ed.), *Journal of Qur'anic Studies* (Edinburgh: Edinburgh University Press, 1999–).

Bell, R., and Watt, W. M., *Introduction to the Qur'an* (Edinburgh: Edinburgh University Press, 1970).

Boullata, I. J., *Literary Structures of Religious Meaning in the Qur'an* (London: Curzon Press, 2000).

Cook, M., *The Koran: A Very Short Introduction* (Oxford: Oxford University Press, 2000).

Draz, M. A., *Introduction to the Qur'an* (London and New York: I.B. Tauris, 2000).

Hawting, G., and Sharif, A., *Approaches to the Qur'an* (London: Routledge, 1993).

Izutsu, T., *The Structure of the Ethical Terms in the Koran: A Study in Semantics* (Tokyo: Keio University, 1959).

Motzki, H., 'The Collection of the Qur'an: A Reconsideration of Western Views in Light of Recent Methodological Developments', *Der Islam* (2001), 2–34.

Nelson, K. L., *The Art of Reciting the Qur'an* (Austin: University of Texas Press, 1985).

Rahman, F., *Major Themes of the Qur'an* (Minneapolis: Bibliotheca Islamica Inc., 1980).

Rippin, A., *Approaches to the History of the Interpretation of the Qur'an* (Oxford: Oxford University Press, 1988).

Robinson, N., *Discovering the Qur'an* (London: SCM Press, 1996).

Tottoli, R., *Biblical Prophets in the Quran and Muslim Literature* (Richmond, Surrey: Curzon, 2002).

Versteegh, C. H. M., *Arabic Grammar and Qur'anic Exegesis in Early Islam* (Leiden: E. J. Brill, 1993).

von Denffer, A., *Ulum al-Qur'an: An Introduction to the Sciences of the Qur'an* (Leicester: Islamic Foundation, 1994).

The Life of Muhammad

Cook, M., *Muhammad*, Past Masters (Oxford: Oxford University Press, 1983).

Guillaume, A., *The Life of Muhammad* (Oxford: Oxford University Press, 2002).

Lings, M., *Muhammad: His Life Based on the Earliest Sources* (Cambridge: Islamic Texts Society, 1991).

Watt, W. Montgomery, *Muhammad: Prophet and Statesman* (Oxford: Oxford University Press, 1974).

Introductions to Islam

Arnold, Thomas W., *The Preaching of Islam* (London: Constable, 1913).

Endress, Gerhard, *An Historical Introduction to Islam*, 2nd edn., Islamic Surveys (Edinburgh: Edinburgh University Press, 2002).

Esposito, John L., *Islam, The Straight Path* (Oxford: Oxford University Press, 1998).

Rahman, Fazlur, *Islam*, 2nd edn. (Chicago: University of Chicago Press, 1979).

Robinson, Neal, *Islam: A Concise Introduction* (London: Curzon, 1999).

Ruthven, Malise, *Islam: A Very Short Introduction* (Oxford: Oxford University Press, 2000).

Arabic Works Cited in Footnotes

Abū Ḥayyān, *al-Baḥr al-Muḥīṭ* (many editions).

Arabic Language Academy, Cairo, *al-Muʿjam al-Wasīṭ* (Istanbul: Dār al-Daʿwa, 1989).

al-Bayḍāwī, *Anwār al-Tanzīl wa Asrār al-Taʾwīl* (many editions).

al-Bukhārī, *Ṣaḥīḥ* (many editions).

al-Fayrūzabādī, *al-Qāmūs al-Muḥīṭ* (many editions).

Ḥassān, Tammām, *al-Lugha al-ʿArabiya Maʿnāhā wa Mabnāhā* (Cairo: Al-Hayʾa al-Miṣriyya al-ʿĀmma, 1973).

Ḥassān, Tammām, *al-Bayān fī Rawāʾiʿ al-Qurʾān* (Cairo: ʿĀlam al-Kutub, 1993).

Ibn ʿAbdul-Salām, ʿIzz al-Dīn, *Majāz al-Qurʾān* (London: Al-Furqān Foundation, 1999).

Ibn al-Jawzī, ʿAbd al-Raḥmān (d. AH 597/1201 CE), *Nuzhat al-Aʿyun al-Nawāẓir fī ʿilm al-Wujūh wa al-Naẓāʾir* (Beirut, 1985 and many edns.).

Ibn Sulaymān, Muqātil (d. AH 150/767 CE), *al-Ashbāh wa al-Naẓāʾir fī al-Qurʾān al-Karīm* (Cairo, 1975).

al-Iṣfahānī, al-Rāghib, *Mufradāt al-Rāghib* (many editions).

Lane, E. W., *Arabic–English Lexicon* (Beirut: Librairie du Liban, 1968).

Mubarrad, Muḥammad ibn Yazīd (d. AH 286/899 CE), *Ma Ittafaqa Lafẓuhu wa Ikhtalafa Maʿnāhu fī al-Qurʾān al-Majīd* (Cairo, AH 1350/1931 CE).

Omar, A. M., and Makram, A. S., *Muʿjam al-Qiraʾāt al-Qurʾānīyya* (Tehran: Intisharāt Uswa, 1999).

Qutb, Sayyid, *Fī Zilāl al-Qurʾān* (Cairo, 1985).

al-Rāzī, Fakhr al-Dīn, *al-Tafsīr al-Kabīr* or *Mafātīḥ al-Ghayb*, 3rd edn. (Beirut: Dar Ihyaʾ al-Turāth al-ʿArabi, n.d.).

al-Ṣaliḥ, Ṣubḥi, *Mabāḥith fī ʿulūm al-Qurʾān* (Beirut, 1981).

Suyūṭī, *Tafsīr al-Jalālayn* (many editions).

al-Tirmidhī, *Jāmiʿ al-Tirmidhī* (many editions).

Zamakhsharī, *al-Kashshāf* (many editions).

Zamakhsharī, *Asās al-Balāgha* (many editions).

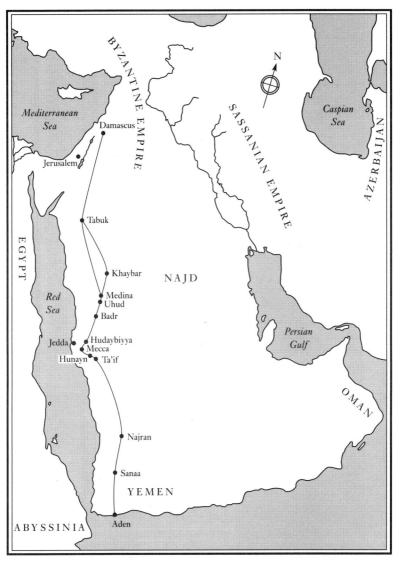

Map of Arabia showing places at the time of the revelation of the Qur'an (612–32 CE), most located along the north–south trade route between Aden and Damascus.

THE QUR'AN

1. THE OPENING

This sura is seen to be a precise table of contents of the Qur'anic message. It is very important in Islamic worship, being an obligatory part of the daily prayer, repeated several times during the day.

[1] In the name of God, the Lord of Mercy,[a] the Giver[b] of Mercy![c] [2] Praise belongs to God, Lord[d] of the Worlds,[e] [3] the Lord of Mercy, the Giver of Mercy, [4] Master of the Day of Judgement. [5] It is You we worship; it is You we ask for help. [6] Guide us to the straight path: [7] the path of those You have blessed, those who incur no anger[f] and who have not gone astray.

[a] Most occurrences of this term *rahman* in the Qur'an are in the context of Him being mighty and majestic as well as merciful. The addition of the word 'Lord' here is intended to convey this aspect of the term.

[b] This term *rahim* is an intensive form suggesting that the quality of giving mercy is inherent in God's nature.

[c] This is the only instance where this formula, present at the start of every sura but one, is counted as the first numbered verse.

[d] The Arabic root *r–b–b* has connotations of caring and nurturing in addition to lordship, and this should be borne in mind wherever the term occurs and is rendered 'lord'.

[e] *Al-'alamin* in Arabic means all the worlds, of mankind, angels, animals, plants, this world, the next, and so forth.

[f] Note that the verb here is not attributed to God.

2. THE COW

*This is a Medinan sura and the longest in the Qur'an, containing material
revealed over several years, and named after the story of the cow which the
Israelites were ordered to slaughter (verses 67 ff.). The sura opens with a
response to the plea for guidance in Sura 1, 'The Opening', dividing mankind
into three groups in their response to this guidance—the believers, the disbelievers, and the hypocrites—and closes confirming the tenets of faith given in
the opening verses (3–5). The addressee shifts as the sura progresses: at various
times the text addresses mankind in general (verses 21 ff.), where they are urged
to serve God who has been so gracious to them (they are reminded that God
created Adam and favoured him over the angels), the Children of Israel
(verses 40 ff.), who are reminded of God's special favours to them and urged to
believe in scriptures that do indeed confirm their own, and the believers (verses
136 ff.), who are given instruction in many areas—prayer, fasting, pilgrimage,
defence, marital law, and financial matters.*

In the name of God, the Lord of Mercy, the Giver of Mercy

¹ *Alif Lam Mim* [a]

² This is the Scripture in which there is no doubt, [b] containing guidance for those who are mindful [c] of God, ³ who believe in the unseen, [d]

---

[a] These are the names of the three Arabic letters *a*, *l*, and *m*. Twenty-nine suras of
the Qur'an begin with separate alphabetical letters like these, from one individual letter
up to five. Various interpretations have been offered. It is sufficient to mention two here:
(1) these letters indicated to the Arabs who first heard the Qur'an that the Qur'an
consists of letters and words of their own language, although it was superior to any
speech of their own, being of divine origin; (2) they are an exclamatory device intended
to arrest the listeners' attention, similar to the custom of starting poems with an
emphatic 'No!' or 'Indeed!' Exegetes normally added, after expounding their theories,
'God knows best.'

[b] The Arabic construction *la rayba fihi* carries more than one meaning, including
'there is nothing dubious about/in it' and 'it is not to be doubted' as regards its origin or
contents.

[c] The root *w–q–y* in this morphological form has the meaning of being mindful or
being wary of something. The opposite of being mindful of God is to ignore Him or
have no reference to Him in your thought, feeling, or action. This is a fundamental
concept about God and the believers' relation to Him. Many translators render the term
as 'those who fear God', but this is an over-expression of the term and does not
correctly convey the meaning of the concept, which is a very common one in the Qur'an.

[d] What is beyond their perception, literally 'absent'—this applies to the nature of
God, the Hereafter, historical information not witnessed, etc.

keep up the prayer,[a] and give[b] out of what We have provided for them; [4]those who believe in the revelation sent down to you [Muhammad], and in what was sent before you, those who have full faith in the Hereafter. [5]Such people are following their Lord's guidance and it is they who will prosper. [6]As for those who disbelieve, it makes no difference whether you warn them or not: they will not believe. [7]God has sealed their hearts and their ears, and their eyes are covered. They will have great torment.[c]

[8]Some people say, 'We believe in God and the Last Day,' when really they do not believe. [9]They seek to deceive God and the believers but they only deceive themselves, though they do not realize it. [10]There is a disease in their hearts to which God has added more: agonizing torment awaits them for their persistent lying. [11]When it is said to them, 'Do not cause corruption in the land,' they say, 'We are only putting things right,' [12]but they are really causing corruption, though they do not realize it. [13]When it is said to them, 'Believe, as the others believe,' they say, 'Should we believe as the fools do?' but they are the fools, though they do not know it. [14]When they meet the believers, they say, 'We believe,' but when they are alone with their evil ones, they say, 'We're really with you; we were only mocking.' [15]God is mocking them, and allowing them more slack to wander blindly in their insolence. [16]They have bought error in exchange for guidance, so their trade reaps no profit, and they are not rightly guided. [17]They are like people who [labour to] kindle a fire: when it lights up everything around them, God takes away all their light, leaving them in utter darkness, unable to see—[18]deaf, dumb, and blind: they will never return—[19]or [like people who, under] a cloudburst from the sky, with its darkness, thunder, and lightning, put their fingers into their ears to keep out the thunderclaps for fear of death—but God surrounds the disbelievers—[20]the lightning almost snatches away their sight: whenever it flashes on

---

[a] This means regular and proper performance of the formal prayer (*salah*), as taught by the Prophet Muhammad.

[b] *Yunfiquna* in the Arabic of the Qur'an literally means 'spend' in good causes, in the way of God.

[c] The basic meaning of *'adhab* is 'to restrain (from doing wrong)', extended to mean anything difficult or painful, punishment, famine (see 23: 78). See *Majaz al-Qur'an*, by 'Izz al-Din Ibn 'Abdul-Salam (London: Al-Furqan Foundation, 1999), 194, and E. W. Lane, *Arabic–English Lexicon* (Beirut: Librairie du Liban, 1968).

them they walk on and when darkness falls around them they stand still. If God so willed, He could take away their hearing and sight: God has power over everything.

²¹ People, worship your Lord, who created you and those before you, so that you may be mindful [of Him] ²² who spread out the earth for you and built the sky; who sent water down from it and with that water produced things for your sustenance. Do not, knowing this, set up rivals to God. ²³ If you have doubts about the revelation We have sent down to Our servant, then produce a single sura like it—enlist whatever supporters*a* you have other than God—if you truly [think you can]. ²⁴ If you cannot do this—and you never will—then beware of the Fire prepared for the disbelievers, whose fuel is men and stones.

²⁵ [Prophet], give those who believe and do good the news that they will have Gardens graced with flowing streams. Whenever they are given sustenance from the fruits of these Gardens, they will say, 'We have been given this before,' because they were provided with something like it.*b* They will have pure spouses and there they will stay.

²⁶ God does not shy from drawing comparisons even with something as small as a gnat or something larger:*c* the believers know it is the truth from their Lord, but the disbelievers say, 'What does God mean by such a comparison?' Through it He makes many go astray and leads many to the right path. But He makes only the rebels go astray: ²⁷ those who break their covenant with God after it has been confirmed, who sever the bonds that God has commanded to be joined, who spread corruption on the earth: these are the losers. ²⁸ How can you ignore God when you were lifeless and He gave you life, when He will cause you to die, then resurrect you to be returned to Him? ²⁹ It was He who created all that is on the earth for you; He turned to the sky and made the seven heavens; it is He who has knowledge of all things.

---

a Literally 'whatever witnesses'. Razi interprets this as referring either to their idols or to their leaders.

b One interpretation is that they enjoy each meal so much that they are delighted to see favourite dishes again; another interpretation is that the food of Paradise resembles the delicacies of this world in appearance.

c Comparisons such as those given here were seen by some as inappropriate for God, and this is an answer to these critics.

³⁰ [Prophet], when your Lord told the angels, 'I am putting a successor^a on earth,' they said, 'How can^b You put someone there who will cause damage and bloodshed when we celebrate Your praise and proclaim Your holiness?' but He said, 'I know things you do not.' ³¹ He taught Adam the names of all things, then He showed them to the angels and said, 'Tell me the names of these if you truly [think you can].' ³² They said, 'May You be glorified! We have knowledge only of what You have taught us. You are the All Knowing and All Wise.' ³³ Then He said, 'Adam, tell them the names of these.' When he told them their names, God said, 'Did I not tell you that I know what is hidden in the heavens and the earth, and that I know what you reveal and what you conceal?'

³⁴ When We told the angels, 'Bow down before Adam,' they all bowed. But not Iblis, who refused and was arrogant: he was one of the disobedient. ³⁵ We said, 'Adam, live with your wife in this garden and both of you eat freely there as you will, but do not go near this tree, or you will both become wrongdoers,' ³⁶ but Satan made them slip, and removed them from the state they were in. We said, 'Get out, all of you! You are each other's enemy.^c On earth you will have a place to stay and livelihood for a time,' ³⁷ then Adam received some words^d from his Lord and He accepted his repentance: He is the Ever Relenting, the Most Merciful. ³⁸ We said, 'Get out, all of you! But when guidance comes from Me, as it certainly will, there will be no fear for those who follow My guidance nor will they grieve—³⁹ those who disbelieve and deny Our messages shall be the inhabitants of the Fire, and there they will remain.'

⁴⁰ Children of Israel, remember how I blessed you. Honour your pledge to Me and I will honour My pledge to you: I am the One you should fear. ⁴¹ Believe in the message I have sent down confirming what you already possess. Do not be the first to disbelieve in it, and

---

^a The term *khalifa* is normally translated as 'vicegerent' or 'deputy'. While this is one meaning of the term, its basic meaning is 'successor'—the Qur'an often talks about generations and individuals who are successors to each other, cf. 6: 165, 7: 129, etc.—or a 'trustee' to whom a responsibility is temporarily given, cf. Moses and Aaron, 7: 142.

^b This is *istifham inkari* in Arabic, i.e. not an interrogative but an exclamatory statement, best rendered in English by 'How can you'. There are numerous examples of this in the Qur'an.

^c Iblis is the enemy of mankind and vice versa. Iblis is also known as Shaytan/Satan.

^d Words teaching Adam how to repent, see 7: 23.

do not sell My messages for a small price: I am the One of whom you should beware. [42] Do not mix truth with falsehood, or hide the truth when you know it. [43] Keep up the prayer, pay the prescribed alms, and bow your head [in worship] with those who bow theirs. [44] How can you tell people to do what is right and forget to do it yourselves, even though you recite the Scripture? Have you no sense? [45] Seek help with steadfastness and prayer—though this is hard indeed for anyone but the humble, [46] who know[a] that they will meet their Lord and that it is to Him they will return.

[47] Children of Israel, remember how I blessed you and favoured you over other people. [48] Guard yourselves from a Day when no soul will stand in place of another, no intercession will be accepted for it, nor any ransom; nor will they be helped. [49] Remember when We saved you from Pharaoh's people, who subjected you to terrible torment, slaughtering your sons and sparing only your women—this was a great trial from your Lord—[50] and when We parted the sea for you, so saving you and drowning Pharaoh's people right before your eyes. [51] We appointed forty nights for Moses [on Mount Sinai] and then, while he was away, you took to worshipping the calf—a terrible wrong. [52] Even then We forgave you, so that you might be thankful.

[53] Remember when We gave Moses the Scripture, and the means to distinguish [right and wrong], so that you might be guided. [54] Moses said to his people, 'My people, you have wronged yourselves by worshipping the calf, so repent to your Maker and kill [the guilty among] you. That is the best you can do in the eyes of your Maker.' He accepted your repentance: He is the Ever Relenting and the Most Merciful. [55] Remember when you said, 'Moses, we will not believe you until we see God face to face.' At that, thunderbolts struck you as you looked on. [56] Then We revived you after you had died, so that you might be thankful. [57] We made the clouds cover you with shade and sent manna and quails down to you, saying, 'Eat the good things We have provided for you.' It was not Us they wronged; they wronged themselves.

[58] Remember when We said, 'Enter this town and eat freely there as you will, but enter its gate humbly and say, "Relieve us!" Then We

---

[a] One of the classical meanings of *zanna* is 'to know' rather than the predominant modern sense of 'to think'. This term is used in the sense of knowledge several times in the Qur'an.

shall forgive you your sins and increase the rewards of those who do good.' [59] But the wrongdoers substituted a different word from the one they had been given. So, because they persistently disobeyed, We sent a plague down from the heavens upon the wrongdoers.

[60] Remember when Moses prayed for water for his people and We said to him, 'Strike the rock with your staff.' Twelve springs gushed out, and each group knew its drinking place. 'Eat and drink the sustenance God has provided and do not act wrongfully in the land, causing corruption.' [61] Remember when you said, 'Moses, we cannot bear to eat only one kind of food, so pray to your Lord to bring out for us some of the earth's produce, its herbs and cucumbers, its garlic, lentils, and onions.' He said, 'Would you exchange better for worse? Go to Egypt and there you will find what you have asked for.' They were struck with humiliation and wretchedness, and they incurred the wrath of God because they persistently rejected His messages and killed prophets contrary to all that is right. All this was because they disobeyed and were lawbreakers.

[62] The [Muslim] believers, the Jews, the Christians, and the Sabians[a] — all those who believe in God and the Last Day and do good — will have their rewards with their Lord. No fear for them, nor will they grieve. [63] Remember when We took your pledge, and made the mountain tower high above you, and said, 'Hold fast to what We have given you and bear its contents in mind, so that you may be conscious of God.' [64] Even after that you turned away. Had it not been for God's favour and mercy on you, you would certainly have been lost. [65] You know about those of you who broke the Sabbath, and so We said to them, 'Be like apes![a] Be outcasts!' [23] We made this an example to those people who were there at the time and to those who came after them, and a lesson to all who are mindful of God.

[67] Remember when Moses said to his people, 'God commands you to sacrifice a cow.' They said, 'Are you making fun of us?' He answered, 'God forbid that I should be so ignorant.' [68] They said, 'Call on your Lord for us, to show us what sort of cow it should be.' He answered, 'God says it should be neither too old nor too young,

[a] The Sabians were a monotheistic religious community. See M. Asad, *The Message of the Qur'an* (Gibraltar: Dar al-Andalus, 1997), 40 n. 49.

[b] This is understood by some as 'physically turn into apes' but in fact it is a figure of speech—the structure 'be apes' is like 'be stones/iron' in 17: 50. Just as the Qur'an describes the disbelievers as blind, deaf, and dumb, here the transgressors are apes.

but in between, so do as you are commanded.' ⁶⁹ They said, 'Call on your Lord for us, to show us what colour it should be.' He answered, 'God says it should be a bright yellow cow, pleasing to the eye.' ⁷⁰ They said, 'Call on your Lord for us, to show us [exactly] what it is: all cows are more or less alike to us. With God's will, we shall be guided.' ⁷¹ He replied, 'It is a perfect and unblemished cow, not trained to till the earth or water the fields.' They said, 'Now you have brought the truth,' and so they slaughtered it, though they almost failed to do so. ⁷² Then, when you [Israelites] killed someone and started to blame one another—although God was to bring what you had concealed to light—⁷³ We said, 'Strike the [body] with a part of [the cow]': thus God brings the dead to life and shows His signs so that you may understand. ⁷⁴ Even after that, your hearts became as hard as rocks, or even harder, for there are rocks from which streams spring out, and some from which water comes when they split open, and others which fall down in awe of God: He is not unaware of what you do.

⁷⁵ So can you [believers] hope that such people will believe you, when some of them used to hear the words of God and then deliberately twist them, even when they understood them? ⁷⁶ When they meet the believers, they say, 'We too believe.' But when they are alone with each other they say, 'How could you tell them about God's revelation [to us]? They will be able to use it to argue against you before your Lord! Have you no sense?' ⁷⁷ Do they not know that God is well aware of what they conceal and what they reveal? ⁷⁸ Some of them are uneducated, and know the Scripture only through wishful thinking. They rely on guesswork. ⁷⁹ So woe to those who write the Scripture with their own hands and then claim, 'This is from God,' in order to make some small gain. Woe to them for what their hands have written! Woe to them for all that they have earned! ⁸⁰ They say, 'The Fire will only touch us for a few days.' Say to them, 'Have you received a promise from God—for God never breaks His promise—or are you saying things about Him of which you have no real knowledge?' ⁸¹ Truly those who do evil and are surrounded by their sins will be the inhabitants of the Fire, there to remain, ⁸² while those who believe and do good deeds will be the inhabitants of the Garden, there to remain.

⁸³ Remember when We took a pledge from the Children of Israel: 'Worship none but God; be good to your parents and kinsfolk, to

orphans and the poor; speak good words to all people; keep up the prayer and pay the prescribed alms.' Then all but a few of you turned away and paid no heed. [84] We took a pledge from you, 'Do not shed one another's blood or drive one another from your homelands.' You acknowledged it at the time, and you can testify to this. [85] Yet here you are, killing one another and driving some of your own people from their homes, helping one another in sin and aggression against them. If they come to you as captives, you still pay to set them free, although you had no right to drive them out. [a] So do you believe in some parts of the Scripture and not in others? The punishment for those of you who do this will be nothing but disgrace in this life, and on the Day of Resurrection they will be condemned to the harshest torment: God is not unaware of what you do. [86] These are the people who buy the life of this world at the price of the Hereafter: their torment will not be lightened, nor will they be helped.

[87] We gave Moses the Scripture and We sent messengers after him in succession. We gave Jesus, son of Mary, clear signs and strengthened him with the Holy Spirit. So how is it that, whenever a messenger brings you something you do not like, you become arrogant, calling some impostors and killing others? [88] They say, 'Our hearts are impenetrably wrapped [against whatever you say],' but God has rejected[b] them for their disbelief: they have little faith. [89] When a Scripture came to them from God confirming what they already had, and when they had been praying for victory against the disbelievers, even when there came to them something they knew [to be true], they disbelieved in it: God rejects those who disbelieve. [90] Low indeed is the price for which they have sold their souls by denying the God-sent truth, out of envy that God should send His bounty to any of His servants He pleases. The disbelievers have ended up with wrath upon wrath, and a humiliating torment awaits them. [91] When it is said to them, 'Believe in God's revelations,' they reply, 'We believe in what was revealed to us,' but they do not believe in what came afterwards, though it is the truth confirming what they

---

[a] Razi: although the Jews fought each other in alliance with different Arab tribes, when their side captured a Jew from another side, they would pay to have them released, as they said this was required by the Torah.

[b] *La'ana* in Arabic dictionaries gives the meaning of *tarada* 'to reject', 'to drive away' rather than 'to curse'.

already have. Say [Muhammad], 'Why did you kill God's prophets in the past if you were true believers? ⁹²Moses brought you clear signs, but then, while he was away, you chose to worship the calf—you did wrong.'

⁹³Remember when We took your pledge, making the mountain tower above you, and said, 'Hold on firmly to what We have given you, and listen to [what We say].' They said, 'We hear and we disobey,' and through their disbelief they were made to drink [the love of] the calf deep into their hearts. ⁹⁴Say, 'How evil are the things your belief commands you to do, if you really are believers!' Say, 'If the last home with God is to be for you alone and no one else, then you should long for death, if your claim is true.' ⁹⁵But they will never long for death, because of what they have stored up with their own hands: God is fully aware of the evildoers. ⁹⁶[Prophet], you are sure to find them clinging to life more eagerly than any other people, even the polytheists. Any of them would wish to be given a life of a thousand years, though even such a long life would not save them from the torment: God sees everything they do.

⁹⁷Say [Prophet], 'If anyone is an enemy of Gabriel—who by God's leave brought down the Qur'an to your heart confirming previous scriptures as a guide and good news for the faithful—⁹⁸if anyone is an enemy of God, His angels and His messengers, of Gabriel and Michael, then God is certainly the enemy of such disbelievers.' ⁹⁹For We have sent down clear messages to you and only those who defy [God] would refuse to believe them. ¹⁰⁰How is it that whenever they make a covenant or a pledge, some of them will throw it away? In fact, most of them do not believe.

¹⁰¹When God sent them a messenger confirming the Scriptures they already had, some of those who had received the Scripture before threw the Book of God over their shoulders as if they had no knowledge, ¹⁰²and followed what the evil ones had fabricated about the Kingdom of Solomon instead. Not that Solomon himself was a disbeliever; it was the evil ones who were disbelievers. They taught people witchcraft and what was revealed in Babylon to the two angels Harut and Marut. Yet these two never taught anyone without first warning him, 'We are sent only to tempt—do not disbelieve.' From these two, they learned what can cause discord between man and wife, although they harm no one with it except by God's leave. They learned what harmed them, not what benefited them, knowing

full well that whoever acquired [this knowledge] would have no share in the Hereafter. Evil indeed is the [price] for which they sold their souls, if only they knew. [103] If they had believed and been mindful of God, their reward from Him would have been far better, if only they knew.

[104] Believers, do not say [to the Prophet], '*Ra'ina*,' but say, '*Unzurna*,'[a] and listen [to him]: an agonizing torment awaits those who ignore [God's words]. [105] Neither those People of the Book who disbelieve nor the idolaters would like anything good to be sent down to you from your Lord, but God chooses for His grace whoever He will: His bounty has no limits. [106] Any revelation We cause to be superseded or forgotten, We replace with something better or similar. Do you [Prophet] not know that God has power over everything? [107] Do you not know that control of the heavens and the earth belongs to Him? You [believers] have no protector or helper but God. [108] Do you wish to demand of your messenger something similar to what was demanded of Moses?[b] Whoever exchanges faith for disbelief has strayed far from the right path. [109] Even after the truth has become clear to them, many of the People of the Book wish they could turn you back to disbelief after you have believed, out of their selfish envy. Forgive and forbear until God brings about His order: He has power over all things. [110] Keep up the prayer and pay the prescribed alms. Whatever good you store up for yourselves, you will find it with God: He sees everything you do.

[111] They also say, 'No one will enter Paradise unless he is a Jew or a Christian.' This is their own wishful thinking. [Prophet], say, 'Produce your evidence if you are telling the truth.' [112] In fact, any who direct themselves[c] wholly to God and do good will have their reward with their Lord: no fear for them, nor will they grieve. [113] The Jews say, 'The Christians have no ground whatsoever to stand on,' and the Christians say, 'The Jews have no ground whatsoever to stand on,' though they both read the Scripture, and those who have no

---

[a] The word *ra'ina* can be used politely as an expression for 'look at us'. However, a group of Jews in Medina hostile to Muhammad subtly changed its pronunciation to imply 'you are foolish' or 'you herd our sheep' in order to abuse the Prophet. So the believers are advised to avoid the word and use *unzurna*, also meaning 'look at us', instead. See 4: 46.

[b] See 2: 55 and 4: 153.

[c] Literally 'their faces'. One meaning of *wajh* (face) is 'direction' and the basic meaning of *aslama* is 'devote'. See note to 2: 128.

knowledge say the same; God will judge between them on the Day of Resurrection concerning their differences.

[114] Who could be more wicked than those who prohibit the mention of God's name in His places of worship[a] and strive to have them deserted? Such people should not enter them without fear. There is disgrace for them in this world and painful punishment in the Hereafter. [115] The East and the West belong to God: wherever you turn, there is His Face.[b] God is all pervading and all knowing.

[116] They[c] have asserted, 'God has a child.' May He be exalted! No! Everything in the heavens and earth belongs to Him, everything devoutly obeys His will. [117] He is the Originator of the heavens and the earth, and when He decrees something, He says only, 'Be,' and it is. [118] Those who have no knowledge also say, 'If only God would speak to us!' or 'If only a miraculous sign would come to us!' People before them said the same things: their hearts are all alike. We have made Our signs clear enough to those who have solid faith. [119] We have sent you [Prophet] with the truth, bearing good news and warning. You will not be responsible for the inhabitants of the Blaze. [120] The Jews and the Christians will never be pleased with you unless you follow their ways. Say, 'God's guidance is the only true guidance.' If you were to follow their desires after the knowledge that has come to you, you would find no one to protect you from God or help you. [121] Those to whom We have given the Scripture, who follow it as it deserves,[d] are the ones who truly believe in it. Those who deny its truth will be the losers.

[122] Children of Israel, remember how I blessed you and favoured you over other people, [123] and beware of a Day when no person can stand in for another. No compensation will be accepted from him, nor intercession benefit him, nor will anyone be helped. [124] When Abraham's Lord tested him with certain commandments, which he fulfilled, He said, 'I will make you a leader of men.' Abraham asked, 'And will You make leaders from my descendants too?' God answered, 'My pledge does not hold for those who do evil.'

---

[a] Razi suggests that this probably alludes to the Jews' objections to the change of *qibla* (direction of prayer) from Jerusalem to Mecca and their efforts to stop people praying towards Mecca in the Prophet's mosque in Medina (see 2: 115 and 142).

[b] Or 'His direction'.

[c] Razi suggests that this refers to the pagan Arabs (see 16: 57) and (some of) the Christians and Jews (see 9: 30).

[d] This can also mean 'who read it as it ought to be read'.

¹²⁵ We made the House^{*a*} a resort and a sanctuary for people, saying, 'Take the spot where Abraham stood as your place of prayer.' We commanded Abraham and Ishmael: 'Purify My House for those who walk round it, those who stay there, and those who bow and prostrate themselves in worship.' ¹²⁶ Abraham said, 'My Lord, make this land secure and provide with produce those of its people who believe in God and the Last Day.' God said, 'As for those who disbelieve, I will grant them enjoyment for a short while and then subject them to the torment of the Fire—an evil destination.'

¹²⁷ As Abraham and Ishmael built up the foundations of the House [they prayed], 'Our Lord, accept [this] from us. You are the All Hearing, the All Knowing. ¹²⁸ Our Lord, make us devoted^{*b*} to You; make our descendants into a community devoted to You. Show us how to worship and accept our repentance, for You are the Ever Relenting, the Most Merciful. ¹²⁹ Our Lord, make a messenger of their own rise up from among them, to recite Your revelations to them, teach them the Scripture and wisdom, and purify them: You are the Mighty, the Wise.'

¹³⁰ Who but a fool would forsake the religion of Abraham? We have chosen him in this world and he will rank among the righteous in the Hereafter. ¹³¹ His Lord said to him, 'Devote yourself to Me.' Abraham replied, 'I devote myself to the Lord of the Universe,' ¹³² and commanded his sons to do the same, as did Jacob: 'My sons, God has chosen [your] religion for you, so make sure you devote yourselves to Him, to your dying moment.'

¹³³ Were you [Jews] there to see when death came upon Jacob? When he said to his sons, 'What will you worship after I am gone?' they replied, 'We shall worship your God and the God of your fathers, Abraham, Ishmael, and Isaac, one single God: we devote ourselves to Him.'^{*c*} ¹³⁴ That community passed away. What they earned belongs to them, and what you earn belongs to you: you will not be answerable for their deeds.

¹³⁵ They say, 'Become Jews or Christians, and you will be rightly

^{*a*} The Ka'ba at Mecca.

^{*b*} *Aslama* here means to devote oneself to the one God alone, so that Abraham will come to his Lord with his heart totally devoted to Him: 3: 64; 26: 89; 37: 84.

^{*c*} 'One single God' reinforces the interpretation of *islam* as 'devotion', one meaning of *aslama* (*al-Mu'jam al-Wasit*).

guided.' Say [Prophet], 'No, [ours is] the religion of Abraham, the upright, who did not worship any god besides God.' ¹³⁶ So [you believers], say, 'We believe in God and in what was sent down to us and what was sent down to Abraham, Ishmael, Isaac, Jacob, and the Tribes, and what was given to Moses, Jesus, and all the prophets by their Lord. We make no distinction between any of them, and we devote ourselves to Him.' ¹³⁷ So if they believe like you do, they will be rightly guided. But if they turn their backs, then they will be entrenched in opposition. God will protect you from them: He is the All Hearing, the All Knowing. And say [believers], ¹³⁸ '[Our life] takes its colour from God, and who gives a better colour than God? It is Him we worship.'

¹³⁹ Say [Prophet] [to the Jews and Christians], 'How can you argue with us about God when He is our Lord and your Lord? Our deeds belong to us, and yours to you. We devote ourselves entirely to Him. ¹⁴⁰ Or are you saying that Abraham, Ishmael, Isaac, Jacob, and the Tribes were Jews or Christians?' [Prophet], ask them, 'Who knows better: you or God? Who could be more wicked than those who hide a testimony [they received] from God? God is not unmindful of what you do.' ¹⁴¹ That community passed away: what they earned belongs to them, and what you earn belongs to you. You will not be answerable for their deeds.

¹⁴² The foolish people will say, 'What has turned them away from the prayer direction they used to face?'ᵃ Say, 'East and West belong to God. He guides whoever He will to the right way.' ¹⁴³ We have made you [believers] into a just community,ᵇ so that you may bear witness [to the truth] before others and so that the Messenger may bear witness [to it] before you. We [previously] made the direction the one you used to face [Prophet] in order [now] to distinguish those who follow the Messenger from those who turn on their heels: that test was hard, except for those God has guided. God would never let your faith go to waste [believers],ᶜ for God is most compassionate and most merciful towards people. ¹⁴⁴ Many a time We have seen you [Prophet] turn your face towards Heaven, so We

---

ᵃ This refers to the change in the Muslims' prayer direction from Jerusalem to Mecca in the second year of the Hijra.

ᵇ Literally 'a middle nation'.

ᶜ This reassured those who asked whether the prayers said towards Jerusalem had been wasted.

are turning you towards a prayer direction that pleases you.[a] Turn your face in the direction of the Sacred Mosque: wherever you [believers] may be, turn your faces to it. Those who were given the Scripture know with certainty that this is the Truth from their Lord: God is not unaware of what they do. [145] Yet even if you brought every proof to those who were given the Scripture, they would not follow your prayer direction, nor will you follow theirs, nor indeed will any of them follow one another's direction. If you [Prophet] were to follow their desires, after the knowledge brought to you, you would be doing wrong. [146] Those We gave Scripture know it as well as they know their own sons, but some of them hide the truth that they know. [147] The truth is from your Lord, so do not be one of those who doubt. [148] Each community has its own direction to which it turns: race to do good deeds and wherever you are, God will bring you together.[b] God has power to do everything.

[149] [Prophet], wherever you may have started out, turn your face in the direction of the Sacred Mosque—this is the truth from your Lord: He is not unaware of what you do—[150] wherever you may have started out, turn your face in the direction of the Sacred Mosque; wherever any of you may be, turn your faces towards it, so that people may have no argument against you,[c] except for the wrong-doers among them. Do not fear them; fear Me, so that I may perfect My favour on you and you may be guided, [151] just as We[d] have sent among you a Messenger of your own to recite Our revelations to you, purify you and teach you the Scripture, wisdom, and [other] things you did not know. [152] So remember Me; I will remember you. Be thankful to Me, and never ungrateful.

[153] You who believe, seek help through steadfastness and prayer, for God is with the steadfast. [154] Do not say that those who are killed in God's cause are dead; they are alive, though you do not realize it. [155] We shall certainly test you with fear and hunger, and loss of

---

[a] The Prophet secretly hoped to be allowed to face the Mosque in Mecca in prayer, as it was so dear to him, being built by Abraham and Ishmael, as seen from verse 127 onwards.

[b] On the Day of Judgement, cf. 5: 48.

[c] Both Jews and polytheists questioned the choice of *qibla* (prayer direction) for their own reasons.

[d] Note the shift in pronoun from singular to plural of majesty (see Introduction, p. xx).

property, lives, and crops. But [Prophet], give good news to those who are steadfast, ¹⁵⁶ those who say, when afflicted with a calamity, 'We belong to God and to Him we shall return.' ¹⁵⁷ These will be given blessings and mercy from their Lord, and it is they who are rightly guided.

¹⁵⁸ Safa and Marwa^{*a*} are among the rites of God, so for those who make major or minor^{*b*} pilgrimage to the House^{*c*} it is no offence to circulate between the two.^{*d*} Anyone who does good of his own accord will be rewarded, for God rewards good deeds, and knows everything. ¹⁵⁹ As for those who hide the proofs and guidance We send down, after We have made them clear to people in the Scripture, God rejects them, and so do others, ¹⁶⁰ unless they repent, make amends, and declare the truth. I will certainly accept their repentance: I am the Ever Relenting, the Most Merciful. ¹⁶¹ As for those who disbelieve and die as disbelievers, God rejects them, as do the angels and all people. ¹⁶² They will remain in this state of rejection: their punishment will not be lightened, nor will they be reprieved.

¹⁶³ Your God is the *one* God: there is no god except Him, the Lord of Mercy, the Giver of Mercy. ¹⁶⁴ In the creation of the heavens and earth; in the alternation of night and day; in the ships that sail the seas with goods for people; in the water which God sends down from the sky to give life to the earth when it has been barren, scattering all kinds of creatures over it; in the changing of the winds and clouds that run their appointed courses between the sky and earth: there are signs in all these for those who use their minds. ¹⁶⁵ Even so, there are some who choose to worship others besides God as rivals to Him, loving them with the love due to God, but the believers have greater love for God. If only the wrongdoers could see—as they will see when they face the punishment—that all power belongs to God, and that God punishes severely. ¹⁶⁶ When those who have been followed disown their followers, when they all see the suffering, when all

---

^{*a*} Two hills adjacent to the Ka'ba between which a pilgrim and visitor should walk up and down in commemoration of what Hagar did in search of water for her baby, Ishmael.

^{*b*} The minor pilgrimage ('*umra*) can be done during the pilgrimage season or at any other time during the year.

^{*c*} The Ka'ba, which is central both to the direction of prayer and to the rites of pilgrimage as established by Abraham at God's command.

^{*d*} The Muslims were reluctant to perform this rite, as the polytheists had installed two idols on these hills. Here it is reclaimed for God.

bonds between them are severed, [167] the followers will say, 'If only we had one last chance, we would disown them as they now disown us.' In this way, God will make them see their deeds as a source of bitter regret; they shall not leave the Fire.

[168] People, eat what is good and lawful from the earth, and do not follow Satan's footsteps, for he is your sworn enemy. [169] He always commands you to do what is evil and indecent, and to say things about God that you do not really know. [170] But when it is said to them, 'Follow the message that God has sent down,' they answer, 'We follow the ways of our fathers.' What! Even though their fathers understood nothing and were not guided? [171] Calling to disbelievers[a] is like a herdsman calling to things that hear nothing but a shout and a cry: they are deaf, dumb, and blind, and they understand nothing. [172] You who believe, eat the good things We have provided for you and be grateful to God, if it is Him that you worship. [173] He has only forbidden you carrion, blood, pig's meat, and animals over which any name other than God's has been invoked. But if anyone is forced to eat such things by hunger, rather than desire or excess, he commits no sin: God is most merciful and forgiving.

[174] As for those who conceal the Scripture that God sent down and sell it for a small price, they only fill their bellies with Fire. God will not speak to them on the Day of Resurrection, nor will He purify them: an agonizing torment awaits them. [175] These are the ones who exchange guidance for error, and forgiveness for torment. What can make them patient in the face of the Fire? [176] This is because God has sent the Scripture with the Truth; those who pursue differences in the Scripture are deeply entrenched in opposition.

[177] Goodness does not consist in turning your face towards East or West. The truly good are those who believe in God and the Last Day, in the angels, the Scripture, and the prophets; who give away some of their wealth, however much they cherish it, to their relatives, to orphans, the needy, travellers and beggars, and to liberate those in bondage; those who keep up the prayer and pay the prescribed alms; who keep pledges whenever they make them; who are steadfast in misfortune, adversity, and times of danger. These are the ones who are true, and it is they who are aware of God.

---

[a] It is also possible to interpret this as referring to the disbelievers calling on their idols, who cannot respond.

[178] You who believe, fair retribution is prescribed for you in cases
of murder: the free man for the free man, the slave for the slave, the
female for the female. [a] But if the guilty is pardoned by his aggrieved
brother, this shall be adhered to fairly, and the culprit shall pay
what is due in a good way. This is an alleviation from your Lord
and an act of mercy. If anyone then exceeds these limits, grievous
suffering awaits him. [179] Fair retribution saves life for you, people of
understanding, so that you may guard yourselves against what is
wrong.

When death approaches one of you and he leaves wealth, [180] it is
prescribed that he should make a proper bequest to parents and close
relatives—a duty incumbent on those who are mindful of God. [181] If
anyone alters the bequest after hearing it, the guilt of the alteration
will fall on them: God is all hearing and all knowing. [182] But if anyone
knows [b] that the testator has made a mistake, or done wrong, and so
puts things right between the parties, he will incur no sin: God is
most forgiving and merciful.

[183] You who believe, fasting is prescribed for you, as it was prescribed for those before you, so that you may be mindful of God.
[184] Fast for a specific number of days, but if one of you is ill, or on a
journey, he should fast on other days later. For those who can fast
only with extreme difficulty, there is a way to compensate—feed a
needy person. But if anyone does good of his own accord, it is better
for him, and fasting is better for you, if only you knew. [185] It was in
the month of Ramadan that the Qur'an was revealed as guidance
for mankind, clear messages giving guidance and distinguishing
between right and wrong. So any one of you who is present that
month should fast, and anyone who is ill or on a journey should
make up for the lost days by fasting on other days later. God wants
ease for you, not hardship. He wants you to complete the prescribed
period and to glorify Him for having guided you, so that you may be
thankful. [186] [Prophet], if My servants ask you about Me, I am near.
I respond to those who call Me, so let them respond to Me, and
believe in Me, so that they may be guided.

---

[a] Before Islam, the Arabs did not observe equality in retribution, but a stronger tribe
would demand more, e.g. a man for a woman, a free man for a slave, or several men for
one man, likewise for financial compensation. The intention of this verse is to insist on
equality.

[b] One meaning of *khafa* is 'to know' (*al-Mu'jam al-Wasit*).

¹⁸⁷ You [believers] are permitted to lie with your wives during the night of the fast: they are [close] as garments to you, as you are to them. God was aware that you were betraying yourselves,ᵃ so He turned to you in mercy and pardoned you: now you can lie with them—seek what God has ordained for you—eat and drink until the white thread of dawn becomes distinct from the black. Then fast until nightfall. Do not lie with them during the nights of your devotional retreat in the mosques: these are the bounds set by God, so do not go near them. In this way God makes His messages clear to people, that they may guard themselves against doing wrong. ¹⁸⁸ Do not consume your property wrongfully, nor use it to bribe judges, intending sinfully and knowingly to consume parts of other people's property.

¹⁸⁹ They ask you [Prophet] about crescent moons. Say, 'They show the times appointed for people, and for the pilgrimage.' Goodness does not consist of entering houses by the back [door];ᵇ the truly good person is the one who is mindful of God. So enter your houses by their [main] doors and be mindful of God so that you may prosper. ¹⁹⁰ Fight in God's cause against those who fight you, but do not overstep the limits:ᶜ God does not love those who overstep the limits. ¹⁹¹ Kill them wherever you encounter them,ᵈ and drive them out from where they drove you out, for persecution is more serious than killing.ᵉ Do not fight them at the Sacred Mosque unless they fight you there. If they do fight you, kill them—this is what such disbelievers deserve— ¹⁹² but if they stop, then God is most forgiving and merciful. ¹⁹³ Fight them until there is no more persecution, and

---

ᵃ Some Muslims admitted to the Prophet that they had spoiled their fast by having sexual relations during the nights of Ramadan.

ᵇ It was the custom of some Arabs on returning from the pilgrimage to enter their houses by the back door, considering this to be an act of piety.

ᶜ The Arabic command *la ta'tadu* is so general that commentators have agreed that it includes prohibition of starting hostilities, fighting non-combatants, disproportionate response to aggression, etc.

ᵈ The Muslims were concerned as to whether it was permitted to retaliate when attacked within the sacred precincts in Mecca when on pilgrimage (see 2: 196 and Razi's *Tafsir*). They are here given permission to fight back wherever they encounter their attackers.

ᵉ 'Persecuting you unlawfully is worse than you killing them in the precincts in self-defence.' The article *al-* in Arabic sometimes takes the place of a pronoun, as here 'their persecution' and 'your killing them' (Tammam Hassan, *al-Bayan*, Cairo, 1993, 118–45); it is not the generic *al-*, cf. 2: 217.

[your]*ᵃ* worship is devoted to God. If they cease hostilities, there can be no [further] hostility, except towards aggressors. ¹⁹⁴ A sacred month for a sacred month: violation of sanctity [calls for] fair retribution. So if anyone commits aggression against you, attack him as he attacked you, but be mindful of God, and know that He is with those who are mindful of Him. ¹⁹⁵ Spend in God's cause: do not contribute to your destruction with your own hands,*ᵇ* but do good, for God loves those who do good.

¹⁹⁶ Complete the pilgrimages, major and minor, for the sake of God. If you are prevented [from doing so], then [send] whatever offering for sacrifice you can afford, and do not shave your heads*ᶜ* until the offering has reached the place of sacrifice. If any of you is ill, or has an ailment of the scalp, he should compensate by fasting, or feeding the poor, or offering sacrifice. In times of peace, anyone wishing to take a break*ᵈ* between the minor pilgrimage and the major one must make whatever offering he can afford. If he lacks the means, he should fast for three days during the pilgrimage, and seven days on his return, making ten days in all. This applies to those whose household is not near the Sacred Mosque. Always be mindful of God, and be aware that He is stern in His retribution.

¹⁹⁷ The pilgrimage takes place during the prescribed months. There should be no indecent speech, misbehaviour, or quarrelling for anyone undertaking the pilgrimage—whatever good you do, God is well aware of it. Provide well for yourselves: the best provision is to be mindful of God—always be mindful of Me, you who have understanding—¹⁹⁸ but it is no offence to seek some bounty from your Lord.*ᵉ* When you surge down from Arafat remember God at the sacred place.*ᶠ* Remember Him: He has guided you. Before that

ᵃ Cf. 8: 39 and note *e* to 2: 191 above.

ᵇ If they are not prepared to pay for what it takes to defend themselves, then they will bring ruin on themselves. The verse is also understood generally to outlaw suicide and other forms of self-harm.

ᶜ Shaving the head is one of the rites performed by male pilgrims after most of the other rites have been completed.

ᵈ This means breaking the restrictions of *ihram* (consecration) technically termed *tamattu'*.

ᵉ It is lawful to trade while on pilgrimage.

ᶠ This is one of the sites of the pilgrimage between Arafat and Mina—a plain called Muzdalifa.

you were astray. [199] Surge down where the rest of the people do, [a] and ask forgiveness of God: He is most forgiving and merciful. [200] When you have completed your rites, remember God as much as you remember your own fathers, or even more. There are some who pray, 'Our Lord, give us good in this world,' and they will have no share in the Hereafter; [201] others pray, 'Our Lord, give us good in this world and in the Hereafter, and protect us from the torment of the Fire.' [202] They will have the share they have worked for: God is swift in reckoning.

[203] Remember God on the appointed days. [b] If anyone is in a hurry to leave after two days, there is no blame on him, nor is there any blame on anyone who stays on, so long as they are mindful of God. Be mindful of God, and remember that you will be gathered to Him. [204] There is [a kind of] man whose views on the life of this world may please you [Prophet], he even calls on God to witness what is in his heart, yet he is the bitterest of opponents. [205] When he leaves, he sets out to spread corruption in the land, destroying crops and live-stock—God does not like corruption. [206] When he is told, 'Beware of God,' his arrogance leads him to sin. Hell is enough for him: a dreadful resting place. [207] But there is also a kind of man who gives his life away to please God, and God is most compassionate to His servants. [208] You who believe, enter wholeheartedly into submission to God [c] and do not follow in Satan's footsteps, for he is your sworn enemy. [209] If you slip back after clear proof has come to you, then be aware that God is almighty and wise.

[210] Are these people waiting for God to come to them in the shadows of the clouds, together with the angels? But the matter would already have been decided by then: [d] all matters are brought back to God. [211] [Prophet], ask the Children of Israel how many clear signs We brought them. If anyone alters God's blessings after he has received them, God is stern in punishment. [212] The life of this world is made to seem glamorous to the disbelievers, and they laugh at those who believe. But those who are mindful of God will be above

---

[a] Some arrogant tribes used to take a different route from the masses.

[b] These come after the day of sacrifice, when two or three days are spent in Mina to perform the rite of stoning the Devil.

[c] *Silm*, which also means 'peace'.

[d] It will be too late for them to repent.

them on the Day of Resurrection: God provides immeasurably for whoever He pleases. [213] Mankind was a single community, then God sent prophets to bring good news and warning, and with them He sent the Scripture with the Truth, to judge between people in their disagreements. It was only those to whom it was given who disagreed about it after clear signs had come to them, because of rivalry between them. So by His leave God guided the believers to the truth they had differed about: God guides whoever He will to a straight path.

[214] Do you suppose that you will enter the Garden without first having suffered like those before you? They were afflicted by misfortune and hardship, and they were so shaken that even [their] messenger and the believers with him cried, 'When will God's help arrive?' Truly, God's help is near. [215] They ask you [Prophet] what they should give. Say, 'Whatever you give should be for parents, close relatives, orphans, the needy, and travellers. God is well aware of whatever good you do.

[216] Fighting is ordained for you, though you dislike it. You may dislike something although it is good for you, or like something although it is bad for you: God knows and you do not.' [217] They ask you [Prophet] about fighting in the prohibited month. Say, 'Fighting in that month is a great offence, but to bar others from God's path, to disbelieve in Him, prevent access to the Sacred Mosque, and expel its people, are still greater offences in God's eyes: persecution is worse than killing.' [a] They will not stop fighting you [believers] until they make you revoke your faith, if they can. If any of you revoke your faith and die as disbelievers, your deeds will come to nothing in this world and the Hereafter, and you will be inhabitants of the Fire, there to remain. [218] But those who have believed, migrated, and striven for God's cause, it is they who can look forward to God's mercy: God is most forgiving and merciful.

[219] They ask you [Prophet] about intoxicants and gambling: say, 'There is great sin in both, and some benefit for people: the sin is greater than the benefit.' They ask you what they should give: say, 'Give what you can spare.' In this way, God makes His messages clear to you, so that you may reflect [220] on this world and the next.

---

[a] To persecute people for believing in God is a worse offence than for the aggrieved party to fight back in the prohibited month. This further explains verse 191.

2: 228 *The Cow* 25

They ask you about [the property of] orphans: say, 'It is good to set things right for them. If you combine their affairs with yours, remember they are your brothers and sisters: God knows those who spoil things and those who improve them. Had He so willed, He could have made you vulnerable too: He is almighty and wise.'

²²¹ Do not marry idolatresses until they believe: a believing slave woman is certainly better than an idolatress, even though she may please you. And do not give your women in marriage to idolaters until they believe: a believing slave is certainly better than an idolater, even though he may please you. Such people call [you] to the Fire, while God calls [you] to the Garden and forgiveness by His leave. He makes His messages clear to people, so that they may bear them in mind.

²²² They ask you [Prophet] about menstruation. Say, 'Menstruation is a painful condition, so keep away from women during it. Do not approach them until they are cleansed; when they are cleansed, you may approach them as God has ordained. ^a God loves those who turn to Him, and He loves those who keep themselves clean. ²²³ Your women are your fields, so go into your fields whichever way you like, ^b and send [something good] ahead for yourselves. Be mindful of God: remember that you will meet Him.' [Prophet], give good news to the believers.

²²⁴ [Believers], do not allow your oaths in God's name to hinder you from doing good, being mindful of God and making peace between people. God hears and knows everything: ²²⁵ He will not call you to account for oaths you have uttered unintentionally, but He will call you to account for what you mean in your hearts. God is most forgiving and forbearing. ²²⁶ For those who swear that they will not approach their wives, there shall be a waiting period of four months: ^c if they go back, remember God will be most forgiving and merciful, ²²⁷ but if they are determined to divorce, remember that God hears and knows all. ²²⁸ Divorced women must wait for three monthly periods before remarrying, and, if they really believe in God and the

---

^a The Arabic expressions used here are clear euphemisms for 'do not have sexual intercourse with them'.

^b When the Muslims emigrated to Medina, they heard from the Jews that a child born from a woman approached from behind would have a squint.

^c Before Islam, husbands could make such an oath and suspend the wife indefinitely. In Islam, if they do not go back after four months, divorce becomes effective.

Last Day, it is not lawful for them to conceal what God has created in their wombs: their husbands are entitled to take them back during this period provided they wish to put things right. Wives have [rights] similar to their [obligations], according to what is recognized to be fair, and husbands have a degree [of right] over them: [both should remember that] God is almighty and wise.

²²⁹ Divorce can happen twice, and [each time] wives either be kept on in an acceptable manner or released in a good way. It is not lawful for you to take back anything that you have given [your wives] except where both fear that they cannot maintain [the marriage] within the bounds set by God: if you [arbiters] suspect that the couple may not be able to do this, then there will be no blame on either of them if the woman opts to give something for her release.^{*a*} These are the bounds set by God: do not overstep them. It is those that overstep God's bounds who are doing wrong. ²³⁰ If a husband re-divorces his wife after the second divorce, she will not be lawful for him until she has taken another husband; if that one divorces her, there will be no blame if she and the first husband return to one another, provided they feel that they can keep within the bounds set by God. These are God's bounds, which He makes clear for those who know.

²³¹ When you divorce women and they have reached their set time, then either keep or release them in a fair manner. Do not hold on to them with intent to harm them and commit aggression: anyone who does this wrongs himself. Do not make a mockery of God's revelations; remember the favour He blessed you with, and the Scripture and wisdom He sent to teach you. Be mindful of God and know that He has full knowledge of everything. ²³² When you divorce women and they have reached their set time, do not prevent them from remarrying their husbands if they both agree to do so in a fair manner.^{*b*} Let those of you who believe in God and the Last Day take this to heart: that is more wholesome and purer for you. God knows and you do not.

²³³ Mothers suckle their children for two whole years, if they wish to complete the term, and clothing and maintenance must be borne by the father in a fair manner. No one should be burdened with more than they can bear: no mother shall be made to suffer harm on

---

^{*a*} By paying back all or part of the dowry in return for divorce.

^{*b*} Sometimes a woman's father or brother would interfere to stop her reconciling with her husband. Here the Qur'an condemns such interference.

account of her child, nor any father on account of his. The same duty is incumbent on the father's heir. [a] If, by mutual consent and consultation, the couple wish to wean [the child], they will not be blamed, nor will there be any blame if you wish to engage a wet nurse, provided you pay as agreed in a fair manner. Be mindful of God, knowing that He sees everything you do.

[234] If any of you die and leave widows, the widows should wait for four months and ten nights before remarrying. When they have completed this set time, you will not be blamed for anything they may reasonably choose to do with themselves. God is fully aware of what you do. [235] You will not be blamed whether you give a hint that you wish to marry these women, or keep it to yourselves—God knows that you intend to propose [b] to them. Do not make a secret arrangement with them; speak to them honourably and do not confirm the marriage tie until the prescribed period reaches its end. Remember that God knows what is in your souls, so be mindful of Him. Remember that God is most forgiving and forbearing.

[236] You will not be blamed if you divorce women when you have not yet consummated the marriage or fixed a dowry for them, but make fair provision for them, the rich according to his means and the poor according to his—this is a duty for those who do good. [237] If you divorce wives before consummating the marriage but after fixing a dowry for them, then give them half of what you had previously fixed, unless they waive [their right], or unless the one who holds the marriage tie waives [his right]. Waiving [your right] is nearer to godliness, so do not forget to be generous towards one another: God sees what you do. [238] Take care to do your prayers, [c] praying in the best way, [d] and stand before God in devotion. [239] If you are in danger, pray when you are out walking or riding; when you are safe again, remember God, for He has taught you what you did not know.

[240] If any of you die and leave widows, make a bequest for them: a year's maintenance and no expulsion from their homes [for that time]. But if they leave of their own accord, you will not be blamed for what they may reasonably choose to do with themselves: God is

[a] If he dies.

[b] *Dhakasa* in classical Arabic meant 'to propose'.

[c] To secure that the parties in such a bitter situation will abide by the Qur'an's teaching they are instructed to pray and stand before God.

[d] Another interpretation is 'including the middle prayer', with various opinions as to which prayer is meant.

almighty and wise. ²⁴¹ Divorced women shall also have such maintenance as is considered fair: this is a duty for those who are mindful of
God. ²⁴² In this way God makes His revelations clear to you, so that
you may grow in understanding.

²⁴³ [Prophet], consider those people who abandoned their homeland in fear of death,ᵃ even though there were thousands of them.
God said to them, 'Die!' and then brought them back to life again;
God shows real favour to people, but most of them are ungrateful.
²⁴⁴ Fightᵇ in God's cause and remember that He is all hearing and all
knowing. ²⁴⁵ Who will give God a good loan, which He will increase
for him many times over? It is God who withholds and God who
gives abundantly, and it is to Him that you will return.

²⁴⁶ [Prophet], consider the leaders of the Children of Israel who
came after Moses, when they said to one of their prophets, 'Set up a
king for us and we shall fight in God's cause.' He said, 'But could it
be that you would not fight, if it were ordained for you?' They said,
'How could we not fight in God's cause when we and our children
have been driven out of our homeland?' Yet when they were commanded to fight, all but a few of them turned away: God has full
knowledge of those who do wrong. ²⁴⁷ Their prophet said to them,
'God has now appointed Talutᶜ to be your king,' but they said, 'How
can he be king over us when we have a greater right to rule than he?
He does not even have great wealth.' He said, 'God has chosen him
over you, and has given him great knowledge and stature. God
grants His authority to whoever He pleases: God is magnanimous,
all knowing.' ²⁴⁸ Their prophet said to them, 'The sign of his authority will be that the Ark [of the Covenant] will come to you. In it there
will be [the gift of] tranquillity from your Lord and relics of the
followers of Moses and Aaron, carried by the angels. There is a sign
in this for you if you believe.'

²⁴⁹ When Talut set out with his forces, he said to them, 'God will
test you with a river. Anyone who drinks from it will not belong with
me, but anyone who refrains from tasting it will belong with me; if
he scoops up just one handful [he will be excused].' But they all
drank [deep] from it, except for a few. When he crossed it with those

---

ᵃ See verse 246 below.

ᵇ After dealing with marital issues, the Qur'an returns to the question of warfare.

ᶜ The Arabic name for Saul.

who had kept faith, they[a] said, 'We have no strength today against Goliath and his warriors.' But those who knew that they were going to meet their Lord said, 'How often a small force has defeated a large army with God's permission! God is with those who are steadfast.' [250] And when they met Goliath and his warriors, they said, 'Our Lord, pour patience on us, make us stand firm, and help us against the disbelievers,' [251] and so with God's permission they defeated them. David killed Goliath, and God gave him sovereignty and wisdom and taught him what He pleased. If God did not drive some back by means of others the earth would be completely corrupt, but God is bountiful to all.

[252] These are the revelations of God which We recite to you [Muhammad] with the truth, and you truly are one of the messengers. [253] We favoured some of these messengers above others. God spoke to some; others He raised in rank; We gave Jesus, son of Mary, Our clear signs and strengthened him with the holy spirit. If God had so willed, their successors would not have fought each other after they had been brought clear signs. But they disagreed: some believed and some disbelieved. If God had so willed, they would not have fought each other, but God does what He will.

[254] You who believe, give from what We have provided for you, before the Day comes when there is no bargaining, no friendship, and no intercession. It is the disbelievers who do wrong. [255] God: there is no god but Him, the Ever Living, the Ever Watchful.[b] Neither slumber nor sleep overtakes Him. All that is in the heavens and in the earth belongs to Him. Who is there that can intercede with Him except by His leave? He knows what is before them and what is behind them, but they do not comprehend any of His knowledge except what He wills. His throne extends over the heavens and the earth; it does not weary Him to preserve them both. He is the Most High, the Tremendous.

[256] There is no compulsion in religion: true guidance has become distinct from error, so whoever rejects false gods and believes in God has grasped the firmest hand-hold, one that will never break. God is all hearing and all knowing. [257] God is the ally of those who believe: He brings them out of the depths of darkness and into the light. As

[a] Those who had drunk the water or some of the few who went with Talut.
[b] Cf. 13: 33.

for the disbelievers, their allies are false gods who take them from the light into the depths of darkness, they are the inhabitants of the Fire, and there they will remain.

²⁵⁸ [Prophet], have you not thought about the man who disputed with Abraham about his Lord, because God had given him power to rule? When Abraham said, 'It is my Lord who gives life and death,' he said, 'I too give life and death.' So Abraham said, 'God brings the sun from the east; so bring it from the west.' The disbeliever was dumbfounded: God does not guide those who do evil.

²⁵⁹ Or take the one who passed by a ruined town. He said, 'How will God give this life when it has died?' So God made him die for a hundred years, and then raised him up, saying, 'How long did you stay like that?' He answered, 'A day, or part of a day.' God said, 'No, you stayed like that for a hundred years. Look at your food and drink: they have not gone bad. Look at your donkey—We will make you a sign for the people—look at the bones: see how We bring them together and clothe them with flesh!' When all became clear to him, he said, 'Now I know that God has power over everything.'

²⁶⁰ And when Abraham said, 'My Lord, show me how You give life to the dead,' he said, 'Do you not believe, then?' 'Yes,' said Abraham, 'but just to put my heart at rest.' So God said, 'Take four birds and train them to come back to you. Then place them on separate hilltops,ᵃ call them back, and they will come flying to you: know that God is all powerful and wise.'

²⁶¹ Those who spend their wealth in God's cause are like grains of corn that produce seven ears, each bearing a hundred grains. God gives multiple increase to whoever He wishes: He is limitless and all knowing. ²⁶² Those who spend their wealth in God's cause and do not follow their spending with reminders of their benevolence or hurtful words will have their rewards with their Lord: no fear for them, nor will they grieve. ²⁶³ A kind word and forgiveness is better than a charitable deed followed by hurtful [words]: God is self-sufficient, forbearing. ²⁶⁴ You who believe, do not cancel out your charitable

ᵃ Most of the classical commentators take the view that Abraham must have had to cut up the birds first if they were really to rise from the dead, rendering this phrase 'then place them separately on hilltops'. However, Abu Muslim thought the important part of the image was that it is as easy for souls to come back to the body as for the birds to come back to Abraham (Razi). Cf. 'To Him you shall return', in many places, e.g. 2: 245 and 285.

deeds with reminders and hurtful words, like someone who spends his wealth only to be seen by people, not believing in God and the Last Day. Such a person is like a rock with earth on it: heavy rain falls and leaves it completely bare. Such people get no rewards for their works: God does not guide the disbelievers. [265] But those who spend their wealth in order to gain God's approval, and as an affirmation of their own faith, are like a garden on a hill: heavy rain falls and it produces double its normal yield; even if no heavy rain falls, it will still be watered by the dew. God sees all that you do. [266] Would any of you like to have a garden of palm trees and vines, graced with flowing streams and all kinds of produce, which, when you are afflicted with old age and feeble offspring, is struck by a fiery whirlwind and burnt down? In this way God makes His messages clear to you, so that you may reflect on them.

[267] You who believe, give charitably from the good things you have acquired and that We have produced for you from the earth. Do not give away the bad things that you yourself would only accept with your eyes closed: remember that God is self-sufficient, worthy of all praise. [268] Satan threatens you with the prospect of poverty and commands you to do foul deeds; God promises you His forgiveness and His abundance: God is limitless and all knowing, [269] and He gives wisdom to whoever He will. Whoever is given wisdom has truly been given much good, but only those with insight bear this in mind. [270] Whatever you may give, or vow to give, God knows it well, and those who do wrong will have no one to help them. [271] If you give charity openly, it is good, but if you keep it secret and give to the needy in private, that is better for you, and it will atone for some of your bad deeds: God is well aware of all that you do. [272] It is not for you [Prophet] to guide them; it is God who guides whoever He will. Whatever charity you give benefits your own soul, provided you do it for the sake of God: whatever you give will be repaid to you in full, and you will not be wronged. [273] [Give] to those needy who are wholly occupied in God's way and cannot travel in the land [for trade]. The unknowing might think them rich because of their self-restraint, but you will recognize them by their characteristic of not begging persistently. God is well aware of any good you give.

[274] Those who give, out of their own possessions, by night and by day, in private and in public, will have their reward with their Lord: no fear for them, nor will they grieve. [275] But those who take usury

will rise up on the Day of Resurrection like someone tormented by Satan's touch. That is because they say, 'Trade and usury are the same,' [276] but God has allowed trade and forbidden usury. Whoever, on receiving God's warning, stops taking usury may keep his past gains—God will be his judge—but whoever goes back to usury will be an inhabitant of the Fire, there to remain. God blights usury, but blesses charitable deeds with multiple increase: He does not love the ungrateful sinner. [277] Those who believe, do good deeds, keep up the prayer, and pay the prescribed alms will have their reward with their Lord: no fear for them, nor will they grieve. [278] You who believe, beware of God: give up any outstanding dues from usury, if you are true believers. [279] If you do not, then be warned of war from God and His Messenger. You shall have your capital if you repent, and without suffering loss or causing others to suffer loss. [280] If the debtor is in difficulty, then delay things until matters become easier for him; still, if you were to write it off as an act of charity, that would be better for you, if only you knew. [281] Beware of a Day when you will be returned to God: every soul will be paid in full for what it has earned, and no one will be wronged.

[282] You who believe, when you contract a debt for a stated term, put it down in writing: have a scribe write it down justly between you. No scribe should refuse to write: let him write as God has taught him, let the debtor dictate, and let him fear God, his Lord, and not diminish [the debt] at all. If the debtor is feeble-minded, weak, or unable to dictate, then let his guardian dictate justly. Call in two men as witnesses. If two men are not there, then call one man and two women out of those you approve as witnesses, so that if one of the two women should forget the other can remind her. Let the witnesses not refuse when they are summoned. Do not disdain to write the debt down, be it small or large, along with the time it falls due: this way is more equitable in God's eyes, more reliable as testimony, and more likely to prevent doubts arising between you. But if the merchandise is there and you hand it over, there is no blame on you if you do not write it down. Have witnesses present whenever you trade with one another, and let no harm be done to either scribe or witness, for if you did cause them harm, it would be a crime on your part. Be mindful of God, and He will teach you: He has full knowledge of everything. [283] If you are on a journey, and cannot find a scribe, something should be handed over as security, but if you

decide to trust one another, then let the one who is trusted fulfil his trust; let him be mindful of God, his Lord. Do not conceal evidence: anyone who does so has a sinful heart, and God is fully aware of everything you do. [284] Whatever is in the heavens and in the earth belongs to God and, whether you reveal or conceal your thoughts, God will call you to account for them. He will forgive whoever He will and punish whoever He will: He has power over all things.

[285] The Messenger believes in what has been sent down to him from his Lord, as do the faithful. They all believe in God, His angels, His scriptures, and His messengers. 'We make no distinction between any of His messengers,' they say, 'We hear and obey. Grant us Your forgiveness, our Lord. To You we all return!' — [286] God does not burden any soul with more than it can bear: each gains whatever good it has done, and suffers its bad — 'Lord, do not take us to task if we forget or make mistakes. Lord, do not burden us as You burdened those before us. Lord, do not burden us with more than we have strength to bear. Pardon us, forgive us, and have mercy on us. You are our Protector, so help us against the disbelievers.'

3. THE FAMILY OF 'IMRAN

A Medinan sura which takes its title from the family of 'Imran mentioned in verse 33. It begins by emphasizing that the Qur'an confirms the earlier scriptures and goes on to say later that the central tenet of faith is devotion to God (verses 19–20). The story of Zachariah, Mary, and Jesus is given in verses 35–64 and the fact that Jesus was unfathered, just as Adam was created without a father, is accentuated. Aspects of the battles of Badr and Uhud are described, especially the latter, where the Muslims disobeyed the Prophet and were defeated. The sura first documents the tension that arose between the Muslims and certain of the Jews and Christians (verses 65–85 and 98–101), then closes by emphasizing the unity of faith and conduct between the Muslims and some of these People of the Book, explaining that these will have their reward from God (verse 199).

In the name of God, the Lord of Mercy, the Giver of Mercy

¹ *Alif Lam Mim*[a]

² God: there is no god but Him, the Ever Living, the Ever Watchful. ³ Step by step, He has sent the Scripture down to you [Prophet] with the Truth, confirming what went before: He sent down the Torah and the Gospel ⁴ earlier as a guide for people and He has sent down the distinction [between right and wrong].[b] Those who deny God's revelations will suffer severe torment: God is almighty and capable of retribution. ⁵ Nothing on earth or in heaven is hidden from God: ⁶ it is He who shapes you all in the womb as He pleases. There is no God but Him, the Mighty, the Wise: ⁷ it is He who has sent this Scripture down to you [Prophet]. Some of its verses are definite in meaning—these are the cornerstone[c] of the Scripture—and others are ambiguous. The perverse at heart eagerly pursue the ambiguities in their attempt to make trouble and to pinpoint a specific meaning—only God knows the true meaning—while those firmly grounded in knowledge say, 'We believe in it: it is all from our Lord'—only those with real perception will take heed—⁸ 'Our Lord,

---

[a] See note to 2: 1.
[b] See also 5: 48; 25: 1.
[c] Literally 'the mother'.

do not let our hearts deviate after You have guided us. Grant us Your mercy: You are the Ever Giving. [9] Our Lord, You will gather all people on the Day of which there is no doubt:[a] God never breaks His promise.'

[10] Neither their possessions nor their children will be any use to the disbelievers against God. The disbelievers will be fuel for the Fire, [11] just as Pharaoh's people and their predecessors denied Our revelations, and God punished them for their sins: God is severe in punishing. [12] [Prophet], say to the disbelievers, 'You will be defeated and driven together into Hell, a foul resting place. [13] You have already seen a sign in the two armies that met in battle, one fighting for God's cause and the other made up of disbelievers. With their own eyes [the former] saw [the latter] to be twice their number,[b] but God helps whoever He will. There truly is a lesson in this for all with eyes to see.'

[14] The love of desirable things is alluring for men—women, children, gold and silver treasures piled up high, horses with fine markings, livestock, and farmland—these may be the joys of this life, but God has the best place to return to. [15] [Prophet], say, 'Would you like me to tell you of things that are better than all of these? Their Lord will give those who are mindful of God Gardens graced with flowing streams, where they will stay with pure spouses and God's good pleasure—God is fully aware of His servants—[16] those who say, "Our Lord, we believe, so forgive us our sins and protect us from suffering in the Fire," [17] those who are steadfast, truthful, truly devout, who give [in God's cause] and pray before dawn for forgiveness.'

[18] God bears witness that there is no god but Him, as do the angels and those who have knowledge. He upholds justice. There is no god but Him, the Almighty, the All Wise. [19] True Religion, in God's eyes, is *islam*: devotion to Him alone.[c] Those who were given the Scripture disagreed out of rivalry, only after they had been given knowledge— if anyone denies God's revelations, God is swift to take account—[20] if they argue with you [Prophet], say, 'I have devoted myself[d] to God alone and so have my followers.' Ask those who were given the

---

[a] And on the day itself there will no longer be any doubt (see 102: 3–8).

[b] This is an allusion to the Battle of Badr, where the Muslim army was vastly outnumbered but still victorious (see 8: 43–4).

[c] See note to 2: 128 above.

[d] Literally 'submitted my face'.

Scripture, as well as those without one, 'Do you too devote your-selves to Him alone?' If they do, they will be guided, but if they turn away, your only duty is to convey the message. God is aware of His servants.

²¹ Give news of agonizing torment to those who ignore God's revelations, who unjustifiably kill prophets, who kill those who command that justice is done: ²² the deeds of such people will come to nothing in this world and in the next and no one will help them. ²³ Have you considered those who were given a share of the Scripture? When they are asked to accept judgement from God's Scripture, some of them turn their backs and walk away, all because they declare, ²⁴ 'The Fire will only touch us for a limited number of days.' The lies they have invented have led them astray in their own religion. ²⁵ How will they fare when We gather them together for a Day of which there is no doubt, when every soul will be paid in full for what it has done, and they will not be wronged?

²⁶ Say, 'God, holder of all control,ᵃ You give control to whoever You will and remove it from whoever You will; You elevate whoever You will and humble whoever You will. All that is good lies in Your hand: You have power over everything. ²⁷ You merge night into day and day into night; You bring the living out of the dead and the dead out of the living; You provide limitlessly for whoever You will.'

²⁸ The believers should not make the disbelievers their allies rather than other believers—anyone who does such a thing will isolate himself completely from God—except when you need to protect yourselves from them. God warns you to beware of Him: the Final Return is to God. ²⁹ Say [Prophet], 'God knows every-thing that is in your hearts, whether you conceal or reveal it; He knows everything in the heavens and earth; God has power over all things.' ³⁰ On the Day when every soul finds all the good it has done present before it, it will wish all the bad it has done to be far, far away. God warns you to beware of Him but God is compassionate towards His servants. ³¹ Say, 'If you love God, follow me, and God will love you and forgive you your sins; God is most forgiving, most merciful.' ³² Say, 'Obey God and the Messenger,' but if they turn away, [know that] God does not love those who ignore [His commands].

ᵃ Or sovereignty.

³³ God chose Adam, Noah, Abraham's family,ᵃ and the family of 'Imran, over all other people, ³⁴ in one line of descent—God hears and knows all. ³⁵ 'Imran's wife said, 'Lord, I have dedicated what is growing in my womb entirely to You; so accept this from me. You are the One who hears and knows all,' ³⁶ but when she gave birth, she said, 'My Lord! I have given birth to a girl'—God knows best what she had given birth to: the male is not like the female—'I name her Mary and I commend her and her offspring to Your protection from the rejected Satan.' ³⁷ Her Lord graciously accepted her and made her grow in goodness, and entrusted her to the charge of Zachariah.

Whenever Zachariah went in to see her in her sanctuary, he found her supplied with provisions. He said, 'Mary, how is it you have these provisions?' and she said, 'They are from God: God provides limitlessly for whoever He will.' ³⁸ There and then Zachariah prayed to his Lord, saying, 'Lord, from Your grace grant me virtuous offspring: You hear every prayer.' ³⁹ The angels called out to him, while he stood praying in the sanctuary, 'God gives you news of John, confirming a Word from God.ᵇ He will be noble and chaste, a prophet, one of the righteous.' ⁴⁰ He said, 'My Lord, how can I have a son when I am so old and my wife is barren?' [An angel] said, 'It will be so: God does whatever He will.' ⁴¹ He said, 'My Lord, give me a sign.' 'Your sign,' [the angel] said, 'is that you will not communicate with anyone for three days, except by gestures. Remember your Lord often; celebrate His glory in the evening and at dawn.'

⁴² The angels said to Mary: 'Mary, God has chosen you and made you pure: He has truly chosen you above all women. ⁴³ Mary, be devout to your Lord, prostrate yourself in worship, bow down with those who pray.' ⁴⁴ This is an account of things beyond your knowledge that We reveal to you [Muhammad]: you were not present among them when theyᶜ cast lots to see which of them should take charge of Mary, you were not present with them when they argued [about her].

⁴⁵ The angels said, 'Mary, God gives you news of a Word from Him, whose name will be the Messiah, Jesus, son of Mary, who will

---

ᵃ This means family in the widest sense of the term.

ᵇ Verse 45 below: Jesus was given the epithet 'a Word from God'. One explanation is that this was because it was God's command that brought him into being, rather than the intervention of a human father (Razi).

ᶜ The priests.

be held in honour in this world and the next, who will be one of those brought near to God. [46] He will speak to people in his infancy[a] and in his adulthood. He will be one of the righteous.' [47] She said, 'My Lord, how can I have a son when no man has touched me?' [The angel] said, 'This is how God creates what He will: when He has ordained something, He only says, "Be", and it is. [48] He will teach him the Scripture and wisdom, the Torah and the Gospel, [49] He will send him as a messenger to the Children of Israel: "I have come to you with a sign from your Lord: I will make a bird for you out of clay, then breathe into it and, with God's permission, it will become a real bird; I will heal the blind and the leper, and bring the dead back to life with God's permission; I will tell you what you may eat and what you may store up in your houses.[b] There truly is a sign for you in this, if you are believers. [50] I have come to confirm the truth of the Torah which preceded me, and to make some things lawful to you which used to be forbidden. I have come to you with a sign from your Lord. Be mindful of God, obey me— [51] God is my Lord and your Lord—so serve Him: that is a straight path." '

[52] When Jesus realized they [still] did not believe, he said, 'Who will help me in God's cause?' The disciples said, 'We will be God's helpers; we believe in God—witness our devotion to Him. [53] Lord, we believe in what You have revealed and we follow the messenger: record us among those who bear witness [to the Truth].' [54] The [disbelievers] schemed but God also schemed; God is the Best of Schemers.

[55] God said, 'Jesus, I will take you back and raise you up to Me: I will purify you of the disbelievers. To the Day of Resurrection I will make those who follow you superior to the disbelievers. Then you will all return to Me and I will judge between you regarding your differences. [56] I will make the disbelievers suffer severely in this world and the next; no one will help them.' [57] God will pay those who believe and do good deeds their reward in full; God does not love evildoers.

[58] We relate to you [Muhammad] this revelation, a decisive statement. [59] In God's eyes Jesus is just like Adam: He created him from

---

[a] Cf. 19: 29–30. The word *mahd* means a place smoothed out for a small child to sleep in. It is not a piece of furniture like a cradle.

[b] Another possible translation is 'to tell you what you eat and what you store . . .'.

dust, said to him, 'Be', and he was. [60] This is the truth from your Lord: do not be one of those who doubt. [61] If anyone disputes this with you now that you have been given this knowledge, say, 'Come, let us gather our sons and your sons, our women and your women, ourselves and yourselves, and let us pray earnestly and invoke God's rejection on those of us who are lying. [62] This is the truth of the matter: there is no god but God; God is the Exalted, the Decider.'[a] [63] If they turn away, [know that] God is well aware of anyone who causes corruption.[b] [64] Say, 'People of the Book, let us arrive at a statement that is common to us all: we worship God alone, we ascribe no partner to Him, and none of us takes others beside God as lords.' If they turn away, say, 'Witness our devotion to Him.'

[65] People of the Book, why do you argue about Abraham when the Torah and the Gospels were not revealed until after his time? Do you not understand? [66] You argue about some things of which you have some knowledge, but why do you argue about things of which you know nothing? God knows and you do not. [67] Abraham was neither a Jew nor a Christian. He was upright and devoted to God, never an idolater, [68] and the people who are closest to him are those who truly follow his ways, this Prophet, and [true] believers—God is close to [true] believers.

[69] Some of the People of the Book would dearly love to lead you [believers] astray, but they only lead themselves astray, though they do not realize it. [70] People of the Book, why do you deny God's revelations when you can see they are true? [71] People of the Book, why do you mix truth with falsehood? Why do you hide the truth when you recognize it? [72] Some of the People of the Book say, 'At the beginning of the day, believe in what has been revealed to these believers [the Muslims], then at the end of the day reject it, so that they too may turn back, [73] but do not sincerely believe in anyone unless he follows your own religion'—[Prophet], tell them, 'True guidance is the guidance of God'—[They say], 'Do not believe that anyone else could be given a revelation similar to what you were given, or that they could use it to argue against you in your Lord's presence.' [Prophet], tell them, 'All grace is in God's hands: He grants it to whoever He will—He is all embracing, all knowing—

---

[a] This translation of the term *hakim* is suggested by Razi.

[b] Corruption of beliefs and all that follows from that.

[74] and He singles out for His mercy whoever He will. His grace is infinite.'

[75] There are people of the Book who, if you [Prophet] entrust them with a heap of gold, will return it to you intact, but there are others of them who, if you entrust them with a single dinar, will not return it to you unless you keep standing over them, because they say, 'We are under no obligation towards the gentiles'—they tell a lie against God and they know it. [76] No indeed! God loves those who keep their pledges and are mindful of Him, [77] but those who sell out God's covenant and their own oaths for a small price will have no share in the life to come. God will neither speak to them nor look at them on the Day of Resurrection—He will not cleanse them [of their sins]—agonizing torment awaits them. [78] There are some who twist the Scripture with their tongues to make you [people] think that what they say is part of the Scripture when it is not; they say it is from God when it is not; they attribute lies to God and they know it.

[79] No person to whom God had given the Scripture, wisdom, and prophethood would ever say to people, 'Be my servants, not God's.' [He would say], 'You should be devoted to God because you have taught the Scripture and studied it closely.' [80] He would never command you to take angels and prophets as lords. How could he command you to be disbelievers after you had devoted yourselves to God?

[81] God took a pledge from the prophets, saying, 'If, after I have bestowed Scripture and wisdom upon you, a messenger comes confirming what you have been given, you must believe in him and support him. Do you affirm this and accept My pledge as binding on you?' They said, 'We do.' He said, 'Then bear witness and I too will bear witness.' [82] Those who turn away after this are the ones who break pledges. [83] Do they seek anything other than submission to God? Everyone in the heavens and earth submits to Him, willingly or unwillingly; they will all be returned to Him.

[84] Say [Muhammad], 'We [Muslims] believe in God and in what has been sent down to us and to Abraham, Ishmael, Isaac, Jacob, and the Tribes. We believe in what has been given to Moses, Jesus, and the prophets from their Lord. We do not make a distinction between any of the [prophets]. It is to Him that we devote ourselves.' [85] If anyone seeks a religion other than *islam*: complete devotion to

God, it will not be accepted from him: he will be one of the losers in the Hereafter. [86] Why would God guide people who deny the truth, after they have believed and acknowledged that the Messenger is true, and after they have been shown clear proof? God does not guide evildoers: [87] such people will be rewarded with rejection by God, by the angels, by all people, [88] and so they will remain, with no relief or respite for their suffering. [89] Not so those who afterwards repent and mend their ways—God is most forgiving and merciful— [90][although] the repentance of those who, having believed, then increase in their disbelief, will not be accepted. They are the ones who have gone [far] astray: [91] those who disbelieve and die disbelievers will not be saved even if they offer enough gold to fill the entire earth. Agonizing torment is in store for them, and there will be no one to help them. [92] None of you [believers] will attain true piety unless you give out of what you cherish: whatever you give, God knows about it very well.

[93] Except for what Israel made unlawful for himself, all food was lawful to the Children of Israel before the Torah was revealed. [a] Say, 'Bring the Torah and read out [the relevant passage] if you are telling the truth. [94] Those who persist in making up lies and attributing them to God are the wrongdoers.' [95] [Prophet], say, 'God speaks the truth, so follow Abraham's religion: he had true faith and he was never an idolater.' [96] The first House [of worship] to be established for mankind was the one at Mecca. [b] It is a blessed place; a source of guidance for all people; [97] there are clear signs in it; it is the place where Abraham stood; whoever enters it is safe. Pilgrimage to the House is a duty owed to God by people who are able to undertake it. Those who reject this [should know that] God has no need of anyone. [98] Say, 'People of the Book, why do you reject God's revelations? God witnesses everything you do.' [99] Say, 'People of the Book, why do you turn the believers away from God's path and try to make it crooked, when you yourselves [should be] witnesses to the [truth]? God is not heedless of anything you do.'

---

[a] The commentators explain that Israel/Jacob (Abraham's grandson) vowed to give up camel flesh and camel milk if he were relieved of his sciatica, and the Jews in Medina argued with Muhammad: 'You claim to be following the religion of Abraham. If this were so you would not be eating camel meat and drinking its milk, as these are forbidden in Abraham's religion.' This verse answers this argument (Razi).

[b] The original reads *Bakkah*, which was an old name for Mecca.

[100] You who believe, some of those who were given the Scripture would turn you into disbelievers if you were to yield to them. [101] How can you disbelieve when God's revelations are being recited to you and His Messenger is living among you? Whoever holds fast to God will be guided to the straight path. [102] You who believe, be mindful of God, as is His due, and make sure you devote yourselves to Him, to your dying moment. [103] Hold fast to God's rope all together; do not split into factions. Remember God's favour to you: you were enemies and then He brought your hearts together and you became brothers by His grace; you were about to fall into a pit of Fire and He saved you from it—in this way God makes His revelations clear to you so that you may be rightly guided. [104] Be[a] a community that calls for what is good, urges what is right, and forbids what is wrong: those who do this are the successful ones. [105] Do not be like those who, after they have been given clear revelation, split into factions and fall into disputes: a terrible punishment awaits such people. [106] On the Day when some faces brighten and others darken, it will be said to those with darkened faces, 'How could you reject your faith after believing? Taste the torment for doing so,' [107] but those with brightened faces will be in God's grace, there to remain. [108] These are God's revelations: We recite them to you [Prophet] with the Truth. God does not will injustice for His creatures. [109] Everything in the heavens and earth belongs to God; it is to Him that all things return.

[110] [Believers], you are the best community singled out for people: you order what is right, forbid what is wrong, and you believe in God. If the People of the Book had also believed, it would have been better for them. For although some of them do believe, most of them are lawbreakers—[111] they will not do you much harm: even if they come out to fight you, they will soon turn tail; they will get no help—[112] and, unless they hold fast to a lifeline from God and from mankind, they are overshadowed by vulnerability wherever they are found. They have drawn God's wrath upon themselves. They are overshadowed by weakness, too, because they have persistently disbelieved in God's revelation and killed prophets without any right, all because of their disobedience and boundless transgression. [113] But they are not all alike. There are some among the People of the Book

---

[a] Razi explains that the preposition *min* in the Arabic, usually translated as 'let there be *among* you', here applies to the whole community, not just part of it.

who are upright, who recite God's revelations during the night, who bow down in worship, [114] who believe in God and the Last Day, who order what is right and forbid what is wrong, who are quick to do good deeds. These people are among the righteous [115] and they will not be denied [the reward] for whatever good deeds they do: God knows exactly who is conscious of Him.

[116] As for those who disbelieve, neither their possessions nor their children will help them against God—they will be companions in the Fire, there to remain— [117] and whatever they give away in this life will be nullified: a frosty wind strikes and destroys the harvest of people who have wronged themselves. It was not God who wronged them; they wronged themselves.

[118] You who believe, do not take for your intimates such outsiders as spare no effort to ruin you and want to see you suffer: their hatred is evident from their mouths, but what their hearts conceal is far worse. We have made Our revelations clear for you; will you not use your reason? [119] This is how it is: here you are, you love them, but they do not love you; you believe in all the Scriptures and when they meet you, they say, 'We believe,' but when they are alone, they bite their fingertips in rage at you. [Prophet], say, 'Die of rage [if you wish]!' God knows exactly what is in everyone's hearts. [120] They grieve at any good that befalls you [believers] and rejoice at your misfortunes. But if you are steadfast and conscious of God, their scheming will not harm you in the least: God encircles everything they do.

[121] [Prophet], remember when you left your home at dawn to assign battle positions to the believers—God hears and knows everything. [122] Remember when two groups of you were about to lose heart and God protected them—let the believers put their trust in God— [123] God helped you at Badr when you were very weak. Be mindful of God, so that you may be grateful. [124] Remember when you said to the believers, 'Will you be satisfied if your Lord reinforces you by sending down three thousand angels? [125] Well, if you are steadfast and mindful of God, your Lord will reinforce you with five thousand swooping angels if the enemy should suddenly attack you!' and God arranged it so, [126] as a message of hope for you [believers] to put your hearts at rest—help comes only from God, the Mighty, the Wise— [127] and in order to cut off the flanks of the disbelievers' army and frustrate them, to make them withdraw in total defeat. [128] Whether

God relents towards them or punishes them is not for you [Prophet] to decide: they are wrongdoers. ¹²⁹ Everything in the heavens and earth belongs to God. He forgives whoever He will and punishes whoever He will: God is most forgiving and merciful.

¹³⁰ You who believe, do not consume usurious interest, doubled and redoubled. Be mindful of God so that you may prosper— ¹³¹ beware of the Fire prepared for those who disbelieve—¹³² and obey God and the Prophet so that you may be given mercy. ¹³³ Hurry towards your Lord's forgiveness and a Garden as wide as the heavens and earth prepared for the righteous, ¹³⁴ who give, both in prosperity and adversity, who restrain their anger and pardon people—God loves those who do good—¹³⁵ those who remember God and implore forgiveness for their sins if they do something shameful or wrong themselves—who forgives sins but God?—and who never knowingly persist in doing wrong. ¹³⁶ The reward for such people is forgiveness from their Lord, and Gardens graced with flowing streams, there to remain. How excellent is the reward of those who labour!

¹³⁷ God's ways have operated before your time: travel through the land, and see what was the end of those who disbelieved. ¹³⁸ This is a clear lesson to people, and guidance and teaching for those who are mindful of God. ¹³⁹ Do not lose heart or despair—if you are true believers you have the upper hand—¹⁴⁰ if you have suffered a blow, they too have suffered one like it.ᵃ We deal out such days among people in turn, for God to find out who truly believes, for Him to choose martyrsᵇ from among you—God does not love evildoers— ¹⁴¹ for Him to cleanse those who believe and for Him to destroy the disbelievers. ¹⁴² Did you think you would enter the Garden without God first proving which of you would struggle for His cause and remain steadfast? ¹⁴³ Before you encountered death, you were hoping for it. Well, now you have seen it with your own eyes.

¹⁴⁴ Muhammad is only a messenger before whom many messengers

ᵃ This part of the sura refers to the Battle of Uhud, where the Muslims were defeated, having disobeyed the Prophet's orders.

ᵇ The noun *shahid* is much more complex than the term 'martyr' chosen to render it in this context. The root *sh–h–d* conveys 'to witness, to be present, to attend', but also 'to testify' or 'to give evidence'. Thus the 'martyrs' here are chosen by God to witness Him in heaven, are given the opportunity to give evidence of the depth of their faith by sacrificing their worldly lives, and will testify with the prophets on the Day of Judgement.

have been and gone. If he died or was killed,[a] would you revert to your old ways? If anyone did so, he would not harm God in the least. God will reward the grateful. [145]No soul may die except with God's permission at a predestined time. If anyone strives for the rewards of this world, We will give him some of them. If anyone strives for the rewards of the Hereafter, We will give him some of them: We will reward the grateful. [146]Many prophets have fought, with large bands of godly men alongside them who, in the face of their sufferings for God's cause, did not lose heart or weaken or surrender—God loves those who are steadfast. [147]All they said was, 'Our Lord, forgive us our sins and our excesses. Make our feet firm, and give us help against the disbelievers,' [148]and so God gave them both the rewards of this world and the excellent rewards of the Hereafter: God loves those who do good.

[149]You who believe, if you obey the disbelievers, they will make you revert to your old ways and you will turn into losers. [150]No indeed! It is God who is your protector: He is the best of helpers. [151]We will strike panic into the disbelievers' hearts because they attribute partners to God although He has sent no authority for this: their shelter will be the Fire—how miserable is the home of the evildoers! [152]God fulfilled His promise to you: you were routing them, with His permission, but then you faltered, disputed the order, and disobeyed, once He had brought you within sight of your goal[b]—some of you desire the gains of this world and others desire the world to come—and then He prevented you from [defeating] them as a punishment. He has now forgiven you: God is most gracious to the believers. [153]You fled without looking back while the Messenger was calling out to you from behind, and God rewarded you with sorrow for sorrow. [He has now forgiven you] so that you may not grieve for what you missed or for what happened to you. God is well aware of everything you do. [154]After sorrow, He caused calm to descend upon some of you—a sleep that overtook you.

Another group, caring only for themselves, entertained false thoughts about God, thoughts more appropriate to pagan ignorance, and said, 'Do we get a say in any of this?' [Prophet], tell them,

[a] In the Battle of Uhud, it was rumoured that Muhammad had been killed.

[b] The archers disobeyed the Prophet's order to remain in their positions until the end. They thought the Muslims had won and dashed to get the booty. This allowed their enemies to regroup and attack, so winning the battle.

'Everything to do with this affair is in God's hands.' They conceal in their hearts things they will not reveal to you. They say, 'If we had had our say in this, none of us would have been killed here.' Tell them, 'Even if you had resolved to stay at home, those who were destined to be killed would still have gone out to meet their deaths.' God did this in order to test everything within you and in order to prove what is in your hearts. God knows your innermost thoughts very well. [155] As for those of you who turned away on the day the two armies met in battle, it was Satan who caused them to slip, through some of their actions. God has now pardoned them: God is most forgiving and forbearing.

[156] You who believe, do not be like those who disbelieved and said of their brothers who went out on a journey or a raid, 'If only they had stayed with us they would not have died or been killed,' for God will make such thoughts a source of anguish in their hearts. It is God who gives life and death; God sees everything you do. [157] Whether you are killed for God's cause or die, God's forgiveness and mercy are better than anything people amass. [158] Whether you die or are killed, it is to God that you will be gathered.

[159] By an act of mercy from God, you [Prophet] were gentle in your dealings with them—had you been harsh, or hard-hearted, they would have dispersed and left you—so pardon them and ask forgiveness for them. Consult with them about matters, then, when you have decided on a course of action, put your trust in God: God loves those who put their trust in Him. [160] If God helps you [believers], no one can overcome you; if He forsakes you, who else can help you? Believers should put their trust in God.

[161] It is inconceivable that a prophet would ever dishonestly take something from the battle gains. Anyone who does so will carry it with him on the Day of Resurrection, when each soul will be fully repaid for what it has done: no one will be wronged. [162] Can the man who pursues God's good pleasure be like the man who has brought God's wrath upon himself and whose home will be Hell—a foul destination? [163] They are in a different class in God's eyes; God sees exactly what they do.

[164] God has been truly gracious to the believers in sending them a Messenger from among their own, to recite His revelations to them, to make them grow in purity, and to teach them the Scripture and wisdom—before that they were clearly astray. [165] Why do you

[believers] say, when a calamity befalls you, even after you have inflicted twice as much damage [on your enemy], 'How did this happen?'? [Prophet], say, 'You brought it upon yourselves.' God has power over everything: [166] what befell you on the day the two armies met in battle happened with God's permission and in order for Him to see who were the true believers and who were the hypocrites who, [167] when it was said to them, 'Come, fight for God's cause, or at least defend yourselves,' answered, 'We would follow you if we knew there was going to be fighting.' On that day they were closer to disbelief than belief. They say with their tongues what is not in their hearts: God knows exactly what they conceal.

[168] As for those who stayed behind, and said of their brothers, 'If only they had listened to us, they would not have been killed,' tell them [Prophet], 'Ward off death from yourselves, if what you say is true.' [169] [Prophet], do not think of those who have been killed in God's way as dead. They are alive with their Lord, well provided for, [170] happy with what God has given them of His favour; rejoicing that for those they have left behind who have yet to join them there is no fear, nor will they grieve; [171] [rejoicing] in God's blessing and favour, and that God will not let the reward of the believers be lost. [172] Those who responded to God and the Messenger after suffering defeat, who do good and remain conscious of God, will have a great reward. [173] Those whose faith only increased when people said, 'Fear your enemy: they have amassed a great army against you,' and who replied, 'God is enough for us: He is the best protector,' [174] returned with grace and bounty from God and no harm befell them. They pursued God's good pleasure. God's favour is great indeed. [175] It is Satan who urges you to fear his followers; do not fear them, but fear Me, if you are true believers.

[176] [Prophet], do not be grieved by those who are quick to disbelieve. They will not harm God in the least; it is God's will that they will have no share in the Hereafter—a terrible torment awaits them. [177] Those who sell their faith for disbelief will not harm God in any way; agonizing torment awaits them. [178] The disbelievers should not think that it is better for them that We give them more time: when We give them more time they become more sinful—a shameful torment awaits them. [179] Nor was it God's aim to leave you as you were, with no separation between the bad and the good.[a] God

---

[a] With hypocrites mixing with them (Razi). See verses 166–7.

would not show you [people] what is hidden: God chooses as His messengers whoever He will. So believe in God and His messengers: if you believe and stay mindful of God, you will have a great reward. [180] Those who are miserly with what God has granted them out of His grace should not think that it is good for them; on the contrary, it is bad for them. Whatever they meanly withhold will be hung around their necks on the Day of Resurrection. It is God who will inherit the heavens and earth: God is well aware of everything you do.

[181] God has certainly heard the words of those who sneer, 'So God is poor, while we are rich'.[a] We shall record everything they say—as well as their killing of prophets in defiance of all that is right—and We shall say to them, 'Taste the torment of the scorching fire. [182] That is on account of what you stored up for yourselves with your own hands: God is never unjust to His servants.' [183] To those who say, 'God has commanded us not to believe in any messenger unless he brings us an offering that fire [from heaven] consumes,' say [Prophet], 'Messengers before me have come to you with clear signs, including the one you mention. If you are sincere, why did you kill them?' [184] If they reject you, so have other messengers been rejected before you, even though they came with clear evidence, written texts and the enlightening Scripture. [185] Every soul will taste death and you will be paid in full only on the Day of Resurrection. Whoever is kept away from the Fire and admitted to the Garden will have triumphed. The present world is only an illusory pleasure: [186] you are sure to be tested through your possessions and persons; you are sure to hear much that is hurtful from those who were given the Scripture before you and from those who associate others with God. If you are steadfast and mindful of God, that is the best course.

[187] God took a pledge from those who were given the Scripture— 'Make it known to people; do not conceal it'—but they tossed the pledge over their shoulders, they bartered it for a small price: what a bad bargain they made! [188] Do not think [Prophet] that those who exult in their actions and seek praise for things they have not done will escape the torment; agonizing torment awaits them.

[189] Control of the heavens and earth belongs to God; God has

---

[a] A retort to 2: 245, which was often cited by the Prophet when asking for financial contributions to the cause.

power over everything. [190] There truly are signs in the creation of the heavens and earth, and in the alternation of night and day, for those with understanding, [191] who remember God standing, sitting, and lying down, who reflect on the creation of the heavens and earth: 'Our Lord! You have not created all this without purpose—You are far above that!—so protect us from the torment of the Fire. [192] Our Lord! You will truly humiliate those You commit to the Fire. The evildoers have no one to help them. [193] Our Lord! We have heard someone calling us to faith—"Believe in your Lord"—and we have believed. Our Lord! Forgive us our sins, wipe out our bad deeds, and grant that we join the righteous when we die. [194] Our Lord! Bestow upon us all that You have promised us through Your messengers— do not humiliate us on the Day of Resurrection—You never break Your promise.' [195] Their Lord has answered them: 'I will not allow the deeds of any one of you to be lost, whether you are male or female, each is like the other [in rewards]. [a] I will certainly wipe out the bad deeds of those who emigrated and were driven out of their homes, who suffered harm for My cause, who fought and were killed. I will certainly admit them to Gardens graced with flowing streams as a reward from God: the best reward is with God.'

[196] [Prophet], do not be deceived by the disbelievers' [lucrative] trading to and fro in the land: [197] this is only a brief enjoyment, after which Hell will be their home—a miserable resting place! [198] But those who were mindful of their Lord will have Gardens graced with flowing streams where they will stay as a reward from God. What God has is best for those who are truly good.

[199] Some of the People of the Book believe in God, in what has been sent down to you and in what was sent down to them: humbling themselves before God, they would never sell God's revelation for a small price. These people will have their rewards with their Lord: God is swift in reckoning. [200] You who believe, be steadfast, more steadfast than others; fortify yourselves; always be mindful of God, so that you may prosper.

---

[a] Literally 'you come from each other', i.e. you are equal.

4. WOMEN

A Medinan sura which takes its title from the many references to women throughout the sura (verses 3–4, 127–30). It gives a number of instructions, urging justice to children and orphans, and mentioning inheritance and marriage laws. The early verses of the sura give rulings on property and inheritance, and so does the verse which concludes the sura. The sura also talks of the tensions between the Muslim community in Medina and some of the People of the Book (verses 44, 61), moving into a general discussion of war: it warns the Muslims to be cautious and to defend the weak and helpless (verses 71–6). Another similar theme is the intrigues of the hypocrites (verses 88–91, 138–46).

In the name of God, the Lord of Mercy, the Giver of Mercy

[1] People, be mindful of your Lord, who created you from a single soul, and from it[a] created its mate, and from the pair of them spread countless men and women far and wide; be mindful of God, in whose name you make requests of one another. Beware of severing the ties of kinship:[b] God is always watching over you. [2] Give orphans their property, do not replace [their] good things with bad, and do not consume their property with your own—a serious crime. [3] If you fear that you will not deal fairly with orphan girls,[c] you may marry whichever [other][d] women seem good to you, two, three, or four. If you fear that you cannot be equitable [to them], then marry only one, or your slave(s):[e] that is more likely to make you avoid bias. [4] Give women their dowry as a gift upon marriage, though if they are happy to give up some of it for you, you may enjoy it with clear conscience.

[5] Do not entrust your property to the feeble-minded. God has made it a means of support for you: make provision for them from it, clothe them, and address them kindly. [6] Test orphans until they reach marriageable age; then, if you find they have sound judgement, hand

---

[a] 'From the same essence'. Razi convincingly reached this conclusion based on comparison with many instances when *min anfusikum* is used in the Qur'an.

[b] Literally 'the womb-relationships', i.e. all those to whom you are related. This expression occurs again in 47: 22.

[c] In pre-Islamic Arabia, some guardians of orphan girls used to marry them in order to take their property (see 4: 127).

[d] This is a widely accepted interpretation.

[e] 'Literally 'what your right hands possess'.

over their property to them. Do not consume it wastefully before they come of age: if the guardian is well off he should abstain from the orphan's property, and if he is poor he should use only what is fair. When you give them their property, call witnesses in; God takes full account of everything you do.

[7] Men shall have a share in what their parents and closest relatives leave, and women shall have a share in what their parents and closest relatives leave, whether the legacy be small or large: this is ordained by God. [8] If other relatives, orphans, or needy people are present at the distribution, give them something too, and speak kindly to them. [9] Let those who would fear for the future of their own helpless children, if they were to die, show the same concern [for orphans]; let them be mindful of God and speak out for justice. [10] Those who consume the property of orphans unjustly are actually swallowing fire into their own bellies: they will burn in the blazing Flame.

[11] Concerning your children, God commands you that a son should have the equivalent share of two daughters. If there are only daughters, two or more should share two-thirds of the inheritance, if one, she should have half. Parents inherit a sixth each if the deceased leaves children; if he leaves no children and his parents are his sole heirs, his mother has a third, unless he has brothers, in which case she has a sixth. [In all cases, the distribution comes] after payment of any bequests or debts. You cannot know which of your parents or your children is closer to you in benefit: this is a law from God, and He is all knowing, all wise. [12] You inherit half of what your wives leave, if they have no children; if they have children, you inherit a quarter. [In all cases, the distribution comes] after payment of any bequests or debts. If you have no children, your wives' share is a quarter; if you have children, your wives get an eighth. [In all cases, the distribution comes] after payment of any bequests or debts. If a man or a woman dies leaving no children or parents,[a] but a single brother or sister, he or she should take one-sixth of the inheritance; if there are more siblings, they share one-third between them. [In all cases, the distribution comes] after payment of any bequests or debts, with no harm done to anyone: this is a commandment from God, and He is all knowing and benign to all. [13] These are the bounds

[a] This is the most generally accepted meaning of the Arabic word *kalala*. There are many others.

set by God: God will admit those who obey Him and His Messenger to Gardens graced with flowing streams, and there they will stay—that is the supreme triumph! [14] But those who disobey God and His Messenger and overstep His limits will be consigned by God to the Fire, and there they will stay—a humiliating torment awaits them!

[15] If any of your women commit a lewd act, call four witnesses from among you, then, if they testify to their guilt, keep the women at home until death comes to them or until God gives them another way out. [a] [16] If two men commit a lewd act, punish them both; if they repent and mend their ways, leave them alone—God is always ready to accept repentance, He is full of mercy. [17] But God only undertakes to accept repentance from those who do evil out of ignorance and soon afterwards repent: these are the ones God will forgive, He is all knowing, all wise. [18] It is not true repentance when people continue to do evil until death confronts them and then say, 'Now I repent,' nor when they die as disbelievers: We have prepared a painful torment for these.

[19] You who believe, it is not lawful for you to inherit women against their will, [b] nor should you treat your wives harshly, hoping to take back some of the dowry you gave them, unless they are guilty of something clearly outrageous. Live with them in accordance with what is fair and kind: if you dislike them, it may well be that you dislike something in which God has put much good. [20] If you wish to replace one wife with another, do not take any of her dowry back, even if you have given her a great amount of gold. [21] How could you take it when this is unjust and a blatant sin? How could you take it when you have lain with each other and they have taken a solemn pledge from you?

[22] Do not marry women that your fathers married—with the exception of what is past—this is indeed a shameful thing to do, loathsome and leading to evil. [23] You are forbidden to take as wives your mothers, daughters, sisters, paternal and maternal aunts, the daughters of brothers and daughters of sisters, your milk-mothers and milk-sisters, [c] your wives' mothers, the stepdaughters in your

---

[a] Through another regulation, or marriage, or any other way. See also end of 65: 2, which uses nearly identical words.

[b] In pre-Islamic Arabia, if a man died leaving a widow, her stepson or another man of his family could inherit her.

[c] Islam regards women who breastfeed other people's infants as their 'milk-mothers', not merely 'wet nurses'.

care—those born of women with whom you have consummated marriage, if you have not consummated the marriage, then you will not be blamed—wives of your begotten sons, two sisters simultaneously—with the exception of what is past: God is most forgiving and merciful—²⁴ women already married, other than your slaves:[a] God has ordained all this for you. Other women are lawful to you, so long as you seek them in marriage, with gifts from your property, looking for wedlock rather than fornication. If you wish to enjoy women through marriage, give them their dowry—this is obligatory—though if you should choose mutually, after fulfilling this obligation, to do otherwise [with the dowry], you will not be blamed: God is all knowing and all wise.

²⁵ If any of you does not have the means to marry a believing free woman, then marry a believing slave—God knows best [the depth of] your faith: you are [all] part of the same family.[b] So marry them with their people's consent and their proper dowries. [Make them] married women, not adulteresses or lovers. If they commit adultery when they are married, their punishment will be half that of free women. Only those of you who fear that they will sin should marry slaves; it is better for you to practise self-restraint. God is most forgiving and merciful, ²⁶ He wishes to make His laws clear to you and guide you to the righteous ways of those who went before you. He wishes to turn towards you in mercy—He is all knowing, all wise—²⁷ He wishes to turn towards you, but those who follow their lusts want you to go far astray. ²⁸ God wishes to lighten your burden; man was created weak.

²⁹ You who believe, do not wrongfully consume each other's wealth but trade by mutual consent. Do not kill each other, for God is merciful to you. ³⁰ If any of you does these things, out of hostility and injustice, We shall make him suffer Fire: that is easy for God. ³¹ But if you avoid the great sins you have been forbidden, We shall wipe out your minor misdeeds and let you in through the entrance of honour. ³² Do not covet what God has given to some of you more than others—men have the portion they have earned[c] and women their

---

[a] Slave women were often unclaimed war captives, who would not be in a position to dissolve any previous marriage. An owner was not permitted to touch a slave woman whose husband was with her (Abu Hanifa, in Razi).

[b] Literally 'you are from one another'.

[c] The preposition *min* here is taken to have an explanatory rather than a partitive function, which would render the translation 'some of what they have earned'.

portion—you should rather ask God for some of His bounty: He has full knowledge of everything. [33] We have appointed heirs for everything that parents and close relatives leave behind, including those to whom you have pledged your hands [in marriage], so give them their share: God is witness to everything.

[34] Husbands should take full care of their wives, with [the bounties] God has given to some more than others and with what they spend out of their own money. Righteous wives are devout and guard what God would have them guard in their husbands' absence. If you fear high-handedness[a] from your wives, remind them [of the teachings of God], then ignore them when you go to bed, then hit them.[b] If they obey you, you have no right to act against them: God is most high and great. [35] If you [believers] fear that a couple may break up, appoint one arbiter from his family and one from hers. Then, if the couple want to put things right, God will bring about a reconciliation between them: He is all knowing, all aware.

[36] Worship God; join nothing with Him. Be good to your parents, to relatives, to orphans, to the needy, to neighbours near and far, to travellers in need, and to your slaves. God does not like arrogant, boastful people, [37] who are miserly and order other people to be the same, hiding the bounty God has given them. We have prepared a humiliating torment for such ungrateful people. [38] [Nor does He like those] who spend their wealth to show off, who do not believe in Him or the Last Day. Whoever has Satan as his companion has an evil companion! [39] What harm would it do them to believe in God and the Last Day, and give charitably from the sustenance God has given them? God knows them well. [40] He does not wrong anyone by as much as the weight of a speck of dust: He doubles any good deed and gives a tremendous reward of His own. [41] What will they do when We bring a witness from each community, with you [Muhammad] as a witness against these people? [42] On that day, those who disbelieved and disobeyed the Prophet will wish that the earth could swallow them up: they will not be able to hide anything from God.

---

[a] The verb *nashaza* from which *nushuz* is derived means 'to become high', 'to rise'. See also verse 128, where the same word is applied to husbands. It applies to a situation where one partner assumes superiority to the other and behaves accordingly.

[b] See Abdel Haleem, *Understanding the Qur'an*, 46–54.

[43] You who believe, do not come anywhere near the prayer if you are intoxicated,[a] until you know what you are saying; nor if you are in a state of major ritual impurity—though you may pass through the mosque—until you have bathed; if you are ill, on a journey, have relieved yourselves, or had intercourse, and cannot find any water, then find some clean sand[b] and wipe your faces and hands with it. God is always ready to pardon and forgive.

[44] [Prophet], have you not considered how those who were given a share of the Scripture purchase misguidance and want you [believers], too, to lose the right path? [45] God knows your enemies best: God is enough to protect and enough to help you. [46] Some Jews distort the meaning of [revealed] words: they say, 'We hear and disobey,' and 'Listen,' [adding the insult] 'May you not hear,' and '*Ra'ina* [Look at us],'[c] twisting it abusively with their tongues so as to disparage religion. If they had said, 'We hear and obey,' 'Listen,' and '*Unzurna* [Look at us],' that would have been better and more proper for them, but God has spurned them for their defiance: they believe very little.

[47] People of the Book, believe in what We have sent down to confirm what you already have, before We wipe out [your sense of] direction,[d] turning you back, or reject you, as We rejected those who broke the Sabbath: God's will is always done. [48] God does not forgive the joining of partners with Him: anything less than that He forgives to whoever He will, but anyone who joins partners with God is lying and committing a tremendous sin. [49] [Prophet], have you considered those who claim purity for themselves? No! God purifies whoever He will: no one will be wronged by as much as the husk of a date stone. [50] See how they invent lies about God, this in itself is a flagrant sin! [51] Have you considered how those given a share of the Scripture, [evidently] now believe in idols and evil powers? They say of the disbelievers, 'They are more rightly guided than the believers.'[e] [52] Those are the ones God has rejected: you [Prophet] will not find

[a] The prohibition of intoxicants was introduced by stages, and they were eventually made completely unlawful. Cf. 2: 219; 5: 90–1.

[b] The term *sa'id* means dust or earth or soil or sand.

[c] Cf. note to 2: 104.

[d] Literally 'obliterate faces'. Another meaning of *wujuh* (faces) is 'directions' (Razi).

[e] This is taken to refer to an actual event in which a group of disbelieving Meccans went to two eminent Jewish figures for counsel on the truth of Muhammad's teachings and were told that the pagans were more rightly guided than the Muslims.

anyone to help those God has rejected. [53] Do they have any share of what He possesses? If they did they would not give away so much as the groove of a date stone. [54] Do they envy [other] people for the bounty God has granted them? We gave the descendants of Abraham the Scripture and wisdom—and We gave them a great kingdom—[55] but some of them believed in it[a] and some turned away from it. Hell blazes fiercely enough. [56] We shall send those who reject Our revelations to the Fire. When their skins have been burned away, We shall replace them with new ones so that they may continue to feel the pain: God is mighty and wise. [57] As for those who believe and do good deeds, We shall admit them into Gardens graced with flowing streams and there they will remain. They will have pure spouses there, and We shall admit them into cool refreshing shade.

[58] God commands you [people] to return things entrusted to you to their rightful owners, and, if you judge between people, to do so with justice: God's instructions to you are excellent, for He hears and sees everything. [59] You who believe, obey God and the Messenger, and those in authority among you. If you are in dispute over any matter, refer it to God and the Messenger, if you truly believe in God and the Last Day: that is better and fairer in the end. [60] Have you [Prophet] considered those who claim to believe in what has been sent down to you, and in what was sent down before you, yet still want to turn to unjust tyrants[b] for judgement, although they have been ordered to reject them? Satan wants to lead them far astray. [61] When they are told, 'Turn to God's revelations and the Messenger [for judgement],' you see the hypocrites turn right away from you [Prophet]. [62] [Let them think:] if disaster strikes them because of what they themselves have done, then they will come to you, swearing by God, 'We only wanted to do good and achieve harmony.' [63] God knows well what is in the hearts of these people, so ignore what they say, instruct them, and speak to them about themselves using penetrating words.

[64] All the messengers We sent were meant to be obeyed, by God's leave. If only [the hypocrites] had come to you [Prophet] when they

---

[a] The pronoun *hi* here refers to either (i) the Scripture or (ii) Abraham.

[b] The Arabic *taghut* is variously interpreted to refer to idols, a specific tyrant, an oracle, or an opponent of the Prophet.

wronged themselves, and begged God's forgiveness, then the Messenger would have asked forgiveness for them and they would have found that God accepts repentance and is most merciful. [65] By your Lord, they will not be true believers until they let you decide between them in all matters of dispute, and find no resistance in their souls to your decisions, accepting them totally—[66] if We had ordered, 'Lay down your lives' or 'Leave your homes,' they would not have done so, except for a few—it would have been far better for them and stronger confirmation of their faith, if they had done as they were told, [67] and We would have given them a rich reward of Our own [68] and guided them to a straight path. [69] Whoever obeys God and the Messenger will be among those He has blessed: the messengers, the truthful, those who bear witness to the truth,[a] and the righteous—what excellent companions these are! [70] That is God's favour. No one knows better than Him.

[71] You who believe, be on your guard. March [to battle] in small groups or as one body. [72] Among you there is the sort of person who is sure to lag behind: if a calamity befalls you, he says, 'God has been gracious to me that I was not there with them,' [73] yet he is sure to say, if you are favoured by God, 'If only I had been with them, I could have made great gains,' as if there had been no ties of affection between you and him. [74] Let those of you who are willing to trade the life of this world for the life to come, fight in God's way. To anyone who fights in God's way, whether killed or victorious, We shall give a great reward. [75] Why should you not fight in God's cause and for those oppressed men, women, and children who cry out, 'Lord, rescue us from this town whose people are oppressors! By Your grace, give us a protector and helper!'? [76] The believers fight for God's cause, while those who reject faith fight for an unjust cause.[b] Fight the allies of Satan: Satan's ploys are truly weak.

[77] [Prophet], have you considered those who were told, 'Restrain yourselves from fighting, perform the prayer, and pay the prescribed alms'? When fighting was ordained for them, some of them feared men as much as, or even more than, they feared God, saying, 'Lord, why have You ordained fighting for us? If only You would give us just a little more time.' Say to them, 'Little is the enjoyment in this

---

[a] Martyrs bear witness to the truth with their lives (Razi).

[b] Again this is the term *taghut*, which has a multitude of meanings. See note to verse 60.

world, the Hereafter is far better for those who are aware of God: you will not be wronged by as much as the fibre in a date stone. [78] Death will overtake you no matter where you may be, even inside high towers.' When good fortune comes their way, they say, 'This is from God,' but when harm befalls them, they say, 'This is from you [Prophet].' Say to them, 'Both come from God.' What is the matter with these people that they can barely understand what they are told? [79] Anything good that happens to you [Prophet] is from God; anything bad is [ultimately] from yourself. We have sent you as a messenger to people; God is sufficient witness. [80] Whoever obeys the Messenger obeys God. If some pay no heed, We have not sent you to be their keeper. [81] They say, 'We obey you,' but as soon as they leave your presence, some of them scheme by night to do other than what you said. God records what they scheme, so leave them alone, and put your trust in God: He is sufficient protector.

[82] Will they not think about this Qur'an? If it had been from anyone other than God, they would have found much inconsistency in it. [83] Whenever news of any matter comes to them, whether concerning peace or war, they spread it about; if they referred it to the Messenger and those in authority among them, those seeking its meaning would have found it out from them. If it were not for God's bounty and mercy towards you, you would almost all have followed Satan.

[84] So [Prophet] fight in God's way. You are accountable only for yourself. Urge the believers on. God may well curb the power of the disbelievers, for He is stronger in might and more terrible in punishment. [85] Whoever speaks for[a] a good cause will share in its benefits and whoever speaks for a bad cause will share in its burden: God controls everything. [86] But [even in battle] when you [believers] are offered a greeting, respond with a better one, or at least return it:[b] God keeps account of everything. [87] He is God: there is no god but Him. He will gather you all together on the Day of Resurrection, about which there is no doubt. Whose word can be truer than God's?

---

[a] It is reported that an individual asked the Prophet to exempt another from going into battle. 'Speaks for' is one of the meanings of *shafaʿa* as explained by Razi, and it is more fitting for the context of urging the believer to fight in God's cause here. The other meaning, 'intercedes', adopted by most translators does not fit with the context.

[b] See 4: 94 and Razi's comment.

[88] [Believers], why are you divided in two about the hypocrites, when God Himself has rejected them because of what they have done? Do you want to guide those God has left to stray? If God leaves anyone to stray, you [Prophet] will never find the way for him. [89] They would dearly like you to reject faith, as they themselves have done, to be like them. So do not take them as allies until they migrate [to Medina] for God's cause. If they turn [on you],*a* then seize and kill them wherever you encounter them.*b* Take none of them as an ally or supporter. [90] But as for those who seek refuge with people with whom you have a treaty, or who come over to you because their hearts forbid them to fight against you or against their own people, God could have given them power over you, and they would have fought you. So if they withdraw and do not fight you, and offer you peace, then God gives you no way against them. [91] You will find others who wish to be safe from you, and from their own people, but whenever they are back in a situation where they are tempted [to fight you], they succumb to it. So if they neither withdraw, nor offer you peace, nor restrain themselves from fighting you, seize and kill them wherever you encounter them: We give you clear authority against such people.

[92] Never should a believer kill another believer, except by mistake. If anyone kills a believer by mistake he must free one Muslim slave and pay compensation to the victim's relatives, unless they charitably forgo it; if the victim belonged to a people at war with you but is a believer, then the compensation is only to free a believing slave; if he belonged to a people with whom you have a treaty, then compensation should be handed over to his relatives, and a believing slave set free. Anyone who lacks the means to do this must fast for two consecutive months by way of repentance to God: God is all knowing, all wise. [93] If anyone kills a believer deliberately, the punishment for him is Hell, and there he will remain: God is angry with him, and rejects him, and has prepared a tremendous torment for him. [94] So, you who believe, be careful when you go to fight in God's way, and do not say to someone who offers you a greeting of peace, 'You are not a believer,'*c* out of desire for the chance gains of this life—God

---

a That 'turn with aggression' is the intended meaning is clear from the context. Cf. 4: 91.

b See 2: 191.

c A Muslim killed someone in battle who had given him the Muslim greeting, thinking that the man was trying to save himself, but the Prophet condemned this.

has plenty of gains for you. You yourself were in the same position [once], but God was gracious to you, so be careful: God is fully aware of what you do.

⁹⁵ Those believers who stay at home, apart from those with an incapacity, are not equal to those who commit themselves and their possessions to striving in God's way. God has raised such people to a rank above those who stay at home—although He has promised all believers a good reward, those who strive are favoured with a tremendous reward above those who stay at home—⁹⁶ high ranks conferred by Him, as well as forgiveness, and mercy: God is most forgiving and merciful.

⁹⁷ When the angels take the souls of those who have wronged themselves,ᵃ they ask them, 'What circumstances were you in?' They reply, 'We were oppressed in this land,' and the angels say, 'But was God's earth not spacious enough for you to migrate to some other place?' These people will have Hell as their refuge, an evil destination, ⁹⁸ but not so the truly helpless men, women, and children who have no means in their power nor any way to leave— ⁹⁹ God may well pardon these, for He is most pardoning and most forgiving. Anyone who migrates for God's cause will find many a refuge and great plenty in the earth, ¹⁰⁰ and if anyone leaves home as a migrant towards God and His Messenger and is then overtaken by death, his reward from God is sure. God is most forgiving and most merciful.

¹⁰¹ When you [believers] are travelling in the land, you will not be blamed for shortening your prayers, if you fear the disbelievers may harm you: they are your sworn enemies. ¹⁰² When you [Prophet] are with the believers, leading them in prayer, let a group of them stand up in prayer with you, taking their weapons with them, and when they have finished their prostration, let them take up their positions at the back. Then let the other group, who have not yet prayed, pray with you, also on their guard and armed with their weapons: the disbelievers would dearly like you to be heedless of your weapons and baggage, in order for them to take you in a single assault. You will not be blamed if you lay aside your arms when you are overtaken by heavy rain or illness, but be on your guard. Indeed, God has prepared a humiliating punishment for the disbelievers. ¹⁰³ After

---

ᵃ By living in a place where they are unable to practise their religion.

performing the ritual prayer, continue to remember God—standing, sitting, and lying on your sides—and once you are safe, keep up regular prayer, for prayer is obligatory for the believers at prescribed times. [104] Do not be faint-hearted in pursuing the enemy: if you are suffering hardship, so are they, but you hope to receive something from God for which they cannot hope. God is all knowing and wise.

[105] We have sent down the Scripture to you [Prophet] with the truth so that you can judge between people in accordance with what God has shown you. Do not be an advocate for those who betray trust.[a] [106] Ask God for forgiveness: He is most forgiving and merciful. [107] Do not argue for those who betray their own souls: God does not love anyone given to treachery and sin. [108] They try to hide themselves from people, but they cannot hide from God. He is with them when they plot at night, saying things that do not please Him: He is fully aware of everything they do. [109] There you [believers] are, arguing on their behalf in this life, but who will argue on their behalf with God on the Day of Resurrection? Who will be their defender? [110] Yet anyone who does evil or wrongs his own soul and then asks God for forgiveness will find Him most forgiving and merciful. [111] He who commits sin does so against his own soul—God is all knowing and wise—[112] and anyone who commits an offence or a sin, and then throws the blame on to some innocent person, has burdened himself with deceit as well as flagrant sin.

[113] If it were not for the grace of God and His mercy to you [Prophet], a party of them would have tried to lead you astray; they only lead themselves astray, and cannot harm you in any way, since God has sent down the Scripture and Wisdom to you, and taught you what you did not know. God's bounty to you is great indeed. [114] There is no good in most of their secret talk, only in commanding charity, or good, or reconciliation between people. To anyone who does these things, seeking to please God, We shall give a rich reward; [115] if anyone opposes the Messenger, after guidance has been made clear to him, and follows a path other than that of the believers, We shall leave him on his chosen path—We shall burn him in Hell, an evil destination.

---

[a] A man from Medina stole a suit of armour and accused a Jew of doing it. He brought his family to ask the Prophet to rule against the Jew and he was about to do this when these verses were revealed (Razi).

[116] God does not forgive the worship of others beside Him—though He does forgive whoever He will for lesser sins—for whoever does this has gone far, far astray. [117] In His place the idolaters invoke only females,[a] and Satan, the rebel [118] God rejected, who said, 'I will certainly take my due share of Your servants; [119] I will mislead them and incite vain desires in them; I will command them to slit the ears of cattle;[b] I will command them to tamper with God's creation.' Whoever chooses Satan as a patron instead of God is utterly ruined: [120] he makes them promises and raises false hopes, but Satan's promises are nothing but delusion. [121] Such people will have Hell for their home and will find no escape from it, [122] but We shall admit those who believe and do good deeds into Gardens graced with flowing streams, there to remain for ever—a true promise from God. Who speaks more truly than God? [123] It will not be according to your hopes or those of the People of the Book: anyone who does wrong will be requited for it and will find no one to protect or help him against God; [124] anyone, male or female, who does good deeds and is a believer, will enter Paradise and will not be wronged by as much as the dip in a date stone. [125] Who could be better in religion than those who direct themselves wholly to God, do good, and follow the religion of Abraham, who was true in faith? God took Abraham as a friend. [126] It is to God that everything in the heavens and earth belongs: God is fully aware of all things.

[127] They ask you [Prophet] for a ruling about women. Say, 'God Himself gives you a ruling about them. You already have what has been recited to you in the Scripture about orphan girls [in your charge] from whom you withhold the prescribed shares [of their inheritance] and whom you wish to marry, and also about helpless children—God instructs you to treat orphans fairly: He is well aware of whatever good you do.'

[128] If a wife fears high-handedness or alienation from her husband, neither of them will be blamed if they come to a peaceful settlement, for peace is best. Although human souls are prone to selfishness, if you do good and are mindful of God, He is well aware of all that you

---

[a] See also 53: 19–20.

[b] An example of pagan superstitious practices: they used to dedicate cattle to their gods by slitting their ears.

do. ¹²⁹ You will never be able to treat your wives with equal fairness, however much you may desire to do so, but do not ignore one wife altogether, leaving her suspended [between marriage and divorce]. If you make amends and remain conscious of God, He is most forgiving and merciful, ¹³⁰ but if husband and wife do separate, God will provide for each out of His plenty: He is infinite in plenty, and all wise. ¹³¹ Everything in the heavens and the earth belongs to God.

We have commanded those who were given the Scripture before you, and We command you, to be mindful of God. Even if you do ignore Him, everything in the heavens and the earth belongs to Him, and He is self-sufficient, worthy of all praise. ¹³² Yes, indeed, everything in the heavens and the earth belongs to God, and He is enough for those who trust in Him. ¹³³ If He so willed, He could remove you altogether and replace you with new people: He has full power to do so. ¹³⁴ If some want the rewards of this world, the rewards of this world and the next are both God's to give: He hears and sees everything.

¹³⁵ You who believe, uphold justice and bear witness to God, even if it is against yourselves, your parents, or your close relatives. Whether the person is rich or poor, God can best take care of both. Refrain from following your own desire, so that you can act justly—if you distort or neglect justice, God is fully aware of what you do. ¹³⁶ You who believe, believe in God and His Messenger and in the Scripture He sent down to His Messenger, as well as what He sent down before. Anyone who does not believe in God, His angels, His Scriptures, His messengers, and the Last Day has gone far, far astray. ¹³⁷ As for those who believe, then reject the faith, then believe again, then reject the faith again and increasingly disbelieve, God will not forgive them, nor will He guide them on any path. ¹³⁸ [Prophet], tell such hypocrites that an agonizing torment awaits them.

¹³⁹ Do those who ally themselves with the disbelievers rather than the believers seek power through them? In reality all power is God's to give. ¹⁴⁰ As He has already revealed to you [believers] in the Scripture, if you hear people denying and ridiculing God's revelation, do not sit with them unless they start to talk of other things, or else you yourselves will become like them:ᵃ God will gather all the hypocrites

---

ᵃ See 6: 68—an earlier, Meccan sura.

and disbelievers together into Hell. [141] The [hypocrites] wait to see what happens to you and, if God brings you success, they say, 'Were we not on your side?' but if the disbelievers have some success, they say to them, 'Did we not have the upper hand over you, and [yet] protect you from the believers?' God will judge between you all on the Day of Resurrection, and He will give the disbelievers no means of overcoming the believers.

[142] The hypocrites try to deceive God, but it is He who causes them to be deceived. When they stand up to pray, they do so sluggishly, showing off in front of people, and remember God only a little, [143] wavering all the time between this and that, belonging neither to one side nor the other. If God leaves someone to stray, you [Prophet] will never find a way for him. [144] You who believe, do not take the disbelievers as allies and protectors instead of the believers: do you want to offer God clear proof against you? [145] The hypocrites will be in the lowest depths of Hell, and you will find no one to help them. [146] Not so those who repent, mend their ways, hold fast to God, and devote their religion entirely to Him: these will be joined with the believers, and God will give the believers a mighty reward. [147] Why should God make you suffer torment if you are thankful and believe in Him? God always rewards gratitude and He knows everything. [148] God does not like bad words to be made public unless someone has been wronged: He is all hearing and all knowing. [149] If you do good, openly or in secret, or if you pardon something bad,[a] then God is most forgiving and powerful.

[150] As for those who ignore God and His messengers and want to make a distinction between them, saying, 'We believe in some but not in others,' seeking a middle way, [151] they are really disbelievers: We have prepared a humiliating punishment for those who disbelieve. [152] But God will give [due] rewards to those who believe in Him and His messengers and make no distinction between any of them. God is most forgiving and merciful.

[153] The People of the Book demand that you [Prophet] make a book physically come down to them from heaven, but they demanded even more than that of Moses when they said, 'Show us God face to face,' and were struck by the thunderbolt for their

---

[a] Razi suggests that this means: if the hypocrites repent, the believers should not taunt them for what they did in the past.

presumption. Even after clear revelations had come down to them, they took the calf as an object of worship, yet We pardoned this, and gave Moses clear authority; [154]We made the mountain tower high above them at their pledge; We said to them, 'Enter the gate[a] humbly,' and, 'Do not break the Sabbath,' and took a solemn pledge from them. [155]And so for breaking their pledge, for rejecting God's revelations, for unjustly killing their prophets, for saying 'Our minds are closed'[b]—No! God has sealed them in their disbelief, so they believe only a little—[156]and because they disbelieved and uttered a terrible slander against Mary, [157]and said, 'We have killed the Messiah, Jesus, son of Mary, the Messenger of God.'

(They did not kill him, nor did they crucify him, though it was made to appear like that to them. Those that disagreed about him are full of doubt, with no knowledge to follow, only supposition: they certainly did not kill him, [158]God raised him up to Himself. God is almighty and wise. [159]There is not one of the People of the Book who will not believe in Jesus before his death, and on the Day of Resurrection he will be a witness against them.)

[160]For the wrongdoings done by the Jews, We forbade them certain good things that had been permitted to them before: for having frequently debarred others from God's path; [161]for taking usury when they had been forbidden to do so; and for wrongfully devouring other people's property. For those of them that reject the truth we have prepared an agonizing torment. [162]But those of them who are well grounded in knowledge and have faith do believe in what has been revealed to you [Muhammad], and in what was revealed before you—those who perform the prayers, pay the prescribed alms, and believe in God and the Last Day—to them We shall give a great reward.

[163]We have sent revelation to you [Prophet] as We did to Noah and the prophets after him, to Abraham, Ishmael, Isaac, Jacob, and the Tribes, to Jesus, Job, Jonah, Aaron, and Solomon—to David We gave the Psalms—[164]to other messengers We have already mentioned to you, and also to some We have not—to Moses God spoke directly—[165]messengers bearing good news and warning, so that mankind would have no excuse before God, once the messengers had been

---

[a] The gate of the town mentioned in 2: 58; 7: 161.
[b] Literally 'our hearts are covered', or 'encased'. Cf. 2: 88.

sent: God is almighty and all wise. [166] But God Himself bears witness to what He has sent down to you—He sent it down with His full knowledge—the angels too bear witness, though God is sufficient witness. [167] Those who have disbelieved and barred others from God's path have gone far astray; [168] God will not forgive those who have disbelieved and do evil, nor will He guide them to any path [169] except that of Hell, where they will remain for ever—this is easy for God.

[170] The Messenger has come to you [people] with the truth from your Lord, so believe—that is best for you—for even if you disbelieve, all that is in the heavens and the earth still belongs to God, and He is all knowing and all wise. [171] People of the Book, do not go to excess in your religion, and do not say anything about God except the truth: the Messiah, Jesus, son of Mary, was nothing more than a messenger of God, His word, conveyed to Mary, a spirit from Him. So believe in God and His messengers and do not speak of a 'Trinity'—stop [this], that is better for you—God is only one God, He is far above having a son, everything in the heavens and earth belongs to Him and He is sufficient protector. [172] The Messiah would never disdain to be a servant of God, nor would the angels who are close to Him. He will gather before Him all those who disdain His worship and are arrogant: [173] to those who believe and do good works He will give due rewards and more of His bounty; to those who are disdainful and arrogant He will give an agonizing torment, and they will find no one besides God to protect or help them.

[174] People, convincing proof has come to you from your Lord and We have sent a clear light down to you. [175] God will admit into His mercy and favour those who believe in Him and hold fast to Him; He will guide them towards Him on a straight path.

[176] They ask you [Prophet] for a ruling. Say, 'God gives you a ruling[a] about inheritance from someone who dies childless with no surviving parents. If a man leaves a sister, she is entitled to half of the inheritance; if she has no child her brother is her sole heir; if there are two sisters, they are entitled to two-thirds of the inheritance between them, but if there are surviving brothers and sisters, the male is entitled to twice the share of the female. God makes this clear to you so that you may not make mistakes: He has full knowledge of everything.'

---

[a] See also verse 12.

5. THE FEAST

The title relates to food, and a central theme of this Medinan sura is the regulation of lawful and unlawful food, obedience to which is part of the pledge between God and the believers (verses 1–5, 87–108). Part of the sura concerns hunting for food during the pilgrimage and respect for the rites of pilgrimage. God had also taken pledges from the Jews and Christians and the section between verses 13 and 86 deals with what these two communities did to their pledges, and with their relationships with the Muslims. The passage from verse 109 to the end deals with the afterlife and the verdict of the messengers on the behaviour of their respective communities. Jesus, in particular, is given prominence here: mention is made of the feast for which his disciples asked him to pray to God, which gives the sura its title, and of his renunciation of any claim to divinity.

In the name of God, the Lord of Mercy, the Giver of Mercy

¹You who believe, fulfil your obligations.[a] Livestock animals are lawful as food for you, with the exception of what is about to be announced. You are forbidden to kill game while you are on pilgrimage—God commands what He will, ²so, you who believe, do not violate the sanctity of God's rites, the Sacred Month, the offerings, their garlands, nor those going to the Sacred House to seek the bounty and pleasure of their Lord—but when you have completed the rites of pilgrimage you may hunt. Do not let your hatred for the people who barred you from the Sacred Mosque induce you to break the law: help one another to do what is right and good; do not help one another towards sin and hostility. Be mindful of God, for His punishment is severe.

³You are forbidden to eat carrion; blood; pig's meat; any animal over which any name other than God's has been invoked; anything strangled, victim of a violent blow or a fall, gored or savaged by a beast of prey, unless you still slaughter it [in the correct manner]; or anything sacrificed on idolatrous altars. You are also forbidden to allot shares [of meat] by drawing marked arrows[b]—a heinous

---

[a] Obligations consequent on accepting the faith, including its dietary prohibitions. See verse 7, 'pledge'.

[b] A pagan Arab custom. Arrows were also used to make other decisions, as in drawing lots, to determine the will of the idols (see verse 90).

practice—the disbelievers have already lost all hope that you will give up your religion. Do not fear them: fear Me. Today I have perfected your religion for you, completed My blessing upon you, and chosen as your religion *islam*: total devotion to God; but if any of you is forced by hunger to eat forbidden food, with no intention of doing wrong, then God is most forgiving and merciful.

⁴They ask you, Prophet, what is lawful for them. Say, 'All good things are lawful for you.' [This includes] what you have taught your birds and beasts of prey to catch, teaching them as God has taught you, so eat what they catch for you, but first pronounce God's name over it. Be mindful of God: He is swift to take account. ⁵Today all good things have been made lawful for you. The food of the People of the Book is lawful for you as your food is lawful for them. So are chaste, believing, women as well as chaste women of the people who were given the Scripture before you, as long as you have given them their dowries and married them, not taking them as lovers or secret mistresses. The deeds of anyone who rejects faith will come to nothing and in the Hereafter he will be one of the losers.

⁶You who believe, when you are about to pray, wash your faces and your hands up to the elbows, wipe your heads, wash your feet up to the ankles and, if required,*ᵃ* wash your whole body. If any of you is sick or on a journey, or has just relieved himself, or had intimate contact with a woman, and can find no water, then take some clean sand and wipe your face and hands with it. God does not wish to place any burden on you: He only wishes to cleanse you and perfect His blessing on you, so that you may be thankful.*ᵇ* ⁷So remember God's blessing on you and the pledge with which you were bound when you said, 'We hear and we obey.' Be mindful of God: God has full knowledge of the secrets of the heart.

⁸You who believe, be steadfast in your devotion to God and bear witness impartially: do not let hatred of others lead you away from

---

ᵃ i.e. after sexual intercourse or discharging semen.

ᵇ 'Perfecting the blessing' is seen in instructing believers to avoid what is unclean in food and to wash before worship. This is also noted in 4: 43, where there is an instruction to wash before the prayer following an instruction to keep away from the pollution of the immoral acts mentioned in the preceding verses.

justice, but adhere to justice, for that is closer to awareness of God. Be mindful of God: God is well aware of all that you do. [9] God has promised forgiveness and a rich reward to those who have faith and do good works; [10] those who reject faith and deny Our revelations will inhabit the blazing Fire.

[11] You who believe, remember God's blessing on you when a certain people were about to raise their hands against you and He restrained them. Be mindful of God: let the believers put their trust in Him.

[12] God took a pledge from the Children of Israel. We appointed twelve leaders among them, and God said, 'I am with you: if you keep up the prayer, pay the prescribed alms, believe in My messengers and support them, and lend God a good loan,[a] I will wipe out your sins and admit you into Gardens graced with flowing streams. After this [pledge] any of you who ignore it will be far from the right path.' [13] But they broke their pledge, so We distanced them [from Us] and hardened their hearts. They distort the meaning of [revealed] words and have forgotten some of what they were told to remember: you [Prophet] will always find treachery in all but a few of them. Overlook this and pardon them—God loves those who do good. [14] We also took a pledge from those who say, 'We are Christians,' but they too forgot some of what they were told to remember, so We stirred up enmity and hatred among them until the Day of Resurrection when God will tell them what they have done.

[15] People of the Book, Our Messenger has come to make clear to you much of what you have kept hidden of the Scripture and to overlook much [you have done]. A light has now come to you from God, and a Scripture making things clear, [16] with which God guides those who follow what pleases Him to the ways of peace, bringing them from darkness out into light, by His will, and guiding them to a straight path. [17] Those who say, 'God is the Messiah, the son of Mary,' are defying the truth. Say, 'If it had been God's will, could anyone have prevented Him from destroying the Messiah, son of Mary, together with his mother and everyone else on earth? Control of the heavens and earth and all that is between them belongs to God: He creates whatever He will[b] and has power over everything.'

---

[a] God repays what is given for His sake, many times over. The Qur'an uses this figure of speech in many instances. See, for example, 57: 18; 64: 17.

[b] Including his creation of Jesus without a father (3: 47 and 59).

¹⁸ The Jews and the Christians say, 'We are the children of God and His beloved ones.' Say, 'Then why does He punish you for your sins? You are merely human beings, part of His creation: He forgives whoever He will and punishes whoever He will. Control of the heavens and earth and all that is between them belongs to Him: all journeys lead to Him.' ¹⁹ People of the Book, Our Messenger comes to you now, after a break in the sequence of messengers, to make things clear for you in case you should say, 'No one has come to give us good news or to warn us.' So someone has come to you to give you good news and warn you: God has the power to do all things.

²⁰ Moses said to his people, 'My people, remember God's blessing on you: how He raised prophets among you and appointed kings for you and gave you what he had not given to any other people. ²¹ My people, go into the holy land which God has ordained for you—do not turn back or you will be the losers.' ²² They said, 'Moses, there is a fearsome people in this land. We will not go there until they leave. If they leave, then we will enter.' ²³ Yet two men whom God had blessed among those who were afraid said, 'Go in to them through the gate and when you go in you will overcome them. If you are true believers, put your trust in God.' ²⁴ They said, 'Moses, we will never enter while they are still there, so you and your Lord go in and fight, and we will stay here.' ²⁵ He said, 'Lord, I have authority over no one except myself and my brother: judge between the two of us and these disobedient people.' ²⁶ God said, 'The land is forbidden to them and for forty years they will wander the earth aimlessly. Do not grieve over those who disobey.'

²⁷ [Prophet], tell them the truth about the story of Adam's two sons: each of them offered a sacrifice, and it was accepted from one and not the other. One said, 'I will kill you,' but the other said, 'God only accepts the sacrifice of those who are mindful of Him—²⁸ if you raise your hand to kill me, I will not raise mine to kill you. I fear God, the Lord of all worlds, ²⁹ and I would rather you were burdened with my sins as well as yours and became an inhabitant of the Fire: such is the evildoers' reward.' ³⁰ But his soul prompted him to kill his brother: he killed him and became one of the losers. ³¹ God sent a raven to scratch up the ground and show him how to cover his brother's corpse and he said, 'Woe is me! Could I not have been like this raven and covered up my brother's body?'—he was filled with

remorse. [32] On account of [his deed], We decreed to the Children of Israel that if anyone kills a person—unless in retribution for murder or spreading corruption in the land—it is as if he kills all mankind, while if any saves a life it is as if he saves the lives of all mankind. Our messengers came to them with clear signs, but many of them continued to commit excesses in the land. [33] Those who wage war against God and His Messenger and strive to spread corruption in the land should be punished by death, crucifixion, the amputation of an alternate hand and foot,[a] or banishment from the land: a disgrace for them in this world, and then a terrible punishment in the Hereafter, [34] unless they repent before you overpower them: in that case bear in mind that God is forgiving and merciful.

[35] You who believe, be mindful of God, seek ways to come closer to Him and strive for His cause, so that you may prosper. [36] If the disbelievers possessed all that is in the earth and twice as much again and offered it to ransom themselves from torment on the Day of Resurrection, it would not be accepted from them: they will have a painful torment. [37] They will wish to come out of the Fire but they will be unable to do so: theirs will be a lasting torment.

[38] Cut off the hands of thieves, whether they are male or female, as punishment for what they have done—a deterrent from God: God is almighty and wise. [39] But if anyone repents after his wrongdoing and makes amends, God will accept his repentance: God is most forgiving, most merciful. [40] Do you [Prophet] not know that control of the heavens and earth belongs solely to God? He punishes whoever He will and forgives whoever He will: God has power over everything.

[41] Messenger, do not be grieved by those who race to surpass one another in disbelief—those who say with their mouths, 'We believe,' but have no faith in their hearts and the Jews who listen eagerly to lies and to those who have not even met you, who distort the meanings of [revealed] words and say [to each other], 'If you are given this ruling, accept it, but if you are not, then beware!'[b]—if God intends

---

[a] Left hand and right foot or vice versa.

[b] According to most interpreters, this refers to a case where an eminent Jewish man and woman committed adultery. The Jewish community did not want to apply the biblical penalty of stoning, so they sent representatives to the Prophet to ask for a ruling, saying, 'If he orders you to apply lashing accept it, but if he orders stoning, do not accept it' (Razi).

some people to be so misguided, you will be powerless against God on their behalf. These are the ones whose hearts God does not intend to cleanse—a disgrace for them in this world, and then a heavy punishment in the Hereafter—[42] they listen eagerly to lies and consume what is unlawful. If they come to you [Prophet] for judgement, you can either judge between them, or decline—if you decline, they will not harm you in any way, but if you do judge between them, judge justly: God loves the just—[43] but why do they come to you for judgement when they have the Torah with God's judgement, and even then still turn away? These are not believers. [44] We revealed the Torah with guidance and light, and the prophets, who had submitted to God, [and] the rabbis and the scholars all judged according to it for the Jews in accordance with that part of God's Scripture which they were entrusted to preserve, and to which they were witnesses. So [Children of Israel] do not fear people, fear Me; do not barter away My messages for a small price; those who do not judge according to what God has sent down are rejecting [God's teachings]. [45] In the Torah We prescribed for them a life for a life, an eye for an eye, a nose for a nose, an ear for an ear, a tooth for a tooth, an equal wound for a wound: if anyone forgoes this out of charity, it will serve as atonement for his bad deeds. Those who do not judge according to what God has revealed are doing grave wrong.

[46] We sent Jesus, son of Mary, in their footsteps, to confirm the Torah that had been sent before him: We gave him the Gospel with guidance, light, and confirmation of the Torah already revealed—a guide and lesson for those who take heed of God. [47] So let the followers of the Gospel judge according to what God has sent down in it. Those who do not judge according to what God has revealed are lawbreakers.

[48] We sent to you [Muhammad] the Scripture with the truth, confirming the Scriptures that came before it, and with final authority over them: so judge between them according to what God has sent down. Do not follow their whims, which deviate from the truth that has come to you. We have assigned a law and a path to each of you. If God had so willed, He would have made you one community, but He wanted to test you through that which He has given you, so race to do good: you will all return to God and He will make clear to you the matters you differed about. [49] So [Prophet] judge between them according to what God has sent down. Do not follow their whims,

and take good care that they do not tempt you away from any of what God has sent down to you. If they turn away, remember that God intends to punish them for some of the sins they have committed: a great many people are lawbreakers— [50] do they want judgement according to the time of pagan ignorance? Is there any better judge than God for those of firm faith?

[51] You who believe, do not take the Jews and Christians as allies:[a] they are allies only to each other. Anyone who takes them as an ally becomes one of them—God does not guide such wrongdoers— [52] yet you [Prophet] will see the perverse at heart rushing to them for protection, saying, 'We are afraid fortune may turn against us.' But God may well bring about a triumph or some other event of His own making: then they will rue the secrets they harboured in their hearts, [53] and the believers will say, 'Are these the men who swore by God using their strongest oaths that they were with you?' All they did was in vain and they have lost everything.

[54] You who believe, if any of you go back on your faith,[b] God will soon replace you with people He loves and who love Him, people who are humble towards the believers, hard on the disbelievers, and who strive in God's way without fearing anyone's reproach. Such is God's favour. He grants it to whoever He will. God has endless bounty and knowledge. [55] Your true allies are God, His Messenger, and the believers—those who keep up the prayer, pay the prescribed alms, and bow down in worship. [56] Those who turn for protection to God, His Messenger, and the believers are God's party: God's party is sure to triumph.

[57] You who believe, do not take as allies those who ridicule your religion and make fun of it—whether people who were given the Scripture before you, or disbelievers—and be mindful of God if you are true believers. [58] When you make the call to prayer, they ridicule it and make fun of it: this is because they are people who do not reason. [59] Say [Prophet], 'People of the Book, do you resent us for any reason other than the fact that we believe in God, in what has been sent down to us, and in what was sent before us, while most of you are disobedient?' [60] Say, 'Shall I tell you who deserves a worse punishment from God than [the one you wish upon] us? Those God

---

[a] i.e. those who are against the Muslim camp, as is clear from the following verses, up to 59. 'Do not turn to them as allies in preference to the Muslims' (see 4: 144).

[b] What is intended in this context is 'by taking them as allies'.

distanced from Himself, was angry with, and condemned as apes and pigs,[a] and those who worship idols: they are worse in rank and have strayed further from the right path.

[61] When they come to you [believers], they say, 'We believe,' but they come disbelieving and leave disbelieving—God knows best what they are hiding. [62] You [Prophet] see many of them rushing into sin and hostility and consuming what is unlawful. How evil their practices are! [63] Why do their rabbis and scholars not forbid them to speak sinfully and consume what is unlawful? How evil their deeds are! [64] The Jews have said, 'God is tight-fisted,' but it is they who are tight-fisted, and they are rejected for what they have said. Truly, God's hands are open wide: He gives as He pleases. What has been sent down to you from your Lord is sure to increase insolence and disbelief in many of them. We have sown enmity and hatred amongst them till the Day of Resurrection. Whenever they kindle the fire of war, God will put it out. They try to spread corruption in the land, but God does not love those who corrupt. [65] If only the People of the Book would believe and be mindful of God, We would take away their sins and bring them into the Gardens of Delight. [66] If they had upheld the Torah and the Gospel and what was sent down to them from their Lord, they would have been given abundance from above and from below: some of them are on the right course, but many of them do evil.

[67] Messenger, proclaim everything that has been sent down to you from your Lord—if you do not, then you will not have communicated His message—and God will protect you from people. God does not guide those who defy Him. [68] Say, 'People of the Book, you have no true basis [for your religion] unless you uphold the Torah, the Gospel, and that which has been sent down to you from your Lord,' but what has been sent down to you [Prophet] from your Lord is sure to increase many of them in their insolence and defiance: do not worry about those who defy [God]. [69] The [Muslim] believers, the Jews, the Sabians,[b] and the Christians—those who believe in God and the Last Day and do good deeds—will have nothing to fear or to regret.

[70] We took a pledge from the Children of Israel, and sent

[a] Tabari (in his commentary on 2: 65) regards this as metaphorical in the sense of 'like apes, pigs'. Compare the metaphorical use of 'blind, deaf, dumb'—2: 18; 5: 71; 8: 22; 43: 40; etc.

[b] See note to 2: 62.

messengers to them. Whenever a messenger brought them anything they did not like, they accused some of lying and put others to death; [71] they thought no harm could come to them and so became blind and deaf [to God]. God turned to them in mercy but many of them again became blind and deaf: God is fully aware of their actions. [72] Those who say, 'God is the Messiah, son of Mary,' although the Messiah himself said, 'Children of Israel, worship God, my Lord and your Lord,' have defied [what he said]: if anyone associates others with God, God will forbid him from the Garden, and Hell will be his home. No one will help such evildoers.

[73] Those people who say that God is the third of three are defying [the truth]: there is only One God. If they persist in what they are saying, a painful punishment will afflict those of them who defy [the truth]. [74] Why do they not turn to God and ask His forgiveness, when God is most forgiving, most merciful? [75] The Messiah, son of Mary, was only a messenger; other messengers had come and gone before him; his mother was a virtuous woman; both ate food [like other mortals]. See how clear We make these signs for them; see how deluded they are. [76] Say, 'How can you worship something other than God, that has no power to do you harm or good? God alone is the All Hearing and All Knowing.' [77] Say, 'People of the Book, do not overstep the bounds of truth in your religion and do not follow the whims of those who went astray before you—they led many others astray themselves, and continue to stray from the right path.'

[78] Those Children of Israel who defied [God] were rejected through the words of David and Jesus, son of Mary, because they disobeyed, they persistently overstepped the limits, [79] they did not forbid each other to do wrong—how vile their deeds were! [80] You [Prophet] see many of them allying themselves with the disbelievers. Terrible is what their souls have stored up for them: God is angry with them and they will remain tormented. [81] If they had believed in God, in the Prophet, and in what has been sent down to him, they would never have allied themselves with the disbelievers, but most of them are rebels.

[82] You [Prophet] are sure to find that the most hostile to the believers are the Jews and those who associate other deities with God; you are sure to find that the closest in affection towards the believers are those who say, 'We are Christians,' for there are among them people devoted

to learning and ascetics. [a] These people are not given to arrogance,
[83] and when they listen to what has been sent down to the Messenger,
you will see their eyes overflowing with tears because they recognize
the truth [in it]. They say, 'Our Lord, we believe, so count us amongst
the witnesses. [84] Why should we not believe in God and in the truth
that has come down to us when we long for our Lord to include us
in the company of the righteous?' [85] For saying this, God has rewarded
them with Gardens graced with flowing streams, and there they
will stay: that is the reward of those who do good. [86] Those who reject
the truth and deny Our messages will be the inhabitants of Hellfire.

[87] You who believe, do not forbid the good things God has made
lawful to you—do not exceed the limits: God does not love those who
exceed the limits—[88] but eat the lawful and good things that God provides for you. Be mindful of God, in whom you believe. [89] God does not
take you [to task] for what is thoughtless in your oaths, [b] only for your
binding oaths: the atonement for breaking an oath is to feed ten poor
people with food equivalent to what you would normally give your own
families, or to clothe them, or to set free a slave—if a person cannot find
the means, he should fast for three days. This is the atonement for
breaking your oaths but you should keep your oaths. In this way God
makes clear His revelations to you, so that you may be thankful.

[90] You who believe, intoxicants and gambling, idolatrous practices,
and [divining with] [c] arrows are repugnant acts—Satan's doing: shun
them so that you may prosper. [91] With intoxicants and gambling,
Satan seeks only to incite enmity and hatred among you, and to stop
you remembering God and prayer. Will you not give them up?
[92] Obey God, obey the Messenger, and always be on your guard: if
you pay no heed, bear in mind that the sole duty of Our Messenger is
to deliver the message clearly. [93] Those who believe and do good
deeds will not be blamed for what they may have consumed [in the
past] [d] as long as they are mindful of God, believe and do good deeds,

---

[a] Most translators render these as 'priests and monks', which are their modern
meanings, not the etymological senses of the words (al-Raghib, *Mufradat*).

[b] Some Muslims swore to renounce the world and not to eat certain good foods or
wear fine clothes, and when told this was wrong, they asked the Prophet what they could
do about their oaths.

[c] See note to verse 3 above.

[d] It was reported that when wine was forbidden, some companions asked the Prophet,
'What about those believers who used to drink and have already died? What state would
they be in?' This is the reply to that question, and it also applies to the living.

then are mindful of God and believe, then are mindful of God and do good deeds: God loves those who do good deeds.

⁹⁴ You who believe, God is sure to test you with game within reach of your hands and spears, to find out who fears Him even though they cannot see Him: from now on, anyone who transgresses will have a painful punishment.ᵃ ⁹⁵ You who believe, do not kill game while you are in the state of consecration [for pilgrimage]. If someone does so intentionally the penalty is an offering of a domestic animal brought to the Ka'ba, equivalent—as judged by two just men among you—to the one he has killed; alternatively, he may atone by feeding the needy or by fasting an equivalent number of days, so that he may taste the full gravity of his deed. God forgives what is past, but if anyone re-offends, God will exact the penalty from him: God is mighty, and capable of exacting the penalty. ⁹⁶ It is permitted for you to catch and eat seafood—an enjoyment for you and the traveller—but hunting game is forbidden while you are in the state of consecration [for pilgrimage]. Be mindful of God to whom you will be gathered.

⁹⁷ God has made the Ka'ba—the Sacred House—a means of support for people;ᵇ and the Sacred Months, the animals for sacrifice and their garlands, for you to know that God has knowledge of all that is in the heavens and earth and that He is fully aware of all things; ⁹⁸ know too that God is severe in punishment yet most forgiving and merciful.ᶜ ⁹⁹ The Messenger's duty is only to deliver the message: God knows what you reveal and what you conceal.

¹⁰⁰ Say [Prophet], 'Bad cannot be likened to good, though you may be dazzled by how abundant the bad is. Be mindful of God, people of understanding, so that you may prosper.' ¹⁰¹ You who believe, do not ask about matters which, if made known to you, might make things difficult for you—if you ask about them while the Qur'an is being revealed, they will be made known to you—God has kept silent

---

ᵃ In the world to come.

ᵇ The Ka'ba is the centre of the pilgrimage, bringing in people from all over the world, where Muslims are allowed to trade—the Sacred Months ensured their safety. The offerings provide a means of livelihood to the poor and needy, and the custom of garlanding an animal gives it special protection. In addition to all these material benefits, there are the spiritual benefits of worshipping God. This is an example of bringing people together in peace (Razi).

ᶜ This is a warning for those who violate these rites and refers back to verse 2 of this sura.

about them: God is most forgiving and forbearing. [102] Before you, some people asked about things, then ignored [the answers]. [103] God did not institute the dedication of such things as *bahira*, *sa'iba*, *wasila*, or *ham*[a] to idols; but the disbelievers invent lies about God. Most of them do not use reason—[104] when it is said to them, 'Come to what God has sent down, and to the Messenger,' they say, 'What we inherited from our forefathers is good enough for us,' even though their forefathers knew nothing and were not guided. [105] You who believe, you are responsible for your own souls; if anyone else goes astray it will not harm you so long as you follow the guidance; you will all return to God, and He will make you realize what you have done.

[106] You who believe, when death approaches any of you, let two just men from among you act as witnesses to the making of a bequest, or two men from another people if you are journeying in the land when death approaches. Keep the two witnesses back after prayer, if you have any doubts, and make them both swear by God, 'We will not sell our testimony for any price, even if a close relative is involved. We will not hide God's testimony, for then we should be doing wrong.' [107] If it is discovered that these two are guilty of perjury, two of those whose rights have been usurped have a better right to bear witness. Let them swear by God, 'Our testimony is truer than theirs. We have said nothing but the truth, for that would make us wrongdoers': [108] that will make it more likely they will give true and proper testimony, or fear that their oaths might be refuted by others afterwards. Be mindful of God and listen; God does not guide those who break His laws.

[109] On the Day when God assembles all the messengers[b] and asks, 'What response did you receive?' they will say, 'We do not have that knowledge: You alone know things that cannot be seen.' [110] Then God will say, 'Jesus, son of Mary! Remember My favour to you and to your mother: how I strengthened you with the holy spirit, so that

---

[a] Different classes of animals liberated from work or use as food, in honour of idols, and venerated by the pagan Arabs.

[b] As Razi rightly stated, it is the habit of the Qur'an, having talked at length on legislation, to follow it with reminders of God's power, stories of earlier prophets, or what happens on the Day of Judgement, in order to motivate people to adhere to the legislation. In this sura, having earlier mentioned the claims of Christians, it seeks further to refute them by showing that Jesus will disown their claims on the Day of Judgement.

you spoke to people in your infancy and as a grown man; how I taught you the Scripture and wisdom, the Torah and the Gospel; how, by My leave, you fashioned the shape of a bird out of clay, breathed into it, and it became, by My leave, a bird; how, by My leave, you healed the blind person and the leper; how, by My leave, you brought the dead back to life; how I restrained the Children of Israel from [harming] you when you brought them clear signs, and those of them who disbelieved said, "This is clearly nothing but sorcery"; [111] and how I inspired the disciples to believe in Me and My messengers—they said, "We believe and bear witness that we devote ourselves [to God]." '[a]

[112] When the disciples said, 'Jesus, son of Mary, can your Lord send down to us a feast from heaven?' he said, 'Be mindful of God if you are true believers.' [113] They said, 'We wish to eat from it; to have our hearts reassured; to know that you have told us the truth; and to be witnesses of it.' [114] Jesus, son of Mary, said, 'Lord, send down to us a feast from heaven so that we can have a festival—the first and last of us—and a sign from You. Provide for us: You are the best provider.' [115] God said, 'I will send it down to you, but anyone who disbelieves after this will be punished with a punishment that I will not inflict on anyone else in the world.'

[116] When God says, 'Jesus, son of Mary, did you say to people, "Take me and my mother as two gods alongside God"?' he will say, 'May You be exalted! I would never say what I had no right to say— if I had said such a thing You would have known it: You know all that is within me, though I do not know what is within You, You alone have full knowledge of things unseen—[117] I told them only what You commanded me to: "Worship God, my Lord and your Lord." I was a witness over them during my time among them. Ever since You took my soul, You alone have been the watcher over them: You are witness to all things [118] and if You punish them, they are Your servants; if You forgive them, You are the Almighty, the Wise.' [119] God will say, 'This is a Day when the truthful will benefit from their truthfulness. They will have Gardens graced with flowing streams, there to remain for ever. God is pleased with them and they with Him: that is the supreme triumph.' [120] Control of the heavens and earth and everything in them belongs to God: He has power over all things.

[a] Cf. 2: 131–3.

6. LIVESTOCK

A Meccan sura which takes its title from verses 136–9. The false claims the polytheists made about livestock are thoroughly refuted. The sura in its entirety makes plain that it is God who creates, controls, and sees everything, and that it is to Him that we turn in times of need. Thus it gives a lengthy refutation of the idolaters' claims.

In the name of God, the Lord of Mercy, the Giver of Mercy

¹Praise belongs to God who created the heavens and the earth and made darkness and light; yet the disbelievers set up equals to their Lord! ²He is the one who created you from clay and specified a term [for you] and another fixed time,*ᵃ* known only to Him; yet you still doubt! ³He is God in the heavens and on earth, He knows your secrets and what you reveal, and He knows what you do; ⁴but every time revelation comes to them from their Lord, they turn their backs on it. ⁵So they denied the truth when it came to them, but the very thing they laughed at will be brought home to them.

⁶Do they not realize how many generations We destroyed before them? We established them in the earth more firmly than you, sent down abundant rain on them from the sky and made running rivers flow at their feet, yet We destroyed them for their misdeeds and raised other generations after them. ⁷Even if We had sent down to you [Prophet] a book inscribed on parchment, and they had touched it with their own hands, the disbelievers would still say, 'This is clearly sorcery.' ⁸They say, 'Why was no angel sent down to [support] him?'*ᵇ* But had We sent down an angel, their judgement would have come at once with no respite given. ⁹Indeed, if We had sent an angel as messenger, We would still have sent him in the form of a man, so increasing their confusion.

¹⁰Messengers have been mocked before you [Muhammad], and those who mocked them were engulfed by the very punishment they had mocked. ¹¹Say, 'Travel throughout the earth and see what fate

---

ᵃ These refer to the specified lifetime of individuals and the Day of Judgement.

ᵇ They always argued against the Prophet that he was only a man, and asked him to produce an angel to support him. Cf. 25: 7.

befell those who rejected the truth.' ¹²Say, 'To whom belongs all that is in the heavens and earth?' Say, 'To God. He has taken it upon Himself to be merciful. He will certainly gather you on the Day of Resurrection, which is beyond all doubt. Those who deceive themselves will not believe. ¹³All that rests by night or by day belongs to Him. He is the All Hearing, the All Knowing.' ¹⁴Say, 'Shall I take for myself a protector other than God, the Creator of the heavens and the earth, who feeds but is not fed?' Say, 'I am commanded to be the first [of you] to devote myself [to Him].' Do not be one of the polytheists. ¹⁵Say, 'I fear the punishment of a dreadful Day if I disobey my Lord. ¹⁶God will have been truly merciful to whoever is spared on that Day: that is the clearest triumph.'

¹⁷If God touches you [Prophet] with affliction, no one can remove it except Him, and if He touches you with good, He has power over all things: ¹⁸He is the Supreme Master over His creatures, the All Wise, the All Aware. ¹⁹Say, 'What counts most as a witness?' Say, 'God is witness between you and me. This Qur'an was revealed for me to warn you [people] and everyone it reaches. Do you really bear witness that there are other gods beside God?' Say, 'I myself do not bear witness [to any such thing].' Say, 'He is only one God, and I disown whatever you join with Him.' ²⁰Those to whom We have given the Scripture know this as well as they know their own sons. Those who deceive themselves will not believe. ²¹Who does greater wrong than someone who fabricates a lie against God or denies His revelation? Those who do such wrong will not prosper. ²²When We gather them all together and say to the polytheists, 'Where are those you claimed were partners with God?' in their utter dismay ²³they will only say, 'By God, our Lord, we have not set up partners beside Him!' ²⁴See how they lie against themselves and how those they invented have deserted them.

²⁵Among them are some who [appear to] listen to you but we have placed covers over their hearts—so they do not understand the Qur'an—and deafness in their ears. Even if they saw every sign they still would not believe in them. So, when they come to you, they argue with you: the disbelievers say, 'These are nothing but ancient fables,' ²⁶and tell others not to listen [to the Qur'an], while they themselves keep away from it. But they ruin no one but themselves, though they fail to realize this. ²⁷If you could only see, when they are made to stand before the Fire, how they will say, 'If only we could be

sent back, we would not reject the revelations of our Lord, but be among the believers.' ²⁸ The truth they used to hide will become all too clear to them. Even if they were brought back, they would only return to the very thing that was forbidden to them—they are such liars! ²⁹ They say, 'There is nothing beyond our life in this world: we shall not be raised from the dead.' ³⁰ If you could only see, when they are made to stand before their Lord, how He will say, 'Is this not real?' They will say, 'Yes indeed, by our Lord.' He will say, 'Then taste the torment for having disbelieved.' ³¹ Lost indeed are those who deny the meeting with their Lord until, when the Hour suddenly arrives, they say, 'Alas for us that we disregarded this!' They will bear their burdens on their backs—how terrible those burdens will be! ³² The life of this world is nothing but a game and a distraction; the Home in the Hereafter is best for those who are aware of God—why will you [people] not understand?

³³ We know well that what they say grieves you [Prophet]. It is not you they disbelieve: they reject God's revelation. ³⁴ Other messengers were disbelieved before you, and they bore their rejection and persecution steadfastly until Our aid arrived—no one can alter God's words. You have already received accounts of these messengers. ³⁵ If you find rejection by the disbelievers so hard to bear, then seek a tunnel into the ground or a ladder into the sky, if you can, and bring them a sign: God could bring them all to guidance if it were His will, so do not join the ignorant. ³⁶ Only those who can hear will respond; as for the dead, God will raise them up, and to Him they will all be returned.

³⁷ They also say, 'Why has no sign been sent down to him from his Lord?' Say, 'God certainly has the power to send down a sign,' though most of them do not know: ³⁸ all the creatures that crawl on the earth and those that fly with their wings are communities like yourselves—We have left nothing out of the Book—and in the end they will be gathered to their Lord. ³⁹ Those who reject Our signs are deaf, dumb, and in total darkness. God leaves whoever He will to stray, and sets whoever He will on a straight path. ⁴⁰ Say, 'Think: if the punishment of God or the Hour should come to you, would you call on anyone other than God, if you are being truthful?' ⁴¹ No indeed, it is on Him that you would call. If it were His will, He could remove whatever harm made you call on Him, and then you would forget what you now associate with Him.

⁴² We sent messengers before you [Prophet] to many communities and afflicted their people with suffering and hardships, so that they might learn humility. ⁴³ If only they had learned humility when suffering came from Us! But no, their hearts became hard and Satan made their foul deeds alluring to them. ⁴⁴ So, when they had forgotten the warning they had received, We opened the gates to everything for them. Then, as they revelled in what they had been given, We struck them suddenly and they were dumbfounded, ⁴⁵ so the evildoers were wiped out: praise be to God, the Lord of the Worlds!

⁴⁶ Say [Prophet], 'Think: if God were to take away your hearing and your sight and seal up your hearts, what god other than He could restore them?' See how We explain Our revelations in various ways, yet still they turn away. ⁴⁷ Say, 'Think: if the punishment of God should come to you, by surprise or openly, would anyone but the evildoers be destroyed?' ⁴⁸ We send messengers only to give good news and to warn, so for those who believe and do good deeds there will be no fear, nor will they grieve. ⁴⁹ As for those who rejected Our signs, torment will afflict them as a result of their defiance. ⁵⁰ Say, 'I do not have the treasures of God, nor do I know the unseen, nor do I tell you that I am an angel. I only follow what is revealed to me.' Say, 'Is a blind person like someone who can see? Why will you not reflect?'

⁵¹ Use the Qur'an to warn those who fear being gathered before their Lord—they will have no one but Him to protect them and no one to intercede—so that they may beware. ⁵² Do not drive away those who call upon their Lord morning and evening, seeking nothing but His Face.*ᵃ* You are in no way accountable for them, nor they for you; if you drove the believers away,*ᵇ* you would become one of the evildoers. ⁵³ We have made some of them a test for others, to make the disbelievers say, 'Is it these men that God has favoured among us?' Does God not know best who are the grateful ones?

⁵⁴ When those who believe in Our revelations come to you [Prophet], say, 'Peace be upon you. Your Lord has taken it on

ᵃ 'His pleasure/approval', or 'to see His face' (see 'The Face, Divine and Human in the Qur'an', in Abdel Haleem, *Understanding the Qur'an*, 107–22); see also 92: 19–21.

ᵇ Cf. 80: 1. The Prophet was torn between his efforts to win over the nobles to save them, and the humble believers, whom the nobles wanted him to get rid of, claiming that they only congregated around him to gain prestige or material benefits. The Prophet here is told that he should not worry about them and so become a wrongdoer by driving away true believers.

Himself to be merciful: if any of you has foolishly done a bad deed, and afterwards repented and mended his ways, God is most forgiving and most merciful.' ⁵⁵ In this way We explain the revelations, so that the way for sinners may be made clear.ᵃ ⁵⁶ Say, 'I am forbidden to worship those you call on other than God.' Say, 'I will not follow your vain desires, for if I did, I would stray from the path and cease to be rightly guided.' ⁵⁷ Say, 'I [base my] stand on clear proof from my Lord, but still you deny it. What you seek to hasten is not within my power. Judgement is for God alone: He tells the truth, and He is the best of judges.' ⁵⁸ Say, 'If what you seek to hasten were within my power, the matter would be settled between you and me, but God knows best who does wrong.' ⁵⁹ He holds the keys to the unseen: no one knows them but Him. He knows all that is in the land and sea. No leaf falls without His knowledge, nor is there a single grain in the darkness of the earth, or anything, fresh or withered, that is not written in a clear Record. ⁶⁰ It is He who calls your souls back by night, knowing what you have done by day, then raises you up again in the daytime until your fixed term is fulfilled. It is to Him that you will return in the end, and He will tell you what you have done. ⁶¹ He is the Supreme Master over His subjects. He sends out recorders to watch over you until, when death overtakes any of you, those sent by Us take his soul—they never fail in their duty. ⁶² Then they will all be returned to God, their true Lord. The Judgement truly belongs to Him, and He is the swiftest of reckoners.

⁶³ Say [Prophet], 'Who is it that saves you from the dark depths of land and sea when you humbly and secretly call to Him [and say], "If He rescues us from this, We shall truly be thankful"?' ⁶⁴ Say, 'God rescues you from this and every distress; yet still you worship others beside Him.' ⁶⁵ Say, 'He has power to send punishment on you from above or from under your very feet, or to divide you into discordant factions and make some taste the violence of others.' See how We explain Our revelation in various ways, so that they may understand, ⁶⁶ yet your people still reject it even though it is the truth. Say, 'I have not been put in charge of you. ⁶⁷ Every prophecy has its fixed time to be fulfilled: you will come to realize this.'

⁶⁸ When you come across people who speak with scorn about Our

---

ᵃ Another interpretation of this verse is that the way of the sinners is hereby made distinct from the way of the righteous.

revelations, turn away from them until they move on to another topic. If Satan should make you forget, then, when you have remembered, do not sit with those who are doing wrong. [69] The righteous are not in any way held accountable for the wrongdoers; their only duty is to remind them, so that they may be mindful of God. [70] Leave to themselves those who take their religion for a mere game and distraction and are deceived by the life of this world but continue to remind them with the [Qur'an], lest any soul be damned by what it has done—it will have no one to protect it from God and no one to intercede; whatever ransom it may offer will not be accepted. Such are those who are damned by their own actions: they will have boiling water to drink and a painful punishment because they used to defy [God].

[71] Say, 'Instead of God, are we to call on what neither profits nor harms us? [Are we to] turn on our heels after God has guided us, like someone bewildered, having been tempted by devils into a deep ravine, [a] though his companions call him to guidance [saying], "Come to us"?' Say, 'God's guidance is the true guidance. We are commanded to devote ourselves to the Lord of the Worlds, [72] to establish regular prayers and be mindful of Him.' It is to Him that you will all be gathered. [73] It is He who created the heavens and the earth for a true purpose. On the Day when He says, 'Be,' it will be: His word is the truth. All control on the Day the Trumpet is blown belongs to Him. He knows the seen and the unseen: He is the All Wise, the All Aware.

[74] Remember when Abraham said to his father, Azar, 'How can you take idols as gods? I see that you and your people have clearly gone astray.' [75] In this way We showed Abraham [God's] mighty dominion over the heavens and the earth, so that he might be a firm believer. [76] When the night grew dark over him he saw a star and said, 'This is my Lord,' but when it set, he said, 'I do not like things that set.' [77] And when he saw the moon rising he said, '*This* is my Lord,' but when it too set, he said, 'If my Lord does not guide me, I shall be one of those who go astray.' [78] Then he saw the sun rising and cried, '*This* is my Lord! This is greater.' But when the sun set, he said, 'My people, I disown all that you worship beside God. [79] I have turned my face as a true believer towards Him who created the heavens and the earth. I am not one of the polytheists.'

---

[a] This interpretation of the literal 'in the land' is preferred by Razi.

⁸⁰His people argued with him, and he said, 'How can you argue with me about God when He has guided me? I do not fear anything you associate with Him: unless my Lord wills [nothing can happen]. My Lord encompasses everything in His knowledge. How can you not take heed? ⁸¹Why should I fear what you associate with Him? Why do you not fear to associate with Him things for which He has sent you no authority? Tell me, if you know the answer, which side has more right to feel secure? ⁸²It is those who have faith, and do not mix their faith with idolatry,ᵃ who will be secure, and it is they who are rightly guided.' ⁸³Such was the argument We gave to Abraham against his people—We raise in rank whoever We will—your Lord is all wise, all knowing.

⁸⁴We gave him Isaac and Jacob, each of whom We guided, as We had guided Noah before, and among his descendants were David, Solomon, Job, Joseph, Moses, and Aaron—in this way We reward those who do good—⁸⁵Zachariah, John, Jesus, and Elias—every one of them was righteous—⁸⁶Ishmael, Elijah, Jonah, and Lot—We favoured each one of them over other people, ⁸⁷and also some of their forefathers, their offspring, and their brothers: We chose them and guided them on a straight path. ⁸⁸Such is God's guidance, with which He guides whichever of His servants He will. If they had associated other gods with Him, all their deeds would have come to nothing. ⁸⁹Those are the ones to whom We gave the Scripture, wisdom, and prophethood. Even if these people now disbelieve in them, We have entrusted them to others who do not disbelieve. ⁹⁰These were the people God guided, '[Prophet], follow the guidance they received.' Say, 'I ask no reward for it from you: it is a lesson for all people.'

⁹¹They have no grasp of God's true measure when they say, 'God has sent nothing down to a mere mortal.' Say, 'Who was it who sent down the Scripture, which Moses brought as a light and a guide to people, which you made into separate sheets, showing some but hiding many? You were taught things that neither you nor your forefathers had known.' Say, 'God [sent it down],' then leave them engrossed in their vain talk. ⁹²This is a blessed Scripture that We have sent down to confirm what came before it and for you to warn

---

ᵃ The Prophet explained *zulm* (evildoing) here to be *shirk* (idolatry), referring to 31: 13.

the Mother of Cities[a] and all around it. Those who believe in the Hereafter believe in this Scripture, and do not neglect their prayers. [93] Who could be more wicked than someone who invents a lie against God, or claims, 'A revelation has come to me,' when no revelation has been sent to him, or says, 'I too can reveal something equal to God's revelation'? If you could only see the wicked in their death agonies, as the angels stretch out their hands [to them], saying, 'Give up your souls. Today you will be repaid with a humiliating punishment for saying false things about God and for arrogantly rejecting His revelations.' [94] [God will say], 'Now you return to Us, alone, as We first created you: you have left behind everything We gave you, nor do We see those intercessors of yours that you claimed were partners of God. All the bonds between you have been severed, and those about whom you made such claims have deserted you.'

[95] It is God who splits open the seed and the fruit stone: He brings out the living from the dead and the dead from the living—that is God—so how can you turn away from the truth? [96] He makes the dawn break; He makes the night for rest; and He made the sun and the moon to a precise measure. That is the design of the Almighty, the All Knowing. [97] It is He who made the stars, so that they can guide you when land and sea are dark: We have made the signs clear for those who have knowledge. [98] It is He who first produced you from a single soul, then gave you a place to stay [in life] and a resting place [after death]. We have made Our revelations clear to those who understand. [99] It is He who sends down water from the sky. With it We produce the shoots of each plant, then bring greenery from it, and from that We bring out grains, one riding on the other in close-packed rows.

From the date palm come clusters of low-hanging dates, and there are gardens of vines, olives, and pomegranates, alike yet different— watch their fruits as they grow and ripen! In all this there are signs for those who would believe. [100] Yet they made the jinn[b] partners with God, though He created them, and without any true knowledge they attribute sons and daughters to Him. Glory be to Him! He is far

---

[a] Mecca.
[b] Unseen beings (sometimes said to appear) made from 'smokeless fire' (see 38: 76; 55: 15).

higher than what they ascribe to Him, [101] the Creator of the heavens and earth! How could He have children when He has no spouse, when He created all things, and has full knowledge of all things? [102] This is God, your Lord, there is no God but Him, the Creator of all things, so worship Him; He is in charge of everything. [103] No vision can take Him in, but He takes in all vision.[a] He is the All Subtle, the All Aware.

[104] Now clear proof has come to you from your Lord: if anyone sees it, that will be to his advantage; if anyone is blind to it, that will be to his loss—[Say], 'I am not your guardian.' [105] This is how We explain Our revelations in various ways—though[b] they will say, 'You [Muhammad] have been studying'—to make them clear for those who know. [106] Follow what has been revealed to you from your Lord, there is no God but Him. Turn away from those who join other gods with Him. [107] If it had been God's will, they would not have done so, but We have not made you their guardian, nor are you their keeper.

[108] [Believers], do not revile those they call on beside God in case they, in their hostility and ignorance, revile God. To each community We make their own actions seem alluring, but in the end they will return to their Lord and He will inform them of all they did. [109] They swear by God with their most solemn oaths that if a miraculous sign came to them they would believe in it. Say [Prophet], 'Signs are in the power of God alone.' What will make you [believers] realize that even if a sign came to them they still would not believe, [110] just as they did not believe the first time? We will make their hearts and their eyes waver, and leave them to flounder in their obstinacy. [111] Even if We sent the angels down to them, and the dead spoke to them, and We gathered all things right in front of them, they still would not believe, unless God so willed, but most of them are ignorant [of this]. [112] In the same way We assigned to each prophet an enemy, evil humans and evil jinn. They suggest alluring words to one another in order to deceive—if it had been your Lord's will, [Prophet], they would not have done this: leave them to their inventions—[113] so that the hearts of those who do not believe in the

---

[a] No human eye is able to see God, but God sees everything we see: this is another illustration of our powerlessness compared with Him.

[b] See Razi; the preposition *li* in Arabic here indicates result rather than purpose.

Hereafter may incline towards their deceit, be pleased with it, and so perpetrate whatever they perpetrate.

[114] [Say], 'Shall I seek any judge other than God, when it is He who has sent down the Scripture, clearly explained, for you [people]?' Those to whom We gave the Scripture know that this is revealed by your Lord [Prophet] with the truth, so do not be one of those who doubt. [115] The words of your Lord are complete in their truth and justice. Nothing can change His words—He is the All Hearing, the All Knowing. [116] If you obeyed most of those on earth, they would lead you away from the path of God. They follow nothing but speculation—they are merely guessing. [117] Your Lord knows best who strays from His path and who is rightly guided.

[118] So [believers] eat any [animal] over which God's name has been pronounced, if you believe in His revelations—[119] why should you not eat such animals when God has already fully explained what He has forbidden you, except when forced by hunger? But many lead others astray by their desires, without any true knowledge: your Lord knows best who oversteps the limit. [120] Avoid committing sin, whether openly or in secret, for those who commit sin will be repaid for what they do, [121] and do not eat anything over which God's name has not been pronounced, for that is breaking the law.

The evil ones incite their followers to argue with you:[a] if you listen to them, you too will become idolaters. [122] Is a dead person brought back to life by Us and given light with which to walk among people comparable to someone trapped in deep darkness who cannot escape? That is how it is. The evil deeds of the disbelievers are made to seem alluring to them, [123] and so We have put chief evildoers in every city to perpetrate their schemes there; but they scheme only against themselves, without realizing it. [124] When a revelation is brought before them they say, 'We shall not believe unless we ourselves are given a revelation as God's messengers were.' But God knows best where to place His messages: humiliation before God and severe torment will befall the evildoers for their scheming. [125] When God wishes to guide someone, He opens their breast to *islam*;[b] when He wishes to lead them astray, He closes and constricts their breast as if they were climbing up to the skies. That is how God makes the foulness of those who do not believe rebound against them.

[a] Saying that nothing is wrong with meat sacrificed to an idol.
[b] Devotion to God (see 2: 131–2).

¹²⁶[Prophet], this is the path of your Lord, made perfectly straight. We have explained Our revelations to those who take heed. ¹²⁷They shall have the Home of Peace with their Lord, and He will take care of them as a reward for their deeds.

¹²⁸On the day He gathers everyone together [saying], 'Company of jinn! You have seduced a great many humans,' their adherents among mankind will say, 'Lord, we have profited from one another, but now we have reached the appointed time You decreed for us.' He will say, 'Your home is the Fire, and there you shall remain'—unless God wills otherwise: [Prophet], your Lord is all wise, all knowing. ¹²⁹In this way, We make some evildoers have power over others through their misdeeds. ¹³⁰'Company of jinn and mankind! Did messengers not come from among you to recite My revelations to you and warn that you would meet this Day?' They will say, 'We testify against ourselves.' The life of this world seduced them but they will testify against themselves that they rejected the truth: ¹³¹your Lord would not destroy a community for its wrongdoing without warning them first. ¹³²Everyone is assigned a rank according to their deeds; your Lord is not unaware of anything they do. ¹³³Your Lord is self-sufficient and full of mercy. If He pleased, He could remove you and put others in your place, just as He produced you from the offspring of other people. ¹³⁴What you are promised is sure to come, and you cannot escape. ¹³⁵[Prophet], say, 'My people, you carry on as you are, and so will I: you will come to realize who will have a happy homecoming in the Hereafter.' The evildoers will not prosper.

¹³⁶They apportion to God a share of the produce and the livestock He created, saying, 'This is for God'—so they claim!—'and this is for our idols.' Their idols' share does not reach God, but God's share does reach their idols: how badly they judge! ¹³⁷In the same way, their idols have induced the pagans to kill their own children,^{*a*} bringing them ruin and confusion in their faith: if God had willed otherwise they would not have done this, so [Prophet] leave them to their own devices. ¹³⁸They also say, 'These cattle and crops are reserved, and only those we allow may eat them'—so they claim! There are some animals they exempt from labour and some over

---

^{*a*} Razi explains that either the jinn or servants of the idols appointed by the pagans suggested this infanticide.

which they do not pronounce God's name [during slaughter], falsely attributing these [regulations] to Him: He will repay them for the falsehoods they invent. [139] They also say, 'The contents of these animals' wombs will be reserved solely for our men and forbidden to our women, though if the offspring is stillborn they may have a share of it.' He will punish them for what they attribute to Him: He is all wise, all aware. [140] Lost indeed are those who kill their own children out of folly, with no basis in knowledge,[a] forbidding what God has provided for them, fabricating lies against Him: they have gone far astray and have heeded no guidance.

[141] It is He who produces both cultivated and wild gardens: date palms, crops of diverse flavours, the olive, the pomegranate, [all] alike yet different. So when they bear fruit, eat it, paying what is due on the day of harvest, but do not be wasteful: God does not like wasteful people. [142] [He gave you] livestock, as beasts of burden and as food. So eat what God has provided for you and do not follow in Satan's footsteps: he is your sworn enemy. [143] [God gave you] eight animals, in [four] pairs: a pair of sheep and a pair of goats—ask them [Prophet], 'Has He forbidden the two males, the two females, or the young in the wombs of the two females? Tell me based on knowledge if you are telling the truth'—[144] a pair of camels and a pair of cattle—ask them [Prophet], 'Has He forbidden the two males, the two females, or the young in the wombs of the two females? Were you present when God gave you these commands?' So who is more wicked than he who fabricates lies against God with no basis in knowledge in order to lead people astray? God does not guide the evildoers.

[145] [Prophet], say, 'In all that has been revealed to me, I find nothing forbidden for people to eat, except for carrion, flowing blood, pig's meat—it is loathsome—or a sinful offering over which any name other than God's has been invoked.' But if someone is forced by hunger, rather than desire or excess, then God is most forgiving and most merciful. [146] We forbade for the Jews every animal with claws, and the fat of cattle and sheep, except what is on their backs and in their intestines, or that which sticks to their bones. This is how We penalized them for their disobedience: We are true to Our word. [147] If they [the disbelievers] accuse you [Prophet] of lying, say,

---

[a] i.e. scriptural evidence, cf. verses 143, 144, and 148.

'Your Lord has all-encompassing mercy, but His punishment cannot be diverted from the evildoers.' [148] The idolaters will say, 'If God had willed, we would not have ascribed partners to Him—nor would our fathers—or have declared anything forbidden.' In the same way, those before them continually denied [the truth] until they tasted Our punishment. Say, 'Have you any knowledge that you can show us? You follow only supposition and tell only lies.' [149] Say, 'The conclusive argument belongs to God alone. Had He so willed He would have guided you all.' [150] Say, 'Bring your witnesses to testify that God has forbidden all this.' If they do testify, do not bear witness with them. Do not follow the whims of those who have denied Our revelation, who do not believe in the Hereafter, and who set up equals with their Lord.

[151] Say, 'Come! I will tell you what your Lord has really forbidden you! Do not ascribe anything as a partner to Him; be good to your parents; do not kill your children in fear of poverty'—We will provide for you and for them—'stay well away from committing indecent deeds, whether openly or in secret; do not take the life God has made sacred, except by right. This is what He commands you to do, so that you may use your reason. [152] Stay well away from the property of orphans, except with the best intentions, until they come of age; give full measure and weight, according to justice'—We do not burden any soul with more than it can bear—'when you speak, be just, even if it concerns a relative; keep any promises you make in God's name. This is what He commands you to do, so that you may take heed'—[153] this is My path, leading straight, so follow it, and do not follow other ways: they will lead you away from it—'This is what He commands you to do, so that you may refrain from wrongdoing.'

[154] Once again,[a] We gave Moses the Scripture, perfecting [Our favour] for those who do good, explaining everything clearly, as guidance and mercy, so that they might believe in the meeting with their Lord. [155] This, too, is a blessed Scripture which We have sent down—follow it and be conscious of your Lord, so that you may receive mercy—[156] lest you say, 'Scriptures were only sent down to two communities before us: we were not aware of what they studied,' [157] or 'If only the Scripture had been sent down to us, we would have

---

[a] This reiterates the statement in verses 91–3 in response to their denial that God has ever sent down any revelation.

been better guided than them.' Now your Lord has brought you clear evidence, guidance, and mercy. Who could be more wrong than someone who rejects God's revelations and turns away from them? We shall repay those who turn away with a painful punishment. [158] Are they waiting for the very angels to come to them, or your Lord Himself, or maybe some of His signs? But on the Day some of your Lord's signs[a] come, no soul will profit from faith if it had none before, or has not already earned some good through its faith. Say, 'Wait if you wish: we too are waiting.'

[159] As for those who have divided their religion and broken up into factions, have nothing to do with them [Prophet]. Their case rests with God: in time He will tell them about their deeds. [160] Whoever has done a good deed will have it ten times to his credit, but whoever has done a bad deed will be repaid only with its equivalent—they will not be wronged. [161] Say, 'My Lord has guided me to a straight path, an upright religion, the faith of Abraham, a man of pure faith. He was not a polytheist.' [162] Say, 'My prayers and sacrifice, my life and death are all for God, Lord of all the Worlds; [163] He has no partner. This is what I am commanded, and I am the first[b] to devote myself to Him.' [164] Say, 'Should I seek a Lord other than God, the Lord of all things?' Each soul is responsible for its own actions; no soul will bear the burden of another. You will all return to your Lord in the end, and He will tell you the truth about your differences. [165] It is He who made you successors[c] on the earth and raises some of you above others in rank, to test you through what He gives you. [Prophet], your Lord is swift in punishment, yet He is most forgiving and merciful.

[a] Signs of the Day of Judgement.
[b] The first 'of you': cf. verse 14 and many others.
[c] See note *a* to 2: 30.

7. THE HEIGHTS

A Meccan sura named after the heights of the barrier which will divide the righteous from the damned on the Day of Judgement (verse 46). The sura begins by addressing the Prophet, reassuring him about his revelations, and closes emphasizing the fact that he merely repeats what is revealed to him. It warns the disbelievers of their fate via numerous stories of corrupt communities of the past, in the hope that the disbelievers may take heed and repent before it is too late. Both subjects also serve to give encouragement to the Prophet and the believers.

In the name of God, the Lord of Mercy, the Giver of Mercy

¹ *Alif Lam Mim Sad*

² This Book has been sent down to you [Prophet]—let there be no anxiety in your heart about it*ᵃ*—so that you may use it to give warning and to remind the believers: ³ 'Follow what has been sent down to you from your Lord; do not follow other masters beside Him. How seldom you take heed!'

⁴ How many towns We have destroyed! Our punishment came to them by night or while they slept in the afternoon: ⁵ their only cry when Our punishment came to them was, 'How wrong we were!' ⁶ We shall certainly question those to whom messengers were sent— and We shall question the messengers themselves—⁷ and with full knowledge, for We were never far from them, We shall tell them what they did. ⁸ On that Day the weighing of deeds will be true and just: those whose good deeds are heavy on the scales will be the ones to prosper, ⁹ and those whose good deeds are light will be the ones who have lost their souls through their wrongful rejection of Our messages.

¹⁰ We established you [people] on the earth and provided you with a means of livelihood there—small thanks you give! ¹¹ We created you, We gave you shape, and then We said to the angels, 'Bow down before Adam,' and they did. But not Iblis: he was not one of those who bowed

---

ᵃ See 6: 33–6; 20: 2.

down. ¹² God said, 'What prevented you from bowing down as I commanded you?' and he said, 'I am better than him: You created me from fire and him from clay.' ¹³ God said, 'Get down from here! This^a is no place for your arrogance. Get out! You are contemptible!' ¹⁴ but Iblis said, 'Give me respite until the Day people are raised from the dead,' ¹⁵ and God replied, 'You have respite.' ¹⁶ And then Iblis said, 'Because You have put me in the wrong, I will lie in wait for them all on Your straight path: ¹⁷ I will come at them—from their front and back, from their right and their left—and You will find that most of them are ungrateful.' ¹⁸ God said, 'Get out! You are disgraced and banished! I swear I shall fill Hell with you and all who follow you! ¹⁹ But you and your wife, Adam, live in the Garden. Both of you eat whatever you like, but do not go near this tree or you will become wrongdoers.'

²⁰ Satan whispered to them to expose their nakedness,^b which had been hidden from them: he said, 'Your Lord only forbade you this tree to prevent you becoming angels or immortals,' ²¹ and he swore to them, 'I am giving you sincere advice'—²² he lured them with lies. Their nakedness became exposed to them when they had eaten from the tree: they began to put together leaves from the Garden to cover themselves. Their Lord called to them, 'Did I not forbid you to approach that tree? Did I not warn you that Satan was your sworn enemy?' ²³ They replied, 'Our Lord, we have wronged our souls: if You do not forgive us and have mercy, we shall be lost.' ²⁴ He said, 'All of you get out! You are each other's enemy.^c On earth you will have a place to stay and livelihood—for a time.' ²⁵ He said, 'There you will live; there you will die; from there you will be brought out.'

²⁶ Children of Adam, We have given you garments to cover your nakedness—and as adornment for you; the garment of God-consciousness is the best of all garments—this is one of God's signs, so that people may take heed. ²⁷ Children of Adam, do not let Satan seduce you—as he did your parents, causing them to leave the Garden, stripping them of their garments^d to expose their nakedness to them—he and his forces can see you when you cannot see them: We have made evil ones allies to those who do not believe.

---

^a The Garden, cf. 20: 117.

^b Conventionally translated as 'private parts', but the Arabic does not necessarily have this meaning.

^c Iblis is the enemy of mankind and vice versa.

^d Of God-consciousness. This is one of the views reported by Razi.

[28] When they do something disgraceful,[a] they say, 'We found our forefathers doing this,' and, 'God has commanded us to do this.' Say [Prophet], 'God does not command disgraceful deeds. How can you say about God things that you do not know [to be true]?' [29] Say, 'My Lord commands righteousness. Direct your worship straight to Him wherever you pray; call on Him; devote your religion entirely to Him. Just as He first created you, so you will come back [to life] again.' [30] Some He has guided and some are doomed to stray: they have taken evil ones rather than God as their masters, thinking that they are rightly guided. [31] Children of Adam, dress well[b] whenever you are at worship, and eat and drink [as We have permitted] but do not be wasteful: God does not like wasteful people. [32] Say [Prophet], 'Who has forbidden the adornment and the nourishment God has provided for His servants?' Say, 'They are given for the benefit of those who believe during the life of this world: they will be theirs alone on the Day of Resurrection.' This is how We make Our revelation clear for those who understand.

[33] Say [Prophet], 'My Lord only forbids disgraceful deeds— whether they be open or hidden—and sin[c] and unjustified aggression, and that you, without His sanction, associate things with Him, and that you say things about Him without knowledge.'[d] [34] There is an appointed term for every people: they cannot hasten it, nor, when their time comes, will they be able to delay it for a single moment.

[35] Children of Adam, when messengers come to you from among yourselves, reciting My revelations to you, for those who are conscious of God and live righteously, there will be no fear, nor will they grieve, [36] but those who reject Our revelations and arrogantly scorn them are the people of the Fire and there they will remain. [37] Who is more wrong than the person who invents lies against God or rejects His revelations? Such people will have what has been decreed for them. Then, when Our angels arrive to take them back, saying,

---

[a] It has been suggested that this could refer to the pagan custom of men and women walking round the Ka'ba naked (Razi).

[b] Literally 'wear your adornment', but this is clearly a reference to clothes and not to jewellery; cf. 7: 26.

[c] Razi identifies this as intoxicants because of their link with 'sin' in 2: 219 and the preceding verse about food.

[d] Revealed knowledge, cf. 6: 148.

'Where are those you used to call on beside God?' they will say, 'They have deserted us.' They will confess that they were dis-believers and [38] God will say, 'Join the crowds of jinn and humans who have gone before you into the Fire.' Every crowd curses its fellow crowd as it enters, then, when they are all gathered inside, the last of them will say of the first, 'Our Lord, it was they who led us astray: give them double punishment in the Fire'—God says, 'Every one of you will have double punishment, though you do not know it'—[39] and the first of them will say to the last, 'You were no better than us: taste the punishment you have earned.'

[40] The gates of Heaven will not be open to those who rejected Our revelations and arrogantly spurned them; even if a thick rope[a] were to pass through the eye of a needle they would not enter the Garden. This is how We punish those who do evil—[41] Hell will be their resting place and their covering, layer upon layer—this is how We punish those who do evil. [42] But those who believe and do good deeds—and We do not burden any soul with more than it can bear—are the people of the Garden and there they will remain. [43] We shall have removed all ill feeling from their hearts; streams will flow at their feet. They will say, 'Praise be to God, who guided us to this: had God not guided us, We would never have found the way. The messengers of our Lord brought the Truth.' A voice will call out to them, 'This is the Garden you have been given as your own on account of your deeds.' [44] The people of the Garden will cry out to the people of the Fire, 'We have found what our Lord promised us to be true. Have you found what your Lord promised you to be true?' and they will answer, 'Yes'. A voice will proclaim from their midst, 'God's rejection [hangs] over the evildoers: [45] those who turned others away from God's path and tried to make it crooked, those who denied the Hereafter.'

[46] A barrier divides the two groups with men on its heights recognizing each group by their marks: they will call out to the people of the Garden, 'Peace be with you!'—they will not have entered, but they will be hoping, [47] and when their glance falls upon the people of the Fire, they will say, 'Our Lord, do not let us join the evildoers!'—[48] and the people of the heights will call out to certain

---

[a] Not 'camel'. The roots of the words for 'camel' and 'thick twisted rope' are the same in Arabic and 'rope' makes more sense here (Razi).

men they recognize by their marks, 'What use have been your great numbers and your false pride? [49] And are these the people you swore God would never bless? [Now these people are being told], "Enter the Garden! You have nothing to fear, nor shall you grieve." '

[50] The people of the Fire will call to the people of Paradise, 'Give us some water, or any of the sustenance God has granted you!' and they will reply, 'God has forbidden both to the disbelievers— [51] those who took their religion for distraction, a mere game, and were deluded by worldly life.' On that Day We shall ignore[a] them, just as they have ignored their meeting with this Day and denied Our Revelations.

[52] We have brought them a Scripture—We have explained it on the basis of true knowledge—as guidance and mercy for those who believe. [53] What are they waiting for but the fulfilment of its [final prophecy]? On the Day it is fulfilled, those who had ignored it will say, 'Our Lord's messenger spoke the truth. Is there anyone to intercede for us now? Or can we be sent back to behave differently from the way we behaved before?' They will really have squandered their souls, and all [the idols] they invented will have deserted them.

[54] Your Lord is God, who created the heavens and earth in six Days, then established Himself on the throne—He makes the night cover the day in swift pursuit; He created the sun, moon, and stars to be subservient to His command; all creation and command belong to Him—exalted be God, Lord of all the worlds! [55] Call on your Lord humbly and privately—He does not like those who transgress His bounds: [56] do not corrupt the earth after it has been set right—call on Him fearing and hoping. The mercy of God is close to those who do good. [57] It is God who sends the winds, bearing good news of His coming grace, and when they have gathered up the heavy clouds, We drive them to a dead land where We cause rain to fall, bringing out all kinds of fruit, just as We shall bring out the dead. Will you not reflect? [58] Vegetation comes out of good land in abundance, by the will of its Lord, but out of bad land only scantily: We explain Our Revelations in various ways to those who give thanks.

[59] We sent Noah to his people. He said, 'My people, serve God: you have no god other than Him. I fear for you the punishment of an awesome Day!' [60] but the prominent leaders of his people said, 'We

---

[a] 'Ignore' is one of the meanings of the Arabic *nasiya* normally translated as 'forget'.

believe you are far astray.' [61] He replied, 'My people, there is nothing astray about me! On the contrary, I am a messenger from the Lord of all the Worlds: [62] I am delivering my Lord's messages to you and giving you sincere advice. I know things from God that you do not. [63] Do you find it so strange that a message would come from your Lord—through a man in your midst—to warn you and make you aware of God so that you may be given mercy?' [64] but they called him a liar. We saved him, and those who were with him, on the Ark; and We drowned those who rejected Our revelations—they were wilfully blind!

[65] To the people of 'Ad We sent their brother, Hud. He said, 'My people, serve God: you have no god other than Him. Will you not take heed?' [66] but the disbelieving leaders of his people said, 'We believe you are a fool,' and 'We think you are a liar.' [67] He said, 'My people, there is nothing foolish about me! On the contrary, I am a messenger from the Lord of all the Worlds: [68] I am delivering my Lord's messages to you. I am your sincere and honest adviser. [69] Do you find it so strange that a message should come from your Lord, through a man in your midst, to warn you? Remember how He made you heirs after Noah's people, and increased your stature: remember God's bounties, so that you may prosper.' [70] They said, 'Have you really come to tell us to serve God alone and to forsake what our forefathers served? If what you say is true, bring us the punishment you threaten.' [71] He said, 'You are already set to receive your Lord's loathing and anger. Are you arguing with me about mere names you and your forefathers invented, names for which God has given no sanction? Just wait; I too am waiting.' [72] We saved him, and those who were with him, through Our mercy; We destroyed those who denied Our revelations and would not believe.

[73] To the people of Thamud We sent their brother, Salih. He said, 'My people, serve God: you have no god other than Him. A clear sign has come to you now from your Lord: this is God's she-camel—a sign for you—so let her graze in God's land and do not harm her in any way, or you will be struck by a painful torment. [74] Remember how He made you heirs after 'Ad and settled you in the land to build yourselves castles on its plains and carve houses out of the mountains: remember God's blessings and do not spread corruption in the land,' [75] but the arrogant leaders among his people said to the believers they thought to be of no account, 'Do you honestly think

that Salih is a messenger from his Lord?' They said, 'Yes. We believe in the message sent through him,' [76] but the arrogant leaders said, 'We reject what you believe in,' [77] and then they hamstrung the camel. They defied their Lord's commandment and said, 'Salih, bring down the punishment you threaten, if you really are a messenger!' [78] An earthquake seized them—by the next morning they were lying dead in their homes—[79] so he turned away from them, saying, 'My people, I delivered my Lord's messages to you and gave you sincere advice, but you did not like those who gave sincere advice.'

[80] We sent Lot and he said to his people, 'How can you practise this outrage? No one in the world has outdone you in this. [81] You lust after men rather than women! You transgress all bounds!' [82] The only response his people gave was to say [to one another], 'Drive them out of your town! These men want to keep themselves chaste!' [83] We saved him and his kinsfolk—apart from his wife who stayed behind—[84] and We showered upon [the rest of] them a rain [of destruction]. Consider the fate of the evildoers.

[85] To the people of Midian We sent their brother, Shu'ayb. He said, 'My people, serve God: you have no god other than Him. A clear sign has come to you from your Lord. Give full measure and weight and do not undervalue people's goods; do not cause corruption in the land after it has been set in order: this is better for you, if you are believers. [86] Do not sit in every pathway, threatening and barring those who believe in God from His way, trying to make it crooked. Remember how you used to be few and He made you multiply. Consider the fate of those who used to spread corruption. [87] If some of you believe the message I bring and others do not, then be patient till God judges between us. He is the best of all judges.'

[88] His people's arrogant leaders said, 'Shu'ayb, we will expel you and your fellow believers from our town unless you return to our religion.' He said, 'What! Even if we detest it? [89] If we were to return to your religion after God has saved us from it, we would be inventing lies about Him: there is no way we could return to it—unless by the will of God our Lord: in His knowledge He comprehends everything. We put our trust in God. Our Lord, expose the truth [and judge] between us and our people, for You are the best judge.' [90] The disbelieving leaders among his people said, 'You will certainly be losers if you follow Shu'ayb'—[91] an earthquake seized them: by the next morning they were lying dead in their homes; [92] it was as if those

who had rejected Shuʿayb had never lived there; it was those who had rejected Shuʿayb who were the losers—[93] so he turned away from them, saying, 'My people, I delivered my Lord's messages to you and gave you sincere advice, so why should I grieve for people who refused to believe?'

[94] Whenever We sent a prophet to a town, We afflicted its disbelieving[a] people with suffering and hardships, so that they might humble themselves [before God], [95] and then We changed their hardship into prosperity, until they multiplied. But then they said, 'Hardship and affluence also befell our forefathers,' and so[b] We took them suddenly, unawares. [96] If the people of those towns had believed and been mindful of God, We would have showered them with blessings from the heavens and earth, but they rejected the truth and so We punished them for their misdeeds.

[97] Do the people of these towns feel secure that Our punishment will not come upon them by night, while they are asleep? [98] Do the people of these towns feel secure that Our punishment will not come upon them by day, while they are at play? [99] Do they feel secure against God's plan? Only the losers feel safe from God's plan. [100] Is it not clear to those who inherit the land from former generations that We can punish them too for their sins if We will? And seal up their hearts so that they cannot hear? [101] We have told you [Prophet] the stories of those towns: messengers came to them, and clear signs, but they would not believe in what they had already rejected—in this way God seals the hearts of disbelievers. [102] We found that most of them did not honour their commitments; We found that most of them were defiant.

[103] After these, We sent Moses to Pharaoh and his leading supporters with Our signs, but they rejected them—consider the fate of those who used to spread corruption. [104] Moses said, 'Pharaoh, I am a messenger from the Lord of all the Worlds, [105] duty-bound to say nothing about God but the truth, and I have brought you a clear sign from your Lord. Let the Children of Israel go with me.' [106] He said, 'Produce this sign you have brought, if you are telling the truth.' [107] So Moses threw his staff and—lo and behold!—it was a snake, clear to all, [108] and then he pulled out his hand and—lo and

---

[a] This is implied in Arabic (Razi).

[b] i.e. because they refused to acknowledge the hardship and affluence as God's signs.

behold!—it was white for all to see. [109] The leaders among Pharaoh's people said, 'This man is a learned sorcerer! [110] He means to drive you out of your land!' Pharaoh said, 'What do you suggest?' [111] They said, 'Delay him and his brother for a while, and send messengers to all the cities [112] to summon every learned sorcerer to you.'

[113] The sorcerers came to Pharaoh and said, 'Shall we be rewarded if we win?' [114] and he replied, 'Yes, and you will join my inner court.' [115] So they said, 'Moses, will you throw first or shall we?' [116] He said, 'You throw,' and they did, casting a spell on people's eyes, striking fear into them, and bringing about great sorcery. [117] Then We inspired Moses, 'Throw your staff,' and—lo and behold!—it devoured their fakery. [118] The truth was confirmed and what they had produced came to nothing: [119] they were defeated there and utterly humiliated. [120] The sorcerers fell to their knees [121] and said, 'We believe in the Lord of the Worlds, [122] the Lord of Moses and Aaron!' [123] but Pharaoh said, 'How dare you believe in Him before I have given you permission? This is a plot you have hatched to drive the people out of this city! Soon you will see: [124] I will cut off your alternate hands and feet[a] and then crucify you all!' [125] They said, 'And so we shall return to our Lord. [126] Your only grievance against us is that we believed in the signs of our Lord when they came to us. Our Lord, pour steadfastness upon us and let us die in devotion to You.'

[127] The leaders among Pharaoh's people said to him, 'But are you going to leave Moses and his people to spread corruption in the land and forsake you and your gods?' He replied, 'We shall kill their male children—sparing only the females. We have complete power over them.' [128] Moses said to his people, 'Turn to God for help and be steadfast: the earth belongs to God—He gives it as their own to whichever of His servants He chooses—and the happy future belongs to those who are mindful of Him,' [129] and they replied, 'We were being persecuted long before you came to us, and since then too.' He said, 'Your Lord may well destroy your enemy and make you successors to the land to see how you behave.'

[130] We inflicted years of drought and crop failure on Pharaoh's people, so that they might take heed, [131] then, when something good came their way, they said, 'This is our due!'—when something bad

---

[a] Left hand and right foot or vice versa.

came, they ascribed it to the evil omen of Moses and those with him, but their 'evil omen' was really from God, though most of them did not realize it. [132] They said, 'We will not believe in you, no matter what signs you produce to cast a spell on us,' [133] and so We let loose on them the flood, locusts, lice, frogs, blood—all clear signs. They were arrogant, wicked people. [134] They would say, whenever a plague struck them, 'Moses, pray to your Lord for us by virtue of the promise He has made to you: if you relieve us of the plague, we will believe you and let the Children of Israel go with you,' [135] but when We relieved them of the plague and gave them a fixed period [in which to fulfil their promise]—lo and behold!—they broke it. [136] And so, because they rejected Our signs and paid them no heed, We exacted retribution from them: We drowned them in the sea [137] and We made those who had been oppressed succeed to both the east and the west of the land that We had blessed—your Lord's good promise to the Children of Israel was fulfilled, because of their patience, and We destroyed everything Pharaoh and his people had made and all that they had constructed.

[138] We took the Children of Israel across the sea, but when they came upon a people who worshipped idols, they said, 'Moses, make a god for us like theirs.' He said, 'You really are foolish people: [139] [the cult] these people practise is doomed to destruction, and what they have been doing is false. [140] Why should I seek any god other than God for you, when He has favoured you over all other people?' [141] Remember how We saved you from Pharaoh's people, who were subjecting you to the worst of sufferings, killing your male children, sparing only your females—that was a mighty ordeal from your Lord.

[142] We appointed thirty nights for Moses, then added ten more: the term set by his Lord was fulfilled in forty nights. Moses said to his brother Aaron, 'Take my place among my people: act rightly and do not follow the way of those who spread corruption.' [143] When Moses came at the time We appointed, and his Lord spoke to him, he said, 'My Lord, show Yourself to me: let me see You!' He said, 'You will never see Me, but look at that mountain: if it remains standing firm, you will see Me.' When his Lord revealed Himself to the mountain, He made it crumble: Moses fell down unconscious. When he recovered, he said, 'Glory be to You! To You I turn in repentance! I am the first to believe!' [144] He said, 'Moses, I have raised you over

other people by [giving you] My messages and speaking to you: hold on to what I have given you; be one of those who give thanks.'

¹⁴⁵ We inscribed everything for him in the Tablets which taught and explained everything, saying, 'Hold on to them firmly and urge your people to hold fast to their excellent teachings. I will show you the end of those who rebel: ¹⁴⁶ those who behave arrogantly on Earth without any right I will turn away from My messages and even if they see every sign they will not believe in them—they will not take the way of right guidance if they see it, but they will take the way of error if they see that. This is because they denied Our signs and paid them no heed: ¹⁴⁷ the deeds of those who denied Our signs and the Meeting of the Hereafter will come to nothing—why should they be repaid for anything other than what they have done?'

¹⁴⁸ In his absence, Moses' people took to worshipping a mere shape that made sounds like a cow—a calf made from their jewellery. Could they not see that it did not speak to them or guide them in any way? Yet they took it for worship: they were evildoers. ¹⁴⁹ When, with much wringing of hands, they perceived that they were doing wrong, they said, 'If our Lord does not have mercy and forgive us, we shall be the losers.' ¹⁵⁰ On his return to his people, angry and aggrieved, Moses said, 'What you have done in my absence is foul and evil. Were you so keen to bring your Lord's judgement forward?' He threw the tablets down and seized his brother by the hair, pulling him towards him. Aaron said, 'Son of my mother, these people overpowered me! They almost killed me! Do not give my enemies reason to rejoice! Do not include me with these evildoers!' ¹⁵¹ Moses said, 'My Lord, forgive me and my brother; accept us into Your mercy: You are the Most Merciful of all who show mercy. ¹⁵² Those who took to worshipping the calf will be afflicted by their Lord's wrath, and by disgrace in this life.' This is the way We repay those who invent such falsehoods, ¹⁵³ but your Lord is most forgiving and most merciful towards those who do wrong, then repent afterwards and truly believe.

¹⁵⁴ When Moses' anger abated, he picked up the Tablets, on which were inscribed guidance and mercy for those who stood in awe of their Lord. ¹⁵⁵ Moses chose from his people seventy men for Our appointment, and when they were seized by trembling, he prayed, 'My Lord, if You had chosen to do so, You could have destroyed them long before this, and me too, so will You now destroy us for

what the foolish among us have done? This is only a trial from You—through it, You cause whoever You will to stray and guide whoever You will—and You are our Protector, so forgive us and have mercy on us. You are the best of those who forgive. [156] Grant us good things in this world and in the life to come. We turn to You.' God said, 'I bring My punishment on whoever I will, but My mercy encompasses all things.

'I shall ordain My mercy for those who are conscious of God and pay the prescribed alms; who believe in Our Revelations; [157] who follow the Messenger—the unlettered[a] prophet they find described in the Torah that is with them, and in the Gospel—who commands them to do right and forbids them to do wrong, who makes good things lawful to them and bad things unlawful, and relieves them of their burdens, and the iron collars[b] that were on them. So it is those who believe him, honour and help him, and who follow the light which has been sent down with him, who will succeed.' [158] Say [Muhammad], 'People, I am the Messenger of God to you all, from Him who has control over the heavens and the earth. There is no God but Him; He gives life and death, so believe in God and His Messenger, the unlettered prophet who believes in God and His words, and follow him so that you may find guidance.'

[159] There is a group among the people of Moses who guide with truth, and who act justly according to it. [160] We divided them into twelve tribes [as distinct] communities, and, when his people asked him for water, inspired Moses to strike the rock with his staff [so that] twelve springs gushed out. Each tribe knew its own drinking place; We gave them the shade of clouds and sent down to them manna and quails [saying], 'Eat the good things We have provided for you.' They did not wrong Us; it was themselves they wronged. [161] When they were told, 'Enter this town and eat freely there as you will, but say, "Relieve us!" and enter its gate humbly: then We shall forgive you your sins, and increase the reward of those who do good,' [162] the wrongdoers among them substituted another saying for that which had been given them, so We sent them a punishment from heaven for their wrongdoing.

---

[a] *Ummi* can mean 'unlettered' or 'gentile'.

[b] Cf. 6: 146. This reference is said by interpreters to refer to the difficult obligations imposed on the Children of Israel.

¹⁶³ [Prophet], ask them about the town by the sea; how its people broke the Sabbath when their fish surfaced for them only on that day, never on weekdays—We tested them in this way: because of their disobedience—¹⁶⁴ how, when some of them asked [their preachers], 'Why do you bother preaching to people God will destroy, or at least punish severely?' [the preachers] answered, 'In order to be free from your Lord's blame, and so that they may perhaps take heed.' ¹⁶⁵ When they ignored [the warning] they were given, We saved those who forbade evil, and punished the wrongdoers severely because of their disobedience. ¹⁶⁶ When, in their arrogance, they persisted in doing what they had been forbidden to do, We said to them, 'Be like apes!ᵃ Be outcasts!' ¹⁶⁷ And then your Lord declared that, until the Day of Resurrection, He would send people against them to inflict terrible suffering on them. Your Lord is swift in punishment but He is most forgiving and merciful.

¹⁶⁸ We dispersed them over the earth in separate communities—some are righteous and some less so: We tested them with blessings and misfortunes, so that they might all return [to righteousness]—¹⁶⁹ and they were succeeded by generations who, although they inherited the Scripture, took the fleeting gains of this lower world, saying, 'We shall be forgiven,' and indeed taking them again if other such gains came their way. Was a pledge not taken from them, written in the Scripture, to say nothing but the truth about God? And they have studied its contents well. For those who are mindful of God, the Hereafter is better. 'Why do you not use your reason?' ¹⁷⁰ But as for those who hold fast to the Scripture and keep up the prayer, We do not deny righteous people their rewards. ¹⁷¹ When We made the mountain loom high above them like a shadow, and they thought it would fall on them, We said, 'Hold fast to what We have given you and remember what it contains so that you may remain conscious of God.'

¹⁷² [Prophet], when your Lord took out the offspring from the loins of the Children of Adam and made them bear witness about themselves, He said, 'Am I not your Lord?' and they replied, 'Yes, we bear witness.' So you cannot say on the Day of Resurrection, 'We were not aware of this,' ¹⁷³ or, 'It was our forefathers who, before us, ascribed partners to God, and we are only the descendants who came

---

ᵃ Cf. note to 2: 65.

after them: will you destroy us because of falsehoods they invented?'
¹⁷⁴ In this way We explain the messages, so that they may turn [to the
right path].

¹⁷⁵ [Prophet], tell them the story of the man to whom We gave Our
messages: he sloughed them off, so Satan took him as his follower
and he went astray—¹⁷⁶ if it had been Our will, We could have used
these signs to raise him high, but instead he clung to the earth and
followed his own desires—he was like a dog that pants with a lolling
tongue whether you drive it away or leave it alone. Such is the image
of those who reject Our signs. Tell them the story so that they may
reflect—¹⁷⁷ how foul is the image of those who reject Our signs! It is
themselves they wrong: ¹⁷⁸ whoever God guides is truly guided, and
whoever God allows to stray is a loser. ¹⁷⁹ We have created many jinn
and people who are destined for Hell, with hearts they do not use for
comprehension, eyes they do not use for sight, ears they do not use
for hearing: they are like cattle, no, even further astray—these are
the ones who are entirely heedless.

¹⁸⁰ The Most Excellent Names belong to God: use them to call on
Him and keep away from those who distort them—they will be
requited for what they do. ¹⁸¹ Among those We created are a group of
people who guide with truth and act justly according to it, ¹⁸² but We
lead those who reject Our messages to ruin, step by step, without
them realizing it. ¹⁸³ I will give them respite, but My plan is sure.
¹⁸⁴ Has it not occurred to them that their companion*a* is not mad but
is giving clear warning? ¹⁸⁵ Have they not contemplated the realm of
the heavens and earth and all that God created, and that the end of
their time might be near? What [other revelation] will they believe in
if they do not believe in this? ¹⁸⁶ No one can guide those God allows
to stray: He leaves them blundering about in their insolence.

¹⁸⁷ They ask you [Prophet] about the Hour, 'When will it happen?'
Say, 'My Lord alone has knowledge of it: He alone will reveal when
its time will come, a time that is hidden*b* from both the heavens and
earth. All too suddenly it will come upon you.' They ask you about
it as if you were eager [to find out]. Say, 'God alone has knowledge
of [when it will come], though most people do not realize it.' ¹⁸⁸ Say
[Prophet], 'I have no control over benefit or harm, even to myself,

---

a This refers to Prophet Muhammad.
b This interpretation of *thaqulat* is given by Suddi (Razi).

except as God may please: if I had knowledge of what is hidden, I would have abundant good things and no harm could touch me. I am no more than a bearer of warning and good news to those who believe.'

[189] It is He who created you all from one soul, and from it made its mate so that he might find comfort in her: when one [of them] lies with his wife and she conceives a light burden, going about freely, then grows heavy, they both pray to God, their Lord, 'If You give us a good child we shall certainly be grateful,' [190] and yet when He gives them a good child they ascribe some of what He has granted them to others. [191] God is far above the partners they set up alongside Him! How can they set up with Him these partners that create nothing and are themselves created, [192] that cannot help them at all, or even help themselves?

[193] If you [believers] call such people to guidance, they do not follow you: it makes no difference whether you call them or remain silent. [194] Those you [idolaters] call upon instead of God are created beings like you. Call upon them, then, and let them respond to you if what you say is true. [195] Do they have feet to walk, hands to strike, eyes to see, or ears to hear? Say [Prophet], 'Call on your "partners"! Scheme against me! Do not spare me! [196] My protector is God: He has revealed the Scripture, and it is He who protects the righteous, [197] but those you call on instead of Him cannot help you or even help themselves.' [198] If you [believers] call such people to guidance, they do not hear. You [Prophet] may observe them looking at you, but they cannot see. [199] Be tolerant and command what is right: pay no attention to foolish people. [200] If Satan should prompt you to do something, seek refuge with God—He is all hearing, all knowing—[201] those who are aware of God think of Him when Satan prompts them to do something and immediately they can see [straight]; [202] the followers of devils[a] are led relentlessly into error by them and cannot stop.

[203] When you do not bring them a fresh revelation, they say, 'But can you not just ask for one?' Say, 'I merely repeat[b] what is revealed to me from my Lord: this revelation brings you knowledge from your Lord, and guidance and mercy for those who believe, [204] so pay

---

[a] *Ikhwan* 'brothers'—cf. 17: 27, where the devils' followers are described as their *ikhwan*.

[b] Cf. 75: 18.

attention and listen quietly when the Qur'an is recited, so that you may be given mercy.' ²⁰⁵[Prophet], remember your Lord inwardly, in all humility and awe, without raising your voice, in the mornings and in the evenings—do not be one of the heedless. ²⁰⁶ The ones who live in the presence of your Lord are not too proud to worship Him: they glorify Him and bow down before Him.

8. BATTLE GAINS

The main part of this Medinan sura is a comment on the Battle of Badr (near Medina), the first fought between the Muslims and their Meccan opponents in the second year after the Migration. The Muslims, some of whom were at first reluctant to fight, won in spite of being vastly outnumbered, and began to question the distribution of the gains. The sura reminds them that it was God who brought about the victory. Verse 41 shows how the gains were to be distributed. It advises Muslims and comments on the role of the hypocrites and on those who always break their treaties (verse 56), ending with a statement about loyalties and alliances.

In the name of God, the Lord of Mercy, the Giver of Mercy

¹ They ask you [Prophet] about [distributing] the battle gains. Say, 'That is a matter for God and His Messenger, so be conscious of God and make things right between you. Obey God and His Messenger if you are true believers: ² true believers are those whose hearts tremble with awe when God is mentioned, whose faith increases when His revelations are recited to them, who put their trust in their Lord, ³ who keep up the prayer and give to others out of what We provide for them. ⁴ Those are the ones who truly believe. They have high standing with their Lord, forgiveness, and generous provision.'

⁵ For it was your Lord [Prophet] who made you venture from your home for a true purpose—though a group of the believers disliked it ⁶ and argued with you about the truth after it had been made clear, as if they were being driven towards a death they could see with their own eyes. ⁷ Remember how God promised you [believers] that one of the two enemy groups[a] would fall to you: you wanted the unarmed group to be yours, but it was God's will to establish the truth according to His Word and to finish off the disbelievers—⁸ to prove the Truth to be true, and the false to be false, much as the guilty might dislike it. ⁹ When you begged your Lord for help, He answered you, 'I will reinforce you with a thousand angels in succession.' ¹⁰ God

---

[a] The Meccan trade caravan or their army.

made this a message of hope to reassure your hearts: help comes only from God, He is mighty and wise. [11] Remember when He gave you sleep[a] as a reassurance from Him, and sent down water from the sky to cleanse you, to remove Satan's pollution from you, to make your hearts strong and your feet firm. [12] Your Lord revealed to the angels: 'I am with you: give the believers firmness; I shall put terror into the hearts of the disbelievers. Strike above their necks and strike their fingertips.' [13] That was because they opposed God and His Messenger, and if anyone opposes God and His Messenger, God punishes them severely—[14] 'That is what you get! Taste that!'—and the torment of the Fire awaits the disbelievers.

[15] Believers, when you meet the disbelievers in battle, never turn your backs on them: [16] if anyone does so on such a day—unless manoeuvring to fight or to join a fighting group—he incurs the wrath of God, and Hell will be his home, a wretched destination! [17] It was not you who killed them but God, and when you [Prophet] threw [sand at them][b] it was not your throw [that defeated them] but God's, to do the believers a favour: God is all seeing and all knowing—[18] 'That is what you get!'—and God will weaken the disbelievers' designs. [19] [Disbelievers], if you were seeking a decision, now you have witnessed one: if you stop here, it will be better for you. If you return, so shall We, and your forces, though greater in number, will be of no use to you. God is with the believers.

[20] Believers, obey God and His Messenger: do not turn away when you are listening to him; [21] do not be like those who say, 'We heard,' though in fact they were not listening—[22] the worst creatures in God's eyes are those who are [wilfully] deaf and dumb, who do not reason. [23] If God had known there was any good in them, He would have made them hear, but even if He had, they would still have turned away and taken no notice. [24] Believers, respond to God and His Messenger when he calls you to that which gives you life. Know that God comes between a man and his heart,[c] and that you will be gathered to Him. [25] Beware of discord that harms not only the wrongdoers among you: know that God is severe in His punishment.

---

[a] On the night before the battle.

[b] Before the battle, the Prophet prayed and threw a handful of sand at the enemy as a symbol of their being defeated.

[c] There are various ways of interpreting this, including that, through death, God separates a man from his heart's desire, i.e. life.

²⁶ Remember when you were few, victimized in the land, afraid that people might catch you, but God sheltered you and strengthened you with His help, and provided you with good things so that you might be grateful. ²⁷ Believers, do not betray God and the Messenger, or knowingly betray [other people's] trust in you. ²⁸ Be aware that your possessions and your children are only a test, and that there is a tremendous reward with God. ²⁹ Believers, if you remain conscious of God, He will give you a criterion [to tell right from wrong] and wipe out your bad deeds, and forgive you: God's favour is great indeed.

³⁰ Remember [Prophet] when the disbelievers plotted to take you captive, kill, or expel you. They schemed and so did God: He is the best of schemers. ³¹ Whenever Our Revelation is recited to them they say, 'We have heard all this before—we could say something like this if we wanted—this is nothing but ancient fables.' ³² They also said, 'God, if this really is the truth from You, then rain stones on us from the heavens, or send us some other painful punishment.' ³³ But God would not send them punishment while you [Prophet] are in their midst, nor would He punish them if they sought forgiveness, ³⁴ yet why should God not punish them when they debar people from the Sacred Mosque, although they are not its [rightful] guardians? Only those conscious of God are its rightful guardians, but most of the disbelievers do not realize this. ³⁵ Their prayers before the House are nothing but whistling and clapping. 'So taste the punishment*a* for your disbelief.' ³⁶ They use their wealth to bar people from the path of God, and they will go on doing so. In the end this will be a source of intense regret for them: they will be overcome and herded towards Hell. ³⁷ God will separate the bad from the good, place the bad on top of one another—heaping them all up together—and put them in Hell. They will be the losers. ³⁸ [Prophet], tell the disbelievers that if they desist their past will be forgiven, but if they persist, they have an example in the fate of those who went before. ³⁹ [Believers], fight them until there is no more persecution, and [your]*b* worship is devoted to God alone: if they desist, then God sees all that they do, ⁴⁰ but if they pay no heed, be sure that God is your protector, the best protector and the best helper.

---

a This could allude to their defeat in the battle.

b Cf. 2: 191–3.

⁴¹ Know that one-fifth of your battle gains belongs to God and the Messenger, to close relatives and orphans, to the needy and travellers, if you believe in God and the revelation We sent down to Our servant on the decisive day, the day when the two forces met in battle. God has power over all things. ⁴² Remember when you were on the near side of the valley, and they were on the far side and the caravan was below you. If you had made an appointment to fight, you would have failed to keep it [but the battle took place] so that God might bring about something already ordained, so that those who were to die might die after seeing a clear proof, and so that those who were to live might live after seeing a clear proof—God is all hearing and all seeing.

⁴³ [Prophet], remember when God made you see them in your sleep as few: if He had shown them to you [believers] as many, you would certainly have lost heart and argued about it, but God saved you. He knows the secrets of the heart. ⁴⁴ When you met He showed them to you as few, and He made you few in their eyes, so that He might bring about what has been ordained: everything goes back to God.

⁴⁵ Believers, when you meet a force in battle, stand firm and keep God firmly in mind, so that you may prosper. ⁴⁶ Obey God and His Messenger, and do not quarrel with one another, or you may lose heart and your spirit may desert you. Be steadfast: God is with the steadfast. ⁴⁷ Do not be like those who came out of their homes full of conceit, showing off to people, and barring others from the way of God—God has full knowledge of all that they do. ⁴⁸ Satan made their foul deeds seem fair to them, and said, 'No one will conquer you today, for I will be right beside you,' but when the armies came within sight of one another he turned on his heels, saying, 'This is where I leave you: I see what you do not, and I fear God—God is severe in His punishment.'

⁴⁹ The hypocrites and those who have sickness in their hearts said, 'These people [the believers] must be deluded by their religion,' but if anyone puts his trust in God, God is mighty and wise. ⁵⁰ If only you [Prophet] could see, when the angels take the souls of the disbelievers, how they strike their faces and backs: it will be said, 'Taste the punishment of the Fire. ⁵¹ This is caused by what your own hands have stored up for you: God is never unjust to His creatures.' ⁵² They are like Pharaoh's people and those before them who ignored

God's signs, so God punished them for their sins: God is strong and severe in His punishment. ⁵³[He did] this because God would never change a favour He had conferred on a people unless they changed what was within themselves. God is all hearing, all knowing. ⁵⁴They are indeed like Pharaoh's people and those before them, who denied the signs of their Lord: We destroyed them for their sins, and We drowned Pharaoh's people—they were all evildoers.

⁵⁵The worst creatures in the sight of God are those who reject Him and will not believe; ⁵⁶who, whenever you [Prophet] make a treaty with them, break it—for they have no fear of God. ⁵⁷If you meet them in battle, make a fearsome example of them to those who come after them, so that they may take heed. ⁷And if you learn of treachery on the part of any people, throw their treaty back at them, for God does not love the treacherous. ⁵⁹The disbelievers should not think they have won—they cannot escape. ⁶⁰Prepare whatever forces you [believers] can muster, including warhorses, to frighten off God's enemies and yours, and warn others unknown to you but known to God. Whatever you give in God's cause will be repaid to you in full, and you will not be wronged. ⁶¹But if they incline towards peace, you [Prophet] must also incline towards it, and put your trust in God: He is the All Hearing, the All Knowing. ⁶²If they intend to deceive you, God is enough for you: it was He who strengthened you with His help, ⁶³and with the believers, and brought their hearts together in friendship. Even if you had given away everything in the earth you could not have done this, but God brought them together: God is mighty and wise. ⁶⁴Prophet, God is enough for you, and for the believers who follow you. ⁶⁵Prophet, urge the believers to fight: if there are twenty of you who are steadfast, they will overcome two hundred, and a hundred of you, if steadfast, will overcome a thousand of the disbelievers, for they are people who do not comprehend. ⁶⁶But God has lightened your burden for now, knowing that there is weakness in you—a steadfast hundred of you will defeat two hundred and a steadfast thousand of you will defeat two thousand, by God's permission: God is with the steadfast.

⁶⁷It is not right for a prophet to take captives before he has

---

ᵃ Translators use 'if you fear', but one of the old meanings of *khafa* is 'to know' and 'to be certain'.

conquered the land.[a] You [people] desire the transient goods of this world, but God desires the Hereafter [for you]—God is mighty and wise—[68] and had it not been preordained by God, a severe punishment would have come upon you for what you have taken. [69] So enjoy[b] in a good and lawful manner the things you have gained in war and be conscious of God: He is forgiving and merciful.

[70] Prophet, tell those you have taken captive, 'If God knows of any good in your hearts, He will give you something better than what has been taken from you, and He will forgive you: God is forgiving and merciful.' [71] But if they mean to betray you, they have betrayed God before, and He has given you mastery over them: He is all knowing, all wise.

[72] Those who believed and emigrated [to Medina] and struggled for God's cause with their possessions and persons, and those who gave refuge and help, are all allies of one another. As for those who believed but did not emigrate, you are not responsible for their protection until they have done so. But if they seek help from you against persecution, it is your duty to assist them, except against people with whom you have a treaty: God sees all that you do.

[73] The disbelievers support one another. If you do not do the same, there will be persecution in the land and great corruption. [74] Those who believed and emigrated, and struggled for God's cause, and those who gave refuge and help—they are the true believers and they will have forgiveness and generous provision. [75] And those who came to believe afterwards, and emigrated and struggled alongside you, they are part of you, but kindred still have prior claim over one another in God's Scripture: God has full knowledge of all things.

---

[a] This interpretation is the one favoured by Razi.
[b] Literally 'eat'.

9. REPENTANCE

A Medinan sura whose title is taken from verse 104. The sura opens by giving notice of the severance of the treaty with the idolaters because they had broken it, but the bulk of the sura deals with preparations and recruitment for the expedition to Tabuk, which took place in the heat of the summer of AH 9 (631 CE). The hypocrites and those who stayed behind and failed to support the Prophet are all censured. This is the only sura not to begin with the formula 'In the name of God, the Lord of Mercy, the Giver of Mercy'; there is an opinion that suras 8 and 9 are in fact just one sura.

¹A release by God and His Messenger from the treaty you [believers] made with the polytheists [is announced]—²you [polytheists] may move freely about the land for four months, but you should bear in mind both that you will not escape God, and that God will disgrace those who ignore [Him].ᵃ ³On the Day of the Great Pilgrimage [there will be] a proclamation from God and His Messenger to all people: 'God and His Messenger are released from [treaty] obligations to the polytheists. It will be better for you [polytheists] if you repent; know that you cannot escape God if you turn away.' [Prophet], warn those who ignore [God] that they will have a painful punishment. ⁴As for those who have honoured the treaty you made with them and who have not supported anyone against you: fulfil your agreement with them to the end of their term. God loves those who are mindful of Him.

⁵When the [four] forbidden months are over, whereverᵇ you find the polytheists,ᶜ kill them, seize them, besiege them, ambush them—but if they turn [to God], maintain the prayer, and pay the prescribed alms, let them go on their way, for God is most forgiving and merciful. ⁶If any one of the polytheists should seek your protection [Prophet], grant it to him so that he may hear the word of God—then take him to a safe place—for they are people with no knowledge. ⁷What sort of treaty could these polytheists make with

---

ᵃ 'Kafara bi (something)' in Arabic can mean 'disown (something)' (al-Mu'jam al-Wasit), so kuffar here could also mean 'those who disown [the treaty]'.

ᵇ Inside or outside the Sanctuary in Mecca. See note d to 2: 191.

ᶜ In this context, this definitely refers to the ones who broke the treaty. The article here is ahdiya (specific) referring to what has already been stated.

God and His Messenger? As for those with whom you made a treaty at the Sacred Mosque, so long as they remain true to you, be true to them; God loves those who are mindful of Him. ⁸[What sort of a treaty could there be] when, if they were to get the upper hand over you, they would not respect any tie with you, of kinship or of treaty? They flatter you with their tongues, but their hearts are against you and most of them are transgressors. ⁹They have sold God's message for a trifling gain, and barred others from His path. How evil their actions are! ¹⁰Where believers are concerned, they respect no tie of kinship or treaty. They are the ones who are committing aggression. ¹¹If they turn to God, keep up the prayer, and pay the prescribed alms, then they are your brothers in faith: We make the messages clear for people who are willing to learn. ¹²But if they break their oath after having made an agreement with you, if they revile your religion, then fight the leaders of disbelief—oaths mean nothing to them—so that they may stop. ¹³How could you not fight a people who have broken their oaths, who tried to drive the Messenger out, who attacked you first? Do you fear them? It is God you should fear if you are true believers. ¹⁴Fight them: God will punish them at your hands, He will disgrace them, He will help you to conquer them, He will heal the believers' feelings ¹⁵and remove the rage from their hearts. God turns to whoever He will in His mercy; God is all knowing and wise. ¹⁶Do you think that you will be left untested*ᵃ* without God identifying which of you would strive for His cause and take no supporters apart from God, His Messenger, and other believers? God is fully aware of all your actions.

¹⁷It is not right that the polytheists should tend God's places of worship while testifying to their own disbelief: the deeds of such people will come to nothing and they will abide in Hell. ¹⁸The only ones who should tend God's places of worship are those who believe in God and the Last Day, who keep up the prayer, who pay the prescribed alms, and who fear no one but God: such people may hope to be among the rightly guided. ¹⁹Do you consider giving water to pilgrims and tending the Sacred Mosque to be equal to the deeds of those who believe in God and the Last Day and who strive in God's path? They are not equal in God's eyes. God does not guide such benighted people. ²⁰Those who believe, who migrated and

---

ᵃ See also 29: 2.

strove hard in God's way with their possessions and their persons, are in God's eyes much higher in rank; it is they who will triumph; [21] and their Lord gives them the good news of His mercy and pleasure, Gardens where they will have lasting bliss [22] and where they will remain for ever: truly, there is a tremendous reward with God.

[23] Believers, do not take your fathers and brothers as allies[a] if they prefer disbelief to faith: those of you who do so are doing wrong. [24] Say [Prophet], 'If your fathers, sons, brothers, wives, tribes, the wealth you have acquired, the trade which you fear will decline, and the dwellings you love are dearer to you than God and His Messenger and the struggle in His cause, then wait until God brings about His punishment.' God does not guide those who break away. [25] God has helped you [believers] on many battlefields, even on the day of the Battle of Hunayn.[b] You were well pleased with your large numbers, but they were of no use to you: the earth seemed to close in on you despite its spaciousness, and you turned tail and fled. [26] Then God sent His calm down to His Messenger and the believers, and He sent down invisible forces. He punished the disbelievers—this is what the disbelievers deserve, [27] but God turns in His mercy to whoever He will. God is most forgiving and merciful.

[28] Believers, those who ascribe partners to God are truly unclean: do not let them come near the Sacred Mosque after this year. If you are afraid you may become poor, [bear in mind that] God will enrich you out of His bounty if He pleases: God is all knowing and wise. [29] Fight those of the People of the Book who do not [truly][c] believe in God and the Last Day, who do not forbid what God and His Messenger have forbidden, who do not obey the rule of justice[d] until they pay the tax[e] and agree to submit.[f] [30] The Jews said, 'Ezra is the

[a] Against the Muslims. Cf. 4: 144.

[b] This took place in a valley between Mecca and Ta'if in the year AH 8/630 CE.

[c] 'Truly' is implied, as it is in many other statements in the Qur'an, e.g. 2: 32; 8: 41; and 65: 3.

[d] The main meaning of the Arabic *dana* is 'he obeyed'. It also means 'behave', and 'follow a way of life or religion' (*Qamus* and Lane).

[e] Etymologically, *jizya* means 'payment in return', related to *jazā* meaning 'reward', i.e. in return for the protection of the Muslim state with all the accruing benefits and exemption from military service, and such taxes on Muslims as *zakah*. This tax was levied only on able-bodied free men who could afford it, and monks were exempted. The amount was generally low (e.g. one dinar per year).

[f] Commentators in the past generally understood *wa hum saghirun* to mean they should be humiliated when paying. However, it is clear from the context that they were unwilling to pay, and the clause simply means they should submit to paying this tax.

son of God,'[a] and the Christians said, 'The Messiah is the son of God': they said this with their own mouths, repeating what earlier disbelievers had said. May God confound them! How far astray they have been led! [31] They take their rabbis, their monks, and Christ, the son of Mary, as lords beside God. But they were commanded to serve only one God: there is no god but Him; He is far above whatever they set up as His partners! [32] They try to extinguish God's light with their mouths, but God insists on bringing His light to its fullness, even if the disbelievers hate it. [33] It is He who has sent His Messenger with guidance and the religion of truth, to show that it is above all [other] religions, however much the polytheists may hate this. [34] Believers, many rabbis and monks wrongfully consume people's possessions and turn people away from God's path! [Prophet], tell those who hoard gold and silver instead of giving in God's cause that they will have a grievous punishment: [35] on the Day it is heated up in Hell's Fire and used to brand their foreheads, sides, and backs, they will be told, 'This is what you hoarded up for yourselves! Now feel the pain of what you hoarded!'

[36] God decrees that there are twelve months—ordained in God's Book on the Day when He created the heavens and earth—four months of which are sacred:[b] this is the correct calculation.[c] Do not wrong your souls in these months—though you may fight the idolaters at any time,[d] if they first fight you—remember that God is with those who are mindful of Him. [37] Postponing sacred months is another act of disobedience by which those who disregard [God] are led astray: they will allow it one year and forbid it in another in order outwardly to conform with the number of God's sacred months, but in doing so they permit what God has forbidden. Their evil deeds are made alluring to them: God does not guide those who disregard [Him].

[38] Believers, why, when it is said to you, 'Go and fight in God's way,' do you dig your heels into the earth? Do you prefer this

---

[a] Clearly this refers to a certain group who, possibly at the time of the Prophet or earlier, made this claim.

[b] These are Rajab, Dhu 'l-Qaʿda, Dhu 'l-Hijjah, and Muharram in the Muslim lunar calendar. Fighting was not allowed during these months (except in self-defence). Cf. 2: 194.

[c] One of the meanings of *din* is 'calculation' or 'reckoning'.

[d] Another interpretation of *kafatan* is 'all together'.

world to the life to come? How small the enjoyment of this world is, compared with the life to come! [39] If you do not go out and fight, God will punish you severely and put others in your place, but you cannot harm Him in any way: God has power over all things. [40] Even if you do not help the Prophet, God helped him when the disbelievers drove him out: when the two of them[a] were in the cave, he [Muhammad] said to his companion, 'Do not worry, God is with us,' and God sent His calm down to him, aided him with forces invisible to you, and brought down the disbelievers' plan. God's plan is higher: God is almighty and wise. [41] So go out, no matter whether you are lightly or heavily armed, and struggle in God's way with your possessions and your persons: this is better for you, if you only knew. [42] They would certainly have followed you [Prophet] if the benefit was within sight and the journey short, but the distance seemed too great for them. They will swear by God, 'If we could, we certainly would go out [to battle] with you,' but they ruin themselves, for God knows that they are lying.

[43] God forgive you [Prophet]! Why did you give them permission to stay at home before it had become clear to you which of them spoke the truth and which were liars? [44] Those who have faith in God and the Last Day do not ask you for exemption from struggle with their possessions and their persons—God knows exactly who is mindful of Him—[45] only those who do not have faith in God and the Last Day ask your permission to stay at home: they have doubt in their hearts and so they waver. [46] If they had really wanted to go out [to battle] with you, they would have made preparations, but God was loath to let them rise up and made them hold back. It was said, 'Stay with those who stay behind.' [47] They would only have given you trouble if they had gone out [to battle] with you: they would have scurried around, trying to sow discord among you, and some of you would willingly have listened to them—God knows exactly who does evil. [48] Indeed, they had tried before that to stir up discord: they devised plots against you [Prophet] until the truth was exposed and God's will triumphed, much to their disgust. [49] Some of them said, 'Give me permission to stay at home: do not trouble me.' They are already in trouble: Hell will engulf the disbelievers. [50] If you

---

[a] The Prophet and his companion Abu Bakr.

[Prophet] have good fortune, it will grieve them, but if misfortune comes your way, they will say to themselves, 'We took precautions for this,' and go away rejoicing. [51] Say, 'Only what God has decreed will happen to us. He is our Master: let the believers put their trust in God.' [52] Say, 'Do you expect something other than one of the two best things to happen to us?[a] We expect God to inflict punishment on you, either from Himself or at our hands. So wait; we too are waiting.' [53] Say, 'Whether you give willingly or unwillingly, what you give will not be accepted, for you are disobedient people.' [54] The only thing that prevents what they give from being accepted is the fact that they disbelieve in God and His Messenger, perform the prayer lazily, and give grudgingly. [55] So [Prophet] do not let their possessions or their children impress you: through these God intends to punish them in this world and for their souls to depart while they disbelieve.

[56] They swear by God that they belong with you [believers], but they do not. They are cowardly: [57] if they could find a place of refuge, or a cave, or somewhere to crawl into, they would run there with great haste. [58] Some of them find fault with you [Prophet] regarding the distribution of alms: they are content if they are given a share, but angry if not. [59] If only they would be content with what God and His Messenger have given them, and say, 'God is enough for us—He will give us some of His bounty and so will His Messenger—to God alone we turn in hope.' [60] Alms are meant only for the poor, the needy, those who administer them, those whose hearts need winning over, to free slaves and help those in debt, for God's cause, and for travellers in need. This is ordained by God; God is all knowing and wise.

[61] There are others who insult the Prophet by saying, 'He will listen to anything.' Say, 'He listens for your own good: he believes in God, trusts the believers, and is a mercy for those of you who believe.' An agonizing torment awaits those who insult God's Messenger. [62] They swear by God in order to please you [believers]: if they were true believers it would be more fitting for them to please God and His Messenger. [63] Do they not know that whoever opposes God and His Messenger will go to the Fire of Hell and stay there? That is the supreme disgrace.

---

[a] Victory or martyrdom.

[64] The hypocrites fear that a sura will be revealed exposing what is in their hearts—say, 'Carry on with your jokes: God will bring about what you fear!'—[65] yet if you were to question them, they would be sure to say, 'We were just chatting, just amusing ourselves.' Say, 'Were you making jokes about God, His Revelations, and His Messenger? [66] Do not try to justify yourselves; you have gone from belief to disbelief.' We may forgive some of you, but We will punish others: they are evildoers. [67] The hypocrites, both men and women, are all the same: they order what is wrong and forbid what is right; they are tight-fisted. They have ignored God, so He has ignored them.[a] The hypocrites are the disobedient ones. [68] God promises the Fire of Hell as a permanent home for the hypocrites, both men and women, and the disbelievers: this is enough for them. God rejects them and a lasting punishment awaits them. [69] 'You[b] are like those who lived before you: they were even stronger than you, with more wealth and children; they enjoyed their share in this life as you have enjoyed yours; like them, you have indulged in idle talk.' Their deeds go to waste in this world and the next; it is they who will lose all in the life to come. [70] Have they never heard the stories about their predecessors, the peoples of Noah, 'Ad, Thamud, Abraham, Midian, and the ruined cities? Their messengers came to them with clear evidence of the truth. It was not God who wronged them; they wronged themselves.

[71] The believers, both men and women, support each other; they order what is right and forbid what is wrong; they keep up the prayer and pay the prescribed alms; they obey God and His Messenger. God will give His mercy to such people—God is almighty and wise—[72] God has promised the believers, both men and women, Gardens graced with flowing streams where they will remain; good, peaceful homes in Gardens of lasting bliss; and—greatest of all—God's good pleasure. That is the supreme triumph.

[73] Prophet, work hard against the disbelievers and the hypocrites, and be tough with them. Hell is their final home—an evil destination! [74] They swear by God that they did not, but they certainly did speak words of disbelief and become disbelievers after having submitted; they tried to do something, though they did not achieve it,

---

[a] See note to 7: 51.
[b] Another example of *iltifat*: God turns to address them.

and being spiteful was their only response to God and His Messenger enriching them out of His bounty. They would be better off turning back [to God]: if they turn away, God will punish them in this world and the Hereafter, and there will be no one on earth to protect or help them.

75 There are some among them who pledged themselves to God, saying, 'If God gives us some of His bounty, we shall certainly give alms and be righteous,' 76 yet when He did give them some of His bounty, they became mean and turned obstinately away. 77 Because they broke their promise to God, because of all the lies they told, He made hypocrisy settle in their hearts until the Day they meet Him. 78 Do they not realize that God knows their secrets and their private discussions? That God knows all that is hidden? 79 They criticize the believers who give freely and those who can only give a little with great effort: they scoff at such people, but it is God who scoffs at them—a painful punishment awaits them. 80 It makes no difference [Prophet] whether you ask forgiveness for them or not: God will not forgive them even if you ask seventy times, because they reject God and His Messenger. God does not guide those who rebel against Him.

81 Those who were left behind rejoiced at their position when God's Messenger set out [for battle]; they hated the thought of striving in God's way with their possessions and their persons. They said to one another, 'Do not go to war in this heat.' Say, 'Hellfire is hotter.' If only they understood! 82 Let them laugh a little; they will weep a lot as a reward for what they have done. 83 So [Prophet], if God brings you back to a group of them, who ask you for permission to go out [to battle], say, 'You will never go out and fight an enemy with me: you chose to sit at home the first time, so remain with those who stay behind now.'

84 Do not hold prayers for any of them if they die, and do not stand by their graves: they disbelieved in God and His Messenger and died rebellious. 85 Do not let their possessions and their children impress you: God means to punish them through these in this world, and [to ensure] that their souls depart while they disbelieve. 86 When a sura is revealed [saying], 'Believe in God and strive hard alongside His Messenger,' their wealthy ask your permission [to be exempt], saying, 'Allow us to stay behind with the others': 87 they prefer to be with those who stay behind. Their hearts have been sealed: they do not

comprehend. [88] But the Messenger and those who believe with him strive hard with their possessions and their persons. The best things belong to them: it is they who will prosper. [89] God has prepared Gardens graced with running streams for them and there they will stay. That is the supreme triumph.

[90] Some of the desert Arabs, too, came to make excuses, asking to be granted exemption. Those who lied to God and His Messenger stayed behind at home. A painful punishment will afflict those of them who disbelieved, [91] but there is no blame attached to the weak, the sick, and those who have no means to spend, provided they are true to God and His Messenger; there is no reason to reproach those who do good—God is most forgiving and merciful—[92] and there is no blame attached to those who came to you [Prophet] for riding animals and to whom you said, 'I cannot find a mount for you': they turned away with their eyes overflowing with tears of grief that they had nothing they could contribute. [93] The ones open to blame are those who asked you for exemption despite their wealth, and who preferred to be with those who stay behind. God has sealed their hearts: they do not understand.

[94] When you return from the expedition they will carry on coming to you [believers] with excuses. Say, 'Do not make excuses. We do not believe you: God has told us about you. God and His Messenger will watch your actions now, and in the end you will be returned to the One who knows the seen and the unseen. He will confront you with what you have done.' [95] When you return to them, they will swear to you by God in order to make you leave them alone—so leave them alone: they are unclean, and Hell will be their home as a reward for their actions—[96] they will swear to you in order to make you accept them, but even if you do accept them, God will not accept people who rebel against Him.

[97] The desert Arabs are the most stubborn of all peoples in their disbelief and hypocrisy. They are the least likely to recognize the limits that God has sent down to His Messenger. God is all knowing and all wise. [98] Some of the desert Arabs consider what they give to be an imposition; they are waiting for fortune to turn against you, but fortune will turn against them. God is all hearing and all knowing. [99] But there are also some desert Arabs who believe in God and the Last Day and consider their contributions as bringing them nearer to God and the prayers of the Messenger: they will indeed

bring them nearer and God will admit them to His mercy. God is most forgiving and merciful.

[100] God will be well pleased with the first emigrants and helpers[a] and those who followed them in good deeds, and they will be well pleased with Him: He has prepared Gardens graced with flowing streams for them, there to remain for ever. That is the supreme triumph.

[101] Some of the desert Arabs around you are hypocrites, as are some of the people of Medina—they are obstinate in their hypocrisy. You [Prophet] do not know them, but We know them well: We shall punish them twice and then they will be returned to [face] a painful punishment [in the Hereafter]. [102] And there are others who have confessed their wrongdoing, who have done some righteous deeds and some bad ones: God may well accept their repentance, for God is most forgiving and merciful. [103] In order to cleanse and purify them [Prophet], accept a gift out of their property [to make amends] and pray for them—your prayer will be a comfort to them. God is all hearing, all knowing. [104] Do they not know that it is God Himself who accepts repentance from His servants and receives what is given freely for His sake, and that He is always ready to accept repentance, most merciful? [105] Say [Prophet], 'Take action! God will see your actions—as will His Messenger and the believers—and then you will be returned to Him who knows what is seen and unseen and He will tell you what you have been doing. [106] And there are others who are waiting for God's decree, either to punish them or to show them mercy. God is all knowing and wise.

[107] Then there are those who built a mosque[b]—in an attempt to cause harm, disbelief, and disunity among the believers—as an outpost for those who fought God and His Messenger before: they swear, 'Our intentions were nothing but good,' but God bears witness that they are liars. [108] [Prophet], never pray in that mosque. You should rather pray in a mosque founded from its first day on consciousness of God: in this mosque there are men who desire to grow in purity—God loves those who seek to purify themselves. [109] Which is better, the person who founds his building on consciousness of

---

[a] The Medinan Muslims who welcomed and supported the emigrants from Mecca.

[b] Abu 'Amir al-Rahib told the hypocrites to build a rival mosque in order to sow dissension in the community.

God and desire for His good pleasure, or the person who founds his building on the brink of a crumbling precipice that will tumble down into the Fire of Hell, taking him with it? God does not guide the evildoers: [110] the building they have founded will always be a source of doubt within their hearts, until their hearts are cut to pieces. God is all knowing and wise.

[111] God has purchased the persons and possessions of the believers in return for the Garden—they fight in God's way: they kill and are killed—this is a true promise given by Him in the Torah, the Gospel, and the Qur'an. Who could be more faithful to his promise than God? So be happy with the bargain you have made: that is the supreme triumph. [112] [The believers are] those who turn to God in repentance; who worship and praise Him; who bow down and prostrate themselves; who order what is good and forbid what is wrong; who observe God's limits. Give glad news to such believers.

[113] The Prophet and the believers should not ask forgiveness for the polytheists—even if they are related to them—after having been shown that they are the inhabitants of the Blaze: [114] Abraham asked forgiveness for his father because he had made a promise to him, but once he realized that his father was an enemy of God, he washed his hands of him. Abraham was tender-hearted and forbearing. [115] God would not condemn those He has already guided for going astray before making entirely clear to them what they should avoid.[a] God has knowledge of everything; [116] control of the heavens and earth belongs to God; He alone gives life and death; you have no ally or helper other than Him.

[117] In His mercy God has turned to the Prophet, and the emigrants and helpers who followed him in the hour of adversity when some hearts almost wavered: He has turned to them; He is most kind and merciful to them. [118] And to the three men who stayed behind: when the earth, for all its spaciousness, closed in around them, when their very souls closed in around them, when they realized that the only refuge from God was with Him, He turned to them in mercy in order for them to return [to Him]. God is the Ever Relenting, the Most Merciful.

[119] You who believe, be mindful of God: stand with those who are

---

[a] This reassured the Muslims who had been praying for their disbelieving ancestors that they would not be blamed for having done this.

true. [120] The people of Medina and their neighbouring desert Arabs should not have held back from following God's Messenger, nor should they have cared about themselves more than him: if ever they suffer any thirst, weariness, or hunger in God's cause, take any step that angers the disbelievers, or cause any harm to an enemy, a good deed is recorded in their favour on account of it—God never wastes the reward of those who do good— [121] if they spend a little or a lot for God's cause, if they traverse a mountain pass, all this is recorded to their credit so that God can reward them in accordance with the best of their deeds.

[122] Yet it is not right for all the believers to go out [to battle] together: out of each community, a group should go out to study the religion, so that they can teach their people when they return and so that they can guard themselves against evil. [123] You who believe, fight the disbelievers near you and let them find you standing firm: be aware that God is with those who are mindful of Him.

[124] When a sura is revealed, some [hypocrites] say, 'Have any of you been strengthened in faith by it?' It certainly does strengthen the faith of those who believe and they rejoice, [125] but, as for the perverse at heart, each new sura adds further to their uncleanness. They die disbelieving. [126] Can they not see that they are afflicted once or twice a year? Yet they neither repent nor take heed. [127] Whenever a sura is revealed, they look at each other and say, 'Is anyone watching you?' and then they turn away—God has turned their hearts away because they are people who will [not] understand.

[128] A Messenger has come to you from among yourselves. Your suffering distresses him: he is deeply concerned for you and full of kindness and mercy towards the believers. [129] If they turn away, [Prophet], say ,'God is enough for me: there is no god but Him; I put my trust in Him; He is the Lord of the Mighty Throne.'

10. JONAH

A Meccan sura which takes its title from the reference to Jonah in verse 98. It stresses God's power, the authenticity of the Qur'an, and the end of the evildoers. God's anger at those who consistently deny the truth of His revelations and signs is made clear, as is the fact that, were it not for His decision to await the Day of Resurrection, His judgement would already have fallen upon them. The Prophet is encouraged to be patient and reminded of the fact that he cannot force people to believe.

In the name of God, the Lord of Mercy, the Giver of Mercy

¹ *Alif Lam Ra*

These are the verses of the wise *a* Book. ²Is it so surprising to people that We have revealed to a man from among them that he should warn people, and give glad news to those who believe, that they are on a sure footing with their Lord? [Yet] those who disbelieve say, 'This man is clearly a sorcerer.'

³Your Lord is God who created the heavens and earth in six Days, *b* then established Himself on the Throne, governing everything; there is no one that can intercede with Him, unless He has first given permission: this is God your Lord so worship Him. How can you not take heed? ⁴It is to Him you shall all return—that is a true promise from God. It was He who created [you] in the first place, and He will do so again, so that He may justly reward those who believe and do good deeds. But the disbelievers will have a drink of scalding water, and agonizing torment because they persistently disbelieved.

⁵It is He who made the sun a shining radiance and the moon a light, determining phases for it so that you might know the number of years and how to calculate time—God did not create all these without a true purpose; He explains His signs to those who understand. ⁶In the succession of night and day, and in what God created

---

a *Hakim* is understood in various ways: to mean 'full of wisdom', to suggest that it gives decisions on matters, and to convey that it is perfected and well formed.

b Not the sort of days we know—see 32: 5; 70: 4.

in the heavens and earth, there truly are signs for those who are aware of Him. [7] Those who do not expect[a] to meet Us and are pleased with the life of this world, contenting themselves with it and paying no heed to Our signs, [8] shall have the Fire for their home because of what they used to do. [9] But as for those who believe and do good deeds, their Lord will guide them because of their faith. Streams will flow at their feet in the Gardens of Bliss. [10] Their prayer in them will be, 'Glory be to You, God!' their greeting, 'Peace,' and the last part of their prayer, 'Praise be to God, Lord of the Worlds.'

[11] If God were to hasten on for people the harm [they have earned] as they wish to hasten on the good, their time would already be up. But We leave those who do not expect to meet Us to wander blindly in their excesses. [12] When trouble befalls man he cries out to Us, whether lying on his side, sitting, or standing, but as soon as We relieve him of his trouble he goes on his way as if he had never cried out to Us. In this way the deeds of such heedless people are made attractive to them. [13] Before you people, We destroyed whole generations when they did wrong—their messengers brought them clear signs but they refused to believe. This is how We repay the guilty. [14] Later We made you their successors in the land, to see how you would behave.

[15] When Our clear revelations are recited to them, those who do not expect to meet with Us say, 'Bring [us] a different Qur'an, or change it.' [Prophet], say, 'It is not for me to change it of my own accord; I only follow what is revealed to me, for I fear the torment of an awesome Day, if I were to disobey my Lord.' [16] Say, 'If God had so willed, I would not have recited it to you, nor would He have made it known to you. I lived a whole lifetime among you before it came to me. How can you not use your reason?'

[17] Who could be more wicked than someone who invents lies against God or denies His revelations? The guilty will never prosper. [18] They worship alongside God things that can neither harm nor benefit them, and say, 'These are our intercessors[b] with God.' Say, 'Do you think you can tell God about something He knows not to exist in the heavens or earth? Glory be to Him! He is far above the partner-gods they associate with Him! [19] All people were originally a

---

[a] Or 'fear' (one of the meanings of *yarjuna*).

[b] See above, verse 3.

single community, but later they differed. If it had not been for a word*a* from your Lord, the preordained judgement would already have been passed between them regarding their differences. ²⁰ They say, 'Why has no miraculous sign been sent down to him from his Lord?' Say [Prophet], 'Only God knows the unseen, so wait—I am waiting too.' ²¹ No sooner do We let people taste some mercy after some hardship has afflicted them, than they begin to scheme against Our revelations. Say, 'God schemes even faster.' Our messengers*b* record all your scheming.

²² He enables you to travel on land and sea until, when you are sailing on ships and rejoicing in the favouring wind, a storm arrives: waves come at those on board from all sides and they feel there is no escape. Then they pray to God, professing sincere devotion to Him, 'If You save us from this we shall be truly thankful.' ²³ Yet no sooner does He save them than, back on land, they behave outrageously against all that is right. People! Your outrageous behaviour only works against yourselves. Take your little enjoyment in this present life, then you will return to Us and We shall confront you with everything you have done.

²⁴ The life of this world is like this: rain that We send down from the sky is absorbed by the plants of the earth, from which humans and animals eat. But when the earth has taken on its finest appearance, and adorns itself, and its people think they have power over it, then the fate We commanded comes to it, by night or by day, and We reduce it to stubble, as if it had not flourished just the day before. This is the way We explain the revelations for those who reflect.

²⁵ But God invites [everyone] to the Home of Peace, and guides whoever He will to a straight path. ²⁶ Those who did well will have the best reward and more besides. Neither darkness nor shame will cover their faces: these are the companions in Paradise, and there they will remain. ²⁷ As for those who did evil, each evil deed will be requited by its equal and humiliation will cover them—no one will protect them against God—as though their faces were covered with veils cut from the darkness of the night. These are the inmates of the Fire, and there they shall remain.

²⁸ On the Day We gather them all together, We shall say to those who associate partners with God, 'Stay in your place, you and your

---

a Postponing judgement.   *b* Angels.

partner-gods.' Then We shall separate them, and their partner-gods will say, 'It was not us you worshipped—²⁹ God is witness enough between us and you—we had no idea that you worshipped us.' ³⁰ Every soul will realize, then and there, what it did in the past. They will be returned to God, their rightful Lord, and their invented [gods] will desert them.

³¹ Say [Prophet], 'Who provides for you from the sky and the earth? Who controls hearing and sight? Who brings forth the living from the dead and the dead from the living, and who governs everything?' They are sure to say, 'God.' Then say, 'So why do you not take heed of Him? ³² That is God, your Lord, the Truth. Apart from the Truth, what is there except error? So how is it that you are dissuaded?' ³³ In this way, your Lord's word about those who defy [the Truth] has been proved—they do not believe. ³⁴ Ask them, 'Can any of your partner-gods originate creation, then bring it back to life again in the end?' Say, 'It is God that originates creation, and then brings it back to life, so how can you be misled?' ³⁵ Say, 'Can any of your partner-gods show the way to the Truth?' Say, 'God shows the way to the Truth. Is someone who shows the way to the Truth more worthy to be followed, or someone who cannot find the way unless he himself is shown? What is the matter with you? How do you judge?' ³⁶ Most of them follow nothing but assumptions, but assumptions can be of no value at all against the Truth: God is well aware of what they do.

³⁷ Nor could this Qur'an have been devised by anyone other than God. It is a confirmation of what was revealed before it and an explanation of the Scripture—let there be no doubt about it—it is from the Lord of the Worlds. ³⁸ Or do they say, 'He has devised it'? Say, 'Then produce a sura like it, and call on anyone you can beside God if you are telling the truth.' ³⁹ But they are denying what they cannot comprehend—its prophecy has yet to be fulfilled for them. In the same way, those before them refused to believe—see what was the end of those evildoers!

⁴⁰ Some of them believe in it, and some do not: your Lord knows best those who cause corruption. ⁴¹ If they do not believe you, [Prophet], say, 'I act for myself, and you for yourselves. You are not responsible for my actions nor am I responsible for yours.' ⁴² Some of them do listen to you: but can you make the deaf hear if they will not use their minds? ⁴³ Some of them look at you: but can you guide the

blind if they will not see? ⁴⁴God does not wrong people at all—it is they who wrong themselves.

⁴⁵On the Day He gathers them together, it will be as if they have stayed [in the world] no longer than a single hour, and they will recognize one another. Those who denied the meeting with God will be the losers, for they did not follow the right guidance. ⁴⁶Whether We let you [Prophet] see some of the punishment We have threatened them with, or cause you to die [first], they will return to Us and God is witness to what they do. ⁴⁷Every community is sent a messenger, and when their messenger comes, *ᵃ* they will be judged justly; they will not be wronged. ⁴⁸They ask, 'When will this promise be fulfilled, if what you say is true?' ⁴⁹Say [Prophet], 'I cannot control any harm or benefit that comes to me, except as God wills. There is an appointed term for every community, and when it is reached they can neither delay nor hasten it, even for a moment.' ⁵⁰Say, 'Think: if His punishment were to come to you, during the night or day, what part of it would the guilty wish to hasten? ⁵¹Will you believe in it, when it actually happens?' It will be said, 'Now [you believe], when [before] you sought to hasten it?' ⁵²It will be said to the evil-doers, 'Taste lasting punishment. Why should you be rewarded for anything but what you did?'

⁵³They ask you [Prophet], 'Is it true?' Say, 'Yes, by my Lord, it is true, and you cannot escape it.' ⁵⁴Every soul that has done evil, if it possessed all that is on the earth, would gladly offer it as ransom. When they see the punishment, they will repent in secret, but they will be judged with justice and will not be wronged. ⁵⁵It is to God that everything in the heavens and the earth truly belongs. His promise is true, but most people do not realize it. ⁵⁶He gives life and takes it, and you will all be returned to Him.

⁵⁷People, a teaching from your Lord has come to you, a healing for what is in [your] hearts, and guidance and mercy for the believers. ⁵⁸Say [Prophet], 'In God's grace and mercy let them rejoice: these are better than all they accumulate.' ⁵⁹Say, 'Think about the provision God has sent down for you, some of which you have made unlawful and some lawful.'*ᵇ* Say, 'Has God given you permission [to do this], or are you inventing lies about God?' ⁶⁰What will those people who

---

ᵃ At the Judgement. The messengers will bear witness, see 39: 69.
ᵇ See 5: 103.

invent lies about Him think on the Day of Resurrection? God is bountiful towards people, but most of them do not give thanks.

⁶¹ In whatever matter you [Prophet] may be engaged and whatever part of the Qur'an you are reciting, whatever work you [people] are doing, We witness you when you are engaged in it. Not even the weight of a speck of dust in the earth or sky escapes your Lord, nor anything lesser or greater: it is all written in a clear record. ⁶²But for those who are on God's side there is no fear, nor shall they grieve. ⁶³For those who believe and are conscious of God, ⁶⁴there is good news in this life and in the Hereafter—there is no changing the words of God—that is truly the supreme triumph. ⁶⁵Do not let their words grieve you [Prophet]. Power belongs entirely to God; He hears all and knows all; ⁶⁶indeed, all who are in the heavens and on the earth belong to Him. Those who call upon others beside God are not really following partner-gods; they are only following assumptions and telling lies. ⁶⁷It is He who made the night so that you can rest in it and the daylight so that you can see—there truly are signs in this for those who hear.

⁶⁸ They say, 'God has children!' May He be exalted! He is the Self-Sufficient One; everything in the heavens and the earth belongs to Him. You have no authority to say this. How dare you say things about God without any knowledge? ⁶⁹Say [Prophet], 'Those who invent lies about God will not prosper.' ⁷⁰They may have a little enjoyment in this world, but then they will return to Us. Then We shall make them taste severe punishment for persisting in blasphemy.

⁷¹Tell them the story of Noah. He said to his people, 'My people, if my presence among you and my reminding you of God's signs is too much for you, then I put my trust in God. Agree on your course of action, you and your partner-gods, and do not be hesitant or secretive about it, then carry out your decision on me and give me no respite. ⁷²But if you turn away, I have asked no reward from you; my reward is with God alone, and I am commanded to be one of those who devote themselves to Him.' ⁷³But they rejected him. We saved him and those with him on the Ark and let them survive; and We drowned those who denied Our revelations—see what was the end of those who were forewarned!

⁷⁴Then, after him, We sent messengers to their peoples bringing them clear signs. But they would not believe in anything they had

already rejected: in this way we seal the hearts of those who are full of hostility. [75] After them We sent Moses and Aaron with Our signs to Pharaoh and his leading supporters, but they acted arrogantly — they were wicked people. [76] When the truth came to them from Us, they said, 'This is blatant sorcery.' [77] Moses said, 'Is this what you say about the Truth when it comes to you? Is this sorcery? Sorcerers never prosper.' [78] They said, 'Have you come to turn us away from the faith we found our fathers following, so that you and your brother gain greatness in this land? We will never believe in you.' [79] And Pharaoh said, 'Bring me every learned sorcerer.' [80] When the sorcerers came, Moses said to them, 'Throw down whatever you have.'[a] [81] When they did so, Moses said, 'Everything you have brought is sorcery and God will show it to be false. God does not support the work of mischief-makers; [82] He will uphold the Truth with His words, even if the evildoers hate it.' [83] But no one believed in Moses except a few of his own people, for fear that Pharaoh and their leaders would persecute them, for Pharaoh was domineering in the land and prone to excess.

[84] Moses said, 'My people, if you have faith in God and are devoted to Him, put your trust in Him.' [85] They said, 'We have put our trust in God. Lord! Do not make us an object of persecution for the oppressors. [86] Save us, in Your mercy, from those who reject [Your message].' [87] We revealed to Moses and his brother: 'House your people in Egypt and make these houses places of worship; keep up the prayer; give good news to the believers!' [88] And Moses said, 'Our Lord, You have given Pharaoh and his chiefs splendour and wealth in this present life and here they are, Lord, leading others astray from Your path. Our Lord, obliterate their wealth and harden their hearts so that they do not believe until they see the agonizing torment.' [89] God said, 'Your prayers are answered, so stay on the right course, and do not follow the path of those who do not know.'

[90] We took the Children of Israel across the sea. Pharaoh and his troops pursued them in arrogance and aggression. But as he was drowning he cried, 'I believe there is no God except the one the Children of Israel believe in. I submit to Him.' [91] 'Now? When you had always been a rebel, and a troublemaker! [92] We shall make your body a sign to all posterity. A great many people fail to

---

[a] Your sticks or staffs — see 20: 66–9.

heed Our signs.' [93] We settled the Children of Israel in a good place and provided good things as sustenance for them. It was only after knowledge had come to them that they began to differ among themselves. Your Lord will judge between them on the Day of Resurrection regarding their differences.

[94] So if you [Prophet] are in doubt about what We have revealed to you, ask those who have been reading the scriptures before you. The Truth has come to you from your Lord, so be in no doubt and do not deny God's signs—[95] then you would become one of the losers. [96] Those against whom your Lord's sentence is passed will not believe, [97] even if every sign comes to them, until they see the agonizing torment. [98] If only a single town had believed and benefited from its belief! Only Jonah's people did so, and when they believed, We relieved them of the punishment of disgrace in the life of this world, and let them enjoy life for a time. [99] Had your Lord willed, all the people on earth would have believed. So can you [Prophet] compel people to believe? [100] No soul can believe except by God's will, and He brings disgrace on those who do not use their reason. [101] Say, 'See what is in the heavens and on the earth.' But what use are signs and warnings to people who will not believe? [102] What are they waiting for but the punishment that came to those before them? Say, 'Wait then, I am waiting too.' [103] In the end We shall save Our messengers and the believers. We take it upon Ourself to save the believers.

[104] [Prophet] say, 'People, even if you are in doubt about my religion, I do not worship those you worship other than God, but I worship God who will cause you to die, and I am commanded to be a believer.' [105] [Prophet], set your face towards religion as a man of pure faith. Do not be one of those who join partners with God; [106] do not pray to any other [god] that can neither benefit nor harm you: if you do, you will be one of the evildoers. [107] If God inflicts harm on you, no one can remove it but Him, and if He intends good for you, no one can turn away His bounty; He grants His bounty to any of His servants that He will. He is the Most Forgiving, the Most Merciful. [108] Say, 'People, the Truth has come to you from your Lord. Whoever follows the right path follows it for his own good, and whoever strays does so to his own loss: I am not your guardian.' [109] [Prophet], follow what is being revealed to you, and be steadfast until God gives His judgement, for He is the Best of Judges.

11. HUD

A Meccan sura named after the prophet Hud whose story is given in verses 50–60. It begins by announcing that the Prophet is sent both to warn and to give good news, and the body of the sura focuses on the warning aspect: God watches over everything and is aware of all that people do (verses 5–6, 111–12, 123). The many stories of past prophets, which serve to warn the disbelievers, also strengthen the heart of the Prophet (verse 120).

In the name of God, the Lord of Mercy, the Giver of Mercy

¹ *Alif Lam Ra*

[This is] a Scripture whose verses are perfected, then set out clearly, from One who is all wise, all aware. ² [Say, Prophet], 'Worship no one but God. I am sent to you from Him to warn and to give good news. ³ Ask your Lord for forgiveness, then turn back to Him. He will grant you wholesome enjoyment until an appointed time, and give His grace to everyone who has merit. But if you turn away, I fear for you that you will suffer on a terrible Day: ⁴ it is to God that you will all return, and He has power over everything.'

⁵ See how they [the disbelievers] wrap themselves up, to hide their feelings from Him. But even when they cover themselves with their clothes, He knows what they conceal and what they reveal: He knows well the innermost secrets of the heart. ⁶ There is not a creature that moves on earth whose provision is not His concern. He knows where it lives and its [final] resting place: it is all [there] in a clear record. ⁷ It is He who created the heavens and the earth in six Days*a* —His rule*b* extends over the waters*c* too—so as to test which of you does best.

Yet [Prophet], if you say to them, 'You will be resurrected after death,' the disbelievers will answer, 'This is clearly nothing but sorcery.' ⁸ If We defer their punishment for a determined time,

---

a See also 22: 47; 32: 4; 41: 9 ff.

b 'Rule' is one of the meanings of the Arabic word *'arsh*, normally translated as 'throne' (*al-Mu'jam al-Wasit*).

c Cf. 21: 30.

they are sure to say, 'What is holding it back?' But on the Day it comes upon them, nothing will divert it from them; what they mocked will be all around them. ⁹How desperate and ungrateful man becomes when We let him taste Our mercy and then withhold it! ¹⁰And if We let him taste mercy after some harm has touched him, he is sure to say, 'Misfortune has gone away from me.' He becomes exultant and boastful! ¹¹Not so those who are steadfast and do good deeds: they will have forgiveness and a great reward.

¹²So [Prophet] are you going to[a] abandon some part of what is revealed to you, and let your heart be oppressed by it, because they say, 'Why is no treasure sent down to him, why has no angel come with him?'? You are only there to warn; it is God who is in charge of everything. ¹³If they say, 'He has invented it himself,' say, 'Then produce ten invented suras like it, and call in whoever you can beside God, if you are truthful.' ¹⁴If they do not answer you, then you will all know that it is sent down containing knowledge from God, and that there is no god but Him. Then will you submit to Him? ¹⁵If any desire [only] the life of this world with all its finery, We shall repay them in full in this life for their deeds—they will be given no less— ¹⁶but such people will have nothing in the Hereafter but the Fire: their work here will be fruitless and their deeds futile. ¹⁷Can they be compared to those who have clear proof from their Lord,[b] recited by a witness from Him,[c] and before it the Book of Moses, as a guide and mercy? These people believe in it, whereas those groups that deny its truth are promised the Fire. So have no doubt about it [Prophet]: it is the Truth from your Lord, though most people do not believe so.

¹⁸Who could do more wrong than someone who invents lies about God? Such people will be brought before their Lord, and the witnesses will say, 'These are the ones that lied about their Lord.' God's rejection is the due of those who do such wrong, ¹⁹who hinder others from God's path, trying to make it crooked, and deny the life to come. ²⁰They will not escape on earth, and there will be no one other than God to protect them. Their punishment will be doubled. They could not hear, and they did not see. ²¹It is they who will have lost

[a] Literally 'Perhaps you will . . .', but this is a challenging figure of speech whose meaning is given here.

[b] The Qur'an.

[c] The Angel Gabriel, see 4: 166.

their souls, and what they invented will have deserted them. [22] There is no doubt they will be the ones to lose most in the life to come. [23] But those who believed, did good deeds, and humbled themselves before their Lord will be companions in Paradise and there they will stay. [24] These two groups are like the blind and the deaf as compared with those who can see and hear well: can they be alike? How can you not take heed?

[25] We sent Noah to his people to say, 'I have come to you to give a clear warning: [26] worship no one but God. I fear for you that you may suffer on a painful Day.' [27] But the prominent disbelievers among his people said, 'We can see that you are nothing but a mortal like ourselves, and it is clear to see that only the vilest among us follow you. We cannot see how you are any better than we are. In fact, we think you are a liar.' [28] He said, 'My people, think: if I did have a clear sign from my Lord, and He had given me grace of His own, though it was hidden from you, could we force you to accept it against your will? [29] My people, I ask no reward for it from you; my reward comes only from God. I will not drive away the faithful: they are sure to meet their Lord. I can see you are foolish. [30] My people, who could help me against God if I drove the faithful away? Will you not take heed? [31] I am not telling you that I hold God's treasures, or have any knowledge of what is hidden, or that I am an angel. Nor do I say that God will not grant any good to those who are despised in your eyes: God Himself knows best what is in their souls. If I did this I would be one of the wrongdoers.' [32] They said, 'Noah! You have argued with us for too long. Bring down on us the punishment you threaten us with, if you are telling the truth.' [33] He said, 'It is God who will bring it down, if He wishes, and you will not be able to escape. [34] My advice will be no use to you if God wishes to leave you to your delusions: He is your Lord and to Him you will be returned.'

[35] If [these disbelievers][a] say, 'He has made this up,' say [Muhammad], 'If I have made this up, I am responsible for my own crime, but I am innocent of the crimes you commit.'

[36] It was revealed to Noah, 'None of your people will believe other than those who have already done so, so do not be distressed by what they do. [37] Build the Ark under Our [watchful] eyes and with Our inspiration. Do not plead with Me for those who have done

---

[a] In Mecca.

evil—they will be drowned.' ³⁸ So he began to build the Ark, and whenever leaders of his people passed by, they laughed at him. He said, 'You may scorn us now, but we will come to scorn you: ³⁹ you will find out who will receive a humiliating punishment, and on whom a lasting suffering will descend.' ⁴⁰ When Our command came, and water gushed up*ᵃ* out of the earth, We said, 'Place on board this Ark a pair of each species, and your own family—except those against whom the sentence has already been passed—and the believers,' though only a few believed with him. ⁴¹ He said, 'Board the Ark. In the name of God it shall sail and anchor. My God is most forgiving and merciful.' ⁴² It sailed with them on waves like mountains, and Noah called out to his son, who stayed behind, 'Come aboard with us, my son, do not stay with the disbelievers.' ⁴³ But he replied, 'I will seek refuge on a mountain to save me from the water.' Noah said, 'Today there is no refuge from God's command, except for those on whom He has mercy.' The waves cut them off from each other and he was among the drowned.

⁴⁴ Then it was said, 'Earth, swallow up your water, and sky, hold back,' and the water subsided, the command was fulfilled. The Ark settled on Mount Judi, and it was said, 'Gone are those evildoing people!' ⁴⁵ Noah called out to his Lord, saying, 'My Lord, my son was one of my family, but Your promise*ᵇ* is true, and You are the most just of all judges.' ⁴⁶ God said, 'Noah, he was not one of your family. What he did was not right. Do not ask Me for things you know nothing about. I am warning you not to be foolish.' ⁴⁷ He said, 'My Lord, I take refuge with You from asking for things I know nothing about. If You do not forgive me, and have mercy on me, I shall be one of the losers.' ⁴⁸ And it was said, 'Noah, descend in peace from Us, with blessings on you and on some of the communities that will spring from those who are with you. There will be others We will allow to enjoy life for a time, but then a painful punishment from Us will afflict them.' ⁴⁹ These accounts are part of what was beyond your knowledge [Muhammad]. We revealed them to you. Neither you nor your people knew them before now, so be patient: the future belongs to those who are aware of God.

⁵⁰ To the 'Ad, We sent their brother, Hud. He said, 'My people,

---

ᵃ Literally 'the furnace boiled over'.
ᵇ To save Noah's family; see verse 40.

worship God. You have no god other than Him; you are only making up lies. [51] I ask no reward from you, my people; my reward comes only from Him who created me. Why do you not use your reason? [52] My people, ask forgiveness from your Lord, and return to Him. He will send down for you rain in abundance from the sky, and give you extra strength. Do not turn away and be lost in your sins.' [53] They replied, 'Hud, you have not brought us any clear evidence. We will not forsake our gods on the strength of your word alone, nor will we believe in you. [54] All we can say is that one of our gods may have inflicted some harm on you.' He said, 'I call God to witness, and you too are my witnesses, that I disown those you set up as partners with God. [55] So plot against me, all of you, and give me no respite. [56] I put my trust in God, my Lord and your Lord. There is no moving creature which He does not control.[a] My Lord's way is straight.' [57] But if they turn away, then say, 'I have conveyed the message with which I was sent to you, and my Lord will bring along another people in your place. You cannot do Him any harm: it is my Lord who protects everything.' [58] And so, when Our judgement came to pass, by Our grace We saved Hud and his fellow believers. We saved them from a severe punishment. [59] These were the 'Ad: they rejected their Lord's signs, disobeyed His messengers, and followed the command of every obstinate tyrant. [60] They were rejected in this life and so they shall be on the Day of Judgement. Yes, the 'Ad denied their Lord—so away with the 'Ad, the people of Hud!

[61] To the Thamud, We sent their brother, Salih. He said, 'My people, worship God. You have no god other than Him. It was He who brought you into being from the earth and made you inhabit it, so ask forgiveness from Him, and turn back to Him: my Lord is near, and ready to answer.' [62] They said, 'Salih, We used to have such great hopes in you. Will you forbid us to worship what our fathers worshipped? We are in grave doubt about what you are asking us to do.' [63] He said, 'My people, just think: if I did have clear proof from my Lord, and if He had given me mercy of His own, who could protect me from God if I disobeyed Him? You would only make my loss greater. [64] My people, this camel belongs to God, a sign for you, so leave it to pasture on God's earth and do not harm it, or you will soon be punished.' [65] But they hamstrung it, so he said, 'Enjoy

---

[a] Literally 'grasp by its forelock'.

life *a* for another three days: ⁶⁶ this warning will not prove false.' And so, when Our command was fulfilled, by Our mercy We saved Salih and his fellow believers from the disgrace of that day. [Prophet], it is your Lord who is the Strong, the Mighty One. ⁶⁷ The blast struck the evildoers and they lay dead in their homes, ⁶⁸ as though they had never lived and flourished there. Yes, the Thamud denied their Lord—so away with the Thamud!

⁶⁹ To Abraham Our messengers brought good news. They said, 'Peace.' He answered, 'Peace,' and without delay he brought in a roasted calf. ⁷⁰ When he saw that their hands did not reach towards the meal, he found this strange and became afraid of them. But they said, 'Do not be afraid. We have been sent against the people of Lot.' ⁷¹ His wife was standing [nearby] and laughed. We gave her good news of Isaac and, after him, of Jacob. ⁷² She said, 'Alas for me! How am I to bear a child when I am an old woman, and my husband here is an old man? That would be a strange thing!' ⁷³ They said, 'Are you astonished at what God ordains? The grace of God and His blessing be upon you, people of this house! For He is worthy of all praise and glory.' ⁷⁴ Then, when the fear left Abraham and the good news came to him, he pleaded with Us for Lot's people, ⁷⁵ for Abraham was forbearing, tender-hearted, and devout. ⁷⁶ 'Abraham, cease your pleading: what your Lord has ordained has come about; punishment is coming to them, which cannot be turned back.'

⁷⁷ And when Our messengers came to Lot, he was anxious for them, feeling powerless to protect them, and said, 'This is a truly terrible day!' ⁷⁸ His people came rushing towards him; they used to commit foul deeds. He said, 'My people, here are my daughters. *b* They are more wholesome for you, so have some fear of God and do not disgrace me with my guests. Is there not a single right-minded man among you?' ⁷⁹ They said, 'You know very well that we have no right to your daughters. You know very well what we want.' ⁸⁰ He said, 'If only I had the strength to stop you or could rely on strong support!' ⁸¹ They [the messengers] said, 'Lot, we are your Lord's messengers. They will not reach you. Leave with your household in the dead of night, and let none of you turn back. Only your wife

---

a Literally 'continue to live in your homes'.

b Some commentators interpret this to refer to the daughters of his people, rather than the prophet's own daughters.

will suffer the fate that befalls the others. Their appointed time is the morning: is the morning not near?' ⁸²And so when what We had ordained came about, We turned their town upside down and rained down stones of baked clay on it, layer upon layer, ⁸³marked from your Lord. It is not far from the evildoers. ᵃ

⁸⁴And to Midian, We sent their brother Shuʿayb. He said, 'My people, worship God. You have no god other than Him. Do not give short measure nor short weight. I see you are prospering, but I fear for you that you will suffer on an overwhelming Day. ⁸⁵My people, in fairness, give full measure and weight. Do not withhold from people things that are rightly theirs, and do not spread corruption in the land. ⁸⁶What lasts with God is best for you, if you are believers: I am not your keeper.' ⁸⁷They said, 'Shuʿayb, does your prayer tell you that we should abandon what our forefathers worshipped and refrain from doing whatever we please with our own property? Indeed you are a tolerant and sensible man.' ⁸⁸He answered, 'My people, can you not see? What if I am acting on clear evidence from my Lord? He Himself has given me good provision: I do not want to do what I am forbidding you to do, I only want to put things right as far as I can. I cannot succeed without God's help: I trust in Him, and always turn to Him. ⁸⁹My people, do not let your opposition to me bring upon you a similar fate to the peoples of Noah or Hud or Salih; the people of Lot are not far away from you. ᵇ ⁹⁰Ask forgiveness from your Lord, and turn to Him in repentance: my Lord is merciful and most loving.'

⁹¹They said, 'Shuʿayb, we do not understand much of what you say, and we find you very weak in our midst. But for your tribe, we would have stoned you, for you have no great status among us.' ⁹²He said, 'My people, is my tribe stronger in your estimation than God? And have you put Him behind you? My Lord surrounds everything you do. ⁹³My people, do whatever is within your power, and I will do likewise. Soon you will know who will receive a disgraceful punishment and who is a liar. Watch out, and so will I.' ⁹⁴When what We had ordained came about, in Our mercy We saved Shuʿayb and his fellow believers, but a mighty blast struck the wrongdoers. By

---

ᵃ This town is not far from the evildoers of Mecca, within their trading range (see 37: 137–8), nor is the punishment far from them.

ᵇ In time or place. See 7: 85; 7: 93.

morning they lay dead in their homes, [95] as if they had never lived and flourished there. Yes, away with the people of Midian, just like the Thamud!

[96] We also sent Moses, with Our signs and clear authority, [97] to Pharaoh and his supporters, but they followed Pharaoh's orders, and Pharaoh's orders were misguided. [98] He will be at the forefront of his people on the Day of Resurrection, leading them down towards the Fire. What a foul drinking place to be led to! [99] They were pursued by God's rejection in this life and will be on the Day of Resurrection, too. What a foul gift to be given!

[100] We relate to you [Muhammad] such accounts of earlier towns: some of them are still standing; some have been mown down; [101] We did not wrong them; they wronged themselves. Their gods, which they called on beside God, were no use to them when what your Lord had ordained came about; they only increased their ruin. [102] Such is the punishment of your Lord for towns in the midst of their sins: His punishment is terrible and severe. [103] There truly is a sign in this for anyone who fears the punishment of the Hereafter. That is a Day in which all people will be gathered together, a Day for all to see. [104] We are delaying it only for a specified period, [105] and when that Day comes, no soul will speak except by His permission, and some of them will be wretched and some happy. [106] The wretched ones will be in the Fire, sighing and groaning, [107] there to remain for as long as the heavens and earth endure, unless your Lord wills otherwise: your Lord carries out whatever He wills. [108] As for those who have been blessed, they will be in Paradise, there to remain as long as the heavens and earth endure, unless your Lord wills otherwise—an unceasing gift. [a]

[109] [Prophet], have no doubt about what these people worship: it is merely what their fathers worshipped before them, and We shall certainly give them their share in full, without any reduction. [110] We gave Moses the Scripture before you, but differences arose about it and if it had not been for a prior word from your Lord, a decision would already have been made between them, though they are in grave doubt about it. [111] Your Lord will give everyone full due for whatever they have done: He is aware of everything they do. [112] So keep to the right course as you have been commanded, together with

---

[a] Literally 'uninterrupted giving'.

those who have turned to God with you. Do not overstep the limits, for He sees everything you do. ¹¹³Do not rely on those who do evil, or the Fire may touch you, and then you will have no one to protect you from God, nor will you be helped.

¹¹⁴[Prophet], keep up the prayer at both ends of the day, and during parts of the night, for good deeds drive evil deeds away—this is a reminder for those who are aware. ¹¹⁵Be steadfast: God does not let the rewards of those who do good go to waste. ¹¹⁶If only there had been, among the generations before your time, people with a remnant of good sense, to forbid corruption on the earth! We saved only a few of them, while the unjust pursued the enjoyment of plenty, and persisted in sin! ¹¹⁷Your Lord would not destroy any town without cause if its people were acting righteously. ¹¹⁸If your Lord had pleased, He would have made all people a single community, but they continue to have their differences—¹¹⁹except those on whom your Lord has mercy—for He created them to be this way, and the word of your Lord is final: 'I shall definitely fill Hell with both jinn and men.'

¹²⁰So [Muhammad], We have told you the stories of the prophets to make your heart firm and in these accounts truth has come to you, as well as lessons and reminders for the believers. ¹²¹Say to those who do not believe, 'Do whatever you can: we too are doing what we can,' ¹²²and 'Wait: we too are waiting.' ¹²³All that is hidden in the heavens and earth belongs to God, and all authority*ᵃ* goes back to Him. So [Prophet], worship Him, and put your trust in Him: your Lord is never unaware of what you [people] are doing.

ᵃ Or 'all things'.

12. JOSEPH

A Meccan sura dealing primarily with the story of Joseph, but framed by a three-verse introduction about the Qur'an and a ten-verse epilogue about the Meccans' response, the punishment met by earlier disbelievers, and encouragement for the Prophet.

In the name of God, the Lord of Mercy, the Giver of Mercy

¹ *Alif Lam Ra*

These are the verses of the Scripture that makes things clear—² We have sent it down as an Arabic Qur'an so that you [people] may understand.

³ We tell you [Prophet] the best of stories in revealing this Qur'an to you.*ᵃ* Before this*ᵇ* you were one of those who knew nothing about them. ⁴ Joseph said to his father, 'Father, I dreamed of eleven stars and the sun and the moon: I saw them all bow down before me,' ⁵ and he replied, 'My son, tell your brothers nothing of this dream, or they may plot to harm you—Satan is man's sworn enemy. ⁶ Your Lord will choose you, teach you to interpret dreams, and perfect His blessing on you and the House of Jacob, just as He perfected it earlier on your forefathers Abraham and Isaac: your Lord is all knowing and wise.'

⁷ There are lessons in the story of Joseph and his brothers for all who seek them. ⁸ The brothers said [to each other], 'Although we are many, Joseph and his brother are dearer to our father than we are—our father is clearly in the wrong.' ⁹ [One of them said], 'Kill Joseph or banish him to another land, and your father's attention will be free to turn to you. After that you can be righteous.' ¹⁰ [Another of them] said, 'Don't kill Joseph, but, if you must, throw him into the hidden depths of a well where some caravan may pick him up.'

¹¹ They said to their father, 'Why don't you trust us with Joseph? We wish him well. ¹² Send him with us tomorrow and he will enjoy

---

ᵃ Many translators add 'though' ('. . . to you, though before this . . .'), thinking that *in* is conditional, when in fact it is for emphasis here, as confirmed by the emphatic *lam* following it.

ᵇ Cf. 11: 49 and 42: 52.

himself and play—we will take good care of him.' [13] He replied, 'The thought of you taking him away with you worries me: I am afraid a wolf may eat him when you're not paying attention.' [14] They said, 'If a wolf were to eat him when there are so many of us, we would truly be losers!'

[15] Then they took him away with them, resolved upon throwing him into the hidden depths of a well—We inspired him, saying, 'You will tell them of all this [at a time] when they do not realize [who you are]!'—[16] and at nightfall they returned to their father weeping. [17] They said, 'We went off racing one another, leaving Joseph behind with our things, and a wolf ate him. You will not believe us, though we are telling the truth!' [18] and they showed him his shirt, deceptively stained with blood. He cried, 'No! Your souls have prompted you to do wrong! But it is best to be patient: from God alone I seek help to bear what you are saying.'

[19] Some travellers came by. They sent someone to draw water and he let down his bucket. 'Good news!' he exclaimed. 'Here is a boy!' They hid him like a piece of merchandise—God was well aware of what they did—[20] and then sold him for a small price, for a few pieces of silver: so little did they value him.

[21] The Egyptian who bought him said to his wife, 'Look after him well! He may be useful to us, or we may adopt him as a son.' In this way We settled Joseph in that land and later taught him how to interpret dreams: God always prevails in His purpose, though most people do not realize it.

[22] When he reached maturity, We gave him judgement and knowledge: this is how We reward those who do good. [23] The woman in whose house he was living tried to seduce him: she bolted the doors and said, 'Come to me,' and he replied, 'God forbid! My master has been good to me; wrongdoers never prosper.' [24] She made for him, and he would have succumbed to her if he had not seen evidence of his Lord—We did this in order to keep evil and indecency away from him, for he was truly one of Our chosen servants. [25] They raced for the door—she tore his shirt from behind—and at the door they met her husband. She said, 'What, other than prison or painful punishment, should be the reward of someone who tried to dishonour your wife?' [26] but he said, 'She tried to seduce me.' A member of her household suggested, 'If his shirt is torn at the front, then it is she who is telling the truth and he who is lying, [27] but if it is torn at the

back, then she is lying and he is telling the truth.' [28] When the husband saw that the shirt was torn at the back, he said, 'This is another instance of women's treachery: your treachery is truly great. [29] Joseph, overlook this; but you [wife], ask forgiveness for your sin—you have done wrong.'

[30] Some women of the city said, 'The governor's wife is trying to seduce her slave! Love for him consumes her heart! It is clear to us that she has gone astray.' [31] When she heard their malicious talk, she prepared a banquet and sent for them, giving each of them a knife. She said to Joseph, 'Come out and show yourself to them!' and when the women saw him, they were stunned by his beauty, and cut their hands, exclaiming, 'Great God! He cannot be mortal! He must be a precious angel!' [32] She said, 'This is the one you blamed me for. I tried to seduce him and he wanted to remain chaste, but if he does not do what I command now, he will be put in prison and degraded.' [33] Joseph said, 'My Lord! I would prefer prison to what these women are calling me to do. If You do not protect me from their treachery, I shall yield to them and do wrong,' [34] and his Lord answered his prayer and protected him from their treachery—He is the All Hearing, the All Knowing.

[35] In the end they[a] thought it best, after seeing all the signs of his innocence, that they should imprison him for a while. [36] Two young men went into prison alongside him. One of them said, 'I dreamed that I was pressing grapes'; the other said, 'I dreamed that I was carrying bread on my head and that the birds were eating it.' [They said], 'Tell us what this means—we can see that you are a knowledgeable[b] man.'

[37] He said, 'I can tell you what you will be fed before any meal arrives:[c] this is part of what my Lord has taught me. I reject the faith of those who disbelieve in God and deny the life to come, [38] and I follow the faith of my forefathers Abraham, Isaac, and Jacob. Because of God's grace to us and to all mankind, we would never worship anything beside God, but most people are ungrateful. [39] Fellow prisoners, would many diverse gods be better than God the One, the All Powerful? [No indeed!] [40] All those you worship instead of Him are mere names you and your forefathers have invented, names

---

[a] The governor and his household.
[b] Razi gives this interpretation of *muhsinin*.
[c] This interpretation is supported by Razi.

for which God has sent down no authority: all command belongs to God alone, and He orders you to worship none but Him: this is the true faith, though most people do not realize it. [41] Fellow prisoners, one of you will serve his master with wine; the other will be crucified and the birds will eat his head. That is the end of the matter on which you asked my opinion.' [42] Joseph said to the one he knew would be saved, 'Mention me to your master,' but Satan made him forget to do this, and so Joseph remained in prison for a number of years.

[43] The king said, 'I dreamed about seven fat cows being eaten by seven lean ones; seven green ears of corn and [seven] others withered. Counsellors, if you can interpret dreams, tell me the meaning of my dream.' [44] They said, 'These are confusing dreams and we are not skilled at dream-interpretation,' [45] but the prisoner who had been freed, at last remembered [Joseph] and said, 'I shall tell you what this means. Give me leave to go.'

[46] 'Truthful Joseph! Tell us the meaning of seven fat cows being eaten by seven lean ones, seven green ears of corn and [seven] others withered, [47] then I can return to the people and inform them.' Joseph said, 'You will sow for seven consecutive years as usual. Store all that you reap, left in the ear, apart from the little you eat. [48] After that will come seven years of hardship which will consume all but a little of what you stored up for them; [49] after that will come a year when the people will have abundant rain and will press grapes.'

[50] The king said, 'Bring him to me,' but when the messenger came to fetch Joseph, he said, 'Go back to your master and ask him about what happened to those women who cut their hands—my Lord knows all about their treachery.' [51] The king asked the women, 'What happened when you tried to seduce Joseph?' They said, 'God forbid! We know nothing bad of him!' and the governor's wife said, 'Now the truth is out: it was I who tried to seduce him—he is an honest man.' [52] [Joseph said, 'This was] for my master to know that I did not betray him behind his back: God does not guide the mischief of the treacherous. [53] I do not pretend to be blameless, for man's very soul incites him to evil unless my Lord shows mercy: He is most forgiving, most merciful.'

[54] The king said, 'Bring him to me: I will have him serve me personally,' and then, once he had spoken with him, 'From now on you will have our trust and favour.' [55] Joseph said, 'Put me in charge of the nation's storehouses: I shall manage them prudently and care-

fully.' ⁵⁶ In this way We settled Joseph in that land to live wherever he wished—We grant Our mercy to whoever We will and do not fail to reward those who do good—⁵⁷ yet the reward of the Hereafter is best for those who believe and are mindful of God.

⁵⁸ Joseph's brothers came and presented themselves before him. He recognized them—though they did not recognize him—⁵⁹ and once he had given them their provisions, he said, 'Bring me the brother [you left with] your father!*ᵃ* Have you not seen me giving generous measure and being the best of hosts? ⁶⁰ You will have no more corn from me if you do not bring him to me, and you will not be permitted to approach me.' ⁶¹ They said, 'We shall do all we can to persuade his father to send him with us, indeed we shall.' ⁶² Joseph said to his servants, 'Put their [traded] goods back into their saddle-bags, so that they may recognize them when they go back to their family, and [be eager to] return.'

⁶³ When they returned to their father, they said, 'Father, we have been denied any more corn, but send our brother back with us and we shall be given another measure. We shall guard him carefully.' ⁶⁴ He said, 'Am I to entrust him to you as I did his brother before? God is the best guardian and the Most Merciful of the merciful.' ⁶⁵ Then, when they opened their packs, they discovered that their goods had been returned to them and they said, 'Father! We need no more [goods to barter]:*ᵇ* look, our goods have been returned to us. We shall get corn for our household; we shall keep our brother safe; we shall be entitled to another camel-load of grain—an extra measure so easily achieved!' ⁶⁶ He said, 'I will never send him with you, not unless you swear by God that you will bring him back to me if that is humanly possible.'*ᶜ* Then, when they had given him their pledge, he said, 'Our words are entrusted to God.' ⁶⁷ He said, 'My sons, do not enter all by one gate—use different gates. But I cannot help you against the will of God: all power is in God's hands. I trust in Him; let everyone put their trust in Him,' ⁶⁸ and, when they entered as their father had told them, it did not help them against the will of God, it merely satisfied a wish of Jacob's. He knew well what We had taught him, though most people do not.

⁶⁹ Then, when they presented themselves before Joseph, he drew

---

ᵃ Or a paternal half-brother (Benjamin).

ᵇ This understanding of the phrase *ma nabghi* is supported by Razi.

ᶜ Literally 'unless you are totally surrounded'. Razi suggests by death or the enemy.

his brother apart*a* and said, 'I am your brother, so do not be saddened by their past actions,' [70] and, once he had given them their provisions, he placed the drinking-cup in his brother's pack. A man called out, 'People of the caravan! You are thieves!' [71] and they turned and said, 'What have you lost?' [72] They replied, 'The king's drinking-cup is missing,' and, 'Whoever returns it will get a camel-load [of grain],' and, 'I give you my word.' [73] They said, 'By God! You must know that we did not come to make mischief in your land: we are no thieves.' [74] They asked them, 'And if we find that you are lying, what penalty shall we apply to you?' [75] and they answered, 'The penalty will be [the enslavement of] the person in whose bag the cup is found: this is how we punish wrongdoers.' [76] [Joseph] began by searching their bags, then his brother's, and he pulled it out from his brother's bag.

In this way We schemed on Joseph's behalf—if God had not willed it so, he could not have detained his brother as a penalty under the king's law—We raise the rank of whoever We will. Above everyone who has knowledge there is the One who is all knowing.

[77] They said, 'If he is a thief then his brother was a thief before him,' but Joseph kept his secrets and did not reveal anything to them. He said, 'You are in a far worse situation. God knows the truth of what you claim.' [78] They said, 'Mighty governor, he has an elderly father. Take one of us in his place. We can see that you are a very good man.' [79] He replied, 'God forbid that we should take anyone other than the person on whom we found our property: that would be unjust of us.' [80] When they lost hope of [persuading] him, they withdrew to confer with each other: the eldest of them said, 'Do you not remember that your father took a solemn pledge from you in the name of God and before that you failed in your duty with regard to Joseph? I will not leave this land until my father gives me leave or God decides for me—He is the best decider—[81] so go back to your father and say, "Your son stole. We can only tell you what we saw. How could we guard against the unforeseen? [82] Ask in the town where we have been; ask the people of the caravan we travelled with: we are telling the truth." '

---

a Literally 'accommodated him' or 'took him as a guest'. Some interpret this as suggesting that the brothers were offered lodgings in pairs and Benjamin, as the odd one out, was given lodging with Joseph; another suggestion is that the two full brothers dined together: either way the sense is that Joseph drew Benjamin apart from the others.

[83] Their father said, 'No! Your souls have prompted you to do wrong! But it is best to be patient: may God bring all of them[a] back to me—He alone is the All Knowing, the All Wise,' [84] and he turned away from them, saying, 'Alas for Joseph!' His eyes clouded over with grief and he was filled with sorrow. [85] They said, 'By God! You will ruin your health if you do not stop thinking of Joseph, or even die.' [86] He said, 'I plead my grief and sorrow before God. I have knowledge from God that you do not have. [87] My sons, go and seek news of Joseph and his brother and do not despair of God's mercy— only disbelievers despair of God's mercy.'

[88] Then, when they presented themselves before Joseph, they said, 'Mighty governor, misfortune has afflicted us and our family. We have brought only a little merchandise, but give us full measure. Be charitable to us: God rewards the charitable.' [89] He said, 'Do you now realize what you did to Joseph and his brother when you were ignorant?' [90] and they cried, 'Could it be that you are Joseph?' He said, 'I am Joseph. This is my brother. God has been gracious to us: God does not deny anyone who is mindful of God and steadfast in adversity the rewards of those who do good.' [91] They said, 'By God! God really did favour you over all of us and we were in the wrong!' [92] but he said, 'You will hear no reproaches today. May God forgive you: He is the Most Merciful of the merciful. [93] Take my shirt and lay it over my father's face: he will recover his sight. Then bring your whole family back to me.'

[94] Then, when the caravan departed, their father said, 'You may think I am senile but I can smell Joseph,' [95] but [people] said, 'By God! You are still lost in that old illusion of yours!' [96] Then, when the bearer of good news came and placed the shirt on to Jacob's face, his eyesight returned and he said, 'Did I not tell you that I have knowledge from God that you do not have?' [97] The [brothers] said, 'Father, ask God to forgive our sins—we were truly in the wrong.' [98] He replied, 'I shall ask my Lord to forgive you: He is the Most Forgiving, the Most Merciful.'

[99] Then, when they presented themselves before Joseph, he drew his parents to him—he said, 'Welcome to Egypt: you will all be safe here, God willing'—[100] and took them up to [his] throne. They all bowed down before him and he said, 'Father, this is the fulfilment of

[a] Razi suggests Joseph, Benjamin, and the eldest son who remained in Egypt.

that dream I had long ago. My Lord has made it come true and has been gracious to me—He released me from prison and He brought you here from the desert—after Satan sowed discord between me and my brothers. My Lord is most subtle in achieving what He will; He is the All Knowing, the Truly Wise. [101] My Lord! You have given me authority; You have taught me to interpret dreams; Creator of the heavens and the earth, You are my protector in this world and in the Hereafter. Let me die in true devotion to You. Join me with the righteous.'

[102] This account is part of what was beyond your knowledge [Muhammad]. We revealed it to you: you were not present with Joseph's brothers when they made their treacherous plans. [103] However eagerly you may want them to, most men will not believe. [104] You ask no reward from them for this: it is a reminder for all people [105] and there are many signs in the heavens and the earth that they pass by and give no heed to—[106] most of them will only believe in God while also joining others with Him. [107] Are they so sure that an overwhelming punishment from God will not fall on them, or that the Last Hour will not come upon them suddenly when they least expect it? [108] Say, 'This is my way. Based on sure knowledge, I, and all who follow me, call [people] to God—glory be to God!—I do not join others with Him.'

[109] All the messengers We sent before you [Muhammad] were men to whom We made revelations, men chosen from the people of their towns. Have the [disbelievers] not travelled through the land and seen the end of those who went before them? Those who are mindful of God prefer the life to come. Do you [people] not use your reason? [110] When the messengers lost all hope and realized that they had been dismissed as liars, Our help came to them: We saved whoever We pleased, but Our punishment will not be turned away from guilty people. [111] There is a lesson in the stories of such people for those who understand. This revelation is no fabrication: it is a confirmation of the truth of what was sent before it; an explanation of everything;[a] a guide and a blessing for those who believe.

---

[a] There are two interpretations of this phrase: (i) 'everything to do with the story of Joseph'; and (ii) 'everything to do with religion'.

13. THUNDER

A Medinan sura that takes its title from the thunder that praises God in verse 13. The sura is distinguished by its moving, poetical description of God's power and knowledge. Muhammad's place in a long tradition of prophets, none of whom could produce miracles on request, is stressed, and his role emphasized: it is only to deliver the message. God is the One who will call people to account for their deeds, and He is the witness for the truth of the message.

In the name of God, the Lord of Mercy, the Giver of Mercy

¹ *Alif Lam Mim Ra*

These are the signs of the Scripture. What your Lord has sent down to you [Prophet] is the truth, yet most people will not believe. ²It is God who raised up the heavens with no visible supports and then established Himself on the throne; He has subjected the sun and the moon each to pursue its course for an appointed time; He regulates all things, and makes the revelations clear so that you may be certain of meeting your Lord; ³it is He who spread out the earth, placed firm mountains and rivers on it, and made two of every kind of fruit; He draws the veil of night over the day. There truly are signs in this for people who reflect. ⁴There are, in the land, neighbouring plots, gardens of vineyards, cornfields, palm trees in clusters or otherwise, all watered with the same water, yet We make some of them taste better than others: there truly are signs in this for people who reason.

⁵If anything can amaze you [Prophet], then you should surely be amazed at their asking, 'What? When we become dust, shall we be created anew?' These are the ones who deny their Lord, who will wear iron collars around their necks and be the inhabitants of the Fire, there to remain. ⁶They ask you to bring on the punishment rather than any promised rewards, though there have been many examples before them—your Lord is full of forgiveness for people, despite their wrongdoing, but He is truly severe in punishment. ⁷The disbelievers say, 'Why has no miracle been sent down to him from his Lord?' But you are only there to give warning: [earlier] communities each had their guide.

[8] God knows what every female bears and how much their wombs shrink or swell—everything has its measure with Him; [9] He knows what is not seen as well as what is seen; He is the Great, the Most High. [10] It makes no difference whether any of you speak secretly or aloud, whether you are hiding under cover of night or skulking about in the day: [11] each person has guardian angels before him and behind, watching over him by God's command. God does not change the condition of a people [for the worse][a] unless they change what is in themselves, but if He wills harm on a people, no one can ward it off— apart from Him, they have no protector.

[12] It is He who shows you the lightning, inspiring fear and hope; He builds up the clouds heavy with rain; [13] the thunder sounds His praises, as do the angels in awe of Him; He sends thunderbolts to strike whoever He will. Yet still they dispute about God—He has mighty plans. [14] The only true prayer is to Him: those they pray to besides Him give them no answer any more than water reaches the mouth of someone who simply stretches out his hands for it—it cannot do so: the prayers of the disbelievers are all in vain. [15] All that are in heaven and earth submit[b] to God alone, willingly or unwillingly, as do their shadows in the mornings and in the evenings.

[16] Say [Prophet], 'Who is Lord of the heavens and the earth?' Say, 'God.' Say, 'Why do you take protectors other than Him, who can neither benefit nor harm even themselves?' Say, 'Are the blind equal to those who can see? And are the depths of darkness equal to the light?' Have the partners they assign to God created anything like His creation? Is their creation indistinguishable from His? Say, 'God is the Creator of all things: He is the One, the All Compelling.' [17] He sends water from the sky that fills riverbeds to overflowing, each according to its measure. The stream carries on its surface a growing layer of froth, like the froth that appears when people melt metals in the fire to make ornaments and tools: in this way God illustrates truth and falsehood—the froth disappears, but what is of benefit to man stays behind—this is how God makes illustrations. [18] There will be the best of rewards for those who respond to their Lord; those who do not respond would willingly give away the earth's contents

---

[a] Cf. 8: 53; 16: 112.

[b] Or 'prostrate': shadows submit to God's laws in nature and also stretch out on the ground as if prostrating. *Sajada* has both meanings.

twice over, if they had it, in order to ransom themselves, so terrible will be their reckoning. Hell will be their home, and their bed wretched.

¹⁹ Can someone who knows that the revelation from your Lord is the Truth be equal to someone who is blind? Only those with understanding will take it to heart; ²⁰ those who fulfil the agreements they make in God's name and do not break their pledges; ²¹ who join together what God commands to be joined; who are in awe of their Lord and fear the harshness of the Reckoning; ²² who remain steadfast through their desire for the face of their Lord; who keep up the prayer; who give secretly and openly from what We have provided for them; who repel evil with good. These will have the reward of the [true] home: ²³ they will enter perpetual gardens, along with their righteous ancestors, spouses, and descendants; the angels will go in to them from every gate, ²⁴ 'Peace be with you, because you have remained steadfast. What an excellent reward is this home of yours!' ²⁵ But there will be rejection for those who break their confirmed agreements made in God's name, who break apart what God has commanded to be joined and who spread corruption on earth: theirs is the dreadful home— ²⁶ God gives abundantly to whoever He will, and sparingly to whoever He will—though they may revel in the life of this world, it is but a fleeting comfort compared with the Life to come.

²⁷ The disbelievers say, 'Why has no miracle been sent down to him from his Lord?' [Prophet], say, 'God leaves whoever He will to stray, and guides to Himself those who turn towards Him, ²⁸ those who have faith and whose hearts find peace in the remembrance of God—truly it is in the remembrance of God that hearts find peace— ²⁹ those who believe and do righteous deeds: joy awaits these, and their final homecoming will be excellent.' ³⁰ So We have sent you [Prophet] to a community—other communities passed away long before them—to recite to them what We reveal to you. Yet they disbelieve in the Lord of Mercy. Say, 'He is my Lord: there is no god but Him. I put my trust in Him and to Him is my return.' ³¹ If there were ever to be a Qur'an with which mountains could be moved, the earth shattered, or the dead made to speak [it would have been this one],ᵃ but everything is truly in God's hands. Do the believers not

---

ᵃ Or '[they still would not believe]'.

realize that if God had so willed, He could have guided all mankind? As for the disbelievers, because of their misdeeds, disaster will not cease to afflict them or fall close to their homes until God's promise is fulfilled: God never fails to keep His promise.

³² Many messengers before you [Muhammad] were mocked, but I granted respite to the disbelievers: in the end, I took them to task—how terrible My punishment was! ³³ Is He who stands over every soul marking its action [in need of any partner]? Yet they ascribe partners to God. Say, 'Name them,' or, 'Can you tell Him about something on the earth He does not know to exist, or are these just empty words?' But the things they devise are made alluring to the disbelievers and they are barred from the [right] path: no one can guide those God leaves to stray. ³⁴ There is a punishment for them in this world, but the punishment of the Hereafter will be harder—no one will defend them against God.

³⁵ Here is a picture of the Garden that those conscious of God have been promised: flowing streams and perpetual food and shade. This is the reward that awaits those who are conscious of God; the disbelievers' reward is the Fire. ³⁶ Those to whom We sent the Scripture rejoice in what has been revealed to you [Prophet]; some factions deny parts of it. Say, 'I am commanded to worship God, and not join anything with Him in worship: to Him I pray and to Him I shall return.' ³⁷ In this way We have sent down the Qur'an to give judgement in the Arabic language. If you were to follow their desires, after the knowledge that has come to you, you would have no one to guard or protect you from God. ³⁸ We sent messengers before you and gave them wives and offspring; no messenger was given the power to produce a miracle except with God's permission. There was a Scripture for every age:*a* ³⁹ God erases or confirms whatever He will, and the source of Scripture is with Him. ⁴⁰ Whether We let you [Prophet] see part of what We threaten them with, or cause you to die [before that], your duty is only to deliver the message: the Reckoning is Ours. ⁴¹ Do they not see how We come to [their] land and shrink its borders? God decides—no one can reverse His decision—and He is swift in reckoning. ⁴² Those before them also schemed, but the overall scheme belongs to God: He knows what each soul does. In the end, the disbelievers will find out who will have the excellent home.

---

a Another interpretation is 'there is a time decreed for everything'.

[43] They say, 'You have not been sent.' Say, 'God is sufficient witness between me and you: all knowledge of the Scripture comes from Him.'[a]

---

[a] Alternatively, 'God—and those who have [true] knowledge of the Scripture—are sufficient witness between us.'

14. ABRAHAM

A Meccan sura named after Abraham (verses 35–41), who prays to God that Mecca may be made prosperous so that its people may be thankful and continue to worship God. The ungrateful are condemned, and the grateful commended, throughout the sura. Abraham also asks that he and his descendants may be protected from idol-worship. This serves to remind the Meccans that they should shun the worship of idols.

In the name of God, the Lord of Mercy, the Giver of Mercy

¹ *Alif Lam Ra*

This is a Scripture which We have sent down to you [Prophet] so that, with their Lord's permission, you may bring people from the depths of darkness into light, to the path of the Almighty, the Praiseworthy One, ² God, to whom everything in the heavens and earth belongs. How terrible the torment of the disbelievers will be! ³ Those who prefer the life of this world over the life to come, who turn others from God's way, trying to make it crooked: such people have gone far astray. ⁴ We have never sent a messenger who did not use his own people's language to make things clear for them. But still God leaves whoever He will to stray, and guides whoever He will: He is the Almighty, the All Wise.

⁵ We sent Moses with Our signs: 'Bring out your people from the depths of darkness into light. Remind them of the Days of God:*ᵃ* there truly are signs in this for every steadfast, thankful person.' ⁶ And so Moses said to his people, 'Remember God's blessing on you when He saved you from Pharaoh's people, who were inflicting terrible suffering on you, slaughtering your sons and sparing only your women—that was a severe test from your Lord! ⁷ Remember that He promised, "If you are thankful, I will give you more, but if you are thankless, My punishment is terrible indeed." ' ⁸ And Moses said, 'Even if you, together with everybody else on earth, are thankless, God is self-sufficient, worthy of all praise.'

ᵃ The times when God singled them out for special favour or tribulation (cf. 2: 30–61).

⁹Have you not heard about those who went before you, the people of Noah, 'Ad, Thamud, and those who lived after them, known only to God? Their messengers came to them with clear proof, but they tried to silence them,ᵃ saying, 'We do not believe the message with which you were sent. We have serious doubts about what you are asking us to do.' ¹⁰Their messengers answered, 'Can there be any doubt about God, the Creator of the heavens and earth? He calls you to Him in order to forgive you your sins and let you enjoy your life until the appointed hour.' But they said, 'You are only men like us. You want to turn us away from what our forefathers used to worship. Bring us clear proof then, [if you can].' ¹¹Their messengers answered, 'True, we are only men like you, but God favours which-ever of His servants He chooses. We cannot bring you any proof unless God permits it, so let the believers put all their trust in Him— ¹²why should we not put our trust in God when it is He who has guided us to this way we follow? We shall certainly bear steadfastly whatever harm you do to us. Let anyone who trusts, trust in God.'

¹³The disbelievers said to their messengers, 'We shall expel you from our land unless you return to our religion.' But their Lord inspired the messengers: 'We shall destroy the evildoers, ¹⁴and leave you to dwell in the land after them. This reward is for those who are in awe of meeting Me, and who heed My warnings.' ¹⁵They asked God to decide, and every obstinate tyrant failed—¹⁶Hell awaits each one; he will be given foul water to drink, ¹⁷which he will try to gulp but scarcely be able to swallow; death will encroach on him from every side, but he will not die; more intense suffering will lie ahead of him. ¹⁸The deeds of those who reject their Lord are like ashes that the wind blows furiously on a stormy day: they have no power over anything they have gained. This is to stray far, far away.

¹⁹[Prophet], do you not see that God created the heavens and the earth for a purpose? He could remove all of you and replace you with a new creation if He wished to: ²⁰that is not difficult for God. ²¹When they all appear before Him, the weak will say to the power-seekers, 'We were your followers. Can you protect us from any of God's punishment?' They will reply, 'If God had guided us, we would have guided you. It makes no difference now whether we rage or endure with patience: there is no escape.' ²²When everything has

---

ᵃ Literally 'they pushed their hands into the prophets' mouths'.

been decided, Satan will say, 'God gave you a true promise. I too made promises but they were false ones: I had no power over you except to call you, and you responded to my call, so do not blame me; blame yourselves. I cannot help you, nor can you help me. I reject the way you associated me with God before.' A bitter torment awaits such wrongdoers, ²³ but those who believed and did good deeds will be brought into Gardens graced with flowing streams, there to remain with their Lord's permission: their greeting there is 'Peace'.

²⁴ [Prophet], do you not see how God makes comparisons? A good word is like a good tree whose root is firm and whose branches are high in the sky, ²⁵ yielding constant fruit by its Lord's leave—God makes such comparisons for people so that they may reflect—²⁶ but an evil word is like a rotten tree, uprooted from the surface of the earth, with no power to endure. ²⁷ God will give firmness to those who believe in the firmly rooted word,ᵃ both in this world and the Hereafter, but the evildoers He leaves to stray: God does whatever He will.

²⁸ [Prophet], do you not see those who, in exchange for God's favour, offer only ingratitude and make their people end up in Hell, the home of ruin, ²⁹ where they burn? What an evil place to stay! ³⁰ They set up [false deities] as God's equals to lead people astray from His path. Say, 'Take your pleasure now, for your destination is the Fire.' ³¹ Tell My servants who have believed to keep up the prayer and give out of what We have provided them, secretly and in public, before a Day comes when there will be no trading or friendship.

³² It is God who created the heavens and earth, who has sent down water from the sky and with it brought forth produce to nourish you; He has made ships useful to you, sailing the sea by His command, and the rivers too; ³³ He has made the sun and the moon useful to you, steady on their paths; He has made the night and day useful to you ³⁴ and given you some of everything you asked Him for. If you tried to count God's favours you could never calculate them: man is truly unjust and ungrateful.

³⁵ Remember when Abraham said, 'Lord, make this town safe! Lord, preserve me and my offspring from idolatry: ³⁶ the [idols] have

---

ᵃ Possibly the Scripture, firmly rooted in knowledge from God.

led many people astray! Anyone who follows me is with me, but as for anyone who disobeys me—You are surely forgiving and merciful. [37] Our Lord, I have established some of my offspring in an uncultivated valley, close to Your Sacred House, Lord, so that they may keep up the prayer. Make people's hearts turn to them, and provide them with produce, so that they may be thankful. [38] Our Lord, You know well what we conceal and what we reveal: nothing at all is hidden from God, on earth or in heaven. [39] Praise be to God, who has granted me Ishmael and Isaac in my old age: my Lord surely hears all requests! [40] Lord, grant that I may keep up the prayer, and so may my offspring. Our Lord, accept my request. [41] Our Lord, forgive me, my parents, and the believers on the Day of Reckoning.'

[42] Do not think [Prophet] that God is unaware of what the disbelievers[a] do: He only gives them respite until a Day when their eyes will stare in terror. [43] They will rush forward, craning their necks, unable to divert their eyes, a gaping void in their hearts. [44] So warn people of the Day when punishment will come to them, and when the disbelievers will say, 'Our Lord, give us a little more time: we shall answer Your call and follow the messengers.' Did you [disbelievers] not swear in the past that your power would have no end? [45] You lived in the same places as others who wronged themselves before, and you were clearly shown how We dealt with them—We gave you many examples. [46] They made their plots, but, even if their plots had been able to move mountains, God had the answer.

[47] So do not think [Prophet] that God will break His promise to His messengers: He is mighty, and capable of retribution. [48] One Day—when the earth is turned into another earth, the heavens into another heaven, and people all appear before God, the One, the Overpowering—[49] you [Prophet] will see the guilty on that Day, bound together in fetters, [50] in garments of pitch, faces covered in fire. [51] [All will be judged] so that God may reward each soul as it deserves: God is swift in His reckoning.

[52] This is a message to all people, so that they may be warned by it, and know that He is the only God, and so that those who have minds may take heed.

---

[a] This is an instance where *dhalimun* means 'disbelievers', see verse 44 and 31: 11, 13.

15. AL-HIJR

A Meccan sura which takes its title from the reference to the people of al-Hijr (verses 80–4). These are an example of the many who disbelieved and rejected their prophets. Each has its own time for punishment so the Prophet should bear patiently, not grieve over what the disbelievers say, and continue with his worship. The sura uses the example of nature and Iblis's insistence on corrupting people to show, in turn, God's grace and the danger Satan personifies.

In the name of God, the Lord of Mercy, the Giver of Mercy

¹ *Alif Lam Ra*

These are the verses of the Scripture, a Qur'an that makes things clear. ² The disbelievers may well come to wish they had submitted to God, ³ so [Prophet] leave them to eat and enjoy themselves. Let [false] hopes distract them: they will come to know. ⁴ Never have We destroyed a community that did not have a set time; ⁵ no community can bring its time forward, nor delay it. ⁶ They say, 'Receiver of this Qur'an! You are definitely mad. ⁷ Why do you not bring us the angels, if you are telling the truth?' ⁸ But We send down the angels only to bring justice and then they will not be reprieved. ⁹ We have sent down the Qur'an Ourself, and We Ourself will guard it. Even before you [Prophet], ¹⁰ We sent messengers among the various communities of old, ¹¹ but they mocked every single messenger that came to them: ¹² in this way We make the message slip through the hearts of evildoers. ¹³ They will not believe in it. That was what happened with the peoples of long ago, ¹⁴ and even if We opened a gateway into Heaven for them and they rose through it, higher and higher, ¹⁵ they would still say, 'Our eyes are hallucinating. We are bewitched.'

¹⁶ We have set constellations up in the sky and made it beautiful for all to see, ¹⁷ and guarded it from every stoned satan:^a ¹⁸ any eavesdropper will be pursued by a clearly visible flame. ¹⁹ As for the earth, We have spread it out, set firm mountains on it, and made everything

---

^a See 72: 8–9.

grow there in due balance. [20] We have provided sustenance in it for you and for all those creatures for whom you do not provide. [21] There is not a thing whose storehouses are not with Us. We send it down only according to a well-defined measure: [22] We send the winds to fertilize, and We bring down water from the sky for you to drink— you do not control its sources. [23] It is We who give life and death; it is We who inherit [everything]. [24] We know exactly those of you who come first and those who come later. [25] [Prophet], it is your Lord who will gather them all together: He is all wise, all knowing.

[26] We created man out of dried clay formed from dark mud— [27] the jinn We created before, from the fire of scorching wind. [28] Your Lord said to the angels, 'I will create a mortal out of dried clay, formed from dark mud. [29] When I have fashioned him and breathed My spirit into him, bow down before him,' [30] and the angels all did so. [31] But not Iblis: he refused to bow down like the others. [32] God said, 'Iblis, why did you not bow down like the others?' [33] and he answered, 'I will not bow to a mortal You created from dried clay, formed from dark mud.' [34] 'Get out of here!' said God. 'You are an outcast, [35] rejected until the Day of Judgement.' [36] Iblis said, 'My Lord, give me respite until the Day when they are raised from the dead.' [37] 'You have respite,' said God, [38] 'until the Day of the Appointed Time.' [39] Iblis then said to God, 'Because You have put me in the wrong, I will lure mankind on earth and put them in the wrong, [40] all except Your devoted servants.' [41] God said, '[Devotion] is a straight path to Me: [42] you will have no power over My servants, only over the ones who go wrong and follow you. [43] Hell is the promised place for all these, [44] with seven gates, each gate having its allotted share of them. [45] But the righteous will be in Gardens with springs— [46] "Enter them in peace and safety!"— [47] and We shall remove any bitterness from their hearts: [they will be like] brothers, sitting on couches, face to face. [48] No weariness will ever touch them there, nor will they ever be expelled.' [49] [Prophet], tell My servants that I am the Forgiving, the Merciful, [50] but My torment is the truly painful one.

[51] Tell them too about Abraham's guests: [52] when they came to him and said, 'Peace,' he said, 'We are afraid of you.' [53] 'Do not be afraid,' they said, 'We bring you good news of a son who will have great knowledge.' [54] He said, 'How can you give me such news when old age has come to me? What sort of news is this?' [55] They said, 'We

have told you the truth, so do not despair.' ⁵⁶He said, 'Who but the misguided despair of the mercy of their Lord?' ⁵⁷and then asked, 'Messengers, what is your errand?' ⁵⁸They replied, 'We have been sent to a people who are guilty.' ⁵⁹But We shall save the household of Lot, ⁶⁰all except his wife: We have decreed that she will be one of those who stay behind.

⁶¹When the messengers came to the household of Lot, ⁶²he said, 'You are strangers.' ⁶³They said, 'We have brought you what they said would never happen: ⁶⁴we have brought you the Truth. We speak truly, ⁶⁵so leave in the dead of the night with your household, and walk behind them. Let none of you look back. Go where you are commanded.' ⁶⁶We made this decree known to him: the last remnants of those people would be wiped out in the morning. ⁶⁷The people of the town came along, revelling, ⁶⁸and he told them, 'These are my guests, do not disgrace me. ⁶⁹Fear God, and do not shame me.' ⁷⁰They answered, 'Have we not told you not to interfere [between us and] anyone else?' ⁷¹He said, 'My daughters are here, if you must.' ⁷²By your life [Prophet], they wandered on in their wild intoxication ⁷³and the blast overtook them at sunrise: ⁷⁴We turned their city upside down and rained on them a shower of clay stones. ⁷⁵There truly is a sign in this for those who can learn—⁷⁶it is still there on the highway—⁷⁷there truly is a sign in this for those who believe.

⁷⁸The forest-dwellers were wrongdoers ⁷⁹and We took retribution on them; both are still there on the highway, plain for all to see. ⁸⁰The people of al-Hijr*ᵃ* also rejected Our messengers: ⁸¹We gave them Our signs, but they turned their backs, ⁸²carved out dwellings in the mountains, and lived in security—⁸³the blast overwhelmed them early in the morning. ⁸⁴What they had gained was of no use to them.

⁸⁵We did not create the heavens and the earth and everything between them without a true purpose: the Hour will certainly come, so [Prophet] bear with them graciously. ⁸⁶Your Lord is the All Knowing Creator. ⁸⁷We have given you the seven oft-recited verses*ᵇ* and the whole glorious Qur'an. ⁸⁸Do not look longingly at the good things We have given some to enjoy. Do not grieve over the

---

ᵃ The tribe of Thamud who lived north of Medina. *Al-Hijr* means 'stone city', like Petra in Jordan.

ᵇ According to most interpreters this refers to *al-Fatiha* 'The Opening' (Sura 1).

[disbelievers], but lower your wings over the believers [89] and say, 'I am here to give plain warning,' [90] like the [warning] We have sent down for those who divide themselves into bands[a] [91] and abuse the Qur'an[b] — [92] by your Lord, We will question them all [93] about their deeds. [94] So proclaim openly what you have been commanded [to say], and ignore the idolaters. [95] We are enough for you against all those who ridicule your message, [96] who set up another god beside God — they will come to know. [97] We are well aware that your heart is weighed down by what they say. [98] Celebrate the glory of your Lord and be among those who bow down to Him: [99] worship your Lord until what is certain comes to you.

[a] This refers to some disbelievers who organized themselves into groups to meet pilgrims and warn them against the Qur'an.

[b] There are two interpretations of the word *'idina* given by Razi. One is 'parts/shreds', the other is 'lies/inventions': 'abuse' covers both.

16. THE BEE

A Meccan sura. It takes its title from the bee (verses 68–9) inspired in its remarkable way by God. This is just one of the numerous examples given in this sura of God's grace and the many things man should be grateful for. The sura condemns the idolaters who attribute God's bounty to other powers and worship false deities. Abraham is given at the end as an example for the Muslim community to follow. Until verse 88, the sura is directed at the polytheists; from verse 90 onwards it teaches the Muslims in various ways. Verse 89 connects the two parts by naming the Prophet as witness to the believers and disbelievers of his community.

In the name of God, the Lord of Mercy, the Giver of Mercy

¹God's Judgement is coming,[a] so do not ask to bring it on sooner. Glory be to Him! He is far above anything they join with Him! ²He sends down angels with inspiration at His command to whichever of His servants He chooses: 'Declare that there is no god but Me. Beware of Me.' ³He created the heavens and earth for a true purpose, and He is far above whatever they join with Him! ⁴He created man from a drop of fluid, and yet man openly challenges Him. ⁵And livestock—He created them for you too. You derive warmth and other benefits from them: you eat some of them; ⁶you find beauty in them when you bring them home to rest and when you drive them out to pasture. ⁷They carry your loads to lands you yourselves could not reach without great hardship—truly your Lord is kind and merciful! —⁸horses, mules, and donkeys for you to ride and use for show, and other things you know nothing about. ⁹God points out the right path, for some of them lead the wrong way: if He wished, He could guide you all.

¹⁰It is He who sends down water for you from the sky. Some of it you drink, and the shrubs that you feed to your animals come from it. ¹¹With it He grows for you corn, olives, palms, vines, and all kinds of fruit. There truly is a sign in this for those who reflect. ¹²By His command He has made the night and day, the sun, moon, and stars all of benefit to you. There truly are signs in this for those who use

---

[a] The Arabic verb *ata* is in the past tense to express inevitability and nearness.

their reason. ¹³He has made of benefit to you the many-coloured things He has multiplied on the earth. There truly are signs in this for those who take heed. ¹⁴It is He who made the sea of benefit to you: you eat fresh fish from it and bring out jewellery to wear; you see the ships cutting through its waves so that you may go in search of His bounty and give thanks. ¹⁵He has made mountains stand firm on the earth, to prevent it shaking under you, and rivers and paths so that you may find your way, ¹⁶and landmarks and stars to guide people. ¹⁷Can He who creates be compared to one who cannot create? Why do you not take heed?

¹⁸If you tried to count God's blessings, you could never take them all in: He is truly most forgiving and most merciful. ¹⁹He knows what you conceal and what you reveal. ²⁰Those they invoke beside God create nothing; they are themselves created. ²¹They are dead, not living. They do not know when they will be raised up. ²²Your God is the One God. As for those who deny the life to come, their hearts refuse to admit the truth and they are arrogant. ²³There is no doubt that God knows what they conceal and what they reveal. He does not love the arrogant.

²⁴When they are asked, 'What has your Lord sent down?' they say, 'Ancient fables.' ²⁵On the Day of Resurrection they will bear the full weight of their own burden, as well as some of the burden of those they misled with no true knowledge. How terrible their burden will be! ²⁶Those who went before them also schemed, but God attacked the very foundations of what they built. The roof fell down on them: punishment came on them from unimagined directions. ²⁷In the end, on the Day of Resurrection, He will shame them, saying, 'Where are these "partners" of Mine that you opposed [Us] for?' Those given knowledge will say, 'Shame and misery on the disbelievers today!' ²⁸Those whose lives the angels take while they are wronging themselves offer submission: 'We were doing no evil.' 'Yes you were: God knows fully everything that you have done, ²⁹so enter the gates of Hell. There you will remain—the home of the arrogant is evil indeed.'

³⁰But when the righteous are asked, 'What has your Lord sent down?' they say, 'All that is good.' There is a reward in this present world for those who do good, but their home in the Hereafter is far better: the home of the righteous is excellent. ³¹They will enter perpetual Gardens graced with flowing streams. There they will

have everything they wish. This is the way God rewards the right-eous, [32] those whose lives the angels take in a state of goodness, saying to them, 'Peace be upon you. Enter the Garden as a reward for what you have done.' [33] Are the disbelievers waiting for the angels to come to them, or your Lord's Judgement? Those who went before them did the same. God did not wrong them—they wronged themselves. [34] So the evil they had done hit them and they were surrounded by the very thing they had mocked.

[35] Those who worshipped others alongside God say, 'If God had willed, we would not have worshipped anything but Him, nor would our fathers. We would not have declared anything forbidden without His sanction.' Those before them said the same. Are the messengers obliged to do anything other than deliver [their message] clearly? [36] We sent a messenger to every community, saying, 'Worship God and shun false gods.' Among them were some God guided; misguidance took hold of others. So travel through the earth and see what was the fate of those who denied the truth. [37] Though you [Prophet] may be eager to guide them, God does not guide those who misguide [others],[a] nor will they have anyone to help them. [38] They have sworn by God with their strongest oaths that He will not raise the dead to life. But He will—it is His binding promise, though most people do not realize it—[39] in order to make clear for them what they have differed about and so that the disbelievers may realize that what they said was false. [40] When We will something to happen, all that We say is, 'Be,' and it is. [41] As for those who emi-grated in God's cause after being wronged, We shall give them a good home in this world, but the reward of the Hereafter will be far greater, if they only knew it. [42] They are the ones who are steadfast and put their trust in their Lord.

[43] [Prophet], all the messengers We sent before you were simply men to whom We had given the Revelation: you [people] can ask those who have knowledge if you do not know. [44] We sent them with clear signs and scriptures. We have sent down the message to you too [Prophet], so that you can explain to people what was sent for them, so that they may reflect.

[45] Are those who plan evil so sure that God will not make the earth swallow them up, that punishment will not come on them from some

------

[a] Cf. verse 25.

unimagined direction, [46] that it will not overtake them suddenly in the midst of their comings and goings—for they cannot frustrate God—[47] or that it will not overtake them gradually? Indeed your Lord is kind and merciful. [48] Do the [disbelievers] not observe the things that God has created, casting their shadows right and left, submitting themselves to God obediently? [49] It is to God that everything in the heavens and earth submits, every beast that moves, even the angels—they are free from arrogance: [50] they fear their Lord above them, and they do as they are commanded.

[51] God said, 'Do not take two gods'—for He is the One God—'I alone am the One that you should hold in awe.' [52] Everything in the heavens and earth belongs to Him: everlasting obedience is His right. Will you heed anyone other than God? [53] Whatever good things you possess come from God, and when hardship afflicts you, it is to Him alone you cry out for help, [54] yet when He has relieved you of your hardship—lo and behold!—some of you attribute partners to your Lord. [55] Let them show ingratitude for the favours We have shown them; 'Enjoy your brief time—soon you will know.'

[56] They set aside part of the sustenance We give them, for [idols] about which they have no true knowledge.[a] By God! You will be questioned about your false invention. [57] They assign daughters to God[b]—may He be exalted!—and prefer [sons] for themselves. [58] When one of them is given news of the birth of a baby girl, his face darkens and he is filled with gloom. [59] In his shame he hides himself away from his people because of the bad news he has been given. Should he keep her and suffer contempt or bury her in the dust? How ill they judge! [60] Those who do not believe in the Hereafter should have the contemptible image, and God should have the highest one.[c] He is the Mighty, the Wise. [61] If God took people to task for the evil they do, He would not leave one living creature on earth, but He reprieves them until an appointed time: when their time comes they cannot delay it for an hour nor can they bring it forward.

[a] The pagan Arabs gave part of their crops and livestock to their deities (6: 136).

[b] Some of the pagan Arabs called angels the daughters of God. This is doubly blasphemous because of the contempt in which daughters were held in a warrior community, to the extent of female infanticide as described below.

[c] Their image of God is that He can only have daughters, though they themselves have contempt for their daughters.

⁶²They attribute to God what they themselves dislike while their own tongues utter the lie that the best*ᵃ* belongs to them. Without doubt it is the Fire that belongs to them: they will be given priority there!*ᵇ*

⁶³By God,*ᶜ* We have sent messengers before you [Muhammad] to other communities, but Satan made their foul deeds seem alluring to them. He is the patron of these present disbelievers*ᵈ* too, and a painful punishment awaits them all. ⁶⁴We have sent down the Scripture to you only to make clear to them what they differ about, and as guidance and mercy to those who believe.

⁶⁵It is God who sends water down from the sky and with it revives the earth when it is dead. There truly is a sign in this for people who listen. ⁶⁶In livestock, too, you have a lesson—We give you a drink from the contents of their bellies, between waste matter and blood, pure milk, sweet to the drinker. ⁶⁷From the fruits of date palms and grapes you take sweet juice*ᵉ* and wholesome provisions. There truly is a sign in this for people who use their reason. ⁶⁸And your Lord inspired the bee, saying, 'Build yourselves houses in the mountains and trees and what people construct. ⁶⁹Then feed on all kinds of fruit and follow the ways made easy for you by your Lord.' From their bellies comes a drink of different colours in which there is healing for people. There truly is a sign in this for those who think.

⁷⁰It is God who has created you and in time will cause you to die. Some of you will be reduced, in old age, to a most abject state, so that, after having knowledge, they will know nothing at all: God is truly all knowing and all powerful. ⁷¹God has given some of you more provision than others. Those who have been given more are unwilling to pass their provision on to the slaves they possess so that they become their equals.*ᶠ* How can they refuse to acknowledge God's blessings? ⁷²And it is God who has given you spouses from amongst yourselves and through them He has given you children and grandchildren and provided you with good things. How can they

---

ᵃ i.e. sons.

ᵇ This meaning of *farata* is supported by Rāzī.

ᶜ The disbelievers used to swear by their idols, so here God swears by Himself.

ᵈ This refers to the disbelievers of Mecca.

ᵉ The Arabic word *sakar* means 'wine', 'juice', or 'vinegar' (*al-Mu'jam al-Wasit*).

ᶠ i.e. 'How can you make idols equal to God if you do not make your own slaves equal to you?' What people have is from God alone and they should acknowledge it.

believe in falsehood and deny God's blessings?[a] 73 What they worship beside God has no power to provide anything for them from the heavens or the earth: they can do nothing. 74 So do not make up images about God: God knows and you do not.

75 God presents this illustration: a slave controlled by his master, with no power over anything, and another man We have supplied with good provision, from which he gives alms privately and openly. Can they be considered equal? All praise belongs to God, but most of them do not recognize this. 76 God presents another illustration: two men, one of them mute, unable to do anything, a burden to his carer—whatever task he directs him to, he achieves nothing good— can he be considered equal to one who commands justice and is on the straight path? 77 All that is hidden from view in the heavens and earth belongs to God. The coming of the Hour of Judgement is like the blink of an eye, or even quicker: God has power over everything. 78 It is God who brought you out of your mothers' wombs knowing nothing, and gave you hearing and sight and minds, so that you might be thankful. 79 Do they not see the birds made to fly through the air in the sky? Nothing holds them up except God. There truly are signs in this for those who believe. 80 It is God who has given you a place of rest in your houses and tents, made from the skins of animals, that you find light [to handle] when you travel and when you set up camp; furnishings and comfort for a while from their wool, fur, and hair. 81 It is God who has given you shade from what He has created, and places of shelter in the mountains; garments to protect you from the heat, and garments to protect you in your wars. In this way He perfects His blessings on you, so that you may devote your-selves to Him. 82 But if they turn away [Prophet], your only duty is to deliver the message clearly. 83 They know God's blessings, but refuse to recognize them: most of them are ungrateful.

84 The day will come when We raise up a witness from every community, when the disbelievers will not be allowed to make excuses or make amends. 85 When the evildoers face punishment it will not be lightened for them nor will they be given any respite. 86 When the idolaters see the partners they joined with God they will say, 'Our Lord, these are the partners we used to invoke beside

---

[a] i.e. claim that the partners they ascribe to God are the ones to give them such blessings.

You.' But the partners will retort, 'You are liars,' [87] and on that Day they will offer total submission to God: their false deities will desert them. [88] Because of the corruption they spread, We shall add torment upon torment for those who disbelieved and barred others from the path of God.

[89] The day will come when We raise up for each community a witness against them, and We shall bring you [Prophet] as a witness against these people, for We have sent the Scripture down to you explaining everything, and as guidance and mercy and good news to those who submit to God.

[90] God commands justice, doing good, and generosity towards relatives and He forbids what is shameful, blameworthy, and oppressive. He teaches you, so that you may take heed. [91] Fulfil any pledge you make in God's name and do not break oaths after you have sworn them, for you have made God your surety: God knows everything you do. [92] Do not use your oaths to deceive each other—like a woman who unravels the thread she has firmly spun—just because one party may be more numerous than another. God tests you with this, and on the Day of the Resurrection He will make clear to you those things you differed about.

[93] If God so willed, He would have made you all one people, but He leaves to stray whoever He will and guides whoever He will. You will be questioned about your deeds. [94] Do not use your oaths to deceive each other lest any foot should slip after being firmly placed and lest you should taste the penalty for having hindered others from the path of God, and suffer terrible torment. [95] Do not sell for a small price any pledge made in God's name: what God has [to give] is better for you, if you only knew. [96] What you have runs out but what God has endures, and We shall certainly reward those who remain steadfast according to the best of their actions. [97] To whoever, male or female, does good deeds and has faith, We shall give a good life and reward them according to the best of their actions.

[98] [Prophet], when you recite the Qur'an, seek God's protection from the outcast, Satan. [99] He has no power over those who believe and trust in their Lord; [100] his power is only over those who ally themselves with him and those who, because of him, join partners with God. [101] When We substitute one revelation for another— and God knows best what He reveals—they say, 'You are just making it up,' but most of them have no knowledge. [102] Say that the Holy

Spirit[a] has brought the Revelation with the Truth step by step from your Lord, to strengthen the believers and as guidance and good news to the devout. [103] We know very well that they say, 'It is a man who teaches him,' but the language of the person they allude to is foreign, while this revelation is in clear Arabic. [104] If people do not believe in God's revelation, God does not guide them, and a painful punishment awaits them. [105] Falsehood is fabricated only by those who do not believe in God's revelation: they are the liars. [106] With the exception of those who are forced to say they do not believe, although their hearts remain firm in faith, those who reject God after believing in Him and open their hearts to disbelief will have the wrath of God upon them and a grievous punishment awaiting them. [107] This is because they love the life of this world more than the one to come, and God does not guide those who reject Him. [108] These are people whose hearts, hearing, and sight have been closed off by God: they are heedless, [109] and there is no doubt that they will be the losers in the Hereafter. [110] But your Lord will be most forgiving and most merciful to those who leave their homes after persecution, then strive and remain steadfast. [111] On the Day when every soul will come pleading for itself, every soul will be paid in full for all its actions — they will not be wronged. [112] God presents the example of a town that was secure and at ease, with provisions coming to it abundantly from all places. Then it became ungrateful for God's blessings, so God afflicted it with the garment of famine and fear, for what its people had done. [113] A messenger who was one of them came to them, but they called him a liar. So punishment overwhelmed them in the midst of their evildoing.

[114] So eat of the good and lawful things God has provided for you and be thankful for His blessings,[b] if it is Him that you worship. [115] He has forbidden you only these things: carrion, blood, pig's meat, and animals over which any name other than God's has been invoked. But if anyone is forced by hunger, not desiring it nor exceeding his immediate need, God is forgiving and merciful towards him. [116] Do not say falsely, 'This is lawful and that is forbidden,' inventing a lie about God: those who invent lies about God will not prosper — [117] they may have a little enjoyment, but painful punishment awaits

---

[a] This refers to the Angel Gabriel.
[b] Unlike the ungrateful people just mentioned.

them. [118] [Prophet], We forbade the Jews what We told you about.[a] We did not wrong them; they wronged themselves. [119] But towards those who do wrong out of ignorance, and afterwards repent and make amends, your Lord is most forgiving and merciful.

[120] Abraham was truly an example: devoutly obedient to God and true in faith. He was not an idolater; [121] he was thankful for the blessings of God who chose him and guided him to a straight path. [122] We gave him blessings in this world, and he is among the righteous in the Hereafter. [123] Then We revealed to you [Muhammad], 'Follow the creed of Abraham, a man of pure faith who was not an idolater.' [124] The Sabbath was made obligatory only for those who differed about it. On the Day of Resurrection your Lord will judge between them as to their differences.

[125] [Prophet], call people to the way of your Lord with wisdom and beautiful teaching. Argue with them in the most courteous way, for your Lord knows best who has strayed from His way and who is rightly guided. [126] If you [people] have to respond to an attack, make your response proportionate, but it is best to stand fast. [127] So [Prophet] be steadfast: your steadfastness comes only from God. Do not grieve over them; do not be distressed by their scheming, [128] for God is with those who are aware of Him and who do good.

[a] In an earlier revelation (see 6: 146).

17. THE NIGHT JOURNEY

A Meccan sura framed by references to the Children of Israel at the beginning, and to Pharaoh at the end. The bulk of the sura deals with the Qur'an as guidance and warning, Muhammad, and the nature of prophecy, especially the fact that he is a human being and incapable himself of producing miracles. It also warns of Iblis's promise to tempt mankind and of the fate of the disbelievers, and it gives a series of commandments (verses 22–39). The Night Journey, which gives the sura its title, is mentioned in verse 1 and again in verse 60. Towards the end of the Meccan period, God caused Muhammad, in the space of a single night, to journey from Mecca to Jerusalem and from there to heaven and back again.

In the name of God, the Lord of Mercy, the Giver of Mercy

¹ Glory to Him who made His servant travel by night from the sacred place of worship*ᵃ* to the furthest place of worship,*ᵇ* whose surroundings We have blessed, to show him some of Our signs: He alone is the All Hearing, the All Seeing. ² We also gave Moses the Scripture, and made it a guide for the Children of Israel. 'Entrust yourselves to no one but Me, ³ you descendants of those We carried with Noah: he was truly a thankful servant.'

⁴ In the Scripture, We declared to the Children of Israel, 'Twice you will spread corruption in the land and become highly arrogant.' ⁵ When the first of these warnings was fulfilled, We sent servants of Ours against you with great force, and they ravaged your homes. That warning was fulfilled, ⁶ but then We allowed you to prevail against your enemy. We increased your wealth and offspring and made you more numerous— ⁷ whether you do good or evil it is for your own soul—and when the second warning was fulfilled [We sent them] to shame your faces and enter the place of worship as they did the first time, and utterly destroy whatever fell into their power. ⁸ Your Lord may yet have mercy on you, but if you do the same again, so shall We: We have made Hell a prison for those who ignore [Our warning].

ᵃ In Mecca.   *ᵇ* In Jerusalem.

⁹ This Qur'an does indeed show the straightest way. It gives the faithful who do right the good news that they will have a great reward and ¹⁰ warns that We have prepared an agonizing punishment for those who do not believe in the world to come. ¹¹ Yet man prays for harm, just as he prays for good: man is ever hasty. ¹² We made the night and the day as two signs, then darkened the night and made the day for seeing, for you to seek your Lord's bounty and to know how to count the years and calculate. We have explained everything in detail. ¹³ We have bound each human being's destiny to his neck. On the Day of Resurrection, We shall bring out a record for each of them, which you will find spread wide open, ¹⁴ 'Read your record. Today your own soul is enough to calculate your account.'

¹⁵ Whoever accepts guidance does so for his own good; whoever strays does so at his own peril. No soul will bear another's burden, nor do We punish until We have sent a messenger. ¹⁶ When We decide to destroy a town, We command those corrupted by wealth [to reform], but they [persist in their] disobedience; Our sentence is passed, and We destroy them utterly. ¹⁷ How many generations We have destroyed since Noah! Your Lord knows and observes the sins of His servants well enough. ¹⁸ If anyone desires [only] the fleeting life, We speed up whatever We will in it, for whoever We wish; then We have prepared Hell for him in which to burn, disgraced and rejected. ¹⁹ But if anyone desires the life to come and strives after it as he should, as a true believer, his striving will be thanked. ²⁰ To both the latter and the former, We give some of your Lord's bounty. [Prophet], your Lord's bounty is not restricted—²¹ see how We have given some more than others—but the Hereafter holds greater ranks and greater favours.

²² Set up *ᵃ* no other god beside God, or you will end up disgraced and forsaken. ²³ Your Lord has commanded that you should worship none but Him, and that you be kind to your parents. If either or both of them reach old age with you, say no word that shows impatience with them, and do not be harsh with them, but speak to them respectfully ²⁴ and, out of mercy, lower your wing in humility towards them and say, 'Lord, have mercy on them, just as they cared for me when I was little.' ²⁵ Your Lord knows best what is in your

---

ᵃ This verb is addressed to mankind as a whole (Razi).

heart. If you are good, He is most forgiving to those who return to Him. ²⁶ Give relatives their due, and the needy, and travellers—do not squander your wealth wastefully: ²⁷ those who squander are the brothers of Satan, and Satan is most ungrateful to his Lord—²⁸ but if, while seeking some bounty that you expect from your Lord, you turn them down, then at least speak some word of comfort to them. ²⁹ Do not be tight-fisted, nor so open-handed that you end up blamed and overwhelmed with regret. ³⁰ Your Lord gives abundantly to whoever He will, and sparingly to whoever He will: He knows and observes His servants thoroughly.

³¹ Do not kill your children for fear of poverty ᵃ—We shall provide for them and for you—killing them is a great sin. ³² And do not go anywhere near adultery: it is an outrage, and an evil path. ³³ Do not take life—which God has made sacred—except by right. If anyone is killed wrongfully, We have given authority to the defender of his rights, but he should not be excessive in taking life, for he is already aided [by God]. ³⁴ Do not go near the orphan's property, except with the best intentions, until he reaches the age of maturity. Honour your pledges: you will be questioned about your pledges. ³⁵ Give full measure when you measure, and weigh with accurate scales: that is better and fairer in the end. ³⁶ Do not follow blindly what you do not know to be true: ears, eyes, and heart, you will be questioned about all these. ³⁷ Do not strut arrogantly about the earth: you cannot break it open, nor match the mountains in height. ³⁸ The evil of all these is hateful to your Lord.

³⁹ [Prophet], this is some of the wisdom your Lord has revealed to you: do not set up another god beside God, or you will be thrown into Hell, blamed and rejected. ⁴⁰ What? Has your Lord favoured you people with sons and taken daughters for Himself from the angels? ᵇ What a monstrous thing for you to say!

⁴¹ We have explained things in various ways in this Qur'an, so that such people might take notice, but it has only turned them further away. ⁴² Say, 'If there were other gods along with Him, as they say there are, then they would have tried to find a way to the Lord of the Throne. ⁴³ Glory to Him! He is far above what they say! ⁴⁴ The seven heavens and the earth and everyone in them glorify Him. There is not a single thing that does not celebrate His praise, though

---

ᵃ See 81: 8–9.   ᵇ See also 16: 57–62.

you do not understand their praise: He is most forbearing, most forgiving.'

⁴⁵[Prophet], when you recite the Qur'an, We put an invisible barrier between you and those who do not believe in the life to come. ⁴⁶We have put covers on their hearts that prevent them from understanding it, and heaviness in their ears. When you mention your Lord in the Qur'an, and Him alone, they turn their backs and run away. ⁴⁷We know best the way they listen, when they listen to you and when they confer in secret, and the wrongdoers say, 'You are only following a man who is bewitched.' ⁴⁸See what they think you are like! But they are lost and cannot find the right way. ⁴⁹They also say, 'What? When we are turned to bones and dust, shall we really be raised up in a new act of creation?' ⁵⁰Say, '[Yes] even if you were [as hard as] stone, or iron, ⁵¹or any other substance you think hard to be raised.' Then they will say, 'Who will bring us back?' Say, 'The One who created you the first time.' Then they will shake their heads at you and say, 'When will that be?' Say, 'It may well be very soon. ⁵²It will be the Day when He calls you, and you answer by praising Him, and you think you have stayed [on earth] only a little while.'

⁵³[Prophet], tell My servants to say what is best.ᵃ Satan sows discord among them: Satan is a sworn enemy of man. ⁵⁴Your Lord has the most knowledge about all of you: if He pleases He will have mercy on you, and if He pleases He will punish you. [Prophet], We did not send you to take charge of them. ⁵⁵Your Lord knows best about everyone in the heavens and the earth. We gave some prophets more than others: We gave David a book of wisdom.ᵇ ⁵⁶Say, 'Call upon those you claim to be deities beside God: they have no power to remove or avert any harm from you.' ⁵⁷Those [angels]ᶜ they pray to seek a way to their Lord themselves, even those who are closest to Him. They hope for His mercy and fear His punishment. The punishment of your Lord is much to be feared: ⁵⁸there is no community We shall not bring to an end, or punish severely, before the Day of Resurrection—this is written in the Book.ᵈ

⁵⁹Nothing prevents Us from sending miraculous signs,ᵉ except

ᵃ In arguing about religion and proving it as God has shown here. See 16: 125; 29: 46.
ᵇ See also 4: 163–6.
ᶜ See verse 40.
ᵈ God's divine Record.
ᵉ See 2: 118 for signs demanded by those without knowledge.

the fact that previous peoples denied them. We gave the people of Thamud the she-camel as a clear sign, yet they maltreated it. We send signs only to give warning. [60][Prophet], We have told you that your Lord knows all about human beings. The vision We showed you[a] was only a test for people, as was the cursed tree [mentioned] in the Qur'an.[b] We warn them, but this only increases their insolence.

[61] When We said to the angels, 'Bow down before Adam,' they all bowed down, but not Iblis. He retorted, 'Why should I bow down to someone You have created out of clay?' [62] and [then] said, 'You see this being You have honoured above me? If You reprieve me until the Day of Resurrection, I will lead all but a few of his descendants by the nose.' [63] God said, 'Go away! Hell will be your reward, and the reward of any of them who follow you—an ample reward. [64] Rouse whichever of them you can with your voice, muster your cavalry and infantry against them, share their wealth and their children with them, and make promises to them—Satan promises nothing but delusion—[65] but you will have no authority over My servants: Your Lord can take care of them well enough.'

[66][People], it is your Lord who makes ships go smoothly for you on the sea so that you can seek His bounty: He is most merciful towards you. [67] When you get into distress at sea, those you pray to beside Him desert you, but when He brings you back safe to land you turn away: man is ever ungrateful. [68] Can you be sure that God will not have you swallowed up into the earth when you are back on land, or that He will not send a sandstorm against you? Then you will find no one to protect you. [69] Or can you be sure that He will not send you back out to sea, and send a violent storm against you to drown you for being so ungrateful? You will find no helper against Us there. [70] We have honoured the children of Adam and carried them by land and sea. We have provided good sustenance for them and favoured them specially above many of those We have created.

[71] On the Day when We summon each community, along with its leader,[c] those who are given their record in their right hand will read

[a] The vision he was shown on the Night Journey.

[b] Said to refer to the tree of Zaqqum in Hell (see 56: 52; 44: 43–6). The eater will curse its fruits (Razi). Both the vision and the tree in Hell were objects of derision for the disbelievers.

[c] See 16: 89.

it with [pleasure].[a] But no one will be wronged in the least: [72] those who were blind in this life will be blind in the Hereafter, and even further off the path. [73] [Prophet], the disbelievers planned to tempt you away from what We revealed to you, so that you would invent some other revelation and attribute it to Us. Then they would have taken you as a friend. [74] If We had not made you stand firm, you would almost have inclined a little towards them. [75] In that case, We should have made you taste a double punishment in this life, and a double punishment after death. Then you would have found no one to help you against Us. [76] They planned to scare you off the land, but they would not have lasted for more than a little while after you. [77] Such was Our way with the messengers We sent before you, and you will find no change in Our ways.

[78] So perform the regular prayers in the period from the time the sun is past its zenith till the darkness of the night, and [recite] the Qur'an at dawn—dawn recitation is always witnessed[b]—[79] and during the night wake up and pray, as an extra offering of your own, so that your Lord may elevate you to a [highly] praised status. [80] Say, 'My Lord, make me go in truthfully, and come out truthfully, and grant me supporting authority from You.' [81] And say, 'The truth has come, and falsehood has passed away: falsehood is bound to pass away.'

[82] We send down the Qur'an as healing and mercy to those who believe; as for those who disbelieve, it only increases their loss. [83] When We favour man he turns arrogantly to one side, but when harm touches him, he falls into despair. [84] Say, 'Everyone does things their own way, but your Lord is fully aware who follows the best-guided path.'

[85] [Prophet], they ask you about the Spirit. Say, 'The Spirit is part of my Lord's domain. You have only been given a little knowledge.' [86] If We pleased, We could take away what We have revealed to you— then you would find no one to plead for you against Us—[87] if it were not for your Lord's mercy: His favour to you has been truly great. [88] Say, 'Even if all mankind and jinn came together to produce something like this Qur'an, they could not produce anything like it, however much they helped each other.' [89] In this Qur'an, We have set

---

[a] Cf. 69: 19–24.
[b] By the angels. See Bukhari, *Sahih*, '*Mawaqit*', 16.

out all kinds of examples for people, yet most of them persist in disbelieving. ⁹⁰ They say, 'We will not believe for you [Muhammad] until you make a spring gush out of the ground for us; ⁹¹ or until you have a garden of date palms and vines, and make rivers pour through them; ⁹² or make the sky fall on us in pieces, as you claimed will happen; or bring God and the angels before us face to face; ⁹³ or have a house made of gold, or ascend into the sky—even then, we will not believe in your ascension until you send a real book down for us to read.' Say, 'Glory to my Lord! Am I anything but a mortal, a messenger?' ⁹⁴ The only thing that has kept these people from believing, when guidance came to them, was that they said, 'How could God have sent a human being as a messenger?' ⁹⁵ Say, 'If there were angels walking about on earth, feeling at home, We would have sent them an angel from Heaven as a messenger.' ⁹⁶ Say, 'God is witness enough between me and you. He knows and observes His servants well.'

⁹⁷ [Prophet], anyone God guides is truly guided, and you will find no protector other than Him for anyone He leaves astray. On the Day of Resurrection We shall gather them, lying on their faces, blind, dumb, and deaf. Hell will be their Home. Whenever the Fire goes down, We shall make it blaze more fiercely for them. ⁹⁸ This is what they will get for rejecting Our signs and saying, 'What? When we are turned to bones and dust, how can we be raised in a new act of creation?' ⁹⁹ Do they not see that God, who created the heavens and earth, can create the likes of them [anew]? He has ordained a time for them—there is no doubt about that—but the evildoers refuse everything except disbelief. ¹⁰⁰ Say, 'If you possessed the very stores of my Lord's bounty, you would hold them back in your fear of spending: man is ever grudging.'

¹⁰¹ In the past, We gave Moses nine clear signs—ask the Children of Israel. When Moses came to [the Egyptians], Pharaoh said to him, 'Moses, I think you are bewitched.' ¹⁰² He said, 'You know very well that only the Lord of the heavens and earth could have sent these signs as clear proof. I think that you, Pharaoh, are doomed.' ¹⁰³ So he wanted to wipe them off the [face of the] earth, but We drowned him and those with him. ¹⁰⁴ After his death, We told the Children of Israel, 'Live in the land, and when the promise of the Hereafter is fulfilled, We shall bring you to the assembly of all people.'

¹⁰⁵ We sent down the Qur'an with the truth, and with the truth it has come down—[Prophet], We sent you only to give good news and

warning—[106] it is a recitation that We have revealed in parts, so that you can recite it to people at intervals; We have sent it down little by little. [107] Say, 'Whether you believe it or not, those who were given knowledge earlier fall down on their faces when it is recited to them, [108] and say, "Glory to our Lord! Our Lord's promise has been fulfilled." [109] They fall down on their faces, weeping, and [the Qur'an] increases their humility.' [110] Say [to them], 'Call on God, or on the Lord of Mercy—whatever names you call Him, the best names belong to Him.' [Prophet], do not be too loud in your prayer, or too quiet, but seek a middle way [111] and say, 'Praise belongs to God, who has no child nor partner in His rule. He is not so weak as to need a protector. Proclaim His limitless greatness!'

18. THE CAVE

A Meccan sura which gets its name from the Sleepers of the Cave, whose story takes a prominent place in the sura (verses 9–26). This sura also deals with two other stories: Moses' meeting with an unidentified figure (verses 60–82), and the story of Dhu 'l-Qarnayn (verses 83–99). A parable is put forward for the people of Mecca: the parable of the luscious gardens belonging to an arrogant and ungrateful man, which God reduces to dust. The sura opens and closes with references to the Qur'an itself.

In the name of God, the Lord of Mercy, the Giver of Mercy

¹ Praise be to God, who sent down the Scripture to His servant and made it unerringly straight, ² warning of severe punishment from Him, and [giving] glad news to the believers who do good deeds—an excellent reward ³ that they will always enjoy. ⁴ It warns those people who assert, 'God has a child.'*ᵃ* ⁵ They have no knowledge about this, nor did their forefathers—it is a monstrous assertion that comes out of their mouths: what they say is nothing but lies. ⁶ But [Prophet] are you going to worry yourself to death over them if they do not believe in this message?

⁷ We have adorned the earth with attractive things so that We may test people to find out which of them do best, ⁸ but We shall reduce all this to barren dust. ⁹ [Prophet], do you find the Companions in the Cave and al-Raqim*ᵇ* so wondrous, among all Our other signs? ¹⁰ When the young men sought refuge in the cave and said, 'Our Lord, grant us Your mercy, and find us a good way out of our ordeal,' ¹¹ We sealed their ears [with sleep] in the cave for years. ¹² Then We woke them so that We could make clear which of the two parties*ᶜ* was better able to work out how long they had been there.

¹³ [Prophet], We shall tell you their story as it really was. They were young men who believed in their Lord, and We gave them more

---

ᵃ Walad in classical Arabic applies to masculine and feminine, singular and plural. As this sura is Meccan, it most probably refers to Meccan claims that the angels are daughters of God.

ᵇ Al-Raqim is variously interpreted as being the name of the mountain in which the cave was situated, the name of their dog, or an inscription bearing their names.

ᶜ See verse 19.

and more guidance. [14] We gave strength to their hearts when they stood up and said, 'Our Lord is the Lord of the heavens and earth. We shall never call upon any god other than Him, for that would be an outrageous thing to do. [15] These people of ours have taken gods other than Him. Why do they not produce clear evidence about them? Who could be more unjust than someone who makes up lies about God? [16] Now that you have left such people, and what they worshipped instead of God, take refuge in the cave. God will shower His mercy on you and make you an easy way out of your ordeal.'

[17] You could have seen the [light of the] sun as it rose, moving away to the right of their cave, and when it set, moving away to the left of them, while they lay in the wide space inside the cave. This is one of God's signs. Those people God guides are rightly guided, but you will find no protector to lead to the right path those He leaves to stray. [18] You would have thought they were awake, though they lay asleep. We turned them over, to the right and the left, with their dog stretching out its forelegs at the entrance. If you had seen them, you would have turned and run away, filled with fear of them.

[19] In time We woke them, and they began to question one another. One of them asked, 'How long have you been here?' and [some] answered, 'A day or part of a day,' but then [others] said, 'Your Lord knows best how long you have been here. One of you go to the city with your silver coins, find out where the best food is there, and bring some back. But be careful not to let anyone know about you. [20] If they found you out, they would stone you or force you to return to their religion, where you would never come to any good.' [21] In this way We brought them to people's attention so that they might know that God's promise [of resurrection] is true and that there is no doubt about the Last Hour, [though] people argue among themselves.

[Some] said, 'Construct a building over them: their Lord knows best about them.' Those who prevailed said, 'We shall build a place of worship over them.' [22] [Some] say, 'The sleepers were three, and their dog made four,' others say, 'They were five, and the dog made six'—guessing in the dark—and some say, 'They were seven, and their dog made eight.'—Say [Prophet], 'My Lord knows best how many they were.' Only a few have real knowledge about them, so do not argue, but stick to what is clear, and do not ask any of these people about them. [23] Do not say of anything, 'I will do that tomorrow,'[a] [24] without adding, 'God willing,' and, whenever you forget, remember your Lord and say, 'May my Lord guide me closer to what is right.'—[25] [Some say], 'The sleepers stayed in their cave for three hundred years,' some added nine more. [26] Say [Prophet], 'God knows best how long they stayed.' His is the knowledge of all that is hidden in the heavens and earth—how well He sees! How well He hears!—and they have no one to protect them other than Him; He does not allow anyone to share His rule.

[27] [Prophet], follow what has been revealed to you of your Lord's Scripture: there is no changing His words, nor can you find any refuge except with Him. [28] Be steadfast along with those who pray to their Lord morning and evening, seeking His approval, and do not let your eyes turn away from them out of desire for the attractions of this worldly life:[b] do not yield to those whose hearts We have made heedless of Our Qur'an, those who follow their own low desires, those whose ways are unbridled. [29] Say, 'Now the truth has come from your Lord: let those who wish to believe in it do so, and let those who wish to reject it do so.' We have prepared a Fire for the wrongdoers that will envelop them from all sides. If they call for relief, they will be relieved with water like molten metal, scalding their faces. What a terrible drink! What a painful resting place! [30] As for those who believe and do good deeds—We do not let the reward of anyone who does a good deed go to waste—[31] they will have Gardens of lasting bliss graced with flowing streams. There they will be adorned with bracelets of gold. There they will wear green garments of fine silk and brocade. There they will be comfortably seated on soft chairs. What a blessed reward! What a pleasant resting place!

[32] Tell them the parable of two men: for one of them We made two gardens of grape vines, surrounded them with date palms, and put corn fields in between; [33] both gardens yielded fruit and did not fail in any way; We made a stream flow through them, [34] and so he had abundant fruit. One day, while talking to his friend, he said, 'I have more wealth and a larger following than you.' [35] He went into his garden and wronged himself by saying, 'I do not think this will ever

[a] When the Prophet was challenged by the Meccans, prompted by the Jews, to explain the story of the Sleepers, he promised to do it 'tomorrow', but did not receive revelation about it for some days afterwards.

[b] The notables of Mecca tried to persuade the Prophet to attend to them and drive away his humble followers.

perish, [36] or that the Last Hour will ever come—even if I were to be taken back to my Lord, I would certainly find something even better there.' [37] His companion retorted, 'Have you no faith in Him who created you from dust, from a small drop of fluid, then shaped you into a man? [38] But, for me, He is God, my Lord, and I will never set up any partner with Him. [39] If only, when you entered your garden, you had said, "This is God's will. There is no power not [given] by God." Although you see I have less wealth and offspring than you, [40] my Lord may well give me something better than your garden, and send thunderbolts on your garden from the sky, so that it becomes a heap of barren dust; [41] or its water may sink so deep into the ground that you will never be able to reach it again.' [42] And so it was: his fruit was completely destroyed, and there he was, wringing his hands over what he had invested in it, as it drooped on its trellises, and saying, 'I wish I had not set up any partner to my Lord.' [43] He had no forces to help him other than God—he could not even help himself. [44] In that situation, the only protection is that of God, the True God: He gives the best rewards and the best outcome.

[45] Tell them, too, what the life of this world is like: We send water down from the skies and the earth's vegetation absorbs it, but soon the plants turn to dry stubble scattered about by the wind—God has power over everything. [46] Wealth and children are the attractions of this worldly life, but lasting good works have a better reward with your Lord and give better grounds for hope. [47] One day We shall make the mountains move, and you will see the earth as an open plain. We shall gather all people together, leaving no one. [48] They will be lined up before your Lord: 'Now you have come to Us as We first created you, although you claimed We had not made any such appointment for you.' [49] The record of their deeds will be laid open and you will see the guilty, dismayed at what they contain, saying, 'Woe to us! What a record this is! It does not leave any deed, small or large, unaccounted for!' They will find everything they ever did laid in front of them: your Lord will not be unjust to anyone.

[50] We said to the angels, 'Bow down before Adam,' and they all bowed down, except Iblis: he was one of the jinn and he disobeyed his Lord's command. Are you [people] going to take him and his offspring as your masters instead of Me, even though they are your enemies? What a bad bargain for the evildoers! [51] I did not make them witnesses to the creation of the heavens and earth, nor to their

own creation; I do not take as My supporters those who lead others astray. ⁵²On that Day, God will say, 'Call on those you claimed were My partners,' and they will call on them but they will not answer; We shall set a deadly gulf between them. ⁵³The evildoers will see the Fire and they will realize that they are about to fall into it: they will find no escape from it.

⁵⁴In this Qur'an We have presented every kind of description for people but man is more contentious than any other creature. ⁵⁵Now that guidance has come to them, what stops these people believing and asking forgiveness of their Lord before the fate of earlier peoples annihilates them and they meet their punishment face to face? ⁵⁶We only send messengers to bring good news and to deliver warning, yet the disbelievers seek to refute the truth with false arguments and make fun of My messages and warnings. ⁵⁷Who could be more wrong than the person who is reminded of his Lord's messages and turns his back on them, ignoring what his hands are storing up for him [in the Hereafter]? We have put covers over their hearts and heaviness in their ears—they cannot understand the Qur'an and although you call them to guidance [Prophet] they will never be guided. ⁵⁸Your Lord is forgiving and merciful: if He took them to task for the wrongs they have done, He would hasten their punishment on. They have an appointed time from which they will have no escape, ⁵⁹[just like] the former communities We destroyed for doing wrong: We set an appointed time for their destruction.

⁶⁰Moses said to his servant, 'I will not rest until I reach the place where the two seas meet, even if it takes me years!' ⁶¹but when they reached the place where the two seas meet, they had forgotten all about their fish, which made its way into the sea and swam away. ⁶²They journeyed on, and then Moses said to his servant, 'Give us our lunch! This journey of ours is very tiring,' ⁶³and [the servant] said, 'Remember when we were resting by the rock? I forgot the fish—Satan made me forget to pay attention to it—and it [must have] made its way into the sea.' 'How strange!' ⁶⁴Moses said, 'Then that was the place we were looking for.' So the two turned back, retraced their footsteps, ⁶⁵and found one of Our servants—a man to whom We had granted Our mercy and whom We had given knowledge of Our own. ⁶⁶Moses said to him, 'May I follow you so that you can teach me some of the right guidance you have been taught?' ⁶⁷The man said, 'You will not be able to bear with me

patiently. [68] How could you be patient in matters beyond your comprehension?' [69] Moses said, 'God willing, you will find me patient. I
will not disobey you in any way.' [70] The man said, 'If you follow me
then, do not query anything I do before I mention it to you myself.'

[71] They travelled on. Then, when they got into a boat, and the man
made a hole in it, Moses said, 'How could you make a hole in it? Do
you want to drown its passengers? What a strange thing to do!' [72] He
replied, 'Did I not tell you that you would never be able to bear with
me patiently?' [73] Moses said, 'Forgive me for forgetting. Do not make
it too hard for me to follow you.' [74] And so they travelled on. Then,
when they met a young boy and the man killed him, Moses said,
'How could you kill an innocent person? He has not killed anyone!
What a terrible thing to do!' [75] He replied, 'Did I not tell you that you
would never be able to bear with me patiently?' [76] Moses said, 'From
now on, if I query anything you do, banish me from your company—
you have put up with enough from me.' [77] And so they travelled on.
Then, when they came to a town and asked the inhabitants for food
but were refused hospitality, they saw a wall there that was on the
point of falling down and the man repaired it. Moses said, 'But if
you had wished you could have taken payment for doing that.' [78] He
said, 'This is where you and I part company. I will tell you the
meaning of the things you could not bear with patiently: [79] the boat
belonged to some needy people who made their living from the sea
and I damaged it because I knew that coming after them was a king
who was seizing every [serviceable] boat by force. [80] The young boy
had parents who were people of faith, and so, fearing he would
trouble them through wickedness and disbelief, [81] we wished that
their Lord should give them another child—purer and more compassionate—in his place. [82] The wall belonged to two young orphans
in the town and there was buried treasure beneath it belonging to
them. Their father had been a righteous man, so your Lord intended
them to reach maturity and then dig up their treasure as a mercy
from your Lord. I did not do [these things] of my own accord: these
are the explanations for those things you could not bear with
patience.'

[83] [Prophet], they ask you about Dhu 'l-Qarnayn.[a] Say, 'I will tell
you something about him.' [84] We established his power in the land,

---

[a] Literally 'the two-horned one', said by some to be Alexander the Great.

and gave him the means to achieve everything. ⁸⁵He travelled on a certain road; ⁸⁶then, when he came to the setting of the sun, he found it setting into a muddy spring. Nearby he found some people and We said, 'Dhu 'l-Qarnayn, you may choose [which of them] to punish or show kindness to.' ⁸⁷He answered, 'We shall punish those who have done evil, and when they are returned to their Lord He will punish them [even more] severely, ⁸⁸while those who believed and did good deeds will have the best of rewards: we shall command them to do what is easy for them.' ⁸⁹He travelled on; ⁹⁰then, when he came to the rising of the sun, he found it rising on a people for whom We had provided no shelter from it. ⁹¹And so it was: We had full knowledge of him.

⁹²He travelled on; ⁹³then, when he reached a place between two mountain barriers, he found beside them a people who could barely understand him. ⁹⁴They said, 'Dhu 'l-Qarnayn, Gog and Magog are ruining this land. Will you build a barrier between them and us if we pay you a tribute?' ⁹⁵He answered, 'The power my Lord has given me is better than any tribute, but if you lend me your strength, I will put up a fortification between you and them: ⁹⁶bring me lumps of iron!' and then, when he had filled the gap between the two mountainsides [he said], 'Work your bellows!' and then, when he had made it glow like fire, he said, 'Bring me molten metal to pour over it!' ⁹⁷Their enemies could not scale the barrier, nor could they pierce it, ⁹⁸and he said, 'This is a mercy from my Lord. But when my Lord's promise is fulfilled, He will raze this barrier to the ground—my Lord's promise always comes true.' ⁹⁹On that Day, We shall let them surge against each other like waves and then the Trumpet will be blown and We shall gather them all together. ¹⁰⁰We shall show Hell to the disbelievers, ¹⁰¹those whose eyes were blind to My signs, those who were unable to hear—¹⁰²did they think that they could take My servants as masters instead of Me?—We have prepared Hell as the disbelievers' resting place.

¹⁰³Say [Prophet], 'Shall we*a* tell you who has the most to lose by their actions, ¹⁰⁴whose efforts in this world are misguided, even when they think they are doing good work? ¹⁰⁵It is those who disbelieve in their Lord's messages and deny that they will meet Him.' Their deeds come to nothing: on the Day of Resurrection We shall

---

a This 'we' presumably refers to the Prophet and his community of believers.

give them no weight. [106] Their recompense for having disbelieved and made fun of My messages and My messengers will be Hell. [107] But those who believe and do good deeds will be given the Gardens of Paradise. [108] There they will remain, never wishing to leave.

[109] Say [Prophet], 'If the whole ocean[a] were ink for writing the words of my Lord, it would run dry before those words were exhausted'—even if We were to add another ocean to it. [110] Say, 'I am only a human being, like you, to whom it has been revealed that your God is One—anyone who fears[b] to meet his Lord should do good deeds and give no one a share in the worship due to his Lord.

[a] The term *bahr* refers to all wide expanses of water.
[b] See note to 10: 7.

19. MARY

A Meccan sura which takes its name from the story of Mary (verses 16–35). It recounts the grace given by God to a number of prophets and tells aspects of their stories. The claim that Jesus is the son of God is firmly denied, as is the assertion of the pagans of Mecca that the angels are God's daughters. From verses 66 to 98 the sura discusses the arrogant assertions of the disbelievers of Mecca. The Prophet is told that God's punishment is coming to them and exhorted not to be impatient for it to arrive or to receive the revelation (verses 64–5).

In the name of God, the Lord of Mercy, the Giver of Mercy

¹*Kaf Ha Ya 'Ayn Sad*

²This is an account of your Lord's grace towards His servant, Zachariah, ³when he called to his Lord secretly, saying, ⁴'Lord, my bones have weakened and my hair is ashen grey, but never, Lord, have I ever prayed to You in vain: ⁵I fear [what] my kinsmen [will do] when I am gone, for my wife is barren, so grant me a successor—a gift from You—⁶to be my heir and the heir of the family of Jacob. Lord, make him well pleasing to You.' ⁷'Zachariah, We bring you good news of a son whose name will be John—We have chosen this name for no one before him.' ⁸He said, 'Lord, how can I have a son when my wife is barren, and I am old and frail?' ⁹He said, 'This is what your Lord has said: "It is easy for Me: I created you, though you were nothing before." '

¹⁰He said, 'Give me a sign, Lord.' He said, 'Your sign is that you will not be able to speak to anyone for three full [days and] nights'—¹¹he went out of the sanctuary to his people and signalled to them to praise God morning and evening.

¹²[We said], 'John, hold on to the Scripture firmly.' While he was still a boy, We granted him wisdom, ¹³tenderness from Us, and purity. He was devout, ¹⁴kind to his parents, not domineering or rebellious. ¹⁵Peace was on him the day he was born, the day he died, and it will be on him the day he is raised to life again.

¹⁶Mention in the Qur'an the story of Mary. She withdrew from

her family to a place to the east [17] and secluded herself away; We sent Our Spirit to appear before her in the form of a perfected man. [18] She said, 'I seek the Lord of Mercy's protection against you: if you have any fear of Him [do not approach]!' [19] but he said, 'I am but a Messenger from your Lord, [come] to announce to you the gift of a pure son.' [20] She said, 'How can I have a son when no man has touched me? I have not been unchaste,' [21] and he said, 'This is what your Lord said: "It is easy for Me—We shall make him a sign to all people, a blessing from Us." ' [22] And so it was ordained: she conceived him. She withdrew to a distant place [23] and, when the pains of childbirth drove her to [cling to] the trunk of a palm tree, she exclaimed, 'I wish I had been long dead and forgotten before all this!' [24] but a voice cried to her from below, 'Do not worry: your Lord has provided a stream at your feet [25] and, if you shake the trunk of the palm tree towards you, it will deliver fresh ripe dates for you, [26] so eat, drink, be glad, and say to anyone you may see: "I have vowed to the Lord of Mercy to abstain[a] from conversation, and I will not talk to anyone today." '

[27] She went back to her people carrying the child, and they said, 'Mary! You must have done something terrible! [28] Sister[b] of Aaron! Your father was not an evil man; your mother was not unchaste!' [29] She pointed at him. They said, 'How can we converse with an infant?'[c] [30] [But] he said: 'I am a servant of God. He has granted me the Scripture; made me a prophet; [31] made me blessed wherever I may be—He commanded me to pray, to give alms as long as I live, [32] to cherish my mother—He did not make me domineering or graceless. [33] Peace was on me the day I was born, and will be on me the day I die and the day I am raised to life again.' [34] Such was Jesus, son of Mary.

[This is] a statement of the Truth about which they are in doubt: [35] it would not befit God to have a child. He is far above that: when He decrees something, He says only, 'Be,' and it is. [36] 'God is my Lord and your Lord, so serve Him: that is a straight path.'[d] [37] But

---

[a] *Sawm* can mean 'abstinence' from food or from speech.

[b] Either she had a brother called Aaron, or was simply of Aaron's tribe: in Arabic 'sister/brother of' can mean 'relation of', e.g. 'brother of Hamdan' meaning 'of the tribe of Hamdan'.

[c] See note to 3: 46. Here again the term *mahd* refers to any level place rather than the concrete 'cradle'.

[d] Some suggest that Muhammad is ordered to make this statement; others that it is Jesus speaking.

factions have differed among themselves. What suffering will come to those who obscure the truth when a dreadful Day arrives! [38] How sharp of hearing, how sharp of sight they will be when they come to Us, although now they are clearly off course! Warn them [Muhammad] of the Day of Remorse when the matter will be decided, [39] for they are heedless and do not believe. [40] It is We who will inherit the earth and all who are on it: they will all be returned to Us.

[41] Mention too, in the Qur'an, the story of Abraham. He was a man of truth, a prophet. [42] He said to his father, 'Father, why do you worship something that can neither hear nor see nor benefit you in any way? [43] Father, knowledge that has not reached you has come to me, so follow me: I will guide you to an even path. [44] Father, do not worship Satan—Satan has rebelled against the Lord of Mercy. [45] Father, I fear that a punishment from the Lord of Mercy may afflict you and that you may become Satan's companion [in Hell].'[a] [46] His father answered, 'Abraham, do you reject my gods? I will stone you if you do not stop this. Keep out of my way!' [47] Abraham said, 'Peace be with you: I will beg my Lord to forgive you—He is always gracious to me— [48] but for now I will leave you, and the idols you all pray to, and I will pray to my Lord and trust that my prayer will not be in vain.' [49] When he left his people and those they served beside God, We granted him Isaac and Jacob and made them both prophets: [50] We granted Our grace to all of them, and gave them a noble reputation.

[51] Mention too, in the Qur'an, the story of Moses. He was specially chosen, a messenger and a prophet: [52] We called to him from the right-hand side of the mountain and brought him close to Us in secret communion; [53] out of Our grace We granted him his brother Aaron as a prophet. [54] Mention too, in the Qur'an, the story of Ishmael. He was true to his promise, a messenger and a prophet. [55] He commanded his household to pray and give alms, and his Lord was well pleased with him. [56] Mention too, in the Qur'an, the story of Idris. He was a man of truth, a prophet. [57] We raised him to a high position.

[58] These were the prophets God blessed—from the seed of Adam, of those We carried in the Ark with Noah, from the seed of Abraham

---

[a] Or 'that you will be a supporter of Satan'.

and Israel—and those We guided and chose. When they heard the revelations of the Lord of Mercy they fell down on their knees and wept, ⁵⁹but there came after them generations who neglected prayer and were driven by their own desires. These will come face to face with their evil, ⁶⁰but those who repent, who believe, who do righteous deeds, will enter Paradise. They will not be wronged in the least: ⁶¹they will enter the Gardens of Lasting Bliss, promised by the Lord of Mercy to His servants—it is not yet seen but truly His promise will be fulfilled. ⁶²There they will hear only peaceful talk, nothing bad; there they will be given provision morning and evening. ⁶³That is the Garden We shall give as their own to those of Our servants who were devout.

⁶⁴[Gabriel said],ᵃ 'We only descend [with revelation] at your Lord's command—everything before us, everything behind us, everything in between, all belongs to Him—your Lord is never forgetful. ⁶⁵He is Lord of the heavens and earth and everything in between so worship Him: be steadfast in worshipping Him. Do you know of anyone equal to Him?'

⁶⁶Man says, 'What? Once I am dead, will I be brought back to life?' ⁶⁷but does he not remember that We created him when he was nothing before? ⁶⁸By your Lord [Prophet] We shall gather them and the devils together and set them on their knees around Hell; ⁶⁹We will seize out of each group those who were most disobedient towards the Lord of Mercy—⁷⁰We know best who most deserves to burn in Hell—⁷¹but every single one of youᵇ will approach it, a decree from your Lord which must be fulfilled. ⁷²We shall save the devout and leave the evildoers there on their knees.

⁷³When Our revelations are recited to them in all their clarity, [all that] the disbelievers say to the believers [is], 'Which side is better situated? Which side has the better following?' ⁷⁴We have destroyed many a generation before them who surpassed them in riches and outward glitter! ⁷⁵Say [Prophet], 'As for the misguided, may the Lord of Mercy lengthen their lives: still, when they are confronted with what they have been warned about—either the punishment [in this life] or the Hour [of Judgement]—they will realize who is worse

---

ᵃ This is a response from Gabriel to the Prophet's request for more frequent visits (see Bukhari, *Sahih*, Book of Tafsir, Sura 19).

ᵇ This is taken to refer either to the disbelievers mentioned here, or to all humanity.

situated and who has the weakest forces.' ⁷⁶But God gives more guidance to those who are guided, and good deeds of lasting merit are best and most rewarding in your Lord's sight. ⁷⁷Have you considered the man who rejects Our revelation, who says, 'I will certainly be given wealth and children'? ⁷⁸Has he penetrated the unknown or received a pledge to that effect from the Lord of Mercy? ⁷⁹No! We shall certainly record what he says and prolong his punishment: ⁸⁰We shall inherit from him all that he speaks of and he will come to Us all alone.

⁸¹They have taken other gods beside God to give them strength, ⁸²but these gods will reject their worship and will even turn against them. ⁸³Have you [Prophet] not considered that We send devils to incite the disbelievers to sin? ⁸⁴There is no need for you to be impatient concerning them: We are counting down their [allotted] time. ⁸⁵On the Day We gather the righteous as an honoured company before the Lord of Mercy ⁸⁶and drive the sinful like a thirsty herd into Hell, ⁸⁷no one will have power to intercede except for those who have permission*ᵃ* from the Lord of Mercy.

⁸⁸The disbelievers say, 'The Lord of Mercy has offspring.'*ᵇ* ⁸⁹How terrible is this thing you assert: ⁹⁰it almost causes the heavens to be torn apart, the earth to split asunder, the mountains to crumble to pieces, ⁹¹that they attribute offspring to the Lord of Mercy. ⁹²It does not befit the Lord of Mercy [to have offspring]: ⁹³there is no one in the heavens or earth who will not come to the Lord of Mercy as a servant—⁹⁴He has counted them all: He has numbered them exactly—⁹⁵and they will each return to Him on the Day of Resurrection all alone.

⁹⁶But the Lord of Mercy will give love to those who believe and do righteous deeds: ⁹⁷We have made it*ᶜ* easy, in your own language [Prophet], so that you may bring glad news to the righteous and warnings to a stubborn people. ⁹⁸How many generations We have destroyed before them! Do you perceive a single one of them now, or hear as much as a whisper?

ᵃ For the meaning of *'ahd* as *idhn* 'permission' see Baydawi. Cf. 10: 3; 78: 38.

ᵇ Many translators say 'a son' here, not realizing that *walad* in classical Arabic means 'child' or 'children'. The discussion here is about the pagans of Mecca, who said that the angels were daughters of God.

ᶜ Either what is said in this sura or the whole Qur'an.

20. TA HA

A Meccan sura that both begins and ends with mention of the Qur'an: it was not sent to the Prophet to cause him grief but is a clear proof from his Lord. The example of Moses is given as a lengthy account in order to encourage the Prophet and show the end of the disbelievers. The destruction of earlier generations is cited as a lesson from which the disbelievers should learn. The Prophet is ordered to be patient and to persevere with his worship.

In the name of God, the Lord of Mercy, the Giver of Mercy

¹ *Ta Ha*[a]

² It was not to distress you [Prophet] that We sent down the Qur'an to you, ³ but as a reminder for those who hold God in awe, ⁴ a revelation from the One who created the earth and the high heaven, ⁵ the Lord of Mercy, established on the throne. ⁶ Everything in the heavens and on earth, everything between them, everything beneath the soil, belongs to Him. ⁷ Whatever you may say aloud, He knows what you keep secret and what is even more hidden. ⁸ God—there is no god but Him—the most excellent names belong to Him.

⁹ Has the story of Moses come to you [Prophet]?[b] ¹⁰ He saw a fire and said to his people, 'Stay here—I can see a fire. Maybe I can bring you a flaming brand from it or find some guidance there.' ¹¹ When he came to the fire, he was summoned, 'Moses! ¹² I am your Lord. Take off your shoes: you are in the sacred valley of Tuwa. ¹³ I have chosen you, so listen to what is being revealed. ¹⁴ I am God; there is no god but Me. So worship Me and keep up the prayer so that you remember Me. ¹⁵ The Hour is coming—though I choose[c] to keep it hidden—for each soul to be rewarded for its labour. ¹⁶ Do not let anyone who does not believe in it and follows his own desires distract you from it, and so bring you to ruin.'

[a] There is an opinion that *ta ha* are not isolated letters but 'O man!' in the Yemeni dialect of 'Akk (Razi). For the significance of the isolated letters as a whole, see note to 2: 1.

[b] This construction is an idiom in Arabic implying 'think well about it' or 'take a lesson from this'.

[c] Abu Muslim interprets *akadu* as *uridu*, 'I wish' or 'I choose' (Razi).

¹⁷'Moses, what is that in your right hand?' ¹⁸'It is my staff,' he said, 'I lean on it; restrain my sheep with it;^a I also have other uses for it.' ¹⁹God said, 'Throw it down, Moses.' ²⁰He threw it down and—lo and behold!—it became a fast-moving snake. ²¹He said, 'Pick it up without fear: We shall turn it back to its former state. ²²Now place your hand under your armpit: it will come out white, though unharmed: that is another sign. ²³We do this to show you some of Our greatest signs. ²⁴Go to Pharaoh, for he has truly become a tyrant.' ²⁵Moses said, 'Lord, lift up my heart ²⁶and ease my task for me. ²⁷Untie my tongue ²⁸so that they may understand my words ²⁹and give me a helper from my family, ³⁰my brother Aaron— ³¹augment my strength through him. ³²Let him share my task ³³so that we can glorify You much ³⁴and remember You often: ³⁵You are always watching over us.'

³⁶God said, 'Moses, your request is granted. ³⁷Indeed We showed you favour before. ³⁸We inspired your mother, saying, ³⁹"Put your child into the chest, then place him in the river. Let the river wash him on to its bank, and he will be taken in by an enemy of Mine and his." I showered you with My love and planned that you should be reared under My watchful eye. ⁴⁰Your sister went out, saying, "I will tell you someone who will nurse him," then We returned you to your mother so that she could rejoice and not grieve. Later you killed a man, but We saved you from distress and tried you with other tests. You stayed among the people of Midian for years, then you came here as I ordained. ⁴¹I have chosen you for Myself. ⁴²Go, you and your brother, with My signs, and make sure that you remember Me. ⁴³Go, both of you, to Pharaoh, for he has exceeded all bounds. ⁴⁴Speak to him gently so that he may take heed, or fear his Lord.'

⁴⁵They said, 'Lord, we fear he will do us great harm or exceed all bounds.' ⁴⁶He said, 'Do not be afraid, I am with you both, hearing and seeing everything. ⁴⁷Go and tell him, "We are your Lord's messengers, so send the Children of Israel with us and do not oppress them. We have brought you a sign from your Lord. Peace be upon whoever follows the right guidance; ⁴⁸it has been revealed to us that punishment falls on whoever rejects the truth and turns his back on it." '

⁴⁹[Pharaoh] said, 'Moses, who is this Lord of yours?' ⁵⁰Moses

---

^a Or 'beat down leaves for my sheep with it'.

said, 'Our Lord is He who gave everything its form, then gave it guidance.' [51] He said, 'What about former generations?' [52] Moses said, 'My Lord alone has knowledge of them, all in a record; my Lord does not err or forget.' [53] It was He who spread out the earth for you and traced routes in it. He sent down water from the sky. With that water We bring forth every kind of plant, [54] so eat, and graze your cattle. There are truly signs in all this for people of understanding. [55] From the earth We created you, into it We shall return you, and from it We shall raise you a second time. [56] We showed Pharaoh all Our signs, but he denied them and refused [to change].

[57] [Pharaoh] said, 'Have you come to drive us from our land with your sorcery, Moses? [58] We will confront you with sorcery to match your own: make an appointment between us which neither of us will fail to keep, in a mutually agreeable place.' [59] He said, 'Your meeting will be on the day of the feast, so let the people be assembled when the sun has risen high.'

[60] Pharaoh withdrew and gathered his resources,[a] then he returned. [61] Moses said to them, 'Beware, do not invent lies against God or He will destroy you with His punishment. Whoever invents lies will fail.' [62] So they discussed their plan among themselves, talking secretly, [63] saying, 'These two men are sorcerers. Their purpose is to drive you out of your land with their sorcery and put an end to your time-honoured way of life. [64] So gather your resources and line up for the contest. Whoever wins today is sure to prosper.' [65] They said, 'Moses, will you throw first or shall we?' [66] 'You throw,' said Moses, and—lo and behold!—through their sorcery, their ropes and staffs seemed to him to be moving. [67] Moses was alarmed, [68] but We said, 'Do not be afraid, you have the upper hand. [69] Throw down what is in your right hand. It will swallow up what they have produced. They have only produced the tricks of a sorcerer, and a sorcerer will not prosper, wherever he goes.'

[70] [So it was, and] the sorcerers threw themselves down in submission. 'We believe,' they said, 'in the Lord of Aaron and Moses.' [71] Pharaoh said, 'Do you believe in him before I have given you permission? This must be your master, the man who taught you witchcraft. I shall certainly cut off your alternate hands and feet,[b]

---

[a] Literally 'his mischief', *kaydahu*. This could refer to his sorcerers or to the plots he made.

[b] See note to 5: 33.

then crucify you on the trunks of palm trees. You will know for certain which of us has the fiercer and more lasting punishment.' [72] They said, 'We shall never prefer you to the clear sign that has come to us, nor to Him who created us. So decide whatever you will: you can only decide matters of this present life—[73] we believe in our Lord, [hoping] He may forgive us our sins and the sorcery that you forced us to practise—God is better and more lasting.'

[74] Hell will be the reward of those who return to their Lord as evildoers: there they will stay, neither living nor dying. [75] But those who return to their Lord as believers with righteous deeds will be rewarded with the highest of ranks, [76] Gardens of lasting bliss graced with flowing streams, and there they will stay. Such is the reward of those who purify themselves.

[77] We revealed to Moses, 'Go out at night with My servants and strike a dry path for them across the sea.[a] Have no fear of being overtaken and do not be dismayed.' [78] Pharaoh pursued them with his armies and was overwhelmed by the sea. [79] Pharaoh truly led his people astray; he did not guide them.

[80] Children of Israel, We rescued you from your enemies. We made a pledge with you on the right-hand side of the mountain. We sent down manna and quails for you, [81] 'Eat from the good things We have provided for you, but do not overstep the bounds, or My wrath will descend on you. Anyone on whom My wrath descends has truly fallen. [82] Yet I am most forgiving towards those who repent, believe, do righteous deeds, and stay on the right path.'

[83] [God said], 'Moses, what has made you come ahead of your people in such haste?'[b] [84] and he said, 'They are following in my footsteps. I rushed to You, Lord, to please You,' [85] but God said, 'We have tested your people in your absence: the Samiri[c] has led them astray.' [86] Moses returned to his people, angry and aggrieved. He said, 'My people, did your Lord not make you a gracious promise? Was my absence too long for you? Did you break your word to me because you wanted anger to fall on you from your Lord?' [87] They said, 'We did not break our word to you deliberately. We were burdened with the weight of people's jewellery, so we threw it [into the

---

[a] *Bahr*, 'sea', means any expanse of water, fresh or salty. Cf. 35: 12.

[b] Moses had left his people in the charge of Aaron to contemplate on Mount Sinai. See 7: 142 ff.

[c] Razi suggests various unsubstantiated identities for the Samiri.

fire], and the Samiri did the same,' [88] but he [used the molten jewellery to] produce an image of a calf which made a lowing sound, and they said, 'This is your god and Moses' god. He has forgotten [his faith].' [89] Did they not see that [the calf] gave them no answer, that it had no power to harm or benefit them? [90] Aaron did say to them, 'My people, this calf is a test for you. Your true Lord is the Lord of Mercy, so follow me and obey my orders,' [91] but they replied, 'We shall not give up our devotion to it until Moses returns to us.'

[92] Moses said, 'When you realized they had gone astray, what prevented you, Aaron, [93] from coming after me? How could you disobey my orders?' [94] He said, 'Son of my mother—let go of my beard and my hair!—I was afraid you would say, "You have caused division among the children of Israel and have not heeded what I said."' [95] Moses said, 'And what was the matter with you, Samiri?' [96] He replied, 'I saw something they did not, and I took in some of the teachings of the Messenger but tossed them aside, and so my soul prompted me to do what I did.' [97] Moses said, 'Get away from here! Your lot in this life is to say, "Do not touch me,"[a] but you have an appointment from which there is no escape. Look at your god which you have kept on worshipping—we shall grind it down[b] and scatter it into the sea. [98] [People], your true god is the One God—there is no god but Him—whose knowledge embraces everything.'

[99] In this way We relate to you [Prophet] stories of what happened before. We have given you Our Qur'an [100] and whoever turns away from it will bear a heavy burden on the Day of Resurrection—[101] it will last indefinitely and be grievous indeed! On that Day [102] when the trumpet is sounded and We gather the sinful, sightless,[c] [103] they will murmur to one another, 'You stayed only ten days [on earth]'—[104] We know best what they say—but the more perceptive of them will say, 'Your stay [on earth] was only a single day.'

[105] They will ask you [Prophet] about the mountains: say, '[On that Day] my Lord will blast them into dust [106] and leave a flat plain, [107] with no peak or trough to be seen. [108] On that Day, people will follow the summoner from whom there is no escape; every voice will be hushed for the Lord of Mercy; only whispers will be heard. [109] On

---

[a] Another interpretation is that the Samiri will become a social outcast.

[b] *Harraka* in classical usage has the meaning 'grind', as used here, rather than 'burn'.

[c] *Zurq* from *azraq*, which means, among other things, 'blind'. Cf. verses 124–6.

that Day, intercession will be useless except from those to whom the Lord of Mercy has granted permission and whose words He approves—[110]He knows what is before and behind them, though they do not comprehend Him—[111]and [all] faces[a] will be humbled before the Living, Ever Watchful One. Those burdened with evil deeds will despair, [112]but whoever has done righteous deeds and believed need have no fear of injustice or deprivation.' [113]We have sent the Qur'an down in the Arabic tongue and given all kinds of warnings in it, so that they may beware or take heed—[114]exalted be God, the one who is truly in control.

[Prophet], do not rush to recite before the revelation is fully complete[b] but say, 'Lord, increase me in knowledge!' [115]We also commanded Adam before you, but he forgot and We found him lacking in constancy. [116]When We said to the angels, 'Bow down before Adam,' they did. But Iblis refused, [117]so We said, 'Adam, this is your enemy, yours and your wife's: do not let him drive you out of the garden and make you miserable. [118]In the garden you will never go hungry, feel naked, [119]be thirsty, or suffer the heat of the sun.' [120]But Satan whispered to Adam, saying, 'Adam, shall I show you the tree of immortality and a kingdom that never decays?' [121]and they both ate from it. They became conscious of their nakedness and began to cover themselves with leaves from the garden. Adam disobeyed his Lord and was led astray—[122]later his Lord brought him close, accepted his repentance, and guided him—[123]God said, 'Get out of the garden as each other's enemy.'[c]

Whoever follows My guidance, when it comes to you [people], will not go astray nor fall into misery, [124]but whoever turns away from it will have a life of great hardship. We shall bring him blind to the Assembly on the Day of Resurrection [125]and he will say, 'Lord, why did You bring me here blind? I was sighted before!' [126]God will say, 'This is how it is: You ignored Our revelations when they came to you, so today you will be ignored.' [127]This is how We reward those who go to excess, and who do not believe in their Lord's revelations. The greatest and most enduring punishment is in the Hereafter.

---

[a] This can also mean 'their faces'.

[b] Muhammad, when repeating to Gabriel each revelation, after the angel delivered it, sometimes in his eagerness started repeating even before Gabriel had finished revealing. See also 75: 16–19.

[c] Both parties, cf. 2: 36 and note.

[128] Do they not draw a lesson from the many generations We destroyed before them, through whose dwelling places they now walk? There truly are signs in this for anyone with understanding!

[129] If it were not for a preordained Word from your Lord [Prophet], they would already have been destroyed. Their time has been set, [130] so [Prophet] be patient with what they say—celebrate the praise of your Lord, before the rising and setting of the sun, celebrate His praise during the night, and at the beginning and end of the day, so that you may find contentment—[131] and do not gaze longingly at what We have given some of them to enjoy, the finery of this present life: We test them through this, but the provision of your Lord is better and more lasting. [132] Order your people[a] to pray, and pray steadfastly yourself. We are not asking you to give Us provision;[b] We provide for you, and the rewards of the Hereafter belong to the devout.

[133] The disbelievers say, 'Why does he not bring us a sign from his Lord?' Have they not been given clear proof confirming what was in the earlier scriptures? [134] If We had destroyed them through punishment before this Messenger came, they would have said, 'Lord, if only You had sent us a messenger before we suffered humiliation and disgrace, we could have followed Your revelations!' [135] [Prophet], say, 'We are all waiting, so you carry on waiting: you will come to learn who has followed the even path, and been rightly guided.'

---

[a] Or 'your family'.　　[b] Cf. 51: 57.

21. THE PROPHETS

A Meccan sura which takes its name from the list of prophets mentioned from verse 48 to verse 91. It stresses that fact that Muhammad is a man like earlier prophets, and has been given the same message to declare the unity of God. It warns the disbelievers of the approaching Judgement from which there is no escape.

In the name of God, the Lord of Mercy, the Giver of Mercy

¹ Ever closer to people draws their reckoning, while they turn away, heedless. ² Whenever any fresh revelation comes to them from their Lord, they listen to it with amusement ³ and frivolous hearts. The evildoers conferred in secret: 'Is this man anything but a mortal like yourselves? Are you going to fall under his spell with your eyes wide open?' ⁴ He said,ᵃ 'My Lord knows everything that is said in the heavens and the earth: He is the All Hearing, the All Knowing.' ⁵ Some say, 'Muddled dreams'; others, 'He made it up'; yet others, 'He is just a poet, let him show us a sign as previous messengers did.' ⁶ But of the communities We destroyed before them not a single one believed. Will these now believe? ⁷ And even before your time [Prophet], all the messengers We sent were only men We inspired— if you [disbelievers] do not know, ask people who know the Scripture—⁸ the bodies We gave them could not do without food, nor were they immortal. ⁹ We fulfilled Our promise to them in the end: We saved them and those We wished to save, and We destroyed those who exceeded all bounds.

¹⁰ And now We have sent down to you [people] a Scripture to remind you. Will you not use your reason? ¹¹ How many communities of evildoers We have destroyed! How many others We have raised up in their places! ¹² When they felt Our might coming upon them, see how they tried to escape it! ¹³ 'Do not try to escape. Go back to your homes and the pleasure you revelled in: you may be questioned.' ¹⁴ They said, 'Woe to us! We were wrong!' ¹⁵ and that cry of theirs did not cease until We made them burnt-off stubble.

ᵃ Here and in verse 112 an alternative reading is the imperative, *qul* ('say').

¹⁶ We did not create the heavens and the earth and everything between them for play. ¹⁷ If We had wished for a pastime, We had it in Us—if We had wished for any such thing. ¹⁸ No! We hurl the truth against falsehood, and truth obliterates it—see how falsehood vanishes away! Woe to you for the way you describe God! ¹⁹ Everyone in the heavens and earth belongs to Him, and those that are with Him are never too proud to worship Him, nor do they grow weary; ²⁰ they glorify Him tirelessly night and day.

²¹ Have they chosen any gods from the earth who can give life to the dead? ²² If there had been in the heavens or earth any gods but Him, both heavens and earth would be in ruins: God, Lord of the Throne, is far above the things they say—²³ He cannot be called to account for anything He does, whereas they will be called to account. ²⁴ Have they chosen to worship other gods instead of Him? Say, 'Bring your proof. This is the Scripture for those who are with me and the Scripture for those who went before me.' But most of them do not recognize the truth, so they pay no heed. ²⁵ We never sent any messenger before you [Muhammad] without revealing to him: 'There is no god but Me, so serve Me.' ²⁶ And they say, 'The Lord of Mercy has taken offspring for Himself.'ᵃ May He be exalted! No! They are only His honoured servants: ²⁷ they do not speak before He speaks and they act by His command. ²⁸ He knows what is before them and what is behind them, and they cannot intercede without His permission—indeed they themselves stand in awe of Him. ²⁹ If any of them were to claim, 'I am a god beside Him,' We would reward him with Hell: this is how We reward evildoers.

³⁰ Are the disbelievers not aware that the heavens and the earth used to be joined together and that We ripped them apart, that We made every living thing from water—will they not believe?—³¹ and We put firm mountains on the earth, lest it should sway under them, and set broad paths on it, so that they might follow the right direction, ³² and We made the sky a well-secured canopy—yet from its wonders they turn away. ³³ It is He who created night and day, the sun and the moon, each floating in its orbit. ³⁴ We have not granted everlasting life to any other human being before you either [Muhammad]—if you die, will [the disbelievers] live for ever?

ᵃ The Meccan polytheists claimed the angels were God's daughters.

³⁵ Every soul is certain to taste death: We test you all through the bad and the good, and to Us you will all return. ³⁶ When the disbelievers see you, they laugh at you: 'Is this the one who talks about your gods?' They reject any talk of the Lord of Mercy.

³⁷ Man was created hasty: I will show you My signs soon, so do not ask Me to hasten them. ³⁸ They say, 'When will this promise be fulfilled, if what you say is true?' ³⁹ If the disbelievers only knew, the time will arrive when they will not be able to ward off the Fire from their faces or their backs, and they will get no help! ⁴⁰ It will come upon them suddenly and stupefy them; they will be powerless to push it away; they will not be reprieved.

⁴¹ Messengers before you [Muhammad] were also ridiculed, but those who mocked them were overwhelmed in the end by the very thing they had mocked. ⁴² Say, 'Who could protect you night and day from the Lord of Mercy?' Yet they turn away when their Lord is mentioned. ⁴³ Do they have gods who can defend them against Us? Their gods have no power to help themselves, nor can they be protected from Us. ⁴⁴ We have allowed these sinners and their forefathers to enjoy life for a long time. But do they not see how We are shrinking their borders? Is it they who will prevail? ⁴⁵ Say, 'I warn you only through the Revelation.' The deaf will not hear the warning call, ⁴⁶ yet if a mere breath of your Lord's punishment touches them, they will be sure to cry, 'Woe to us! We were wrong!' ⁴⁷ We will set up scales of justice for the Day of Resurrection so that no one can be wronged in the least, and if there should be even the weight of a mustard seed, We shall bring it out—We take excellent account!

⁴⁸ We gave Moses and Aaron [the Scripture] that distinguishes right from wrong, a light and a reminder for those who are mindful of God, ⁴⁹ those who stand in awe of their Lord, though He is unseen, and who fear the Hour. ⁵⁰ This [Qur'an] too is a blessed message We have sent down—are you [people] going to deny it? ⁵¹ Long ago We bestowed right judgement on Abraham and We knew him well. ⁵² He said to his father and his people, 'What are these images to which you are so devoted?' ⁵³ They replied, 'We found our fathers worshipping them.' ⁵⁴ He said, 'You and your fathers have clearly gone astray.' ⁵⁵ They asked, 'Have you brought us the truth or are you just playing about?' ⁵⁶ He said, 'Listen! Your true Lord is the Lord of the heavens and the earth, He who created them, and I am a

witness to this. [57] By God I shall certainly plot against your idols as soon as you have turned your backs!' [58] He broke them all into pieces, but left the biggest one for them to return to. [59] They said, 'Who has done this to our gods? How wicked he must be!' [60] Some said, 'We heard a youth called Abraham talking about them.' [61] They said, 'Bring him before the eyes of the people, so that they may witness [his trial].' [62] They asked, 'Was it you, Abraham, who did this to our gods?' [63] He said, 'No, it was done by this big one. Ask them, if they can talk.' [64] They turned to one another, saying, 'It is you who are in the wrong,' [65] but then they lapsed again and said, 'You know very well these gods cannot speak.' [66] Abraham said, 'How can you worship what can neither benefit nor harm you, instead of God? [67] Shame on you and on the things you worship instead of God. Have you no sense?' [68] They said, 'Burn him and avenge your gods, if you are going to do the right thing.' [69] But We said, 'Fire, be cool and safe for Abraham.' [70] They planned to harm him, but We made them suffer the greatest loss. [71] We saved him and Lot [and sent them] to the land We blessed for all people, [72] and We gave him Isaac and Jacob as an additional gift, and made each of them righteous. [73] We made all of them leaders, guiding others by Our command, and We inspired them to do good works, to keep up the prayer, and to give alms: they were Our true worshippers. [74] We gave Lot sound judgement and knowledge and saved him from the community who practised obscenities—they were people who broke God's law! [75] We admitted him to Our mercy; he was a righteous man.

[76] Long before that, We answered Noah when he cried out to Us. We saved him and his family from the great calamity [77] and We helped him against the people who rejected Our signs: they were evil people, so We drowned them all.

[78] And remember David and Solomon, when they gave judgement regarding the field into which sheep strayed by night and grazed. We witnessed their judgement [79] and made Solomon understand the case [better], though We gave sound judgement and knowledge to both of them. We made the mountains and the birds celebrate Our praises with David—We did all these things—[80] We taught him how to make coats of mail for the benefit of you [people], to protect you in your wars, but are you grateful for this? [81] We harnessed the stormy wind for Solomon, so that it sped by his command to the land We had blessed—We have knowledge of all things—[82] and We made some of

the jinn[a] subservient to him, to dive for him and do other works besides. We were watching over them.

[83] Remember Job, when he cried to his Lord, 'Suffering has truly afflicted me, but you are the Most Merciful of the merciful.' [84] We answered him, removed his suffering, and restored his family to him, along with more like them, as an act of grace from Us and a reminder for all who serve Us. [85] And remember Ishmael, Idris, and Dhu'l-Kifl:[b] they were all steadfast. [86] We admitted them to Our mercy; they were truly righteous. [87] And remember the man with the whale,[c] when he went off angrily, thinking We had no power over him, but then he cried out in the deep darkness, 'There is no God but You, glory be to You, I was wrong.' [88] We answered him and saved him from distress: this is how We save the faithful. [89] Remember Zachariah, when he cried to his Lord, 'My Lord, do not leave me childless, though You are the best of heirs.' [90] We answered him—We gave him John, and cured his wife of barrenness—they were always keen to do good deeds. They called upon Us out of longing and awe, and humbled themselves before Us. [91] Remember the one who guarded her chastity.[d] We breathed into her from Our Spirit and made her and her son a sign for all people.

[92] [Messengers],[e] this community of yours is one single community and I am your Lord, so serve Me. [93] They have torn their unity apart, but they will all return to Us. [94] If anyone does good deeds and is a believer, his efforts will not be rejected: We record them for him. [95] No community destroyed by Us can escape its return,[f] [96] and when the peoples of Gog and Magog are let loose and swarm swiftly from every highland, [97] when the True Promise draws near, the disbelievers' eyes will stare in terror, and they will say, 'Woe to us! We were not aware of this at all. We were wrong.' [98] You [disbelievers] and what you worship instead of God will be fuel for Hell: that is where you will go—[99] if these [idols] had been real gods they would not have gone there—you will all stay there. [100] There

---

[a] Cf. 34: 12–13.

[b] Some commentators suggest this refers to the prophet Ezekiel. See *Encyclopaedia of Islam* under *Dhu'l-Kifl.*

[c] Jonah. Cf. 37: 139–48.

[d] Mary. Cf. 66: 12.

[e] Cf. 23: 51–3.

[f] Other interpretations are: they will not return to the world; they will not turn away from their misdeeds.

the disbelievers will be groaning piteously, but the [idols] will hear nothing.

[101] But those for whom We have decreed Paradise will be kept far from Hell—[102] they will not hear a murmur from it—and endlessly they will enjoy everything their souls desire. [103] They will have no fear of the great Terror:[a] the angels will receive them with the words, 'This is the Day you were promised!' [104] On that Day, We shall roll up the skies as a writer rolls up [his] scrolls. We shall reproduce creation just as We produced it the first time: this is Our binding promise. We shall certainly do all these things.

[105] We wrote in the Psalms, as We did in [earlier] Scripture: 'My righteous servants will inherit the earth.' [106] There truly is a message in this for the servants of God! [107] It was only as a mercy that We sent you [Prophet] to all people.[b] [108] Say, 'It is revealed to me that your God is one God—will you submit to Him?' [109] But if they turn away, say, 'I have proclaimed the message fairly to you all. I do not know whether the judgement you are promised is near or far, [110] but He knows what you reveal and conceal. [111] I do not know: this [time] may well be a test for you, and enjoyment for a while.' [112] He said,[c] 'My Lord, pass the true judgement.' And, 'Our Lord is the Lord of Mercy. We seek His assistance against what you [disbelievers] say.'

[a] The Day of Judgement.
[b] Or 'We sent you [Prophet] only as a mercy to all people'.
[c] See note to verse 4.

22. THE PILGRIMAGE

A Medinan sura that gets its title from the reference to the sacred rite of the pilgrimage first enacted by Abraham (verse 27). This theme is introduced by the condemnation of those who bar the believers from access to the Sacred Mosque and is followed by permission to fight when attacked. The sura begins with the Day of Judgement and castigates those who worship useless idols, describing them later as powerless to create even a fly. The sura ends by urging the Muslims to persevere in following the faith of Abraham.

In the name of God, the Lord of Mercy, the Giver of Mercy

¹ People, be mindful of your Lord, for the earthquake of the Last Hour will be a mighty thing: ² on the Day you see it, every nursing mother will think no more of her baby, every pregnant female will miscarry, you will think people are drunk when they are not, so severe will be God's torment. ³ Yet still there are some who, with no knowledge, argue about God, who follow every devilish rebel ⁴ fated to lead astray those who take his side and guide them to the suffering of the blazing flame.

⁵ People, remember, if you doubt the Resurrection, that We created you from dust, then a drop of fluid, then a clinging form, then a lump of flesh, both shaped and unshaped: We mean to make Our power clear to you. Whatever We choose We cause to remain in the womb for an appointed time, then We bring you forth as infants and then you grow and reach maturity. Some die young and some are left to live on to such an age that they forget all they once knew. You sometimes see the earth lifeless, yet when We send down water it stirs and swells and produces every kind of joyous growth: ⁶ this is because God is the Truth; He brings the dead back to life; and He has power over everything.

⁷ There is no doubt that the Last Hour is bound to come, nor that God will raise the dead from their graves, ⁸ yet still there are some who, with no knowledge or guidance or any book of enlightenment, argue about God, ⁹ turning scornfully aside to lead others away from God's path. Disgrace in this world awaits such a person and, on the Day of Resurrection, We shall make him taste the suffering of the

Fire. ¹⁰[It will be said], 'This is for what you have stored up with your own hands: God is never unjust to His creatures.'

¹¹ There are also some who serve God with unsteady faith: if something good comes their way, they are satisfied, but if they are tested, they revert to their old ways, losing both this world and the next: that is the clearest loss.¹² Instead of God, they call upon what can neither harm nor help them—that is straying far away—¹³ or invoke one whose harm is closer than his help: an evil master and an evil companion. ¹⁴ But God will admit those who believe and do good deeds to Gardens graced with flowing streams. God does whatever He wishes. ¹⁵ Anyone who thinks that God will not support him in this world and the next should stretch a rope up to the sky, climb all the way up it,ᵃ and see whether this strategy removes the cause of his anger. ¹⁶ In this way, We send the Qur'an down as clear messages, and God guides whoever He will.

¹⁷ God will judge between the believers, those who follow the Jewish faith, the Sabians,ᵇ the Christians, the Magians,ᶜ and the idolaters on the Day of Resurrection; God witnesses all things. ¹⁸ Do you not realize [Prophet] that everything in the heavens and earth bows down to God: the sun, the moon, the stars, the mountains, the trees, and the animals? So do many human beings, though for many others punishment is well deserved. Anyone disgraced by God will have no one to honour him: God does whatever He will. ¹⁹ These two kinds of people disagree about their Lord. Garments of fire will be tailored for those who disbelieve; scalding water will be poured over their heads, ²⁰ melting their insides as well as their skins; ²¹ iron rods will be prepared for them; ²² whenever, in their anguish, they try to escape, they will be pushed back in and told, 'Taste the suffering of the Fire.' ²³ But God will admit those who believe and do good deeds to Gardens graced with flowing streams; there they will be adorned with golden bracelets and pearls; there they will have silken garments. ²⁴ They were guided to good speech and to the path of the One Worthy of all Praise.

ᵃ See also 6: 35. Another interpretation of this verse is 'stretch a rope up to the ceiling and hang himself'.

ᵇ See note to 2: 62.

ᶜ Followers of an ancient Persian and Median religion, based on monotheism, identified with Zoroastrians.

²⁵ As for the disbelievers, who bar others from God's path and from the Sacred Mosque—which We made for all people, residents and visitors alike—and who try to violate it with wrongdoing, We shall make them taste a painful punishment. ²⁶ We showed Abraham the site of the House, saying, 'Do not assign partners to Me. Purify My House for those who circle around it, those who stand to pray, and those who bow and prostrate themselves. ²⁷ Proclaim the Pilgrimage to all people. They will come to you on foot and on every kind of swift mount, emerging from every deep mountain pass ²⁸ to attain benefits and celebrate God's name, on specified days, over the livestock He has provided for them—feed yourselves and the poor and unfortunate—²⁹ so let the pilgrims perform their acts of cleansing, fulfil their vows, and circle around the Ancient House.' ³⁰ All this [is ordained by God]: anyone who honours the sacred ordinances of God will have good rewards from his Lord.

Livestock have been made lawful to you, except for what has been explicitly forbidden. Shun the filth of idolatrous beliefs and practices and shun false utterances. *ᵃ* ³¹ Devote yourselves to God and assign Him no partners, for the person who does so is like someone who has been hurled down from the skies and snatched up by the birds or flung to a distant place by the wind. ³² All this [is ordained by God]: anyone who honours God's rites shows the piety of his heart. ³³ Livestock are useful to you until the set time. Then their place of sacrifice is near the Ancient House: ³⁴ We appointed acts of devotion for every community for them to celebrate God's name over the livestock He provided for them: your God is One, so devote yourselves to Him. [Prophet], give good news to the humble ³⁵ whose hearts fill with awe whenever God is mentioned, who endure whatever happens to them with patience, who keep up the prayer, who give to others out of Our provision to them.

³⁶ We have made camels *ᵇ* part of God's sacred rites for you. There is much good in them for you, so invoke God's name over them as they are lined up for sacrifice, then, when they have fallen down dead, feed yourselves and those who do not ask, as well as those who do. We have subjected them to you in this way so that you may be thankful. ³⁷ It is neither their meat nor their blood that reaches God

---

ᵃ Dedicating animals to idols.

ᵇ The term *budn* can refer to either camels or cows.

but your piety. He has subjected them to you in this way so that you may glorify God for having guided you.

Give good news to those who do good: [38] God will defend the believers; God does not love the unfaithful or the ungrateful. [39] Those who have been attacked are permitted to take up arms because they have been wronged—God has the power to help them—[40] those who have been driven unjustly from their homes only for saying, 'Our Lord is God.' If God did not repel some people by means of others, many monasteries, churches, synagogues, and mosques, where God's name is much invoked, would have been destroyed. God is sure to help those who help His cause—God is strong and mighty—[41] those who, when We establish them in the land, keep up the prayer, pay the prescribed alms, command what is right, and forbid what is wrong: God controls the outcome of all events.

[42] If they reject you [Prophet], so did the people of Noah before them, and those of ʿAd, Thamud, [43] Abraham, Lot, [44] Midian. Moses was called a liar. I gave the disbelievers time, but in the end I punished them. How I condemned them! [45] How many towns steeped in wrongdoing We have destroyed and left in total ruin; how many deserted wells; how many lofty palaces! [46] Have these people [of Mecca] not travelled through the land to make their hearts understand and let their ears hear? It is not people's eyes that are blind, but their hearts within their breasts.

[47] They will challenge you [Prophet] to hasten the punishment. God will not fail in His promise—a Day with your Lord is like a thousand years by your reckoning. [48] To many a town steeped in wrongdoing I gave more time and then struck them down: they all return to Me in the end.

[49] Say [Prophet], 'People, I am sent only to give you clear warning.' [50] Those who believe and do good deeds will be forgiven and given a rich reward, [51] but those who strive to oppose Our messages and try in vain to defeat Us are destined for the Blaze. [52] We have never sent any messenger or prophet before you [Muhammad] into whose wishes Satan did not insinuate something, but God removes[a] what Satan insinuates and then God affirms His message. God is all

---

[a] The basic meaning of *nasakha* is 'removed' rather than 'abrogated' (*al-Muʿjam al-Wasit*).

knowing and wise: ⁵³ He makes Satan's insinuations a temptation only for the sick at heart and those whose hearts are hardened— the evildoers are profoundly opposed [to the Truth]—⁵⁴ and He causes those given knowledge to realize that this Revelation is your Lord's Truth, so that they may believe in it and humble their hearts to Him: God guides the faithful to the straight path. ⁵⁵ The disbelievers will remain in doubt about it until the Hour suddenly overpowers them; until the punishment descends on them on a Day devoid of all hope. ⁵⁶ On that Day control will belong to God: He will judge between them. Those who believe and do good deeds will be admitted to Gardens of Delight, ⁵⁷ while those who disbelieve and reject Our revelations will receive a humiliating punishment.

⁵⁸ He will give a generous provision to those who migrated in God's way and died or were killed: He is the Best Provider. ⁵⁹ He will admit them to a place that will please them: God is all knowing and most forbearing. ⁶⁰ So it will be. God will help those who retaliate against an aggressive act merely with its like and are then wronged again: God is pardoning and most forgiving. ⁶¹ So it will be, because God makes night pass into day, and day into night, and He is all hearing and all seeing. ⁶² So it will be, because it is God alone who is the Truth, and whatever else they invoke is sheer falsehood: it is God who is the Most High, the Most Great.

⁶³ Have you not considered [Prophet] that God sends water down from the sky and the next morning the earth becomes green? God is truly most subtle, all aware; ⁶⁴ everything in the heavens and earth belongs to Him; God alone is self-sufficient, worthy of all praise. ⁶⁵ Have you not considered that God has made everything on the earth of service to you? That ships sail the sea by His command? That He keeps the heavens from falling down on the earth without His permission? God is most compassionate and most merciful to mankind—⁶⁶ it is He who gave you [people] life, will cause you to die, then will give you life again—but man is ungrateful.

⁶⁷ We have appointed acts of devotion for every community to observe, so do not let them argue with you [Prophet] about this matter. Call them to your Lord—you are on the right path—⁶⁸ and if they argue with you, say, 'God is well aware of what you are doing.' ⁶⁹ On the Day of Resurrection, God will judge between you regarding your differences. ⁷⁰ Are you [Prophet] not aware that God knows

all that is in the heavens and earth? All this is written in a Record; this is easy for God.

⁷¹ Yet beside God they serve that for which He has sent no authority and of which they have no knowledge:ᵃ the evildoers will have no one to help them. ⁷² [Prophet], you can see the hostility on the faces of the disbelievers when Our messages are recited clearly to them: it is almost as if they are going to attack those who recite Our messages to them. Say, 'Shall I tell you what is far worse than what you feel now? The Fire that God has promised the disbelievers! What a dismal end!' ⁷³ People, here is an illustration, so listen carefully: those you call on beside God could not, even if they combined all their forces, create a fly, and if a fly took something away from them, they would not be able to retrieve it. How feeble are the petitioners and how feeble are those they petition! ⁷⁴ They have no comprehension of God's true measure: God is truly most strong and mighty.

⁷⁵ God chooses messengers from among the angels and from among men. God is all hearing, all seeing: ⁷⁶ He knows what lies before and behind them. All matters return to Him. ⁷⁷ Believers, bow down, prostrate yourselves, worship your Lord, and do good so that you may succeed. ⁷⁸ Strive hard for God as is His due: He has chosen you and placed no hardship in your religion, the faith of your forefather Abraham. God has called you Muslimsᵇ—both in the past and in this [message]—so that the Messenger can bear witness about you and so that you can bear witness about other people. So keep up the prayer, give the prescribed alms, and seek refuge in God: He is your protector—an excellent protector and an excellent helper.

ᵃ i.e. 'scriptural knowledge'.　　ᵇ i.e. 'devoted to God'.

23. THE BELIEVERS

A Meccan sura which stresses that the believers are the ones who will succeed, whereas the disbelievers will be punished for their arrogance and derision. Several proofs are given of God's Oneness and His power, and the inevitability of the Resurrection is emphasized.

In the name of God, the Lord of Mercy, the Giver of Mercy

[1] The believers will succeed: [2] those who pray humbly, [3] who shun idle talk, [4] who pay the prescribed alms, [5] who guard their chastity [6] except with their spouses or their slaves[a] — with these they are not to blame, [7] but anyone who seeks more than this is exceeding the limits — [8] who are faithful to their trusts and pledges [9] and who keep up their prayers, [10] will rightly be given [11] Paradise as their own,[b] there to remain.

[12] We created man from an essence of clay, [13] then We placed him as a drop of fluid in a safe place, [14] then We developed that drop into a clinging form, and We developed that form into a lump of flesh, and We developed that lump into bones, and We clothed those bones with flesh, and later We developed him into other forms[c] — glory be to God, the best of creators! — [15] then you will die [16] and then, on the Day of Resurrection, you will be raised up again.

[17] We created seven levels[d] above you — We are never unmindful of Our creation — [18] We sent water down from the sky in due measure and lodged it in the earth — We have the power to take it all away if We so wish — [19] with it We produced for you gardens of date palms and vines, with many fruits there for you to eat, [20] and a tree, growing out of Mount Sinai, that produces oil and seasoning for your food. [21] There is a lesson for you in livestock: We produce milk for you to drink from their bellies. And they have many other benefits: you eat them [22] and you ride on them, as you do in ships.

---

[a] Cf. 4: 25.

[b] Literally 'will be the heirs to "inherit" Paradise', but they do not inherit from anyone who dies.

[c] Razi quotes Ibn 'Abbas to explain 'other forms' as referring to all the various stages of infancy, childhood, and maturity — cf. 22: 5; 40: 67.

[d] *Tara'iq*: 'levels (of heaven)' or 'highways' (Razi).

²³ We sent Noah to his people. He said, 'My people, serve God, for He is your only god. Will you not heed Him?' ²⁴ But the leading disbelievers among his people said, 'He is merely a mortal like you, trying to gain some superiority over you. God would have sent down angels if He had wished; besides, we never heard of anything like this from our forefathers. ²⁵ He is just a madman, so let's wait and see what happens to him.' ²⁶ Noah said, 'My Lord, help me! They call me a liar,' ²⁷ and so We revealed to him: 'Build the Ark under Our watchful eye and according to Our revelation. When Our command comes and water gushes up out of the earth,ᵃ take pairs of every species on board, and your family, except for those on whom the sentence has already been passed—do not plead with me for the evildoers: they will be drowned—²⁸ and when you and your companions are settled on the Ark, say, "Praise be to God, who delivered us from a wicked people," ²⁹ and say, "My Lord, let me land with Your blessing: it is You who provide the best landings".' ³⁰ There are signs in all this: We have always put [people] to the test.

³¹ Then We raised another generation after them, ³² and sent one of their own as a messenger—'Serve God, for He is your only god. Will you not heed Him?' ³³ But the leading disbelievers among his people, who denied the Meeting in the Hereafter, to whom We had granted ease and plenty in this life, said, 'He is just a mortal like you—he eats what you eat and drinks what you drink—³⁴ and you will really be losers if you obey a mortal like yourselves. ³⁵ How can he promise you that after you die and become dust and bones you will be brought out alive? ³⁶ What you are promised is very far-fetched. ³⁷ There is only the life of this world: we die, we live,ᵇ but we will never be resurrected. ³⁸ He is just a man making lies up about God. We will never believe in him.' ³⁹ The prophet said, 'My Lord, help me! They call me a liar,' ⁴⁰ and so God said, 'Soon they will be filled with regret.' ⁴¹ The blast justly struck them and We swept them away like scum—away with the evildoers!—⁴² We raised other generations after them—⁴³ no community can advance or delay its time—⁴⁴ and We sent Our messengers in succession: whenever a messenger came to a community they invariably called him a liar, so We

---

ᵃ Literally 'the furnace boils over'.
ᵇ Razi interprets this order to mean successive generations.

destroyed them one after the other and made them into cautionary tales—away with the disbelievers!

⁴⁵ Then We sent Moses and his brother Aaron—with Our signs and clear authority—⁴⁶ to Pharaoh and his prominent leaders, but they responded with arrogance. They were a haughty people. ⁴⁷ They said, 'Are we to believe in two mortals like us? And their people are our servants?' ⁴⁸ and so they called them both liars: they became another ruined people. ⁴⁹ We gave Moses the Scripture, so that they might be rightly guided. ⁵⁰ We made the son of Mary and his mother a sign; We gave them shelter on a peaceful hillside with flowing water. *ᵃ*

⁵¹ Messengers, eat good things and do good deeds: I am well aware of what you do. ⁵² This community of yours is one—and I am your Lord: be mindful of Me—⁵³ but they have split their community into sects, each rejoicing in their own. ⁵⁴ So [Muhammad] leave them for a while steeped [in their ignorance]. ⁵⁵ Do they reckon that, by giving them wealth and sons, ⁵⁶ We race to give them good things? They really have no idea! ⁵⁷ Those who stand in awe of their Lord, ⁵⁸ who believe in His messages, ⁵⁹ who do not ascribe partners to Him, ⁶⁰ who always give with hearts that tremble at the thought that they must return to Him, ⁶¹ are the ones who race toward good things, and they will be the first to get them. ⁶² We do not burden any soul with more than it can bear—We have a Record that tells the truth—they will not be wronged. ⁶³ But the disbelievers' hearts are steeped [in ignorance of] all this; and besides, there are other things besides this that they do. ⁶⁴ When We bring Our punishment on the pursuers of pleasure, they will cry for help: ⁶⁵ 'Do not cry out today: you will get no help from Us. ⁶⁶ Time and time again My messages were recited to you, but you turned arrogantly on your heels, ⁶⁷ and spent the evening making fun of [the Qur'an].'

⁶⁸ Have they not contemplated the Word of God? Has something come to them that did not come to their forefathers? ⁶⁹ Do they not recognize their Messenger? So why do they reject him? ⁷⁰ Why do they say he is possessed? He has brought them the truth and most of them hate it, ⁷¹ but if the truth were in accordance with their desires, the heavens, the earth, and everyone in them would disintegrate. We have brought them their Reminder and they turn away from it.

ᵃ Where Mary gave birth; see Baydawi.

⁷²Do you [Prophet] ask them for any reward? Your Lord's is the best reward: He is the Best of Providers. ⁷³You call them to a straight path ⁷⁴and those who do not believe in the Hereafter turn away from that path. ⁷⁵Even if We were to show them mercy and relieve them of distress, they would blindly persist in their transgression. ⁷⁶We have already afflicted them, yet they did not submit to their Lord: they will not humble themselves ⁷⁷until We open a gate to severe punishment for them—then they will be plunged into utter despair.

⁷⁸It is God who endowed you with hearing, sight, and hearts— how seldom you are grateful! ⁷⁹It is He who made you multiply on earth. You will be gathered to Him: ⁸⁰it is He who gives life and death; the alternation of night and day depends on Him; will you not use your minds? ⁸¹But, like others before them, ⁸²they say, 'What? When we die and turn to dust and bones, shall we really be resurrected? ⁸³We have heard such promises before, and so did our fore-fathers. These are just ancient fables.' ⁸⁴Say [Prophet], 'Who owns the earth and all who live in it, if you know [so much]?' ⁸⁵and they will reply, 'God.' Say, 'Will you not take heed?' ⁸⁶Say, 'Who is the Lord of the seven heavens? Who is the Lord of the Mighty Throne?' ⁸⁷and they will reply, 'God.' Say, 'Will you not be mindful?' ⁸⁸Say, 'Who holds control of everything in His hand? Who protects, while there is no protection against Him, if you know [so much]?' ⁸⁹and they will reply, 'God.' Say, 'Then how can you be so deluded?' ⁹⁰The fact is, We brought them the truth and they are lying. ⁹¹God has never had a child. Nor is there any god beside Him—if there were, each god would have taken his creation aside and tried to overcome the others. May God be exalted above what they describe! ⁹²He knows what is not seen as well as what is seen; He is far above any partner they claim for Him. ⁹³Say, 'Lord, if You are going to show me the punishment You have promised them, ⁹⁴then Lord, do not include me among the evildoers!' ⁹⁵We certainly are able to show you the punishment We have promised them. ⁹⁶Repel evil with good— We are well aware of what they attribute to Us—⁹⁷and say, 'Lord, I take refuge with You from the goadings of the evil ones; ⁹⁸I seek refuge with you, Lord, so that they may not come near me.'

⁹⁹When death comes to one of them, he cries, 'My Lord, let me return ¹⁰⁰so as to make amends for the things I neglected.' Never! This will not go beyond his words: a barrier stands behind such people until the very Day they are resurrected. ¹⁰¹On that Day when

the Trumpet is blown, the ties between them will be as nothing and they will not ask about each other: [102] those whose good deeds weigh heavy will be successful, [103] but those whose balance is light will have lost their souls for ever and will stay in Hell—[104] the Fire will scorch their faces and their lips will be twisted in pain. [105] 'Were My messages not recited over and over to you and still you rejected them?' [106] They will say, 'Lord, misfortune overcame us and we went astray. [107] Lord, take us away from this and if we go back to our old ways, then we will be evildoers.' [108] He will say, 'Away with you! In you go! Do not speak to Me! [109] Among My servants there were those who said, "Lord, We believe: forgive us and have mercy on us: You are the most merciful of all." [110] But you kept on laughing at them: so intent were you on laughing at them that it made you forget My warning. [111] Today I have rewarded them for their patience: it is they who will succeed.' [112] He will say, 'How many years were you on earth?' [113] and they will reply, 'We stayed a day or a part of a day, but ask those who keep count.' [114] He will say, 'You only stayed a little, if only you knew. [115] Did you think We created you in vain, and that you would not be brought back to Us?'

[116] Exalted be God, the true King, there is no god but Him, the Lord of the Glorious Throne! [117] Whoever prays to another god alongside Him—a god for whose existence he has no evidence—will face his reckoning with his Lord. Those who reject the truth will not succeed. [118] Say [Prophet], 'Lord, forgive and have mercy: You are the most merciful of all.'

24. LIGHT

This Medinan sura clarifies several regulations for the Muslim community, mainly to do with marriage, modesty, obedience to the Prophet, and appropriate behaviour in the household. The initial context is the false accusation of adultery made against 'A'isha, the Prophet's wife, who was left behind after wandering away from the caravan in search of a dropped necklace, and was escorted back to Medina by a fellow Muslim, Safwan, giving rise to gossip. The sura is named after the Verse of Light (verses 35–6) where God's light is contrasted to the darkness in which the disbelievers find themselves engulfed.

In the name of God, the Lord of Mercy, the Giver of Mercy

¹ This is a sura We have sent down and made obligatory: We have sent down clear revelations in it, so that you may take heed. ² Strike the adulteress and the adulterer *a* one hundred times.*b* Do not let compassion for them keep you from carrying out God's law—if you believe in God and the Last Day—and ensure that a group of believers witnesses the punishment. ³ The adulterer is only [fit] to marry*c* an adulteress or an idolatress, and the adulteress is only [fit] to marry an adulterer or an idolater: such behaviour is forbidden to believers. ⁴ As for those who accuse chaste women of fornication, and then fail to provide four witnesses, strike them eighty times, and reject their testimony ever afterwards: they are the lawbreakers, ⁵ except for those who repent later and make amends: God is most forgiving and merciful.

⁶ As for those who accuse their own wives of adultery, but have no other witnesses, let each one four times call God to witness that he is telling the truth, ⁷ and, the fifth time, call God to reject him if he is lying; ⁸ punishment shall be averted from his wife if she in turn four times calls God to witness that her husband is lying ⁹ and, the fifth time, calls God to reject her if he is telling the truth.

---

a The crime of *zina* in Arabic covers all extramarital sexual intercourse between a man and a woman.

b *Jalada* in Arabic means 'hit the skin' with the hand or anything else. There are reports that people used shoes, clothes, etc. (Bukhari, *Hudud* 4).

c This is not an injunction but a statement of fact, emphasizing the guilt of both. There is another opinion that *yankihu* is used in its original sense of 'copulate'. Whichever translation is used, this is not part of the punishment but a condemnation of the crime.

¹⁰ If it were not for God's bounty and mercy towards you, if it were not that God accepts repentance and is wise . . .!ᵃ ¹¹ It was a group from among you that concocted the lieᵇ—do not consider it a misfortune for you [people]; it was a good thing—and every one of them will be charged with the sin he has earned. He who took the greatest part in it will have a painful punishment. ¹² When you heard the lie, why did believing men and women not think well of their own people and declare, 'This is obviously a lie'? ¹³ And why did the accusers not bring four witnesses to it? If they cannot produce such witnesses, they are the liars in God's eyes. ¹⁴ If it were not for God's bounty and mercy towards you in this world and the next, you would already have been afflicted by terrible suffering for indulging in such talk. ¹⁵ When you took it up with your tongues, and spoke with your mouths things you did not know [to be true], you thought it was trivial but to God it was very serious. ¹⁶ When you heard the lie, why did you not say, 'We should not repeat this—God forbid!—It is a monstrous slander'? ¹⁷ God warns you never to do anything like this again, if you are true believers. ¹⁸ God makes His messages clear to you: God is all knowing, all wise. ¹⁹ A painful punishment waits in this world and the next for those who like indecency to spread among the believers: God knows and you do not. ²⁰ If it were not for God's bounty and mercy and the fact that He is compassionate and merciful . . .! ²¹ Believers, do not follow in Satan's footsteps—if you do so, he will urge you to indecency and evil. If it were not for God's bounty and mercy towards you, none of you would have become pure. God purifies whoever He will: God is all hearing, all seeing.

²² Those who have been graced with bounty and plenty should not swear that they will [no longer] give to kinsmen, the poor, those who emigrated in God's way:ᶜ let them pardon and forgive. Do you not wish that God should forgive you? God is most forgiving and merciful.

ᵃ The statement 'If it were not for God's bounty and mercy' is repeated four times in this context, but the concluding clauses are suspended in verses 10 and 20. This rhetorical suspense works in English and in Arabic.

ᵇ This alludes to the accusation made against ʿA'isha, the Prophet's wife.

ᶜ Abu Bakr, father of ʿA'isha, who used to support a relative called Mistah, swore, when Mistah participated in spreading the rumour, that he would never support Mistah again.

²³ Those who accuse honourable but unwary believing women are rejected by God, in this life and the next. A painful punishment awaits them ²⁴ on the Day when their own tongues, hands, and feet will testify against them about what they have done—²⁵ on that Day, God will pay them their just due in full—and they will realize that God is the Truth that makes everything clear. ²⁶ Corrupt women are for corrupt men, and corrupt men are for corrupt women; good women are for good men and good men are for good women. The good are innocent of what has been said against them; they will have forgiveness and a generous reward.

²⁷ Believers, do not enter other people's houses until you have asked permission to do so and greeted those inside—that is best for you: perhaps you will bear this in mind. ²⁸ If you find no one in, do not enter unless you have been given permission to do so. If you are told, 'Go away', then do so—that is more proper for you. God knows well what you do. ²⁹ You will not be blamed for entering houses where no one lives, and which could provide you with some useful service. God knows everything you do openly and everything you conceal. ³⁰ [Prophet], tell believing men to lower their gaze and guard their private parts: that is purer for them. God is well aware of everything they do. ³¹ And tell believing women that they should lower their gaze, guard their private parts, and not flaunt their charms beyond what [it is acceptable] to reveal;*ᵃ* they should let their headscarves fall to cover their necklines and not reveal their charms except to their husbands, their fathers, their husbands' fathers, their sons, their husbands' sons, their brothers' sons, their sisters' sons, their womenfolk, their slaves, such men as attend them who have no sexual desire, or children who are not yet aware of women's nakedness; they should not stamp their feet so as to draw attention to any hidden charms. Believers, all of you, turn to God so that you may prosper.

³² Marry off*ᵇ* the single among you and those of your male and female slaves who are fit [for marriage].*ᶜ* If they are poor, God will

ᵃ Literally 'beyond what [ordinarily] shows'. This phrase is ambiguous in Arabic. Recourse is commonly made to the *hadith* (prophetic tradition), which uses the same verb *dhahara* in the sense of its being permissible for a woman to show only her face and her hands in front of strangers.

ᵇ There is another reading that translates as 'marry'.

ᶜ Or 'righteous'.

provide for them from His bounty: for God's bounty is infinite and He is all knowing. ³³ Those who are unable to marry should keep chaste until God gives to them enough out of His bounty. If any of your slaves wish to pay for their freedom, make a contract with them accordingly, if you know they have good in them, and give them some of the wealth God has given you; do not force your slave-girls into prostitution, when they themselves wish to remain honourable, in your quest for the short-term gains of this world, although if they are forced, God will be forgiving and merciful to them.

³⁴ We have sent verses down to you [people] clarifying the right path, examples of those who passed away before you, and advice for those who are mindful of God.

³⁵ God is the Light of the heavens and earth. His Light is like this: there is a niche, and in it a lamp, the lamp inside a glass, a glass like a glittering star, fuelled from a blessed olive tree from neither east nor west, whose oil almost gives light even when no fire touches it—light upon light—God guides whoever He will to his Light; God draws such comparisons for people; God has full knowledge of everything—³⁶ shining out in houses of worship. God has ordained that they be raised high and that His name be remembered in them, with men in them celebrating His glory morning and evening: ³⁷ men[a] who are not distracted, either by commerce or profit, from remembering God, keeping up the prayer, and paying the prescribed alms, fearing a day when hearts and eyes will turn over, ³⁸ hoping that God will reward them according to the best of their actions, and that He will give them more of His bounty. God provides limitlessly for anyone He will.

³⁹ But the deeds of those who disbelieve are like a mirage in a desert: the thirsty person thinks there will be water but, when he gets there, he finds only God, who pays him his account in full—God is swift in reckoning. ⁴⁰ Or like shadows in a deep sea covered by wave upon wave, with clouds above—layer upon layer of darkness—if he holds out his hand, he is scarcely able to see it. The one to whom God gives no light has no light at all.

⁴¹ [Prophet], do you not see that all those who are in the heavens and earth praise God, as do the birds with wings outstretched? Each knows its [own way] of prayer and glorification: God has full

---

[a] Cf. 62: 11, which makes reference to worshippers who are distracted by trade.

knowledge of what they do. [42] Control of the heavens and earth belongs to God: and to God is the final return. [43] Do you not see that God drives the clouds, then gathers them together and piles them up until you see rain pour from their midst? He sends hail down from [such] mountains in the sky, pouring it on whoever He wishes and diverting it from whoever He wishes—the flash of its lightning almost snatches sight away. [44] God alternates night and day—there truly is a lesson in this for those who have eyes to see— [45] and God created each animal out of [its own] fluid:*a* some of them crawl on their bellies, some walk on two legs, and some on four. God creates whatever He will; God has power over everything.

[46] We have sent verses that clarify the right path: God guides whoever He will to a straight path. [47] They say, 'We believe in God and the Messenger; we obey,' but then some of them turn away— these people are not true believers [48] and when they are summoned to God and His Messenger in order for him to judge between them, some of them turn away. [49] If they had the truth [on their side], they would come willingly [to the Prophet]. [50] Do they have sickness in their hearts? Are they full of doubts? Do they fear that God and His Messenger might deal with them unjustly? No, it is they who are the unjust ones. [51] When the true believers are summoned to God and His Messenger in order for him to judge between them, they say, 'We hear and we obey.' These are the ones who will prosper: [52] whoever obeys God and His Messenger, stands in awe of God, and keeps his duty to Him will be triumphant. [53] [The others] solemnly swear by God that if you [Prophet] commanded them, they would march out—tell them, 'Do not swear: it is reasonable obedience that is required, and God is aware of everything you do.' [54] Say, 'Obey God; obey the Messenger. If you turn away, [know that] he is responsible for the duty placed upon him, and you are responsible for the duty placed upon you. If you obey him, you will be rightly guided, but the Messenger's duty is only to deliver the message clearly.'

[55] God has made a promise to those among you who believe and do good deeds: He will make them successors to the land, as He did those who came before them; He will strengthen the religion He has chosen for them; He will grant them security to replace their fear.

---

a This *ma'* is not 'water', which would have the generic *al-* (cf. 21: 30), but is for each animal a special, essential fluid (e.g. semen), and so each creature is different, as is clear from what follows.

'They worship Me and do not join anything with Me.' Whoever still chooses to disbelieve is truly rebellious—⁵⁶[people], keep up the prayer, pay the prescribed alms, and obey the Messenger, so that you may be given mercy. ⁵⁷Do not think [Prophet] that the disbelievers can escape God on earth; the Fire will be their final home, an evil end.

⁵⁸Believers, your slaves and any who have not yet reached puberty should ask your permission to come in at three times of day: before the dawn prayer; when you lay your garments aside in the midday heat; and after the evening prayer—these are your three times for privacy. At other times, there is no blame on you or them if you move around each other freely. This is how God makes messages clear: God is all knowing, all wise. ⁵⁹When your children reach puberty, they should [always] ask your permission to enter, like their elders do. This is how God makes His messages clear to you: God is all knowing, all wise. ⁶⁰No blame will be attached to elderly women who do not desire sex, if they take off their outer garments without flaunting their charms, but it is preferable for them not to do this: God is all hearing, all seeing.

⁶¹No blame will be attached to the blind, the lame, the sick.ᵃ Whether you eat in your own houses, or those of your fathers, your mothers, your brothers, your sisters, your paternal uncles, your paternal aunts, your maternal uncles, your maternal aunts, houses you have the keys for, or any of your friends' houses, you will not be blamed: you will not be blamed whether you eat in company or separately.ᵇ When you enter any house, greet one another with a greeting of blessing and goodness as enjoined by God. This is how God makes His messages clear to you so that you may understand.

⁶²The true believers are those who believe in God and His Messenger, who, when they are gathered with him on a communal matter, do not depart until they have asked his permission—those who ask your permission [Prophet] are the ones who truly believe in God and His Messenger. When they ask your permission to attend to their private affairs, allow whoever you see fit and ask God to forgive

---

ᵃ Commentators state that the blind etc. refrained from eating with the healthy, or that the healthy refused to eat with them, and many link this statement to the following one.

ᵇ Some commentators take this to be a qualification of 4: 29, which was interpreted by some Muslims as a prohibition on eating at each other's houses without invitation.

them. God is most forgiving and merciful. [63] [People], do not regard the Messenger's summons to you like one of you summoning another—God is well aware of those of you who steal away surreptitiously—and those who go against his order should beware lest a trial afflict them or they receive a painful punishment.

[64] Everything in the heavens and earth belongs to God: He knows what state you are in—on the Day when all are returned to Him, He will tell them everything they have done—God has full knowledge of everything.

25. THE [SCRIPTURE THAT] SHOWS
THE DIFFERENCE

A Meccan sura that starts with a denunciation of polytheism, then deals with the disbelievers' arguments against the Prophet, the Qur'an, and the Day of Judgement. It warns them of their fate, citing examples of earlier peoples. The sura describes the power and grace of God, and ends with the qualities of true believers (verses 63–76).

In the name of God, the Lord of Mercy, the Giver of Mercy

¹ Exalted*ᵃ* is He who has sent the [scripture that] shows the difference*ᵇ* down to His servant so that he may warn all people. ² It is He who has control over the heavens and earth and has no offspring—no one shares control with Him—and who created all things and made them to an exact measure. ³ Yet the disbelievers take as their gods things beneath Him that create nothing, and are themselves created, that can neither harm nor help themselves, and have no control over death, life, or resurrection.

⁴ The disbelievers say, 'This can only be a lie he has forged with the help of others'—they themselves have done great wrong and told lies—⁵ and they say, 'It is just fables of the ancients, which he has had written down: they are dictated to him morning and evening.' ⁶ Say, 'It was sent down by Him who knows the secrets of the heavens and earth. He is all forgiving, all merciful.' ⁷ They also say, 'What sort of messenger is this? He eats food and walks about in the marketplaces. Why has no angel been sent down to help him with his warnings? ⁸ Why has he not been given treasure or a garden to supply his food?' and the evildoers say, 'The man you follow is simply under a spell.' ⁹ See what they liken you to! In doing so they have gone astray; they cannot find the right way. ¹⁰ Exalted is He who can, if He wishes, give you better things than these: Gardens graced with flowing streams, and palaces too. ¹¹ It is actually the coming of the Hour that they

---

ᵃ This meaning of *tabarak* is supported by Razi and is more appropriate here than 'blessed'.

ᵇ *Al-furqan*, another name for the Qur'an. The word means 'that which differentiates right from wrong'.

reject: We have prepared a blazing fire for those who reject the Hour. [12] When it sees them from a distance, they will hear it raging and roaring, [13] and when they are hurled into a narrow part of it, chained together, they will cry out for death. [14] 'Do not cry out this day for one death, but for many.' [15] Say, 'Which is better, this or the lasting Garden that those who are mindful of God have been promised as their reward and journey's end?' [16] There they will find everything they wish for, and there they will stay. [Prophet], this is a binding promise from your Lord. [17] On the Day He gathers them all together with those they worship beside Him, He will say, 'Was it you [false gods] who led these creatures of Mine astray, or did they stray from the path by themselves?' [18] They will say, 'May You be exalted! We ourselves would never take masters other than You! But You granted them and their forefathers pleasures in this life, until they forgot Your Reminder and were ruined.' [19] [God will say], 'Now your gods have denounced what you say as lies: you cannot avoid the punishment; you will not get any help.' If any of you commits such evil, We shall make him taste agonizing punishment.

[20] No messenger have We sent before you [Muhammad] who did not eat food and walk about in the marketplace. But We have made some of you a means of testing others—will you stand fast? Your Lord is always watching. [21] Those who do not fear to meet Us say, 'Why are the angels not sent down to us?' or 'Why can we not see our Lord?' They are too proud of themselves and too insolent. [22] There will be no good news for the guilty on the day they see the angels. The angels will say, 'You cannot cross the forbidden barrier,'[a] [23] and We shall turn to the deeds they have done and scatter them like dust. [24] But the companions in the Garden will have a better home on that Day, and a fairer place to rest. [25] On the Day when the sky and its clouds are split apart and the angels sent down in streams, [26] on that Day, true authority belongs to the Lord of Mercy. It will be a grievous Day for the disbelievers. [27] On that Day the evildoer will bite his own hand and say, 'If only I had taken the same path as the Messenger. [28] Woe is me! If only I had not taken so and so as a friend—[29] he led me away from the Revelation after it reached me. Satan has always betrayed mankind.'

[30] The Messenger has said, 'Lord, my people treat this Qur'an

---

[a] Cf. 23: 100.

as something to be shunned,' [31] but We have always appointed adversaries from the wicked, for every prophet: Your Lord is sufficient guide and helper. [32] The disbelievers also say, 'Why was the Qur'an not sent down to him all at once?' We sent it in this way to strengthen your heart [Prophet]; We gave it to you in gradual revelation. [33] They cannot put any argument to you without Our bringing you the truth and the best explanation. [34] It is those driven [falling], on their faces,[a] to Hell who will be in the worst place—they are the furthest from the right path.

[35] We gave Moses the Book and appointed his brother Aaron to help him. [36] We said, 'Go, both of you, to the people who have rejected Our signs.' Later We destroyed those people utterly. [37] The people of Noah, too: when they rejected their messengers, We drowned them and made them an example to all people. We have prepared a painful punishment for the evildoers, [38] as for the people of 'Ad, Thamud, and al-Rass, and many generations in between. [39] To each of them We gave warnings, and each of them We destroyed completely. [40] These disbelievers must have passed by the town that was destroyed by the terrible rain[b]—did they not see it? Yet they do not expect to be raised from the dead. [41] Whenever they see you [Prophet] they ridicule you—'Is this the one God has sent as a messenger? [42] He might almost have led us astray from our gods if we had not stood so firmly by them.' When they see the punishment, they will know who is furthest from the path. [43] Think [Prophet] of the man who has taken his own passion as a god: are you to be his guardian? [44] Do you think that most of them hear or understand? They are just like cattle—no, they are further from the path.

[45] Have you not considered how your Lord lengthens the shade? If He had willed, He could have made it stand still—We made the sun its indicator—[46] but We gradually draw it towards Us, little by little. [47] It is He who made the night a garment for you, and sleep a rest, and made the day like a resurrection. [48] It is He who sends the winds as heralds of good news before His Mercy.[c] We send down pure water from the sky, [49] so that We can revive a dead land with it, and We give it as a drink to many animals and people We have created—[50] many times We have repeated this to people so that they might take heed, but most persist in their ingratitude—[51] had it been Our will,

a Cf. 67: 22.   b See 15: 74, 76.   c The rain.

We would have sent a warner to every town—⁵²so do not give in to the disbelievers: strive hard against them with this Qur'an.

⁵³It is He who released the two bodies of flowing water, one sweet and fresh and the other salty and bitter, and put an insurmountable barrier between them. ⁵⁴It is He who creates human beings from fluid, then makes them kin by blood and marriage: your Lord is all powerful! ⁵⁵Yet instead of God they worship things that can neither benefit nor harm them: the disbeliever has always turned his back on his Lord. ⁵⁶We sent you only to give good news and warning. ⁵⁷Say, 'I am not asking for any reward for it, but anyone who wishes should take a path to his Lord.' ⁵⁸Put your trust in the Living [God] who never dies, and celebrate His praise. He knows the sins of His servants well enough. ⁵⁹It is He who created the heavens and earth and what is between them in six Days,ᵃ and then established Himself on the throne. He is the Lord of Mercy; He is the Best Informed.ᵇ ⁶⁰Yet when they are told, 'Bow down before the Lord of Mercy,' they say, 'What is the Lord of Mercy? Should we bow down before anything you command?' and they turn even further away. ⁶¹Exalted is He who put constellations in the heavens, a radiant light, and an illuminating moon—⁶²it is He who made the night and day follow each other—so anyone who wishes may be mindful or show gratitude.

⁶³The servants of the Lord of Mercy are those who walk humbly on the earth, and who, when the foolish address them, reply, 'Peace'; ⁶⁴those who spend the night bowed down or standing, worshipping their Lord, ⁶⁵who plead, 'Our Lord, turn away from us the suffering of Hell, for it is a dreadful torment to suffer—⁶⁶it is an evil home, a foul resting place.' ⁶⁷They are those who are neither wasteful nor niggardly when they spend, but keep to a just balance; ⁶⁸those who never invoke any other deity beside God, nor take a life, which God has made sacred, except in the pursuit of justice, nor commit adultery.

(Whoever does this will face the penalties [for all these]: ⁶⁹their torment will be doubled on the Day of Resurrection, and they will remain in torment, disgraced, ⁷⁰except those who repent, believe,

---

ᵃ Cf. 41: 9–12.

ᵇ Other readings of this phrase include 'ask someone who knows' or 'ask anyone how well informed He is', but the expression *fas'al*, 'ask someone', at the beginning of the phrase is a rhetorical device suggesting the truth of the statement and need not be translated literally.

and do good deeds: God will change the evil deeds of such people into good ones: He is most forgiving, most merciful. [71] People who repent and do good deeds truly return to God.)—[72]

[The servants of the Lord of Mercy are] those who do not give false testimony, and who, when they see some frivolity, pass by with dignity; [73] who, when reminded of their Lord's signs, do not turn a deaf ear and a blind eye to them; [74] those who pray, 'Our Lord, give us joy in our spouses and offspring. Make us good examples to those who are aware of You'—[75] these servants will be rewarded with the highest place in Paradise for their steadfastness. There they will be met with greetings and peace. [76] There they will stay—a happy home and resting place! [77] [Prophet, tell the disbelievers], 'What are you to my Lord without your supplication? But since you have written off the truth as lies, the inevitable will happen.'[a]

[a] The punishment (cf. 4: 147).

26. THE POETS

A Meccan sura which takes it name from the reference to poets in verse 224. It talks about the disbelievers who belittle the Qur'an, and gives examples of God's power and grace in nature. It recounts several stories of earlier prophets, the reactions of their followers, and punishments that afflicted them, ending by confirming the divine origin of the Qur'an. It is not something brought down by the jinn, nor is it poetry.

In the name of God, the Lord of Mercy, the Giver of Mercy

¹ *Ta Sin Mim*

² These are the verses of the Scripture that makes things clear:
³ [Prophet], are you going to worry yourself to death because they will not believe? ⁴ If We had wished, We could have sent them down a sign from heaven, at which they would bow their heads in utter humility. ⁵ Whenever they are brought a new revelation from the Lord of Mercy, they turn away: ⁶ they deny it, but the truth of what they scorned will soon hit them. ⁷ Do they not see the earth, and what noble kinds of thing We grow in it? ⁸ There truly is a sign in this, though most of them do not believe: ⁹ your Lord alone is the Almighty, the Merciful.

¹⁰ Your Lord called to Moses: 'Go to those wrongdoers, ¹¹ the people of Pharaoh. Will they not take heed?' ¹² Moses said, 'My Lord, I fear they will call me a liar, ¹³ and I will feel stressed and tongue-tied, so send Aaron too; ¹⁴ besides, they have a charge*ᵃ* against me, and I fear they may kill me.' ¹⁵ God said, 'No [they will not]. Go, both of you, with Our signs—We shall be with you, listening. ¹⁶ Go, both of you, to Pharaoh and say, "We bring a message from the Lord of the Worlds: ¹⁷ let the Children of Israel leave with us." '

¹⁸ Pharaoh said, 'Did we not bring you up as a child among us? Did you not stay with us for many years? ¹⁹ And then you committed that crime of yours: you were so ungrateful.' ²⁰ Moses replied, 'I was

---

ᵃ Cf. 28: 15–20.

misguided when I did it [21] and I fled from you in fear; then my Lord gave me wisdom and made me one of His messengers. [22] And is this—that you have enslaved the Children of Israel—the favour with which you reproach me?'

[23] Pharaoh asked, 'What is this "Lord of the Worlds"?' [24] Moses replied, 'He is the Lord of the heavens and earth and everything between them, if you would only have faith!' [25] Pharaoh said to those present, 'Do you hear what he says?' [26] Moses said, 'He is your Lord and the Lord of your forefathers.' [27] Pharaoh said, 'This messenger who has been sent to you is truly possessed.' [28] Moses continued, 'Lord of the East and West and everything between them, if you would only use your reason!' [29] But Pharaoh said [to him], 'If you take any god other than me, I will throw you into prison,' [30] and Moses asked, 'Even if I show you something convincing?' [31] 'Show it then,' said Pharaoh, 'if you are telling the truth.' [32] So Moses threw down his staff and—lo and behold!—it became a snake for everyone to see. [33] Then he drew out his hand and—lo and behold!—it was white for the onlookers to see. [34] Pharaoh said to the counsellors around him, 'This man is a learned sorcerer! [35] He means to use his sorcery to drive you out of your land! What do you suggest?' [36] They answered, 'Delay him and his brother for a while, and send messengers to all the cities [37] to summon every accomplished sorcerer to come to you.' [38] The sorcerers were [to be] assembled at the appointed time on a certain day [39] and the people were asked, [40] 'Are you all coming? We may follow the sorcerers if they win!'

[41] When the sorcerers came, they said to Pharaoh, 'Shall we be rewarded if we win?' [42] and he said, 'Yes, and you will join my inner court.' [43] Moses said to them, 'Throw down whatever you will.' [44] They threw their ropes and staffs, saying, 'By Pharaoh's might, we shall be victorious.' [45] But Moses threw his staff and—lo and behold!—it swallowed up their trickery [46] and the sorcerers fell down on their knees, [47] exclaiming, 'We believe in the Lord of the Worlds, [48] the Lord of Moses and Aaron.' [49] Pharaoh said, 'How dare you believe in him before I have given you permission? He must be the master who taught you sorcery! Soon you will see: I will cut off your alternate hands and feet[a] and then crucify the lot of you!' [50] 'That will do us no harm,' they said, 'for we are sure to return to our

---

[a] See note to 5: 33.

Lord. [51] We hope that our Lord will forgive us our sins, as we were the first to believe.'

[52] Then We revealed Our will to Moses, 'Leave with My servants by night, for you will be pursued!' [53] Pharaoh sent messengers into the cities, proclaiming, [54] 'These people are a puny band—[55] they have enraged us—[56] and we are a large army, fully prepared.' [57] So it was that We made them leave their gardens and their springs, [58] their treasures and their noble dwellings—[59] We gave [such] things [later][a] to the Children of Israel. [60] Pharaoh and his people pursued them at sunrise, [61] and as soon as the two sides came in sight of one another, Moses' followers said, 'We shall definitely be caught.' [62] Moses said, 'No, my Lord is with me: He will guide me,' [63] and We revealed to Moses: 'Strike the sea with your staff.' It parted—each side like a mighty mountain—[64] and We brought the others to that place: [65] We saved Moses and all his companions, [66] and drowned the rest. [67] There truly is a sign in this, though most of them do not believe: [68] your Lord alone is the Almighty, the Merciful.

[69] Tell them the story of Abraham, [70] when he asked his father and his people, 'What do you worship?' [71] They said, 'We worship idols, and are constantly in attendance on them.' [72] He asked, 'Do they hear you when you call? [73] Do they help or harm you?' [74] They replied, 'No, but this is what we saw our fathers doing.' [75] Abraham said, 'Those idols you have worshipped, [76] you and your forefathers, [77] are my enemies; not so the Lord of the Worlds, [78] who created me. It is He who guides me; [79] He who gives me food and drink; [80] He who cures me when I am ill; [81] He who will make me die and then give me life again; [82] and He who will, I hope, forgive my faults on the Day of Judgement. [83] My Lord, grant me wisdom; join me with the righteous; [84] give me a good name among later generations; [85] make me one of those given the Garden of Bliss—[86] forgive my father, for he is one of those who have gone astray—[87] and do not disgrace me on the Day when all people are resurrected: [88] the Day when neither wealth nor children can help, [89] when the only one who will be saved is the one who comes before God with a heart devoted to Him.'

[90] When the Garden is brought near to the righteous [91] and the Fire is placed in full view of the misguided, [92] it will be said to them,

---

[a] Cf. 7: 137.

'Where are those you worshipped [93] beside God? Can they help you now, or even help themselves?' [94] and then they will all be hurled into Hell, together with those that misled them, [95] and all Iblis's supporters. [a] [96] There they will say to their gods, as they bicker among themselves, [97] 'We were clearly misguided [98] when we made you equal with the Lord of the Worlds. [99] It was the evildoers who led us astray, [100] and now we have no intercessor [101] and no true friend. [102] If only we could live our lives again, we would be true believers!' [103] There truly is a sign in this, though most of them do not believe: [104] your Lord alone is the Almighty, the Merciful.

[105] The people of Noah, too, called the messengers liars. [106] Their brother Noah said to them, 'Will you not be mindful of God? [107] I am a faithful messenger sent to you: [108] be mindful of God and obey me. [109] I ask no reward of you, for my only reward is with the Lord of the Worlds: [110] be mindful of God and obey me.' [111] They answered, 'Why should we believe you when the worst sort of people follow you?' [112] He said, 'What knowledge do I have of what they used to do? [113] It is for my Lord alone to bring them to account—if only you could see—[114] I will not drive believers away. [115] I am here only to give people a clear warning.' [116] So they said, 'Noah, if you do not stop this, you will be stoned.' [117] He said, 'My Lord, my people have rejected me, [118] so make a firm judgement between me and them, and save me and my believing followers.' [119] So We saved him and his followers in the fully laden ship, [120] and drowned the rest. [121] There truly is a sign in this, though most of them do not believe: [122] your Lord alone is the Almighty, the Merciful.

[123] The people of 'Ad, too, called the messengers liars. [124] Their brother Hud said to them, 'Will you not be mindful of God? [125] I am a faithful messenger sent to you: [126] be mindful of God and obey me. [127] I ask no reward of you, for my only reward is with the Lord of the Worlds. [128] How can you be so vain that you set up monuments on every high place? [129] Do you build fortresses because you hope to be immortal? [130] Why do you act like tyrants whenever you attack someone? [131] Be mindful of God and obey me; [132] be mindful of Him who has provided you with everything you know—[133] He has given you livestock, sons, [134] gardens, springs—[135] for I truly fear that the torment of a grievous day will overtake you.' [136] They replied, 'It makes

---

[a] See note to 37: 173.

no difference to us whether you warn us or not, [137] for we only do what our forefathers used to do: [138] we shall not be punished.' [139] They denounced him as a liar, and so We destroyed them. There truly is a sign in this, though most of them do not believe: [140] your Lord alone is the Almighty, the Merciful.

[141] The people of Thamud, too, called the messengers liars. [142] Their brother Salih said to them, 'Will you not be mindful of God? [143] I am a faithful messenger to you: [144] be mindful of God and obey me. [145] I ask no reward from you, for my only reward is with the Lord of the Worlds. [146] [Do you think] you will be left secure for ever in what you have here—[147] gardens, springs, [148] fields, palm trees laden with fruit—[149] carving your fine houses from the mountains? [150] Be mindful of God and obey me: [151] do not obey those who are given to excess [152] and who spread corruption in the land instead of doing what is right.' [153] They said, 'You are bewitched! [154] You are nothing but a man like us. Show us a sign, if you are telling the truth.' [155] He said, 'Here is a camel. She should have her turn to drink and so should you, each on a specified day, [156] so do not harm her, or the punishment of a terrible day will befall you.' [157] But they hamstrung her. In the morning they had cause to regret it: [158] the punishment fell upon them. There truly is a sign in this, though most of them will not believe: [159] your Lord alone is the Almighty, the Merciful.

[160] The people of Lot, too, called the messengers liars. [161] Their brother Lot said to them, 'Will you not be mindful of God? [162] I am a faithful messenger to you: [163] be mindful of God and obey me. [164] I ask no reward from you, for my only reward is with the Lord of the Worlds. [165] Must you, unlike [other] people, lust after males [166] and abandon the wives that God has created for you? You are exceeding all bounds,' [167] but they replied, 'Lot! If you do not stop this, you will be driven away.' [168] So he said, 'I loathe what you do: [169] Lord, save me and my family from what they are doing.' [170] We saved him and all his family, [171] except for an old woman who stayed behind, [172] then We destroyed the others, [173] and poured a rain of destruction down upon them—how dreadful that rain was for those who had been forewarned. [174] There truly is a sign in this, though most of them will not believe: [175] your Lord alone is the Almighty, the Merciful.

[176] The forest-dwellers, too, called the messengers liars. [177] Shu'ayb said to them, 'Will you not be mindful of God? [178] I am a faithful

messenger to you: [179] be mindful of God and obey me. [180] I ask no reward of you, for my only reward is with the Lord of the Worlds. [181] Give full measure: do not sell others short. [182] Weigh with correct scales: [183] do not deprive people of what is theirs. Do not spread corruption on earth. [184] Be mindful of God who created you and former generations,' [185] but they replied, 'You are bewitched! [186] You are nothing but a man like us. In fact we think you are a liar. [187] Make bits of the heavens fall down on us, if you are telling the truth.' [188] He said, 'My Lord knows best what you do.' [189] They called him a liar, and so the punishment of the Day of Shadow came upon them—it was a terrible day. [190] There truly is a sign in this, though most of them will not believe: [191] your Lord alone is the Almighty, the Merciful.

[192] Truly, this Qur'an has been sent down by the Lord of the Worlds: [193] the Trustworthy Spirit[a] brought it down [194] to your heart [Prophet], so that you could bring warning [195] in a clear Arabic tongue. [196] This was foretold in the scriptures of earlier religions. [197] Is it not proof enough for them that the learned men of the Children of Israel have recognized it? [198] If We had sent it down to someone who was not an Arab,[b] [199] and he had recited it to them, they still would not have believed in it. [200] So We make it pass straight through the hearts of the guilty: [201] they will not believe in it until they see the grievous punishment, [202] which will suddenly hit them when they are not expecting it, [203] and then they will say, 'Can we have more time?' [204] How can they ask that Our punishment be brought to them sooner? [205] Think, if we let them enjoy this life for some years [206] and then the promised punishment came upon them, [207] what good would their past enjoyment be to them? [208] Never have We destroyed a town without sending down messengers to warn it, [209] as a reminder from Us: We are never unjust.

[210] It was not the jinn[c] who brought down this Qur'an: [211] it is neither in their interests nor in their power, [212] indeed they are prevented from overhearing it. [213] So [Prophet] do not invoke any gods beside God, or you will incur punishment. [214] Warn your nearest kinsfolk [215] and lower your wing tenderly over the believers who

---

[a] Generally understood to mean the Angel Gabriel.

[b] This alludes to the refusal of many Meccan Arabs to believe that revelation could come to a man from among themselves.

[c] Cf. 72: 8–9; 37: 7–10.

follow you. [216] If they disobey you, say, 'I bear no responsibility for your actions.' [217] Put your trust in the Almighty, the Merciful, [218] who sees you when you stand up [for prayer] [219] and sees your movements among the worshippers: [220] He is the All Hearing, the All Knowing. [221] Shall I tell you who the jinn come down to? [222] They come down to every lying sinner [223] who readily lends an ear to them, and most of them are liars: [224] only those who are lost in error follow the poets. [225] Do you not see how they rove aimlessly in every valley; [226] how they never follow their words with actions? [227] Not so those [poets] who believe, do good deeds, remember God often, and defend themselves after they have been wronged. The evildoers will find out what they will return to.

27. THE ANTS

A Meccan sura which takes its title from the ants mentioned in the Solomon story (verses 18–19). It both opens and closes by describing the Qur'an as joyful news for the believers and a warning for others. It gives stories of past prophets and the destruction of the communities that disbelieved in them. Illustrations are given of the nature of God's power, contrasted with the total lack of power of the 'partners' they worship beside Him, and descriptions are given of the Day of Judgement for those who deny it.

In the name of God, the Lord of Mercy, the Giver of Mercy

¹ *Ta Sin*

These are the verses of the Qur'an—a scripture that makes things clear, ²a guide and joyful news for the believers ³who keep up the prayer, pay the prescribed alms, and believe firmly in the life to come. ⁴As for those who do not believe in the life to come, We have made their deeds seem alluring to them, so they wander blindly: ⁵it is they who will have the worst suffering, and will be the ones to lose most in the life to come. ⁶You [Prophet] receive the Qur'an from One who is all wise, all knowing.

⁷Moses said to his family, 'I have seen a fire. I will bring you news from there, or a burning stick for you to warm yourselves.' ⁸When he reached the fire, a voice called: 'Blessed is the person near this fire*ᵃ* and those around it;*ᵇ* may God be exalted, the Lord of the Worlds. ⁹Moses, I am God, the Mighty, the Wise. ¹⁰Throw down your staff,' but when he saw it moving like a snake, he turned and fled. 'Moses, do not be afraid! The messengers need have no fear in My presence, ¹¹I am truly most forgiving and merciful to those who do wrong,*ᶜ* and then replace their evil with good. ¹²Put your hand inside your cloak and it will come out white, but unharmed. These are among

---

ᵃ Moses or God. Literally 'in this fire' (*fi al-nari*). Zamakhshari interprets *fi* as 'near', while Qatada and Zajjaj understand *nar* 'fire' to mean *nur* 'light' (Razi).

ᵇ The angels.

ᶜ Cf. 28: 15. This is an allusion to a man Moses killed in Egypt.

the nine signs that you will show Pharaoh and his people; they have really gone too far.'

¹³ But when Our enlightening signs came to them, they said, 'This is clearly [just] sorcery!' ¹⁴ They denied them—in their wickedness and their pride—even though their souls acknowledged them as true. See how those who spread corruption met their end!

¹⁵ We gave knowledge to David and Solomon, and they both said, 'Praise be to God, who has favoured us over many of His believing servants.' ¹⁶ Solomon succeeded David. He said, 'People, we have been taught the speech of birds, and we have been given a share of everything: this is a clearly a great favour.' ¹⁷ Solomon's hosts of jinn, men, and birds were marshalled in ordered ranks before him, ¹⁸ and when they came to the Valley of the Ants, one ant said, 'Ants! Go into your homes, in case Solomon and his hosts inadvertently crush you.' ¹⁹ Solomon smiled broadly at its words and said, 'Lord, inspire me to be thankful for the blessings You have granted me and my parents, and to do good deeds that please You; admit me by Your grace into the ranks of Your righteous servants.'

²⁰ Solomon inspected the birds and said, 'Why do I not see the hoopoe? Is he absent? ²¹ I will punish him severely, or kill him, unless he brings me a convincing excuse for his absence.' ²² But the hoopoe did not stay away long: he came and said, 'I have learned something you did not know: I come to you from Sheba with firm news. ²³ I found a woman ruling over the people, who has been given a share of everything—she has a magnificent throne—²⁴ [but] I found that she and her people worshipped the sun instead of God. Satan has made their deeds seem alluring to them, and diverted them from the right path: they cannot find the right path. ²⁵ Should they not worship God, who brings forth what is hidden in the heavens and earth and knows both what you people conceal and what you declare? ²⁶ He is God, there is no god but Him, the Lord of the mighty throne.' ²⁷ Solomon said, 'We shall see whether you are telling the truth or lying. ²⁸ Take this letter of mine and deliver it to them, then withdraw and see what answer they send back.'

²⁹ The Queen of Sheba said, 'Counsellors, a gracious letter has been delivered to me. ³⁰ It is from Solomon, and it says, "In the name of God, the Lord of Mercy, the Giver of Mercy, ³¹ do not put yourselves above me, and come to me in submission to God." ' ³² She said, 'Counsellors, give me your counsel in the matter I now face: I

only ever decide on matters in your presence.' [33] They replied, 'We possess great force and power in war, but you are in command, so consider what orders to give us.' [34] She said, 'Whenever kings go into a city, they ruin it and humiliate its leaders—that is what they do— [35] but I am going to send them a gift, then see what answer my envoy brings back.'

[36] When her envoy came to Solomon, Solomon said, 'What! Are you offering me wealth? What God has given me is better than what He has given you, though you rejoice in this gift of yours. [37] Go back to your people: we shall certainly come upon them with irresistible forces, and drive them, disgraced and humbled, from their land.' [38] Then he said, 'Counsellors, which of you can bring me her throne before they come to me in submission?' [39] A powerful and crafty jinn replied, 'I will bring it to you before you can even rise from your place. I am strong and trustworthy enough,' [40] but one of them who had some knowledge of the Book said, 'I will bring it to you in the twinkling of an eye.'

When Solomon saw it set before him, he said, 'This is a favour from my Lord, to test whether I am grateful or not: if anyone is grateful, it is for his own good, if anyone is ungrateful, then my Lord is self-sufficient and most generous.' [41] Then he said, 'Disguise her throne, and we shall see whether or not she recognizes it.' [42] When she arrived, she was asked, 'Is this your throne?' She replied, 'It looks like it.' [Solomon said], 'We were given knowledge before her, and we devoted ourselves to God— [43] she was prevented by what she worshipped instead of God, for she came from a disbelieving people.' [44] Then it was said to her, 'Enter the hall,' but when she saw it, she thought it was a deep pool of water, and bared her legs. Solomon explained, 'It is just a hall paved with glass,' and she said, 'My Lord, I have wronged myself: I devote myself, with Solomon, to God, the Lord of the Worlds.'

[45] To the people of Thamud We sent their brother, Salih, saying, 'Worship God alone,' but they split into two rival factions. [46] Salih said, 'My people, why do you rush to bring [forward] what is bad rather than good? Why do you not ask forgiveness of God, so that you may be given mercy?' [47] They said, 'We see you and your followers as an evil omen.' He replied, 'God will decide on any omen you may see: you people are being put to the test.' [48] There were nine men in the city who spread corruption in the land and did nothing

that was good. [49] They said, 'Swear by God: we shall attack this man and his household in the night, then say to his next of kin, "We did not witness the destruction of his household. We are telling the truth." ' [50] So they devised their evil plan, but We too made a plan of which they were unaware. [51] See how their scheming ended: We destroyed them utterly, along with all their people. [52] As a result of their evil deeds, their homes are desolate ruins—there truly is a sign in this for those who know—[53] but We saved those who believed and were mindful of God.

[54] We also sent Lot to his people. He said to them, 'How can you commit this outrage with your eyes wide open? [55] How can you lust after men instead of women? What fools you are!' [56] The only answer his people gave was to say, 'Expel Lot's followers from your town! These men mean to stay chaste!' [57] We saved him and his family—except for his wife: We made her stay behind—[58] and We brought [an awesome] rain down on them. How dreadful that rain was for those who had been warned!

[59] Say [Prophet], 'Praise be to God and peace on the servants He has chosen.[a] Who is better: God, or those they set up as partners with Him? [60] Who created the heavens and earth? Who sends down water from the sky for you—with which We cause gardens of delight to grow: you have no power to make the trees grow in them—is it another god beside God? No! But they are people who take others to be equal with God. [61] Who is it that made the earth a stable place to live? Who made rivers flow through it? Who set immovable mountains on it and created a barrier between the fresh and salt water? Is it another god beside God? No! But most of them do not know. [62] Who is it that answers the distressed when they call upon Him? Who removes their suffering? Who makes you successors in the earth? Is it another god beside God? Little notice you take! [63] Who is it that guides you through the darkness on land and sea? Who sends the winds as heralds of good news before His mercy?[b] Is it another god beside God? God is far above the partners they put beside him! [64] Who is it that creates life and reproduces it? Who is it that gives you provision from the heavens and earth? Is it another god beside God?' Say, 'Show me your evidence then, if what you say is true.'

---

[a] As messengers, see e.g. 3: 33.
[b] i.e. rain.

⁶⁵ Say, 'No one in the heavens or on earth knows the unseen except God.' They do not know when they will be raised from the dead: ⁶⁶ their knowledge cannot comprehend the Hereafter; they are in doubt about it; they are blind to it. ⁶⁷ So the disbelievers say, 'What! When we and our forefathers have become dust, shall we be brought back to life again? ⁶⁸ We have heard such promises before, and so did our forefathers. These are just ancient fables.' ⁶⁹ [Prophet], say, 'Travel through the earth and see how the evildoers ended up.' ⁷⁰ [Prophet], do not grieve over them; do not be distressed by their schemes. ⁷¹ They also say, 'When will this promise be fulfilled if what you say is true?' ⁷² Say, 'Maybe some of what you seek to hasten is near at hand.' ⁷³ Your Lord is bountiful to people, though most of them are ungrateful. ⁷⁴ He knows everything their hearts conceal and everything they reveal: ⁷⁵ there is nothing hidden in the heavens or on earth that is not recorded in a clear Book.

⁷⁶ Truly, this Qur'an explains to the Children of Israel most of what they differ about, ⁷⁷ and it is guidance and grace for those who believe. ⁷⁸ Truly, your Lord will judge between them in His wisdom—He is the Almighty, the All Knowing—⁷⁹ so [Prophet], put your trust in God, you are on the path of clear truth. ⁸⁰ You cannot make the dead hear, you cannot make the deaf listen to your call when they turn their backs and leave, ⁸¹ you cannot guide the blind out of their error: you cannot make anyone hear you except those who believe in Our signs and submit to them. ⁸² When the verdict is given against them, We shall bring a creature out of the earth, which will tell them that people had no faith in Our revelations. ⁸³ The Day will come when We gather from every community a crowd of those who disbelieved in Our signs and they will be led in separate groups ⁸⁴ until, when they come before Him, He will say, 'Did you deny My messages without even taking them in? Or what were you doing?' ⁸⁵ The verdict will be given against them because of their wrongdoing: they will not speak.

⁸⁶ Did they not see that We gave them the night for rest, and the day for light? There truly are signs in this for those who believe. ⁸⁷ On the Day that the Trumpet sounds, everyone in heaven and on earth will be terrified—except such as God wills—and will come to Him in utter humility. ⁸⁸ You will see the mountains and think they are firmly fixed, but they will float away like clouds. This is the handiwork of God who has perfected all things. He is fully aware of

what you do: ⁸⁹ whoever comes with a good deed will be rewarded with something better, and be secure from the terrors of that day, ⁹⁰ but whoever comes with evil deeds will be cast face downwards into the Fire. 'Are you rewarded for anything except what you have done?' ⁹¹ Say [Prophet], 'I am commanded to serve the Lord of this town,^a which He has made inviolable, and to whom everything belongs; I am commanded to be one of those devoted to Him; ⁹² I am commanded to recite the Qur'an.' Whoever chooses to follow the right path does so for his own good. Say to whoever deviates from it, 'I am only here to warn.' ⁹³ Say, 'Praise belongs to God: He will show you His signs so that you will recognize them.' Your Lord is never unmindful of what you do.

^a Mecca.

28. THE STORY

A Meccan sura which centres on the story of Moses and takes its title from the reference to the story told by Moses in verse 25. Its main theme is the bad end that comes to those who are arrogant and spread corruption, like Pharaoh and Qarun—polytheism is denounced at various points throughout the sura—and a link is made between these and the disbelievers of Mecca. The Prophet is reminded that he cannot make everyone believe (verse 56) and should remain steadfast (verse 87).

In the name of God, the Lord of Mercy, the Giver of Mercy

¹ *Ta Sin Mim*

² These are the verses of the Scripture that makes things clear:
³ We recount to you [Prophet] part of the story of Moses and Pharaoh, setting out the truth for people who believe. ⁴ Pharaoh made himself high and mighty in the land and divided the people into different groups: one group he oppressed, slaughtering their sons and sparing their women—he was one of those who spread corruption—⁵ but We wished to favour those who were oppressed in that land, to make them leaders, the ones to survive, ⁶ to establish them in the land, and through them show Pharaoh, Haman, and their armies the very thing they feared.
⁷ We inspired Moses' mother, saying, 'Suckle him, and then, when you fear for his safety, put him in the river: do not be afraid, and do not grieve, for We shall return him to you and make him a messenger.' ⁸ Pharaoh's household picked him up—later to*ᵃ* become an enemy and a source of grief for them: Pharaoh, Haman, and their armies were wrongdoers—⁹ and Pharaoh's wife said, 'Here is a joy to behold for me and for you! Do not kill him: he may be of use to us, or we may adopt him as a son.' They did not realize what they were doing. ¹⁰ The next day, Moses' mother felt a void in her heart—if We had not strengthened it to make her one of those who believe, she would have revealed everything about him—¹¹ and she said to his sister, 'Follow him.' So she watched him from a distance, without

---

ᵃ Li here indicates consequence rather than purpose.

them knowing. [12] We had ordained that he would refuse to feed from wet nurses. His sister approached them and said, 'Shall I tell you about a household which could bring him up for you and take good care of him?' [13] We restored him to his mother in this way, so that she might be comforted, not grieve, and know that God's promise is true, though most of them do not know.

[14] When Moses reached full maturity and manhood, We gave him wisdom and knowledge: this is how We reward those who do good. [15] He entered the city, unnoticed by its people, and found two men fighting: one from his own people, the other an enemy. The one from his own people cried out to him for help against the enemy. Moses struck him with his fist and killed him. He said, 'This must be Satan's work: clearly he is a misleading enemy.' [16] He said, 'Lord, I have wronged myself. Forgive me,' so He forgave him; He is truly the Most Forgiving, the Most Merciful. [17] He said, 'My Lord, because of the blessings You have bestowed upon me, I shall never support those who do evil.'

[18] Next morning, he was walking in the city, fearful and vigilant, when suddenly the man he had helped the day before cried out to him for help. Moses said, 'You are clearly a troublemaker.' [19] As he was about to attack the man who was an enemy to both of them, the man said, 'Moses, are you going to kill me as you killed that person yesterday? You clearly want to be a tyrant in the land; you do not intend to put things right.' [20] Then a man came running from the furthest part of the city and said, 'Moses, the authorities are talking about killing you, so leave—this is my sincere advice.' [21] So Moses left the city, fearful and vigilant, and prayed, 'My Lord, save me from people who do wrong.'

[22] As he made his way towards Midian, he was saying, 'May my Lord guide me to the right way.' [23] When he arrived at Midian's waters, he found a group of men watering [their flocks], and beside them two women keeping their flocks back, so he said, 'What is the matter with you two?' They said, 'We cannot water [our flocks] until the shepherds take their sheep away: our father is a very old man.' [24] He watered their flocks for them, withdrew into the shade, and prayed, 'My Lord, I am in dire need of whatever good thing You may send me,' [25] and then one of the two women approached him, walking shyly, and said, 'My father is asking for you: he wants to reward you for watering our flocks for us.'

When Moses came to him and told him his story, the old man said, 'Do not be afraid, you are safe now from people who do wrong.' [26] One of the women said, 'Father, hire him: a strong, trustworthy man is the best to hire.' [27] The father said, 'I would like to marry you to one of these daughters of mine, on condition that you serve me for eight years: if you complete ten, it will be of your own free will. I do not intend to make things difficult for you: God willing, you will find I am a fair man.' [28] Moses said, 'Let that be the agreement between us—whichever of the two terms I fulfil, let there be no injustice to me—may God be witness to what we say.'

[29] Once Moses had fulfilled the term and was travelling with his family, he caught sight of a fire on the side of the mountain and said to his family, 'Wait! I have seen a fire. I will bring you news from there, or a burning stick for you to warm yourselves.' [30] But when he reached it, a voice called out to him from the right-hand side of the valley, from a tree on the blessed ground: 'Moses, I am God, the Lord of the Worlds. [31] Throw down your staff.' When he saw his staff moving like a snake, he fled in fear and would not return. Again [he was called]: 'Moses! Draw near! Do not be afraid, for you are one of those who are safe. [32] Put your hand inside your shirt and it will come out white but unharmed—hold your arm close to your side, free from all fear. These shall be two signs from your Lord to Pharaoh and his chiefs; they are truly wicked people.' [33] Moses said, 'My Lord, I killed one of their men, and I fear that they may kill me. [34] My brother Aaron is more eloquent than I: send him with me to help me and confirm my words—I fear they may call me a liar.' [35] God said, 'We shall strengthen you through your brother; We shall give you both power so that they cannot touch you. With Our signs you, and those who follow you, will triumph.'

[36] But when Moses came to them with Our clear signs, they said, 'These are mere conjuring tricks; we never heard this from our forefathers.' [37] Moses said, 'My Lord knows best who comes with guidance from Him and who will have the final Home: wrongdoers will never succeed.' [38] Pharaoh said, 'Counsellors, you have no other god that I know of except me. Haman, light me a fire to bake clay bricks, then build me a tall building so that I may climb up to Moses' God: I am convinced that he is lying.'

[39] Pharaoh and his armies behaved arrogantly in the land with no

right—they thought they would not be brought back to Us—[40] so We seized him and his armies and threw them into the sea. See what became of the wrongdoers! [41] We made them leaders calling [others] only to the Fire: on the Day of Resurrection they will not be helped. [42] We made Our rejection pursue them in this world, and on the Day of Resurrection they will be among the despised. [43] After We had destroyed the earlier generations, We gave Moses the Scripture to provide insight, guidance, and mercy for people, so that they might take heed.

[44] You [Muhammad] were not present on the western side of the mountain when We gave Our command to Moses: you were not there—[45] We have brought into being many generations who lived long lives!—you did not live among the people of Midian or recite Our Revelation to them—We have always sent messengers to people—[46] nor were you present on the side of Mount Sinai when We called out to Moses. But you too have been sent as an act of grace from your Lord, to give warning to a people to whom no warner has come before, so that they may take heed, [47] and may not say, if a disaster should befall them as a result of what they have done with their own hands, 'Lord, if only You had sent us a messenger, we might have followed Your message and become believers.' [48] Even now that Our truth has come to them, they say, 'Why has he not been given signs like those given to Moses?' Did they not also deny the truth that was given to Moses before? They say, 'Two kinds of sorcery, helping each other,' and, 'We refuse to accept either of them.' [49] Say [Muhammad], 'Then produce a book from God that gives better guidance than these two and I will follow it, if you are telling the truth.' [50] If they do not respond to you, you will know that they follow only their own desires. Who is further astray than the one who follows his own desires with no guidance from God? Truly God does not guide those who do wrong.

[51] We have caused Our Word to come to them so that they may be mindful. [52] Those to whom We gave the Scripture before believe in it,[a] [53] and, when it is recited to them, say, 'We believe in it, it is the truth from our Lord. Before it came we had already devoted ourselves to Him.' [54] They will be given their rewards twice over because they are steadfast, repel evil with good, give to others out of what

---

[a] The Qur'an.

We have provided for them, [55] and turn away whenever they hear frivolous talk, saying, 'We have our deeds and you have yours. Peace be with you! We do not seek the company of ignorant people.'

[56] You [Prophet] cannot guide everyone you love to the truth; it is God who guides whoever He will. He knows best those who will follow guidance. [57] They say, 'If we were to follow guidance with you [Prophet], we would be driven from our land.' Have We not established for them a secure sanctuary[a] where every kind of produce is brought, as a provision from Us? But most of them do not comprehend. [58] We have destroyed many a community that once revelled in its wanton wealth and easy living: since then their dwelling places have barely been inhabited—We are the only heir. [59] Your Lord would never destroy towns without first raising a messenger in their capital to recite Our messages to them, nor would We destroy towns unless their inhabitants were evildoers. [60] Whatever things you have been given for the life of this world are merely [temporary] gratification and vanity: that which is with God is better and more lasting—will you not use your reason?

[61] Can the person who will see the fulfilment of the good promise We gave him be compared to someone We have given some enjoyments for this worldly life but who, on the Day of Resurrection, will face punishment? [62] The Day will come when God will call them, saying, 'Where now are those you allege are My partners?' [63] and those [ringleaders] against whom the verdict will be passed will say, 'Our Lord, these are the ones we caused to deviate. We caused them to deviate as we ourselves deviated, but now we disown them before You, they did not really serve us.' [64] It will then be said to them, 'Now call those you worshipped as partners,' and they will call them but receive no answer. They will see the suffering and wish they had followed guidance. [65] On that Day He will call them, saying, 'How did you respond to My messengers?' [66] All arguments will seem obscure to them on that Day; they will not be able to consult one another. [67] Yet anyone who has repented, believed, and done good deeds can hope to find himself among the successful. [68] Your Lord creates what He pleases and chooses those He will—they have no choice—so glory be to God, and may He be exalted above the partners they ascribe to Him! [69] Your Lord knows what their hearts

[a] Mecca.

conceal and what they reveal. [70]He is God; there is no god but Him; all praise belongs to Him in this world and the next; His is the Judgement; and to Him you shall be returned.

[71]Say [Prophet], 'Just think, if God were to cast perpetual night over you until the Day of Resurrection, what god other than He could bring you light? Do you not listen?' [72]Say, 'Just think, if God were to cast perpetual day over you until the Day of Resurrection, what god other than He could give you night in which to rest? Do you not see? [73]In His mercy He has given you night and day, so that you may rest and seek His bounty and be grateful.' [74]The Day will come when He will call out to them, saying, 'Where are the partners you claimed for Me?' [75]We shall call a witness from every community, and say, 'Produce your evidence,' and then they will know that truth belongs to God alone; the gods they invented will forsake them.

[76]Qarun was one of Moses' people, but he oppressed them. We had given him such treasures that even their keys would have weighed down a whole company of strong men. His people said to him, 'Do not gloat, for God does not like people who gloat. [77]Seek the life to come by means of what God has granted you, but do not neglect your rightful share in this world. Do good to others as God has done good to you. Do not seek to spread corruption in the land, for God does not love those who do this,' [78]but he answered, 'This wealth was given to me on account of the knowledge I possess.' Did he not know that God had destroyed many generations before him, who had greater power than him and built up greater wealth? The guilty are not [even] questioned about their sins.[a] [79]He went out among his people in all his pomp, and those whose aim was the life of this world said, 'If only we had been given something like what Qarun has been given: he really is a very fortunate man,' [80]but those who were given knowledge said, 'Alas for you! God's reward is better for those who believe and do good deeds: only those who are steadfast will attain this.' [81]We caused the earth to swallow him and his home: he had no one to help him against God, nor could he defend himself. [82]The next day, those who had, the day before, wished to be

---

[a] There are a number of interpretations of this verse, the most likely, according to Razi, being that the guilty will not be granted the privilege of being questioned about their sins, nor will they be given the opportunity to provide excuses.

in his place exclaimed, 'Alas [for you, Qarun]! It is God alone who gives what He will, abundantly or sparingly, to whichever He will of His creatures: if God had not been gracious to us, He would have caused the earth to swallow us too.' Alas indeed! Those who deny the truth will never prosper.

[83] We grant the Home in the Hereafter to those who do not seek superiority on earth or spread corruption: the happy ending is awarded to those who are mindful of God. [84] Whoever comes before God with a good deed will receive a better reward; whoever comes with an evil deed will be punished only for what he has done. [85] He who has made the Qur'an binding on you [Prophet] will bring you back home.[a] So say, 'My Lord knows best who has brought true guidance and who is blatantly astray.' [86] You yourself could not have expected the Scripture to be sent to you; it came only as a mercy from your Lord. So give no help to the disbelievers. [87] Do not let them turn you away from God's revelations after they have been revealed to you. Call people to your Lord. Never become one of those who ascribe partners to God. [88] Do not call out to another god beside God, for there is no god but Him. Everything will perish except His Face. His is the Judgement and to Him you shall all be brought back.

[a] To Him. Cf. verse 83. Various commentators take this to refer to Mecca or to the life to come.

29. THE SPIDER

A Meccan sura that takes its title from the illustration of the spider in verse 41. The sura stresses that believers will be tested and that they should remain steadfast. The misconceptions of disbelievers regarding the nature of revelation and the Prophet are addressed. References are made to earlier prophets and details given of the punishments brought on those who denied them.

In the name of God, the Lord of Mercy, the Giver of Mercy

¹ *Alif Lam Mim*

² Do people think they will be left alone after saying 'We believe' without being put to the test? ³ We tested those who went before them: God will certainly mark out which ones are truthful and which are lying. ⁴ Do the evildoers think they can escape us? How ill they judge! ⁵ But as for those who strive for their meeting with God, God's appointed time is bound to come; He is the All Seeing, the All Knowing. ⁶ Those who exert themselves do so for their own benefit—God does not need His creatures—⁷ We shall certainly blot out the misdeeds of those who believe and do good deeds, and We shall reward them according to the best of their actions. ⁸ We have commanded people to be good to their parents, but do not obey them if they strive to make you serve, beside Me, anything of which you have no knowledge: you will all return to Me, and I shall inform you of what you have done. ⁹ We shall be sure to admit those who believe and do good deeds to the ranks of the righteous.

¹⁰ There are some people who say, 'We believe in God,' but, when they suffer for His cause, they think that human persecution is as severe as God's punishment—yet, if any help comes to you [Prophet] from your Lord, they will say, 'We have always been with you'. Does God not know best what is in everyone's hearts?—¹¹ God will be sure to mark out which ones are the believers, and which the hypocrites. ¹² Those who disbelieve say to the believers, 'Follow our path and we shall take the consequences for your sins,' yet they will not do so—they are liars. ¹³ They will bear their own burdens and

others besides: they will be questioned about their false assertions on the Day of Resurrection.

¹⁴ We sent Noah out to his people. He lived among them for fifty years short of a thousand and they were doing evil when the Flood overwhelmed them. ¹⁵ We saved him and those with him on the Ark. We made this a sign for all people.

¹⁶ We also sent Abraham. He said to his people, 'Serve God and be mindful of Him: that is better for you, if only you knew. ¹⁷ What you worship instead of God are mere idols; what you invent is nothing but falsehood. Those you serve instead of God have no power to give you provisions, so seek provisions from God, serve Him, and give Him thanks: you will all be returned to Him. ¹⁸ If you say this is a lie, [be warned that] other communities before you said the same. The messenger's only duty is to give clear warning.'

¹⁹ Do they not see that God brings life into being and reproduces it? Truly this is easy for God. ²⁰ Say, 'Travel throughout the earth and see how He brings life into being: He will bring the next life into being. God has power over all things. ²¹ He punishes whoever He will and shows mercy to whoever He will. You will all be returned to Him. ²² You cannot escape Him on earth or in the heavens; you will have no one to protect or help you besides God.' ²³ Those who deny God's Revelation and their meeting with Him have no hope of receiving My grace: they will have a grievous punishment.

²⁴ The only answer Abraham's people gave was, 'Kill him or burn him!' but God saved him from the Fire: there truly are signs in this for people who believe. ²⁵ Abraham said to them, 'You have chosen idols instead of God but your love for them will only last for the present life: on the Day of Resurrection, you will disown and reject one another. Hell will be your home and no one will help you.' ²⁶ Lot believed him, and said, 'I will flee to my Lord: He is the Almighty, the All Wise.' ²⁷ We gave Isaac and Jacob to Abraham, and placed prophethood and Scripture among his offspring. We gave him his rewards in this world, and in the life to come he will be among the righteous.

²⁸ And Lot: when He said to his people, 'You practise outrageous acts that no people before you have ever committed. ²⁹ How can you lust after men, waylay travellers, and commit evil in your gatherings?' the only answer his people gave was, 'Bring God's punishment

down on us, if what you say is true.' ³⁰ So he prayed, 'My Lord, help
me against these people who spread corruption.' ³¹ When Our messengers brought the good news [of the birth of a son] to Abraham, ^{*a*}
they told him, 'We are about to destroy the people of that town.
They are wrongdoers.' ³² Abraham said, 'But Lot lives there.' They
answered, 'We know who lives there better than you do. We shall save
him and his household, except for his wife: she will be one of those
who stay behind.' ³³ When Our messengers came to Lot, he was
troubled and distressed on their account. They said, 'Have no fear or
grief: we shall certainly save you and your household, except for your
wife—she will be one of those who stay behind—³⁴ and we shall send
a punishment from heaven down on the people of this town because
they violate [God's order].' ³⁵ We left some [of the town] there as a
clear sign for those who use their reason.

³⁶ To the people of Midian We sent their brother Shu'ayb. He said,
'My people, serve God and think ahead to the Last Day. Do not
commit evil and spread corruption in the land.' ³⁷ They rejected him
and so the earthquake overtook them. When morning came, they
were lying dead in their homes. ³⁸ [Remember] the tribes of 'Ad and
Thamud: their history is made clear to you by [what is left of] their
dwelling places. Satan made their foul deeds seem alluring to them
and barred them from the right way, though they were capable of
seeing. ³⁹ [Remember] Qarun and Pharaoh and Haman: Moses
brought them clear signs, but they behaved arrogantly on earth.
They could not escape Us ⁴⁰ and We punished each one of them for
their sins: some We struck with a violent storm; some were overcome
by a sudden blast; some We made the earth swallow; and some We
drowned. It was not God who wronged them; they wronged themselves. ⁴¹ Those who take protectors other than God can be compared to spiders building themselves houses—the spider's is the
frailest of all houses—if only they could understand. ⁴² God knows
what things they call upon beside Him: He is the Mighty, the Wise.
⁴³ Such are the comparisons We draw for people, though only the
wise can grasp them. ⁴⁴ God has created the heavens and earth for a
true purpose. There truly is a sign in this for those who believe.

⁴⁵ [Prophet], recite what has been revealed to you of the Scripture;
keep up the prayer: prayer restrains outrageous and unacceptable

---

^{*a*} Cf. e.g. 51: 28.

behaviour. Remembering God is greater: God knows everything you are doing. [46] [Believers], argue only in the best way with the People of the Book, except with those of them who act unjustly. Say, 'We believe in what was revealed to us and in what was revealed to you; our God and your God are one [and the same]; we are devoted to Him.' [47] This is the way [Muhammad] We sent the Scripture to you. Those to whom We had already given Scripture[a] believe in [the Qur'an] and so do some of these people. No one refuses to acknowledge Our revelations but those who reject [the Truth].

[48] You never recited any Scripture before We revealed this one to you; you never wrote one down with your hand. If you had done so, those who follow falsehood might have had cause to doubt. [49] But no, [this Qur'an] is a revelation that is clear to the hearts of those endowed with knowledge. Only the evildoers refuse to acknowledge Our revelations. [50] They say, 'Why have no miracles been sent to him by his Lord?' Say, 'Miracles lie in God's hands; I am simply here to warn you plainly.' [51] Do they not think it is enough that We have sent down to you the Scripture that is recited to them? There is a mercy in this and a lesson for believing people. [52] Say, 'God is sufficient witness between me and you: He knows what is in the heavens and earth. Those who believe in false deities and deny God will be the losers.'

[53] They challenge you to hasten the punishment: they would already have received a punishment if God had not set a time for it, and indeed it will come to them suddenly and catch them unawares. [54] They challenge you to hasten the punishment: Hell will encompass all those who deny the truth, [55] on the Day when punishment overwhelms them from above and from below their very feet, and they will be told, 'Now taste the punishment for what you used to do.'

[56] My believing servants! My earth is vast, so worship Me and Me alone. [57] Every soul will taste death, then it is to Us that you will be returned. [58] We shall lodge those who believed and did good deeds in lofty dwellings, in the Garden graced with flowing streams, there to remain. How excellent is the reward of those who labour, [59] those who are steadfast, those who put their trust in their Lord! [60] How many are the creatures who do not have their sustenance stored up:

---

[a] According to some commentators this refers to those Jews and Christians at the time of the Prophet who believed in him.

God sustains them and you: He alone is the All Hearing, the All Knowing. ⁶¹ If you ask the disbelievers who created the heavens and earth and who harnessed the sun and moon, they are sure to say, 'God.' Then why do they turn away from Him? ⁶² It is God who gives abundantly to whichever of His servants He will, and sparingly to whichever He will. He has full knowledge of everything. ⁶³ If you ask them, 'Who sends water down from the sky and gives life with it to the earth after it has died?' they are sure to say, 'God.' Say, 'Praise be to God!' Truly, most of them do not use their reason.

⁶⁴ The life of this world is merely an amusement and a diversion; the true life is in the Hereafter, if only they knew. ⁶⁵ Whenever they go on board a ship they call on God, and dedicate their faith to Him alone, but once He has delivered them safely back to land, see how they ascribe partners to Him. ⁶⁶ Let them show their ingratitude for what We have given them; let them take their enjoyment. Soon they will know. ⁶⁷ Can they not see that We have granted them a secure sanctuary*ᵃ* though all around them people are snatched away? Then how can they believe in what is false and deny God's blessing? ⁶⁸ Who could be more wicked than the person who invents lies about God, or denies the truth when it comes to him? Is Hell not the home for the disbelievers? ⁶⁹ But We shall be sure to guide to Our ways those who strive hard for Our cause: God is with those who do good.

ᵃ Mecca.

30. THE BYZANTINES

A Meccan sura which opens with a reference to the defeat of the Byzantines at the hands of the Persians (613–14 CE) in Syria, and the subsequent victory of the Byzantines in 624 CE. The sura urges people to reflect on the creation of themselves, the heavens and earth, and all God's wonders. God's power to give life to a barren land is repeated as an indication both of His ability to raise the dead and of His mercy to mankind. The disbelievers are warned to believe before it is too late; the Prophet is urged to persevere and to ignore the taunts of the disbelievers.

In the name of God, the Lord of Mercy, the Giver of Mercy

¹ *Alif Lam Mim*

² The Byzantines have been defeated ³ in a nearby land. They will reverse their defeat with a victory ⁴ in a few years' time *ᵃ* — God is in command, first and last. On that day, the believers will rejoice ⁵ at God's help. He helps whoever He pleases: He is the Mighty, the Merciful. ⁶ This is God's promise: God never breaks His promise, but most people do not know; ⁷ they only know the outer surface of this present life and are heedless of the life to come. ⁸ Have they not thought about their own selves? *ᵇ* God did not create the heavens and earth and everything between them without a serious purpose and an appointed time, yet many people deny that they will meet their Lord.

⁹ Have they not travelled through the land and seen how their predecessors met their end? They were mightier than them: they cultivated the earth more and built more upon it. Their own messengers also came to them with clear signs: God did not wrong them; they wronged themselves. ¹⁰ The evildoers met a terrible end for rejecting and [repeatedly] mocking God's revelations. ¹¹ God brings creation into being; in the end He will reproduce it and it is to Him you will be recalled.

¹² On the Day the Hour arrives, the guilty will despair ¹³ and they

---

ᵃ When fortunes were reversed and the Byzantines won a victory, this was to please the believers. This was also the year of the Muslim victory at Badr. The earlier defeat of the Byzantines had been viewed by the Meccan pagans as a victory for paganism.

ᵇ Or 'within' themselves.

will have no intercessors among those partners they ascribed to God. They will deny these partners. ¹⁴ When the Hour arrives, on that Day they will be separated: ¹⁵ those who believed and did good deeds will delight in a Garden, ¹⁶ while those who disbelieved and denied Our messages and the meeting of the Hereafter will be brought for punishment.

¹⁷ So celebrate God's glory in the evening, in the morning— ¹⁸ praise is due to Him in the heavens and the earth—in the late afternoon, and at midday. ¹⁹ He brings the living out of the dead and the dead out of the living. He gives life to the earth after death, and you will be brought out in the same way. ²⁰ One of His signs is that He created you from dust and—lo and behold!—you became human and scattered far and wide. ²¹ Another of His signs is that He created spouses from among yourselves for you to live with in tranquillity: He ordained love and kindness between you. There truly are signs in this for those who reflect. ²² Another of His signs is that He created the heavens and earth, the diversity of your languages and colours. There truly are signs in this for those who know. ²³ Among His signs are your sleep, by night and by day, and your seeking His bounty. There truly are signs in this for those who can hear. ²⁴ Among His signs, too, are that He shows you the lightning that terrifies and inspires hope; that He sends water down from the sky to restore the earth to life after death. There truly are signs in this for those who use their reason. ²⁵ Among His signs, too, is the fact that the heavens and the earth stand firm by His command. In the end, you will all emerge when He calls you from the earth. ²⁶ Everyone in the heavens and earth belongs to Him, and all are obedient to Him. ²⁷ He is the One who originates creation and will do it again—this is even easier for Him. He is above all comparison in the heavens and earth; He is the Almighty, the All Wise.

²⁸ He gives you this example, drawn from your own lives: do you make your slaves full partners with an equal share in what We have given you? Do you fear them as you fear each other? This is how We make Our messages clear to those who use their reason. ²⁹ And still the polytheists follow their own desires without any knowledge. Who can guide those God leaves to stray, who have no one to help them? ³⁰ So [Prophet] as a man of pure faith, stand firm in your devotion to *a*

a Literally 'set your face to'.

the religion. This is the natural disposition God instilled in man-kind—there is no altering God's creation—and this is the right religion, though most people do not realize it. ³¹ Turn to Him alone, all of you. Be mindful of Him; keep up the prayer; do not join those who ascribe partners to God ³² [or] those who divide their religion into sects, with each party rejoicing in their own. ³³ When something bad happens to people, they cry to their Lord and turn to Him for help, but no sooner does He let them taste His blessing than—lo and behold!—some of them ascribe partners to their Lord, ³⁴ showing no gratitude for what We have given them. 'Take your pleasure! You will come to understand.' ³⁵ Did We send them down any authority that sanctions the partners they ascribe to God?

³⁶ When We give people a taste of Our blessing, they rejoice, but when something bad happens to them—because of their own actions—they fall into utter despair. ³⁷ Do they not see that God gives abundantly to whoever He will and sparingly [to whoever He will]? There truly are signs in this for those who believe. ³⁸ So give their due to the near relative, the needy, and the wayfarer—that is best for those whose goal is God's countenance: these are the ones who will prosper. ³⁹ Whatever you lend out in usury to gain value through other people's wealth will not increase in God's eyes, but whatever you give in charity, in your desire for God's countenance, will earn multiple rewards. ⁴⁰ It is God who created you and provided for you, who will cause you to die and give you life again. Which of your 'partners' can do any one of these things? Glory be to God, and exalted be He above the partners they attribute to Him. ⁴¹ Corruption has appeared on land and sea as a result of people's actions and He will make them taste the consequences of some of their own actions so that they may turn back. ⁴² Say, 'Travel through the land, and see how those before you met their end—most of them were idolaters.' ⁴³ [Prophet], stand firm in your devotion to the upright religion, before an irresistible Day comes from God. On that Day, mankind will be divided: ⁴⁴ those who rejected the truth will bear the burden of that rejection, and those who did good deeds will have made good provision for themselves. ⁴⁵ From His bounty God will reward those who believe and do good deeds; He does not like those who reject the truth.

⁴⁶ Another of His signs is that He sends out the winds bearing good news, giving you a taste of His grace, making the ships sail at

His command, enabling you to [journey in] search of His bounty so that you may be grateful. [47] Before you [Muhammad], We sent messengers, each to their own people: they brought them clear proofs and then We punished the evildoers. We make it Our duty to help the believers. [48] It is God who sends out the winds; they stir up the clouds; He spreads them over the skies as He pleases; He makes them break up and you see the rain falling from them. See how they rejoice when He makes it fall upon whichever of His servants He wishes, [49] though before it is sent they may have lost all hope. [50] Look, then, at the imprints of God's mercy, how He restores the earth to life after death: this same God is the one who will return people to life after death—He has power over all things. [51] Yet they will continue in their disbelief, even if We send a [scorching] wind and they see their crops turn yellow: [52] you [Prophet] cannot make the dead hear and you cannot make the deaf hear your call when they turn their backs and leave; [53] you cannot lead the blind out of their error: the only ones you can make hear you are those who believe in Our revelations and devote themselves to Us. [54] It is God who creates you weak, then gives you strength, then weakness after strength, together with your grey hair: He creates what He will; He is the All Knowing, All Powerful.

[55] On the Day the Hour comes, the guilty will swear they lingered no more than an hour—they have always been deluded—[56] but those endowed with knowledge and faith will say, 'In accordance with God's decree, you actually lingered till the Day of Resurrection: this is the Day of Resurrection, yet you did not know.' [57] On that Day the evildoers' excuses will be of no use to them: they will not be allowed to make amends.

[58] In this Qur'an We have set every kind of illustration before people, yet if you [Prophet] brought them a miracle, the disbelievers would still say, 'You [prophets] deal only in falsehood.' [59] In this way God seals the hearts of those who do not know, [60] so be patient, for God's promise is true: do not let those with no firm beliefs discourage you.

31. LUQMAN

A Meccan sura that takes its title from Luqman the Wise, whose counsel to his son is related in verses 13–19. The sura opens with a description of the believers, and it condemns those who attempt to lead others away from guidance. It extols God's power and warns the disbelievers of the consequences of their actions. The Prophet is told not to be saddened by their disbelief.

In the name of God, the Lord of Mercy, the Giver of Mercy

¹ *Alif Lam Mim*

² These are the verses of the wise Scripture, ³ [with] guidance and mercy for those who do good, ⁴ who keep up the prayer, pay the prescribed alms, and are certain of the Hereafter. ⁵ These are rightly guided by their Lord, and it is they who will prosper. ⁶ But there is the sort of person who pays for distracting tales, intending, without any knowledge, to lead others from God's way, and to hold it up to ridicule.ᵃ There will be humiliating punishment for him! ⁷ When Our verses are recited to him, he turns away disdainfully as if he had not heard them, as if there were heaviness in his ears. Tell him that there will be a grievous punishment! ⁸ But for those who believe and do righteous deeds, there will be Gardens of bliss ⁹ where they will stay: that is God's true promise, and He is the Almighty, the All Wise. ¹⁰ He created the heavens without any visible support, and He placed firm mountains on the earth—in case it should shake under you—and He spread all kinds of animals around it. We sent down water from the sky, with which We made every kind of good plant grow: ¹¹ all this is God's creation. Now, show Me what these others have created. No, the disbelievers are clearly astray.

¹² We endowed Luqman with wisdom: 'Be thankful to God: whoever gives thanks benefits his own soul, and as for those who are thankless—God is self-sufficient, worthy of all praise.' ¹³ Luqman counselled his son, 'My son, do not attribute any partners to God: attributing partners to Him is a terrible wrong.'

ᵃ Understood to refer to al-Nadr ibn al-Harith, who bought some ancient Persian stories to distract the people of Quraysh from listening to the Qur'an.

¹⁴ We have commanded people to be good to their parents. Their mothers carried them, with strain upon strain, and it takes two years to wean them. Give thanks to Me and to your parents—all will return to Me. ¹⁵ But if they strive to make you associate with Me anything about which you have no knowledge,ᵃ then do not obey them. Yet keep their company in this life according to what is right, ʳand follow the path of those who turn to Me. You will all return to Me in the end, and I will tell you everything that you have done.

¹⁶ [And Luqman continued], 'My son, if even the weight of a mustard seed were hidden in a rock or anywhere in the heavens or earth, God would bring it [to light], for He is all subtle and all aware. ¹⁷ Keep up the prayer, my son; command what is right; forbid what is wrong; bear anything that happens to you steadfastly: these are things to be aspired to. ¹⁸ Do not turn your nose up at people, nor walk about the place arrogantly, for God does not love arrogant or boastful people. ¹⁹ Go at a moderate pace and lower your voice, for the ugliest of all voices is the braying of asses.'

²⁰ [People], do you not see how God has made what is in the heavens and on the earth useful to you, and has lavished His blessings on you both outwardly and inwardly? Yet some people argue about God, without knowledge or guidance or an illuminating scripture. ²¹ When they are told, 'Follow what God has sent down,' they say: 'We shall follow what we saw our forefathers following.' What! Even if Satan is calling them to the suffering of the Blazing Flame? ²² Whoever directs himselfᵇ wholly to God and does good work has grasped the surest handhold, for the outcome of everything is with God. ²³ As for those who refuse to do this, do not let their refusal sadden you [Prophet]—they will return to Us and We shall tell them what they have done: God knows all that hearts contain—²⁴ We let them enjoy themselves for a little while, but We shall drive them to a harsh punishment. ²⁵ If you ask them who created the heavens and earth, they are sure to say, 'God.' Say, 'Praise belongs to God,' but most of them do not understand. ²⁶ Everything in the heavens and earth belongs to God. God is self-sufficient and worthy of all praise. ²⁷ If all the trees on earth were pens and all the seas, with seven more seas besides, [were ink,] still God's words would not run out: God is almighty and all wise. ²⁸ Creating and resurrecting all of you is just

ᵃ i.e. scriptural proof.   ᵇ Literally 'his face'.

like creating or resurrecting a single soul: God is all hearing and all seeing.

²⁹[Prophet], do you not see that God causes the night to merge into day and the day to merge into night; that He has subjected the sun and the moon, each to run its course for a stated term; that He is aware of everything you [people] do? ³⁰This is because God is the Truth, and what they invoke beside Him is false. He is the Most High, Most Great. ³¹[Prophet], do you not see that ships sail through the sea, by the grace of God, to show you [people] some of His wonders? Truly there are signs in this for every steadfast, thankful person. ³²When the waves loom over those on board like giant shadows they call out to God, devoting their religion entirely to Him. But, when He has delivered them safely to land, some of them waver—only a treacherous, thankless person refuses to acknowledge Our signs. ³³People, be mindful of your Lord and fear a day when no parent will take the place of their child, nor a child take the place of their parent, in any way. God's promise is true, so do not let the present life delude you, nor let the Deceiver delude you about God. ³⁴Knowledge of the Hour [of Resurrection] belongs to God; it is He who sends down rain and He who knows what is hidden in the womb. No soul knows what it will reap tomorrow, and no soul knows in what land it will die; it is God who is all knowing and all aware.

32. BOWING DOWN IN WORSHIP

A Meccan sura which takes its title from the bowing down of true believers in worship in verse 15. The truth of the Qur'an is emphasized at the beginning of the sura, and the Prophet is urged at the end of the sura to pay no attention to the disbelievers who cannot see the significance of God's signs.

In the name of God, the Lord of Mercy, the Giver of Mercy

¹ *Alif Lam Mim*

² This scripture, free from all doubt, has been sent down from the Lord of the Worlds. ³ Yet they say, 'Muhammad has made it up.' No indeed! It is the Truth from your Lord [Prophet], for you to warn a people who have had no one to warn them before, so that they may be guided. ⁴ It is God who created the heavens and the earth and everything between them in six Days. Then He established Himself on the Throne. You [people] have no one but Him to protect you and no one to intercede for you, so why do you not take heed? ⁵ He runs everything, from the heavens to the earth, and everything will ascend to Him in the end, on a Day that will measure a thousand years in your reckoning. ⁶ Such is He who knows all that is unseen as well as what is seen, the Almighty, the Merciful, ⁷ who gave everything its perfect form. He first created man from clay, ⁸ then made his descendants from an extract of underrated fluid.ᵃ ⁹ Then He moulded him; He breathed His Spirit into him; He gave you hearing, sight, and minds. How seldom you are grateful! ¹⁰ They say, 'What? When we have disappeared into the earth, shall we really be created anew?' In fact, they deny the meeting with their Lord. ¹¹ Say, 'The Angel of Death put in charge of you will reclaim you, and then you will be brought back to your Lord.'

¹² [Prophet], if only you could see the wrongdoers hang their heads before their Lord: 'Our Lord, now that we have seen and heard, send us back and we shall do good. [Now] we are convinced.' ¹³ 'If it had been Our will, We could certainly have given every soul its true guidance, but My words have come true. "I shall be sure to

---

ᵃ Semen.

fill Hell with jinn and men together." ¹⁴ So since you ignored the meeting on this Day of yours, now We shall ignore you: taste the lasting suffering for all you have done.'

¹⁵ The only people who truly believe in Our messages are those who, when they are reminded of them, bow down in worship, celebrate their Lord's praises, and do not think themselves above this. ¹⁶ Their sides shun their beds in order to pray to their Lord in fear and hope; they give to others some of what We have given them. ¹⁷ No soul knows what joy is kept hidden in store for them as a reward for what they have done. ¹⁸ So, is someone who believes equal to someone who defies God? No, they are not equal. ¹⁹ Those who believe and do good deeds will have Gardens awaiting them as their home and as a reward for what they have done. ²⁰ As for those who defy God, their home will be the Fire. Whenever they try to escape it, they will be driven back into it, and they will be told, 'Taste the torment of the Fire, which you persistently denied.' ²¹ We shall certainly make them taste a nearer torment [in this life] prior to the greater torment, so that perhaps they may return [to the right path]. ²² Who does more wrong than someone who, when messages from his Lord are recited to him, turns away from them? We shall inflict retribution on the guilty.

²³ We gave Moses the Scripture—so [Muhammad] do not doubt that you are receiving it—and We made it a guide for the Children of Israel. ²⁴ When they became steadfast and believed firmly in Our messages, We raised leaders among them, guiding them according to Our command. ²⁵ [Prophet], it is your Lord who will judge between them on the Day of Resurrection concerning their differences.

²⁶ Is it not a lesson for them [to see] how many generations We destroyed before them, in whose homes they now walk? There truly are signs in this—do they not hear? ²⁷ Do they not consider how We drive rain to the barren land, and with it produce vegetation from which their cattle and they themselves eat? Do they not see? ²⁸ And they say, 'When will this Decision be, if you are telling the truth?' ²⁹ Say, 'On the Day of Decision it will be no use for the disbelievers to believe; they will be granted no respite.' ³⁰ So [Prophet], turn away from them and wait: they too are waiting.

33. THE JOINT FORCES

A Medinan sura which gets its title from the incident of the Battle of the Trench in AH 5/627 CE (verses 9–27), when the joint forces of various tribes of disbelievers besieged Medina. The believers dug a ditch, which the disbelievers were unable to cross, and eventually the enemy retreated in disarray. This is mentioned in order to remind the believers of God's goodness to them, so that they may obey the numerous instructions given in the sura, starting with the regulation of adoption and including proper conduct towards the Prophet and his wives. The hypocrites are warned to stop their bad behaviour.

In the name of God, the Lord of Mercy, the Giver of Mercy

¹ Prophet, be mindful of God and do not give in to the disbelievers and the hypocrites: God is all knowing, all wise. ² Follow what your Lord reveals to you: God is well aware of all your actions. ³ Put your trust in God: God is enough to trust. ⁴ God does not put two hearts within a man's breast. He does not turn the wives you reject and compare to your mothers' backs *a* into your real mothers; nor does He make your adopted sons into real sons. These are only words from your mouths, while God speaks the truth and guides people to the right path.

⁵ Name your adopted sons after their real fathers: this is more equitable in God's eyes—if you do not know who their fathers are [they are your] 'brothers-in-religion' and protégés. *b* You will not be blamed if you make a mistake, only for what your hearts deliberately intend; God is most forgiving and merciful. ⁶ The Prophet is more caring towards the believers than they are themselves, while his wives are their mothers. *c* In God's Scripture, blood-relatives have a stronger claim than other believers and emigrants, though you may still bestow gifts on your friends. All this is written in the Scripture.

---

a In pre-Islamic Arabia the husband sometimes said to his wife, 'From now on, you are to me like my mother's back,' by which he meant that he refused to have further conjugal relations with her, yet did not divorce her and so give her the freedom to remarry (see 58: 1–4).

b *Mawla* in Arabic has many meanings, including 'protégé', 'client', 'companion'.

c The Prophet's wives were given the title 'Mothers of the Believers'. Cf. verse 53.

⁷ We took a solemn pledge from the prophets—from you [Muhammad], from Noah, from Abraham, from Moses, from Jesus, son of Mary—We took a solemn pledge from all of them: ⁸ God will question the truthful about their sincerity, and He has prepared a painful punishment for those who reject the truth.

⁹ You who believe, remember God's goodness to you when mighty armies massed against you: We sent a violent wind and invisible forces against them. God sees all that you do. ¹⁰ They massed against you from above and below; your eyes rolled [with fear], your hearts rose into your throats, and you thought [ill] thoughts of God. ¹¹ There the believers were sorely tested and deeply shaken: ¹² the hypocrites and the sick at heart said, 'God and His Messenger promised us nothing but delusions!' ¹³ Some of them said, 'People of Yathrib,ᵃ you will not be able to withstand [the attack], so go back!' Some of them asked the Prophet's permission to leave, saying, 'Our houses are exposed,' even though they were not—they just wanted to run away: ¹⁴ had the city been invaded from all sides, and the enemy invited them to rebel, they would have done so almost without hesitation. ¹⁵ Yet they had already promised God that they would not turn tail and flee, and a promise to God will be answered for. ¹⁶ [Prophet], say, 'Running away will not benefit you. If you manage to escape death or slaughter, you will only be permitted to enjoy [life] for a short while.' ¹⁷ Say, 'If God wishes to harm you, who can protect you? If God wishes to show you mercy, who can prevent Him?' They will find no one but God to protect or help them.

¹⁸ God knows exactly who among you hinder others, who [secretly] say to their brothers, 'Come and join us,' who hardly ever come out to fight, ¹⁹ who begrudge you [believers] any help. When fear comes,ᵇ you [Prophet] see them looking at you with rolling eyes like someone in their death throes; when fear has passed, they attack you with sharp tongues and begrudge you any good. Such men do not believe, and God brings their deeds to nothing. That is all too easy for God. ²⁰ They think the joint forces have not gone, and if the joint forces did come again they would wish they were in the desert, wandering among the Bedouin and seeking news about you [from a safe distance]. Even if they were with you [believers], they would

ᵃ The pre-Islamic name for Medina.
ᵇ This specifically refers to fear felt in battle in this context (*al-Mu'jam al-Wasit*).

hardly fight at all. [21] The Messenger of God is an excellent model for those of you who put your hope in God and the Last Day and remember Him often.

[22] When the believers saw the joint forces, they said, 'This is what God and His Messenger promised us: the promise of God and His Messenger is true,' and this only served to increase their faith and submission to God. [23] There are men among the believers who honoured their pledge to God: some of them have fulfilled it by death, and some are still waiting. They have not changed in the least. [24] [Such trials are ordained] so that God may reward the truthful for their honesty and punish the hypocrites, if He so wills, or He may relent towards them, for God is forgiving and merciful. [25] God sent back the disbelievers[a] along with their rage—they gained no benefit—and spared the believers from fighting. He is strong and mighty. [26] He brought those People of the Book who supported them down from their strongholds and put terror into their hearts. Some of them you [believers] killed and some you took captive. [27] He passed on to you their land, their houses, their possessions, and a land where you had not set foot: God has power over everything.

[28] Prophet, say to your wives,[b] 'If your desire is for the present life and its finery, then come, I will make provision for you and release you with kindness, [29] but if you desire God, His Messenger, and the Final Home, then remember that God has prepared great rewards for those of you who do good.' [30] Wives of the Prophet, if any of you does something clearly outrageous, she will be doubly punished— that is easy for God—[31] but if any of you is obedient to God and His Messenger and does good deeds, know that We shall give her a double reward and have prepared a generous provision for her. [32] Wives of the Prophet, you are not like any other woman. If you truly fear God, do not speak too softly in case the sick at heart should lust after you, but speak in an appropriate manner; [33] stay at home, and do not flaunt your attractions as they used to in the pagan past; keep up the prayer, give the prescribed alms, and obey God and His Messenger. God wishes to keep uncleanness away from you, people of the [Prophet's] House, and make you completely pure. [34] Remember

---

[a] This refers to the sandstorm that caused the disbelievers to go back without success.

[b] Some of the Prophet's wives decided to ask him for more provision, seeing that he had become leader of a new state.

what is recited in your houses of God's revelations and wisdom, for God is all subtle, all aware.

³⁵For men and women who are devoted to God—believing men and women, obedient men and women, truthful men and women, steadfast men and women, humble men and women, charitable men and women, fasting men and women, chaste men and women, men and women who remember God often—God has prepared forgiveness and a rich reward.

³⁶When God and His Messenger have decided on a matter that concerns them, it is not fitting for any believing man or woman to claim freedom of choice in that matter: whoever disobeys God and His Messenger is far astray. ³⁷When you [Prophet] said to the man who had been favoured by God and by you, 'Keep your wife and be mindful of God,' you hid in your heart what God would later reveal: you were afraid of people, but it is more fitting that you fear God. After Zayd divorced her,^a We gave her to you in marriage so that there might be no fault in believers marrying the wives of their adopted sons after they had divorced them. God's command must be carried out: ³⁸the Prophet is not at fault for what God has ordained for him. This was God's practice with those who went before— God's command must be fulfilled—³⁹[and with all] those who deliver God's messages and fear only Him and no other: God's reckoning is enough. ⁴⁰Muhammad is not the father of any one of you men; he is God's Messenger and the seal of the prophets: God knows everything. ⁴¹Believers, remember God often ⁴²and glorify Him morning and evening: ⁴³it is He who blesses you, as do His angels, in order to lead you out of the depths of darkness into the light. He is ever merciful towards the believers—⁴⁴when they meet Him they will be greeted with 'Peace'—and He has prepared a generous reward for them.

⁴⁵Prophet, We have sent you as a witness, as a bearer of good news and warning, ⁴⁶as one who calls people to God by His leave, as a light-giving lamp. ⁴⁷Give the believers the good news that great bounty awaits them from God. ⁴⁸Do not give in to the disbelievers and the hypocrites: ignore the harm they cause you and put your trust in God. God is enough to trust.

^a The Prophet married Zayd, his adopted son, to Zaynab, his own cousin. Zayd later divorced her and the Prophet took her as his own wife. This sura shows the marriage to be lawful since adoption does not create blood relations that preclude marriage.

⁴⁹ Believers, you have no right to expect a waiting period when you marry believing women and then divorce them before you have touched them: make provision for them and release them in an honourable way. ⁵⁰ Prophet, We have made lawful for you the wives whose dowries you have paid, and any slaves God has assigned to you through war, and the daughters of your uncles and aunts on your father's and mother's sides, who migrated with you. Also any believing woman who offers herself [without dowry] to the Prophet and whom the Prophet wishes to wed—this only applies to you [Prophet] and not the rest of the believers: We know exactly what We have made obligatory for them concerning their wives and slave-girls—so you should not be blamed: God is most forgiving, most merciful. ⁵¹ You may make any of [your women] wait and receive any of them as you wish, but you will not be at fault if you invite one whose turn you have previously set aside: this way it is more likely that they will be satisfied and will not be distressed. All will be content with what you have given them. God knows what is in your hearts: God is all knowing, forbearing. ⁵² You [Prophet] are not permitted to take any further wives, nor to exchange the wives you have for others, even if these attract you with their beauty. But this does not apply to your slave-girls: God is watchful over all.

⁵³ Believers, do not enter the Prophet's apartments for a meal unless you are given permission to do so; do not linger until [a meal] is ready. When you are invited, enter; then, when you have taken your meal, depart. Do not stay on and talk for that would offend the Prophet, though he would shrink from asking you to leave. God does not shrink from the truth. When you ask his wives for something, do so from behind a screen: this is purer both for your hearts and for theirs. It is not right for you to offend God's Messenger, just as you should never marry his wives after him: that would be grievous in God's eyes. ⁵⁴ God has full knowledge of all things, whether you reveal them or not. ⁵⁵ The Prophet's wives are not to blame [if they are seen by] their fathers, their sons, their brothers, their brothers' sons, their sisters' sons, their women, or their slaves. [Wives of the Prophet], be mindful of God. God observes everything. ⁵⁶ God and His angels bless the Prophet—so, you who believe, bless him too and give him greetings of peace. ⁵⁷ Those who insult God and His Messen-

ger will be rejected by God in this world and the next—He has prepared a humiliating punishment for them—[58] and those who undeservedly insult believing men and women will bear the guilt of slander and obvious sin.

[59] Prophet, tell your wives, your daughters, and women believers to make their outer garments hang low over them[a] so as to be recognized and not insulted: God is most forgiving, most merciful. [60] If the hypocrites, the sick at heart, and those who spread lies in the city do not desist, We shall rouse you [Prophet] against them, and then they will only be your neighbours in this city for a short while. [61] They will be rejected wherever they are found, and then seized and killed. [62] This has been God's practice with those who went before. You will find no change in God's practices.

[63] People ask you about the Hour. Say, 'God alone has knowledge of it.' How could you [Prophet] know? The Hour may well be near. [64] God has rejected the disbelievers and prepared a blazing fire for them. [65] There they will live, with no one to befriend or support them. [66] On the Day when their faces are being turned about in the Fire, they will say, 'If only we had obeyed God and the Messenger,' [67] and 'Lord! We obeyed our masters and our chiefs, and they led us astray. [68] Lord! Give them a double punishment and reject them completely.'

[69] Believers, do not be like those who insulted Moses—God cleared him of their allegations and he was highly honoured in God's eyes. [70] Believers, be mindful of God, speak in a direct fashion and to good purpose, [71] and He will put your deeds right for you and forgive you your sins. Whoever obeys God and His Messenger will truly achieve a great triumph. [72] We offered the Trust[b] to the heavens, the earth, and the mountains, yet they refused to undertake it and were afraid of it; mankind undertook it—they have always been inept[c] and foolish. [73] God will punish the hypocrites and the idolaters, both men and women, and turn with mercy to the believers, both men and women: God is most forgiving, most merciful.

[a] The Arabic idiom *adna al-jilbab* means 'make it hang low', not 'wrap around' as other translators have assumed (*al-Mu'jam al-Wasit*).

[b] [Of reason and moral responsibility]

[c] The meaning of *dhalama* is 'put something out of its place'.

34. SHEBA

A Meccan sura that takes its name from the people of Sheba who were blessed, and then punished for their ingratitude (verses 15–21). The Prophet is first encouraged through references to David and Solomon and how God favoured them. The disbelievers of Mecca are warned through a description of the punishment that awaits them on the Day of Resurrection. Two references are made to their accusing the Prophet of madness (verses 8 and 46) and this charge is thoroughly refuted.

In the name of God, the Lord of Mercy, the Giver of Mercy

[1]Praise be to God, to whom belongs all that is in the heavens and earth, and praise be to Him in the life to come. He is the All Wise, the All Aware. [2]He knows all that goes into the earth and all that comes out of it; He knows all that comes down from the heavens and all that goes up to them. He is the Merciful, the Forgiving. [3]Still, the disbelievers say, 'The Last Hour will never come upon us.' Say, 'Yes indeed [it will]. By Him who knows the unseen! Not even the weight of a speck of dust in the heavens or earth escapes His knowledge, nor anything smaller or greater. It is all recorded in a clear Record [4]so that He can reward those who believe and do good deeds: they will have forgiveness and generous provision.' [5]But as for those who work against Our Revelations, seeking to undermine them, there will be a torment of painful suffering.

[6][Prophet], those who have been given knowledge can see that what has been sent to you from your Lord is the truth, and that it leads to the path of the Almighty, worthy of all praise. [7]But the disbelievers say, 'Shall we show you a man who claims that, when you have been utterly torn to pieces, you will be raised in a new creation? [8]Has he invented a lie about God? Is he mad?' No! It is those who do not believe in the life to come who will suffer torment, for they are in gross error. [9]Do they not think about what is in front of them and behind them in the heavens and earth? If We wished, We could make the earth swallow them, or make fragments from the heavens fall down upon them. There truly is a sign in this for every servant who turns back to God in repentance.

[10] We graced David with Our favour. We said, 'You mountains, echo God's praises together with him, and you birds, too.' We softened iron for him, [11] saying, 'Make coats of chain mail and measure the links well.' [We said to his people], 'Do good, for I see everything you do.' [12] And [We subjected] the wind for Solomon. Its outward journey took a month, and its return journey likewise. We made a fountain of molten brass flow for him, and some of the jinn worked under his control with his Lord's command. If one of them deviated from Our command, We let him taste the suffering of the blazing flame. [13] They made him whatever he wanted—palaces,[a] statues, basins as large as water troughs, gigantic cauldrons. We said, 'Work thankfully, family of David, for few of my servants are truly thankful.' [14] Then, when We decreed Solomon's death, the jinn did not know about it until an earthworm gnawed away at his stick— when he fell down they realized he was dead—for if they had known what was hidden they would not have continued their demeaning labour.

[15] There was a sign for the people of Sheba, too, in their dwelling place: two gardens, one on the right, one on the left: 'Eat from what your Lord has provided for you and give Him thanks, for your land is good, and your Lord most forgiving.' [16] But they paid no heed, so We let loose on them a flood from the dam and replaced their two gardens with others that yielded bitter fruit, tamarisk bushes, and a few lote trees.[b] [17] In this way We punished them for their ingratitude— would We punish anyone but the ungrateful? [18] Also, We had placed, between them and the towns We had blessed, other towns within sight of one another to which they could travel easily—'Travel safely in this land by night and by day'—[19] but [still] they complained, 'Our Lord has made the distance between our staging posts so long!'[c] They wronged themselves and, in the end, We made their fate a byword, and scattered them in countless fragments. There truly are signs in this for every patient, thankful person. [20] Satan was proved right in his opinion of them, for they all followed him—except for a group of believers—[21] even though he had no authority over them.

---

[a] *Mihrab* refers to a number of fine edifices, including palaces (*al-Mu'jam al-Wasit*).

[b] Lote tree: a thorny tree, also known as Christ-thorn, with edible fruit.

[c] For this reading see A. H. Omar and A. S. Makram, *Mu'jam al-Qira'at al-Qur'aniyya* (Tehran, 1999), under this verse reference. This seems to make better sense than the other reading 'Lord, make our journeys further apart'.

But [We aim] to distinguish those who believe in the life to come from those who doubt it: [Prophet], your Lord observes everything.

²² Say, 'Pray to your so-called gods beside God. They do not control even the weight of a speck of dust in heaven or earth, nor do they have any share in them, nor are any of them any help to God. ²³ Intercession will not work with Him, except through those to whom He gives permission.' They will be asked, after the terror is lifted from their hearts [on the Day of Judgement], 'What did your Lord speak?' and they will answer, 'The Truth. He is the Most High, the Most Great.' ²⁴ Say [Prophet], 'Who gives you sustenance from the heavens and earth?' Say, 'God does,' and '[One party of us] must be rightly guided and the other clearly astray.' ²⁵ Say, 'You will not be questioned about our sins, nor will we be questioned about what you do.' ²⁶ Say, 'Our Lord will gather us together, then He will judge justly between us; He alone is the All Knowing Judge.' ²⁷ Say, 'Show me those you joined to Him as partners. No indeed! He alone is God, the Almighty, the All Wise.' ²⁸ We have sent you [Prophet] only to bring good news and warning to people, but most of them do not understand. ²⁹ And they say, 'If what you say is true, when will this promise be fulfilled?' ³⁰ Say, 'You have an appointment for a Day which you cannot put off nor bring forward, even by a single moment.'*a*

³¹ The disbelievers say, 'We will believe neither this Qur'an nor the Scriptures that came before it.' If only you could see [Prophet] how the wrongdoers will be made to stand before their Lord, hurling reproaches at one another. Those who were oppressed will say to the oppressors, 'If it were not for you, we would have been believers.' ³² The oppressors will say to them, 'Was it we who prevented you from following right guidance after it had reached you? No! You yourselves were sinners.' ³³ The oppressed will say to them, 'No, it was your scheming, night and day, ordering us to disbelieve in God and set up rivals to Him.' When they see the punishment, they will fall silent with regret, and We shall put iron collars on the disbelievers' necks. Why should they be rewarded for anything other than what they have done? ³⁴ Never have We sent a warner to a community without those among them who were corrupted by

---

a Not 'an hour' (*al-Mu'jam al-Wasit*).

wealth saying, 'We do not believe in the message you have been sent with.' [35] They would say, 'We have greater wealth and more children than you, and we shall not be punished.' [36] Say [Prophet], 'My Lord gives in abundance to whoever He will and sparingly to whoever He will, though most people do not understand. [37] Neither wealth nor children will bring you nearer to Us, but those who believe and do good deeds will have multiple rewards for what they have done, and will live safely in the lofty dwellings of Paradise, [38] whereas those who work against Our messages, seeking to undermine them, will be summoned to punishment.' [39] Say, 'My Lord gives in abundance to whichever of His servants He will, and sparingly to whichever He will; He will replace whatever you give in alms; He is the best of providers.'

[40] On the Day He gathers them all together, He will say to the angels, 'Was it you these people worshipped?' [41] They will reply, 'May You be exalted! You are our supporter against them! Really, they worshipped the jinn and most of them believed in them.' [42] 'So today neither of you has any power to benefit or harm the other,' We shall tell the evildoers, 'Taste the torment of the fire which you called a lie.' [43] When Our messages are recited to them, clear as they are, they say, 'This is only a man who wants to turn you away from what your forefathers worshipped,' and, 'This [Qur'an] is nothing but lies he has made up.' When the Truth comes to the disbelievers, they say, 'This is just plain sorcery,' [44] though We have not given them any books to study nor sent any warner before you. [45] Those who lived before them also denied the truth—these people have not attained even a tenth of what We gave their predecessors—they, too, rejected My messengers, and how terrible My condemnation was!

[46] Say [Prophet], 'I advise you to do one thing only: stand before God, in pairs or singly, and think: there is no sign of madness in your companion [the Prophet]—he is only warning you before severe suffering arrives.' [47] Say, 'If I have asked you for any reward, you can keep it. It is God alone who will reward me: He is witness to everything.' [48] Say, 'My Lord hurls the Truth down [before you]. He has full knowledge of all that is unseen.' [49] Say, 'The Truth has come; falsehood is powerless.'[a] [50] Say, 'If I go astray, that is my loss, and if I

---

[a] The Arabic expression *la yubdi' wa-la yu'id* is an idiom meaning 'powerless'. See Zamakhshari, *Asas al-Balagha*.

am rightly guided, it is through what my Lord has revealed to me. He is all hearing, and ever near.'

⁵¹[Prophet], if you could only see their terror:[a] there will be no escape when they are seized from a nearby place; ⁵²they will say, 'Now we believe in it,'[b] but how can they reach it from such a distant place—⁵³they denied it all in the past, and threw conjecture[c] from a far-off place—when a barrier has been placed between them and what they desire,[d] just as was done with their kind before? They were deep in doubt and suspicion.

[a] On the Day of Resurrection.
[b] The Truth.
[c] About God and the Hereafter.
[d] To be allowed to go back to the world and believe and do good deeds, cf. 35: 37.

35. THE CREATOR

A Meccan sura that affirms God's power and Creation and contrasts this with the powerlessness and uselessness of the 'partners' set up by the idolaters. The sura warns the idolaters of their punishment and comforts the Prophet through mention of previous messengers who were also rejected as liars. The great rewards that await believers are described.

In the name of God, the Lord of Mercy, the Giver of Mercy

¹ Praise be to God, Creator of the heavens and earth, who made angels messengers with two, three, four [pairs of] wings. He adds to creation as He will: God has power over everything. ² No one can withhold the blessing God opens up for people, nor can anyone but Him release whatever He withholds: He is the Almighty, the All Wise. ³ People, remember God's grace towards you. Is there any creator other than God to give you sustenance from the heavens and earth? There is no god but Him. How can you turn away?

⁴ If they call you a liar [Prophet], many messengers before you were also called liars: it is to God that all things will be returned. ⁵ People! God's promise is true, so do not let the present life deceive you. Do not let the Deceiver deceive you about God: ⁶ Satan is your enemy—so treat him as an enemy—and invites his followers only to enter the blazing fire. ⁷ Those who disbelieve will be punished severely; those who believe and do good deeds will be forgiven, and richly rewarded. ⁸ What about those whose evil deeds are made alluring to them so that they think they are good? God leaves whoever He will to stray and guides whoever He will. [Prophet], do not waste your soul away with regret for them: God knows exactly what they do.

⁹ It is God who sends forth the winds; they raise up the clouds; We drive them to a dead land and with them revive the earth after its death: such will be the Resurrection. ¹⁰ If anyone desires power, all power belongs to God; good words rise up to Him and He lifts up the righteous deed, but a severe punishment awaits those who plot evil and their plotting will come to nothing. ¹¹ It is God who created you from dust and later from a drop of fluid; then He made you into

two sexes; no female conceives or gives birth without His knowledge; no person grows old or has his life cut short, except in accordance with a Record: all this is easy for God.

¹² The two bodies of water are not alike—one is palatable, sweet, and pleasant to drink, the other salty and bitter—yet from each you eat fresh fish and extract ornaments to wear, and in each you see the ships ploughing their course so that you may seek God's bounty and be grateful. ¹³ He makes the night merge into the day and the day into the night; He has subjected the sun and the moon—each runs for an appointed term. Such is God your Lord: all control belongs to Him. Those you invoke beside Him do not even control the skin of a date stone; ¹⁴ if you call them they cannot hear you; if they could hear, they could not answer you; on the Day of Resurrection they will disown your idolatry. None can inform you [Prophet] like the one who is all aware.

¹⁵ People, it is you who stand in need of God—God needs nothing and is worthy of all praise—¹⁶ if He wills, He can do away with you and bring in a new creation, ¹⁷ that is not difficult for God. ¹⁸ No burdened soul will bear the burden of another: even if a heavily laden soul should cry for help, none of its load will be carried, not even by a close relative. But you [Prophet] can only warn those who fear their Lord, though they cannot see Him, and keep up the prayer—whoever purifies himself does so for his own benefit—everything ends up with God. ¹⁹ The blind and the seeing are not alike, ²⁰ nor are darkness and light; ²¹ shade and heat are not alike, ²² nor are the living and the dead. God makes anyone He wills hear [His message]: you cannot make those in their graves hear. ²³ You are only here to warn them—²⁴ We have sent you with the Truth as a bearer of good news and warning—every community has been sent a warner. ²⁵ If they call you a liar, their predecessors did the same: messengers came to them with clear signs, scriptures, and enlightening revelation ²⁶ and afterwards I seized the disbelievers—how terrible My punishment was!

²⁷ Have you [Prophet] not considered that God sends water down from the sky and that We produce with it fruits of varied colours? That there are in the mountains layers of white and red of various hues, and jet black? ²⁸ That there are various colours among human beings, wild animals, and livestock too? It is those of His servants who have knowledge who stand in true awe of God. God is almighty,

most forgiving. ²⁹ Those who recite God's scripture, keep up the prayer, give secretly and openly from what We have provided for them, may hope for trade that will never decline: ³⁰ He will repay them in full, and give them extra from His bounty. He is most forgiving, most appreciative.

³¹ The Scripture We have revealed to you [Prophet] is the Truth and confirms the scriptures that preceded it. God is well informed about His servants, He sees everything. ³² We gave the Scripture as a heritage to Our chosen servants: some of them wronged their own souls, some stayed between [right and wrong], and some, by God's leave, were foremost in good deeds. That is the greatest favour: ³³ they will enter lasting Gardens where they will be adorned with bracelets of gold and pearls, where they will wear silk garments. ³⁴ They will say, 'Praise be to God, who has separated us from all sorrow! Our Lord is truly most forgiving, most appreciative: ³⁵ He has, in His bounty, settled us in the everlasting Home where no toil or fatigue will touch us.' ³⁶ But those who reject the truth will stay in Hellfire, where they will neither be finished off by death, nor be relieved from Hell's torment: this is how We reward hardened disbelievers. ³⁷ They will cry out loud in Hell, 'Lord, let us out, and we will do righteous deeds, not what we did before.' 'Did We not give you a life long enough to take warning if you were going to? The warner came to you, now taste the punishment.' The evildoers will have nobody to help them.

³⁸ God knows all that is hidden in the heavens and earth; He knows the thoughts contained in the heart; ³⁹ it is He who made you [people] successors to the land. Anyone who denies the truth will bear the consequences of his denial: their Lord's loathing for them will be increased by it and their denial will only add to their loss. ⁴⁰ Say, 'Consider those "partners" of yours that you call upon beside God. Show me! What part of the earth did they create? What share of the heavens do they possess?' Have We given them a book that contains clear evidence? No indeed! The idolaters promise each other only delusion.

⁴¹ God keeps the heavens and earth from vanishing; if they did vanish, no one else could stop them. God is most forbearing, most forgiving. ⁴² [The idolaters] swore their most solemn oath that, if someone came to warn them, they would be more rightly guided than any other community, but when someone did come they turned

yet further away, [43] became more arrogant in the land, and intensified their plotting of evil—the plotting of evil only rebounds on those who plot. Do they expect anything different from what happened to earlier people? You will never find any change in God's practice; you will never find any deviation there. [44] Have they not travelled in the land and seen how those before them met their end, although they were superior to them in strength? God is not to be frustrated by anything in the heavens or on the earth: He is all knowing, all powerful. [45] If God were to punish people [at once] for the wrong they have done, there would not be a single creature left on the surface of the earth. He gives them respite for a stated time and, whenever their time comes, God has been watching His servants.

36. *YA SIN*

A Meccan sura that emphasizes the divine source of the Qur'an and defends it from the charge of being poetry made by man (verses 5–6, 69–70). It warns of the fate of men who are stubborn and always mock God's revelations. They are reminded of the punishment that befell earlier generations, and of God's power as shown in His Creation. The end of the sura gives strong arguments for the reality of the Resurrection.

In the name of God, the Lord of Mercy, the Giver of Mercy

¹ *Ya Sin*

² By the wise*ᵃ* Qur'an, ³ you [Muhammad] are truly one of the messengers sent ⁴ on a straight path, ⁵ with a revelation from the Almighty, the Lord of Mercy, ⁶ to warn a people whose forefathers were not warned, and so they are unaware. ⁷ The verdict has been passed against most of them, for they refuse to believe. ⁸ [It is as if] we had placed [iron] collars around their necks, right up to their chins so that their heads are forced up. ⁹ We have set barriers before and behind them, blocking their vision: they cannot see. ¹⁰ It is all the same to them whether you warn them or not: they will not believe. ¹¹ You can warn only those who will follow the Qur'an and hold the Merciful One in awe, though they cannot see Him: give such people the glad news of forgiveness and a noble reward. ¹² We shall certainly bring the dead back to life, and We record what they send ahead of them as well as what they leave behind: We keep an account of everything in a clear Record.

¹³ Give them the example of the people to whose town messengers came. ¹⁴ We sent two messengers but they rejected both. Then We reinforced them with a third. ¹⁵ They said, 'Truly, we are messengers to you,' ¹⁶ but they answered, 'You are only men like ourselves. The Lord of Mercy has sent nothing; you are just lying.' They said, 'Our Lord knows that we have been sent to you. ¹⁷ Our duty is only to deliver the message to you,' ¹⁸ but they answered, 'We think you are

---

ᵃ See note to 10: 1.

an evil omen. If you do not stop, we shall stone you, and inflict a painful punishment on you.' [19] The messengers said, 'The evil omen is within yourselves. Why do you take it as an evil omen when you are reminded of the Truth? You are going too far!' [20] Then, from the furthest part of the city, a man came running. He said, 'My people, follow the messengers. [21] Follow them: they are not asking you to pay them and they are rightly guided. [22] Why should I not worship the One who created me? It is to Him that you will be returned. [23] How could I take beside Him any other gods, whose intercession will not help me and who would not be able to save me if the Lord of Mercy wished to harm me? [24] Then I would clearly be in the wrong. [25] I believe in your Lord, so listen to me.'

[26] He was told, 'Enter the Garden,'[a] so he said, 'If only my people knew [27] how my Lord has forgiven me and set me among the highly honoured.' [28] After him We did not send any army from heaven against his people, nor were We about to: [29] there was just one blast, and they fell down lifeless.

[30] Alas for human beings! Whenever a messenger comes to them they ridicule him. [31] Do they not see how many generations We have destroyed before them, none of whom will ever come back to them?[b] [32] [Yet] all of them will be brought before Us. [33] There is a sign for them in the lifeless earth. We give it life and We produce grain from it for them to eat. [34] We have put gardens of date palms and grapes in the earth, and We have made springs of water gush out of it [35] so that they could eat its fruit. It was not their own hands that made all this. How can they not give thanks? [36] Glory be to Him who created all the pairs[c] of things that the earth produces, as well as themselves and other things they do not know about. [37] The night is also a sign for them: We strip the daylight from it, and—lo and behold!—they are in darkness. [38] The sun, too, runs its determined course laid down for it by the Almighty, the All Knowing. [39] We have determined phases for the moon until finally it becomes like an old date-stalk. [40] The sun cannot overtake the moon, nor can the night outrun the day: each floats in [its own] orbit.

[41] Another sign for them is that We carried their seed in the laden

---

[a] The implication may be that he was martyred.

[b] Another interpretation of this phrase is 'none of them can trace [their genealogies] back to them', i.e. God wiped out the entire line.

[c] Or 'varieties'.

Ark, ⁴²and We have made similar things for them to ride in. ⁴³If We wished, We could drown them, and there would be no one to help them: they could not be saved. ⁴⁴Only by Our mercy could they be rescued to enjoy life for a while. ⁴⁵Yet when they are told, 'Beware of what lies before and behind you, so that you may be given mercy,' ⁴⁶they ignore every single sign that comes to them from their Lord, ⁴⁷and when they are told, 'Give to others out of what God has provided for you,' the disbelievers say to the believers, 'Why should we feed those that God could feed if He wanted? You must be deeply misguided.'

⁴⁸And they say, 'When will this promise be fulfilled, if what you say is true?' ⁴⁹But all they are waiting for is a single blast that will overtake them while they are still arguing with each other. ⁵⁰They will have no time to make bequests, nor will they have the chance to return to their own people.

⁵¹The Trumpet will be sounded and—lo and behold!—they will rush out to their Lord from their graves. ⁵²They will say, 'Alas for us! Who has resurrected us from our resting places?' [They will be told], 'This is what the Lord of Mercy promised, and the messengers told the truth.' ⁵³It was just one single blast and then—lo and behold!— they were all brought before Us. ⁵⁴'Today, no soul will be wronged in the least: you will only be repaid for your deeds. ⁵⁵The people of Paradise today are happily occupied—⁵⁶they and their spouses— seated on couches in the shade. ⁵⁷There they have fruit and whatever they ask for. ⁵⁸"Peace," a word from the Lord of Mercy. ⁵⁹But step aside today, you guilty ones. ⁶⁰Children of Adam, did I not command you not to serve Satan, for he was your sworn enemy, ⁶¹but to serve Me? This is the straight path. ⁶²He has led great numbers of you astray. Could you not understand? ⁶³So this is the Fire that you were warned against. ⁶⁴Enter it today, because you went on ignoring [my commands].'

⁶⁵On that Day We shall seal up their mouths, but their hands will speak to Us, and their feet bear witness to everything they have done. ⁶⁶If it had been Our will, We could have taken away their sight. They would have striven to find the way, but how could they have seen it? ⁶⁷If it had been Our will, We could have paralysed them where they stood, so that they could not move forward or backward. ⁶⁸If We extend anyone's life, We reverse his development. Can they not use their reason?

⁶⁹ We have not taught the Prophet poetry,ᵃ nor could he everᵇ have been a poet. ⁷⁰ This is a revelation, an illuminating Qur'an to warn anyone who is truly alive, so that God's verdict may be passed against the disbelievers.

⁷¹ Can they not see how, among the things made by Our hands, We have created livestock they control, ⁷² and made them obedient, so that some can be used for riding, some for food, ⁷³ some for other benefits, and some for drink? Will they not give thanks? ⁷⁴ Yet they have taken other gods beside God to help them, ⁷⁵ though these could not do so even if they called a whole army of them together! ⁷⁶ So [Prophet] do not be distressed at what they say: We know what they conceal and what they reveal.

⁷⁷ Can man not see that We created him from a drop of fluid? Yet—lo and behold!—he disputes openly, ⁷⁸ producing arguments against Us, forgetting his own creation. He says, 'Who can give life back to bones after they have decayed?' ⁷⁹ Say, 'He who created them in the first place will give them life again: He has full knowledge of every act of creation. ⁸⁰ It is He who produces fire for you out of the green tree—lo and behold!—from this you kindle fire. ⁸¹ Is He who created the heavens and earth not able to create the likes of these people? Of course He is! He is the All Knowing Creator: ⁸² when He wills something to be, His way is to say, "Be"—and it is! ⁸³ So glory be to Him in whose Hand lies control over all things. It is to Him that you will all be brought back.'

ᵃ Some of the Arabs dismissed the Qur'an as poetry.

ᵇ This is a classical meaning of *yanbaghi*.

37. RANGED IN ROWS[a]

The central point of this Meccan sura is the unity of God (verses 4 and 180–2) and the refutation of the pagan belief that the angels were daughters of God and worthy of worship. The angels themselves are quoted to refute this (verses 164–6). The prophethood of Muhammad, and the Hereafter, are also affirmed. There are two supporting sections: the scenes in the Hereafter (verses 19–68) and the stories of earlier prophets (verses 75–148).

In the name of God, the Lord of Mercy, the Giver of Mercy

[1] By those [angels] ranged in rows, [2] who rebuke reproachfully [3] and recite God's word, [4] truly your God is One, [5] Lord of the heavens and earth and everything between them, Lord of every sunrise. [6] We have adorned the sky with stars, [7] and made them a safeguard against every rebellious devil: [8] they cannot eavesdrop on the Higher Assembly—pelted from every side, [9] driven away, they are perpetually tormented—[10] if any [of them] stealthily snatches away a fragment,[b] he will be pursued by a piercing flame.

[11] So [Prophet], ask the disbelievers: is it harder to create them than other beings We have created?[c] We created them from sticky clay. [12] You marvel as they scoff, [13] take no heed when they are warned, [14] and resort to ridicule when they see a sign, [15] saying, 'This is no more than blatant sorcery.' [16] 'What! After we have died and become dust and bones, shall we really be raised up again, [17] along with our forefathers?' [18] Say, 'Yes indeed, and you will be humiliated.' [19] One blast and—lo and behold!—they will look [20] and say, 'Woe to us! This is the Day of Judgement.' [21] [It will be said], 'This is the Day of Decision, which you used to deny. [22] [Angels], gather together those who did wrong, and others like them, as well as whatever they worshipped [23] beside God, lead them all to the path of Hell, and [24] halt them for questioning: [25] "Why do you not support each other now?" '—[26] no indeed! They will be in complete submission on that Day—[27] and they will turn on one another accusingly.

---

[a] Cf. 37: 165–6; 78: 38.   [b] Of something he overheard.   [c] Cf. 40: 57.

[28] They will say, 'You came to us from a position of power.'[a] [29] They will say, 'No! It was you who would not believe—[30] we had no power over you—and you were already exceeding all limits. [31] Our Lord's sentence on us is just and we must all taste the punishment. [32] We led you astray as we ourselves were astray.' [33] On that Day they will all share the torment: [34] this is how We deal with the guilty. [35] Whenever it was said to them, 'There is no deity but God,' they became arrogant, [36] and said, 'Are we to forsake our gods for a mad poet?' [37] 'No: he brought the truth and confirmed the earlier messengers; [38] you will taste the painful torment, [39] and be repaid only according to your deeds.'

[40] Not so God's true servants. [41] They will have familiar provisions[b]—[42] fruits—and will be honoured [43] in gardens of delight; [44] seated on couches, facing one another. [45] A drink will be passed round among them from a flowing spring: [46] white, delicious to those who taste it, [47] causing no headiness or intoxication. [48] With them will be spouses—modest of gaze and beautiful of eye—[49] like protected eggs.[c]

[50] They will turn to one another with questions: [51] one will say, 'I had a close companion on earth [52] who used to ask me, "Do you really believe that [53] after we die and become dust and bone, we shall be brought for judgement?" ' [54] Then he will say, 'Shall we look for him?' [55] He will look down and see him in the midst of the Fire, [56] and say to him, 'By God, you almost brought me to ruin! [57] Had it not been for the grace of my Lord, I would also have been taken to Hell.' [58] Then he will say [to his blessed companions], 'Are we never to die again after our earlier death? [59] Shall we never suffer? [60] This truly is the supreme triumph!' [61] Everyone should strive to attain this. [62] Is this the better welcome, or the tree of Zaqqum, [63] which we have made a test for the evildoers? [64] This tree grows in the heart of the blazing Fire,[d] [65] and its fruits are like devils' heads. [66] They will fill their bellies eating from it; [67] then drink scalding water on top of it;

---

[a] The Arabic expression 'from the right-hand side' conveys the meaning of being in the right or approaching from the most honourable angle, or with power and influence (see verse 30).

[b] See 2: 25.

[c] Arabs described beautiful women as being as precious as the ostrich eggs they protected from the dust with feathers.

[d] The disbelievers said, scornfully, 'How can there be a tree in the Fire?'

[68] then return to the blazing Fire. [69] They found their forefathers astray, [70] and rushed to follow in their footsteps—before the disbelievers [of Mecca], [71] most men in the past went astray, [72] even though We sent messengers to warn them.[73] See how those who were warned met their end! [74] Not so the true servants of God.

[75] Noah cried to Us, and how excellent was Our response! [76] We saved him and his people from great distress, [77] We let his offspring remain on the earth, [78] We let him be praised by later generations: [79] 'Peace be upon Noah among all the nations!' [80] This is how We reward those who do good: [81] he was truly one of Our faithful servants. [82] We drowned the rest.

[83] Abraham was of the same faith: [84] he came to his Lord with a devoted heart. [85] He said to his father and his people, 'What are you worshipping? [86] Do you choose false gods instead of the true God? [87] So what is your opinion about the Lord of all the Worlds?' [88] then he looked up to the stars. [89] He said, 'I am sick,' [90] so [his people] turned away from him and left. [91] He turned to their gods and said, [92] 'Why do you not speak?' [93] then he turned and struck them with his right arm. [94] His people hurried towards him, [95] but he said, 'How can you worship things you carve with your own hands, [96] when it is God who has created you and all your handiwork?' [97] They said, 'Build a pyre and throw him into the blazing fire.' [98] They wanted to harm him, but We humiliated them.

[99] He said, 'I will go to my Lord: He is sure to guide me. [100] Lord, grant me a righteous son,' [101] so We gave him the good news that he would have a patient son. [102] When the boy was old enough to work with his father, Abraham said, 'My son, I have seen myself sacrificing you in a dream. What do you think?' He said, 'Father, do as you are commanded and, God willing, you will find me steadfast.' [103] When they had both submitted to God, and he had laid his son down on his face, [104] We called out to him, 'Abraham, [105] you have fulfilled the dream.' This is how We reward those who do good— [106] it was a test to prove [their true characters]— [107] We ransomed his son with a momentous sacrifice, [108] and We let him be praised by succeeding generations: [109] 'Peace be upon Abraham!' [110] This is how We reward those who do good: [111] truly he was one of Our faithful servants.

[112] We gave Abraham the good news of Isaac—a prophet and a righteous man—[113] and blessed him and Isaac too: some of their

offspring were good, but some clearly wronged themselves. ¹¹⁴ We also bestowed Our favour on Moses and Aaron: ¹¹⁵ We saved them and their people from great distress; ¹¹⁶ We helped them to their final triumph; ¹¹⁷ We gave them the Scripture that makes things clear; ¹¹⁸ We guided them to the right path; ¹¹⁹ We let them be praised by succeeding generations: ¹²⁰ 'Peace be upon Moses and Aaron!' ¹²¹ This is how We reward those who do good: ¹²² truly they were among Our faithful servants.

¹²³ Elias too was one of the messengers. ¹²⁴ He said to his people, 'Have you no fear of God? ¹²⁵ How can you invoke Baal and forsake the Most Gracious Creator, ¹²⁶ God, your Lord and the Lord of your forefathers?' ¹²⁷ but they rejected him. They will be brought to punishment[a] as a consequence; ¹²⁸ not so the true servants of God. ¹²⁹ We let him be praised by succeeding generations: ¹³⁰ 'Peace be to Elias!' ¹³¹ This is how We reward those who do good: ¹³² truly he was one of Our faithful servants.

¹³³ Lot was also one of the messengers. ¹³⁴ We saved him and all his people—¹³⁵ except for an old woman who stayed behind—¹³⁶ and We destroyed the rest. ¹³⁷ You [people] pass by their ruins morning ¹³⁸ and night: will you not take heed? ¹³⁹ Jonah too was one of the messengers. ¹⁴⁰ He fled to the overloaded ship. ¹⁴¹ They cast lots, he suffered defeat, ¹⁴² and a great fish swallowed him, for he had committed blameworthy acts. ¹⁴³ If he had not been one of those who glorified God, ¹⁴⁴ he would have stayed in its belly until the Day when all are raised up, ¹⁴⁵ but We cast him out, sick, on to a barren shore, ¹⁴⁶ and made a gourd tree grow above him. ¹⁴⁷ We sent him to a hundred thousand people or more. ¹⁴⁸ They believed, so We let them live out their lives.[b]

¹⁴⁹ Now [Muhammad], ask the disbelievers: is it true that your Lord has daughters, while they choose sons for themselves?[c] ¹⁵⁰ Did they actually see Us create the angels as females? ¹⁵¹ No indeed! It is one of their lies when they say, ¹⁵² 'God has begotten.' How they lie! ¹⁵³ Did He truly choose daughters in preference to sons? ¹⁵⁴ What is the matter with you? How do you form your judgements? ¹⁵⁵ Do you

---

[a] It is inaccurate to say 'brought to account', since this would apply to everyone, including the true servants of God.

[b] One of the classical meanings of *matta'a* is 'to give long life'.

[c] The pagan Arabs were ashamed to have daughters themselves, yet attributed daughters to God.

not reflect? [156] Do you perhaps have clear authority? [157] Bring your scriptures, if you are telling the truth. [158] They claim that He has kinship with the jinn, yet the jinn themselves know that they will be brought before Him. [159] God is far above what they attribute to Him—[160] the true servants of God do not do such things—[161] and neither you nor what you worship [162] can lure away from God any [163] except those who will burn in Hell. [164] [The angels say], 'Every single one of us has his appointed place: [165] we are ranged in ranks. [166] We glorify God.'[a]

[167] [The disbelievers] used to say, [168] 'If only we had a scripture like previous people, [169] we would be true servants of God,' [170] yet now they reject [the Qur'an]. They will soon realize. [171] Our word has already been given to Our servants the messengers: [172] it is they who will be helped, [173] and the ones who support[b] Our cause will be the winners. [174] So [Prophet] turn away from the disbelievers for a while. [175] Watch them: they will soon see. [176] Do they really wish to hasten Our punishment? [177] When it descends on their courtyards, how terrible that morning will be for those who were warned! [178] [Prophet], turn away from the disbelievers for a while. [179] Watch them: they will soon see. [180] Your Lord, the Lord of Glory, is far above what they attribute to Him. [181] Peace be upon the messengers [182] and praise be to God the Lord of all the Worlds.

---

[a] This is the rebuke by the angels referred to in verse 2.

[b] In classical Arabic *jund* means 'supporters', not just 'armies'.

38. SĀD

This Meccan sura mentions previous prophets in support and encouragement for Muhammad, and makes a clear link between the arrogance displayed by the disbelievers of Mecca, previous generations, and Iblis, the original rebel. The first and last verses assert the truth and nobility of the Qur'an.

In the name of God, the Lord of Mercy, the Giver of Mercy

¹ *Sad*

By the noble*ᵃ* Qur'an! ²The disbelievers are steeped in arrogance and hostility. ³How many generations We have destroyed before them! They all cried out, once it was too late to escape. ⁴The disbelievers think it strange that a prophet of their own people has come to warn them: they say, 'He is just a lying sorcerer. ⁵How can he claim that all the gods are but one God? What a peculiar thing [to claim]!' ⁶Their leaders depart, saying, 'Walk away! Stay faithful to your gods! That is what you must do. ⁷We did not hear any such claim in the last religion:*ᵇ* it is all an invention. ⁸Was the message sent only to him out of all of us?'

In fact they doubt My warning; in fact they have not tasted My punishment yet. ⁹Do they possess the treasures of your Lord's bounty, the Mighty, the All Giving? ¹⁰Do they control the heavens and earth and everything between? Let them climb their ropes:*ᶜ* ¹¹their armed alliance will be crushed. ¹²The people of Noah, 'Ad, and firmly supported*ᵈ* Pharaoh rejected their prophets before them. ¹³Thamud, the people of Lot, and the Forest-Dwellers each formed opposition [against theirs]. ¹⁴They all rejected the messengers and they were deservedly struck by My punishment: ¹⁵all the disbelievers here are waiting for is a single blast that cannot be

---

ᵃ The Arabic expression *dhu'al-dhikr* means 'possessing renown, nobility, or eminence' (cf. verse 67). Other translations give 'containing the Remembrance/Reminder' and so on.

ᵇ An allusion to the Christian Trinity.

ᶜ Cf. note to 22: 15.

ᵈ *Dhu'l-awtad* literally means 'with his pegs', but is understood here metaphorically, to indicate something firmly fixed; cf. its use with reference to mountains in 78: 7.

postponed. ¹⁶ They say, 'Our Lord! Advance us our share of punishment before the Day of Reckoning!' ¹⁷ Bear their words patiently [Prophet].

Remember Our servant David, a man of strength who always turned to Us: ¹⁸ We made the mountains join him in glorifying Us at sunset and sunrise; ¹⁹ and the birds, too, in flocks, all echoed his praise. ²⁰ We strengthened his kingdom; We gave him wisdom and a decisive way of speaking. ²¹ Have you heard the story of the two litigants who climbed into his private quarters? ²² When they reached David, he took fright, but they said, 'Do not be afraid. We are two litigants, one of whom has wronged the other: judge between us fairly—do not be unjust—and guide us to the right path. ²³ This is my brother. He had ninety-nine ewes and I just the one, and he said, "Let me take charge of her," and overpowered me with his words.' ²⁴ David said, 'He has done you wrong by demanding to add your ewe to his flock. Many partners treat each other unfairly. Those who sincerely believe and do good deeds do not do this, but these are very few.'

[Then] David realized that We had been testing him,ᵃ so he asked his Lord for forgiveness, fell down on his knees, and repented: ²⁵ We forgave him [his misdeed]. His reward will be nearness to Us, a good place to return to. ²⁶ 'David, We have given you mastery over the land. Judge fairly between people. Do not follow your desires, lest they divert you from God's path: those who wander from His path will have a painful torment because they ignore the Day of Reckoning.'

²⁷ It was not without purpose that We created the heavens and the earth and everything in between. That may be what the disbelievers assume—how they will suffer from the Fire!—²⁸ but would We treat those who believe and do good deeds and those who spread corruption on earth as equal? Would We treat those who are aware of God and those who recklessly break all bounds in the same way? ²⁹ This is a blessed Scripture which We sent down to you [Muhammad], for people to think about its messages, and for those with understanding to take heed.

³⁰ We gave David Solomon. He was an excellent servant who

ᵃ This is allegedly an allusion to David's acquisition of another man's wife to add to his own numerous wives.

always turned to God. [31] When well-bred light-footed horses were paraded before him near the close of day, [32] he kept saying, 'My love of fine things is part of my remembering my Lord!' until [the horses] disappeared from sight—[33] 'Bring them back!' [he said] and started to stroke their legs and necks.[a] [34] We certainly tested Solomon, reducing him to a mere skeleton on his throne.[b] [35] He turned to Us and prayed: 'Lord forgive me! Grant me such power as no one after me will have—You are the Most Generous Provider.' [36] So We gave him power over the wind, which at his request ran gently wherever he willed, [37] and the jinn[c]—every kind of builder and diver [38] and others chained in fetters. [39] 'This is Our gift, so give or withhold as you wish without account.' [40] His reward will be nearness to Us, a good place to return to.

[41] Bring to mind Our servant Job who cried to his Lord, 'Satan has afflicted me with weariness and suffering.' [42] 'Stamp your foot! Here is cool water for you to wash in and drink,' [43] and We restored his family to him, with many more like them: a sign of Our mercy and a lesson to all who understand. [44] 'Take a small bunch of grass in your hand, and strike [her] with that so as not to break your oath.'[d] We found him patient in adversity; an excellent servant! He, too, always turned to God.

[45] Remember Our servants Abraham, Isaac, and Jacob, all men of strength and vision. [46] We caused them to be devoted to Us[e] through their sincere remembrance of the Final Home: [47] with Us they will be among the elect, the truly good. [48] And remember Our servants Ishmael, Elisha, and Dhu 'l-Kifl,[f] each of them truly good. [49] This is a lesson.

The devout will have a good place to return to: [50] Gardens of lasting bliss with gates wide open. [51] They will be comfortably

---

[a] Another interpretation is that the horses distracted Solomon from remembering his Lord and that he slaughtered the horses in anger at his having forgotten the afternoon prayer.

[b] According to Razi, quoting linguistic usage in Arabic, this is interpreted to mean that Solomon became so ill that he was like a walking skeleton.

[c] See 34: 12–13.

[d] Qur'anic commentators explain that, when his wife blasphemed, Job swore that if he recovered from his illness, he would beat her with one hundred lashes. When he recovered, however, he regretted his hasty oath, so God gave him this instruction.

[e] Alternatively, 'We made them pure'.

[f] See note to 21: 85.

seated; they will call for abundant fruit and drink; ⁵²they will have well-matched [wives] with modest gaze. ⁵³'This is what you are promised for the Day of Reckoning: ⁵⁴Our provision for you will never end.'

⁵⁵But the evildoers will have the worst place to return to: ⁵⁶Hell to burn in, an evil place to stay—⁵⁷all this will be theirs: let them taste it—a scalding, dark, foul fluid, ⁵⁸and other such torments. ⁵⁹[It will be said], 'Here is another crowd of people rushing headlong to join you.' [The response will be], 'They are not welcome! They will burn in the Fire.' ⁶⁰They will say to them, 'You are not welcome! It was you who brought this on us, an evil place to stay,' ⁶¹adding, 'Our Lord, give double punishment to those who brought this upon us.' ⁶²They will say, 'Why do we not see those we thought were bad ⁶³and took as a laughing-stock? Have our eyes missed them?' ⁶⁴This is how it will be: the inhabitants of the Fire will blame one another in this way.

⁶⁵[Prophet] say, 'I am only here to give warning. There is no god but God the One, the All Powerful, ⁶⁶Lord of the heavens and earth and everything between, the Almighty, the Most Forgiving.' ⁶⁷Say, 'This message is a mighty one, ⁶⁸yet you ignore it. ⁶⁹I have no knowledge of what those on high discuss:ᵃ ⁷⁰it is only revealed to me that I am here to give clear warning.'

⁷¹Your Lord said to the angels, 'I will create a man from clay. ⁷²When I have shaped him and breathed My Spirit into him, kneel down before him.' ⁷³The angels all bowed down together, ⁷⁴but not Iblis, who was too proud. He became a rebel. ⁷⁵God said, 'Iblis, what prevents you from bowing down to the man I have made with My own hands? Are you too high and mighty?' ⁷⁶Iblis said, 'I am better than him: You made me from fire, and him from clay.' ⁷⁷'Get out of here! You are rejected: ⁷⁸My rejection will follow you till the Day of Judgement!' ⁷⁹but Iblis said, 'My Lord, grant me respite until the Day when they are raised from the dead,' ⁸⁰so He said, 'You have respite ⁸¹till the Appointed Day.' ⁸²Iblis said, 'I swear by Your might! I will tempt all ⁸³but Your true servants.' ⁸⁴God said, 'This is the truth—I speak only the truth—⁸⁵I will fill Hell with you and all those that follow you.'

ᵃ Cf. 2: 30.

⁸⁶[Prophet], say, 'I ask no reward from you for this, nor do I claim to be what I am not: ⁸⁷this is only a warning for all people. ⁸⁸In time you will certainly come to know its truth.'

39. THE THRONGS

A Meccan sura, whose title is taken from its concluding verses. The main focus of the sura is the contrast between those who follow the true faith, and those who ascribe partners to God. The sura emphasizes that people are free to choose whether to believe or disbelieve (verse 41), but urges them in the strongest possible terms to turn to the right path while there is still time to repent (verses 53–61).

In the name of God, the Lord of Mercy, the Giver of Mercy

¹ This Scripture is sent down from God the Mighty, the Wise. ² It is We who sent down the Scripture to you [Prophet] with the Truth, so worship God with your total devotion: ³ true devotion is due to God alone. [As for] those who choose other protectors beside Him, saying, 'We only worship them because they bring us nearer to God,' God Himself will judge between them regarding their differences. God does not guide any ungrateful liar. ⁴ God could have chosen any of His creation He willed for offspring, but He is far above this! He is the One, the Almighty. ⁵ He created the heavens and earth for a true purpose; He wraps the night around the day and the day around the night; He has subjected the sun and moon to run their courses for an appointed time; He is truly the Mighty, the Forgiving.

⁶ He created you all from a single being, from which He made its mate; He gave you*ᵃ* four kinds of livestock in pairs;*ᵇ* He creates you in your mothers' wombs, in one stage after another, in threefold depths of darkness. Such is God, your Lord; He holds control, there is no god but Him. How can you turn away? ⁷ If you are ungrateful, remember God has no need of you, yet He is not pleased by ingratitude in His servants; if you are grateful, He is pleased [to see] it in you. No soul will bear another's burden. You will return to your Lord in the end and He will inform you of what you have done: He knows well what is in the depths of [your] hearts.

⁸ When man suffers some affliction, he prays to his Lord and turns

---

ᵃ Literally 'sent down', i.e. in the Scripture, cf. 6: 142–4.

ᵇ There has been some confusion over numbering here, leading some translators to render this passage 'eight pairs'. In fact, the correct translation is either 'eight head' or 'four pairs'. Cf. 6: 143–4.

to Him, but once he has been granted a favour from God, he forgets the One he had been praying to and sets up rivals to God, to make others stray from His path. Say, 'Enjoy your ingratitude for a little while: you will be one of the inhabitants of the Fire.' ⁹ What about someone who worships devoutly during the night, bowing down, standing in prayer, ever mindful of the life to come, hoping for his Lord's mercy? Say, 'How can those who know be equal to those who do not know?' Only those who have understanding will take heed.

¹⁰ Say, '[God says], believing servants, be mindful of your Lord! Those who do good in this world will have a good reward—God's earth is wide*ᵃ*—and those who persevere patiently will be given a full and unstinting reward.' ¹¹ Say, 'I have been commanded to serve God, dedicating my worship entirely to Him. ¹² I have been commanded to be the first to submit.' ¹³ Say, 'I fear the torment of a terrible Day if I disobey my Lord.' ¹⁴ Say, 'It is God I serve, dedicating my worship entirely to Him—¹⁵ you may serve whatever you please beside Him.' Say, 'The true losers are the ones who will lose themselves and their people on the Day of Resurrection: that is the most obvious loss. ¹⁶ Their only shade will be the Fire above them and below.' This is how God puts fear into His servants: My servants, beware of Me.

¹⁷ There is good news for those who shun the worship of false gods and turn to God, so [Prophet] give good news to My servants ¹⁸ who listen to what is said and follow what is best. These are the ones God has guided; these are the people of understanding. ¹⁹ What about the one who has been sentenced to punishment? Can you [Prophet] rescue those already in the Fire? ²⁰ But those who are mindful of their Lord will have lofty dwellings built for them, one above the other, graced with flowing streams. This is a promise from God: God does not break His promise.

²¹ Have you not considered that God sends water down from the sky, guides it along to form springs in the earth, and then, with it, brings forth vegetation of various colours, which later withers, turns yellow before your eyes, and is crumbled to dust at His command? There is truly a reminder in this for those who have understanding.

²² What about the one whose heart God has opened in devotion to

---

ᵃ See 29: 56–60.

Him, so that he walks in light from his Lord? Alas for those whose hearts harden at the mention of God! They have clearly lost their way. ²³ God has sent down the most beautiful of all teachings: a Scripture that is consistent and draws comparisons; that causes the skins of those in awe of their Lord to shiver. Then their skins and their hearts soften at the mention of God: such is God's guidance. He guides with it whoever He will; no one can guide those God leaves to stray.

²⁴ What about the one who will only have his bare face to protect him from his terrible suffering on the Day of Resurrection? It will be said to the evildoers, 'Taste what you have earned.' ²⁵ Others before them also disbelieved, and the punishment fell on them unawares: ²⁶ God gave them the punishment of disgrace in this world to taste; the punishment will be even harder in the Hereafter, if only they knew.

²⁷ In this Qur'an, We have put forward all kinds of illustration for people, so that they may take heed—²⁸ an Arabic Qur'an, free from any distortion—so that people may be mindful. ²⁹ God puts forward this illustration: can a man who has for his masters several partners at odds with each other be considered equal to a man devoted wholly to one master? All praise belongs to God, though most of them do not know.

³⁰ You [Prophet] will certainly die, and so will they, ³¹ and, on the Day of Resurrection, you will dispute with one another in the presence of your Lord. ³² So who could be more wrong than the person who invents a lie about God and rejects the truth when it comes to him? Is there not ample punishment for the disbelievers in Hell? ³³ It is the one who brings the truth and the one who accepts it as true who are mindful of God: ³⁴ they will have everything they wish for with their Lord. Such is the reward of those who do good: ³⁵ God will absolve them even of their worst deeds and will reward them according to their best.

³⁶ Is God not enough for His servant? Yet they threaten you [Prophet] with those they worship other than Him. If God allows someone to stray he has no one to guide him; ³⁷ if God guides someone no one can lead him astray. Is God not mighty and capable of retribution? ³⁸ If you [Prophet] ask them who created the heavens and earth, they are sure to answer, 'God,' so say, 'Consider those you invoke beside Him: if God wished to harm me, could they undo that

harm? If God wished to show me mercy, could they withhold that mercy?' Say, 'God is enough for me: all those who trust should put their trust in Him.' [39] Say, 'My people, do whatever is in your power—and so will I. You will find out [40] who will suffer humiliation;[a] and on whom a lasting torment will descend.'

[41] We have sent the Scripture down to you [Prophet] with the Truth for people. Whoever follows the guidance does so for his own benefit, whoever strays away from it does so at his own peril: you are not in charge of them. [42] God takes the souls of the dead and the souls of the living while they sleep—He keeps hold of those whose death He has ordained and sends the others back until their appointed time—there truly are signs in this for those who reflect. [43] Yet they take intercessors beside God! Say, 'Even though these have no power or understanding?' [44] Say, 'All intercession belongs to God alone; He holds control of the heavens and the earth; you will all return to Him.'

[45] The hearts of those who do not believe in the Hereafter shrink with aversion whenever God is mentioned on His own, but they rejoice when gods other than Him are mentioned. [46] Say, 'God! Creator of the heavens and earth! Knower of all that is hidden and all that is open, You will judge between Your servants regarding their differences.' [47] If the evildoers possessed the earth's assets twice over they would offer them to ransom themselves from the terrible suffering on the Day of Resurrection: God will show them something they had not reckoned with, [48] the evil of their deeds will become plain to them, and they will be overwhelmed by that at which they used to laugh.

[49] When man suffers some affliction, he cries out to Us, but when We favour him with Our blessing, he says, 'All this has been given to me because of my knowledge'—it is only a test, though most of them do not know it. [50] Those who lived before them said the same. What they earned was of no use to them; [51] they suffered its evil effects. Today's wrongdoers will also suffer the evil effects of their deeds: they will not escape. [52] Do they not know that God provides abundantly for anyone He will and gives sparingly to anyone He will? There truly are signs in this for those who believe.

[53] Say, '[God says], My servants who have harmed yourselves by

---

a In this world; the lasting torment will be in the Hereafter.

your own excess, do not despair of God's mercy. God forgives all sins: He is truly the Most Forgiving, the Most Merciful. ⁵⁴ Turn to your Lord. Submit to Him before the punishment overtakes you and you can no longer be helped. ⁵⁵ Follow the best teaching sent down to you from your Lord, before the punishment suddenly takes you, unawares, ⁵⁶ and your soul says, "Woe is me for having neglected what is due to God, and having been one of those who scoffed!" ⁵⁷ Or it says, "If God had guided me, I would have joined the righteous!" ⁵⁸ Or, faced by punishment, it says, "If only I could have another chance, I would join those who do good!" ⁵⁹ No indeed! My messages came to you and you rejected them: you were arrogant and rejected the truth.'

⁶⁰ On the Day of Resurrection, you [Prophet] will see those who told lies against God, their faces darkened. Is there not ample punishment for the arrogant in Hell? ⁶¹ But God will deliver those who took heed of Him to their place of safety: no harm will touch them, nor will they grieve. ⁶² God is the Creator of all things; He has charge of everything; ⁶³ the keys of the heavens and earth are His. Those who have rejected the revelations of God will be the losers.

⁶⁴ Say, 'Do you order me to worship someone other than God, you foolish people?' ⁶⁵ It has already been revealed to you [Prophet] and to those before you: 'If you ascribe any partner to God, all your work will come to nothing: you will be one if the losers. ⁶⁶ You should worship God alone and be one of those who are grateful to Him.' ⁶⁷ These people have no grasp of God's true measure. On the Day of Resurrection, the whole earth will be in His grip. The heavens will be rolled up in His right hand—Glory be to Him! He is far above the partners they ascribe to Him!—⁶⁸ the Trumpet will be sounded, and everyone in the heavens and earth will fall down senseless except those God spares. It will be sounded once again and they will be on their feet, looking on. ⁶⁹ The earth will shine with the light of its Lord; the Record of Deeds will be laid open; the prophets and witnesses will be brought in. Fair judgement will be given between them: they will not be wronged ⁷⁰ and every soul will be repaid in full for what it has done. He knows best what they do.

⁷¹ Those who rejected the Truth will be led to Hell in their throngs. When they arrive, its gates will open and its keepers will say to them, 'Were you not sent your own messengers to recite the revelations of your Lord to you and warn you that you would meet this Day?' and

they will say, 'Yes indeed we were.' But the sentence of punishment will have been passed against those who rejected the truth. [72] It will be said: 'Enter the gates of Hell: there you will remain. How evil is the abode of the arrogant!'

[73] But those who were mindful of their Lord will be led in throngs to the Garden. When they arrive, they will find its gates wide open, and its keepers will say to them, 'Peace be upon you. You have been good. Come in: you are here to stay,' [74] and they will say, 'Praise be to God who has kept His promise to us and given us this land as our own. Now we may live wherever we please in the Garden.' How excellent is the reward of those who labour! [75] You [Prophet] will see the angels surrounding the Throne, glorifying their Lord with praise. True judgement will have been passed between them, and it will be said, 'Praise be to God, the Lord of the Worlds.'

40. THE FORGIVING ONE

A Meccan sura with two recurring themes: disputing God's truth (verses 4, 35, 69) and calling upon Him (verses 14, 49, 50, 60, 65, 73). In the opening verses God is described as the Forgiver, Accepter of repentance, severe in punishment, and this dual aspect is exemplified in the sura. The central section of the sura deals with the story of Pharaoh and Moses (verses 23–54): the destruction of one and victory of the other are stated in verses 45 and 51. The Prophet is, in his turn, urged to be steadfast and to ignore the taunts of the disbelievers (verses 55 and 77).

In the name of God, the Lord of Mercy, the Giver of Mercy

¹ *Ha Mim*

² This Scripture is sent down from God, the Almighty, the All Knowing, ³ Forgiver of sins and Accepter of repentance, severe in punishment, infinite in bounty. There is no god but Him; to Him is the ultimate return. ⁴ It is only the disbelievers who dispute God's revelations. [Prophet], do not be deceived by their movements back and forth across the land,ᵃ ⁵ for the people of Noah and those who formed opposition after them also rejected the truth: every community schemed to destroy its messenger and strove to refute truth with falsehood; but it was I who destroyed them. How terrible My punishment was! ⁶ In this way your Lord's sentence was passed against the disbelievers; they will be the inhabitants of the Fire.

⁷ Those [angels] who carry the Throne and those who surround it celebrate the praise of their Lord and have faith in Him. They beg forgiveness for the believers: 'Our Lord, You embrace all things in mercy and knowledge, so forgive those who turn to You and follow Your path. Save them from the pains of Hell ⁸ and admit them, Lord, to the lasting Garden You have promised to them, together with their righteous ancestors,ᵇ spouses, and offspring: You alone are the Almighty, the All Wise. ⁹ Protect them from all evil deeds: those You

---

ᵃ Making wealth by trading.

ᵇ The word *aba'* includes male and female ancestors. Father and mother are called *abawan*.

protect from [the punishment for] evil deeds will receive Your mercy—that is the supreme triumph.' [10] But those who disbelieved will be told: 'When you were called to the faith and rejected it, God's disgust with you was even greater then than the self-disgust you feel [today].' [11] They will say, 'Our Lord, twice You have caused us to be lifeless[a] and twice You have brought us to life. Now we recognize our sins. Is there any way out?' [12] [They will be told], 'This is all because when God alone was invoked you rejected this, yet when others were associated with Him you believed [in them].' Judgement belongs to God the Most High, the Most Great.

[13] It is He who shows you [people] His signs and sends water down from the sky to sustain you, though only those who turn to God will take heed. [14] So call upon God and dedicate your religion to Him alone, however hateful this may be to the disbelievers: [15] He is exalted in rank, the Lord of the Throne. He sends revelations with His teachings to whichever of His servants He will, in order to warn of the Day of Meeting, [16] the Day when they will come out and nothing about them will be concealed from God. 'Who has control today?' 'God, the One, the All Powerful. [17] Today each soul will be rewarded with whatever it has earned: today no injustice will be done. God is swift in reckoning.'

[18] Warn them [Prophet] of the ever-approaching Day, when people's hearts will rise into their throats and choke them. The evildoer will have no friends, nor any intercessor to be heeded. [19] God is aware of the most furtive of glances, and of all that hearts conceal: [20] God will judge with truth, while those they invoke beside Him will not judge at all. God is indeed the All Hearing, the All Seeing.

[21] Have they not travelled through the land and seen how those who lived before them met their end? They were stronger than them and made a more impressive mark upon the land, yet God destroyed them for their sins—they had no one to defend them against Him—[22] because messengers repeatedly came to them with clear signs and still they rejected them. God seized them: He is truly full of strength, severe in punishment.

---

[a] Literally 'dead', leading some commentators to interpret this as referring to one's initial death, followed shortly thereafter by a second 'death' after questioning in the grave. The more generally accepted view, however, is that earthly life is both preceded and succeeded by a state of lifelessness. The two acts of giving life therefore refer to birth and resurrection.

²³ We sent Moses with Our signs and clear authority ²⁴ to Pharaoh, Haman, and Korah and they said, 'Sorcerer! Liar!' ²⁵ When he brought the truth to them from Us, they said, 'Kill the sons of those who believe with him, spare only their women'—the scheming of those who reject the truth can only go wrong—²⁶ and Pharaoh said, 'Leave me to kill Moses—let him call upon his Lord!—for I fear he may cause you to change your religion, or spread disorder in the land.' ²⁷ Moses said, 'I seek refuge with my Lord and yours from every tyrant who refuses to believe in the Day of Reckoning.'

²⁸ A secret believer from Pharaoh's family said, 'How can you kill a man just for saying, "My Lord is God"? He has brought you clear signs from your Lord—if he is a liar, on his own head be it—and if he is truthful, then at least some of what he has threatened will happen to you. God does not guide any rebellious, outrageous liar. ²⁹ My people, as masters in the land you have the power today, but who will help us against God's might if it comes upon us?' But Pharaoh said, 'I have told you what I think; I am guiding you along the right path.'

³⁰ The believer said, 'My people, I fear your fate will be the fate of those others who opposed [their prophets]: ³¹ the fate of the people of Noah, ʿAd, Thamud, and those who came after them—God never wills injustice on His creatures. ³² My people, I fear for you on the Day you will cry out to one another, ³³ the Day you will turn tail and flee with no one to defend you from God! Whoever God leaves to stray will have no one to guide him. ³⁴ Joseph came to you before with clear signs, but you never ceased to doubt the message he brought you. When he died, you said, "God will not send another messenger." '

In this way God leaves the doubting rebels to stray—³⁵ those who, with no authority to do so, dispute God's messages are doing something that is loathed by God and by those who believe. In this way God seals up the heart of every arrogant tyrant. ³⁶ Pharaoh said, 'Haman, build me a tall tower so that I may reach the ropes*a* that lead ³⁷ to the heavens to look for this God of Moses. I am convinced that he is lying.' In this way the evil of Pharaoh's deed was made alluring to him and he was barred from the right path—his scheming led only to ruin.

³⁸ The believer said, 'My people, follow me! I will guide you to

---

a Cf. 22: 15, where *sabab* has the meaning 'rope'.

the right path. [39] My people, the life of this world is only a brief enjoyment; it is the Hereafter that is the lasting home. [40] Whoever does evil will be repaid with its like; whoever does good and believes, be it a man or a woman, will enter Paradise and be provided for without measure. [41] My people, why do I call you to salvation when you call me to the Fire? [42] You call me to disbelieve in God and to associate with Him things of which I have no knowledge; I call you to the Mighty, the Forgiving One. [43] There is no doubt that what you call me to serve is not fit to be invoked either in this world or the Hereafter: our return is to God alone, and it will be the rebels who will inhabit the Fire. [44] [One Day] you will remember what I am saying to you now, so I commit my case to God: God is well aware of His servants.' [45] So God saved him from the harm they planned.

A terrible punishment encompassed Pharaoh's people; [46] they will be brought before the Fire morning and evening.[a] On the Day the Hour comes, it will be said, 'Throw Pharaoh's people into the worst torment.' [47] In the Fire they will quarrel with one another: the weak will say to the haughty, 'We were your followers, so can you now relieve us from some share of the Fire?' [48] but they will say, 'We are all in this together. God has judged between His creatures.' [49] Those in the Fire will say to the keepers of Hell, 'Ask your Lord to lessen our suffering for one day,' [50] but they will say, 'Did your messengers not come to you with clear evidence of the truth?' They will say, 'Yes they did,' and the keeper will say, 'You can plead, then, but the pleas of disbelievers will always be in vain.'

[51] We support Our messengers and the believers in the present life and on the Day when witnesses arise. [52] On the Day when excuses will not profit the evildoers, their fate will be rejection and they will have the worst of homes. [53] We gave Moses guidance and passed down the Scripture to the Children of Israel, [54] as a guide and a reminder to people of understanding. [55] So be patient, Prophet, for what God has promised is sure to come. Ask forgiveness for your sins; praise your Lord morning and evening.[b] [56] As for those who, with no authority to do so, dispute God's messages, there is nothing in their hearts but a thirst for a greatness they will never attain. Seek refuge in God, for He is the All Hearing, the All Seeing.

---

[a] 'Morning and evening' can convey a sense of 'all the time'.
[b] See preceding note.

⁵⁷ The creation of the heavens and earth is greater by far than the creation of mankind, though most people do not know it. ⁵⁸ The blind and the sighted are not equal, just as those who believe and do good works and those who do evil are not equal: how seldom you reflect! ⁵⁹ The Final Hour is sure to come, without doubt, but most people do not believe. ⁶⁰ Your Lord says, 'Call on Me and I will answer you; those who are too proud to serve Me will enter Hell humiliated.'

⁶¹ It is God who has given you the night in which to rest and the day in which to see. God is truly bountiful to people, but most people do not give thanks. ⁶² Such is God your Lord, the Creator of all things: there is no god but Him. How can you be so deluded? ⁶³ This is how deluded those who deny God's messages are. ⁶⁴ It is God who has given you the earth for a dwelling place and the heavens for a canopy. He shaped you, formed you well, and provided you with good things. Such is God your Lord, so glory be to Him, the Lord of the Worlds. ⁶⁵ He is the Living One and there is no god but Him, so call on Him, and dedicate your religion entirely to Him. Praise be to God, the Lord of the Worlds.

⁶⁶ Say [Prophet], 'Since clear evidence has come to me from my Lord I am forbidden to serve those you call upon beside God: I am commanded to submit to the Lord of the Worlds.' ⁶⁷ It is He who created you from dust, then from a drop of fluid, then from a tiny, clinging form, then He brought you forth as infants, then He allowed you to reach maturity, then He let you grow old—though some of you die sooner—and reach your appointed term so that you may reflect. ⁶⁸ It is He who gives life and death, and when He ordains a thing, He says only 'Be' and it is.

⁶⁹ [Prophet], do you see how deluded those who dispute God's messages are—⁷⁰ those who reject the Scripture and the messages We have sent through Our messengers? They will find out ⁷¹ when, with iron collars and chains around their necks, they are dragged ⁷² into scalding water, and then burned in the Fire, ⁷³ and asked, 'Where now are those you called upon ⁷⁴ beside God?' They will say, 'They have abandoned us: those we called upon before were really nothing at all.' 'This is how God lets disbelievers go astray, ⁷⁵ all because on earth you revelled in untruth and ran wild. ⁷⁶ Enter the gates of Hell, there to remain—an evil home for the arrogant.'

⁷⁷ So be patient [Prophet], for God's promise is sure: whether We

show you part of what We have promised them[a] in this life or whether We take your soul back to Us first, it is to Us that they will be returned. [78] We have sent other messengers before you—some We have mentioned to you and some We have not—and no messenger could bring about a sign except with God's permission. When [the Day] God ordained comes, just judgement will be passed between them: there and then, those who followed falsehood will be lost.

[79] It is God who provides livestock for you, some for riding and some for your food; [80] you have other benefits in them too. You can reach any destination you wish on them: they carry you, as ships carry you [on the sea]. [81] He shows you His signs: which of God's signs do you still ignore?

[82] Have they not travelled through the land and seen how those who lived before them met their end? They were more numerous than them, stronger than them, and made a more impressive mark on the land, yet what they achieved was of no use to them at all. [83] When messengers came to them with clear signs, they revelled in the knowledge they had, and so they were engulfed by the very punishment they mocked: [84] when they saw Our punishment, they said, 'We believe in God alone; we reject any partner we ascribed to Him,' [85] but believing after seeing Our punishment did not benefit them at all—this has always been God's way of dealing with His creatures—there and then the disbelievers were lost.

---

[a] The disbelievers.

41. [VERSES] MADE DISTINCT

This Meccan sura deals with the obduracy of the disbelievers, the truthfulness of the Qur'an, the unity of God, and the inevitability of Resurrection. The title refers to a term used to describe the Qur'an in verse 3 and again in verse 44. The sura makes several references to the senses (verses 5, 20–2, 44) which the disbelievers shut off from perceiving the Truth in this world, and which will then testify against their 'owners' on the Day of Resurrection, and it describes the arrogance displayed by people when all is well, contrasted with their humility and despair when difficulties strike (verses 49–51).

In the name of God, the Lord of Mercy, the Giver of Mercy

¹ *Ha Mim*

² A revelation from the Lord of Mercy, the Giver of Mercy; ³ a Scripture whose verses are made distinct as a proclamation in Arabic for people who understand, ⁴ giving good news and warning. Yet most of them turn away and so do not hear. ⁵ They say, 'Our hearts are encased against [the faith] you call us to; our ears are heavy; there is a barrier between us and you. So you do whatever you want, and so shall we.' ⁶ Say [Prophet], 'I am only a mortal like you, [but] it has been revealed to me that your God is One. Take the straight path to Him and seek His forgiveness. Woe to the idolaters, ⁷ who do not pay the prescribed alms and refuse to believe in the world to come! ⁸ Those who believe and do good deeds will have a reward that never fails.'

⁹ Say, 'How can you disregard the One who created the earth in two Days?ᵃ How can you set up other gods as His equals? He is the Lord of all the worlds!' ¹⁰ He placed solid mountains on it, blessed it, measured out its varied provisions for all who seek them—all in four Days. ¹¹ Then He turned to the sky, which was smoke—He said to it and the earth, 'Come into being, willingly or not,' and they said, 'We come willingly'—¹² and in two Days He formed seven heavens, and assigned an order to each. We have made the nearest one beautifully

---

ᵃ Commentators include these two days in the four mentioned in verse 10, so that the total is six days; see 32: 4. God's Days are not like ours; see 22: 47.

illuminated and secure. Such is the design of the Almighty, the All Knowing.

¹³ If they turn away, say, 'I have warned you about a blast like the one which struck 'Ad and Thamud: ¹⁴ when their messengers came to them, from all angles,ᵃ saying, "Serve no one but God," they said, "If our Lord had wished, He would have sent down angels. We do not believe in the message with which you have been sent." ¹⁵ The people of 'Ad behaved arrogantly throughout the land without any right, saying, "Who could be stronger than us?" Did they not realize that God, who created them, was stronger than them?' They continued to reject Our message, ¹⁶ so We let a roaring wind loose on them for a few disastrous days to make them taste the punishment of shame in this world; more shameful still will be the punishment of the life to come, and they will not be helped. ¹⁷ As for Thamud, We gave them guidance but they preferred blindness, so they were struck by a blast of humiliating punishment for their misdeeds. ¹⁸ We saved those who believed and were mindful of God.

¹⁹ On the Day when God's enemies are gathered up for the Fire and driven onward, ²⁰ their ears, eyes, and skins will, when they reach it, testify against them for their misdeeds. ²¹ They will say to their skins, 'Why did you testify against us?' and their skins will reply, 'God, who gave speech to everything, has given us speech—it was He who created you the first time and to Him you have been returned—²² yet you did not try to hide yourselves from your ears, eyes, and skin to prevent them from testifying against you. You thought that God did not know about much of what you were doing, ²³ so it was the thoughts you entertained about your Lord that led to your ruin, and you became losers.' ²⁴ The Fire will still be their home, even if they resign themselves to patience, and if they pray to be allowed to make amends, they will not be given permission to do so.

²⁵ We have appointed, for the disbelievers, companionsᵇ who make their past and present seem fair and right to them, but the sentence has already been passed on them, along with generations of jinn and men before them: they were losers. ²⁶ The disbelievers say, 'Do not listen to this Qur'an; drown it in frivolous talk: you may gain the

---

ᵃ Literally 'from before and from behind', i.e. using all angles of argument. The messengers tried every method to persuade their people of the truth of their message.

ᵇ See 43: 36; 50: 27 ff.

upper hand.' ²⁷We shall certainly give the disbelievers a taste of severe punishment. We shall repay them according to their worst deeds—²⁸ that is the reward of the enemies of God—the Fire will be their lasting home, a payment for their rejection of Our revelations. ²⁹The disbelievers will say, 'Our Lord, show us those jinn and men who misled us and we shall trample them underfoot, so that they may be among the lowest of the low.' ³⁰As for those who say, 'Our Lord is God,' and take the straight path towards Him, the angels come down to them and say, 'Have no fear or grief, but rejoice in the good news of Paradise, which you have been promised. ³¹We are your allies in this world and in the world to come, where you will have everything you desire and ask for ³²as a welcoming gift from the Most Forgiving, Most Merciful One.'

³³Who speaks better than someone who calls people to God, does what is right, and says, 'I am one of those devoted to God'? ³⁴Good and evil cannot be equal. [Prophet], repel evil with what is better and your enemy will become as close as an old and valued friend, ³⁵but only those who are steadfast in patience, only those who are blessed with great righteousness, will attain to such goodness. ³⁶If a prompting from Satan should stir you, seek refuge with God: He is the All Hearing and the All Knowing.

³⁷The night, the day, the sun, the moon, are only a few of His signs. Do not bow down in worship to the sun or the moon, but bow down to God who created them, if it is truly Him that you worship. ³⁸If the disbelievers are too arrogant, [remember, Prophet, that] those who are with your Lord glorify Him tirelessly night and day. ³⁹Another of His signs is this: you see the earth lying desolate, but when We send water down on to it, it stirs and grows. He who gives it life will certainly give life to the dead. He has power over everything.

⁴⁰Those who distort the meaning of Our message are not hidden from Us. Is he who is hurled into the Fire better, or he who comes through safely on the Day of Resurrection? Do whatever you want, God certainly sees everything you do. ⁴¹Those who reject the Qur'an when it comes to them—though it is an unassailable Scripture ⁴²which falsehood cannot touch from any angle, a Revelation sent down from the Wise One, Worthy of All Praise—⁴³[should remember that] you [Prophet] are not told anything that the previous messengers were not told: your Lord is a Lord of forgiveness, but also of painful punishment. ⁴⁴If We had made it a foreign

Qur'an, they would have said, 'If only its verses were clear! What? Foreign speech to an Arab?' Say, 'It is guidance and healing for those who have faith, but the ears of the disbelievers are heavy, they are blind to it, it is as if they are being called from a distant place.' [45] We gave the Scripture to Moses but disputes arose about it—if it were not for a decree that had already been issued, they would already have been judged—and still they are doubtful and suspicious of it.

[46] Whoever does good does it for his own soul and whoever does evil does it against his own soul: your Lord is never unjust to His creatures. [47] Knowledge of the Hour belongs solely to Him and no fruit comes out of its sheath, nor does any female conceive or give birth, without His knowledge. On the Day He asks them, 'Where are My partners?' they will answer, 'We admit to You that none of us can see [them]': [48] the gods they invoked before will have vanished away; they will know that there is no escape.

[49] Man never tires of asking for good, but if evil touches him he loses all hope and becomes despondent. [50] Whenever We let him taste some of Our mercy after he has been afflicted, he is sure to say, 'This is all my own doing: I do not think the Hour will ever come, but even if I were to be taken back to my Lord, the best reward would await me with Him.' We shall most certainly inform the disbelievers of what they have done and give them a taste of severe punishment. [51] Whenever We are gracious to man, he goes away haughtily, but, as soon as evil touches him, he turns to prolonged prayer. [52] Say [Prophet], 'Have you ever thought, what if this revelation really is from God and you still reject it? Who could be more astray than someone who cuts himself off so far [from God]?' [53] We shall show them Our signs in every region of the earth and in themselves, until it becomes clear to them that this is the Truth. Is it not enough that your Lord witnesses everything? [54] Truly, they doubt that they will meet their Lord; truly He encompasses[a] everything.

---

[a] This is *muhit*, a metaphor in Arabic for having full knowledge and full power over everything.

42. CONSULTATION

*A Meccan sura that takes its name from verse 38, where the practice of consultation (*shura*) is listed as one characteristic of the Muslim community. The sura discusses man's habit of creating division and disharmony in matters of religion, and God's all-prevailing power, wisdom, and final decision. The unity of religion is stressed (verse 13) as is the continuity of the prophets (verse 3). The Prophet is reminded that he cannot compel people to believe, that they will be judged according to their deeds, and that he is only there to deliver the message. The nature of revelation is described in verses 51–3.*

In the name of God, the Lord of Mercy, the Giver of Mercy

¹ *Ha Mim* ² *'Ayn Sin Qaf*

³ This is how God, the Mighty, the Wise, sends revelation to you [Prophet] as He did to those before you. ⁴ All that is in the heavens and earth belongs to Him: He is the Exalted, the Almighty. ⁵ The heavens are almost broken apart from above as the angels proclaim the praises of their Lord and ask forgiveness for those on earth. God is indeed the Most Forgiving, the Most Merciful. ⁶ As for those who take protectors other than Him, God is watching them; you are not responsible for them.

⁷ So We have revealed an Arabic Qur'an to you, in order that you may warn the capital city*ᵃ* and all who live nearby. And warn [especially] about the Day of Gathering, of which there is no doubt, when some shall be in the Garden and some in the blazing Flame. ⁸ If God had so pleased, He could have made them a single community, but He admits to His mercy whoever He will; the evildoers will have no one to protect or help them. ⁹ How can they take protectors other than Him? God alone is the Protector; He gives life to the dead; He has power over all things. ¹⁰ Whatever you may differ about is for God to judge. [Say], 'Such is God, my Lord. In Him I trust and to Him I turn, ¹¹ the Creator of the heavens and earth.' He made mates for you from among yourselves—and for the animals too—so that

---

ᵃ Literally 'the mother of cities', Mecca.

you may multiply. There is nothing like Him: He is the All Hearing, the All Seeing. [12] The keys of the heavens and the earth are His; He provides abundantly or sparingly for whoever He will; He has full knowledge of all things.

[13] In matters of faith, He has laid down for you [people] the same commandment that He gave Noah, which We have revealed to you [Muhammad] and which We enjoined on Abraham and Moses and Jesus: 'Uphold the faith and do not divide into factions within it'— what you [Prophet] call upon the idolaters to do is hard for them; God chooses whoever He pleases for Himself and guides towards Himself those who turn to Him. [14] They divided, out of rivalry, only after knowledge had come to them, and, if it had not been for a decree already passed by your Lord to reprieve them until an appointed time, they would already have been judged. Those after them, who inherited the Scripture, are in disquieting doubt about it. [15] So [Prophet] call people to that faith and follow the straight path as you have been commanded. Do not go by what they desire, but say, 'I believe in whatever Scripture God has sent down. I am commanded to bring justice between you. God is our Lord and your Lord—to us our deeds and to you yours, so let there be no argument between us and you—God will gather us together, and to Him we shall return.' [16] As for those who argue about God after He has been acknowledged, their argument has no weight with their Lord: anger will fall upon them and agonizing torment awaits them. [17] It is God who has sent down the Scripture with Truth and the Balance.[a] How can you [Prophet] tell? The Last Hour may well be near: [18] those who do not believe in it seek to hasten it, but the believers stand in awe of it. They know it to be the Truth; those who argue about the Hour are far, far astray.

[19] God is most subtle towards His creatures; He provides [bountifully] for whoever He will; He is the Powerful, the Almighty. [20] If anyone desires a harvest in the life to come, We shall increase it for him; if anyone desires a harvest in this world, We shall give him a share of it, but in the Hereafter he will have no share. [21] How can they believe in others who ordain for them things which God has not sanctioned in the practice of their faith? If it were not for God's

---

[a] The balance of justice and of nature; cf. verse 27.

decree concerning the final Decision, judgement would already have been made between them. The evildoers will have a grievous punishment—[22] you will see them fearful because of what they have done: punishment is bound to fall on them—but those who believe and do good deeds will be in the flowering meadows of the Gardens. They will have whatever they wish from their Lord: this is the great bounty; [23] it is of this that God gives good news to His servants who believe and do good deeds.

Say [Prophet], 'I ask no reward from you for this, only the affection due to kin.'[a] If anyone does good, We shall increase it for him; God is most forgiving and most appreciative. [24] How can they say, 'He has invented a lie about God'? If God so willed, He could seal your heart and blot out lies: God confirms the Truth with His words. He has full knowledge of what is in the heart—[25] it is He who accepts repentance from His servants and pardons bad deeds—He knows everything you do. [26] He responds to those who believe and do good deeds, and gives them more of His bounty; agonizing torment awaits the disbelievers. [27] If God were to grant His plentiful provision to [all] His creatures, they would act insolently on earth, but He sends down in due measure whatever He will, for He is well aware of His servants and watchful over them: [28] it is He who sends rain after they have lost hope, and spreads His mercy far and wide. He is the Protector, Worthy of All Praise.

[29] Among His signs is the creation of the heavens and earth and all the living creatures He has scattered throughout them: He has the power to gather them all together whenever He will. [30] Whatever misfortune befalls you [people], it is because of what your own hands have done—God forgives much—[31] you cannot escape Him anywhere on earth: you have no protector or helper other than God. [32] Among His signs are the ships, sailing like floating mountains: [33] if He willed, He could bring the wind to a standstill and they would lie motionless on the surface of the sea—there truly are signs in this for anyone who is steadfast and thankful—[34] or He could cause them to be wrecked on account of what their passengers have done—God pardons much—[35] to let those who argue about Our messages know that there is no escape for them.

[36] What you have been given is only the fleeting enjoyment of this

---

[a] Or 'I only do this out of affection for you as kin!'

world. Far better and more lasting is what God will give to those who believe and trust in their Lord; [37] who shun great sins and gross indecencies; who forgive when they are angry; [38] respond to their Lord and keep up the prayer; conduct their affairs by mutual consultation; give to others out of what We have provided for them; [39] and defend themselves when they are oppressed. [40] Let harm be requited by an equal harm, though anyone who forgives and puts things right will have his reward from God Himself—He does not like those who do wrong. [41] There is no cause to act against anyone who defends himself after being wronged, [42] but there is cause to act against those who oppress people and transgress in the land against all justice—they will have an agonizing punishment—[43] though if a person is patient and forgives, this is one of the greatest things.

[44] Anyone God allows to stray will have no one else to protect him: you [Prophet] will see the wrongdoers, when they face the punishment, exclaiming, 'Is there any way of going back?' [45] You will see them exposed to the Fire, abject in humiliation, glancing furtively while those who believed exclaim, 'The losers are the ones who have lost themselves and their people on the Day of Resurrection.' Truly the evildoers will remain in lasting torment; [46] they will have no allies to help them against God; there is no way [forward] for those God allows to stray.

[47] So [people] respond to your Lord before there comes a Day that cannot, against God's will, be averted—you will have no refuge on that Day, and no possibility of denying [your sins]. If they still turn away [remember that] [48] We have not sent you [Prophet] to be their keeper: your only duty is to deliver the message. When We give man a taste of Our mercy, he rejoices in it, but if some harm befalls him on account of what he has done with his own hands, then he is ungrateful. [49] God has control of the heavens and the earth; He creates whatever He will—He grants female offspring to whoever He will, [50] male to whoever He will, or both male and female, and He makes whoever He will barren; He is all knowing and all powerful.

[51] It is not granted to any mortal that God should speak to him except through revelation or from behind a veil, or by sending a messenger to reveal by His command what He will: He is exalted and wise. [52] So We have revealed a spirit[a] to you [Prophet] by Our

---

[a] A life-giving message.

command: you knew neither the Scripture nor the faith, but We made it a light, guiding with it whoever We will of Our servants. You give guidance to the straight path, [53] the path of God, to whom belongs all that is in the heavens and earth: truly everything will return to God.

43. ORNAMENTS OF GOLD

A Meccan sura named after the gold ornaments mentioned in verse 35, and alluded to again in verse 53: in both instances God is refuting the claim of the disbelievers that a true prophet would be rich. The fact that the angels are not God's daughters but His obedient servants is emphasized again and again (cf. verses 15–20, 60). Similarly, the idea that Jesus could be the son of God is thoroughly denied (verses 57–9).

In the name of God, the Lord of Mercy, the Giver of Mercy

¹ *Ha Mim*

² By the Scripture that makes things clear, ³ We have made the Qur'an in Arabic so that you [people] may understand. ⁴ It is truly exalted in the Source of Scripture*ᵃ* kept with Us, and full of wisdom.

⁵ Should We ignore you and turn this revelation away from you because you are insolent people? ⁶ We have sent many a prophet to earlier people ⁷ and they mocked every one of them, ⁸ so We have destroyed mightier people than the [disbelievers of Mecca] and their example has gone down in history. ⁹ If you [Prophet] ask them, 'Who created the heavens and earth?' they are sure to say, 'They were created by the Almighty, the All Knowing.' ¹⁰ It is He who smoothed out the earth for you and traced out routes on it for you to find your way, ¹¹ who sends water down from the sky in due measure—We resurrect dead land with it, and likewise you will be resurrected from the grave—¹² who created every kind of thing, who gave you ships and animals to ride on ¹³ so that you may remember your Lord's grace when you are seated on them and say, 'Glory be to Him who has given us control over this; we could not have done it by ourselves. ¹⁴ Truly it is to our Lord that we are returning.'

¹⁵ Yet they assign some of His own servants to Him as offspring!*ᵇ* Man is clearly ungrateful! ¹⁶ Has He taken daughters for Himself and favoured you with sons? ¹⁷ When one of them is given news of the

---

ᵃ Literally 'mother of Scripture', identified with the 'Preserved Tablet'. Cf. 13: 39; 85: 22.

ᵇ The Meccan pagans considered the angels to be daughters of God, yet they were dismissive of their own daughters.

birth of a daughter, such as he so readily ascribes to the Lord of Mercy, his face grows dark and he is filled with gloom— [18] 'Someone who is brought up amongst trinkets, who cannot put together a clear argument?'[a] [19] They consider the angels—God's servants—to be female. Did they witness their creation? Their claim will be put on record and they will be questioned about it.

[20] They say, 'If the Lord of Mercy had willed it, we would not have worshipped them,' but they do not know that—all they do is lie!— [21] or have We perhaps given them a book before this one, to which they hold fast? [22] No indeed! They say, 'We saw our fathers following this tradition; we are guided by their footsteps.' [23] Whenever We sent a messenger before you to warn a township, those corrupted by wealth said, in the same way, 'We saw our fathers following this tradition; we are only following in their footsteps.' [24] The messenger said, 'Even though I bring you a truer religion than what you saw your fathers following?' and they replied, 'But we do not believe the message you bring.' [25] We punished them; think about how those who rejected the Truth met their end. [26] Abraham said to his father and his people, 'I renounce what you worship. [27] I worship only Him who created me, and it is He who will guide me,' [28] and he bequeathed these words to his descendants so that they might return [to God].

[29] I have let these people and their fathers enjoy long lives, and now I have given them the Truth and a messenger to make things clear: [30] yet when the Truth came to them, they said, 'This is sorcery. We do not believe in it,' [31] and they said, 'Why was this Qur'an not sent down to a distinguished man, from either of the two cities?'[b] [32] Are they the ones who share out your Lord's grace? We are the ones who give them their share of livelihood in this world and We have raised some of them above others in rank, so that some may take others into service: your Lord's grace is better than anything they accumulate. [33] If it were not that all mankind might have become a single nation [of disbelievers], We could have given all those who disbelieve in the Lord of Mercy houses with roofs of silver, sweeping staircases to ascend, [34] massive gates, couches to sit on, [35] and golden ornaments. All of these are mere enjoyments of this life; your Lord

---

[a] This was the pre-Islamic opinion. One poet boasted that he was inspired by a male, rather than a female, *shaytan*.

[b] Mecca or Ta'if, the two main cities of the region.

reserves the next life for those who take heed of Him. ³⁶ We assign an evil one as a comrade for whoever turns away from the revelations of the Lord of Mercy: ³⁷ evil ones bar people from the right path, even though they may think they are well guided. ³⁸ When such a person comes to Us, he will say [to his comrade], 'If only you had been as far away from me as east is from west. What an evil comrade!' ³⁹ [It will be said to them], 'You have done wrong. Having partners in punishment will not console you today.'

⁴⁰ Can you [Prophet] make the deaf hear? Or guide either the blind or those who are in gross error? ⁴¹ Either We shall take you away and punish them—indeed We will—⁴² or We shall let you witness the punishment We threatened them with; We have full power over them. ⁴³ Hold fast to what has been revealed to you—you truly are on the right path—⁴⁴ for it is an honour*a* for you and your people; you will all be questioned. ⁴⁵ Ask the prophets We sent before you: 'Did We ever appoint any gods to be worshipped beside the Lord of Mercy?'

⁴⁶ We sent Moses to Pharaoh and his courtiers and he said, 'I am truly a messenger from the Lord of the Worlds,' ⁴⁷ but when he presented Our signs to them, they laughed, ⁴⁸ even though each sign We showed them was greater than the previous one. We inflicted torment on them so that they might return to the right path. ⁴⁹ They said, 'Sorcerer, call on your Lord for us, by virtue of His pledge to you: we shall certainly accept guidance,' ⁵⁰ but as soon as We relieved their torment they broke their word. ⁵¹ Pharaoh proclaimed to his people, 'My people, is the Kingdom of Egypt not mine? And these rivers that flow at my feet, are they not mine? Do you not see? ⁵² Am I not better than this contemptible wretch who can scarcely express himself? ⁵³ Why has he not been given any gold bracelets? Why have no angels come to accompany him?' ⁵⁴ In this way he persuaded his people and they obeyed him—they were perverse people. ⁵⁵ When they provoked Us, We punished and drowned them all: ⁵⁶ We made them a lesson and an example for later people.

⁵⁷ When the son of Mary is cited as an example, your people [Prophet] laugh and jeer, ⁵⁸ saying, 'Are our gods*b* better or him?'—

---

a *Dhikr* can mean 'renown' or 'reminder':

b The angels, whom they worshipped as the daughters of God and superior to Jesus, whom they considered to be a god worshipped by Christians as the Son of God.

they cite him only to challenge you: they are a contentious people— [59] but he is only a servant We favoured and made an example for the Children of Israel: [60] if it had been Our will, We could have made you angels,[a] succeeding one another on earth.

[61] This [Qur'an] gives knowledge of the Hour:[b] do not doubt it. Follow Me for this is the right path; [62] do not let Satan hinder you, for he is your sworn enemy. [63] When Jesus came with clear signs he said, 'I have brought you wisdom; I have come to clear up some of your differences for you. Be mindful of God and obey me: [64] God is my Lord and your Lord. Serve Him: this is the straight path.' [65] Yet still the different factions among them disagreed—woe to the evildoers: they will suffer the torment of a grievous day!—[66] what are they waiting for but the Hour, which will come upon them suddenly and take them unawares? [67] On that Day, friends will become each other's enemies. Not so the righteous—[68] 'My servants, there is no fear for you today, nor shall you grieve'—[69] those who believed in Our revelations and devoted themselves to Us. [70] 'Enter Paradise, you and your spouses: you will be filled with joy.' [71] Dishes and goblets of gold will be passed around them with all that their souls desire and their eyes delight in. 'There you will remain: [72] this is the Garden you are given as your own, because of what you used to do, [73] and there is abundant fruit in it for you to eat.' [74] But the evildoers will remain in Hell's punishment, [75] from which there is no relief: they will remain in utter despair. [76] We never wronged them; they were the ones who did wrong. [77] They will cry, 'Malik,[c] if only your Lord would finish us off,' but he will answer, 'No! You are here to stay.' [78] We have brought you the Truth but most of you despise it.

[79] Have these disbelievers thought up some scheme? We too have been scheming. [80] Do they think We cannot hear their secret talk and their private counsel? Yes we can: Our messengers are at their sides, recording everything.

[81] Say [Prophet], 'If the Lord of Mercy [truly] had offspring I would be the first to worship [them],[d] but—[82] exalted be the Lord of

[a] Just as God was able to create Jesus without a father.

[b] Alternatively, the pronoun *hu* can also be seen to refer to Jesus: '[Jesus] gives knowledge of the Hour'.

[c] The angel in charge of Hell.

[d] Another interpretation is 'If the Lord of Mercy had a son I would be the first to worship him' (Razi).

the heavens and earth, the Lord of the Throne—He is far above their false descriptions.' [83] Leave them to wade in deeper and play about, until they face the Day they have been promised. [84] It is He who is God in heaven and God on earth; He is the All Wise, the All Knowing; [85] He is exalted; control of the heavens and earth and everything between them belongs to Him; He has knowledge of the Hour; you will all be returned to Him. [86] Those gods they invoke beside Him have no power of intercession, unlike those[a] who bore witness to the truth and recognized it. [87] If you [Prophet] ask them who created them they are sure to say, 'God,' so why are they so deluded? [88] The Prophet has said, 'My Lord, truly these are people who do not believe,' [89] but turn away from them and say, 'Peace': they will come to know.

[a] Those who have God's permission. Cf. 20: 109.

44. SMOKE

A Meccan sura that takes its title from verse 10, which describes a smoke-filled day, taken by many to refer to the Day of Judgement. The sura highlights the mercy that is the Qur'an, addresses the obduracy of the powerful and wealthy oppressors, and draws comparisons between the people of Pharaoh, Tubba', and the Meccans. The people of Paradise will enjoy heavenly bliss while those who were mighty in this world will suffer the torments of Hell.

In the name of God, the Lord of Mercy, the Giver of Mercy

¹ *Ha Mim*

² By the Scripture that makes things clear, ³ truly We sent it down on a blessed night—We have always sent warnings—⁴ a night when every matter of wisdom was made distinct at Our command—⁵ we have always sent messages to man—⁶ as a mercy [Prophet] from your Lord who sees and knows all: ⁷ Lord of the heavens and the earth and everything between—if only you people were firm believers—⁸ there is no god but Him: He gives life and death—He is your Lord and the Lord of your forefathers—⁹ yet in [their state of] doubt they take nothing seriously.ᵃ

¹⁰ [Prophet], watch out for the Dayᵇ when the sky brings forth clouds of smoke for all to see. ¹¹ It will envelop the people. They will cry, 'This is a terrible torment! ¹² Lord relieve us from this torment! We believe!' ¹³ How will this [sudden] faith benefit them? When a prophet came to warn them plainly, ¹⁴ they turned their backs on him, saying, 'He is tutored! He is possessed!' ¹⁵ We shall hold the torment back for a while ᶜ—you are sure to return [to Us]—¹⁶ and on the Day We seize [them] mightily We shall exact retribution.

ᵃ Literally 'in doubt they play'.

ᵇ Some interpret this as referring to an actual event that occurred in the lifetime of the Prophet—a drought and famine in Mecca during which hunger caused eyes to mist over when the sufferers looked at the sky—but it seems more likely to refer to the Day of Judgement.

ᶜ If this passage is taken to refer to the Day of Judgement, here the torment is relieved rather than held back, and the people return to disbelief rather than to God.

¹⁷ We tested the people of Pharaoh before them: a noble messenger was sent to them, ¹⁸ saying, 'Hand the servants of God over to me! I am a faithful messenger who has been sent to you. ¹⁹ Do not consider yourselves to be above God! I come to you with clear authority. ²⁰ I seek refuge in my Lord and yours against your insults!^a ²¹ If you do not believe me, just let me be.'

²² [Moses] cried to his Lord, 'These people are evildoers!' ²³ [God replied], 'Escape in the night with My servants, for you are sure to be pursued. ²⁴ Leave the sea behind you parted and their army will be drowned.' ²⁵ Many a garden and spring they left behind, ²⁶ many a cornfield and noble building, ²⁷ many a thing in which they had delighted: ²⁸ We gave these to another people to inherit. ²⁹ Neither heavens nor earth shed a tear for them, nor were they given any time. ³⁰ We saved the Children of Israel from their degrading suffering ³¹ at the hands of Pharaoh: he was a tyrant who exceeded all bounds. ³² We chose them knowingly above others: ³³ We gave them revelations in which there was a clear test.

³⁴ These people here^b assert, ³⁵ 'There is nothing beyond our one death: we will not be resurrected. ³⁶ Bring back our forefathers, if what you say is true.' ³⁷ Are they better than the people of Tubba'^c and those who flourished before them? We destroyed them all—they were guilty. ³⁸ We were not playing a pointless game when We created the heavens and earth and everything between; ³⁹ We created them for a true purpose, but most people do not comprehend.

⁴⁰ The Day of Decision is the time appointed for all; ⁴¹ a Day when no friend can take another's place. ⁴² No one will receive any help except for those to whom God shows mercy: He is the Mighty, the Merciful Lord. ⁴³ The tree of Zaqqum ⁴⁴ will be food for the sinners: ⁴⁵ [hot] as molten metal. It boils in their bellies ⁴⁶ like seething water. ⁴⁷ 'Take him! Thrust him into the depths of Hell! ⁴⁸ Pour scalding water over his head as punishment!' ⁴⁹ 'Taste this, you powerful, respected man! ⁵⁰ This is what you doubted.' ⁵¹ But those mindful of God will be in a safe place ⁵² amid Gardens and springs, ⁵³ clothed in silk and fine brocade, facing one another: ⁵⁴ so it will be. We shall wed

---

^a One of the meanings of *rajama* is 'abuse' or 'cast aspersions'; another is 'to stone'; another is 'to expel'.

^b The Meccans.

^c Honorific title of the King of Yemen given to a succession of powerful kings who ruled over southern Arabia in ancient times.

them to maidens with large, dark eyes. [55] Secure and contented, they will call for every kind of fruit. [56] After the one death they will taste death no more. God will guard them from the torment of Hell, [57] a bounty from your Lord. That is the supreme triumph.

[58] We have made this Qur'an easy to understand—in your own language [Prophet]—so that they may take heed. [59] So wait; the disbelievers too are waiting.

45. KNEELING

A Meccan sura that takes its title from verse 28, where the kneeling posture of all communities on the Day of Judgement is described. The sura addresses some of the arguments put forward by those sceptical of the truthfulness of the Qur'an. Emphasis is placed on the signs of God's existence discernible in nature, and on the painful punishment that awaits the doubters on the Day of Judgement. The misguided arrogance of the disbelievers (verses 8 and 31) is contrasted with God's true greatness (verse 37); references to God's wisdom and majesty open and close the sura.

In the name of God, the Lord of Mercy, the Giver of Mercy

¹ *Ha Mim*

²This Scripture is sent down from God, the Mighty, the Wise. ³There are signs in the heavens and the earth for those who believe: ⁴in the creation of you, in the creatures God scattered on earth, there are signs for people of sure faith; ⁵in the alternation of night and day, in the rain God provides, sending it down from the sky and reviving the dead earth with it, and in His shifting of the winds there are signs for those who use their reason. ⁶These are God's signs that We recount to you [Prophet, to show] the Truth.

If they deny God and His revelations, what message will they believe in? ⁷Woe to every lying sinful person ⁸who hears God's revelations being recited to him, yet persists in his arrogance as if he had never heard them—[Prophet] bring him news of a painful torment!—⁹who, if he knows anything about Our revelations, ridicules it! Such people will have a humiliating torment: ¹⁰Hell lurks behind them and their gains will not benefit them, nor will those beings they took as protectors beside God: a tremendous torment awaits them. ¹¹This is true guidance; those who reject their Lord's revelations will have a woeful torment.

¹²It is God who subjected the sea for you—ships sail on it by His command so that you can seek His bounty and give Him thanks—¹³He has subjected all that is in the heavens and the earth for your benefit, as a gift from Him. There truly are signs in this for those who reflect.

¹⁴ Tell the believers to forgive those who do not fear God's days [of punishment]ᵃ—He will requite people for what they have done. ¹⁵ Whoever does good benefits himself, and whoever does evil harms himself, and you will all be returned to your Lord.

¹⁶ We gave scripture, wisdom, and prophethood to the Children of Israel; We provided them with good things and favoured them above others; ¹⁷ We gave them clear proof in matters [of religion]. They differed among themselves out of mutual rivalry, only after knowledge came to them: on the Day of Resurrection your Lord will judge between them regarding their differences. ¹⁸ Now We have set you [Muhammad] on a clear religious path, so follow it. Do not follow the desires of those who lack [true] knowledge—¹⁹ they cannot help you against God in any way. Wrongdoers only have each other to protect them; the righteous have God Himself as their protector. ²⁰ This [revelation] is a means of insight for people, a source of guidance and mercy for those of sure faith.

²¹ Do those who commit evil deeds really think that We will deal with them in the same way as those who believe and do righteous deeds, that they will be alike in their living and their dying? How badly they judge! ²² God created the heavens and earth for a true purpose: to reward each soul according to its deeds. They will not be wronged. ²³ [Prophet], consider the one who has taken his own desire as a god, whom God allows to stray in the face of knowledge, sealing his ears and heart and covering his eyes—who can guide such a person after God [has done this]? Will you [people] not take heed?

²⁴ They say, 'There is only our life in this world: we die, we live, nothing but time destroys us.' They have no knowledge of this; they only follow guesswork: their only argument, ²⁵ when Our clear revelations are recited to them, is to say, 'Bring back our forefathers if what you say is true.' ²⁶ [Prophet], say, 'It is God who gives you life, then causes you to die, and then He gathers you all to the Day of Resurrection of which there is no doubt, though most people do not comprehend.'

²⁷ Control of everything in the heavens and the earth belongs to God. When the Hour comes, those who follow falsehood will be the losers on that Day. ²⁸ You will see every community kneeling.

ᵃ 'God's days' (plural) here suggests the days on which God delivers His punishment in this world, not the Day of Judgement (singular).

Every community will be summoned to its record: 'Today you will be repaid for what you did. ²⁹ Here is Our record that tells the truth about you: We have been recording everything you do.' ³⁰ Those who believed and did good deeds will be admitted by their Lord into His mercy—that is the clearest triumph—³¹ but those who disbelieved [will be asked]: 'When My revelations were recited to you, were you not arrogant and persistent in wicked deeds? ³² When it was said to you, "God's promise is true: there is no doubt about the Hour," did you not reply, "We know nothing of the Hour. This is only conjecture in our opinion. We are not convinced"?' ³³ The evil of their actions will then become clear to them. The punishment they mocked will engulf them. ³⁴ It will be said, 'Today We shall ignore you just as you ignored your appointment with this Day. The Fire will be your home and no one will help you, ³⁵ because you received God's revelations with ridicule and were deceived by worldly life.' They will not be brought out of the Fire on that Day, nor will they be given the chance to make amends.

³⁶ So praise be to God, Lord of the heavens and earth, Lord of the worlds. ³⁷ True greatness in the heavens and the earth is rightfully His: He is the Mighty, the Wise.

46. THE SAND DUNES

A Meccan sura. The title refers to the sand dunes mentioned in verse 21, where the people of 'Ad used to live, and where they were destroyed when they rejected the warning of their prophet. It reflects one of the major themes of this sura: the inescapable punishment that awaits those who deny the truth and the Resurrection. Emphasis is placed on the fact that communities more established than the Meccans' have been destroyed, and that even the jinn believe in the Qur'an before the disbelievers of Mecca do. Finally, the Prophet is encouraged to be steadfast and await God's judgement on the disbelievers.

In the name of God, the Lord of Mercy, the Giver of Mercy

¹ *Ha Mim*

² This Scripture is sent down from God, the Almighty, the Wise. ³ It was for a true purpose and a specific term that We created heaven and earth and everything in between, yet those who deny the truth ignore the warning they have been given. ⁴ Say [Prophet], 'Consider those you pray to other than God: show me which part of the earth they created or which share of the heavens they own; bring me a previous scripture or some vestige of divine knowledge—if what you say is true.' ⁵ Who could be more wrong than a person who calls on those other than God, those who will not answer him till the Day of Resurrection, those who are unaware of his prayers, ⁶ those who, when all mankind is gathered, will become his enemies and disown his worship?

⁷ When Our revelations are recited to them in all their clarity, the disbelievers say of the Truth that has reached them, 'This is clearly sorcery,' ⁸ or they say, 'He has invented it himself.' Say [Prophet], 'If I have really invented it, there is nothing you can do to save me from God. He knows best what you say amongst yourselves about it; He is sufficient as a witness between me and you; He is the Most Forgiving, the Most Merciful.' ⁹ Say, 'I am not the first of God's messengers. I do not know what will be done with me or you; I only follow what is revealed to me; I only warn plainly.' ¹⁰ Say, 'Have you thought: what if this Qur'an really is from God and you reject it? What if one of the Children of Israel testifies to its similarity [to

earlier scripture] and believes in it, and yet you are too proud to [do the same]? God certainly does not guide evildoers.'

¹¹ Those who disbelieve say of the believers, 'If there were any good in this Qur'an, they would not have believed in it before we did,'^a and, since they refuse to be guided by it, they say, 'This is an ancient fabrication.' ¹² Yet the scripture of Moses was revealed before it as a guide and a mercy, and this is a scripture confirming it in the Arabic language to warn those who do evil and bring good news for those who do good. ¹³ There is no fear for those who say, 'Our lord is God,' and then follow the straight path, nor shall they grieve: ¹⁴ they are the people of Paradise, there to remain as a reward for what they were doing.

¹⁵ We have commanded man to be good to his parents: his mother struggled to carry him and struggled to give birth to him—his bearing and weaning took a full thirty months. When he has grown to manhood and reached the age of forty he [may] say, 'Lord, help me to be truly grateful for Your favours to me and to my parents; help me to do good work that pleases You; make my offspring good. I turn to You; I am one of those who devote themselves to You.' ¹⁶ We accept from such people the best of what they do and We overlook their bad deeds. They will be among the people of Paradise—the true promise that has been given to them.

¹⁷ But some say to their parents, 'What? Are you really warning me that I shall be raised alive from my grave, when so many generations have already passed and gone before me?' His parents implore God for help; they say, 'Alas for you! Believe! God's promise is true,' but still he replies, 'These are nothing but ancient fables.' ¹⁸ The verdict has been passed on such people, along with all the communities that went before them, jinn and human: they are lost. ¹⁹ Everyone will be ranked according to their deeds and God will repay them in full for their deeds: they will not be wronged. ²⁰ On the Day when those who deny the truth are brought before the Fire, it will be said to them, 'You squandered the good things you were given in your earthly life, you took your fill of pleasure there, so on this Day a punishment of shame is yours: you were arrogant on earth without any right, and exceeded all limits.'

---

^a The disbelievers had particular difficulty in accepting the fact that some of those who believed in Islam were people they considered to be humble riff-raff.

²¹ Mention [Hud] of the tribe of 'Ad: he warned his people among the sand dunes—other warners have come and gone both before and after him—'Worship no one but God: I fear for you, that you will be punished on a terrible Day,' ²² but they said, 'Have you come to turn us away from our gods? If what you say is true, bring down that punishment you threaten us with!' ²³ He said, 'Only God knows when it will come: I simply convey to you the message I am sent with. I can see you are an insolent people.' ²⁴ When they saw a cloud approaching their valley, they said, 'This cloud will give us rain!' 'No indeed! It is what you wanted to hasten: a storm-wind bearing a painful punishment ²⁵ which will destroy everything by its Lord's command.' In the morning there was nothing to see except their ruined dwellings: this is how We repay the guilty.

²⁶ We had established them in a way we have not established you [people of Mecca]; We gave them hearing, sight, and hearts, yet their hearing, sight, and hearts were of no use to them, since they denied God's revelations. They were overwhelmed by the punishment they had mocked. ²⁷ We have also destroyed other communities that once flourished around you—We had given them various signs so that they might return to the right way—²⁸ so why did their gods not help them, those they set up as gods beside God to bring them nearer to Him? No indeed! They failed them utterly: it was all a lie of their own making.

²⁹ We sent a group of jinn to you [Prophet] to listen to the Qur'an. When they heard it, they said to one another, 'Be quiet!' Then when it was finished they turned to their community and gave them warning. ³⁰ They said, 'Our people, we have been listening to a Scripture that came after Moses, confirming previous scriptures, giving guidance to the truth and the straight path. ³¹ Our people, respond to the one who calls you to God. Believe in Him: He will forgive you your sins and protect you from a painful punishment.' ³² Those who fail to respond to God's call cannot escape God's power anywhere on earth, nor will they have any protector against Him: such people have clearly gone far astray.

³³ Do the disbelievers not understand that God, who created the heavens and earth and did not tire in doing so, has the power to bring the dead back to life? Yes indeed! He has power over everything. ³⁴ On the Day the disbelievers are brought before Hell [it will be said to them], 'Is this not real?' 'Yes, by our Lord,' they will reply

and He will say, 'Then taste the punishment for having denied the truth.'

³⁵ Be steadfast [Muhammad], like those messengers of firm resolve. [a] Do not seek to hasten the punishment for the disbelievers: on the Day they see what they had been warned about, it will seem to them that they lingered no more than a single hour of a single day [in this life]. This is a warning. Shall any be destroyed except the defiant?

---

[a] Noah, Abraham, Moses, Jesus, and Muhammad are traditionally termed 'the messengers of firm resolve' for their tenacity in preaching God's message.

47. MUHAMMAD

A Medinan sura that deals with issues of war, those who try to prevent conversion to Islam and the carrying out of God's commands (a common theme in the Medinan suras), and the fate of the hypocrites. It specifically mentions the iniquity of those who expelled the Prophet from Mecca, it describes the futility of the disbelievers' attempts to oppose God and His Prophet, and it urges the Muslims to obey God in all matters, lest their good deeds come to nothing on the Day of Judgement like those of the disbelievers and hypocrites. It takes its title from the mention of Muhammad's name in verse 2.

In the name of God, the Lord of Mercy, the Giver of Mercy

[1] God will bring to nothing the deeds of those who disbelieve and bar others from the way of God, [2] but He will overlook the bad deeds of those who have faith, do good deeds, and believe in what has been sent down to Muhammad—the truth from their Lord—and He will put them into a good state. [3] This is because the disbelievers follow falsehood, while the believers follow the truth from their Lord. In this way God shows people their true type.

[4] When you meet the disbelievers in battle, strike them in the neck, and once they are defeated, bind any captives firmly—later you can release them by grace[a] or by ransom—until the toils of war have ended. That [is the way]. God could have defeated them Himself if He had willed, but His purpose is to test some of you by means of others. He will not let the deeds of those who are killed for His cause come to nothing; [5] He will guide them and put them into a good state; [6] He will admit them into the Garden He has already made known to them. [7] You who believe! If you help God, He will help you and make you stand firm.

[8] As for the disbelievers, how wretched will be their state! God has brought their deeds to nothing. [9] It is because they hate what God has sent down that He has caused their deeds to go to waste. [10] Have they not travelled the earth and seen how those before them met their end? God destroyed them utterly: a similar fate awaits the

---

[a] Commentators highlight the fact that 'by grace' is the first of the two options given here, concluding that this is the preferred or recommended course of action.

disbelievers. [11] That is because God protects the believers while the disbelievers have no one to protect them: [12] God will admit those who believe and do good deeds to Gardens graced with flowing streams; the disbelievers may take their fill of pleasure in this world, and eat as cattle do, but the Fire will be their home. [13] We have destroyed many a town stronger than your own [Prophet]—the town which [chose to] expel you—and they had no one to help them.

[14] Can those who follow clear proof from their Lord be compared to those whose foul deeds are made to seem alluring to them, those who follow their own desires? [15] Here is a picture of the Garden promised to the pious: rivers of water for ever pure, rivers of milk for ever fresh, rivers of wine, a delight for those who drink, rivers of honey clarified and pure, [all] flow in it; there they will find fruit of every kind; and they will find forgiveness from their Lord. How can this be compared to the fate of those stuck in the Fire, given boiling water to drink that tears their bowels?

[16] Some of these people listen to you [Prophet], but, once they leave your presence, they sneer at those who have been given knowledge, saying, 'What was that he just said?' These are the ones whose hearts God has sealed, those who follow their own desires. [17] God has increased the guidance of those who follow the right path, and given them their awareness [of Him]. [18] What are the disbelievers waiting for, other than the Hour which will come upon them unawares? Its signs are already here, but once the Hour has actually arrived, what use will it be then to take heed? [19] So [Prophet], bear in mind[a] that there is no god but God, and ask forgiveness for your sins and for the sins of believing men and women. God knows whenever any of you move, and whenever any of you stay still.

[20] Those who believe ask why no sura [about fighting] has been sent down. Yet when a decisive sura [that mentions fighting] is sent down, you can see the sick at heart looking at you [Prophet] and visibly fainting at the prospect of death—[21] obedience and fitting words would be better for them; it would also be better for them to be true to God when the decision to fight has been made. [22] 'If you turn away now, could it be that you will go on to spread corruption all over the land and break your ties of kinship?'[b] [23] These are the

---

[a] Literally 'know'.

[b] A reference to the pretext given, by some who refused to fight, that fighting breaks ties of kinship.

ones God has rejected, making their ears deaf and their eyes blind.
²⁴ Will they not contemplate the Qur'an? Do they have locks on their
hearts? ²⁵ Those who turn on their heels after being shown guidance*ᵃ*
are duped and tempted by Satan; ²⁶ they say to those who hate what
God has sent down, 'We will obey you in some matters'*ᵇ* — God
knows their secret schemes.

²⁷ How will they feel when the angels take them in death and beat
their faces and their backs ²⁸ because they practised things that
incurred God's wrath, and disdained to please Him? He makes their
deeds go to waste.

²⁹ Do the corrupt at heart assume that God will not expose their
malice? ³⁰ We could even point them out to you [Prophet] if We
wished, and then you could identify them by their marks, but you
will know them anyway by the tone of their speech. God knows
everything you [people] do. ³¹ We shall test you to see which of you
strive your hardest and remain firm; We shall test the sincerity of
your assertions. ³² Those who disbelieve, bar others from God's path,
and oppose the Messenger when they have been shown guidance, do
not harm God in any way. He will make their deeds go to waste —
³³ believers, obey God and the Messenger: do not let your deeds go to
waste — ³⁴ God will not forgive those who disbelieve, bar others from
God's path, and die as disbelievers.

³⁵ So [believers] do not lose heart and cry out for peace. It is you
who have the upper hand: God is with you. He will not begrudge
you the reward for your [good] deeds: ³⁶ the life of this world is only a
game, a pastime, but if you believe and are mindful of God, He will
recompense you. He does not ask you to give up all your possessions — ³⁷ you would be grudging if He were to press you for them
and He would bring your ill-will to light — ³⁸ though even when you
are called upon to give [a little] for the sake of God, some of you will
be grudging. Whoever is grudging is so only towards himself: God
is the source of wealth and you are the needy ones. He will substitute
other people for you if you turn away, and they will not be like you.

ᵃ Said to refer to some of the Jews in Medina (Razi).

ᵇ For instance, they will agree that Muhammad is not a prophet but will not agree to
idol worship or denial of the Resurrection (Razi).

48. TRIUMPH

A Medinan sura that takes its title from verse 1 and makes reference to the occasion when the Prophet had a vision that he and his followers would be performing pilgrimage to Mecca (verse 27). They set out, but the Meccans decided to bar them at Hudaybiyya from reaching the town and sent emissaries to have discussions with the Prophet. In the end the Prophet signed a treaty that he and the believers would not enter Mecca that year, but would do so the next year. Seeing the long-term significance of this treaty, in the interests of peace he agreed to a truce of ten years during which time, if any Meccan went over to his side, he would return him to the Meccans, but if any of his people went over to the Meccans, they would not return them. Throughout the sura the Prophet is assured that this treaty that God has given him is a great breakthrough (cf. verses 1–3, 18–21, 27). The believers are reassured that their self-restraint and obedience to the Prophet were inspired by God (verses 4–5, 24–6). The sura condemns both the hypocrites in Medina (verse 6) and the idolaters of Mecca (verses 6 and 26) and closes by praising the believers (verse 29).

In the name of God, the Lord of Mercy, the Giver of Mercy

¹ Truly We have opened up a path to clear triumph for you [Prophet], ² so that God may forgive you your past and future sins, complete His grace upon you, guide you to a straight path, ³ and help you mightily. ⁴ It was He who made His tranquillity descend into the hearts of the believers,[a] to add faith to their faith—the forces of the heavens and earth belong to Him; He is all knowing and all wise—⁵ so as to admit believing men and women into Gardens graced with flowing streams, there to remain, absolving their bad deeds—a great triumph in God's eyes—⁶ and to torment the hypocritical and idolatrous men and women who harbour evil thoughts about God[b]—it is they who will be encircled by evil!—who carry the burden of God's anger, whom God has rejected and for whom He has prepared Hell, an evil destination! ⁷ The forces of heaven and earth belong to God; He is almighty and all wise. ⁸ We have sent you [Prophet] to bring good news and to give warning, ⁹ so that you

---

[a] When they pledged to accept the Prophet's decision. See verse 18.

[b] See verse 12.

[people] may believe in God and His Messenger, support Him, honour Him, and praise Him morning and evening.

¹⁰ Those who pledge loyalty to you [Prophet] are actually pledging loyalty to God Himself—God's hand is placed on theirs*—and anyone who breaks his pledge does so to his own detriment: God will give a great reward to the one who fulfils his pledge to Him. ¹¹ The desert Arabs who stayed behind will say to you, 'We were busy with our property and our families: ask forgiveness for us,' but they say with their tongues what is not in their hearts. Say, 'Whether it is God's will to do you harm or good, who can intervene for you?' No! God is fully aware of everything you [people] do. ¹² No! You thought that the Messenger and the believers would never return to their families and this thought warmed your hearts. Your thoughts are evil, for you are corrupt people: ¹³ We have prepared a blazing Fire for those who do not believe in God and His Messenger. ¹⁴ Control of the heavens and earth belongs to God and He forgives whoever He will and punishes whoever He will: God is most forgiving and merciful.

¹⁵ When you [believers] set off for somewhere that promises war gains, those who [previously] stayed behind will say, 'Let us come with you.' They want to change God's words, but tell them [Prophet], 'You may not come with us: God has said this before.' They will reply, 'You begrudge us out of jealousy.' How little they understand!

¹⁶ Tell the desert Arabs who stayed behind, 'You will be called to face a people of great might in war and to fight them, unless they surrender: if you obey, God will reward you well, but if you turn away, as you have done before, He will punish you heavily—¹⁷ the blind, the lame, and the sick will not be blamed.' God will admit anyone who obeys Him and His Messenger to Gardens graced with flowing streams; He will painfully punish anyone who turns away.

¹⁸ God was pleased with the believers when they swore allegiance to you [Prophet] under the tree: He knew what was in their hearts and so He sent tranquillity down to them and rewarded them with a speedy triumph ¹⁹ and with many future gains—God is mighty and wise: ²⁰ He has promised you [people] many future gains—He has

---

a Loyalty was pledged by everybody placing their right hands on top of the Prophet's.

hastened this gain for you: He has held back the hands of hostile people from you as a sign for the faithful—and He will guide you to a straight path. ²¹ There are many other gains [to come], over which you have no power. God has full control over them: God has power over all things.

²² If the disbelievers had fought against you, they would have taken flight, with no one to protect or support them: ²³ such was God's practice in the past and you will find no change in God's practices. ²⁴ In the valley of Mecca it was He who held their hands back from you and your hands back from them after He gave you the advantage over them*ᵃ*—God sees all that you do. ²⁵ They were the ones who disbelieved, who barred you from the Sacred Mosque, and who prevented the offering from reaching its place of sacrifice. If there had not been among them, unknown to you, believing men and women whom you would have trampled underfoot, inadvertently incurring guilt on their account—God brings whoever He will into His mercy—if the [believers] had been clearly separated, We would have inflicted a painful punishment on the disbelievers. ²⁶ While the disbelievers had fury in their hearts—the fury of ignorance—God sent His tranquillity down on to His Messenger and the believers and made binding on them [their] promise to obey God,*ᵇ* for that was more appropriate and fitting for them. God has full knowledge of all things.

²⁷ God has truly fulfilled His Messenger's vision: 'God willing, you will most certainly enter the Sacred Mosque in safety, shaven-headed or with cropped hair,*ᶜ* without fear!'—God knew what you did not—and He has also granted you a speedy triumph. ²⁸ It was He who sent His Messenger with guidance and the religion of Truth to show that it is above every [other] religion. God suffices as a witness: ²⁹ Muhammad is the Messenger of God.

Those who follow him are harsh towards the disbelievers and compassionate towards each other. You see them kneeling and prostrating, seeking God's bounty and His good pleasure: on their faces they bear the marks of their prostrations. They are pictured in the Torah and the Gospel as being like a seed that puts forth its

---

ᵃ A detachment of eighty Meccan fighters attacked the Prophet's camp but were captured. The Prophet released them after the treaty was signed.

ᵇ The promise they made under the tree at Hudaybiyya (see verse 18).

ᶜ These are some of the final rites of pilgrimage.

shoot, becomes strong, grows thick, and rises on its stem to the delight of its sowers. So God infuriates the disbelievers through them; God promises forgiveness and a great reward to those who believe and do righteous deeds.

49. THE PRIVATE QUARTERS

This Medinan sura takes its title from the reference to the Prophet's private quarters in verse 4. It guides the believers on how to behave with proper respect towards their leader (verses 1–5), and with mutual respect and trust towards each other (verses 9–12). The sura stresses the unity of mankind and God's intention that people should live together in harmony (verse 13). It criticizes the desert Arabs for their presumptuous attitude to their faith and to God (verses 14–18).

In the name of God, the Lord of Mercy, the Giver of Mercy

[1] Believers, do not push yourselves forward in the presence of God and His Messenger—be mindful of God: He hears and knows all— [2] believers, do not raise your voices above the Prophet's, do not raise your voice when speaking to him as you do to one another, or your [good] deeds may be cancelled out without you knowing. [3] It is those who lower their voices in the presence of God's Messenger whose hearts God has proved to be aware—they will have forgiveness, and a great reward— [4] but most of those who shout to you [Prophet] from outside your private quarters lack understanding. [5] It would have been better for them if they had waited patiently for you to come out to them: God is all forgiving and merciful.

[6] Believers, if a troublemaker brings you news, check it first, in case you wrong others unwittingly and later regret what you have done, [7] and be aware that it is God's Messenger who is among you: in many matters you would certainly suffer if he were to follow your wishes. God has endeared faith to you and made it beautiful to your hearts; He has made disbelief, mischief, and disobedience hateful to you. These are the people who are rightly guided [8] through God's favour and blessing: God is all knowing and all wise.

[9] If two groups of the believers fight, you [believers] should try to reconcile them; if one of them is [clearly] oppressing the other, fight the oppressors until they submit to God's command, then make a just and even-handed reconciliation between the two of them: God loves those who are even-handed. [10] The believers are brothers, so make peace between your two brothers and be mindful of God, so that you may be given mercy.

[11] Believers, no one group of men should jeer at another, who may after all be better than them; no one group of women should jeer at another, who may after all be better than them; do not speak ill of one another; do not use offensive nicknames for one another. How bad it is to be called a mischief-maker[a] after accepting faith! Those who do not repent of this behaviour are evildoers. [12] Believers, do not indulge many of your suspicions—some suspicions are sinful—and do not spy on one another or speak ill of people behind their backs: would any of you like to eat the flesh of your dead brother? No, you would hate it. So be mindful of God: God is ever relenting, most merciful. [13] People, We created you all from a single man and a single woman, and made you into nations and tribes so that you should get to know one another. In God's eyes, the most honoured of you are the ones most aware of Him: God is all knowing, all aware.

[14] The desert Arabs say, 'We have faith.' [Prophet], tell them, 'You do not have faith. What you should say instead is, "We have submitted," for faith has not yet entered your hearts.' If you obey God and His Messenger, He will not diminish any of your deeds: He is most forgiving and most merciful. [15] The true believers are the ones who have faith in God and His Messenger and leave all doubt behind, the ones who have struggled with their possessions and their persons in God's way: they are the ones who are true. [16] Say, 'Do you presume to teach God about your religion, when God knows everything in the heavens and earth, and He has full knowledge of all things?' [17] They think they have done you [Prophet] a favour by submitting. Say, 'Do not consider your submission a favour to me; it is God who has done you a favour, by guiding you to faith, if you are truly sincere.' [18] God knows the secrets of the heavens and earth: He is fully aware of everything you do.

---

[a] Those who cause trouble by doing any of the above actions will have earned the name of 'mischief-maker' (Razi).

50. QAF

A Meccan sura which deals predominantly with the Resurrection and the Day of Judgement. Reference is made to previous generations of disbelievers (verses 12–14), both to warn the disbelievers in Mecca and to reassure the Prophet. Creation is cited as an indication of God's ability to bring the dead to life again (verses 3–11), and emphasis is placed on the powerlessness of man on the Day of Resurrection (verses 20–30). The sura both opens and closes with mention of the Qur'an.

In the name of God, the Lord of Mercy, the Giver of Mercy

¹*Qaf*

By the glorious Qur'an!*ᵃ* ²The disbelievers are amazed that a warner has come from among them and they say, 'How strange! ³To come back [to life] after we have died and become dust? That is too far-fetched.' ⁴Yet We know very well what the earth takes away from them: We keep a comprehensive record. ⁵But the disbelievers deny the truth when it comes to them; they are in a state of confusion. ⁶Do they not see the sky above them—how We have built and adorned it, with no rifts in it; ⁷how We spread out the earth and put solid mountains on it, and caused every kind of joyous plant to grow in it, ⁸as a lesson and reminder for every servant who turns to God; ⁹and how We send blessed water down from the sky and grow with it gardens, the harvest grain, ¹⁰and tall palm trees laden with clusters of dates, ¹¹as a provision for everyone; how with water We give [new] life to a land that is dead? This is how the dead will emerge [from their graves]. ¹²The people of Noah disbelieved long before these disbelievers, as did the people of Rass, Thamud, ¹³'Ad, Pharaoh, Lot, ¹⁴the Forest-Dwellers, Tubba': all of these people disbelieved their messengers, and so My warning was realized.

¹⁵So were We incapable of the first creation? No indeed! Yet they doubt a second creation. ¹⁶We created man—We know what his soul whispers to him: We are closer to him than his jugular vein—¹⁷with

---

ᵃ That which is sworn—that mankind will be raised from the dead—is omitted but is evident from the verses that follow (cf. 37: 1; 89: 1–4).

two receptors[a] set to record, one on his right side and one on his left, [18] he does not utter a single word without an ever-present watcher. [19] The throes of death will bring the Truth with them: 'This is what you tried to escape.'

[20] The Trumpet will be sounded: 'This is the Day [you were] warned of.' [21] Each person will arrive attended by an [angel] to drive him on and another to bear witness: [22] 'You paid no attention to this Day; but today We have removed your veil and your sight is sharp.' [23] The person's attendant will say, 'Here is what I have prepared'—[24] 'Hurl[b] every obstinate disbeliever into Hell, [25] everyone who hindered good, was aggressive, caused others to doubt, [26] and set up other gods alongside God. Hurl him into severe punishment!'—[27] and his [evil][c] companion will say, 'Lord, I did not make him transgress; he had already gone far astray himself.' [28] God will say, 'Do not argue in My presence. I sent you a warning [29] and My word cannot be changed: I am not unjust to any creature.' [30] We shall say to Hell on that day, 'Are you full?' and it will reply, 'Are there no more?' [31] But Paradise will be brought close to the righteous and will no longer be distant: [32] 'This is what you were promised—this is for everyone who turned often to God and kept Him in mind, [33] who held the Most Gracious in awe, though He is unseen, who comes before Him with a heart turned to Him in devotion—[34] so enter it in peace. This is the Day of everlasting Life.' [35] They will have all that they wish for there, and We have more for them.

[36] We have destroyed even mightier generations before these disbelievers: they searched throughout the land, but could they find any escape? [37] There truly is in this a reminder for whoever has a heart, whoever listens attentively. [38] We created the heavens, the earth, and everything between, in six Days, without tiring. [39] [Prophet], bear everything they say with patience; celebrate the praise of your Lord before the rising and setting of the sun; [40] proclaim His praise in the night and at the end of every prayer;[d] [41] listen out for the Day when the caller will call from a nearby place. [42] They will come out [from

---

[a] Usually taken to mean 'recording angels'.

[b] This verb is in the dual, taken to be addressed either to both recording angels, or to two of the angels who guard Hell.

[c] Cf. 4: 38.

[d] Literally 'prostration', *sujud*. This is a figure of speech in which the part stands for the whole.

their graves] on that Day, the Day when they hear the mighty blast in reality. [43] It is We who give life and death; the final return will be to Us [44] on the Day when the earth will be torn apart, letting them rush out—that gathering will be quite easy for Us. [45] We know best what the disbelievers say. You [Prophet] are not there to force them: so remind, with this Qur'an, those who fear My warning.

51. SCATTERING [WINDS]

A Meccan sura that gives several of the signs of nature as proof of the Resurrection, among them the scattering winds that give the sura its title (verse 1). The disbelievers are reminded of the fate that befell previous rebellious generations and the Prophet is urged to carry on reminding.

In the name of God, the Lord of Mercy, the Giver of Mercy

¹By those [winds] that scatter far and wide,ᵃ ²and those that are heavily laden,ᵇ ³that speed freely, ⁴that distribute [rain] as ordained! ⁵What you [people] are promised is true: ⁶the Judgement will come. ⁷By the sky with its orbits! ⁸What you say is inconsistent: ⁹those who turn away from itᶜ are [truly] deceived. ¹⁰Perish the liars, ¹¹those steeped in error and unaware! ¹²They ask, 'When is this Judgement Day coming?' ¹³On a Day when they will be punished by the Fire, ¹⁴'Taste the punishment, this is what you wished to hasten.' ¹⁵The righteous will be in Gardens with [flowing] springs. ¹⁶They will receive their Lord's gifts because of the good they did before: ¹⁷sleeping only little at night, ¹⁸praying at dawn for God's forgiveness, ¹⁹giving a rightful share of their wealth for the beggar and the deprived. ²⁰On earth there are signs for those with sure faith—²¹and in yourselves too, do you not see?—²²in the sky is your sustenance and all that you are promised.ᵈ ²³By the Lord of the heavens and earth! All this is true, as true as your ability to speak.

²⁴[Muhammad], have you heard the story of the honoured guests of Abraham? ²⁵They went in to see him and said, 'Peace.' 'Peace,' he said, [adding to himself] 'These people are strangers.' ²⁶He turned quickly to his household, brought out a fat calf, ²⁷and placed it before them. 'Will you not eat?' he said, ²⁸beginning to be afraid, but they said, 'Do not be afraid.' They gave him good news of a son who would be gifted with knowledge. ²⁹His wife then entered with a loud cry, struck her face,ᵉ and said, 'A barren old

---

ᵃ See 15: 22; this is a benevolent scattering (unlike the one in 18: 45).
ᵇ With rain.   ᶜ Judgement.
ᵈ The punishment and Final Judgement/Destiny/physical and spiritual sustenance.
ᵉ In her incredulity and embarrassment.

woman?'*a* ³⁰ but they said, 'It will be so. These are your Lord's words, and He is the Wise, the All Knowing.' ³¹ Abraham said, 'What is your errand, messengers?' ³² They said, 'We are sent to a people lost in sin, ³³ to bring rocks of clay, ³⁴ selected by your Lord for those who exceed all bounds.' ³⁵ We brought out such believers as were there— ³⁶ We found only one household devoted to God— ³⁷ and left the town to be a sign for those who fear the painful punishment.

³⁸ There is another sign in Moses: We sent him to Pharaoh with clear authority. ³⁹ Pharaoh turned away with his supporters, saying, 'This is a sorcerer, or maybe a madman,' ⁴⁰ so We seized him and his forces and threw them into the sea: he was to blame. ⁴¹ There is another sign in the 'Ad: We sent the life-destroying wind against them ⁴² and it reduced everything it came up against to dust. ⁴³ And also in the Thamud: it was said to them, 'Make the most of your lives for a while,' ⁴⁴ but they rebelled against their Lord's command, so the blast took them. They looked on helplessly: ⁴⁵ they could not even remain standing, let alone defend themselves. ⁴⁶ Before that We destroyed the people of Noah. They were a truly sinful people! ⁴⁷ We built the heavens with Our power and made them vast, ⁴⁸ We spread out the earth—how well We smoothed it out!— ⁴⁹ and We created pairs of all things so that you [people] might take note.

⁵⁰ [So, say to them, Prophet], 'Quickly turn to God—I am sent by Him to give you clear warning— ⁵¹ and do not set up any other god alongside Him. I am sent by Him to give you clear warning!' ⁵² Every previous people to whom a messenger was sent also said, 'A sorcerer, or maybe a madman!' ⁵³ Did they tell one another to do this? No! They are a people who exceed all bounds, ⁵⁴ so ignore them [Prophet]—you are not to blame— ⁵⁵ and go on reminding [people], it is good for those who believe to be reminded.

⁵⁶ I created jinn and mankind only to worship Me: ⁵⁷ I want no provision from them, nor do I want them to feed Me— ⁵⁸ God is the Provider, the Lord of Power, the Ever Mighty. ⁵⁹ The evildoers, like their predecessors, will have a share of punishment—they need not ask Me to hasten it— ⁶⁰ and woe betide those who deny the truth on the Day they have been promised.

a See 11: 72.

52. THE MOUNTAIN

A Meccan sura which addresses many of the arguments put to the Prophet by the disbelievers of Mecca (verses 29–49). The bliss that will be enjoyed by the believers is contrasted to the torments of Hell, and the Prophet is urged to bide his time, to continue to deliver his message, and to wait with confidence for God's judgement. God swears by, among other things, Mount Sinai, from which the sura takes its title, that the Day of Judgement is inevitable.

In the name of God, the Lord of Mercy, the Giver of Mercy

¹By the mountain,ᵃ ²by a Scripture inscribed ³in unrolled parchment, ⁴by the much-visited House,ᵇ ⁵by the raised canopy,ᶜ ⁶by the ocean ever filled, ⁷[Prophet], your Lord's punishment is coming— ⁸it cannot be put off— ⁹on the Day when the sky sways back and forth ¹⁰and the mountains float away.ᵈ ¹¹Woe on that Day to those who deny the Truth, ¹²who amuse themselves with idle chatter: ¹³on that Day they will be thrust into the Fire of Hell. ¹⁴'This is the Fire you used to deny: ¹⁵so is this sorcery? Do you still not see it? ¹⁶Burn in it—it makes no difference whether you bear it patiently or not— now you are being repaid for what you have done.'

¹⁷Those who were mindful of God are in Gardens and in bliss, ¹⁸rejoicing in their Lord's gifts: He has saved them from the torment of the Blaze, ¹⁹'Eat and drink with healthy enjoyment as a reward for what you have done.' ²⁰They are comfortably seatedᵉ on couches arranged in rows; We pair them with beautiful-eyed maidens; ²¹We unite the believers with their offspring who followed them in faith— We do not deny them any of the rewards for their deeds: each person is in pledge for his own deeds—²²We provide them with any fruit or meat they desire. ²³They pass around a cup which does not lead to any idle talk or sin. ²⁴Devoted youths like hidden pearlsᶠ wait on

---

ᵃ Mount Sinai, see 95: 2; 23: 20.
ᵇ Understood to refer to the Ka'ba in Mecca.
ᶜ The sky.
ᵈ See 27: 88.
ᵉ *Ittaka'a* means 'to sit, well supported' (*al-Mu'jam al-Wasit*) (cf. 55: 54, 76).
ᶠ The choicest pearls were kept hidden for their protection and only removed from safekeeping on very special occasions.

them. [25] They turn to one another and say, [26] 'When we were still with our families [on earth] we used to live in fear—[27] God has been gracious to us and saved us from the torment of intense heat—[28] We used to pray to Him: He is the Good, the Merciful One.' [29] So [Prophet] remind [people].

By the grace of your Lord [Prophet], you are neither oracle nor madman. [30] If[a] they say, 'He is only a poet: we shall await his fate,' [31] say, 'Wait if you wish; I too am waiting'—[32] does their reason really tell them to do this, or are they simply insolent people? [33] If they say, 'He has made it up himself'—they certainly do not believe—[34] let them produce one like it, if what they say is true. [35] Were they created without any agent? Were they the creators? [36] Did they create the heavens and the earth? No! They do not have faith. [37] Do they possess your Lord's treasures or have control over them? [38] Do they have a ladder to climb, in order to eavesdrop [on Heaven's secrets]? Let their eavesdropper produce clear proof. [39] Does God have daughters while you have sons?[b] [40] Do you [Prophet] demand a payment from them that would burden them with debt? [41] Do they have [access to] the unseen? Could they write it down? [42] Do they think they can ensnare you? It is the disbelievers who have been ensnared. [43] Do they really have another god beside God? God is far above anything they set alongside Him.

[44] Even if they saw a piece of heaven falling down on them,[c] they would say, 'Just a heap of clouds,' [45] so leave them, Prophet, until they face the Day when they will be thunderstruck, [46] the Day when their snares will be of no use to them, when they will get no help. [47] Another punishment awaits the evildoers, though most of them do not realize it. [48] Wait patiently [Prophet] for your Lord's judgement: you are under Our watchful eye. Celebrate the praise of your Lord when you rise. [49] Glorify Him at night and at the fading of the stars.

---

[a] Eleven verses in this section begin with 'or', which is powerful in Arabic argumentation. The Qur'an surveys all their arguments, one by one, with equal emphasis. Thus it uses *am* ('or') which indicates equivalence in Arabic. We have omitted the conjunction.

[b] This refers to the pagan belief that the angels were the daughters of God and to their habit of denigrating the birth of their own daughters.

[c] The Meccans challenged the Prophet to bring the heavens down on them, if he were truly God's Messenger. Cf. 17: 92.

53. THE STAR

A Meccan sura that confirms the divine source of the Prophet's message and refers to his ascension to heaven during the Night Journey (verses 1–18). The sura refutes the claims of the disbelievers about the goddesses and the angels (verses 19–28), and the third paragraph lists several truths about God's power. The sura closes with a warning of the imminent Day of Judgement.

In the name of God, the Lord of Mercy, the Giver of Mercy

¹By the setting star!ᵃ ²Your companionᵇ has not strayed; he is not deluded; ³he does not speak from his own desire. ⁴The Qur'an is nothing less than a revelation that is sent to him. ⁵It was taught to him by [an angel]ᶜ with mighty powers ⁶and great strength, who stood ⁷on the highest horizon ⁸and then approached—coming down ⁹until he was two bow-lengths away or even closer—¹⁰and revealed to God's servant what he revealed. ¹¹[The Prophet's] own heart did not distort what he saw. ¹²Are you going to dispute with him what he saw with his own eyes? ¹³A second time he saw him: ¹⁴by the lote tree beyond which none may passᵈ ¹⁵near the Garden of Return, ¹⁶when the tree was covered in nameless splendour.ᵉ ¹⁷His sight never wavered, nor was it too bold, ¹⁸and he saw some of the greatest signs of his Lord.

¹⁹[Disbelievers], consider al-Lat and al-'Uzza, ²⁰and the third one, Manatᶠ—²¹are you to have the male and He the female? ²²That would be a most unjust distribution!ᵍ—²³these are nothing but names you have invented yourselves, you and your forefathers. God has sent no authority for them. Even though their Lord has already brought them guidance, such people merely follow guesswork and

---

ᵃ Sirius (cf. verse 49).

ᵇ Muhammad.

ᶜ This refers to the Angel Gabriel.

ᵈ Cf. 56: 28.

ᵉ Something unimaginable.

ᶠ Names of Arabian pagan goddesses.

ᵍ Because the pagan Arabs regarded daughters as a humiliation, the Qur'an argues with them according to their own logic that it was particularly illogical of them to attribute daughters to God. See also 16: 57–62; 43: 16–20.

the whims of their souls. [24] Should man have everything he wishes for, [a] [25] when the present life and the life to come belong only to God? [26] There are many angels in heaven whose intercession will be of no use until God gives permission to those He will, whose words He will accept. [27] Those who deny the life to come give the angels female names. [28] They have no knowledge to base this on: they merely follow guesswork. Guesswork cannot prevail against the truth. [29] So [Prophet] ignore those who turn away from Our revelation, who want only the life of this world. [30] Their knowledge does not go beyond that. Your Lord knows best who strays from His path and who follows guidance. [31] Everything in the heavens and earth belongs to God. He will repay those who do evil according to their deeds, and reward, with what is best, those who do good. [32] As for those who avoid grave sins and foul acts, though they may commit small sins, your Lord is ample in forgiveness. He has been aware of you from the time He produced you from the earth and from your hiding places in your mothers' wombs, so do not assert your own goodness: [b] He knows best who is mindful of Him.

[33] [Prophet], consider that man who turned away: [34] he only gave a little and then he stopped. [35] Does he have knowledge of the Unseen? Can he see [the Hereafter]? [36] Has he not been told what was written in the Scriptures of Moses [37] and Abraham who fulfilled his duty: [38] that no soul shall bear the burden of another; [39] that man will only have what he has worked towards; [40] that his labour will be seen [41] and that in the end he will be repaid in full for it; [42] that the final goal is your Lord; [43] that it is He who makes people laugh and weep; [44] that it is He who gives death and life; [45] that He Himself created the two sexes, male and female, [46] from an ejected drop of sperm; [47] that He will undertake the second Creation; [48] that it is He who gives wealth and possessions; [49] that He is the Lord of Sirius; [c] [50] that it was He who destroyed, in their entirety, ancient 'Ad [51] and Thamud, [52] and before them the people of Noah who were even more unjust and insolent; [53] that it was He who brought down the ruined cities [54] and enveloped them in the punishment He ordained for them? [55] Which then of your Lord's blessings do you deny?

---

[a] The disbelievers claimed that they worshipped their goddesses in order that these might intercede for them with God, or bring them closer to Him. Cf. 6: 94; 39: 3.

[b] Cf. 32: 10; 50: 4.

[c] The star worshipped by the pagan Arabs.

⁵⁶ This is a warning just like the warnings sent in former times. ⁵⁷ The imminent Hour draws near ⁵⁸ and only God can disclose it. ⁵⁹ Do you [people] marvel at this? ⁶⁰ Why do you laugh instead of weeping? ⁶¹ Why do you pay no heed? ⁶² Bow down before God and worship.

54. THE MOON

A Meccan sura dealing mainly with the punishment dealt out to previous generations of disbelievers. These are presented as a warning to the disbelievers of Mecca, with the refrain 'Will anyone take heed?' running throughout the sura. Finally the treatment of the disbelievers on the Day of Judgement is contrasted to the everlasting bliss the believers will enjoy. The title is taken from verse 1 and is a reference to the Day of Resurrection.

In the name of God, the Lord of Mercy, the Giver of Mercy

¹ The Hour draws near; the moon is split in two.[a]

² Whenever the disbelievers see a sign, they turn away and say, 'Same old sorcery!' ³ They reject the truth and follow their own desires—everything is recorded[b]—⁴ although warning tales that should have restrained them have come down to them—⁵ far-reaching wisdom—but these warnings do not help: ⁶ so [Prophet] turn away from them. On the Day the Summoner will summon them to a horrific event, ⁷ eyes downcast, they will come out of their graves like swarming locusts ⁸ rushing towards the Summoner. The disbelievers will cry, 'This is a stern day!'

⁹ The people of Noah rejected the truth before them: they rejected Our servant, saying, 'He is mad!' Noah was rejected, ¹⁰ and so he called upon his Lord, 'I am defeated: help me!' ¹¹ So We opened the gates of the sky with torrential water, ¹² burst the earth with gushing springs: the waters met for a preordained purpose.¹³ We carried him along on a vessel of planks and nails ¹⁴ that floated under Our watchful eye, a reward for the one who had been rejected. ¹⁵ We have left this[c] as a sign: will anyone take heed? ¹⁶ How [terrible] was My punishment and [the fulfilment of] My warnings! ¹⁷ We have made it easy to learn lessons from the Qur'an: will anyone take heed?

---

[a] One of the signs of the Day of Judgement. The Arabic uses the past tense, as if that Day were already here, to help the reader/listener imagine how it will be. Some traditional commentators hold the view that this describes an actual event at the time of the Prophet, but it clearly refers to the end of the world: cf. the same expression with reference to the sky, 55: 37; 84: 1.

[b] Literally 'fixed' in the divine records.

[c] 'This tale' or 'this ship'.

¹⁸ The people of ʿAd also rejected the truth. How [terrible] was My punishment and [the fulfilment of] My warnings! ¹⁹ We released a howling wind against them on a day of terrible disaster; ²⁰ it swept people away like uprooted palm trunks. ²¹ How [terrible] was My punishment and [the fulfilment of] My warnings! ²² We have made it easy to learn lessons from the Qurʾan: will anyone take heed?

²³ The people of Thamud also rejected the warnings: ²⁴ they said, 'What? A man? Why should we follow a lone man from amongst ourselves? That would be misguided; quite insane! ²⁵ Would a message be given to him alone out of all of us? No, he is an insolent liar!' ²⁶ 'Tomorrow they will know who is the insolent liar, ²⁷ for We shall send them a she-camel to test them: so watch them [Salih] and be patient. ²⁸ Tell them the water is to be shared between them: *a* each one should drink in turn.' ²⁹ But they called their companion, who took a sword and hamstrung the camel. ³⁰ How [terrible] was My punishment and [the fulfilment of] My warnings! ³¹ We released a single mighty blast against them; they ended up like a fence-maker's dry sticks. ³² We have made it easy to learn lessons from the Qurʾan: will anyone take heed?

³³ The people of Lot rejected the warnings. ³⁴ We released a stone-bearing wind against them, all except the family of Lot. We saved them before dawn ³⁵ as a favour from Us: this is how We reward the thankful. ³⁶ He warned them of Our onslaught, but they dismissed the warning—³⁷ they even demanded his guests from him—so We sealed their eyes—'Taste My [terrible] punishment and [the fulfilment of] My warnings!'—³⁸ and early in the morning a punishment seized them that still remains—³⁹ 'Taste My [terrible] punishment and [the fulfilment of] My warnings!' ⁴⁰ We have made it easy to learn lessons from the Qurʾan: will anyone take heed?

⁴¹ The people of Pharaoh also received warnings. ⁴² They rejected all Our signs so We seized them with all Our might and power.

⁴³ 'Are your disbelievers *b* any better than these? Were you given an exemption in the Scripture?' ⁴⁴ Do they perhaps say, 'We are a great army and we shall be victorious'? ⁴⁵ Their forces will be routed and they will turn tail and flee. *c* ⁴⁶ But the Hour is their appointed time—

---

a And the she-camel (see 26: 155).

b Of Mecca.

c The Prophet repeated this verse at the Battle of Badr.

the Hour is most severe and bitter: [47] truly the wicked are misguided and quite insane[a] —[48] on the Day when they are dragged in Hell, their faces down. 'Feel the touch of Hell.' [49] We have created all things in due measure; [50] when We ordain something it happens at once, in the blink of an eye; [51] We have destroyed the likes of you in the past. Will anyone take heed?

[52] Everything they do is noted in their records: [53] every action, great or small, is recorded. [54] The righteous will live securely among Gardens and rivers, [55] secure in the presence of an all-powerful Sovereign.

[a] See verse 24 above.

55. THE LORD OF MERCY

A Medinan sura that highlights God's wonders in this world, describes the end of the world, and paints an evocative picture of the delights of Paradise. Hell is briefly contrasted (verses 43–4) with the joys that await the righteous. The sura is characterized by the refrain 'Which, then, of your Lord's blessings do you both deny?' which runs throughout. The sura divides mankind and jinn into three classes: the disbelievers (verses 41–5), the best of believers (verses 46–61), and the ordinary believers (verses 62–77).

In the name of God, the Lord of Mercy, the Giver of Mercy

¹ It is the Lord of Mercy ² who taught the Qur'an.*ᵃ* ³ He created man ⁴ and taught him to communicate.*ᵇ* ⁵ The sun and the moon follow their calculated courses; ⁶ the plants and the trees submit*ᶜ* to His designs; ⁷ He has raised up the sky. He has set the balance ⁸ so that you may not exceed in the balance—⁹ weigh with justice—and do not fall short in the balance. ¹⁰ He set down the Earth for His creatures, ¹¹ with its fruits, its palm trees with sheathed clusters, ¹² its husked grain, its fragrant plants. ¹³ Which, then, of your Lord's blessings do you both*ᵈ* deny?

¹⁴ He created mankind out of dried clay, like pottery, ¹⁵ the jinn out of smokeless fire. ¹⁶ Which, then, of your Lord's blessings do you both deny?

¹⁷ He is Lord of the two risings and Lord of the two settings.*ᵉ* ¹⁸ Which, then, of your Lord's blessings do you both deny?

¹⁹ He released the two bodies of [fresh and salt] water. They meet, ²⁰ yet there is a barrier between them they do not cross. ²¹ Which, then, of your Lord's blessings do you both deny?

²² Pearls come forth from them: large ones, and small, brilliant ones.*ᶠ* ²³ Which, then, of your Lord's blessings do you both deny?

ᵃ One interpretation is that *qur'an* here means 'to read', cf. 96: 1.

ᵇ *Bayan* (communication) involves both expressing oneself and understanding what has been expressed by others, including the Qur'an, which is called *bayan* and *mubin*.

ᶜ *Sajada* means 'to submit' and consequently also 'to bow down' or 'to prostrate oneself'.

ᵈ Mankind and jinn.

ᵉ This refers to the rising and setting of the sun and the moon, or, alternatively, their furthest points of sunrise and sunset in summer and winter.

ᶠ See Abdel Haleem, *Understanding the Qur'an*, 170–1.

²⁴ His are the moving ships that float high as mountains on the sea. ²⁵ Which, then, of your Lord's blessings do you both deny?

²⁶ Everyone on earth perishes; ²⁷ all that remains is the Face*ᵃ* of your Lord, full of majesty, bestowing honour. ²⁸ Which, then, of your Lord's blessings do you both deny?

²⁹ Everyone in heaven and earth entreats Him; every day He is at work.*ᵇ* ³⁰ Which, then, of your Lord's blessings do you both deny?

³¹ We shall attend to you two huge armies*ᶜ* [of jinn and mankind]. ³² Which, then, of your Lord's blessings do you both deny?

³³ Jinn and mankind, if you can pass beyond the regions of heaven and earth, then do so: you will not pass without Our authority. ³⁴ Which, then, of your Lord's blessings do you both deny?

³⁵ A flash of fire and smoke will be released upon you and no one will come to your aid. ³⁶ Which, then, of your Lord's blessings do you both deny?

³⁷ When the sky is torn apart and turns crimson, like red hide. ³⁸ Which, then, of your Lord's blessings do you both deny?

³⁹ On that Day neither mankind nor jinn will be asked about their sins. ⁴⁰ Which, then, of your Lord's blessings do you both deny?

⁴¹ The guilty will be known by their mark and will be seized by their foreheads and their feet. ⁴² Which, then, of your Lord's blessings do you both deny?

⁴³ This is the Hell the guilty deny, ⁴⁴ but they will go round between its flames and scalding water. ⁴⁵ Which, then, of your Lord's blessings do you both deny?

⁴⁶ There are two gardens for those who fear [the time when they will] stand before their Lord. ⁴⁷ Which, then, of your Lord's blessings do you both deny?

⁴⁸ With shading branches. ⁴⁹ Which, then, of your Lord's blessings do you both deny?

⁵⁰ With a pair of flowing springs. ⁵¹ Which, then, of your Lord's blessings do you both deny?

⁵² With every kind of fruit in pairs. ⁵³ Which, then, of your Lord's blessings do you both deny?

ᵃ Abdel Haleem, *Understanding the Qur'an*, ch. 9.

ᵇ Literally 'in some matter'. The Prophet was asked, 'What is this matter?' He replied, 'He forgives a sin or removes a distress.'

ᶜ *Thaqal* is a mighty or heavy army: all their forces.

[54] They will sit on couches upholstered with brocade, the fruit of both gardens within easy reach. [55] Which, then, of your Lord's blessings do you both deny?

[56] There will be maidens restraining their glances, untouched beforehand by man or jinn. [57] Which, then, of your Lord's blessings do you both deny?

[58] Like rubies and brilliant pearls. [59] Which, then, of your Lord's blessings do you both deny?

[60] Shall the reward of good be anything but good? [61] Which, then, of your Lord's blessings do you both deny?

[62] There are two other gardens below these two. [a] [63] Which, then, of your Lord's blessings do you both deny?

[64] Both of deepest green. [65] Which, then, of your Lord's blessings do you both deny?

[66] With a pair of gushing springs. [67] Which, then, of your Lord's blessings do you both deny?

[68] With fruits—date palms and pomegranate trees. [69] Which, then, of your Lord's blessings do you both deny?

[70] There are good-natured, beautiful maidens. [71] Which, then, of your Lord's blessings do you both deny?

[72] Dark-eyed, sheltered in pavilions. [73] Which, then, of your Lord's blessings do you both deny?

[74] Untouched beforehand by man or jinn. [75] Which, then, of your Lord's blessings do you both deny?

[76] They will all sit on green cushions and fine carpets. [77] Which, then, of your Lord's blessings do you both deny? [78] Blessed is the name of your Lord, full of majesty, bestowing honour.

[a] Paradise exists in two ranks: the higher level for the truly favoured, and this lower level described for the less exalted pious. This cosmology of hell, lower paradise, upper paradise is repeated in the following sura: 56: 7–56.

56. THAT WHICH IS COMING

A Meccan sura whose central message is stated in its opening verses, from which the sura takes its title: the Day of Judgement is inevitable and it will sort men into the humiliated and the richly rewarded. As in the previous sura, people are divided into three classes: those brought near to God (the best of the believers), those on the right (the ordinary believers), and those on the left (the disbelievers). Ample proof is given of the depth of God's power and consequently His ability to bring about the Resurrection (verses 57–72).

In the name of God, the Lord of Mercy, the Giver of Mercy

[1] When that which is coming arrives, [2] no one will be able to deny it has come, [3] bringing low and raising high. [4] When the earth is shaken violently [5] and the mountains are ground to powder [6] and turn to scattered dust, [7] then you will be sorted into three classes. [8] Those on the Right—what people they are! [9] Those on the Left—what people they are! [10] And those in front—ahead indeed! [11] For these will be the ones brought nearest to God [12] in Gardens of Bliss: [13] many from the past [14] and a few from later generations. [15] On couches of well-woven cloth [16] they will sit facing each other; [17] everlasting youths will go round among them [18] with glasses, flagons, and a pure liquid [19] that causes no headache or intoxication; [20] [there will be] any fruit they want; [21] the meat of any bird they like; [22] and beautiful companions [23] like hidden pearls: [24] a reward for what they used to do. [25] They will hear no idle or sinful talk there, [26] only clean and wholesome[a] speech.

[27] Those on the Right, what people they are! [28] They will dwell amid thornless lote trees [29] and clustered acacia [30] with spreading shade, [31] constantly flowing water, [32] abundant fruits, [33] unfailing, unforbidden, [34] with incomparable companions[b] [35] We have specially created—[36] virginal, [37] loving, of matching age—[38] for those on the Right, [39] many from the past [40] and many from later generations.

[41] But those on the Left, what people they are! [42] They will dwell

---

[a] *Salam* is used adjectivally here (Razi). Another interpretation is 'Peace! Peace!'

[b] Alternatively 'couches raised high'. See Razi for both these interpretations.

amid scorching wind and scalding water ⁴³in the shadow of black smoke, ⁴⁴neither cool nor refreshing. ⁴⁵Before, they overindulged in luxury ⁴⁶and persisted in great sin, ⁴⁷always saying, 'What? When we are dead and have become dust and bones, shall we then be raised up? ⁴⁸And our earliest forefathers too?' ⁴⁹Say [Prophet], 'The earliest and latest generations ⁵⁰will all be gathered on a predetermined Day ⁵¹and you who have gone astray and denied the truth ⁵²will eat from the bitter tree of Zaqqum, ⁵³filling your bellies with it, ⁵⁴and drink scalding water, ⁵⁵lapping it like thirsty camels.' ⁵⁶This will be their welcome on the Day of Judgement.

⁵⁷We created you: will you not believe? ⁵⁸Consider [the semen] you eject—⁵⁹do you create it yourselves or are We the Creator? ⁶⁰We ordained death to be among you. Nothing could stop Us ⁶¹if We intended to change you and recreate you in a way unknown to you. ⁶²You have learned how you were first created: will you not reflect? ⁶³Consider the seeds you sow in the ground—⁶⁴is it you who make them grow or We? ⁶⁵If We wished, We could turn your harvest into chaff and leave you to wail, ⁶⁶'We are burdened with debt; ⁶⁷we are bereft.' ⁶⁸Consider the water you drink—⁶⁹was it you who brought it down from the rain-cloud or We? ⁷⁰If We wanted, We could make it bitter: will you not be thankful? ⁷¹Consider the fire you kindle—⁷²is it you who make the wood for it grow or We? ⁷³We made it a reminder and useful to those who kindle it,[a] ⁷⁴so [Prophet] glorify the name of your Lord, the Supreme.

⁷⁵I swear by the positions of the stars—⁷⁶a mighty oath, if you only knew—⁷⁷that this is truly a noble Qur'an, ⁷⁸in a protected Record ⁷⁹that only the purified can touch, ⁸⁰sent down from the Lord of all being. ⁸¹How can you scorn this statement? ⁸²And how, in return for the livelihood you are given, can you deny it? ⁸³When the soul of a dying man comes up to his throat ⁸⁴while you gaze on—⁸⁵We are nearer to him than you, though you do not see Us—⁸⁶why, if you are not to be judged, ⁸⁷do you not restore his soul to him, if what you say is true? ⁸⁸If that dying person is one of those who will be brought near to God, ⁸⁹he will have rest, ease, and a Garden of Bliss; ⁹⁰if he is one of those on the Right, ⁹¹[he will hear], 'Peace be

---

[a] This interpretation of *muqwin* is supported by Razi. The alternatives to 'those who kindle it' are 'the desert-dwellers' or 'the travellers'.

on you,' from his companions on the Right; ⁹²but if he is one of those who denied the truth and went astray, ⁹³he will be welcomed with scalding water. ⁹⁴He will burn in Hell.

⁹⁵This is the certain truth: ⁹⁶[Prophet], glorify the name of your Lord the Supreme.

57. IRON

A Medinan sura that urges the believers to spend in God's cause and uphold justice—the sura takes its title from the iron mentioned in verse 25. The all-pervasiveness of God's power, knowledge, control, and glory is affirmed to encourage the believers to right action, and the fate of the hypocrites is described. Previous prophets are mentioned (verses 26–7), especially Noah, Abraham, and Jesus, showing the response they received. The sura closes with a reference to the People of the Book.

In the name of God, the Lord of Mercy, the Giver of Mercy

¹ Everything in the heavens and earth glorifies God—He is the Almighty, the Wise. ² Control of the heavens and earth belongs to Him; He gives life and death; He has power over all things. ³ He is the First and the Last;*a* the Outer and the Inner; He has knowledge of all things. ⁴ It was He who created the heavens and earth in six Days and then established Himself on the throne. He knows what enters the earth and what comes out of it; what descends from the sky and what ascends to it. He is with you wherever you are; He sees all that you do; ⁵ control of the heavens and earth belongs to Him. Everything is brought back to God. ⁶ He makes night merge into day and day into night. He knows what is in every heart.

⁷ Believe in God and His Messenger, and give out of what He has made pass down to you: those of you who believe and give will have a great reward. ⁸ Why should you not believe in God when the Messenger calls you to believe in your Lord, and He has already made a pledge with you, if you have faith? ⁹ It is He who has sent down clear revelations to His Servant, so that He may bring you from the depths of darkness into light; God is truly kind and merciful to you. ¹⁰ Why should you not give for God's cause when God alone will inherit what is in the heavens and earth? Those who gave and fought before the victory*b* are not like others: they are greater in rank than

---

a Theologians add, 'without a beginning and without an end'.

b The surrender of Mecca.

those who gave and fought afterwards. But God has promised a good reward to all of them: God is fully aware of all that you do.

¹¹ Who will make God a good loan? He will double it for him and reward him generously. ¹² On the Day when you [Prophet] see the believers, both men and women, with their light streaming out ahead of them and to their right, [they will be told], 'The good news for you today is that there are Gardens graced with flowing streams where you will stay: that is truly the supreme triumph!' ¹³ On the same Day, the hypocrites, both men and women, will say to the believers, 'Wait for us! Let us have some of your light!' They will be told, 'Go back and look for a light.' A wall with a door will be erected between them: inside it lies mercy, outside lies punishment. ¹⁴ The hypocrites will call out to the believers, 'Were we not with you?' They will reply, 'Yes. But you allowed yourselves to be tempted, you were hesitant, doubtful, deceived by false hopes until God's command came—the Deceiver tricked you about God—¹⁵ today no ransom will be accepted from you or from the disbelievers. Your home is the Fire—that is where you belong—a miserable destination!'

¹⁶ Is it not time for believers to humble their hearts to the remembrance of God and the Truth that has been revealed, and not to be like those who received the Scripture before them, whose time was extended but whose hearts hardened and many of whom were lawbreakers? ¹⁷ Remember that God revives the earth after it dies; We have made Our revelation clear to you so that you may use your reason. ¹⁸ Charitable men and women who make a good loan to God will have it doubled and have a generous reward. ¹⁹ Those who believe in God and His messengers are the truthful ones who will bear witness before their Lord: they will have their reward and their light. But those who disbelieve and deny Our revelations are the inhabitants of Hell. ²⁰ Bear in mind that the present life is just a game, a diversion, an attraction, a cause of boasting among you, of rivalry in wealth and children. It is like plants that spring up after the rain: their growth at first delights the sowers, but then you see them wither away, turn yellow, and become stubble. There is terrible punishment in the next life as well as forgiveness and approval from God; the life of this world is only an illusory pleasure. ²¹ So race one another for your Lord's forgiveness and a Garden as wide as the heavens and earth, prepared for those who believe in God and His

messengers: that is God's bounty, which he bestows on whoever He pleases. God's bounty is infinite.

[22] No misfortune can happen, either in the earth or in yourselves, that was not set down in writing before We brought it into being—that is easy for God—[23] so you need not grieve for what you miss or be overjoyed by what you gain. [24] God does not love the conceited, the boastful, those who are miserly, and who tell other people to be miserly. If anyone turns away, remember that God is self-sufficient and worthy of praise. [25] We sent Our messengers with clear signs, the Scripture and the Balance, so that people could uphold justice: We also sent iron, with its mighty strength and many uses for mankind, so that God could mark out those who would secretly[a] help Him and His messengers. Truly God is powerful, almighty.

[26] We sent Noah and Abraham, and gave prophethood and scripture to their offspring: among them there were some who were rightly guided, but many were lawbreakers. [27] We sent other messengers to follow in their footsteps. After those We sent Jesus, son of Mary: We gave him the Gospel and put compassion and mercy into the hearts of his followers. But monasticism was something they invented—We did not ordain it for them, only that they should seek God's pleasure—and even so, they did not observe it properly. So We gave a reward to those of them who believed, but many of them broke the rules. [28] Believers, be mindful of God and have faith in His Messenger: He will give you a double share of His mercy; He will provide a light to help you walk; He will forgive you—God is most forgiving, most merciful. [29] The People of the Book should know that they have no power over any of God's grace and that grace is in the hand of God alone: He gives it to whoever He will. God's grace is truly immense.

[a] *Bi 'l-ghaybi* means 'in the unseen'. This could apply to God or His helpers.

58. THE DISPUTE

A Medinan sura which disallows a specific pagan divorce practice: the sura takes its title from the dispute referred to in verse 1 between a wife who had been divorced in this manner and the Prophet. The sura supports the woman. It goes on to state that those who oppose God and His messenger, who secretly ally themselves with Satan, who lie in their oaths and make intrigues against the Prophet, will be defeated and suffer humiliation both in this world and in the next (verses 5 and 20), while those on God's side will triumph (verse 22).

In the name of God, the Lord of Mercy, the Giver of Mercy

¹ God has heard the words of the woman who disputed with you [Prophet] about her husband and complained to God: God has heard what you both had to say. He is all hearing, all seeing. ² Even if any of you say to their wives, 'You are to me like my mother's back,'ᵃ they are not their mothers; their only mothers are those who gave birth to them. What they say is certainly blameworthy and false, but God is pardoning and forgiving. ³ Those of you who say such a thing to their wives, then go back on what they have said, must free a slave before the couple may touch one another again—this is what you are commanded to do, and God is fully aware of what you do—⁴ but anyone who does not have the means should fast continuously for two months before they touch each other, and anyone unable to do this should feed sixty needy people. This is so that you may have faith in God and His Messenger. These are the bounds set by God: grievous suffering awaits those who ignore them. ⁵ Those who oppose God and His Messenger will be brought low, like those before them. We have revealed clear messages, and a humiliating punishment awaits those who ignore them, ⁶ on the Day when God will raise everyone and make them aware of what they have done. God has taken account of it all, though they may have forgotten: He witnesses everything.

ᵃ The pagan Arabs used to separate themselves from their wives by saying, 'You are to me like my mother's back,' which deprived the wife of her marital rights, yet prevented her from marrying again. Khawla, daughter of Tha'laba, against whom such a form of divorce was pronounced, complained to the Prophet and he said to her, 'You are unlawful to him now.' This revelation came as a result, changing the rule about such cruel treatment of wives (cf. 33: 4).

⁷Do you not see [Prophet] that God knows everything in the heavens and earth? There is no secret conversation between three people where He is not the fourth, nor between five where He is not the sixth, nor between less or more than that without Him being with them, wherever they may be. On the Day of Resurrection, He will show them what they have done: God truly has full knowledge of everything. ⁸Have you not seen how those who have been forbidden to hold secret conversations go back afterwards and hold them, and conspire with one another in what is sinful, hostile, and disobedient to the Messenger? When they come to you they greet you with words God never used to greet you, and say inwardly, 'Why does God not punish us for what we say?' Hell will be punishment enough for them: they will burn there—an evil destination.

⁹You who believe, when you converse in secret, do not do so in a way that is sinful, hostile, and disobedient to the Messenger, but in a way that is good and mindful [of God]. Be mindful of God, to whom you will all be gathered. ¹⁰[Any other kind of] secret conversation is the work of Satan, designed to cause grief to the believers, though it cannot harm them in the least, unless God permits it. Let the believers put their trust in God.

¹¹You who believe, if you are told to make room for one another in your assemblies, then do so, and God will make room for you, and if you are told to rise up, do so: God will raise up, by many degrees, those of you who believe and those who have been given knowledge: He is fully aware of what you do. ¹²You who believe, when you come to speak privately with the Messenger, offer something in charity before your conversation: that is better for you and purer. If you do not have the means, God is most forgiving and merciful.

¹³Were you afraid[a] to give charity before consulting the Prophet? Since you did not give charity, and God has relented towards you, you should [at least] observe your prayers, pay the prescribed alms, and obey God and His Messenger: God is well aware of your actions.

¹⁴Have you not seen [Prophet] those who give their loyalty to people with whom God is angry? They are neither with you nor with

---

[a] *Ashfaqtum* is in the past tense. There is a lapse of time between verses 12 and 13 during which those who used to plague the Prophet with questions did not come forward at all, because of having to pay to charity each time. Verse 13 relaxed this requirement.

them, and knowingly swear to lies. ¹⁵ God has prepared a severe torment for them: what they do is truly evil. ¹⁶ They have used their oaths to cover up [their false deeds], and barred others from the path of God. A humiliating torment awaits them—¹⁷ neither their wealth nor their children will be of any use to them against God—they will be the inhabitants of Hell, where they will remain. ¹⁸ On the Day God raises them all from the dead, they will swear before Him as they swear before you now, thinking that it will help them. What liars they are! ¹⁹ Satan has gained control over them and made them forget God. They are on Satan's side, and Satan's side will be the losers: ²⁰ those who oppose God and His Messenger will be among the most humiliated. ²¹ God has written, 'I shall most certainly win, I and My messengers.' God is powerful and almighty.

²² [Prophet], you will not find people who truly believe in God and the Last Day giving their loyalty to those who oppose God and His Messenger, even though they may be their fathers, sons, brothers, or other relations. These are the people in whose hearts God has inscribed faith, and whom He has strengthened with His spirit: He will let them enter Gardens graced with flowing streams, where they will stay. God is well pleased with them, and they with Him. They are on God's side, and God's side will be the one to prosper.

59. THE GATHERING [OF FORCES]

A Medinan sura, the bulk of which is taken to refer to the Jewish clan of Banu al-Nadir, who originally agreed with the Prophet that they would fight neither for nor against him, yet, after the Meccan defeat of the Muslims in the Battle of Uhud, made an alliance with the Meccans. They also tried to kill the Prophet while he was in their area. He asked them to leave and they agreed, but Ibn Ubayy, the head of the 'hypocrites' of Medina, promised them that, if they fought the Muslims, he and his camp would fight with them (verses 11– 13), and, if they had to leave Medina, he and his camp would leave with them. Because the Banu al-Nadir had repeatedly broken their agreements, the Muslims besieged them in Medina (in AH 4/626 CE), Ibn Ubayy did not keep his promise, and the Banu al-Nadir agreed to leave, some going to Syria and some to Khaybar. In this sura, God stresses that any victory is of His making, and any gains should be distributed in accordance with His instructions (verses 6– 10). The end of the sura, consequently, emphasizes obedience and awe towards God (verses 21–4). The sura takes its name from the gathering of forces in verse 2.

In the name of God, the Lord of Mercy, the Giver of Mercy

¹Everything in the heavens and earth glorifies God; He is the Almighty, the Wise. ²It was He who drove those of the People of the Book who broke faith[a] out from their homes at the first gathering of forces—you [believers] never thought they would go, and they themselves thought their fortifications would protect them against God. God came up on them from where they least expected and put panic into their hearts: they brought ruin to their homes by their own hands, as well as the hands of the believers. Learn from this, all of you with insight! ³If God had not decreed exile for them, He would have punished them [even more severely] in this world. In the Hereafter they will have the punishment of the Fire ⁴because they set themselves against God and His Messenger: God is stern in punishment towards anyone who sets himself against Him.

⁵Whatever you [believers] may have done to [their] palm trees— cutting them down or leaving them standing on their roots—was

[a] They were unfaithful to their agreements with the Prophet (see the introduction to this sura).

done by God's leave, so that He might disgrace those who defied Him. [6] You [believers] did not have to spur on your horses or your camels for whatever gains God turned over to His Messenger from them. God gives authority to His messengers over whoever He will: God has power over all things. [7] Whatever gains God has turned over to His Messenger from the inhabitants of the villages belong to God, the Messenger, kinsfolk, orphans, the needy, the traveller in need—this is so that they do not just circulate among those of you who are rich—so accept whatever the Messenger gives you, and abstain from whatever he forbids you. Be mindful of God: God is severe in punishment.

[8] The poor emigrants who were driven from their homes and possessions, who seek God's favour and approval, those who help God and His Messenger—these are the ones who are true—[shall have a share]. [9] Those who were already firmly established in their homes [in Medina], and firmly rooted in faith, show love for those who migrated to them for refuge and harbour no desire in their hearts for what has been given to them. They give them preference over themselves, even if they too are poor: those who are saved from their own souls' greed are truly successful. [10] Those who came after them say, 'Lord, forgive us our sins and the sins of our brothers who believed before us, and leave no malice in our hearts towards those who believe. Lord, You are truly compassionate and merciful.'

[11] Have you [Prophet] considered the hypocrites who say to their fellows, the faithless among the People of the Book, 'If you are driven out, we shall go with you—we would never listen to anyone who sought to harm you—and if you are attacked, we shall certainly come to your aid'? God bears witness that they are in fact liars: [12] if they are driven out, they will never leave with them; if they are attacked, they will never help them. Even if they did come to their aid, they would soon turn tail and flee, and in the end they would have no help. [13] Fear of you [believers] is more intense in their hearts than fear of God because they are people devoid of understanding. [14] Even united they would never fight you, except from within fortified strongholds or behind high walls. There is much hostility between them. You think they are united but their hearts are divided because they are people devoid of reason. [15] Like those who went just before them,[a] they have tasted the result of their conduct and a

[a] This probably refers to the Banu Qaynuqa, another Jewish tribe banished for their treachery. It could also refer to the pagans at Badr.

painful punishment awaits them. [16] Like Satan, who says to man, 'Do not believe!' but when man disbelieves, says, 'I disown you; I fear God, the Lord of the Worlds,' [17] both will end up in the Fire, there to remain. That is the reward of evildoers.

[18] You who believe! Be mindful of God, and let every soul consider carefully what it sends ahead for tomorrow; be mindful of God, for God is well aware of everything you do. [19] Do not be like those who forget God, so God causes them to forget their own souls: they are the rebellious ones—[20] there is no comparison between the inhabitants of the Fire and the inhabitants of Paradise—and the inhabitants of Paradise are the successful ones. [21] If We had sent this Qur'an down to a mountain, you [Prophet] would have seen it humbled and split apart in its awe of God: We offer people such imagery so that they may reflect.

[22] He is God: there is no other god but Him. It is He who knows what is hidden as well as what is in the open, He is the Lord of Mercy, the Giver of Mercy. [23] He is God: there is no other god but Him, the Controller,[a] the Holy One, Source of Peace, Granter of Security, Guardian over all, the Almighty, the Compeller, to whom all greatness belongs; God is far above anything they consider to be His partner. [24] He is God: the Creator, the Originator, the Fashioner. The best names belong to Him. Everything in the heavens and earth glorifies Him: He is the Almighty, the Wise.

[a] Or King/Sovereign.

60. WOMEN TESTED

A Medinan sura, revealed between the Treaty of Hudaybiyya and the conquest of Mecca, which takes its title from verse 10: instructions are given on how to deal with women who leave Mecca and join the Muslims, and the procedure for wives who leave Medina for Mecca (verses 10–11). The Muslims are instructed on the appropriate allocation of their loyalties (verses 1–3, 7–9, 13) and Abraham is cited for them as an example to learn from (verses 4–6).

In the name of God, the Lord of Mercy, the Giver of Mercy

¹ You who believe, do not take My enemies and yours as your allies, showing them friendship when they have rejected the truth you have received, and have driven you and the Messenger out simply because you believe in God, your Lord*ᵃ*—not if you truly emigrated in order to strive for My cause and seek My good pleasure. You secretly show them friendship—I know all you conceal and all you reveal— but any of you who do this are straying from the right path. ² If they gain the upper hand over you, they will revert to being your enemies and stretch out their hands and tongues to harm you; it is their dearest wish that you may renounce your faith.

³ Neither your kinsfolk nor your children will be any use to you on the Day of Resurrection: He will separate you out. God sees everything you do. ⁴ You have a good example in Abraham and his companions, when they said to their people, 'We disown you and what you worship beside God! We renounce you! Until you believe in God alone, the enmity and hatred that has arisen between us will endure!'—except when Abraham said to his father, 'I will pray for forgiveness for you though I cannot protect you from God'—[they prayed] ⁵ 'Lord, we have put our trust in You; we turn to You; You are our final destination. Lord, do not expose us to mistreatment [at the hands of] the disbelievers. Forgive us, Lord, for You are the

ᵃ A Muslim in Medina, Hatib bin Abi Balta'a, who had family and property in Mecca, sent a secret letter to the Meccan leaders telling them that the Prophet was preparing to march on their town, and warning them to take precautions. The letter was intercepted, and when the Prophet asked him to explain his action, he said that he only wanted the Meccans to protect his family and property.

Almighty, the All Wise.' ⁶ Truly, they are a good example for you [believers] to follow, a good example for those who fear God and the Last Day. If anyone turns away, [remember] God is self-sufficing and worthy of all praise.

⁷ God may still bring about affection between you and your present enemies—God is all powerful, God is most forgiving and merciful—⁸ and He does not forbid you to deal kindly and justly with anyone who has not fought you for your faith or driven you out of your homes: God loves the just. ⁹ But God forbids you to take as allies those who have fought against you for your faith, driven you out of your homes, and helped others to drive you out: any of you who take them as allies will truly be wrongdoers.

¹⁰ You who believe, test the believing women when they come to you as emigrants—God knows best about their faith—and if you are sure of their belief, do not send them back to the disbelievers: they are not lawful wives for them, nor are the disbelievers their lawful husbands. Give the disbelievers whatever dowries they have paid—if you choose to marry them, there is no blame on you once you have payed their dowries—and do not yourselves hold on to marriage ties with disbelieving women. Ask for repayment of the dowries you have paid, and let the disbelievers do the same. This is God's judgement: He judges between you, God is all knowing and wise. ¹¹ If any of you have wives who leave you for the disbelievers, and if the community subsequently acquires [gains] from them, then pay those whose wives have deserted them the equivalent of whatever dowry they paid. Be mindful of God, in whom you believe.

¹² Prophet, when believing women come and pledge to you that they will not ascribe any partner to God, nor steal, nor commit adultery, nor kill their children, nor lie about who has fathered their children,ᵃ nor disobey you in any righteous thing, then you should accept their pledge of allegiance and pray to God to forgive them: God is most forgiving and merciful.

¹³ You who believe, do not take as allies those with whom God is angry: they despair of the life to come as the disbelievers despair of those buried in their graves.

ᵃ This is a common interpretation of the idiom 'what is between their hands and their feet' (Razi).

61. SOLID LINES

A Medinan sura encouraging the believers to stick together in support of God's cause (thus the title of the sura, cf. verse 4). It criticizes those who broke their word (verse 3) and those who argued against the faith (verses 7–8). Moses and Jesus are cited as examples of prophets whose communities were divided: the rebellious were left to stray and the faithful granted success (verses 5–6, 14). The rewards of those who strive in God's cause are described in some detail (verses 11–13).

In the name of God, the Lord of Mercy, the Giver of Mercy

¹Everything in the heavens and earth glorifies God—He is the Almighty, the Wise. ²You who believe, why do you say things and then do not do them?ᵃ ³It is most hateful to God that you say things and then do not do them; ⁴God truly loves those who fight in solid lines for His cause, like a well-compacted wall.

⁵Moses said to his people, 'My people, why do you hurt me when you know that I am sent to you by God?' When they went astray, God left their hearts to stray: God does not guide rebellious people. ⁶Jesus, son of Mary, said, 'Children of Israel, I am sent to you by God, confirming the Torah that came before me and bringing good news of a messenger to follow me whose name will be Ahmad.'ᵇ Yet when he came to them with clear signs, they said, 'This is obviously sorcery.'

⁷Who could be more wrong than someone who invents lies against God when called to submit to Him? God does not guide the wrong-doers: ⁸they wish to put His light out with their mouths. But He will perfect His light, even though the disbelievers hate it; ⁹it is He who sent His Messenger with guidance and the religion of truth to show that it is above all [other] religions, even though the idolaters hate it.

¹⁰You who believe, shall I show you a bargainᶜ that will save you from painful punishment? ¹¹Have faith in God and His Messenger and struggle for His cause with your possessions and your persons—

ᵃ Some asked to fight, but when God ordained fighting they failed to do so.

ᵇ Ahmad, like Muhammad, means 'praised' (for his good character).

ᶜ Literally 'a trade'.

that is better for you, if only you knew—¹²and He will forgive your sins, admit you into Gardens graced with flowing streams, into pleasant dwellings in the Gardens of Eternity. That is the supreme triumph. ¹³And He will give you something else that will really please you: His help and an imminent breakthrough. [Prophet], give the faithful the good news. ¹⁴You who believe, be God's helpers. As Jesus, son of Mary, said to the disciples, 'Who will come with me to help God?' The disciples said, 'We shall be God's helpers.' Some of the Children of Israel believed and some disbelieved: We supported the believers against their enemy and they were the ones who came out on top.

62. THE DAY OF CONGREGATION

A Medinan sura which takes its title from the instruction to the believers to observe the Friday prayer promptly and reliably when called (verses 9–11). The sura reminds the Muslims of God's grace in granting them a prophet and the chance to grow spiritually (verses 2–4). Those who do not act in accordance with the knowledge they have been given are criticized (verses 5–8).

In the name of God, the Lord of Mercy, the Giver of Mercy

¹Everything in the heavens and earth glorifies God, the Controller, the Holy One, the Almighty, the Wise. ²It is He who raised a messenger, among the people who had no Scripture, to recite His revelations to them, to make them grow spiritually and teach them the Scripture and wisdom—before that they were clearly astray—³to them and others yet to join them. He is the Almighty, the Wise: ⁴such is God's favour that He grants it to whoever He will; God's favour is immense. ⁵Those who have been charged with to obey the Torah, but do not do so, are like asses*ᵃ* carrying books: how base such people are who disobey God's revelations! God does not guide people who do wrong.

⁶Say [Prophet], 'You who follow the Jewish faith, if you truly claim that out of all people you alone are friends of God, then you should be hoping for death.' ⁷But because of what they have stored up for themselves with their own hands they would never hope for death—God knows the wrongdoers very well—⁸so say, 'The death you run away from will come to meet you and you will be returned to the One who knows the unseen as well as the seen: He will tell you everything you have done.'

⁹Believers! When the call to prayer is made on the day of congregation, go quickly to the prayer*ᵇ* and leave off your trading—that is better for you, if only you knew—¹⁰then when the prayer has ended, disperse in the land and seek out God's bounty. Remember God often so that you may prosper. ¹¹Yet they scatter towards trade or

---

ᵃ Literally 'an ass', but the plural English construction requires the plural.

ᵇ This is one of the meanings of *dhikr Allah* (*al-Mu'jam al-Wasit*).

entertainment whenever they observe it, and leave you [Prophet] standing there.[a] Say, 'God's gift is better than any entertainment or trade: God is the best provider.'

[a] This refers to two occasions. During congregational prayers at a time of famine, a caravan arrived and some of the worshippers rushed out, leaving the Prophet standing on the *minbar* (pulpit). On another occasion, worshippers rushed out because there was a band playing for a wedding.

63. THE HYPOCRITES

A Medinan sura which warns the believers about the treachery of the hypocrites and describes their behaviour in some depth. A specific occasion on which the hypocrites tried to stop anyone donating money to believers is described (verses 7–8) and God calls on the Muslims to compensate for this by giving more of their own funds to the needy (verses 9–11).

In the name of God, the Lord of Mercy, the Giver of Mercy

¹When the hypocrites come to you [Prophet], they say, 'We bear witness that you are the Messenger of God.' God knows that you truly are His Messenger and He bears witness that the hypocrites are liars—²they use their oaths as a cover and so bar others from God's way: what they have been doing is truly evil—³because they professed faith and then rejected it. So their hearts have been sealed and they do not understand. ⁴When you see them [Prophet], their outward appearance pleases you; when they speak, you listen to what they say. But they are like propped-up timbers—they think every cry they hear is against them—and they are the enemy. Beware of them. May God confound them! How devious they are!

⁵They turn their heads away in disdain when they are told, 'Come, so that the Messenger of God may ask forgiveness for you,' and you see them walking away arrogantly. ⁶It makes no difference whether you ask forgiveness for them or not, God will not forgive them: God does not guide such treacherous people. ⁷They are the ones who say, 'Give nothing to those who follow God's Messenger, until they abandon him', but to God belong the treasures of the heavens and earth, though the hypocrites do not understand this. ⁸They say, 'Once we return to Medina the powerful will drive out the weak,' but power belongs to God, to His Messenger, and to the believers, though the hypocrites do not understand this.

⁹Believers, do not let your wealth and your children distract you from remembering God: those who do so will be the ones who lose. ¹⁰Give out of what We have provided for you, before death comes to

one of you and he says, 'My Lord, if You would only reprieve me for a little while, I would give in charity and become one of the righteous.' [11] God does not reprieve a soul when its turn comes: God is fully aware of what you do.

64. MUTUAL NEGLECT

A Medinan sura that gets its title from verse 9. The sura opens with a description of God's power, wisdom, and knowledge (verses 1–4). The disbelievers are reminded of the end of those who disbelieved before them (verses 5–6), and their denial of the Resurrection is strongly refuted (verse 7). The believers are urged to be wary but forgiving of the enemies they may have within their own families (verses 14–15) and warned to remain steadfast and to spend in God's cause (verses 8–10, 16–18).

In the name of God, the Lord of Mercy, the Giver of Mercy

¹ Everything that is in the heavens and earth glorifies God; all control and praise belong to Him; He has power over everything. ² It is He who created you, yet some of you believe and some do not: God sees everything you do. ³ He created the heavens and earth for a true purpose; He formed you and formed you well: you will all return to Him. ⁴ He knows what is in the heavens and earth; He knows what you conceal and what you reveal; God knows very well the secrets of every heart.

⁵ [Disbelievers], have you not heard about those who disbelieved before you? They tasted the evil consequences of their conduct, and a painful punishment awaits them ⁶ because their messengers came to them with clear signs, yet they said, 'Should we take guidance from mere mortals?', rejected the message, and turned away. But God had no need for them: He is all sufficient, worthy of all praise.

⁷ The disbelievers claim they will not be raised from the dead. Say [Prophet], 'Yes indeed! I swear by my Lord! You will be raised and then you will be informed about everything you have done: an easy matter for God.'

⁸ So believe in God, in His Messenger, and in the light*ᵃ* We have sent down: God is fully aware of what you do. ⁹ When He gathers you for the Day of Gathering, the Day of mutual neglect,*ᵇ* He will

---

ᵃ The Qur'an.

ᵇ The Arabic *taghabun* is reciprocal from *ghabina*, 'to neglect or forget'. Everyone will be so preoccupied with their own fate that they will neglect everyone else (cf. 70: 10–11; 80: 34–7).

cancel the sins of those who believed in Him and acted righteously: He will admit them into Gardens graced with flowing streams, there to remain for ever—the supreme triumph. [10]But those who disbelieved and rejected Our signs will be the inhabitants of the Fire, there to remain—a miserable destination!

[11]Misfortunes can only happen with God's permission[a]—He will guide the heart of anyone who believes in Him: God knows all things—[12]so obey God and the Messenger. If you turn away, remember that Our Messenger's duty is only to make plain his message. [13]God! There is no god but Him, so let the faithful put their trust in Him. [14]Believers, even among your wives and your children you have some enemies—beware of them—but if you overlook their offences, forgive them, pardon them: God [too] is all forgiving, all merciful.

[15]Your wealth and your children are only a test for you. There is great reward with God: [16]be mindful of God as much as you can; hear and obey; be charitable—it is for your own good. Those who are saved from their own meanness will be the prosperous ones: [17]if you make a generous loan to God He will multiply it for you and forgive you. God is ever thankful and forbearing; [18]He knows the unseen, as well as the seen; He is the Almighty, the Wise.

[a] Abu Muslim gives the explanation that some of the believers' families tried to dissuade them from emigrating and from *jihad* because they feared for their safety (Razi). See verse 14.

65. DIVORCE

A Medinan sura that outlines regulations concerning divorce (verses 1–7). The sura strongly urges people to observe God's regulations and guidance. To reinforce this they are reminded of the fate of earlier disobedient peoples and the rewards of the obedient. God's power and knowledge are emphasized at the end (verse 12).

In the name of God, the Lord of Mercy, the Giver of Mercy

[1] Prophet, when any of you intend to divorce women, do so at a time when their prescribed waiting period can properly start,[a] and calculate the period carefully: be mindful of God, your Lord. Do not drive them out of their homes—nor should they themselves leave—unless they commit a flagrant indecency. These are the limits set by God—whoever oversteps God's limits wrongs his own soul—for you cannot know what new situation God may perhaps bring about. [2] When they have completed their appointed term, either keep them honourably, or release them honourably. Call two just witnesses from your people and establish witness for the sake of God. Anyone who believes in God and the Last Day should heed this: God will find a way out for those who are mindful of Him, [3] and will provide for them from an unexpected source; God will be enough for those who put their trust in Him. God achieves His purpose; God has set a due measure for everything. [4] If you are in doubt, the period of waiting will be three months for those women who have ceased menstruating and for those who have not reached menstruation; the waiting period of those who are pregnant will be until they deliver their burden: God makes things easy for those who are mindful of Him. [5] This is God's command, which He has sent down to you. God will wipe out the sinful deeds and increase the rewards of anyone who is mindful of Him.

[6] House the wives you are divorcing according to your means, in the same way you house yourselves, and do not harass them so as to make their lives difficult. If they are pregnant, maintain them

[a] The waiting period starts properly after menstruation and before intercourse is resumed, and lasts for three menstrual cycles.

until they are delivered of their burdens; if they suckle your infants, pay them for it. Consult together in a good way—if you find it difficult, another woman may suckle the child for the father[a]—[7] and let the wealthy man spend according to his wealth. But let him whose provision is restricted spend according to what God has given him: God does not burden any person with more than He has given them—after hardship, God will bring ease.

[8] Many a town that insolently opposed the command of its Lord and His messengers We have brought sternly to account: We punished them severely [9] to make them taste the ill effect of their conduct—the result of their conduct was ruin. [10] God has prepared a severe punishment for them.

So, you who have understanding, you who believe, beware of God. He has sent you the Qur'an [11] and a messenger—reciting to you God's revelations that make things clear—to bring those who believe and do righteous deeds from darkness into light: God will admit those who believe in Him and do righteous deeds into Gardens graced with flowing streams, where they will remain for ever—He has made good provision for them.

[12] It is God who created seven heavens and a similar [number] of earths. His command[b] descends throughout them. So you should realize that He has power over all things and that His knowledge encompasses everything.

---

[a] In Islamic law it is the father's responsibility to pay for his child to be fed.

[b] Or 'His revelation'.

66. PROHIBITION

A Medinan sura that discusses episodes in the Prophet's home life. It chides two of the Prophet's wives for an incident when a confidence was betrayed (verses 3–5) and urges all believers to submit themselves to God and to guard themselves and their families against Hellfire (verses 6–8). The sura closes by giving examples of believing and disbelieving women (verses 10–12).

In the name of God, the Lord of Mercy, the Giver of Mercy

[1] Prophet, why do you prohibit what God has made lawful to you[a] in your desire to please your wives? Yet God is forgiving and merciful: [2] He has ordained a way for you [believers] to release you from [such] oaths[b]—God is your helper: He is the All Knowing, the Wise.

[3] The Prophet told something in confidence to one of his wives and she disclosed it [to another wife]—God made this known to him so he confirmed part of it, keeping the rest to himself—so he confronted her with what she had done. She asked, 'Who told you about this?' and he replied, 'The All Knowing, the All Aware told me.' [4] If both of you [wives] repent to God—for your hearts have deviated—[all will be well]; if you collaborate against him, [be warned that] God will aid him, as will Gabriel and all righteous believers, and the angels will stand behind him. [5] His Lord may well replace you with better wives if the Prophet decides to divorce any of you: wives who are devoted to God, true believers, devout, who turn to Him in repentance and worship Him, given to fasting, whether previously married or virgins.

[6] Believers, guard yourselves and your families against a Fire fuelled by people and stones, and guarded by angels, stern and strong; angels who never disobey God's commands to them, but do as they are ordered: [7] 'You who disbelieve, make no excuses today: you are only being repaid for what you used to do.'

[8] Believers, turn to God in sincere repentance. Your Lord may well

---

[a] The Prophet had made an oath to abstain from something: either honey or conjugal relations with one or more of his wives. Razi gives several stories to explain this.

[b] See 5: 89. If a Muslim swears an oath which may be counter to what is right, he is allowed release, provided he gives expiation.

cancel your bad deeds for you and admit you into Gardens graced with flowing streams, on a Day when God will not disgrace the Prophet or those who have believed with him. With their lights streaming out ahead of them and to their right, they will say, 'Lord, perfect our lights for us and forgive us: You have power over everything.'

[9] Prophet, strive hard against the disbelievers and the hypocrites. Deal with them sternly. Hell will be their home, an evil destination! [10] God has given examples of disbelievers: the wives of Noah and Lot who married two of Our righteous servants but failed[a] them. Their husbands could not help them against God: it was said, 'Both of you enter the Fire with the others.' [11] God has also given examples of believers: Pharaoh's wife, who said, 'Lord, build a house in Your Garden for me:[b] save me from Pharaoh and his actions; save me from the evildoers,' [12] and Mary, daughter of 'Imran. She guarded her chastity, so We breathed Our spirit into her. She accepted the truth of her Lord's words and Scriptures: she was truly devout.

[a] Literally 'betrayed'.
[b] Literally 'build me a house with You in the Garden'.

67. CONTROL ^a

A Meccan sura that challenges the disbelievers with declarations of God's total power over them, and everything else, in this world and the next. It describes the regret the disbelievers will express on the Day of Resurrection (verses 9–10, 27).

In the name of God, the Lord of Mercy, the Giver of Mercy

¹ Exalted^b is He who holds all control in His hands; who has power over all things; ² who created death; who created life to test you [people] and reveal which of you performs best—He is the Mighty, the Forgiving; ³ who created the seven heavens, one above the other. You will not see any flaw in what the Lord of Mercy creates. Look around you! Can you see any flaw? ⁴ Look again! And again! All you will achieve is to tire out your eyes.

⁵ We have adorned the lowest heaven with lamps and made them missiles for stoning devils^c. We have prepared the torment of a blazing fire for them. ⁶ For those who deny their Lord We have prepared the torment of Hell: an evil destination. ⁷ They will hear it drawing in its breath when they are thrown in. It blazes forth, ⁸ almost bursting with rage. Its keepers will ask every group that is thrown in, 'Did no one come to warn you?' ⁹ They will reply, 'Yes, a warner did come to us, but we did not believe him. We said, "God has revealed nothing: you are greatly misguided".' ¹⁰ They will say, 'If only we had listened, or reasoned, we would not now be with the inhabitants of the blazing fire,' and ¹¹ they will confess their sins. Away with the inhabitants of the blazing fire! ¹² But there is forgiveness and a great reward for those who fear their Lord though they cannot see Him.

¹³ He knows the contents of every heart, whether you keep your words secret or state them openly. ¹⁴ How could He who created not know His own creation, when He is the Most Subtle, the All Aware? ¹⁵ It is He who has made the earth manageable for you—travel its

^a Or 'Sovereignty'.

^b This meaning of *tabarak* is supported by Razi and is more appropriate here than 'blessed'.

^c Cf. 37: 6–10.

regions; eat His provision—and to Him you will be resurrected. [16] Are you sure that He who is in Heaven will not make the earth swallow you up with a violent shudder? [17] Are you sure that He who is in Heaven will not send a whirlwind to pelt you with stones?

You will come to know what My warning means. [18] Those who went before them also disbelieved—how terrible was My condemnation! [19] Do they not see the birds above them spreading and closing their wings? It is only the Lord of Mercy who holds them up: He watches over everything. [20] Who can defend you except for the Lord of Mercy? The disbelievers are truly deluded. [21] Who can provide for you if He withholds His provision? Yet they persist in their insolence and their avoidance of the Truth. [22] Who is better guided: someone who falls on his face, or someone who walks steadily on a straight path?

[23] Say [Prophet], 'It is He who brought you into being, He who endowed you with hearing, sight, and understanding—what small thanks you give!' [24] Say, 'It is He who scattered you throughout the earth, He to whom you will be gathered.' [25] They say, 'If what you say is true, when will this promise be fulfilled?' [26] Say, 'God alone has knowledge of this: my only duty is to give clear warning.' [27] When they see it close at hand, the disbelievers' faces will be gloomy, and it will be said, 'This is what you were calling for.' [28] Say, 'Just think—regardless of whether God destroys me and my followers[a] or has mercy on us—who will protect the disbelievers from an agonizing torment?' [29] Say, 'He is the Lord of Mercy; we believe in Him; we put our trust in Him. You will come to know in time who is in obvious error.' [30] Say, 'Just think: who can give you flowing water if all your water sinks deep into the earth?'

[a] Reports state that the Meccans were hoping that the Prophet would die, so that they could be rid of him once and for all.

68. THE PEN

An early Meccan sura that deals with the accusation that Muhammad was not God's Messenger but merely mad (verses 2–6). The arrogance of those who assume that, because they have some of the good things in this life, they can reject the Revelation, is rebutted (verses 10–16). Examples are given of those who came to regret their arrogance (verses 17–33). The Prophet is urged to remain steadfast (verses 48–52).

In the name of God, the Lord of Mercy, the Giver of Mercy

¹ *Nun*

By the pen! By all they write![a] ² Your Lord's grace[b] does not make you [Prophet] a madman: ³ you will have a never-ending reward— ⁴ truly you have a noble character—⁵ and soon you will see, as will they, ⁶ which of you is afflicted with madness. ⁷ Your Lord knows best who strays from His path and who is rightly guided. ⁸ So do not yield to those who deny the truth—⁹ they want you to compromise with them and then they will compromise with you—¹⁰ do not yield to any contemptible swearer, ¹¹ to any backbiter, slander-monger, ¹² or hinderer of good, to anyone who is sinful, aggressive, ¹³ coarse, and on top of all that, ill-bred.[c] ¹⁴ Just because he has wealth and sons, ¹⁵ when our revelations are recited to him, he says, 'These are just ancient fables.' ¹⁶ We shall brand him on the snout!

¹⁷ We have tried them as We tried the owners of a certain garden, who swore that they would harvest its fruits in the morning ¹⁸ and made no allowance [for the Will of God]:[d] ¹⁹ a disaster from your Lord struck the garden as they slept ²⁰ and by morning it was

---

[a] This could refer to the angels and what they write down of people's deeds or to the generic pen and what people write, thus swearing by the ability to write with which God endowed human beings. Cf. 96: 4–5.

[b] Receiving God's revelation. See esp. 15: 6 for the accusation of madness, which occurs countless times with reference to various prophets in the Qur'an. Another interpretation is 'by God's grace . . .'.

[c] This is said to refer to al-Walid ibn al-Mughira, a staunch opponent of the Prophet.

[d] Or '[for the poor]'.

stripped bare, a desolate land. ²¹ Still they called each other at day-break, ²² 'Go early to your field if you wish to gather all its fruits,' ²³ and went off, whispering, ²⁴ 'Make sure no poor person enters the garden today!'—²⁵ they left early, bent on their purpose—²⁶ but when they saw the garden, they said, 'We must have lost our way! ²⁷ No—we are ruined!' ²⁸ The wisest of them said, 'Did I not say to you, "Will you not glorify God?" '—²⁹ they said, 'Glory be to God, Our Lord! Truly, we were doing wrong!'—³⁰ and then they turned to each other in mutual reproach. ³¹ They said, 'Alas for us! We have done terrible wrong, ³² but maybe our Lord will give us something better in its place: we truly turn to Him in hope.' ³³ Such is the punishment [in this life], but greater still is the punishment in the Hereafter, if only they knew.

³⁴ There will be Gardens of bliss for those who are mindful of God. ³⁵ Should We treat those who submit to Us as We treat those who do evil? ³⁶ What is the matter with you? On what basis do you judge? ³⁷ Do you have a Scripture that tells you ³⁸ that you will be granted whatever you choose? ³⁹ Have you received from Us solemn oaths, binding to the Day of Resurrection, that you will get whatever you yourselves decide? ⁴⁰ Ask them [Prophet] which of them will guarantee this. ⁴¹ Do they have 'partners' [beside God]? Let them produce their 'partners', if what they say is true. ⁴² On the Day when matters become dire,*ᵃ* they will be invited to prostrate themselves but will be prevented*ᵇ* from doing so, ⁴³ and their eyes will be down-cast and they will be overwhelmed with shame: they were invited to prostrate themselves when they were safe [but refused].

⁴⁴ So [Prophet] leave those who reject this revelation to Me: We shall lead them on, step by step, to their ruin, in ways beyond their knowledge; ⁴⁵ I will allow them more time, for My plan is powerful. ⁴⁶ Do you demand some reward from them that would burden them with debt? ⁴⁷ Do they have knowledge of the unseen that enables them to write down the future? ⁴⁸ Wait patiently [Prophet] for your Lord's judgement: do not be like the man in the whale who called out in distress: ⁴⁹ if his Lord's grace had not reached him, he would have been left, abandoned and blameworthy, on the barren shore,

---

ᵃ This is the meaning of the Arabic expression 'when shins are bared'.

ᵇ Baydawi suggests that this is because the time for obedience is over, or because they are somehow unable to do so (*Tafsir*).

[50] but his Lord chose him and made him one of the Righteous. [51] The disbelievers almost strike you down with their looks when they hear the Qur'an. They say, 'He must be mad!' [52] but truly it is nothing other than a Reminder for all peoples.

69. THE INEVITABLE HOUR

A Meccan sura that describes punishment in this life (verses 4–12) and the next (verses 13–18). The bliss to be enjoyed by the believers is eloquently contrasted with the torments of hell (verses 19–37). From verse 38 onwards, God affirms the Truth of the Qur'an and the Prophet.

In the name of God, the Lord of Mercy, the Giver of Mercy

¹ The Inevitable Hour! ² What is the Inevitable Hour? ³ What will explain to you what the Inevitable Hour is?

⁴ The people of Thamud and 'Ad denied that the crashing blow*ᵃ* would come: ⁵ Thamud was destroyed by a deafening blast; ⁶ 'Ad was destroyed by a furious wind ⁷ that God let loose against them for seven consecutive nights, eight consecutive days, so that you could have seen its people lying dead like hollow palm-trunks. ⁸ Can you see any trace of them now? ⁹ Pharaoh, too, and those before him, and the ruined cities: these people committed grave sins and disobeyed the messenger of their Lord, so He seized them with an ever-tightening grip. ¹⁰ But when the Flood rose high, ¹¹ We saved you in the floating ship, ¹² making that event a reminder for you: attentive ears may take heed.

¹³ When the Trumpet is sounded a single time, ¹⁴ when the earth and its mountains are raised high and then crushed with a single blow, ¹⁵ on that Day the Great Event will come to pass. ¹⁶ The sky will be torn apart, on that Day, it will be so frail. ¹⁷ The angels will appear by its sides and, on that Day, eight of them will bear the throne of your Lord above them. ¹⁸ On that Day you will be brought to judgement and none of your secrets will remain hidden. ¹⁹ He who is given his Record in his right hand will say, 'Here is my Record, read it. ²⁰ I knew I would meet my Reckoning,' ²¹ and so he will have a pleasant life ²² in a lofty Garden, ²³ with clustered fruit within his reach. ²⁴ It will be said, 'Eat and drink to your heart's content as a reward for what you have done in days gone by.' ²⁵ But he who is given his Record in his left hand will say, 'If only I had never been given any

ᵃ Cf. the sura of this name (Sura 101).

Record ²⁶ and knew nothing of my Reckoning. ²⁷ How I wish death had been the end of me. ²⁸ My wealth has been no use to me, ²⁹ and my power has vanished.' ³⁰ 'Take him, put a collar on him, ³¹ lead him to burn in the blazing Fire, ³² and [bind him] in a chain seventy metres*ᵃ* long: ³³ he would not believe in Almighty God, ³⁴ he never encouraged feeding the hungry, ³⁵ so today he has no real friend here, ³⁶ and the only food he has is the filth ³⁷ that only sinners eat.'

³⁸ So I swear by what you can see ³⁹ and by what you cannot see: ⁴⁰ this [Qur'an] is the speech of an honoured messenger, ⁴¹ not the words of a poet—how little you believe!—⁴² nor the words of a soothsayer—how little you reflect! ⁴³ This [Qur'an] is a message sent down from the Lord of the Worlds: ⁴⁴ if [the Prophet] had attributed some fabrication to Us, ⁴⁵ We would certainly have seized his right hand ⁴⁶ and cut off his lifeblood,*ᵇ* ⁴⁷ and none of you could have defended him. ⁴⁸ This [Qur'an] is a reminder for those who are aware of God. ⁴⁹ We know that some of you consider it to be lies—⁵⁰ this will be a source of bitter regret for the disbelievers—⁵¹ but it is in fact the certain truth. ⁵² So [Prophet] glorify the name of your Lord, the Almighty.

ᵃ A *dhira'* is an arm's-length.

ᵇ Literally 'artery'.

70. THE WAYS OF ASCENT

A Meccan sura that describes the Day of Judgement (verses 8–18). One of the opponents of the Prophet challenged him to hasten the punishment they had been threatened with (verse 1), so the foolishness of the disbelievers in denying the Resurrection (verse 6) is exposed (verses 36–44). The people who will be granted the Garden are described (verses 22–35). The title is a reference to the paths through which angels ascend to God, mentioned in verses 3–4.

In the name of God, the Lord of Mercy, the Giver of Mercy

¹ A man [mockingly] demanded the punishment. ² It will fall on the disbelievers—none can deflect it—³ from God, the Lord of the Ways of Ascent, ⁴ by which the angels and the Spirit ascend to Him, on a Day that lasts fifty thousand years. ⁵ So be patient, [Prophet], as befits you. ⁶ The disbelievers think it is distant, ⁷ but We know it to be close. ⁸ On a Day when the heavens will be like molten brass ⁹ and the mountains like tufts of wool, ¹⁰ when no friend will care about his friend, ¹¹ even when they are within sight of one another: the guilty person will wish he could save himself from the suffering of that Day by sacrificing his sons, ¹² his spouse, his brother, ¹³ the kinsfolk who gave him shelter, ¹⁴ and everyone on earth, if it could save him. ¹⁵ But no! There is a raging flame ¹⁶ that strips away the skin, ¹⁷ and it will claim everyone who rejects the truth, turns away, ¹⁸ amasses wealth and hoards it.

¹⁹ Man was truly created anxious: ²⁰ he is fretful when misfortune touches him, ²¹ but tight-fisted when good fortune comes his way. ²² Not so those who pray ²³ and are constant in their prayers; ²⁴ who give a due share of their wealth ²⁵ to beggars and the deprived; ²⁶ who believe in the Day of Judgement ²⁷ and fear the punishment of their Lord—²⁸ none may feel wholly secure from it—²⁹ who guard their chastity ³⁰ from all but their spouses or their slaves—there is no blame attached to [relations with] these, ³¹ but those whose desires exceed this limit are truly transgressors—³² who are faithful to their trusts and their pledges; ³³ who give honest testimony ³⁴ and are steadfast in their prayers. ³⁵ They will be honoured in Gardens of bliss.

³⁶ What is wrong with the disbelievers? Why do they rush to peer at you [Prophet], ³⁷ from right and left, in crowds? ³⁸ Does every one of them expect to enter a Garden of bliss? ³⁹ No! We created them from the substance they know,ᵃ ⁴⁰ and, by the Lord of every sunrise and sunset, We have the power ⁴¹ to substitute for them others better than they are—nothing can prevent Us from doing this. ⁴² So leave them to wallow in idle talk, until they come face to face with their promised Day, ⁴³ the Day they will rush out of their graves as if rallying to a flag, ⁴⁴ eyes downcast and covered in shame: this is how their promised Day will be.

ᵃ They deny the Resurrection, and this points out to them that God has the power to create them from such a small beginning and that He can bring about the Resurrection. Cf. 56: 56–62.

71. NOAH

A Meccan sura giving further details of the life of Noah before the Flood, to encourage the Prophet and warn the disbelievers.

In the name of God, the Lord of Mercy, the Giver of Mercy

¹ We sent Noah to his people: 'Warn your people, before a painful punishment comes to them.' ² And so he said, 'My people, I am here to warn you plainly. ³ Serve God, be mindful of Him and obey me. ⁴ He will forgive you your sins and spare you until your appointed time—when God's appointed time arrives it cannot be postponed. If only you understood!'

⁵ He said, 'My Lord, I have called my people night and day, ⁶ but the more I call them, the further they run away: ⁷ every time I call them, so that You may forgive them, they thrust their fingers into their ears, wrap themselves in their garments, persist in their rejection, and grow more insolent and arrogant. ⁸ I have tried calling them openly. ⁹ I have tried preaching to them in public and speaking to them in private. ¹⁰ I said, "Ask forgiveness of your Lord: He is ever forgiving. ¹¹ He will send down abundant rain from the sky for you; ¹² He will give you wealth and sons; He will provide you with gardens and rivers. ¹³ What is the matter with you? Why will you not fear God's majesty, ¹⁴ when He has created you stage by stage?ᵃ ¹⁵ Have you ever wondered how God created seven heavens, one above the other, ¹⁶ placed the moon as a light in them and the sun as a lamp, ¹⁷ how God made you spring forth from the earth like a plant, ¹⁸ how He will return you into it and then bring you out again, ¹⁹ and how He has spread the Earth out for you ²⁰ to walk along its spacious paths?" '

²¹ Noah said, 'My Lord, they have disobeyed me and followed those whose riches and children only increase their losses; ²² they have hatched a mighty plot, ²³ saying to each other, "Do not renounce your gods! ²⁴ Do not renounce Wadd, Suwaʻ, Yaghuth, Yaʻuq, or

---

ᵃ See 22: 5; 23: 12–15.

Nasr!"*ᵃ* They have led many astray. Lord, bring nothing but destruction*ᵇ* down on the evildoers!'

²⁵ They were drowned and sent to Hell for their evildoings: they found no one to help them against God. ²⁶ And Noah said, 'Lord, do not leave any of the disbelievers on the earth—²⁷ if you leave them they will lead Your servants astray and beget only sinners and disbelievers—²⁸ Lord, forgive me, my parents, and whoever enters my house as a believer. Forgive believing men and women but bring nothing but ruin down on the evildoers!'

ᵃ Names of idols.
ᵇ See *al-Mu'jam al-Wasit* for this meaning of *dalal*.

72. THE JINN

A Meccan sura that gives an account of what a group of jinn said when they overheard a recitation of the Qur'an and realized its truth (verses 1–15). This is a lesson to the Meccan Arabs, who are also told that the Prophet can help them only by delivering the Message—God is the All Powerful One (verses 16–28). The disbelievers are threatened with what they will meet on the Day of Judgement (verses 23–7).

In the name of God, the Lord of Mercy, the Giver of Mercy

¹ Say [Prophet], 'It has been revealed to me that a group of jinn once listened in and said, "We have heard a wondrous Qur'an, ² that gives guidance to the right path, and we have come to believe. We shall never set up partners with our Lord. ³ He has neither spouse nor child—He is far above this in majesty! ⁴ Outrageous things have been said about God by the foolish among us, ⁵ although we had thought that no man or jinn would [dare to] tell a lie about Him. ⁶ Men have sought refuge with the jinn in the past, but they only misguided them further. ⁷ They thought, as you did, that God would never raise anyone from the dead. ⁸ We tried to reach heaven, but discovered it to be full of stern guards and shooting stars—⁹ we used to sit in places there, listening,ᵃ but anyone trying to listen now will find a shooting star lying in wait for him—¹⁰ [so now] we do not know whether those who live on earth are due for misfortune, or whether their Lord intends to guide them. ¹¹ Some of us are righteous and others less so: we follow different paths. ¹² We know we can never frustrate God on earth; we can never escape Him. ¹³ We came to believe when we heard the guidance: whoever believes in his Lord need fear no loss nor injustice. ¹⁴ Some of us submit to Him and others go the wrong way: those who submit to God have found wise guidance, ¹⁵ but those who go wrong will be fuel for Hellfire." '

¹⁶ If theyᵇ had taken to the right way, We would have given them

---

ᵃ They were listening for hints of what might come next, but in verse 10 they say they are no longer able to know the future (cf. verse 26 below).

ᵇ The Meccan Arabs.

abundant water to drink—[17] a test for them[a]—but anyone who turns away from his Lord's Revelation will be sent by Him to spiralling torment. [18] Places of worship are for God alone—so do not pray to anyone other than God—[19] yet when God's Servant[b] stood up to pray to Him, they pressed in on him. [20] Say, 'I pray to my Lord alone; I set up no partner with Him.' [21] Say, 'I have no control over any harm or good that may befall you.' [22] Say, 'No one can protect me from God: I have no refuge except in Him; [23] I only deliver [what I receive] from God and only His messages.'

Whoever disobeys God and His Messenger will have Hell's Fire as his permanent home: [24] when they are confronted by what they have been promised, they will realize who has the weaker protector and the smaller number. [25] Say, 'I do not know whether what you have been promised is near, or whether a distant time has been appointed for it by my Lord.' [26] He is the One who knows what is hidden. [27] He does not disclose it except to a messenger of His choosing. He sends watchers to go in front and behind [28] to ensure that each of His messengers delivers his Lord's message: He is all around them, and He takes account of everything.

---

[a] In the Qur'an, plenty is as great a test as privation (see 21: 35), if not greater (see 10: 21–2).

[b] Muhammad.

73. ENFOLDED

A sura that is part very early Meccan, part Medinan (verse 20). This verse describes how God relaxed the early regime of devotion first imposed on the Prophet (in verses 1–9) to prepare him for the weighty message. The Prophet is urged to be patient (verses 10–11), told of the punishment that awaits the Meccan disbelievers in Hell (verses 12–14), and reminded of the punishment that befell Pharaoh in this life (verses 15–16).

In the name of God, the Lord of Mercy, the Giver of Mercy

¹ You [Prophet], enfolded in your cloak! ² Keep vigil throughout the night, all but a small part of it, ³ half, or a little less, ⁴ or a little more; recite the Qur'an slowly and distinctly: ⁵ We shall send a momentous message down to you. ⁶ Night prayer makes a deeper impression and sharpens words—⁷ you are kept busy for long periods of the day—⁸ so celebrate the name of your Lord and devote yourself wholeheartedly to Him. ⁹ He is Lord of the east and west, there is no god but Him, so take Him as your Protector, ¹⁰ patiently endure what they say, ignore them politely, ¹¹ and leave to Me those who deny the truth and live in comfort. Bear with them for a little while; ¹² We have fetters, a blazing fire, ¹³ food that chokes, and agonizing torment in store for them ¹⁴ on the Day when the earth and the mountains will shake. The mountains will become a heap of loose sand.

¹⁵ We have sent a messenger to you [people] to be your witness, just as We sent a messenger to Pharaoh, ¹⁶ but Pharaoh disobeyed the messenger and so We inflicted a heavy punishment on him. ¹⁷ So if you disbelieve, how can you guard yourselves against a Day that will turn children's hair grey, ¹⁸ a Day when the sky will be torn apart? God's promise will certainly be fulfilled. ¹⁹ This is a reminder. Let whoever wishes take the way to his Lord.

²⁰ [Prophet], your Lord is well aware that you sometimes spend nearly two-thirds of the night at prayer—sometimes half, sometimes a third—as do some of your followers. God determines the division of night and day. He knows that you will not be able to keep a measure of it and He has relented towards all of you, so recite as much of the Qur'an as is easy for you. He knows that some of you

will be sick, some of you travelling through the land seeking God's bounty, some of you fighting in God's way: recite as much as is easy for you, keep up the prayer, pay the prescribed alms, and make God a good loan. Whatever good you store up for yourselves will be improved and increased for you. Ask God for His forgiveness, He is most forgiving, most merciful.

74. WRAPPED IN HIS CLOAK

After his first encounter with the Angel of Revelation in the Cave of Hira, the Prophet went home trembling and asked his wife to cover him with his cloak. The first verses of this Meccan sura were then revealed (verses 1–7). The sura goes on, in a section from a later period, to remind the obstinate disbelievers of their fate on the Day of Judgement (verses 8–10) and a specific opponent of the Prophet is singled out (verses 11–31). The end of the sura (verses 39–53) exposes the foolishness of the disbelievers' attitude to the Revelation and the Day of Resurrection.

In the name of God, the Lord of Mercy, the Giver of Mercy

¹ You, wrapped in your cloak, ² arise and give warning! ³ Proclaim the greatness of your Lord; ⁴ cleanse yourself;*a* ⁵ keep away from all filth;*b* ⁶ do not be overwhelmed and weaken;*c* ⁷ be steadfast in your Lord's cause.

⁸ When the Trumpet sounds, ⁹ that will be a Day of anguish for the disbelievers. ¹⁰ They will have no ease. ¹¹ [Prophet], leave Me to deal with the one I created helpless,*d* ¹² then gave vast wealth, ¹³ and sons by his side, ¹⁴ making everything easy for him—¹⁵ yet he still hopes I will give him more. ¹⁶ No! He has been stubbornly hostile to Our revelation: ¹⁷ I will inflict a spiralling torment on him. ¹⁸ He planned and plotted—¹⁹ devilishly he plotted! ²⁰ ferociously he plotted!—²¹ and looked ²² and frowned and scowled ²³ and turned away and behaved arrogantly ²⁴ and said, 'This is just old sorcery, ²⁵ just the talk of a mortal!'

²⁶ I will throw him into the scorching Fire. ²⁷ What will explain to you what the scorching Fire is? ²⁸ It spares nothing and leaves nothing; ²⁹ it scorches the flesh of humans; ³⁰ there are nineteen in charge of it—³¹ none other than angels appointed by Us to guard

---

a Literally 'clean your garments' (see Razi for this idiomatic usage of *thiyab*).

b Or 'from all idolatry'.

c An alternative translation would be 'do not give, hoping only to receive'. The translation given above is based on Mujahid's understanding of *manna* as 'to weaken'. See Razi for this interpretation, which seems much more appropriate to the context.

d Al-Walid ibn al-Mughira, one of the Prophet's obstinate opponents.

Hellfire—and We have made their number*a* a test for the disbelievers. So those who have been given the Scripture will be certain
and those who believe will have their faith increased: neither those
who have been given the Scripture nor the believers will have any
doubts, but the sick at heart and the disbelievers will say, 'What
could God mean by this image?' God leaves whoever He will to stray
and guides whoever He will—no one knows your Lord's forces
except Him—this [description] is a warning to mortals. ³²Yes—by
the moon! ³³By the departing night! ³⁴By the shining dawn! ³⁵It is
one of the mightiest things, ³⁶a warning to all mortals, ³⁷to those of
you who choose to go ahead and those who lag behind.

³⁸Every soul is held in pledge for its deeds, ³⁹but the Companions
of the Right will stay ⁴⁰in Gardens and ask ⁴¹about the guilty.
⁴²'What drove you to the Scorching Fire?' [they will ask] ⁴³and they
will answer, 'We did not pray; ⁴⁴we did not feed the poor; ⁴⁵we
indulged with others [in mocking the believers]; ⁴⁶we denied the
Day of Judgement ⁴⁷until the Certain End came upon us.' ⁴⁸No
intercessor's plea will benefit them now.

⁴⁹What is the matter with them? Why do they turn away from the
warning, ⁵⁰like frightened asses ⁵¹fleeing from a lion? ⁵²Each one of
them demands that a scripture be sent down to him and unrolled
before his very eyes—⁵³No! Truly they have no fear of the life to
come—⁵⁴but truly this is a reminder. ⁵⁵Let whoever wishes to take
heed do so: ⁵⁶they will only take heed if God so wishes. He is the
Lord who should be heeded, the Lord of forgiveness.

---

a Some have taken this literally to allude to a special significance of the number 19,
but it is much more likely to be *'idda* in the meaning of 'number, group' (*al-Mu'jam
al-Wasit*).

75. THE RESURRECTION

A Meccan sura, dealing with the Day of Resurrection and man's denial of that Day. God's power over mankind is convincingly described in several vignettes (verses 3–4, 26–30, 34–40). The third paragraph instructs the Prophet on appropriate reception of the revelation (verses 16–19), and thereby serves to emphasize that the Qur'an is indeed God's word.

In the name of God, the Lord of Mercy, the Giver of Mercy

¹By[a] the Day of Resurrection ²and by the self-reproaching soul! ³Does man think We shall not put his bones back together? ⁴In fact, We can reshape his very fingertips. ⁵Yet man wants to deny what is ahead of him: ⁶he says, 'So, when will this Day of Resurrection be?'

⁷When eyes are dazzled ⁸and the moon eclipsed, ⁹when the sun and the moon are brought together, ¹⁰on that Day man will say, 'Where can I escape?' ¹¹Truly, there is no refuge: ¹²they will all return to your Lord on that Day. ¹³On that Day, man will be told what he put first and what he put last. ¹⁴Truly, man is a clear witness against himself, ¹⁵despite all the excuses he may put forward.

¹⁶[Prophet], do not rush your tongue in an attempt to hasten [your memorization of] the Revelation: ¹⁷We shall make sure of its safe collection and recitation. ¹⁸When We have recited it, repeat the recitation ¹⁹and We shall make it clear.

²⁰Truly you [people] love this fleeting world ²¹and neglect the life to come. ²²On that Day there will be radiant faces, ²³looking towards their Lord, ²⁴and on that Day there will be the sad and despairing faces ²⁵of those who realize that a great calamity is about to befall them.

²⁶Truly, when the soul reaches the collarbone; ²⁷when it is said, 'Could any charm-healer save him now?'; ²⁸when he knows it is the final parting; ²⁹when his legs are brought together;[b] ³⁰on that day he will be driven towards your Lord. ³¹He neither believed nor prayed,

---

[a] This is preceded by a phrase which can be rendered either 'I swear' or 'I do not swear' (i.e. there is no need for me to swear), depending on how *la* is read.

[b] This is taken to refer to when a corpse is wrapped in the shroud.

³² but denied the truth and turned away, ³³ walking back to his people with a conceited swagger.

³⁴ Closer and closer it comes. ³⁵ Closer and closer still. ³⁶ Does man think he will be left alone? ³⁷ Was he not just a drop of spilt-out sperm, ³⁸ which became a clinging form, which God shaped in due proportion, ³⁹ fashioning from it the two sexes, male and female? ⁴⁰ Does He who can do this not have the power to bring the dead back to life?

76. MAN

A Medinan sura that speaks of how man is tested (verses 2–3) and what the results will be for the evildoers (verse 4) and for the righteous (verses 5–22). The Prophet is urged to persevere in his devotion and to bear with patience (verses 23–6).

In the name of God, the Lord of Mercy, the Giver of Mercy

¹ Was there not a period of time when man was nothing to speak of?[a] ² We created man from a drop of mingled fluid to put him to the test; We gave him hearing and sight; ³ We guided him to the right path, whether he was grateful or not.

⁴ We have prepared chains, iron collars, and blazing Fire for the disbelievers, but ⁵ the righteous will have a drink mixed with *kafur*,[b] ⁶ a spring for God's servants, which flows abundantly at their wish. ⁷ They fulfil their vows; they fear a day of widespread woes; ⁸ they give food to the poor, the orphan, and the captive, though they love it themselves, ⁹ saying, 'We feed you for the sake of God alone: We seek neither recompense nor thanks from you. ¹⁰ We fear the Day of our Lord—a woefully grim Day.' ¹¹ So God will save them from the woes of that Day, give them radiance and gladness, ¹² and reward them, for their steadfastness, with a Garden and silken robes. ¹³ They will sit on couches, feeling neither scorching heat nor biting cold, ¹⁴ with shady [branches] spread above them and clusters of fruit hanging close at hand. ¹⁵ They will be served with silver plates ¹⁶ and gleaming silver goblets according to their fancy, ¹⁷ and they will be given a drink infused with ginger ¹⁸ from a spring called Salsabil. ¹⁹ Everlasting youths will attend them—if you could see them, you would think they were scattered pearls, ²⁰ and if you were to look around, you would see a vast, blissful kingdom—²¹ and they will wear garments of green silk and brocade. They will be adorned with silver bracelets. Their Lord will give them a pure drink.

---

[a] Literally 'Has there not come over man a period of time when he was not mentioned?' This refers to the time before a person is born, the point being that he was nothing, then God created him, just as He will bring him to life again for Judgement.

[b] A fragrant herb.

²²[It will be said], 'This is your reward. Your endeavours are appreciated.'

²³ We Ourself have sent down this Qur'an to you [Prophet] in gradual revelation. ²⁴ Await your Lord's Judgement with patience; do not yield to any of these sinners and disbelievers; ²⁵ remember the name of your Lord at dawn and in the evening; ²⁶ bow down before Him, and glorify Him at length by night.

²⁷ These people love the fleeting life. They put aside [all thoughts of] a Heavy Day. ²⁸ Yet We created them; We strengthened their constitution; if We please, We can replace such people completely.

²⁹ This is a reminder. Let whoever wishes, take the way to his Lord. ³⁰ But you will only wish to do so if God wills—God is all knowing, all wise—³¹ He admits whoever He will into His Mercy and has prepared a painful punishment for the disbelievers.

77. [WINDS] SENT FORTH^a

*A Meccan sura that describes the Day of Decision—its inevitability, argu-
ments for its coming, and the events that will presage the Judgement, as well as
the fates of believers and disbelievers.*

In the name of God, the Lord of Mercy, the Giver of Mercy

¹ By the [winds] sent forth in swift succession, ² violently storming,
³ scattering far and wide, ⁴ carefully distinguishing [their targets],
⁵ delivering a message ⁶ that excuses or warns, ⁷ what you are promised will come to pass. ⁸ When the stars are dimmed ⁹ and the sky
torn apart, ¹⁰ when the mountains are turned to dust ¹¹ and the messengers given their appointed time^b—¹² for what Day has all this
been set? ¹³ The Day of Decision. ¹⁴ What will explain to you what
the Day of Decision is? ¹⁵ Woe, on that Day, to those who denied the
truth! ¹⁶ Did We not destroy earlier generations? ¹⁷ We shall make
later generations follow them: ¹⁸ this is how We deal with sinners.
¹⁹ Woe, on that Day, to those who denied the truth!

²⁰ Did We not make you from a humble fluid ²¹ which We housed in
a safe lodging ²² for a determined period? ²³ We determine [it]: how
excellently We determine! ²⁴ Woe, on that Day, to those who denied
the truth! ²⁵ Did We not make the earth a home ²⁶ for the living and
the dead? ²⁷ Did We not place firm, lofty mountains on it and provide
you with sweet water? ²⁸ Woe, on that Day, to those who denied the
truth!

²⁹ They will be told, 'Go to that which you used to deny! ³⁰ Go to a
shadow of smoke!' It rises in three columns; ³¹ no shade does it give,
nor relief from the flame; ³² it shoots out sparks as large as tree-
trunks^c ³³ and as bright as copper.^d ³⁴ Woe, on that Day, to those who
denied the truth! ³⁵ On that Day they will be speechless, ³⁶ and they

---

^a See 30: 48–51 and many other instances.

^b To give testimony for their communities (Razi).

^c An alternative meaning of *qasr* is 'palaces, castles', but this meaning of 'tree-trunks'
seems to fit better (Razi).

^d Commonly translated as 'camels', but 'copper' (reported by Razi) is a more
convincing alternative.

will be given no chance to offer any excuses. [37] Woe, on that Day, to those who denied the truth! [38] [They will be told], 'This is the Day of Decision: We have gathered you and earlier generations. [39] If you have any plots against Me, try them now.' [40] Woe, on that Day, to those who denied the truth! [41] But those who took heed of God will enjoy cool shade, springs, [42] and any fruit they desire. [43] [They will be told], 'Eat and drink to your hearts' content as a reward for your deeds: [44] this is how We reward those who do good.' [45] Woe, on that Day, to those who denied the truth!

[46] [You may] eat and enjoy yourselves for a short while, evildoers that you are. [47] Woe, on that Day, to those who denied the truth! [48] When they are told, 'Bow down in prayer,' they do not do it. [49] Woe, on that Day, to those who denied the truth! [50] In what revelation, after this, will they believe?

78. THE ANNOUNCEMENT[a]

A Meccan sura. The disbelievers often asked incredulously about the Resurrection. This sura gives evidence of God's power, then explains what will happen on the Day of Resurrection, and the respective fates of believers and disbelievers.

In the name of God, the Lord of Mercy, the Giver of Mercy

[1] What are they asking about? [2] The momentous announcement [3] about which they differ. [4] They will find out. [5] In the end they will find out. [6] Did We not make the earth smooth, [7] and make the mountains to keep it stable?[b] [8] Did We not create you in pairs, [9] give you sleep for rest, [10] the night as a cover, [11] and the day for your livelihood? [12] Did We not build seven strong [heavens] above you, [13] and make a blazing lamp? [14] Did We not send water pouring down from the clouds [15] to bring forth with it grain, plants, [16] and luxuriant gardens? [17] A time has been appointed for the Day of Decision: [18] a Day when the Trumpet will sound and you will come forward in crowds, [19] when the sky will open up like wide portals, [20] when the mountains will vanish like a mirage. [21] Hell lies in wait, [22] a home for transgressors [23] to stay in for a long, long time, [24] where they will taste no coolness nor drink [25] except one that is scalding and dark[c] — [26] a fitting requital, [27] for they did not fear a reckoning, [28] and they rejected Our messages as lies. [29] We have recorded everything in a Record. [30] 'Taste this: more torment is all you will get from Us.'

[31] For those who were aware of God there is supreme fulfilment: [32] private gardens, vineyards, [33] high-breasted companions of matching age, [34] and an overflowing cup. [35] There they will hear no vain talk or lie: [36] a reward from your Lord, a fitting gift [37] from your Lord, the Lord of the heavens and earth and everything between, the Lord of Mercy.

They will have no authority from Him to speak. [38] On the Day

---

[a] Of the Resurrection and Judgement.
[b] Literally 'and the mountains [as its] pegs'.
[c] Cf. 38: 57.

when the Spirit[a] and the angels stand in rows, they will not speak except for those to whom the Lord of Mercy gives permission, who will say only what is right. [39] That is the Day of Truth. So whoever wishes to do so should take the path that leads to his Lord. [40] We have warned you of imminent suffering, on the Day when every person will see what their own hands have sent ahead for them, when the disbeliever will say, 'If only I were dust!'[b]

[a] The Angel Gabriel

[b] In this world, they have often said, 'What, when we are dust, shall we be raised again?'

79. THE FORCEFUL CHARGERS

A Meccan sura, the main theme of which is the possibility and inevitability of the Resurrection, its results, and its timing. The story of Moses and Pharaoh acts as encouragement to the Prophet and a warning to the disbelievers.

In the name of God, the Lord of Mercy, the Giver of Mercy

¹By the forceful chargers[a] ²raring to go, ³sweeping ahead at full stretch, ⁴overtaking swiftly ⁵to bring the matter to an end, ⁶on the Day when the blast reverberates ⁷and the second blast follows, ⁸hearts will tremble ⁹and eyes will be downcast. ¹⁰They[b] say, 'What? shall we be brought back to life, ¹¹after we have turned into decayed bones?' and they say, ¹²'Such a return is impossible!' ¹³But all it will take is a single blast, ¹⁴and they will be back above ground.

¹⁵Have you [Prophet] heard the story of Moses? ¹⁶His Lord called out to him in the sacred valley of Tuwa: ¹⁷'Go to Pharaoh, for he has exceeded all bounds, ¹⁸and ask him, "Do you want to purify yourself [of sin]? ¹⁹Do you want me to guide you to your Lord, so that you may hold Him in awe?"' ²⁰Moses showed him the great sign, ²¹but he denied it and refused [the faith]. ²²He turned away and hastily ²³gathered his people, proclaiming, ²⁴'I am your supreme lord,' ²⁵so God condemned him to punishment in the life to come as well as in this life: ²⁶there truly is a lesson in this for anyone who stands in awe of God.

²⁷Which is harder to create: you people or the sky that He built, ²⁸raising it high and perfecting it, ²⁹giving darkness to its night and bringing out its morning brightness, ³⁰and the earth that He spread out, ³¹bringing waters and pastures out of it, ³²and setting firm mountains [on it] ³³for you and your animals to enjoy? ³⁴When the

---

[a] There are various interpretations of *nazi'at*. One is that they are angels coming to take the souls at death, which is a fitting oath, as this is a fearful event that cannot be avoided, just as the hour of doom cannot be avoided. Another is that they are horses going out on a military expedition, making the hearts of the enemy tremble. In my opinion this is the most likely (see Sura 100). The suddenness and feeling of alarm in this scene is a symbolic anticipation of the suddenness and shock that will accompany the end of the world.

[b] The disbelievers of Mecca.

great overwhelming event arrives [35] on the Day that man remembers what he has done [36] and Hell is there for all to see, [37] for anyone who has transgressed [38] and preferred the present life [39] Hell will be home: [40] for anyone who feared the meeting with his Lord and restrained himself from base desires, [41] Paradise will be home.

[42] They ask you [Prophet] about the Hour, [43] saying, 'When will it arrive?', but how can you tell [them]? [44] Its time is known only to your Lord; [45] you are only sent to warn those who fear it. [46] On the Day they see it, it will seem they lingered [in this life] an evening at most, or a morning.[a]

[a] Cf. 46: 35.

80. HE FROWNED

A Meccan sura. While the Prophet was speaking to some disbelieving notables, hoping to convert them, a blind Muslim man came up to learn from him, but in his eagerness to attract the disbelievers to Islam, the Prophet frowned at him. The Prophet is then reproached and told not to concern himself with the disbelievers. In the second paragraph there is a condemnation of man's ingratitude: man becomes self-satisfied and forgets his origin and his final return to God.

In the name of God, the Lord of Mercy, the Giver of Mercy

¹He frowned and turned away ²when the blind man came to him— ³for all you know,ᵃ he might have grown in spirit, ⁴or benefited from being taught. ⁵For the self-satisfied one ⁶you go out of your way— ⁷though you are not to be blamed for his lack of spiritual growth— ⁸but from the one who has come to you full of eagerness ⁹and awe ¹⁰you allow yourself to be distracted. ¹¹No indeed! This [Qur'an] is a lesson ¹²from which those who wish to be taught should learn, ¹³[written] on honoured, ¹⁴exalted, pure pages, ¹⁵by the hands of ¹⁶noble and virtuous scribes.

¹⁷Woe to man! How ungrateful he is! ¹⁸From what thing does God create him? ¹⁹He creates him from a droplet, He proportions him, ²⁰He makes the way easy for him, ²¹then He causes him to die and be buried. ²²When He wills, He will raise him up again. ²³Yet manᵇ does not fulfil God's commands. ²⁴Let man consider the food he eats! ²⁵Weᶜ pour down abundant water ²⁶and cause the soil to split open. ²⁷We make grain grow, ²⁸and vines, fresh vegetation, ²⁹olive trees, date palms, ³⁰luscious gardens, ³¹fruits, and fodder: ³²all for you and your livestock to enjoy.

³³When the Deafening Blast comes—³⁴the Day man will flee from his own brother, ³⁵his mother, his father, ³⁶his wife, his children;

ᵃ The shift from talking about the Prophet to addressing him directly reinforces the reproach.

ᵇ Some commentators take this to refer only to disbelievers.

ᶜ This is a shift to the plural of divine majesty to emphasize the magnitude of the action; see *iltifat* in Introduction, p. xx.

[37] each of them will be absorbed in concerns of their own on that Day. [38] On that Day some faces will be beaming, [39] laughing, and rejoicing, [40] but some faces will be dust-stained [41] and covered in darkness—[42] such will be the disbelievers, the licentious.

81. SHROUDED IN DARKNESS

A Meccan sura stressing the fact that people will be confronted by their deeds on Judgement Day, asserting the truth of the Qur'an, and calling people to the right path. It opens with a powerful description of events on that Day, and the title of the sura is taken from this description.

In the name of God, the Lord of Mercy, the Giver of Mercy

¹ When the sun is shrouded in darkness, ² when the stars are dimmed, ³ when the mountains are set in motion, ⁴ when pregnant camels are abandoned, ⁵ when wild beasts are herded together, ⁶ when the seas boil over, ⁷ when souls are sorted into classes, ⁸ when the baby girl buried alive is asked ⁹ for what sin she was killed,*ᵃ* ¹⁰ when the records of deeds are spread open, ¹¹ when the sky is peeled away, ¹² when Hell is made to blaze ¹³ and Paradise brought near; ¹⁴ then every soul will know what it has brought about.

¹⁵ I swear by the planets ¹⁶ that recede, move, and hide, ¹⁷ by the night that descends, ¹⁸ by the dawn that softly breathes: ¹⁹ this is the speech of a noble messenger,*ᵇ* ²⁰ who possesses great strength and is held in honour by the Lord of the Throne—²¹ he is obeyed there and worthy of trust. ²² Your companion*ᶜ* is not mad: ²³ he did see him*ᵈ* on the clear horizon. ²⁴ He does not withhold what is revealed to him from beyond. ²⁵ This is not the word of an outcast devil.

²⁶ So where are you [people] going? ²⁷ This is a message for all people; ²⁸ for those who wish to take the straight path. ²⁹ But you will only wish to do so by the will of God, the Lord of all people.

ᵃ Cf. 16: 58–9. The pagan Arab habit of female infanticide.

ᵇ Gabriel.

ᶜ Addressed to the Meccans. The companion is the Prophet.

ᵈ Gabriel.

82. TORN APART

A Meccan sura dealing with man's ingratitude and his failure to concede that the Day of Judgement will come. Again, the sura opens with a powerful description of events on the Day of Judgement and the title is taken from this description.

In the name of God, the Lord of Mercy, the Giver of Mercy

[1] When the sky is torn apart, [2] when the stars are scattered, [3] when the seas burst forth, [4] when graves turn inside out; [5] each soul will know what it has done and what it has left undone. [6] Mankind, what has lured you away from God, [7] your generous Lord who created you, shaped you, proportioned you, [8] in whatever form He chose? [9] Yet you still take the Judgement to be a lie! [10] Over you stand [11] watchers, noble recorders [12] who know what you do: [13] the good will live in bliss, [14] and the wicked will burn in the Fire. [15] They will enter it on the Day of Judgement [16] and they will find no escape. [17] What will explain to you what the Day of Judgement is? [18] Yes! What will explain to you what the Day of Judgement is? [19] The Day when no soul will be able to do anything for another; on that Day, command will belong to God.[a]

---

[a] Or 'everything is up to God'.

83. THOSE WHO GIVE SHORT MEASURE

A Meccan sura. The practice of cheating appears to have been prevalent in Mecca, and is strongly condemned here and elsewhere in the Qur'an (e.g. 11: 84–8; 7: 85). In the sura the fate of the cheats and disbelievers is contrasted with the delight in store for the good.

In the name of God, the Lord of Mercy, the Giver of Mercy

¹ Woe to those who give short measure, ² who demand of other people full measure for themselves, ³ but give less than they should when it is they who weigh or measure for others! ⁴ Do these people not realize that they will be raised up ⁵ on a mighty Day, ⁶ a Day when everyone will stand before the Lord of the Worlds? ⁷ No indeed! The list of the wicked is in Sijjin[a] — ⁸ what will explain to you what Sijjin is? — ⁹ a clearly numbered list. ¹⁰ Woe on that day to the deniers, ¹¹ those who deny the Day of Judgement! ¹² Only the evil aggressor denies it: ¹³ when Our revelations are recited to him, he says, 'Ancient fables!' ¹⁴ No indeed! Their hearts are encrusted with what they have done. ¹⁵ No indeed! On that Day they will be screened off from their Lord, ¹⁶ they will burn in Hell, ¹⁷ and they will be told, 'This is what you called a lie.'

¹⁸ No indeed! The list of the truly good is in 'Illiyyin[b] — ¹⁹ what will explain to you what 'Illiyyin is? — ²⁰ a clearly written list, ²¹ witnessed by those brought near.[c] ²² The truly good will live in bliss, ²³ seated on couches, gazing around. ²⁴ You will recognize on their faces the radiance of bliss. ²⁵ They will be served a sealed nectar, ²⁶ its seal [perfumed with] a fragrant herb[d] — let those who strive, strive for this — ²⁷ mixed with the water of Tasnim,[e] ²⁸ a spring from which those brought near will drink. ²⁹ The wicked used to laugh at the believers — ³⁰ they would wink at one another when the believers

---

[a] The root of this word, *s–j–n*, is the same as the one for *sijn* meaning 'prison'. The form is intensive.

[b] The root of this word, *'–l–w*, relates to height. The form is intensive.

[c] The elect. See also verse 28.

[d] One meaning of *misk* (also 'musk').

[e] The root of this word, *s–n–m*, suggests height and opulence.

passed by them, [31] joke about them when they got back to their own people, [32] and say, when they saw them, 'These people are misguided,' [33] though they were not sent to be their keepers—[34] so today*a* the believers are laughing at the disbelievers [35] as they sit on couches, gazing around. [36] Have the disbelievers [not] been repaid for their deeds?

---

a This is in the present tense, as if described on that Day.

84. RIPPED APART

A Meccan sura dealing with the inevitability of man's meeting with his Lord on the Day of Judgement. The obedience of the sky and earth is contrasted with the disobedience of the disbelievers. The reaction of the believers and of the disbelievers on the Day of Judgement is described. The title is taken from the description of events on that Day in the opening verse.

In the name of God, the Lord of Mercy, the Giver of Mercy

[1] When the sky is ripped apart, [2] in rightful obedience to its Lord's command; [3] when the earth is levelled out, [4] casts out its contents, and becomes empty, [5] in rightful obedience to its Lord's command, [6] you humans, toiling laboriously towards your Lord, will meet Him. [7] Whoever is given his record in his right hand [8] will have an easy reckoning [9] and return to his people well pleased, [10] but whoever is given his record from behind his back [11] will cry out for destruction: [12] he will burn in the blazing Fire. [13] He used to live among his people well pleased. [14] He thought he would never return [to his Lord]— [15] indeed he will! His Lord was watching him. [16] I swear by the glow of sunset, [17] by the night and what it covers, [18] by the full moon, [19] you will progress from stage to stage.[a]

[20] So why do they not believe? [21] Why, when the Qur'an is read to them, do they not prostrate themselves in prayer? [22] The disbelievers reject the Qur'an—[23] God knows best what they keep hidden inside—[24] so give them news of a painful torment. [25] But those who believe and do good deeds will have a never-ending reward.

[a] As the sun sets, followed by darkness, which is then illuminated by the moon, you will move by stages from death to resurrection.

85. THE CONSTELLATIONS

This Meccan sura strengthened the heart of the Prophet and his followers by referring to the fate of those who tortured earlier believers. The title expresses God's power over the whole universe, from the stars in the sky to the evildoers referred to in this sura. Indeed, His all-encompassing power is a recurring theme throughout the sura.

In the name of God, the Lord of Mercy, the Giver of Mercy

¹ By the sky with its constellations, ² by the promised Day, ³ by the Witness[a] and that which is witnessed, ⁴ damned were the makers of the trench,[b] ⁵ the makers of the fuel-stoked fire! ⁶ They sat down ⁷ to watch what they were doing to the believers. ⁸ Their only grievance against them was their faith in God, the Mighty, the Praiseworthy, ⁹ to whom all control over the heavens and earth belongs: God is witness over all things.

¹⁰ For those who persecute believing men and women, and do not repent afterwards, there will be the torment of Hell and burning. ¹¹ But for those who believe and do good deeds there will be Gardens graced with flowing streams: that is the great triumph. ¹² [Prophet], your Lord's punishment is truly stern—¹³ it is He who brings people to life, and will restore them to life again—¹⁴ and He is the Most Forgiving, the Most Loving. ¹⁵ The Lord of the Glorious Throne, ¹⁶ He does whatever He will. ¹⁷ Have you [not] heard the stories of the forces ¹⁸ of Pharaoh and Thamud? ¹⁹ Yet still the disbelievers persist in denial. ²⁰ God surrounds them all.

²¹ This is truly a glorious Qur'an ²² written on a preserved Tablet.[c]

---

[a] God.

[b] Various suggestions are made as to who these trench-makers were, among others, that they were those commanded to make a trench by a Jewish ruler of sixth-century Yemen in order to torture Christians, also that the passage could refer to Nimrod's treatment of Abraham (Razi).

[c] God keeps this with Him.

86. THE NIGHT-COMER

A Meccan sura that focuses on a series of examples of things coming out: the piercing night-star, spurting semen, the baby that bursts out of the womb, and plants that sprout out of the ground. All of these are used to illustrate resurrection from the grave.

In the name of God, the Lord of Mercy, the Giver of Mercy

¹By the sky and the night-comer—²What will explain to you what the night-comer is? ³The piercing star—⁴there is a watcher over every soul.

⁵Man should reflect on what he was created from. ⁶He is created from spurting fluid, ⁷then he*ᵃ* emerges from between the backbone and breastbone:*ᵇ* ⁸God is certainly able to bring him back to life. ⁹On the Day when secrets are laid bare ¹⁰he will have no power and no one to help him.

¹¹By the sky and its recurring rain, ¹²by the earth that bursts forth! ¹³This is truly a decisive statement; ¹⁴it is not something to be taken lightly. ¹⁵They plot and scheme, ¹⁶but so do I: ¹⁷[Prophet], let the disbelievers be for their short while.

ᵃ The pronoun here is taken to refer to the person rather than the fluid.

ᵇ Of the mother, where she carries the baby. He emerges from the womb as he will emerge from the grave.

87. THE MOST HIGH

A Meccan sura reassuring the Prophet that God will help him and urging him to continue with his mission. The temporary nature of this world is highlighted through mention of the short life of green pasture (cf. 10: 24; 18: 45).

In the name of God, the Lord of Mercy, the Giver of Mercy

[1] [Prophet], glorify the name of your Lord the Most High, [2] who created [all things] in due proportion; [3] who determined their destinies and guided them; [4] who brought out the green pasture [5] then made it dark debris. [6] [Prophet], We shall teach you [the Qur'an] and you will not forget—[7] unless God wishes; He knows both what is open and what is hidden—[8] We shall show you the easy way. [9] So give warning, if warning will help.[a] [10] Those who stand in awe of God will heed the warning, [11] but it will be ignored by the most wicked, [12] who will enter the Great Fire, [13] where they will neither die nor live.[b] [14] The triumphant ones will be those who purify themselves, [15] remember the name of their Lord, and pray. [16] Yet you [people] prefer the life of this world, [17] even though the Hereafter is better and more lasting. [18] All this is in the earlier scriptures, [19] the scriptures of Abraham and Moses.

[a] Razi cites many instances in the Qur'an where this structure conveys the meaning 'warn [everyone], whether [or not] warning will help'.

[b] They will neither be granted the respite of death, nor be able to enjoy their continued state of life (Razi).

88. THE OVERWHELMING EVENT

This Meccan sura serves to warn the disbelievers, encourage the Prophet and the believers, and absolve him of responsibility for the disbelievers. The title comes from the description of events on the Day of Judgement in the first verse, and the downcast faces of the disbelievers on that Day are contrasted with the radiant faces of the believers.

In the name of God, the Lord of Mercy, the Giver of Mercy

¹ Have you heard tell*ᵃ* [Prophet] about the Overwhelming Event? ² On that Day, there will be downcast faces, ³ toiling and weary, ⁴ as they enter the blazing Fire ⁵ and are forced to drink from a boiling spring, ⁶ with no food for them except bitter dry thorns ⁷ that neither nourish nor satisfy hunger. ⁸ On that Day there will also be faces radiant with bliss, ⁹ well pleased with their labour, ¹⁰ in a lofty garden, ¹¹ where they will hear no idle talk, ¹² with a flowing spring, ¹³ raised couches, ¹⁴ goblets placed before them, ¹⁵ cushions set in rows, ¹⁶ and carpets spread. ¹⁷ Do the disbelievers not see how rain clouds*ᵇ* are formed, ¹⁸ how the heavens are lifted, ¹⁹ how the mountains are raised high, ²⁰ how the earth is spread out?

²¹ So [Prophet] warn them: your only task is to give warning, ²² you are not there to control them. ²³ As for those who turn away and disbelieve, God will inflict the greatest torment upon them. They will finally come before Us, ²⁴ and We shall call them to account.

ᵃ An Arabic convention to draw attention to what follows.

ᵇ The word *ibl* can mean 'camel' as well as 'rain cloud'. However, the latter is better in this context amongst all the other geographical images presented. Rain is often used to illustrate the concept of resurrection.

89. DAYBREAK

A Meccan sura in which God emphasizes (by oath) that the tyrants of the Prophet's time will be like those He dealt with in the past. The sura compares the destiny of the ungrateful with that of the souls at peace.

In the name of God, the Lord of Mercy, the Giver of Mercy

¹By the Daybreak, ²by the Ten Nights,*ᵃ* ³by the even and the odd,*ᵇ* ⁴by the passing night*ᶜ*—⁵is this oath strong enough for a rational person?

⁶Have you [Prophet] considered how your Lord dealt with the people of 'Ad,*ᵈ* ⁷of Iram, the city of lofty pillars, ⁸whose like has never been built in any land, ⁹and the Thamud,*ᵉ* who hewed into the rocks in the valley, ¹⁰and the mighty and powerful*ᶠ* Pharaoh? ¹¹All of them committed excesses in their lands, ¹²and spread corruption there: ¹³your Lord let a scourge of punishment loose on them. ¹⁴Your Lord is always watchful.

¹⁵The nature of man*ᵍ* is that, when his Lord tries him through honour and blessings, he says, 'My Lord has honoured me,' ¹⁶but when He tries him through the restriction of his provision, he says, 'My Lord has humiliated me.' ¹⁷No indeed! You [people] do not honour orphans, ¹⁸you do not urge one another to feed the poor,

ᵃ This refers to the first ten nights of the month of Dhu 'l-Hijjah, sacred before and after the Prophet's time, which culminate in the Hajj pilgrimage.

ᵇ This has been interpreted in many ways: as a reference to numbers (as translated here); or e.g. as the multiple (God's creation) and the One (God Himself).

ᶜ The complement of this oath is left unmentioned, to be understood from what follows. The commentators use this to complete the oath with 'they will be punished' based on the context of what follows. The omission reinforces the oath, as one has to think more carefully in order to grasp it, a device known in Arabic rhetoric as *hadhf al-jawab* (cf. 38: 1; 50: 1).

ᵈ See 26: 123 ff.

ᵉ See 26: 141 ff.

ᶠ *Dhu'l-awtad*, 'of the stakes', is explained as a Bedouin expression conveying strength and power. Another interpretation is that Pharaoh used stakes as implements of torture.

ᵍ *Insan* 'man' occurs sixty-five times in the Qur'an. It applies to both men and women, as of course does the generic 'man' in English.

¹⁹ you consume inheritance[a] greedily, ²⁰ and you love wealth with a passion. ²¹ No indeed! When the earth is pounded to dust, pounded and pounded, ²² when your Lord comes with the angels, rank upon rank, ²³ when Hell is that Day brought near—on that Day man will take heed, but what good will that be to him then? ²⁴ He will say, 'Would that I had provided for this life to come!' ²⁵ On that Day, no one will punish as He punishes, ²⁶ and no one will bind as He binds. ²⁷ '[But] you, soul at peace:[b] ²⁸ return to your Lord well pleased and well pleasing; ²⁹ go in among My servants; ³⁰ and into My Garden.'

[a] This could refer to the inheritance of orphans (see 4: 2 and 4: 10) or inheritance generally.

[b] At peace through remembering God in this life and the next (cf. 13: 28), unlike the disbeliever who only takes heed on the Day of Judgement, when it will not benefit him. There is *iltifat* here: the sinners are mentioned in the third person while the honoured are addressed directly by their Lord.

90. THE CITY

Revealed in Mecca. The point of this sura is that man is created to work and be judged. He should therefore seek to do good deeds rather than indulge in arrogance and wastefulness.

In the name of God, the Lord of Mercy, the Giver of Mercy

[1] I swear by this city[a] —[2] you [Prophet] are an inhabitant of this city [3] by parent and offspring—[4] that We have created man for toil and trial. [5] Does he think that no one will have power over him? [6] 'I have squandered great wealth,' he says. [7] Does he think no one observes him? [8] Did We not give him eyes, [9] a tongue, lips, [10] and point out to him the two clear ways [of good and evil]? [11] Yet he has not attempted the steep path. [12] What will explain to you what the steep path is? [13] It is to free a slave, [14] to feed at a time of hunger [15] an orphaned relative [16] or a poor person in distress—[17] and to be one of those who believe and urge one another to steadfastness and compassion. [18] Those who do this will be on the right-hand side, [19] but those who disbelieve in Our revelations will be on the left-hand side, [20] and the Fire will close in on them.

[a] Mecca.

91. THE SUN

A Meccan sura, the central theme of which is purifying or corrupting the soul, with the tribe of Thamud given as an example of corruption.

In the name of God, the Lord of Mercy, the Giver of Mercy

[1] By the sun in its morning brightness [2] and by the moon as it follows it, [3] by the day as it displays the sun's glory [4] and by the night as it conceals it, [5] by the sky and how He built it [6] and by the earth and how He spread it, [7] by the soul and how He formed it [8] and inspired it [to know] its own rebellion and piety! [9] The one who purifies his soul succeeds [10] and the one who corrupts it fails. [11] In their arrogant cruelty, the people of Thamud[a] called [their messenger] a liar, [12] when the most wicked man among them rose [against him].[b] [13] The messenger of God said to them, 'This is God's camel, let it drink,' [14] but they called him a liar and hamstrung her. Their Lord destroyed them for their crime and levelled them. [15] He did not hesitate[c] to punish[d] them.

[a] See e.g. 7: 73–9 (on the tribe of Thamud).

[b] Cf. 54: 29.

[c] Literally 'he does not fear'.

[d] One of the lexical meanings of *'uqba* is *jaza*', here 'to punish'.

92. THE NIGHT

A Meccan sura showing the consequences of the paths people choose and emphasizing God's guidance and warning.

In the name of God, the Lord of Mercy, the Giver of Mercy

[1] By the enshrouding night, [2] by the radiant day, [3] by the creation of male and female! [4] The ways you take differ greatly. [5] There is the one who gives, who is mindful of God, [6] who testifies to goodness—[7] We shall smooth his way towards ease. [8] There is the one who is miserly, who is self-satisfied, [9] who denies goodness—[10] We shall smooth his way towards hardship [11] and his wealth will not help him as he falls.

[12] Our part is to provide guidance—[13] this world and the next belong to Us—[14] so I warn you about the raging Fire, [15] in which none but the most wicked one will burn, [16] who denied [the truth], and turned away. [17] The most pious one will be spared this—[18] who gives his wealth away as self-purification, [19] not to return a favour to anyone [20] but for the sake of his Lord the Most High [a]—[21] and he will be well pleased.

***

[a] Literally 'for the sake of the Face of his Lord'.

93. THE MORNING BRIGHTNESS

An early Meccan sura addressed to the Prophet, to reassure him, when he had not received revelation for some time, that his Lord had not forsaken him.

In the name of God, the Lord of Mercy, the Giver of Mercy

[1] By the morning brightness [2] and by the night when it grows still, [3] your Lord has not forsaken you [Prophet], nor does He hate you, [4] and the future will be better for you than the past; [5] your Lord is sure to give you so much that you will be well satisfied. [6] Did He not find you an orphan and shelter you? [7] Did He not find you lost and guide you? [8] Did He not find you in need and make you self-sufficient?

[9] So do not be harsh with the orphan [10] and do not chide the one who asks for help; [11] talk about the blessings of your Lord.

94. RELIEF

This Meccan sura, addressed to the Prophet, is a continuation of the reassurance and encouragement given in Sura 93.

In the name of God, the Lord of Mercy, the Giver of Mercy

[1] Did We not relieve your heart for you [Prophet], [2] and remove the burden [3] that weighed so heavily on your back, [4] and raise your reputation high? [5] So truly where there is hardship there is also ease; [6] truly where there is hardship there is also ease. [7] The moment you are freed [of one task] work on, [8] and turn to your Lord with your requests.

95. THE FIG

A Meccan sura questioning how man can deny the Judgement, and empha-
sizing the importance of faith and good deeds.

In the name of God, the Lord of Mercy, the Giver of Mercy

¹By the fig, by the olive, ²by Mount Sinai, ³by this safe town,*ᵃ*
⁴We create man in the finest state ⁵then reduce him to the lowest of
the low, ⁶except those who believe and do good deeds—⁷they will
have an unfailing reward. After this, what makes you deny the
Judgement?*ᵇ* ⁸Is God not the best of judges?

ᵃ Mecca.
ᵇ Or 'who could show that you [Prophet] are lying about the Judgement?' (Razi)

96. THE CLINGING FORM^a

A Meccan sura named after the term 'alaq in verse 2. The first five verses are known to be the first revelation of the Qur'an when the Prophet was instructed to read. The second part came later to show that man transgresses when he becomes self-satisfied (as exemplified by a specific individual, Abu Jahl).

In the name of God, the Lord of Mercy, the Giver of Mercy

¹Read! In the name of your Lord who created: ²He created man^b from a clinging form. ³Read! Your Lord is the Most Bountiful One ⁴who taught by [means of] the pen, ⁵who taught man what he did not know.

⁶But man exceeds all bounds ⁷when he thinks he is self-sufficient: ⁸[Prophet], all will return to your Lord. ⁹Have you seen the man who forbids ¹⁰[Our] servant to pray? ¹¹Have you seen whether he is rightly guided, ¹²or encourages true piety? ¹³Have you seen whether he denies the truth and turns away from it? ¹⁴Does he not realize that God sees all? ¹⁵No! If he does not stop, We shall drag him by his forehead^c—¹⁶his lying, sinful forehead. ¹⁷Let him summon his comrades; ¹⁸We shall summon the guards of Hell. ¹⁹No! Do not obey him [Prophet]: bow down^d in worship and draw close.

---

^a A stage in the development of a foetus (cf. 22: 5), i.e. embryo. *'Alaq* can also mean anything that clings: a clot of blood, a leech, even a lump of mud. All these meanings involve the basic idea of clinging or sticking. Clinging indicates a state of total dependence in contrast with verse 7.

^b See note to 89: 15.

^c In Hell. Many translators give 'forelock' instead of 'forehead' (cf. 54: 48). His head is sinful, not his forelock.

^d *Sujud* is a position in the Muslim prayer with head, hands, knees, and toes on the ground, but not the rest of the body as in 'prostration'.

97. THE NIGHT OF GLORY

This Meccan sura celebrates the night when the first revelation of the Qur'an was sent down.

In the name of God, the Lord of Mercy, the Giver of Mercy

[1] We sent it down on the Night of Glory. [2] What will explain to you what that Night of Glory is? [3] The Night of Glory is better than a thousand months; [4] on that night the angels and the Spirit[a] descend again and again with their Lord's permission on every task; [5] [there is] peace that night until the break of dawn.

[a] The Angel Gabriel.

98. CLEAR EVIDENCE

A Medinan sura that takes its title from the clear evidence demanded by the disbelievers before they will believe. It spells out the basic tenets of faith, and contrasts the Fire of Hell with the lasting bliss that will be enjoyed by the faithful.

In the name of God, the Lord of Mercy, the Giver of Mercy

[1] The disbelievers—those of the People of the Book who disbelieve and the idolaters—were not about to change their ways until they were sent clear evidence, [2] a messenger from God, reading out pages [blessed with] purity, [3] containing true scriptures. [4] Those who were given the Scripture became divided only after they were sent this clear evidence, [5] though all they were ordered to do was worship God alone, sincerely devoting their religion to Him as people of true faith, keep up the prayer, and pay the prescribed alms, for that is the true religion. [6] The disbelievers—those of the People of the Book who disbelieve and the idolaters—will have the Fire of Hell, there to remain for ever. They are the worst of creation.

[7] Those who believe and do good deeds are the best of creation. [8] Their reward is with their Lord: Gardens of everlasting bliss graced with flowing streams. God is well pleased with them and they with Him. All this is for those who stand in awe of their Lord.

99. THE EARTHQUAKE

A Medinan sura, one of a series of suras that deal with scenes from the Day of Judgement. Compare Suras 81, 82, 101, and others.

In the name of God, the Lord of Mercy, the Giver of Mercy

[1] When the earth is shaken violently in its [last] quaking, [2] when the earth throws out its burdens,[a] [3] when man cries, 'What is happening to it?'; [4] on that Day, it will tell all [5] because your Lord will inspire it [to do so]. [6] On that Day, people will come forward in separate groups to be shown their deeds: [7] whoever has done an atom's-weight of good will see it, [8] but whoever has done an atom's-weight of evil will see that.

[a] This refers to the dead being thrown out of their graves.

100. THE CHARGING STEEDS

An early Meccan sura in which God swears by the warhorses He has subjected to man's use[a] that man is ungrateful and misguided.

In the name of God, the Lord of Mercy, the Giver of Mercy

[1] By the charging steeds that pant [2] and strike sparks with their hooves, [3] who make dawn raids, [4] raising a cloud of dust, [5] and plunging into the midst of the enemy, [6] man is ungrateful to his Lord—[7] and He is witness to this[b]—[8] he is truly excessive in his love of wealth.

[9] Does he not know that when the contents of graves burst forth, [10] when the secrets of men's hearts are uncovered, on that Day, [11] their Lord will be fully aware of them all?

---

[a] Cf. 36: 71–2; 43: 12–13.

[b] Or man will by his own actions be a witness against himself on the Day of Judgement.

101. THE CRASHING BLOW

A Meccan sura which gives some scenes from the Resurrection and Judgement.

In the name of God, the Lord of Mercy, the Giver of Mercy

¹ The Crashing Blow! ² What is the Crashing Blow? ³ What will explain to you what the Crashing Blow is? ⁴ On a Day when people will be like scattered moths ⁵ and the mountains like tufts of wool, ⁶ the one whose good deeds are heavy on the scales ⁷ will have a pleasant life, ⁸ but the one whose good deeds are light ⁹ will have the Bottomless Pit for his home *a* — ¹⁰ what will explain to you what that is? — ¹¹ a blazing fire.

a Literally 'his mother is the bottomless pit'.

102. STRIVING FOR MORE

A Meccan sura which criticizes man's preoccupation with worldly wealth and stresses that he will be brought to account on the Day of Resurrection.

In the name of God, the Lord of Mercy, the Giver of Mercy

¹ Striving for more distracts you ² until you go into your graves. *ᵃ* ³ No indeed! You will come to know. ⁴ No indeed! In the end you will come to know. ⁵ No indeed! If only you knew for certain. ⁶ You will most definitely see Hellfire, ⁷ you will see it with the eye of certainty. ⁸ On that Day, you will be asked about your pleasures.

ᵃ Literally 'until you visit the graves'. Their stay in the grave is like a short visit (cf. 46: 35).

103. THE DECLINING DAY [a]

A Meccan sura showing the way to salvation. The image of a declining day suggests the stage in the day, or in life, when only a short while is left for those wishing to make up for lost time.

In the name of God, the Lord of Mercy, the Giver of Mercy

[1] I swear by the declining day [2] that man is [deep] in loss, [3] except for those who believe, do good deeds, urge one another to the truth, and urge one another to steadfastness.

---

[a] Other interpretations of the title include 'Time' and 'The Flight of Time'.

104. THE BACKBITER

A Meccan sura that condemns the greedy backbiter and gives a description of Hell.

In the name of God, the Lord of Mercy, the Giver of Mercy

[1] Woe to every fault-finding backbiter[a] [2] who amasses riches, counting them over, [3] thinking they will make him live for ever. [4] No indeed! He will be thrust into the Crusher! [5] What will explain to you what the Crusher is? [6] It is God's Fire, made to blaze, [7] which rises over people's hearts. [8] It closes in on them [9] in towering columns.[b]

[a] Said to refer either to al-Akhnas ibn Shurayq or to al-Walid ibn al-Mughira (cf. note to 74: 11).
[b] Cf. 77: 30–3.

105. THE ELEPHANT

This sura is a reference to events that happened in 570 CE, the year of the Prophet's birth, when the army of Abraha (a Christian ruler of Yemen), which included war elephants, marched to attack Mecca, destroy the Ka'ba, and divert pilgrims to the new cathedral in San'a. The destruction of this army is cited here to encourage the believers and warn the disbelievers.

In the name of God, the Lord of Mercy, the Giver of Mercy

¹ Do you [Prophet] not see how your Lord dealt with the army of the elephant? ² Did He not utterly confound their plans? ³ He sent ranks of birds against them, ⁴ pelting them with pellets of hard-baked clay: ⁵ He made them [like] cropped stubble.

106. QURAYSH

This Meccan sura connects grammatically with the previous one's account of how God defeated the threat to Mecca posed by Abraha, so making it safe for the tribe of Quraysh to continue their trading journeys.

In the name of God, the Lord of Mercy, the Giver of Mercy

¹[He did this] to make the Quraysh feel secure, ²secure in their winter and summer journeys. *a* ³So let them worship the Lord of this House: *b* ⁴who provides them with food to ward off hunger, safety to ward off fear.

---

a Their two annual trade caravans—to Yemen in winter and to Syria in summer—on which the prosperity of the Quraysh depended.

b The Ka'ba.

107. COMMON KINDNESSES

A Meccan sura which states that denying the Judgement leads to cruelty to orphans, praying only for show, and begrudging even common kindnesses.

In the name of God, the Lord of Mercy, the Giver of Mercy

[1][Prophet], have you considered the person who denies the Judgement? [2]It is he who pushes aside the orphan [3]and does not urge others to feed the needy. [4]So woe to those who pray [5]but are heedless of their prayer; [6]those who are all show [7]and forbid common kindnesses.

108. ABUNDANCE

When the Prophet lost his last son, an opponent who hated him taunted him with being 'cut off' without posterity. This Meccan sura comes to reassure the Prophet and as a retort to his enemy.

In the name of God, the Lord of Mercy, the Giver of Mercy

[1] We have truly given abundance[a] to you [Prophet]—[2] pray to your Lord and make your sacrifice to Him alone—[3] it is the one who hates you who has been cut off.

---

[a] The word *kawthar*, 'abundance', is also interpreted here as referring to a specific river in Paradise.

109. THE DISBELIEVERS

Some of the Meccan idolaters suggested to the Prophet as a compromise that he should worship their gods for a year and they should worship his for a year. This was the reply.

In the name of God, the Lord of Mercy, the Giver of Mercy

[1] Say [Prophet], 'Disbelievers: [2] I do not worship what you worship, [3] you do not worship what I worship, [4] I will never worship what you worship, [5] you will never worship what I worship: [a] [6] you have your religion and I have mine.'

[a] If you keep to your present gods (see Zamakhshari, *al-Kashshaf*, vol. iv).

110. HELP

A Medinan sura said to be one of the last revelations the Prophet received before his death.

In the name of God, the Lord of Mercy, the Giver of Mercy

[1] When God's help comes and He opens up[a] your way [Prophet], [2] when you see people embracing God's faith in crowds, [3] celebrate the praise of your Lord and ask His forgiveness: He is always ready to accept repentance.

---

[a] This sura is mainly understood by interpreters to refer to the surrender of Mecca to the Prophet. Accordingly many translate the word *fath* as 'victory', although there was no fighting. See also Sura 48, *Surat al-Fath*. *Fath* in classical Arabic means 'opening' or 'decision'. In a prayer, the Prophet says, 'Lord, open the gates of your Mercy for me.' Sura 1 is called *al-Fatiha*, as it opens the Qur'an. In 7: 89, *iftah* means 'decide between us and our enemy'.

111. PALM FIBRE

This sura refers to an uncle of the Prophet who opposed him fiercely, as did his wife. He insulted the Prophet with 'Tabbak yadak' ('may your hands be ruined'). This Meccan sura is the retort.

In the name of God, the Lord of Mercy, the Giver of Mercy

[1] May the hands of Abu Lahab be ruined! May he be ruined too! [2] Neither his wealth nor his gains will help him: [3] he will burn in the Flaming Fire,[a] [4] and so will his wife, the firewood-carrier,[b] [5] with a palm-fibre rope around her neck.

---

[a] Abu Lahab means 'Flame Man' and this verse contains a pun on this name.

[b] She used to tie bunches of thorns with ropes of twisted palm fibre and throw them into the Prophet's path.

112. PURITY [OF FAITH]

This sura is unusual in having as its title a term not mentioned in the body of the sura. Ikhlas *conveys the meaning of sincerity in one's religion and total dedication to the One true God. Because of the importance of this theme in Islam, the Prophet said that this sura, despite its brevity, was equal to one-third of the Qur'an.*

In the name of God, the Lord of Mercy, the Giver of Mercy

[1] Say, 'He is God the One, [2] God the eternal.[a] [3] He fathered no one nor was He fathered. [4] No one is comparable to Him.'

---

[a] *Samad*: other commonly held interpretations include 'self-sufficient' and 'sought by all' (Razi).

113. DAYBREAK

A Meccan sura used as an invocation against evil.

In the name of God, the Lord of Mercy, the Giver of Mercy

¹ Say [Prophet], 'I seek refuge with the Lord of daybreak ² against the evil in what He has created, ³ the evil in the night when darkness gathers, ⁴ the evil in witches when they blow on knots,ᵃ ⁵ the evil in the envier when he envies.'

ᵃ Said to be a means of practising witchcraft and casting spells.

114. PEOPLE

Another Meccan sura commonly used as an invocation against evil.

In the name of God, the Lord of Mercy, the Giver of Mercy

[1] Say, 'I seek refuge with the Lord of people, [2] the Controller[a] of people, [3] the God of people, [4] against the evil of the slinking whisperer—[5] who whispers into the hearts of people—[6] whether they be jinn or people.'

[a] Or 'King' or 'Master'.

INDEX

Aaron (Moses' brother) 104; blessed
288; God's guidance 86; grace 193; as
messenger 134, 229; mission to the
Egyptians 232; Moses requests his
support from God 247; as Moses'
spokesman 197; receives the
Scriptures 205; rejection by
disbelievers 217; and the worship of
the golden calf 200

Abdul Muttalib (Muhammad's
grandfather) x, xxxvii

Abdullah (Muhammad's father) x, xxxvii

Abel (Adam's son) 70

Abraha (Christian ruler of Yemen),
threatens Mecca 437, 438

Abraham xvii, 122, 348; as an example
368–9; builds the Ka'ba x, 17 n. *a*,
18 n. *c*; ceases to pray on behalf of his
disbelieving father 126; condemns
idolatry 205–6, 234, 253, 317, and is
blessed with the birth of Isaac 287;
devotion to God 14–15, 16, 292;
dialogue with God xx; as
encouragement to believers to be
mindful of God 359, 361; example
166, 209; faith 41; forbidden to plead
for Lot's people 141; grace 193;
guests, and the destruction of Lot's
people 343–4; monotheism 85–6;
prayers for the prosperity of Mecca
158, 160–1; questioning of the
prophecy of Isaac's birth 163–4;
receives the same message as that given
to Muhammad 312; rite of pilgrimage
209, 211; standing before God 39

Abraham, people 212; chosen by God 37

Abraham, wife, and the prophecy of
Isaac's birth 141, 343–4

Abu Bakr: father of 'A'isha 120, 221 n. *c*,
flees from Mecca and hides in a cave
xxx; Rightly Guided Caliph xiii;
preservation of the Qur'an xvi, xxxvii

Abu Hanifa, women permitted to be
judges xxv

Abu Lahab (uncle and opponent of
Muhammad), condemnation 443

Abu Talib (Muhammad's uncle) x, xi,
xxxvii

'Ad (Hud's people) 159, 212; arrogance
290; condemnation 254;
wronged themselves 122; destruction
229, 327, 329, 348; disbelief 99,
139–40, as example to those who
disbelieved 340, 344; disbelief 159;
punishment 303, 308, 351;
punishment denied 387; rejection of
Hud 235–6; corruption condemned
420

Adam: angels submit to 94–5; chosen
by God 37; creation and favoured
over the angels 4, 7; disobedience 95,
201; without a father as was
Jesus 34, 38–9

'*adhab* 5 n. *c*

adna al-jilbab 271 n. *b*

adoption 266

adultery 220–1, 221–2; forbidden 177;
marriage rather than adultery 53;
punishments for 71 n. *b*

advocacy, forbidden in the event of the
betrayal of trust 61

afterlife 67, 82, 87, 285–7; contrast with
temporal life 256

Ahmad (name of Muhammad) 370

'A'isha (Muhammad's wife), accused of
adultery falsely 220, 221

'*alaq* 428 n. *a*

Alexander the Great, identification with
Dhu 'l-Qarnayn 188 n. *a*

Ali, Abdullah Ysuf, translation of the
Qur'an xxviii, xxxviii

'Ali (Rightly Guided Caliph) xiii

al-'alamin 3 n. *e*

allies, disbelieving relatives not to be
allies [against Muslims] 118

almsgiving xix, 30–2, 120, 177, 259, 422,
424, 425; charitable spending
(*yunfiquna*) 5 n. *b*; commanded before
it is too late 374–5; commendation
61; before conversations between
believers and Muhammad 363;
continuation 221; during pilgrimages

almsgiving (*cont.*):
24; as marks of belief 19; rewards for
377; standing of blood-relatives in calls
upon believers 266
am 346 n. *a*
Amina (Muhammad's mother) x, xxxvii
amr xxxi
angels 380; ascent to God 389; blessing
239 n. *b*; as bringers of justice 162;
creation 277; dealing out of
punishment to disbelievers 333; deny
being worshipped 275; disbelievers'
claims about refuted 347–8; encourage
believers 309; as gatekeepers of Hell
397–8; gender xxxiii, as the daughters
of God 169 n. *b*, 177, 183 n. *a*, 195, 204
n. *a*, denial of the pagan belief 346 n. *b*,
refutation 191, 285, 288–9, 347 n. *g*,
348, seen as God's servants 316–17,
318 n. *b*, 319; guardian angels 154; lack
of arrogance 169; as messengers of
God 166; prayers for the salvation of
believers 301–2; as receptors of men at
the Day of Judgement 341; record
people's deeds in writing 384 n. *a*;
role on the Day of Judgement 228,
387; subordination to Adam 4, 7, 94–5,
163, 179, 186, 201, 293; worshipped as
gods x
anger, attribution 3 n. *f*
animals: garlanding 77; *see also* creation;
livestock
ansar xii
anxiety 389
apostasy 24, 63, 173
Arabian peninsula, spread of Islam xiii
Arabic: structures and idioms, effects on
translation xxxi–xxxii; use in the
Qur'an for clarity 311, 316, 323, 328;
use in Scripture 307, 310
Arabs: desert Arabs 124, 125, 127,
condemned for disbelief 335,
presumptuousness 339; idolatry 169
n. *a*, 169 n. *b*; Meccan Arabs, reactions
to the Qur'an 393–4; refusal to believe
revelation of the Qur'an through
Muhammad 237; pagan Arabs, divorce
practices disallowed 362 n. *a*
Arafat 22, 22 n. *f*
Arberry, Arthur J., translation of the
Qur'an xxviii, xxxviii
Ark [of the Covenant] 28

arrogant, condemnation 245
'arsh 136 n. *b*
Asad, Muhammad (Leopold Weiss),
translation of the Qur'an xxviii–xxix,
xxxviii
asbab al-nuzul xxii, xxii n. 16
Ascension to Heaven, and Night Journey
xi, xxxvii, 175, 179, 347
ashfaqtum 363 n. *a*
'Ashura, Day xiii
'associate' xvii
ata 166 n. *a*
awe, given to God alone 365, 367
awliya xxxi
ayas xvii; contents and construction xxii;
introductory 3 n. *c*
ayat (signs) of God xvii
Azar (father of Abraham) 85

Badr (battle) xii, xxxvii, 34, 35, 43, 257
n. *a*; distribution of battle gains 110,
112–13, 115; pagans 366 n. *a*
bahira 78
bahr 190 n. *a*
Banu Nadir (Jewish clan) 365, 366–7
Banu Qaynuqa (Jewish clan) 366 n. *a*
Al-Baqara (sura) 4–33
battle, conduct 111, 113, 114
battle gains, distribution 110, 112–13,
115
bayan 353 n. *b*
Baydawi xxxv
beliefs; corruption 39; impossibility of
forcing belief 128, 131–2, 135;
Muhammad to recognize that he
cannot compel belief but deliver
God's message only 311, 314;
refutation of false beliefs of the
polytheists
believers 225, 261, 262; acceptance of the
Qur'an 239, 248–9, 430; afterlife 176;
angels pray on their behalf 301–2;
blessings 416, 430; description 389;
and disbelievers 305, alliances with
disbelievers sometimes permitted 36;
encouraged by angels 309;
exhortations to worship of God 214;
fate 94, 96, 97–8, 122, on the Day of
Resurrection 405; forgiveness to
relatives who oppose their faith 376,
377; and God 43–8, as God's allies
364, God's guidance of 195, 325,

God's providence for 158–61, 217, and God's revelation 42–3, response to God 4–6, 18–19, 111–12, solidarity in defence of God's cause 370, submission to God and defence against Hellfire 380–1, urged to spend in God's cause and uphold justice 359–61, worship of God 264, 265; and hypocrites, divisions between on the Day of Judgement 360; judgement 64, 138; justification 243–4; lack of action criticized 372; mutual respect 338–9; nature 73, known by God 277, 279, 280; and polytheists 295–9; praised 337; prosperity 224; qualities 227, 230–1; reactions to the Day of Judgement contrasted with those of disbelievers 419; record held in their right hands at the Day of Judgement 387; religious practices in daily life 269; respect towards Muhammad 338; rewards 35, 45, 155, 210, 212, 213, 251, 265, 269, 271, 272, 277, 279, 313, 326, 370–1, 401–2, 404, at the Day of Judgement 352, contrasted with the punishments of disbelievers 387, in Paradise 185, 190, 286, 321, 322–3, 328, 341, compared to the disbelievers' life in Hell 345–6, in war for their faithfulness 335–6; salvation 83 n. *b*, 207, 221; success 215; supported by God 304; sustenance by God 256; testing and constancy 252; to be attended to in preference to attempts to convert disbelievers 409; triumph on the Day of Judgement 418; true believers 339; *see also* disbelievers

Benjamin (Joseph's brother) 150 n. *a*

bequests 20, 78; payment 51

bi 'l-ghaybi 361 n. *a*

birth 302 n. *a*

bribes, forbidden 21

broadcasting, use of the Qur'an ix–x

brothers: inheritances 66; property shares 51

burning bush 239–40, 247; revelation to Moses 196–7

Byzantines 257

Cain (Adam's son) 70

calendar xi–xii, xxxvii

camel: hamstrung by the people of Thamud 351, 423; sign invoked by Salih 236

camels, dedication and use 211–12

captives, treatment 115

charity, *see* almsgiving

chastity 389

children: fathers' responsibilities for 379; property shares 51; respect for adults' privacy 225; weaning when parents divorce 26–7; *see also* orphans; parents; relatives

Children of Israel: as disbelievers 7–14, 23, 103–6, during the desert wanderings 199–200, of the Scriptures 143; exodus 134–5, 181, 322; God's guidance 265; and kingship 28–9; oppression in Egypt 245, 303; rebelliousness 175; religious differences among 325; response to God 4, 16; worship of calf 104; *see also* Jews and Judaism; People of the Book

Christianity x

Christians 9; belief in Muhammad 255 n. *a*; claims disowned by Jesus on the Day of Judgement 78–9; factions among 29; as People of the Book xviii, and Islamic relations with xxiv–xxv, xxxvii; relations with Muslims 34, 39–42, and pledges from God 67, 68, 69–76; *see also* People of the Book

chronology, lack of xvi, xix

combatants, and non-combatants 60

commerce, *see* trade

common kindnesses, neglect, the result of denial of Judgement 439

consecration (*ihram*) 22 n. *d*

consultation (*shura*) 311, 314

contexts: effects on understanding xxx–xxxi, importance for interpretation of the Qur'an xxi–xxii, xxiv

contrasts xx

the corrupt, identification 333

corruption spreaders condemned 245

covetousness 53–4

Crashing Blow 433

creation 203, 204, 209; benefits for man 166–7, 169, 170, 171; days 307; and God, as the activity of God 223–4, 229–30, 253, 257, 258–9, 295, 296, 357, creation (*cont.*):

basis in God alone 277, 278, as evidence of God's ability to resurrect the dead 340, 341–2, as illustrative of God's power 215, 261, 262–3, 281, 282, as manifestation of the power of God 264, not to be worshipped in place of God 309, under God's providence 313; levels 305; obedience on the Day of Judgement contrasted with the disobedience of disbelievers 415; as promptings to belief 344; purposeful nature 322; wonders 257, 258–9, 353; *see also* animals; insects; nature

dana 118 n. *d*

daughters: denigration of the birth of daughters by pagans condemned 346 n. *b*; property shares 51; regarded as a disgrace by the pagan Arabs 317, attributed to God 288 n. *c*, 347 n. *g*, 348

David: cited as encouragement to Muhammad 272, 273; given knowledge by God 240; given sovereignty and wisdom by God 29; God's guidance 86; prophetic status 178, 206; and the Psalms 65; repentance when tested 291

Dawood, N. J. xxii n. 17, xxiv, xxxviii; translation of the Qur'an xxviii, xxx

day, and night, as evidence of God's creative power 282

Day of Gathering, *see* Day of Judgement

Day of Judgement 78–9, 78 n. *b*, 80, 90, 137, 143, 179–80, 181, 186, 187, 200–1, 201–2, 207–8, 209, 213, 213–14, 239, 243–4, 258, 340, 354, 411, 412, 431, 432, 433; arrival 319; barriers between righteous and the damned 94, 97–8; condemnation of disbelievers for arrogance 328; condemnation for those who give short measure 413–14; creation's obedience contrasted with the disobedience of disbelievers 415; as the Day of Decision 403–4; denial, by the disbelievers 272, and its consequences 439; description 389, 390; disbelievers' rejections denounced 227–8; divisions between believers and disbelievers 259, 260;

divisions between believers and hypocrites 360; divisions of mankind 356–8; imminence 347, 349; inevitability 203, 274, 311, 312, 314, 325–6, 345, 346, 387; length 264; men's behaviour 409–10; punishment of the Meccan disbelievers 351–2; reactions of believers and disbelievers 234–5, 419; reality 285–6; receptors witness against men 341; signs 350; timing 343; timing not known to any save God 271; tyranny condemned 421; *see also* Day of Resurrection; Final Judgement

Day of Resurrection 58, 172, 178, 230, 399–400, 405–6; description 299–300, as being smoke-filled 321; disbelievers' regrets 382; fate of disbelievers 296; fate of the idolaters and the righteous 167–8; judgement and rewards 176; man's powerlessness 341; punishment for the Meccan disbelievers 272; *see also* Day of Judgement; Resurrection

days, declining days, and the need for repentance 435

Days of God 158

dead: disgorged from graves on the Day of Judgement 431, 432; resurrection 30; *see also* Resurrection

death 58; determination by God 80, 84; inevitability 204

debts: conduct regarding 32; payment 51; written records, and women's status xxv–xxvi

destiny, God's control 267

Devil, *see* Satan

devils, rebellious devils, restraint and punishment 285–6

devotional practices, relaxation by God as preparation for the full weight of the Qur'an 395

dhahara 222 n. *a*

dhalama 271 n. *b*

dhikr 318 n. *a*

dhira' 388 n. *a*

dhu al-dhikr 290 n. *a*

dhu 'l-awtad 290 n. *d*, 420 n. *f*

Dhu 'l-Hijjah, month 420 n. *a*

Dhu 'l-Kifl: goodness 292; prophetic status 207

Dhu 'l-Qarnayn 183, 188–9

dialogue xx

dietary laws 19, 41, 67–8, 76, 76–8, 89, 90–1, 173

disbelievers: activities known to God 136; alliances with believers, condemnation 363–4, sometimes permitted 36; amazement at the Resurrection 340; arguments rejected 227–30; arrogance contrasted with God's pride in creation 324, 326; arrogance linked with those of previous generations and of Satan 290–1; attempts to oppose God and Muhammad futile 331; and believers 305; belittling of the Qur'an 232; challenged as to their questioning of God's power would be 382–3; claim that a true prophet would be wealthy denied 316, 317–18; claims about goddesses and angels refuted 347–8; classification 353, 354–5; condemnation 239, 243–4, 410; abandonment by God 158–61, those who lead others astray 261; consignment to Hell 341; denial of the Day of Judgement 272; destruction 228–9, 231, because of their rejection of the truth of the Qur'an and the Resurrection 327–8, 329–30; disobedience, contrasted with the obedience of creation 415, ordained by God 187; disputes between the oppressors and the oppressed at the Day of Judgement 274–5; disputes in Hell 293; eternal torment 418; eventual punishment 202; as evildoers, fate delayed by God until the Final Judgement 128–9, 130; as examples to those who disbelieve currently 340, 341; exhorted to believe 257; failure to see the significance of God's signs 264; fate 94, 95–108, 111, 112, 113–14, 122–3, 155–7, on the Day of Resurrection 405–6; foolishness in denying the Resurrection 389, 390; and God's revelation 42–3; good actions outweighed by bad faith 331–2; hearts hardened by God 133–4, 185; judgement 63–4, 66, 136–43, 203, 205, 207, 207–8; lack of belief in God as creator 256; lack of success in war dictated by God 336; life in Hell compared to the believers' bliss in Paradise 345–6; misconceptions

regarding revelation and Muhammad's nature 252, 255, 256; nature known by God 277, 280; not to be helped by believers 251; obduracy 307–9, 310; prayers ineffective 154; punishment 35, 36, 41, 45, 48, 153, 194–5, 210, 212, 215, 216–19, 265, 301, 324, 325–6, 377, 395, 397–8, 402, 403–4, in the afterlife 185, 189–90, for barring believers from Mecca 209, 211, contrasted with the rewards of believers 387, on the Day of Judgement 271, 304, 305, 393, 394, inevitability 289, for opposition to God and Muhammad 362, 363, 364, of previous generations, seen as a warning to disbelievers in the present 350–1, shown in the story of Moses 196; reactions to the Day of Judgement contrasted with those of believers 419; reactions to the giving of the Scriptures 24; record held in their left hands at the Day of Judgement 387–8; rejection of prophets and punishment 162; relations with God 42–8; reminded of the fate of previous generations of disbelievers 343–4, 376; repentance, *see* repentance; response to God 4, 5–6, 7–14, 18–19; rewards 279, 313, scoffing met with punishment at the Day of Judgement 285–6, 286–7; guided by own desires 325; stubbornness and mocking of God's revelations 281–3; terror at the Day of Judgement 276; as those who are not in God's light 223; to be left to God's judgement and not to Muhammad's preaching 385–6; to be left to their own devices 409; torturers condemned 416; unjust nature 224; *see also* believers; Meccan disbelievers; polytheists

disbelieving communities, punishment 379

disputes, arbitration 56–7

divorce xix, 52; attempts at reconciliation 54; pagan divorce practices disallowed 362; regulations 278–9; and remarriage 25–8, 266 n. *a*; settlements 62–3, 270; and women's status xxv; *see also* marriage

doubters, *see* disbelievers

dowries 26 n. *a*, 27, 50; payment 53; reclamation 52
drawing lots 76
dying 357–8

eating 225
education xiv *n.* 4; use of the Qur'an ix
Elias: blessing 288; God's guidance 86
Elijah, God's guidance 86
Elisha, goodness 292
elisions xxxi
Embassies, Year of xxxvii
emigrants 115
Eve (Adam's wife), disobedience 95
evidence, suppression 33
evil, invocation against 445, 446
evil ones, assigned as companions to disbelievers 318
evildoers, *see* disbelievers
exodus 8–9, 234; Moses' people refuse to enter the holy land 70
Ezekiel 207 n. *b*
Ezra, ascribed divine sonship 119

fair dealings 177
faith: arguers against faith criticized 370; evidence for 430; freedom, but choice determines fate in the Hereafter 295; purity 444; unity 34, 39
faithful, the success 370
faithfulness, as marks of belief 19
fas'al 230 n. *b*
fasting 20; during pilgrimages 22
fath 442 n. *a*
fathers: responsibility for children 379; *see also* parents; relatives
al-Fatiha ix, 3, 164 n. *b*, 442 n. *a*
al-Fayruzabadi xxxiii
the Feast 67, 79
feeble-minded, provision for 51
Final Judgement xvii, xix, 36, 131–3; condemnation of the polytheists 130–1; Day of 161; and the delay of the condemnation of evil doers 128–9, 130; timing 107; *see also* Day of Judgement
finance xviii
fishing, during the pilgrimage 77
the fly 214
foetuses, development 428 n. *a*
food, hunting, during the pilgrimage 67

forceful chargers 407
Forest-Dwellers: arrogance 290; disbelief as example to those who disbelieve currently 340; rejection of Shu'ayb 236–7
Friday prayer, observance 372–3
al-Furqan (Qur'an) xx, 227 n. *b*

Gabriel (angel) 12, 429; accompanies Muhammad on the Night Journey and Ascension to Heaven xi; as the Holy Spirit 173; revelation of the Qur'an ix, xiv, xv, 137 n. *c*, 201 n. *b*, 237, 347, 411, in obedience to God 194
gambling 24, 76
Garden, *see* Paradise
gardens, parable of the luscious gardens 183, 185–6
generalizations xxi
God: all-pervasiveness 359; believers' mindfulness of 4 n. *c*; beneficence in granting night and day 250; bounty 166–71, 179, 182; calling upon 301, 302, 304, 305; commands, carrying out 331; creates Adam and expels him from Eden 7; as creator 98, 128–9, 153, 154, 213, 215, 229–30, 253, 256, 257, 258–9, 261, 262–3, 264, 295, 296, 307–8, 309, 313, 357, 400, 403, 405, and also as fulfiller of needs 80–9, and His praise 223–4, of man 401, 402, for man's benefit 166–7, 169, 170, 171, and man's ingratitude 409, proof of the Resurrection 209, purpose in creation 327; as decider of victory in war and distributor of booty 365, 366; discrimination when judging believers and disbelievers 291; disobedience towards forbidden 269; as the dispenser of forgiveness and punishment 301, 302; encourages Muhammad 425, 426; exhortation to the Children of Israel 7–14; existence discernible in nature 324; Face 354; gives guidance and warning to men 424; goodness to believers, as reinforcement of his instructions 266, 267–8; grace 361, as revelation 384 n. *b*, shown in nature 162–3; grammatical uses when speaking about xx; invocation 3; as judge 66, 427; justness 237; as lord of the elements

154; mercy 322; Mercy to Muslims in sending of Muhammad 372; munificence 305, 306, 312–13, 314, 316; Names 107; nature as unseen 4 n. *d*; omnipotence 214, 311–12, 376, 416, 418, stressed in relation to disbelievers 382–3; omniscience 136, 143, 144, 226, 263, 272, 310, 363, 367, 376, in awarding blessing and punishment 348; Oneness 119, 227, 251, 274, 393, 394, 444, and creative activity 295, and power 215, 218, without offspring 195, 319–20; only God to be given awe 365, 367; only God to be worshipped 295; pledges given to Jews and Christians 67, 69–76; power 128, 239, 242–3, and creation 281, 282, 284, contrasted with the powerlessness and uselessness of the 'partners' 277–8, 279–80, extolled 261, and grace 227, and grace in nature 232, and knowledge 153–7, and providence 63–4, truths about 347, 348; and predestination 249–50; pride in creation, contrasted with disbelievers' arrogance 324, 326; as protector of the righteous 325; providence 223, 275; punishment of the People of the Book who broke faith with Muhammad 365–6; relations with xix, believers and disbelievers 5–6, 7–14, 18–19, 29–31, 33, 43–8, 158–61; relaxes devotional demands 395; revelation 42; sole worship demanded 441; sovereignty 36; speech xx; submission to God as central tenet of faith 34, 35–6; supremacy 18; tests claims to truth 267; truth disputed 301, 303, 305; uniqueness 166, 169; unity xvii, xx–xxi, 203–4, 208, 213, 285, 289, 293, 307; unity disputed by disbelievers 290; wisdom and majesty 324, 326; wish that mankind should live in harmony 339; wonders, in the world 353–4

goddesses, disbelievers' claims about refuted 347–8
Gog 189, 207
gold ornaments 316, 317, 318
golden calf 8, 12, 65, 104, 200
Goliath (Philistine leader killed by David) 29

grammar xix–xx
graves 434
guidance: for both believers and disbelievers 325; God to provide 424; groups responding to 4; plea 3, 4
guilty, trial 250 n. *a*

hadhf al-jawab 420 n. *c*
hadith 222 n. *a*
hafiz ix
Hagar 18 n. *a*
Hajj pilgrimage 420; infected by polytheism x
hakim 39 n. *a*, 128 n. *a*
ham' 78
Haman: arrogance 254; condemnation 245, 247; disbelief 303
harraka 200 n. *b*
Harut (angel) 12
Hasan (son of 'Ali) xiii
Hayyan, Abu xxxv
heads, shaving 22 n. *c*
Hell 35, 46, 52, 167, 175, 176, 194, 219, 230, 436; capacity 341; contrasted with Paradise 353, 354; description 356–7, 397–8; disbelievers' life compared to the believers' bliss in Paradise 345–6; engulfs sinners 255; entry of disbelievers into 299–300; filling with jinn and men 144; life 293; nature 159, 160; as place of punishment 319; as reward for disbelievers 97, 122, 163, 189, 190, 199, 207, 265, 279, 324, 332, 334, 363, 382, 405, 408; and the Tree of Zaqqum 179, 286, 322, 357; unremitting nature of punishment in Hell 304
Hereafter, *see* afterlife
al-Hijr, people of: disbelief 162, 164; *see also* Thamud's people
Hijra (Migration) xi–xii, xvii, xxxvii
Hira, Cave xi, 397
homosexuality 52; condemnation 242, 253–4, 351; Lot condemns 236
hoopoe, dialogue with Solomon xx, 240
Hour, the *see* Day of Judgement
household behaviour 220, 222, 225
houses, entering 21
Hud (prophet) 98–9, 159, 329; rejection 235–6; role as prophet invoked as an

Hud (prophet) (*cont.*):
  encouragement to Muhammad 136, 139–40
Hudaybiyya (treaty) xxxvii, 334–7, 368
humble, commendation 211
Hunayn (battle) xxxvii, 118
hunting: during the pilgrimage 67; forbidden during the pilgrimage 77
Husayn (son of 'Ali) xiii
husbands, property shares 51
hypocrites: alliances with forbidden 58–9; bad behaviour censured 266, 271; and believers, divisions between on the Day of Judgement 360; condemnation for joking about God 122; criticisms 374; failure to support Muhammad leads to censure 116; fate 331; intrigues 50; judgement 63–4; Medinan hypocrites condemned 334; *munafiqun* xviii; response to God's guidance 4

ibl 419 n. *b*
Iblis, *see* Satan
Ibn 'Abbas 215 n. *c*
Ibn Mandhur xxxiii
Ibn Taymiyya, intertextuality in the Qur'an xxx
Ibn Ubayy (head of the 'hypocrites' of Medina) 365, 366
'*idina* 165 n. *b*
idle talk, condemnation 122
idolaters: attempts to persuade Muhammad to worship their gods 441; castigation 209, 210, 213, 214; condemnation, for denying God's bounty 166–7, 169; Medinan idolaters condemned 334, 336
idolatry x, 62, 76; Abraham condemns 205–6, 253, 287, 317; condemnation 207, 259; refuted in face of God's power and creation 277–8, 279–80; rejection 234–5, 237; to be avoided 158, 160–1
Idris: grace 193; prophetic status 207
iftah 442 n. *a*
ihram (consecration) 22 n. *d*
ikhlas 444
'Illiyyin 413
iltifat xx, xxxv
impurity, avoidance when praying 55
'Imran, family 34, 37

infanticide: female 169, 411 n. *a*; as a result of the fear of poverty, forbidden 177
inheritances 50, 51, 54, 66; misappropriation condemned 420
insan 420 n. *g*
insects: ants, and Solomon 239, 240; bees, activity as evidence of God's inspiration 166, 170
interfaith relations xxiv–xxv
international relations xviii
intertextuality xxx
intoxicants and intoxication 24, 55, 76–7, 96 n. *c*
Iram, tyranny condemned 420
iron 359, 361
Isaac (Abraham's son) 15, 161, 193, 206, 253; birth prophesied 141, 163–4, 254; devotion to God 292; God's guidance 86
Ishmael (Abraham's son) 15, 18 n. *a*, 161; builds the mosque in Mecca 17 n. *a*; God's guidance 86; goodness 292; grace 193; prophetic status 207; sacrifice 287
Islam: acceptance by Meccans xxxvii; conversions, attempts to prevent 331; nature xxiv; spread xiii, xxxvii
Islamic arts and sciences, basis in the Qur'an ix
Isma'il (seventh imam) xiii
istifham inkari 7 n. *b*
ittaka'a 345 n. *e*

Jacob xvii, 145–6, 149, 151, 193, 206, 253; birth prophesied 141; God's guidance 86; obedience to God 15, 292
jaza' 118 n. *e*
Jerusalem xi; Night Journey xxxvii, 175; prayers towards 14 n. *a*
Jesus xvii, 371; birth and mission 34, 37, 37–9; Christian beliefs in his divinity seen as false 69; confirmation of the Torah 72; creation by God 217; disownment of Christian claims on the Day of Judgement 78–9; divinity denied 75, 119, 133, 191, 192, 316, 318–19; divisions among his people 370; as encouragement to believers to be mindful of God 359, 361; foretells the coming of Muhammad under the name of Ahmad 370; God's guidance

86; as prophet 11, 29, 66; receipt of the same message as that given to Muhammad 312; renunciation of claims to divinity 67; as a sign for all people 207; as son of God xxxiii; taken by God 65

Jews and Judaism x; belief in Muhammad 255 n. *a*; criticized for spiritual presumption 372; dietary regulations 91, 174; distortion of the Scriptures 55–6; granted tolerance xii; as People of the Book xviii, and Islamic relations with xxiv–xxv, xxxvii; pledges from God and relations with Muslims 67, 68, 69–76; refusal to enter the holy land during the exodus wanderings 70; relations with Muslims 34, 39–41; *see also* Children of Israel; People of the Book

jihad xxxi

jinn: belief in the Qur'an 327, 329; classification 353, 354; condemnation 308; creation 163, not needed by God 344; not the revealers of the Qur'an 232, 237, 238; reactions to the Qur'an 393; as servants of Solomon 292; subservience to God 289; used as workers for Solomon 273; worshipped by disbelievers 275

jizya 118 n. *e*

Job: blessing after affliction 292; God's guidance 86; prophetic status 206–7

John (son of Zachariah) 191, 207; God's guidance 86

joking, joking about God condemned 122

Jonah 128, 135, 288; God's guidance 86; prophetic status 207; shown God's mercy 385–6

Jonah's people, repentance 135

Joseph xvii, 145–52; God's guidance 86; rejection by disbelievers 303

judgement, *see* Day of Judgement; Final Judgement

judges, bribing forbidden 21; women as judges xxv, xxvi

justice: administration 56, by Muhammad for the People of the Book 72, 72–3; bearing witness impartially 68–9

Ka'ba 77, 345; building by Abraham and Ishmael 15; building and pilgrimages

to x; centrality to *qibla* and rites of pilgrimage 18 n. *c*; guardians 112; pilgrims' disgraceful acts 96 n. *a*

kafur 401 n. *b*

Karbala (battle) xiii

kawthar 440 n. *a*

Khadija (Muhammad's wife) x–xi, xxxvii

khalifa (successor) 7 n. *a*

al-Khattab, 'Umar ibn, conversion to Islam xxxvii

kingship, in Israel 28–9

kinship ties 50

knowing (*zanna*) 8 n. *a*

Korah, disbelief 303

Koran, *see* Qur'an

la yubdi' wa-la yu'id 275 n. *a*

al-Lat (Arabian pagan goddess) 347

learning/knowing xiv n. 4

legal texts xviii–xix

legislation, reinforcements 78 n. *b*

lesbian acts 52

life saving 71

Light, Verse 220, 223

livestock: creation for man's benefit 166, 170, 284; dedication and use 211; intended for man's use 215; polytheists' regulations refuted 90–1; *see also* animals

loans xxvi

Lot 141–2; blessing 288; condemns homosexuality 253–4; God's guidance 86; as messenger 100; rejection 236, 242; salvation and prophetic status 164, 206; seeks refuge in God 253

Lot, people 212; arrogance 290; disbelief as example to those who disbelieve currently 340, 344; as disbelievers 141–2; punishment 351

Lot, wife, disbelief 381

lote trees 273, 347

Luqman the Wise 261, 262

Luther, Martin xxxvii

Madina, *see* Medina

Magians 210, 210 n. *c*

Magog 189, 207

Malik (angel in charge of Hell) 319

Manat (pagan diety) 347

man: birth and resurrection 417;

man: birth and resurrection (*cont.*):
creation 163, 166, 171, 215, 305, and ability to communicate 353, created for toil and trial 422; denial of the Day of Resurrection 399–400; disputes creation by God 284; homosexual acts 52; ingratitude condemned 409, 412; obsession with wealth condemned 434, 436; self-satisfaction 428; testing 183, 298, 401–2; *see also* mankind

mankind: creation 264, not needed by God 344; divisions at the Day of Judgement 356–8; God's knowledge about as shown by the receptors at the Day of Judgement 340–1; need of God 278; powerlessness on the Day of Resurrection 341; unity and harmony among 339; *see also* men

marriage xviii, 220, 222–3; blessing by God 258; commendation of 53; forbidden degrees 52–3; intermarriage between Muslims and women of the People of the Book 68; intermarriage with pagans forbidden 25; intermarriage with those of other faiths xxv; Muhammad's conduct dictated by God 270; remarriage and divorce 25–8, 266 n. *a*; treatment of believing and disbelieving women and their marriage dowries 369; *see also* divorce

martyrdom 282 n. *a*

martyrs: testimony 44 n. *b*

Marut (angel) 12

Marwa 18

Mary (mother of Jesus) 34, 37–8, 65, 66, 75, 191–2, 207, 217; belief 381; denial of Christian claims for her divinity 79

matta'a 288 n. *b*

mawla 266 n. *b*

Mecca x; attacked by the army of Abraha 437, 438; believers barred from when on pilgrimage 209, 211; establishment by God 249; God warns 87; as guarantee of God's oath 422, 427; as one of the two cities 317 n. *b*; pilgrimages 41, ordinances governing 21–3; as point of departure in the Night Journey 175; prayers towards 14 n. *a*, 17; prosperity prayed for by Abraham 158, 160–1; sacred character

does not deny believers the right of self-defence xxiii; as sanctuary 256; surrender 359 n. *b*; surrender to Muhammad 442; warnings to 311

Meccan disbelievers 170 n. *d*; arguments answered 345, 346; assertions denied 191; claims that the angels are God's daughters 183 n. *a*; condemned along with the arrogant 245; denial of the Resurrection 407; opposition to Muhammad's teachings xi; punishment 272, 351–2; *see also* disbelievers

Meccans 321; attacks on Muhammad and his followers allow engagement in self-defence xxii–xxiii; conversion to Islam xii; iniquitous behaviour of those who attempted to expel Muhammad 331; religious beliefs prior to conversion to Islam xvii; Resurrection denied 322; tardiness in believing in the Qur'an 327

mediation 58

Medina x, xi–xii; besieged by disbelievers at the Battle of the Trench 266; Muhammad's death xiii

Medinans, commended for believing acts 127

menstruation, sexual intercourse forbidden during 25

messengers: as commissioned by God 306; mocked 80, 82; persistence in testifying to disbelievers 308; rejection 173; rejection by disbelievers 168; role 159, 176; *see also* prophets

Michael (archangel) 12

Midianites 122, 212; condemnation for the rejection of Shu'ayb 254; as disbelievers 100–1, 142–3

migrants 60

Migration (Hijra) xi–xii, xvii, xxxvii

mihrab 273 n. *a*

milk-mothers 52

milk-sisters 52

min 42 n. *a*

min anfusikum 50 n. *a*

Mina 22 n. *f*, 23 n. *b*

minbar 373 n. *a*

mindfulness (*w-q-y*) 4 n. *c*

miracles 178–9

mischief-makers, condemned as evildoers 339

misdeeds, minor misdeeds cancelled by God 53

Mistah (relative of 'A'isha) 221 n. *c*

modesty 220, 222, 225

monasticism 361

monotheism 92, 93

moon: crescent moons, and the timing of pilgrimages 21; rising and setting 353; splitting in two at the Day of Judgement 350; and sun, as evidence of God's creative power 282; worship x; *see also* sun

Moses xvii, 8–9, 11, 12, 64, 65, 175, 245–8, 348; blessing 288; commissioning at the burning bush 239–40; divisions among his people 370; as encouragement to Muhammad 143, 407; God's guidance 86; and the Golden calf 196–200; grace 193; guiltlessness before God 271; and the Jews' refusal to enter the holy land during the exodus wanderings 70; meeting with unidentified figure 183, 187–8; as messenger 101–5, 134; mission to Pharaoh's people 232–4, 322; and the plagues 318; as prophet 229, 254; receipt of the same message as that given to Muhammad 312; receives the Scriptures 205, 265, 310; rejection 212; rejection by disbelievers 217; rejection by Pharaoh and his people 344; reminds the Children of Israel of God's providence 158; sister 245–6; victory 301, 302–4

Moses, mother 245–6

mosques: first mosque built at Yathrib xii; mosque built by hypocrites condemned 125–6; those qualified to tend 117–18

mothers: property shares 51; *see also* relatives

Mount Judi (resting place for Noah's Ark) 139

Mount of Mercy xii

Mount Sinai 9, 12, 65, 248; God swears by 345

mubin 353 n. *b*

Mufradat 76 n. *a*

muhajirun xii

Muhammad ix, x–xiii, xxxvii; accused of being mad 272, 275, 384; allowed self-defence against Meccan attacks xxii–xxiii; assured of abundance from God, in place of the loss of his last son 440; believers' respect for 270–1; comforted in face of accusations of his being a liar 277, 278; commanded to be faithful to God 237–8; commanded to persist in his proclamations 346; commanded to preach God's word 344; commanded to read 428; commended to the support of his followers as a sign of their loyalty to God 334–5; defence before the disbelievers 275; disbelievers' rejections denounced 227, 229; disobedience towards forbidden 269; divine commission to reveal the Qur'an 281; divine source of his message 347; encouragement by God 425, 426; encouragement 128, 135, 152, 162–5, 196, 202, 327, 330, by the examples of earlier prophets 290, 291–2, perseverance and patience 191, 194, 384, 385–6, 401, 402, and ignore the taunts of disbelievers 301, 304, 305–6, remain close to God 309, through references to David and Solomon 272, 273; as encouragement to believers to be mindful of God 359; exhortation to constancy 254–5; exhorted not to be saddened by disbelief 261, 262; exhorted to remain steadfast in the face of disbelief 243–4; exhorted to follow God's clear religious path 325; exhorted to obey God 269; exhorted to pay no attention to disbelievers 264; exhorted to persevere 257, 258–9; flees from Mecca and hides in a cave xxx; followers, indignant at the treaty made at Hudaybiyya 334, 336; home life 380; instructed on recitation of the Qur'an 399; instructed to speak to believers and disbelievers 274; insults condemned 121; lacking in miraculous powers 181; madness denied by God 411; marriages 270; as 'Messenger' xv; as model for believers 268; name mentioned 331; obedience towards 56–7, 58, 61, 220, 224; opponents and

Muhammad (*cont.*):
their reward 23; as Prophet 44–5; prophetic character xvii, 203, 205, 208, affirmation 285, and lack of miraculous powers 175; rebuked for attention to disbelieving nobles and inattention to a blind enquirer 409; reminded that he cannot convert everyone and should remain steadfast 245, 248, 249; revelation of the Qur'an xiv–xv; revelations, and their truths 94, 107–9; role 153, 156, as the messenger of God to the People of the Book 70, in warning and giving good news 136, 137, 143–4; sending by God 17; sending as God's grace 372; tempting by disbelievers 180; testimony to the Meccan Arabs 394; truth affirmed by God 387, 388; vision of pilgrimage to Mecca 334, 336; witness 166, 172; as witness against the polytheists 172; wives, believers' conduct towards 266, instructions to 268–9

Mujahid 397 n. *c*

munafiqun (hypocrites) xviii

muqwin 357 n. *a*

murder 71; of believers by believers 59–60; fair retribution for 20; forbidden 53, 177

Muslims 214; exhorted to obey God in all things lest their good deeds come to nothing 331, 333; instructions for 172–4; as the just 16; migrate to Abyssinia seeking refuge from persecution xi, xxxvii; not to ally themselves with their Meccan enemies 368, 369; relations with Jews and Christians 15–16, 34, 39–42, 67, 68, 69–76; spiritual growth as grace from God 372; tensions with the People of the Book 50, 55–6

mutual neglect, among those being judged on the Day of Judgement 376

Muzdalifa, plain 22 n. *f*

al-Nadr ibn al-Harith, condemnation for attempting to mislead others 261 n. *a*

nahr xxxii

nar 239 n. *a*

nasakha 212 n. *a*

nashaza 54 n. *a*

nazi'at 407 n. *a*

needy, neglect, the result of denial of Judgement 439

night, and day, as evidence of God's creative power 282

Night of Glory 429

Night Journey and Ascension to Heaven xi, xxxvii, 175, 179, 347

night-comer 417

Nimrod 416 n. *b*

Noah xvii, 175; chosen by God 37; contemporaries condemned 122; dialogue with God xx; as encouragement to believers to be mindful of God 359, 361; God's guidance 86; preaching and prayer for the destruction of disbelievers before the Flood 391–2; as prophet 98–9, 133, 159, 216; receipt of the same message as that given to Muhammad 312; rejection 235; role as prophet invoked as an encouragement to Muhammad 138–9; salvation 287, 350; salvation and rejection by his own people 253

Noah, people 212; arrogance 290; destruction 229, 348; disbelief as example to those who disbelieve currently 340, 344; as disbelievers 159, 216; punishment 301, 303; rejection of Noah and their punishment 350

Noah, wife, disbelief 381

Noah's Ark 138–9, 216, 253, 282–3, 387

nobles, salvation 83 n. *b*

non-combatants, and combatants 60

oathbreaking: atonement for 76; criticisms 370; forbidden 172; God prevents Job from oathbreaking 292

oathtaking 25; release from 380

obedience: given to God alone 365, 367; to Muhammad 56–7, 58, 61, 220, 224

oppressed, defence, permits the taking up of arms xxii

oppression, punishments for 314

orphans: care 425; cruelty to, the result of denial of Judgement 439; orphan girls, treatment 62; property 177, and its disposal 50–1, management 25, 92; *see also* children

pagans: intermarriage with forbidden 25; Meccan pagans, dispute about the angels as daughters of God 195, rejoicing at the defeat of the Byzantines by the Persians 257 n. *a*

Palmer, E. H., translation of the Qur'an xxvii, xxxviii

Paradise 51–2, 167–8; admission to Paradise includes absolution from bad deeds 334; believers' bliss compared to the disbelievers' life in Hell 345–6; contrast between the two levels of Paradise 354–5; description 356, and seen as the reward of believers 332; entry into 13, 300; entry into Paradise preceded by persecution 24; life 283, 286, 292–3; nature in the light of Arabic structures and idioms xxxi–xxxii; as the objective of believers 360–1; resting place for believers 97; as reward of believers 6, 35, 44, 49, 56, 122, 124, 125, 126, 129, 143, 155, 156, 160, 163, 185, 190, 199, 210, 213, 215, 228, 251, 255, 258, 261, 265, 279, 319, 322–3, 328, 341, 343, 379, 385, 401–2, 408, 413, 416; as reward for truthful Christians 76, 79; as the reward of the godly 62; as the reward of those who repent 194

paragraphs, use in translation xxxiv

parents: property shares 51; relations with as the mark of believers and disbelievers 328; respect for except in the case of disbelief 262; respect for 176; respect for and obedience to 252; *see also* children; fathers; mothers; relatives

peace xviii

pearls 353; treatment 345 n. *f*

the pen xiv n. 4

People of the Book xviii; and God's grace 359, 361; lack of faithfulness to treaty leads God to drive them from their homes 365–6; misdeeds 64–5, 66, 430; rebels to be fought 118–19; relations with xxiv–xxv; rewards for faith 49; tensions with Muslims 50, 55–6; *see also* Children of Israel; Christians; Jews and Judaism

'Perfecting the blessing' 68 n. *b*

persecution 17–18; contrasted with God's punishment 252

Persians, attacks on the Byzantines 257

personal responsibility 176, 398; in choosing good or evil 424; in conduct 325; on the Day of Judgement 322; and final rewards 348; in matters of belief 14, 15, 16, 311, 314, 345; for sin 252–3

Pharaoh: arrogance 254, 290; condemnation 245, 247–8; destruction 301, 302–4; disbelief 134, 143, 197–9; dreams, interpreted by Joseph 148; drowning 181; punishment 318, 387, 395; rejects God's word brought by Moses 232–4; rejects Moses 101–2, 217, 240; as reminder to disbelievers 407; tyranny condemned 420

Pharaoh, people: condemnation 416; disbelief as example to those who disbelieve currently 340, 343; punishment 351

Pharaoh, wife, belief 381

Pharaoh's people: destruction 229; as disbelievers 101–3, 114, 134, 143; punishment 318; reject Moses 217, 240, 247–8; rejection of God's word 233–4; summoned to repent by a believer 303–4; testing through the mission of Moses 322; treatment of the Children of Israel and death in the Red Sea 8; *see also* Pharaoh; Pharaoh, people

Pickthall, Muhammad Marmaduke, translation of the Qur'an xxvii–xxviii, xxxviii

pilgrimages: hunting for food 67; hunting forbidden but fishing allowed 77; minor pilgrimages ('*umra*) 18, 18 n. *b*; ordinances governing 21–3; rite, as enacted by Abraham 209, 211

pledges 172, 177; observance 155, as marks of belief 19; as received from God 67, 69–76; taken from the Jews by God 74–5

plenty, as a test 394

poets 232, 238

polygamy 50

polytheism x, xvii; advocation by parents condemned 252; among Hud's people 140; condemnation 176, 204, 254, 256, 258, 259, 318, 320, and the Final Judgement 129, 130–1; condemned by Luqman 261; denial 257–8, 274; denunciation 227, 228, 229, 230, 245,

polytheism (*cont.*):
249, 250, 251; forbidden 177, 178; Muhammad's opposition to xi; rejection 239, 242–3, 284, 312, 327, 329; worthless nature 133

polytheists: beliefs refuted 92, 93; condemnation for denying God's bounty 166–72; contrasted with believers 295–9; false beliefs refuted 80–9; not to tend mosques 117–18; prayers on behalf of hostile relatives condemned 126; relations with in the event of persecution xxiii–xxiv; treaty obligations with 116–17; uncleanness 118; *see also* disbelievers

prayer direction (*qibla*) 14 n. *a*, 16–17, 18 n. *c*, 19

prayers 254–5; avoidance of impurity 55; cleansing before prayer 68; conduct during war 60–1; when in danger 27; formal prayer (*salah*) 5 n. *a*; as marks of belief 19; rewards in the Hereafter 23

praying for show, the result of denial of Judgement 439

predestination 203, 249–50, 252, 253, 264, 297; God decides between believers and disbelievers 259, 260

pride 177

privacy, respect for 225

privation, as a test 394 n. *a*

pronouns, use xxxii–xxxiii

property 50; disposal 50–1, 51–2, 53, 54; management for orphans 92; protection xxvi; restoration 56; right use of personal property 21

prophets xvii–xviii; God's affirmation, after removing Satan's insinuations from their messages 212–13; Children of Israel's treatment of 11–12; continuity 311, 312; disbelievers in the prophets condemned 252, 253–4, 255, 256; as encouragement to believers to be mindful of God 359, 361; examples used as support and encouragement for Muhammad 290, 291–2; followers and their reactions 232–7; grace 191, 193–4; as messengers 203, 205–7; as *muslim* xxiv; perseverance in spite of rejection 162–5; rejection 281–2; rejection by

disbelievers 216–17, 219, 228–9, and their consequent destruction 239, 239–40, 241–2; rejection by the people of 'Ad 327, 329; rejection as liars 277, 278; revelations to 65; role 56; role an encouragement to Muhammad 136, 138–44; sending by God 29; stories 287–8; wealth discounted as a measure of a prophet's truth 316, 317–18; *see also* messengers

providence, God's control 275, 361

punctuation xxxiv–xxxv

punishments: for adultery 71 n. *b*; eternal nature in the afterlife 200; for persecution of Muslims by the People of the Book 71; for theft 71; in this life and the Hereafter 387

Qarun: arrogance 254; condemnation 245, 250–1

qasr 403 n. *c*

qibla (prayer direction) 14 n. *a*, 16–17, 18 n. *c*, 19

Queen of Sheba 240–1; dialogue xx

Qur'an ix–x, xxxvii–xxxviii; acceptance 248–9; authenticity 128; belittling 232; as both joyful news and warning 239; canonization xvi n. 8; compilation xv–xvi; consistency as evidence of its origin 58; disbelievers mock 217; disbelievers' rejections denounced 227, 230; divine origins xiv n. 3, 131, 162, 232, 237, not poetry made by man 281, 284; ease of understanding 350, 351; effects upon believers 297; extent 190; final revelation xiii; first revelation on the Night of Glory 429; as a gift revealed from God 279; gives knowledge about the Hour of Judgement 319; as God's word 399; as guidance 175, 176–82, 187, 201; interpretation xxi–xxvi; Koran xxvi; mercy 321; opponents warned of punishment 165; as reading 353 n. *a*; recitation 180; rejection by disbelievers 415; responses to determine fate at the Day of Judgement 137; revelation xi, xiv–xv, 170, 181–2, 183, 196, 200, 201, 203, 205, 210, 213, 255, 347, 357, 379; revelation questioned by disbelievers 229; role 145; structure xvi–xvii;

stylistic features xix–xxi; themes xvii–xix; translations, conventions used xxix–xxxvi, in English xxvi–xxix; truth 94, 264, 307, 309, 324, 411, affirmed by God 387, 388, disbelievers' rejection and their destruction 327–8, 329, and nobility 290, 294; *see also* ayas; suras

Quraysh (tribe), trading journeys 438

r-b-b 3 n. *d*
al-Raghib 76 n. *a*
rahim 3 n. *b*
rahman 3 n. *a*
rain, illustrative of the concept of resurrection 419 n. *b*
ra'ina 13, 55
Ramadan: obligations xix; observances 20–1
al-Raqim 183
al-Rass, people: destruction 229; disbelief as example to those who disbelieve currently 340
al-Razi, Fakhr al-Din xxxv, xxxvi
reading xiv, xiv n. 4, xv
rebellious, allowed to stray 370
reconciliation, commendation 61
refugees, Muslim refugees, to be rewarded by God 366
refugees from persecution, rewards 168, 173
relatives: prayers on behalf of hostile relatives condemned 126; treatment 172; *see also* children; fathers; mothers; parents
religion, unity 311, 312
religious divisions 311, 312
religious tolerance 29; at Yathrib xii
remarriage, *see* divorce; marriage
repentance 52, 125, 295, 297, 299; disbelievers' repentance, when faced by Hell 382; and entry to Paradise 194; essential that it take place before the Day of Judgement 302, 306, 321, 421; in the face of God's punishment in this life 384–5; futility at the arrival of the Hour 332; God's transformation of those who repent 230–1; and its rewards 249; urged on by the decline of the day 435
Resurrection xvii, xviii, 30, 168, 277, 302 n. *a*, 340, 433; affirmation 376;

assurance 178; coming 417; creation as evidence of God's ability to resurrect the dead 340, 341–2; denied by the Meccans 322; disbelievers' denial questioned 264, 389, 390; disbelievers reject 216, 243; inevitability 215, 218–19, 307, 407; mistaken beliefs about 393; proof seen in the creative power of God 209; reality 281, 283, 427; truth, disbelievers' rejection and their destruction 327–8, 329–30; winds as illustration 343; *see also* Day of Resurrection
retaliation xix
retribution 177
revelation 311, 314–15
rhetorical questions xxxii
righteous, commendation and entry into Paradise 167–8
Rightly Guided Caliphs xiii
rivers, in Paradise xxxii
Rodwell, J. M., translation of the Qur'an xxvii, xxxviii
Ross, Alexander, translation of the Qur'an xxvii, xxxvii

Sabbath, obligatory nature 174
Sabians 9 n. *a*, 74, 210
Sacred Months 77; observance 119
sacrifices, offering for, during pilgrimages 22
Safa 18
safe conduct xxiv
Safwan (companion of 'A'isha), falsely suspected of adultery 220
sa'iba 78
sa'id 55 n. *b*
sajada 154 n. *b*
salah (formal prayer) 5 n. *a*
salam 356 n. *a*
Sale, George, translation of the Qur'an xxxviii
Salih: dialogue xx; as messenger 99–100, 159; rejection 236, 241–2, 351; role as prophet invoked as an encouragement to Muhammad 140–1; *see also* Thamud, people
Salsabil (spring in Paradise) 401
samad 444 n. *a*
al-Samiri (induced some of the Children of Israel to worship golden calf) 199, 200

sand dunes, place of destruction of the people of 'Ad 327, 329

Satan 23, 85; as the ally of disbelievers 362, 363, 364; as an evil companion 54; arrogance linked with that of Meccan disbelievers 290; disobedience 7, 186; disowns men whom he has misled 367; duping of Medinan Jews into rejecting Muhammad 333; incites enmity and hatred through intoxicants and gambling 76; insinuation of evil into the messages of the prophets 212–13; invocation against 446; as a liar 277; as man's enemy 178, 179, 228, 319; opinion of the people of Sheba 273–4; as patron of idolaters 170; personification of danger through temptation 162, 163; power 172; promises false 160; rebelliousness 193; refusal to be subservient to man 94–5, 293; stoning 23 n. *b*; supporters to be flung into Hell 235; as tempter 31, 56, 108, 175, 201, 283, of 'Ad and Thamud 254, of believers 19, 47, of disbelievers in battle 113, of the people of the Queen of Sheba 240; ungratefulness 176; weakness 57; worship condemned 62

Saul (Talut) (king) 28–9

sawm 192 n. *a*

Scriptures: comparison between good and evil words 160; confirmation by the Qur'an 34, 40; as gift to the Children of Israel 175, 265; given to Moses 310; given to Moses and Aaron 205; Jewish attitudes towards 72; Jewish scriptures, as containing the same message as the Qur'an 418; meaning as a whole known to God alone 34; non-Islamic scriptures xxiv; origins in God 92–3; reactions to 24; revelation after Abraham 39; revelation by Moses before the revelation of the Qur'an 328; treatment by disbelievers 48; *see also* Torah

self-defence xxi; allowable 314; permission xii, 212; permits the taking up of arms xxii–xxiii; permitted during pilgrimage 21–2, 24; to be kept in proportion 174

self-destruction 22 n. *b*

senses, testimony against disbelievers at the Day of Judgement 307, 308

'sent down' xv

sexual intercourse 25; during Ramadan 20–1

shafa'a 58 n. *a*

shahid (martyr) 44 n. *b*

Shayan, *see* Satan

Sheba, people 272, 273–4

Shi'is xiii

ships 354; given by God for man's benefit 324; as signs of God's providence 313

shirk (polytheism) xvii

short measure, cheating by giving short measure condemned 413–14

Shu'ayb, as messenger 100–1; rejection 236–7, 254; role as prophet invoked as an encouragement to Muhammad 142–3

shura (consultation) 311, 314

Sijjin 413

silm 23 n. *c*

sin, committing 61

Sirius (star worshipped by the Arabs) 347, 348

sisters: inheritances 66; property shares 51

skies: collapse, as evidence of judgement 346; creation, as evidence of God's power 340

slaves 258; denied provisions by the disbelievers 170; marriage with 50 n. *e*, 53; respect for their owners' privacy 225; treatment 223

Sleepers of the Cave 183–5

smoke, as reference to the Day of Judgement 321

Solomon 12; blessing 291–2; cited as encouragement to Muhammad 272, 273; dialogue xx; God's guidance 86; prophetic status 206; and the Queen of Sheba 239, 240–1

sons, property shares 51

souls: corruption 423; creation 50; peace 421; purification 423; testing 33

spider 252, 254

spiritual and temporal rewards 249, 312–13, 313–14

successor (*khalifa*) 7 n. *a*

suicide 22 n. *b*

sujud 428 n. *d*

Summoner, activity at the Day of Judgement 350

sun: and moon, as evidence of God's creative power 282; pagan worship x; rising and setting 353; *see also* moon

Sunnis xiii

suras ix, xvi–xvii; alphabetical introductions 4 n. *a*; contents xix; introductions xxxv; introductory formula 116; Meccan and Medinan suras xvii–xix; Meccan suras 80, 94, 128, 136, 145, 158, 162, 166, 183, 191, 196, 203, 215, 227, 232, 239, 245, 252, 257, 261, 264, 272, 277, 281, 285, 290, 295, 301, 307, 311, 316, 321, 324, 327, 340, 343, 345, 347, 350, 356, 382, 384, 387, 389, 391, 393, 395, 399, 403, 405, 407, 409, 411, 412, 413, 415, 416, 417, 418, 419, 420, 422, 423, 424, 425, 426, 427, 428, 429, 430, 431, 432, 433, 434, 435, 436, 438, 439, 440, 441, 443, 445, 446; Medinan suras 4, 34, 50, 67, 110, 116, 153, 209, 220, 266, 331, 334, 338, 353, 359, 362, 365, 368, 370, 372, 374, 376, 378, 380, 395, 401, 442; punctuation xxxiv–xxxv; revelation, and the response of disbelievers 127; see also *al-Fatiha*

Suyuti ix

'sword verse' xxiii–xxiv

Syria x

ta ha 196 n. *a*

tabarak 227 n. *a*, 382 n. *b*

Tabari 74 n. *a*

Tabuk, expedition to xxxvii

taghut 56 n. *b*

Ta'if, as one of the two cities 317 n. *b*

Talut (Saul) (King) 28–9

tamattu' 22 n. *d*

taqwa xxxi

Tasnim, water 413

taxation 118

temporal life, contrast with afterlife 256

temporal and spiritual rewards 249, 312–13, 313–14

testimonies, in court, and women's status xxv–xxvi

Thamud, people 122, 159, 212; arrogance 290; arrogance and corruption of soul 423; condemnation 254, 416; destruction 229, 348; dialogue xx; as disbelievers 99–100, 140–1, 159, 179, 340, 343; punishment 303, 308, 351; punishment denied 387; rejection of Salih 236, 241–2; tyranny condemned 420; *see also* Salih

thaqal 354 n. *c*

theft, punishments for 71

Torah: confirmation by Jesus 72; *see also* Scriptures

torments, as punishment for Egyptian disbelief 318

trade and trading xviii, 53, 301 n. *a*; allowed by God 32–3; permitted on pilgrimages 22 n. *e*

travel, under God's providence 313

treaties, treaty obligations with polytheists 116–17

treaty obligations 115

Trench (battle) xii, xxxvii, 266, 267–8

Trinity 290 n. *b*; belief in the Trinity forbidden 66; denial 75

trust, given to mankind 61

truth, God tests claims to truth 267

Tubba', people 321, 322; disbelief 340

tyrants, condemnation by God 420–1

Uhud (battle) xii, xxxvii, 34, 44 n. *a*, 45–7, 365

'Umar (Rightly Guided Caliph) xiii

Umayyads xiii

ummi 105 n. *a*

unzurna 13, 13 n. *a*, 55

'uqba 423 n. *d*

usury: condemnation 31–2, 259; forbidden 44

'Uthman (Rightly Guided Caliph) xiii; preservation of the Qur'an xvi, xxxvii

'Uthmanic Codex xvi

al-'Uzza (Arabian pagan goddess) 347

w-q-y (mindfulness) 4 n. *c*

walad xxxiii, 183 n. *a*, 195 n. *b*

al-Walid ibn al-Mughira 384 n. *c*, 397

war xviii, xxiii, xxiv

war elephants, presence in the army of Abraha 437

war and warfare: conduct 28, 57–9, 60–1, 331; disbelievers' lack of success dictated by God 336; disbelievers refuse to fight in case this should break

war and warfare: (*cont.*):
  kinship ties 332; persistence in war commanded by God in God's cause 333; rewards given to believers for faithfulness in the conduct of war 335–6; sacred duty of fighting in God's way and condemnation of those who hold back 119–20, 123–4, 126, 127; self-defence in the sacred months 119
warfare 50
warhorses, God's oath concerning 432
warnings, to be given by Muhammad, even where they are ignored 418
wasila 78
water, fresh and salt water established by God 353
Ways of Ascent 389
wealth: display forbidden 54; hoarding forbidden 119
wealthy: arrogance reprimanded 384; condemnation for preferring their possessions to fighting in God's cause 123–4; obduracy and punishment 321
weights: fair weights 142; use of correct weights commanded 237
Weiss, Leopold (Muhammad Asad), translation of the Qur'an xxviii–xxix
widows, remarriage 27
winds 403; scattering winds, as proof of the Resurrection 343
witchcraft, invocation against 445
wives: conduct towards 266; fair treatment of 62–3; property shares 51
women: beautiful women as precious as ostrich eggs 286 n. *c*; believing and disbelieving women 380, 381; in childbirth 154; clothing 271; divorced women, and provision for 28; inheritance of women as property forbidden 52; lewd acts between 52; marriage 50; regulations concerning 50; relatives' prevention of

reconcilation with divorced husbands forbidden 26 n. *b*; status xxv–xxvi; status as witnesses 32; treatment 62–3, of believing and disbelieving women and their marriage dowries 369, during divorce 378–9, when convicted of adultery 53, within marriage 52, 54; with whom marriage is forbidden 52–3
words: classical meanings xxxiii; meanings determined by contexts xxx–xxxi
world, end 353, 354
worldly existence, transitory nature 360
worship: kneeling posture used for 324, 325; postures in worship 428
writing, significance for the Qur'an xv n. 6
writing ability 384 n. *a*
wrongdoers, protected only by each other 325
wujuh 55 n. *d*
wujuh al-Qur'an xxx–xxxi

Yamama (battle) xvi
yankihu 220 n. *c*
Yathrib, *see* Medina
Year of Grief xi
Yemen x
yunfiquna (charitable spending) 5 n. *b*

Zachariah 191; God's guidance 86; prophetic status 207
zakah 118 n. *e*
zanna (act of knowing) 8 n. *a*
Zaqqum, Tree of 179, 286, 322, 357
Zayd (Muhammad's adopted son) 269
Zaynab (Muhammad's cousin) 269 n. *a*
zina 220 n. *a*
Zoroastrians 210, 210 n. *c*
zurq 200 n. *c*